Approaches to Language and Culture

T0270638

Anthropological Linguistics

Edited by
Svenja Völkel and Nico Nassenstein

Advisory board

Kate Burridge
N. J. Enfield
Birgit Hellwig
Paul Kockelman
Simon Overall
Jack Sidnell
James Slotta

Volume 1

Approaches to Language and Culture

—

Edited by
Svenja Völkel and Nico Nassenstein

DE GRUYTER
MOUTON

ISBN 978-3-11-152271-5
e-ISBN (PDF) 978-3-11-072662-6
e-ISBN (EPUB) 978-3-11-072715-9
ISSN 2701-987X

Library of Congress Control Number: 2022935771

Bibliographic information published by the Deutsche Nationalbibliothek
The Deutsche Nationalbibliothek lists this publication in the Deutsche Nationalbibliografie;
detailed bibliographic data are available on the internet at http://dnb.dnb.de.

© 2024 Walter de Gruyter GmbH, Berlin/Boston
This volume is text- and page-identical with the hardback published in 2022.
Cover image: _jure/iStock/Getty Images Plus
Typsetting: Integra Software Services Pvt.

www.degruyter.com

Preface

In Europe, and especially in Germany, there are (at the present time) only a few research institutions devoted to the study of language and culture in diverse linguistic and sociocultural contexts (beyond Europe). This book is part of a larger project aimed at establishing a Center for Anthropological Linguistics/ Linguistic Anthropology at the Johannes Gutenberg University of Mainz in the future – in research projects, in teaching (both linguistics and anthropology), in interdisciplinary working groups, and through the launch of a new and exciting book series "*Anthropological Linguistics*".

We are very grateful to all the contributors to this volume for accepting our invitation to participate in this project and for sharing their expertise and years of experience with us – and with all readers. However, without the valuable comments of many colleagues, anonymous reviewers, and kind readers and their insightful ideas and advice, this project would never have taken shape. Our heartfelt thanks go to all of them, as well as to the many colleagues in our departments (Department of English and Linguistics and Department of Anthropology and African Studies, respectively) for their support, interest, and stimulating intellectual atmosphere. The Center for Intercultural Studies (ZIS) at Johannes Gutenberg University Mainz is thanked for providing generous financial support and a platform for international cooperation.

As the first volume, i.e., the present book, is now about to be published, we must thank Birgit Sievers, Natalie Fecher, and Kirstin Boergen of De Gruyter Mouton for their support and interest in our project: without their approval, enthusiasm, and hard work, this new book series would not see the light of day. We are already looking forward to the exciting volumes in preparation, and we appreciate the effort and precise work of many colleagues who choose this series and who plan to base the results of their research with us.

Mary Chambers is sincerely thanked for proofreading some of the contributions; any remaining inaccuracies and errors are on our account. We thank our (patient) families and loved ones who have had to put up with long absences while this project got off the ground – and is still getting off the ground. We invite all readers, interested colleagues, and students to join us on this exciting journey within the new book series!

https://doi.org/10.1515/9783110726626-202

Contents

Part I: Outlining anthropological linguistics

Part II: Fields of research

Part III: **Areal perspectives**

Part IV: **Outlook**

List of figures

https://doi.org/10.1515/9783110726626-204

List of tables

https://doi.org/10.1515/9783110726626-205

Part I: **Outlining anthropological linguistics**

Nico Nassenstein & Svenja Völkel

1 Studying the relationship of language and culture: Scope and directions

The interplay between language and culture has fascinated researchers from various disciplines since the work of Franz Boas (1858–1942) or even Wilhelm von Humboldt (1767–1835) and Johann Gottfried Herder (1744–1803). Since then, an interdisciplinary field has developed at the intersection of cultural/social anthropology and linguistics, referred to as either "anthropological linguistics" or "linguistic anthropology" (henceforth AL/LA), along with a few other (competing) denominations (to be discussed below). The broad field of research that focuses on language and culture encompasses several research traditions that approach the subject from different perspectives, the most important of which are discussed in this introduction. Although it is a common feature of all humans to use language for the purpose of social interaction, the world's languages exhibit a high degree of variation at all linguistic levels (see, e.g., Evans and Levinson 2009 for a concise overview). Cultural-historical factors have a considerable impact on this cross-linguistic variation, interacting with the constraints of human cognition which set the framework for diversification. Societies provide different cultural contexts in which languages are embedded. Individual languages serve to express culture-specific ideas, they are associated with cultural identity, and they are a medium for social interaction within a specific community; language choice, linguistic forms, and verbal practices convey cultural meaning. The overarching research goal of anthropological linguistics or linguistic anthropology, therefore, is to examine the ways in which and the extent to which cultural aspects affect cross-linguistic diversity and language change. The emergence of the study of language and culture, its fusion into an interdisciplinary field combining methods and features of linguistics and social/cultural anthropology, its overlap with neighboring subdisciplines of linguistics, and the topics addressed in this book are discussed in the following sections.

Nico Nassenstein, Johannes Gutenberg University of Mainz/Germany,
e-mail: nnassens@uni-mainz.de
Svenja Völkel, Johannes Gutenberg University of Mainz/Germany,
e-mail: svenja.voelkel@uni-mainz.de

https://doi.org/10.1515/9783110726626-001

1 "Language" and "culture" and their complex relationship

Examining the interaction between language and culture requires two basic considerations. First, it is necessary to define what is meant by the two multifaceted terms "language" and "culture", respectively, and how scholars have filled these key terms with meaning in their work. And second, it must be specified in what ways these basic entities interact and intertwine when brought together.

In anthropology, there are several contested definitions of "culture", the discipline's key concept of analysis. They advocate either a more fixed understanding of a cultural system or a more fluid interpretation that encompasses the shared values, norms, and rules of behavior of a group[1] – both emphasizing different aspects, contrasting them with a more systemic or a more praxeological approach, and advocating different points of view. Some concepts of culture are more or less criticized, and some scholars even question the relevance of culture as a conceptual entity altogether. However, it is by no means superfluous to the study of language in a given cultural context, and certain concepts of culture are related to certain approaches in AL/LA, e.g., "culture as a system of practices" and "culture as shared cognition", as will be shown in Section 3. Duranti (1997: 23–50) and Foley (1997: 12–24) provide detailed discussions of theories of culture used in and relevant to AL/LA.

As with culture, there are different understandings of language. First, Saussure's distinction between *langue* (language as a sign system) vs. *parole* (the utterance- and use-related dimension of language) can be related to the idea of "language as a structural system" vs. "language as practice", where practice can also be translated as "speech/speaking", which contributed to the development of a practice-oriented approach in AL/LA (e.g., Hymes in 1968;[2] see also Dimmendaal, this volume). However, this distinction is not without problems, as is also evident in the work of numerous scholars. The formal grammatical system of each language also evolved from common practices and is subject to constant change, even if this is often less obvious (and understood as a slower process) than in the case of conversational practices and the explicit negotiation of linguistic forms and practices as a (direct) consequence of socio-cultural change

---

1 We avoid long literature lists here; the relevant works are known or easily accessible to all interested readers. For an overview, see Darnell (1997) and Lentz (2017).
2 Hymes (1972) came up with the concept of "communicative competence", which was a criticism of the Chomskyan idea of purely structural or linguistic competence.

(think of examples such as language policy, which can lead to the emergence of specific subversive speech styles, e.g., as described by Kerswill and Wiese 2022, or marriage rituals, which can then trigger specific verbal avoidance styles; see Fleming, this volume, Mitchell 2015). Moreover, the distinction between language (as a formal system) and related varieties, dialects, etc. is notoriously problematic and ultimately arbitrary, reflecting political or social choices rather than an inherent logic of variation or subordination. The object of research, therefore, is, in a Saussurian sense, the study of all the languages of the world as well as language varieties and particular genres and ways of speaking (Hymes 1989). While typological comparisons that reveal cross-linguistic variation require etic parameters, describing language varieties and genres as relevant to the speech community and analyzing language against a cultural background require an emic perspective (see, e.g., in-depth studies by Senft 2010, Völkel 2010; based on Hymes 1968, see also Dimmendaal 2022 for a theoretical discussion). Finally, different subfields of the study of "language" require fine-grained and specific approaches that are not applicable in any other subfield, i.e., different segmentation and descriptive models must be applied in the analysis of phonetics and phonology, morphology, and syntax as compared to semantics and pragmatics, where the context of use and meaning are studied.

Apart from the academic debates on the definition of the basic concepts of "language" and "culture", Underhill and Głaz (this volume) point to yet another issue. Language-specific terms for "language" and "culture" (e.g., *Sprache* and *Kultur* in German, or *język* and *kultura* in Polish) are conceptually not exact equivalents but describe different emic understandings of the two basic entities.

Finally, there is the question of how language and culture are related. Culture, taken in a broad sense as "any form of non-instinctive, patterned behavior that is transmitted via social learning across generations and supported by rules or norms" (Enfield and Sidnell, this volume), also includes the knowledge and practice of language. This suggests that language is part of culture. However, the situation is even more complex as all aspects of culture (social, political, economic, legal, religious, etc.) are linguistically mediated (i.e., expressed, negotiated, transmitted, etc.) and thus languages always have a cultural component. As Enfield, Kockelman, and Sidnell (2014: 15) aptly conclude, language and culture are neither separable from each other, nor can they be considered as a single entity. Just as language is part of culture, culture is contained in language. The relationship between the two is considered complex, as evidenced by the wide variety of research in the field. There are examples of culture shaping language, language expressing cultural identity, language representing or being understood as cultural practice, cultural concepts being encoded in language, language being a tool to convey cultural values, the socialization process determining language acquisition, and more.

Enfield and Sidnell (this volume) distinguish some fundamental kinds of approaches regarding the relationship between language and culture. Apart from approaches which deny a significant relationship (e.g., in formal linguistics, which assumes that languages are innate universal manifestations of the human mind) and which are strongly questioned in AL/LA, there are several approaches arguing for a relationship between language and culture. Basically, a distinction can be made between two kinds of relationships: first, cultural concepts embodied in language structure (which are shared by all speakers speaking the language), and second, cultural perspectives expressed in linguistic practices (which are shared by most people in a social group but which allow for variation). While the first is associated with "linguistic relativity" in the tradition of Franz Boas, Edward Sapir, and Benjamin Lee Whorf, the latter emphasis on ways of communication is associated with Dell Hymes, Joel Sherzer, and Richard Baumann (both approaches are to be discussed in Section 3).

Despite or even because of all these fundamental issues, it is important not to get lost in theoretical considerations but to investigate the interplay between language and culture step by step in multiple contexts and from various perspectives.

2 The interdisciplinary field of anthropological linguistics/linguistic anthropology

The interdisciplinary field of anthropological linguistics (AL) or linguistic anthropology (LA) has several features that are characteristic of work at the intersection of two disciplines. Scholars are grounded in different disciplines, they approach the topic from different perspectives, and they may even use different labels for their research area. Proceeding from different perspectives and being anchored in different disciplines often means also using different methodological procedures. This will become clear in the following sections.

2.1 "Anthropological linguistics", "linguistic anthropology" – or "ethnolinguistics"?

In the United States, "linguistic anthropology" is firmly established as one of the four traditional fields of anthropology, namely archaeology, biological or physical anthropology, cultural or social anthropology, and linguistic anthropology.

This entrenchment of LA as a subfield of anthropology can be traced back to Franz Boas, who is generally regarded as the founder of this interdisciplinary field (for a brief overview of early studies in North America, see also Jim and Webster, this volume). In other parts of the world (e.g., Europe and Australia), it is less systematically anchored, and scholars who study language in its cultural context are located in various departments, primarily linguistics departments, affiliated with language typology or work in African linguistics, Ancient American studies, and less often also in East Asian studies, and so forth. The field of AL/LA is generally then considered a subfield of linguistics to be distinguished from other linguistic subfields such as psycholinguistics, neurolinguistics, or sociolinguistics, and accordingly, it is more commonly referred to as "anthropological linguistics". For example, Duranti (1997) and Ahearn (2012) both use the term LA, while Foley (1997) refers to it as AL. In Europe, where cultural anthropology is often referred to as ethnology, there is another terminological variant, namely "ethnolinguistics" (in French "ethnolinguistique" and in German "Ethnolinguistik"), analogous to other thematic anthropological fields and so-called ethno-sciences such as ethnobotany, ethnomedicine, and ethnomusicology (Hunn 2006). In contrast to the distinction between AL versus LA, the term "ethnolinguistics" subsumes both perspectives, i.e., both linguistics and cultural anthropology use the same term to describe their respective sub-disciplines. However, the term "ethnolinguistics" is used less and less frequently and appears only in a few influential additions to the growing body of literature on AL/LA (for instance in Senft 2013, and in the discussion in Dimmendaal 2022, who notes that this "is still the preferred term for this field in some parts of Europe, as against the Anglo-American label 'anthropological linguistics'", referring to discussions of the term in Bouquiaux 2004, Bouquiaux and Thomas 2013, and others).[3]

In this context, it is important to emphasize that the choice of the title of the present volume (*Approaches to Language and Culture*) connects the dots of both perspectives without implying that we favor one over the other (AL/LA). Rather, we view the two terms as alternative labels for the same interdisciplinary field[4] –

3 In connection with the popularization of the Anglo-American designation "cultural/social anthropology" instead of the German "*Ethnologie*" (see, e.g., numerous institutional renamings of German departments), various reasons play a role, such as the increasing importance of English as the dominant scientific lingua franca and the avoidance of the not uncontroversial meta-reference to Greek "ἔθνος" in the designations of departments, schools, and academic infrastructure. The newly emerged field that studies language and culture is therefore more appropriately called LA or AL, as most scholars suggest.
4 Sharifian (2015: 3, explanations added by the present authors) remarks that "the difficulty in defining both terms [i.e., "language" and "culture", see Section 1] has partly contributed to

and as mutually constitutive, bridging gaps within the same field that stem from different disciplinary and innate starting points or core perspectives. To gain a comprehensive understanding of the interplay between language and culture, it is necessary to approach research topics from both perspectives – from an anthropological and a linguistic one. We therefore strongly recommend that dialogue between disciplines and between approaches be sought, and that this "*Anthropological Linguistics*" book series be seen as a welcome and inspiring platform for such interdisciplinary discourse, as a place for exchange and debate, and as a breeding ground for advances in theory-building alongside any (ethnographic) empirical findings.

2.2 Approaching the field from different perspectives

A rough overview of paradigm shifts in American AL/LA can be sketched as follows. Historically, the emergence of the AL/LA discipline has its roots in the historical linguistics of Native American (First Nation) languages and their genetic classification and relatedness. Likewise, early studies had a focus on salient differences in linguistic and cultural features. The first paradigm shift occurred when, instead of historical linguistics, a linguistic relativity inspired by Franz Boas, Edward Sapir, and Benjamin Lee Whorf came to the fore in the early 20th century, along with more holistic attempts at the documentation of language (then still in written form), but predominantly with a shift to culturally shaped grammatical categories and their functions. We can count the focus on language as cultural practice that began to emerge in the 1960s as a second paradigm shift; speech events and the ethnography of speech were henceforth at the center of linguistic anthropologists' analyses. We consider recent work in which colleagues view anthropological issues through a linguistic lens as a third paradigm, examining, for example, political discourse, sexuality and queerness, race and racialization, prestige and privilege (to name a few topics), with a focus on linguistic practices. This latter kind of studies focuses strongly on multilingual/multicultural settings in western urban contexts, and thus there is a broad intersection with sociolinguistic research (to be discussed in Section 3.2).

These paradigm shifts are reflected in the majority of research topics addressed at these times. However, this in no way means that earlier approaches (and related core issues) were no longer relevant for AL/LA research. The different

---

the immature development of a unified sub-discipline for the study of language and culture". This often goes along with a delimitation from other approaches.

approaches address distinct aspects of the interplay of language and culture. The relevance of multiple approaches in AL/LA can be seen in the comprehensive definitions of the field and in the broad range of topics in the most authoritative introductions and handbooks that provide a comprehensive overview of AL/LA, as well as in this first volume of the present series. Figure 1.1 gives an overview of some statements defining AL/LA.

Anthropological linguistics is that sub-field of linguistics which is concerned with the place of language in its wider social and cultural context, its role in forging and sustaining cultural practices and social structures. [...] Anthropological linguistics views language through the prism of the core anthropological concept, culture, and, as such, seeks to uncover the meaning behind the use, misuse or non-use of language, its different forms, registers and styles.
(Foley 1997: 3)

The subdiscipline of linguistic anthropology in the [...] broader reading [...] of the term – perhaps best labeled the *anthropology of language* – encompasses any work that attempts to answer the research questions of anthropology [...] by focusing on the structure, use, development and/or evolution of language.
(Enfield, Kockelman & Sidnell 2014: 3)

[...] redefining the study of language and culture as one of the major subfields of anthropology [...] linguistic anthropology will be presented as the study of language as a cultural resource and speaking as a cultural practice. As an inherently interdisciplinary field, it relies on and expands existing methods in other disciplines, linguistics and anthropology in particular, with the general goal of providing an understanding of the multifarious aspects of language as a set of cultural practices,
[...]
(Duranti 1997: 2-3)

For the linguistic anthropologist, every aspect of language is socially influenced and culturally meaningful. To use language, therefore, is to engage in a form of social action laden with cultural values.
(Ahearn 2012: 12)

Figure 1.1: Statements defining anthropological linguistics/linguistic anthropology.

Optimally, anthropological-linguistic research requires methodological knowledge and skills, as well as training in both of the disciplines of social/cultural anthropology and linguistics. This includes familiarity with the methods of anthropological fieldwork, i.e., participant observation and ethnographic approaches in particular, as well as linguistic analysis, i.e., linguistic segmentation, interlinearization, and so on. In practice, however, most scholars are better trained or more rooted in one of the two disciplines and approach the interface from one perspective or the other. This means that there are anthropologists who are interested in language as a research object and linguists who are interested in the cultural context of language. These different perspectives often go hand in hand with two major research approaches (as described in Section 1: studies focusing on a. cultural concepts embodied in language structure, and b. cultural perspectives expressed in linguistic practices) and their related topics.[5]

Scholars with a predominantly anthropological background often study speaking as a cultural practice; more specifically, this involves the description of speech styles and verbal practices in different culturally significant contexts (known as the ethnography of communication, formerly called "ethnography of speaking" by Hymes 1968) and their analysis in terms of linguistic features and conversational patterns (conversation analysis is a crucial method for identifying fine-grained patterns such as turn-taking principles, repair strategies, and pauses, e.g., Sidnell and Stivers 2012, Meyer and Quasinowski, this volume). These ethnopragmatic studies (i.e., cultural meaning in verbal interaction) take into account the social roles of speech event participants (e.g., Fleming, this volume), the social function and meaning of communicative practices, and the cultural environment of verbal interaction. Such ethnographic descriptions are concerned with speech styles such as ritual speech[6] (e.g., Senft and Basso 2009, Tavárez, this volume) or transgressive speech (such as swearing and cursing; e.g., Nassenstein and Storch 2020), registers such as honorifics, culture-specific genres (e.g., Senft 2010, Meyer and Quasinowski, this volume), language varieties associated with a certain social group such as children's and carers' communicative strategies in socialization processes (e.g., child language and child-directed speech; see Hellwig, this volume) or the emergence of communicative styles among young people (e.g., Nassenstein and Hollington 2015 on African youth languages, or Dimmendaal, this volume), as well as the ideologies associated with languages or language varieties. Linguistic interaction

---

5 Most studies in cognitive anthropological linguistics, for instance, include cross-linguistic comparison and typological variation, i.e., they proceed from a macro-level perspective on language. By contrast, conversational studies in anthropological linguistics focus instead on a micro-level, investigating language-internal variation and interactional patterns between individual speech act participants. This distinction is often associated with a focus on language as a structural system vs. language as practice, although all linguistic phenomena have ultimately developed out of practice – whether more or less consciously or even deliberately driven, or underlying faster or slower processes of change. However, the linguistic outcome does not always reflect cultural parameters, but is more generally dependent on historical contingencies based on social, political, and environmental factors (Bickel 2015).

6 Tavárez (2014: 496) defines ritual as a practice of study as "the repetitive and highly creative performance of multilayered symbolic acts by individuals or groups in order to secure a number of pragmatic aims" (also drawing on the work of Evans-Pritchard 1940 and Tambiah 1979).

and communicative practices also address issues that go beyond speaking in the narrow sense. They also include the "unspoken" (see Mitchell and Storch, this volume), visual-gestural modalities such as sign languages (see Mohr and Bauer, this volume), or written genres (a topic that has been less addressed by anthropologists, who often work with predominantly oral societies, long considered the most profitable research contexts in linguistic and anthropological work).

Scholars with a more linguistic background are also concerned with more formal or structural aspects of language, examining cultural conceptualizations encoded in metaphors, in the classification of semantic fields (e.g., color terminologies, kinship terminologies, or body nomenclature), and even in grammatical forms (e.g., noun classes, evidential markers, numeral classification, or possessive classification[7]). This research generally proceeds from typological considerations that reveal the range of cross-linguistic variation. The question that follows is whether structural features of language express underlying cultural concepts. Cultural notions of kinship, for instance, are reflected in linguistic forms such as the classificatory system of referential kinship terminologies, e.g., hierarchical family structures in Tongan (Völkel 2010, 2016) or moiety belonging in Njamal (Burling 1970).[8] In contrast to communicative features which are statistically representative for a particular group of persons, the linguistic aspects studied in this field are the fundamental structural features of a language, which in general are less negotiable, are subject to slower change (than nonconventionalized linguistic characteristics), and the speakers are usually less aware of them and their underlying concepts (particularly as compared to alternative language structures; see for instance Silverstein 1981 on different degrees of awareness of native speakers). Ethnosemantic and ethnosyntactic topics (i.e., cultural meaning in lexical semantic domains and grammatical features) are addressed in multiple chapters of this volume, e.g., time and space (da Silva Sinha,

---

7 Numeral classifiers, for instance, distinguish nominal entities by their form rather than by their number (Lucy 1992). A basic distinction in possessive constructions is made between alienable and inalienable possession, i.e., different kinds of relationships between possessor and possessee characterized by [+/- closeness] between possessor and possessum, or [+/- control] of the possessor (e.g., Heine 1997; see also Völkel 2010, Aikhenvald, this volume, or Ameka and Amha, this volume, for specific underlying cultural concepts).
8 Culturally relevant concepts are often not only expressed in linguistic structures but also in non-verbal ways (e.g., by cultural artefacts as shown by da Silva Sinha, this volume, or by behaviors).

this volume), emotion (Ponsonnet, this volume), perception and color, possessive and nominal categorization constructions (Ameka and Amha, this volume), person indexicals, including honorific registers (Fleming, this volume), and simulative and perspective marking constructions (Aikhenvald, this volume), to name some examples. A detailed discussion of research topics in AL/LA follows in Section 4.1.

Despite the distinction of these two major approaches to the interdisciplinary field, they should not be regarded as competing but as complementary if one seeks a comprehensive understanding of the interplay between language and culture. They focus on different aspects of language and contribute distinct AL/LA insights (theoretical frameworks and adjacent disciplines are to be discussed in Section 3). Cultural notions of kinship, for instance, are reflected in the lexico-semantic categorization of referential kinship terminologies (see above), in conceptual patterns of kin metaphors and idioms (see also Aikhenvald, this volume for the use of kin terms with non-humans), in their use and context of use, and in aspects of lexical or semantic change (e.g., through language contact or negotiations of family structures). Furthermore, cultural notions of kinship are expressed in linguistic or conversational practices (often along with non-linguistic behaviors). These include social deixis encoding kinship relations (honorifics, e.g., avoidance registers used with taboo relatives such as in-laws in Australian Aboriginal societies, e.g., Haviland 1978, Dixon 1980, or in African societies, e.g., Herbert 1990, Treis 2005, Mitchell 2015), as well as linguistic features associated with communication between certain relatives (e.g., between grandparents and grandchildren in so-called "joking relationships", e.g., Radcliff-Brown 1940, Barnard 1987). Fleming (this volume) categorizes restriction-free or joking relationships as "characterized by an extreme of permissive interpersonal license", while avoidance or taboo relationships are "associated with extreme reticence and respectful non-engagement". The linguistic expression of these different relationships (in the form of registers, speech volume, (in)direct address, and so forth) is usually accompanied by non-linguistic behaviors (such as avoidance of physical contact or privileges, e.g., Völkel 2010, 2022).

All these aspects together certainly provide a more comprehensive picture of kinship from an anthropological-linguistic perspective. Cultural meaning is expressed on all linguistic levels (lexicon-semantics, pragmatics and even grammar), in language as structural system (focus on *langue*) and in language as communicative practice (focus on *parole*); it differs across languages (synchronic perspective), and it is subject to change (diachronic perspective).

2.3 The importance of language for anthropology and of culture for linguistics

Senft (2013) and Widlok (2020) stress the importance of (the knowledge and consideration of) local languages[9] as a tool in anthropological field research. Competence in the local language in a research context allows for a qualitatively more extensive means and way of participation (during participant observation and verbal interaction with the community). In addition to this, local languages provide deeper insights into emic concepts. Since languages differ on all linguistic levels, using a language of wider communication (LWC) such as English or another lingua franca means switching to a different conceptual system, identifying with a different language and speech community, and the like. This becomes clear if we consider language not only as a research tool, but as an anthropological-linguistic research topic in itself.

Similarly, one can emphasize the importance of familiarity with the cultural environment in linguistic research. Without knowledge and consideration of culture-specific ideas and behaviors, one will never fully understand and may even misinterpret linguistic data. Studies in intercultural communication provide multiple examples of misunderstandings, if awareness of cultural and linguistic differences is missing (e.g., Agar 1994, Heringer 2004). In order to understand, for instance, the conversational patterns in Aboriginal court contexts, one needs to be aware of the relevant participants in the speech event and their social relationships to each other. Here, even the role of bystanders and their social standing is crucial for interpersonal verbal dynamics and their right to knowledge sharing (Walsh 1994). Other important aspects with an impact on (anthropological-)linguistic research are culture-specific practices of knowledge sharing and politeness.[10] Linguists need to be aware that the field for anthropological linguists is more than a site of/with native speakers and a place where one can easily access language data. To study language in its cultural context requires a deeper cultural understanding from an emic perspective. Documentary and descriptive

---

9 The term "local language" is by no means intended to include a derogatory notion here, but is used for (any) language in local contexts of research, regardless of language family and degree of alphabetization etc.

10 To give an example here: After an initial descriptive linguistic field trip focusing on formal aspects of an indigenous language, a young researcher complained that several interlocutors had "lied" to him and provided "wrong" or insufficient data. This illustrates that linguistic data is worthless without an understanding of the conversational practices of the particular speech community. How and with whom is knowledge shared? Why do people give "wrong information", and can it be called "lying" in the Western sense if it is common local practice to agree or to answer at least something for reasons of politeness or shame?

research in anthropological linguistics therefore goes beyond the mere collection of language data or the purely formal description of languages without embedding linguistic subtleties into their cultural context. This means taking into account the local and sociocultural context of data collection and analyzing the linguistic data against this background.

3 The study of language and culture and its adjacent fields of research

The two major approaches of AL/LA have interfaces with other disciplines, namely cognitive science, sociolinguistics, pragmatics, and semiotics. The overlaps between the different research strands, their directions and theoretical frameworks are addressed in the following subsections.

3.1 Anthropological linguistics and cognitive science

A further basic component which is often part of the research on language and culture is cognition. This connects anthropological linguistics with the interdisciplinary network of cognitive sciences (comprising, among other areas, linguistics, cultural anthropology, psychology, and neuroscience; see Bender 2013 for detailed information), or more precisely, cognitive (ethno-)linguistics or cultural linguistics, and cognitive anthropology or cross-cultural psychology.

The fundamental question to be answered is whether there is a relationship between language and thought. Some scholars hold the view that the mind is independent from individual languages. Conceptual patterns of thought are regarded as innate and thus shared by all humans. This is a universalist notion of cognition. Another view is that different languages go together with distinct ways of thinking or even distinct worldviews (*Weltansicht*, as designated by Wilhelm von Humboldt). This relativist notion of cognition, going back to Edward Sapir (1884–1939) and Benjamin Lee Whorf (1897–1941), is known as "linguistic relativity".[11] Research on lexico-semantic fields such as color, kinship,

---

[11] This principle is sometimes also called the Sapir-Whorf hypothesis, but this description is misleading, as neither Sapir nor Whorf made a joint statement, nor did they formulate a hypothesis. For recent studies in this field (and a critical view on Sapir's and Whorf's observations), see Malotki (1983), who was then criticized by Lucy (1992) for not having fully understood Sapir's and Whorf's analysis of Hopi time, for instance. See also Foley (1997: 177–178).

and space has brought evidence to support both views. From a radical point of view, the two perspectives contradict each other. However, there are less extreme, more compatible views, namely scholars studying universal aspects of cognition without denying variation in other aspects. Wierzbicka (1992), for instance, has focused on the universal core concepts of kinship, such as the prototypical characteristics of motherhood. On the other hand, ethnosemantic studies investigate cross-linguistic variation in kinship terminologies. Speakers of Tongan, for instance, have one term for father and father's brother (*tamai*), contrasted with a separate term for mother's brother (*tu'asina*). This categorization, called the bifurcate-merging Hawaiian type, differs from the so-called lineal Eskimo type in English, which has one term for father (*father*) and another for father's brother and mother's brother (*uncle*). Thus, Tongan native speakers have a different mental representation of their family relationships – the father's brother being somehow similar to the father and different from the mother's brother (Völkel 2016).

Just like the universalist perspective, the relativist view that specific languages have an impact on conceptual patterns of thought is also formulated to different extremes. First, in relation to the way language interacts with thinking: A structural correspondence between language and thought in a deterministic sense ("language determines thinking") has been strongly questioned. A weaker formulation ("language has an impact on thinking"), which also allows for structural differences in language and thought, however, is much less controversially discussed. Second, in terms of what kind of thinking is affected by language: A distinction is made between "thinking for speaking", i.e., the activation of mental concepts (e.g., gender, animacy, or alienability) that are relevant in a language immediately prior to language production, and the notion that language can highlight properties in non-linguistic thought or even create mental concepts (e.g., Wolff and Holmes 2011, Casasanto 2017). To investigate the latter type of relationship between language and thought, Brown and Levinson (1993: 1) emphasize the need for non-linguistic data on unconscious conceptual parameters that drive behavior. These data usually come from experimental tasks (e.g., the recognition task) performed in the field and are later compared to the semantic parameters of the participants' language. The research group around Stephen Levinson at the Max Planck Institute in Nijmegen/NL has shown in several studies on space that there is a correlation between the dominant frame of reference of a language and the spatial perception of its speakers (e.g., Levinson 1996). However, there is not always a structural correspondence between language and thought. Moreover, the link between language and cognition is not unidirectional.

Gary Palmer and Farzad Sharifian have combined the cognitive-linguistic perspective with research in linguistic and cognitive anthropology (more precisely,

Boasian linguistics, ethnosemantics, and the Hymesian "ethnography of speaking"), exploring the interface between language, culture, and conceptualization under the heading "Cultural Linguistics" (Palmer 1996, Sharifian 2011). The focus of investigation is on culture-specific conceptual patterns encoded in linguistic features, such as metaphors or categorizations. Cultural concepts are cognitive representations widely shared across a cultural group but not necessarily by all members in all their components. These collective cognitive patterns of knowledge emerge from interactions of the group members, they are constantly negotiated and dynamic, they are passed on in the socialization process (i.e., language acquisition means socialization into a culture-specific worldview), and they provide a common ground for linguistic and non-linguistic interaction. The emic Tongan concepts of *mana* and *tapu*, for instance, form the underlying conceptual pattern of linguistic practices (honorific registers which can be regarded as a system of verbal taboo), as well as non-linguistic practices (taboos avoiding physical touch) (see, for instance, Völkel 2021). Thus, language not only affects thought, but cognitive concepts also leave their traces in language. However, not all conceptualizations or even worldviews encoded in language correspond to current views, as illustrated by the example of sunrise/sunset (often ascribed to Jerzy Bartmiński). The underlying notion of these linguistic expressions is that of an Earth at the center of the universe, around which the sun revolves, although this idea has been disproved since the Copernican Revolution. In this case, language and thought have evolved differently. All these approaches and examples show how complex and diverse the connections between language, culture, and cognition are.

3.2 Anthropological linguistics and sociolinguistics

Anthropological linguistics and sociolinguistics are both linguistic subdisciplines which study language as embedded in its sociocultural context. Language is regarded as a tool of social interaction and the research focus is on the interplay of socio-cultural parameters and linguistic variation. Despite this shared fundamental view on language and a certain thematic overlap, the two interdisciplinary linguistic subfields also differ in various aspects. While anthropological linguists have an anthropological approach to linguistic research, sociolinguistics is shaped by the connection with sociology. Traditionally, sociology and cultural anthropology have different research perspectives, which comes with an interest in distinct aspects of social life. In their studies, they focus on different societies and languages, and conventionally, they use different empirical approaches and methods of investigation.

Foley (1997: 4) provides a vivid example to illustrate the key differences, using the bilingual context of a contemporary Yimas village in Papua New Guinea where people speak Yimas (a Papuan language) and Tok Pisin (a creole and the country's lingua franca). A variationist-sociolinguistic investigation comparable to William Labov's study of social markers (i.e., linguistic variants statistically correlating with social subgroups of speakers such as men vs. women or older vs. younger people; see Labov 1972) would conduct a quantitative correlation analysis. Here the choice of language (Yimas vs. Tok Pisin) is the dependent variable, while age, gender, or other social characteristics of speakers are independent variables. This investigation would show that the use of Yimas vs. Tok Pisin correlates with age and gender: older people tend to speak Yimas and younger ones Tok Pisin; women tend to use Yimas and men Tok Pisin. Anthropological linguists, in contrast, focus more on cultural aspects determining language choice, for which qualitative linguistic-anthropological field research is necessary. The research outcome could be summarized as follows: Yimas is the language of village life (the domain of women) and of the traditional way of life (the domain of older people), while Tok Pisin is the language of political and economic interaction with other ethnic groups (the domain of males) and of the modern world (the domain of younger people). Although the variationist-sociolinguistic research approach is highly quantitative, in contrast to the predominantly qualitative approach in anthropological linguistics, there are other more qualitatively oriented sociolinguistic subfields (see below) that also primarily use field research with participant observation, the core method of cultural anthropology. Apart from the methodological approach, these two linguistic subdisciplines also differ in terms of their thematic research focus. While sociolinguistic studies are mainly interested in the relationship between social parameters and language-internal variation, anthropological linguists primarily investigate the relationship between cultural aspects and cross-linguistic variation. Furthermore, they also focus on different research locations. Labov (1972), for instance, conducted his research with English native speakers in New York City, and Milroy and Milroy (1978) with English native speakers in Belfast/UK, both locations in Western societies (the traditional object of research in most social sciences, including sociology and also sociolinguistics) and both varieties of a major Indo-European language (the most studied field of linguistic research). Generalizing statements in social sciences have, therefore, often been criticized for their cultural bias, being representative only for so-called WEIRD people (i.e., those of "Western, Educated, Industrialized, Rich and Democratic" societies; see Henrich, Heine, and Norenzayan 2010). Likewise, cross-linguistic statements do not hold if they are based on an overrepresented number of Indo-European languages. Scholars working in cultural anthropology and anthropological linguistics, in contrast, are traditionally interested in (rural areas of) non-Western small-scale societies, such as the Yimas people studied by William Foley. The Labovian approach to variationist sociolinguistics (based on specific variables and their occurrence with specific "speaker types") was criticized from the 1980s onwards due to the alleged stability of these variables (ethnicity, age, gender) at a time when fluidity and performativity of self-ascriptions of identity came into focus, and "identity" was to be understood as a more flexible concept (see Austin 1962, Butler 1988, Robinson 2003, to name a few); with the "second wave" in sociolinguistics, social network ties between speakers were brought into focus (e.g., Milroy and Milroy 1985 in their famous neighborhood study). There was a shift from stable speaker types and their variables to speakers' weak and strong ties to other speakers in processes of innovation. Penelope Eckert then eventually initiated a "third wave", in which she stressed the importance of both linguistic and extralinguistic "styles" of speakers, drawing on pragmatic performativity and also on sociocultural frames and representations – a clear overlap with modern linguistic anthropology, which studies agentive speakers and their cultural-situational "ways of speaking" and registers. According to Eckert (2012: 87), and in contrast to early variationists like Labov, "variation does not simply reflect, but also constructs, social meaning and hence is a force in social change". Thus, the greatest overlap is in the area of interactional sociolinguistics and linguistic anthropology, studying conversational practices and discourse strategies as being characteristic of a particular language, language variety, or a specific genre. Here, the two interdisciplinary fields have converged more and more in terms of research methods and research topics. Sociolinguists use qualitative field research methods to study language use in specific subgroups of Western societies (e.g., youth and emergent language practices, political language and discourse, or corporate language practices). In a globally connected world, there are a variety of multilingual and multicultural environments that make the study of language and culture even more complex. There are multiple subcultures within a society and people with multi-ethnic backgrounds. Thus, the contact between language and culture is not only a matter of negotiation between people of different cultural and linguistic groups, but often an "intrapersonal" process. Such issues (e.g., multiethnic political discourse in the United States or online communication between Tongans in Tonga and relatives living overseas) are now studied by anthropological linguists and sociolinguists alike. In addition, anthropological linguists have traditionally conducted long-term anthropological research to familiarize themselves with a culture, in which they were not socialized prior to the research. There is now an increasing number of indigenous researchers who study their own culture and language, much like sociolinguists. Thus, the lines between sociolinguistics and anthropological linguistics get more and more fuzzy.[12]

4 About this book

In the following two subsections, core themes and geographic areas of the volume are identified and discussed in terms of broader anthropological-linguistic directions and movements (which explains the order in which they are mentioned, although this sometimes differs from the order in which they appear in the book). This section is intended to illustrate that the effort involved in assembling a volume that brings together numerous established key themes with (often new) empirical contexts of individual scholars is not a haphazard approach, but an attempt to introduce the field of studies that focus on language and culture.

4.1 Topics of research on language and culture

Language is a crucial means of social interaction; cultural ideas and practices are therefore reflected in linguistic forms and ways of use. Thus, to a certain extent, cross-linguistic variation is rooted in the different cultural environments of speakers.

As a consequence, the fact that a large number of the world's languages, currently numbering around 6,500–7,000, are endangered, raises the question of what impact this language loss has on cultural diversity and which socio-political situations cause or favor language endangerment. As humanity, we must then ask ourselves the question of how we seek to address and face this issue. Since the late 90s, there has been an increase of interest in the topic of endangerment and "language death", as it was often labeled in those earlier studies, which has resulted in multiple documentary and descriptive research incentives on un-/understudied and particularly endangered languages while they (and their speakers) are

---

12 It seems that as the two sub-disciplines slowly shift in content and focus in contemporary linguistic anthropology (especially in North America), they are converging and also moving away, to some extent, from "classical" topics and approaches. Some other topics have not per se been sociolinguistic topics, but they have increasingly been approached from a linguistic-anthropological angle (style, stance, positionality, identity, and ideology). In contrast with Foley (1997) and Duranti (1997), Ahearn (2012) includes many sociolinguistic topics in her introductory overview of AL/LA.

still available. Bradley (Chapter 3, this volume) presents some of the main causes of language endangerment and several strategies for language maintenance or reclamation. As we can see from various studies on these topics, the situational contexts of language contact are extremely diverse, and people display diverging attitudes, interests, and goals which they link to individual languages, an aspect that Kroskrity addresses in his chapter on language ideologies and social identities (Chapter 5, this volume). More precisely, political and economic interests have an impact on people's beliefs, feelings, and conceptions about language, and such language ideologies play an important role in the construction of a speaker's or a group's social identity. Due to their different cultural situations, language ideologies, and social identities, communities also deal with their individual contexts of language endangerment in multiple ways, which may result in language loss (ranging from deliberate language shift to powerful language and social identity erasure) or reclamation. In contrast to language loss on the one hand, there are phenomena of emerging languages, language varieties, and speech styles (also called "language birth") on the other hand. In specific language contact situations where speakers do not share a common language, so-called pidgins and creoles have emerged. Other examples are the development of English, French, Portuguese, and Spanish language varieties in various parts around the world (mainly embedded in processes of imperialism and colonialism). Dimmendaal (Chapter 4, this volume) focuses, in particular, on the creation of new communicative styles, i.e., the interactional dimension of speech styles as used in particular contexts and/or by particular audiences, in the expanding Indo-European languages but also in other indigenous and minority languages. In multilingual and multicultural contexts, the research focus is often on contact phenomena (including cases of "signs of difference" or differentiation; see Gal and Irvine 2019). Hoenigman (2012) provides an example of a "language battle" in a situation of spirit possession in a Sepik society (Papua New Guinea), where the lingua franca (Tok Pisin) vs. the local Papuan language (Awiakay) is associated with changing language ideologies among speakers. Apart from language death and language birth, there are multiple other less extreme outcomes of language change within the broad field of language and culture contact, such as code-switching between languages and the transfer of linguistic features from one language onto another. They, however, are not particularly addressed in separate chapters of this volume, but other topics in Part I of this book certainly allow for an impression of what it means to live with multiple languages, which differ conceptually and reflect different cultural ideas and practices.

The interplay of language and culture starts at birth. Children are socialized in a particular social environment to become "competent" members of their community. This includes the acquisition of social ideas and behaviors as well as language, a fundamental tool for social interaction (see Hymes 1972 on "communicative competence"). Not only does socialization take place through verbal interaction, but the acquisition of language is also essentially part of socialization. Hellwig (Chapter 2, this volume) focuses on three aspects in anthropological-linguistic research, namely the learning environment of children (e.g., ways of interaction and conversational partners), ideologies of language development, and properties of input for language learning (e.g., child-directed speech). All these aspects have an impact on one's language acquisition process. Most theories on linguistic stages and ages of first language acquisition, for instance, have been developed based on the much-better studied major European languages. Therefore, we still need to overcome this research bias in order to obtain deeper cross-linguistic and cross-cultural insights into language acquisition and language socialization. In the socialization process, humans adopt culture-specific perspectives which are also attested in conversational practices and even linguistic forms, as shown in the following paragraphs.

Much of our linguistic interaction follows specific rules and principles which are more or less conventionalized or even ritualized. Despite some universal patterns, most of them are highly language- and culture-specific in form and function. The speech event of greeting, for instance, consists of greeting and re-greeting to establish social contact, but the linguistic formulas of greetings differ across languages and cultures, as is also the case for farewell utterances. Within a society, language use depends primarily on the situation, the speakers, and their social relationship with other participants in the speech event. This includes genres, registers, sociolects, dialects, etc. In anthropological linguistics, these topics of linguistic interaction have been described in ethnographies of communication and studied through conversation analysis (CA). In this volume, Meyer and Quasinowski (Chapter 6) focus on conversational organization ("candidate universals" of social interaction in CA, turn-taking, etc.) and genre. Genres are particular modes of speaking or writing, e.g., fairy tales, letters, poems, or prayers, but there are also new genres which have emerged in the context of digital media, such as text messages or social media chats. Apart from these formal and ritualistic uses of language, genres also include embedded elements in the course of ordinary verbal interaction, such as jokes, proverbs, gossip, or swearing. Tavárez (Chapter 8, this volume) addresses ritual speech; verbal practice is part of ritual activities which are understood as events of highly patterned and carefully calibrated bodily and verbal performances. Social order and authority play a central role here. Thus, Tavárez focuses on language ideologies and local epistemologies, historical narratives and ritual authority, ritual practices and social order, and ritual labor, non-human actors, and materiality. Language behavior also includes silence and omissions, topics avoided or left out in interaction – or "the unspoken", as labeled by Mitchell and Storch (Chapter 9, this volume). Each society has topics (conceptual domains, e.g., personal names, death, sex, or the supernatural) which are not talked about for various reasons such as shame, tactfulness, or danger, i.e., the fear of negative consequences. Such verbal taboos often go hand in hand with the avoidance of physical contact. In language, we find different ways of working around them (e.g., through avoidance registers or conventionalized euphemisms) which are more or less ritualized. This affects the degree of negotiability and dynamics. Mitchell and Storch provide anthropological-linguistic insights into taboo and avoidance, silence and euphemistic censorship, and practices of breaking this silence and filling the void. Another aspect which has caught attention in anthropological-linguistic research is the multimodality of language. Apart from the acoustic cues, communicative practice also takes place on a visual level. Mohr and Bauer (Chapter 7, this volume) focus on manual co-speech signals such as gestures and manual signs in sign languages. The multimodal approach to language accounts for the interaction of speech, gestures, gaze, posture, and other modes in the meaning-making process. Situational contexts and cultural conventions are also important aspects to be considered in multimodal interaction for an understanding of the semiotic diversity of language. Cross-linguistic studies provide insights into commonalities and differences in gestural forms across various cultural contexts, and research on language contact phenomena (e.g., borrowing, code-switching, and code-blending, to name but a few) are enriched by multimodal accounts, as Mohr and Bauer show.

Further areas of research on language and culture deal with semantic domains (e.g., space, time, emotion, kinship, senses, body nomenclature, and color) or grammatical forms (e.g., numeral classifiers, noun classes, and possessive classifiers) and their underlying conceptualizations, or, more broadly, with the issue of how we perceive or classify the world linguistically. The broad field of social indexicality, i.e., the non-referential encoding of social identities and relationships, is described by Fleming (Chapter 10, this volume). These linguistic signs are phonological, morphological, or lexical alternations which index sociocultural meanings such as gender, kin relationships, or stratification, i.e., absolute/personal or relational/interpersonal characteristics which may be associated with taboo, respect, or other social behavioral requirements. In contrast with statistical or frequency-based linguistic alternations (also called "social markers") which are associated with certain social groups (e.g., male vs. female speakers, or younger vs. older speakers), Fleming focuses on social indexicals, which are categorical encodings of social identities or relationships (also labeled "social deixis"; e.g., gender deixis or honorific vocabularies). They may differ according to the interactional role of the socially indexed person in a given context. Da Silva Sinha

(Chapter 11, this volume) addresses the domain of time, which is often linked to space as the source domain of metaphorical mapping (locating events in time). Language (e.g., metaphors, grammatical tenses, and lexical time references) and cultural artefacts (e.g., calendars or clocks) provide information on how people conceptualize time. Although all languages and cultures have ways of thinking and communicating about time and space, there is cross-linguistic/-cultural variation. A major distinction can be made between languages/societies with a metric time concept (using calendars and clock times) and those with event-based concepts of time. Another fundamental domain of human experience and interaction described in this volume is emotion. Ponsonnet (Chapter 12, this volume) gives an overview of the anthropological-linguistic research on the relationship between language and emotion, including the language of emotion (lexicon) and emotionally loaded linguistic practices (together with social correlates of these practices). The aim is to study cross-linguistic and cross-cultural commonalities and differences and to learn about the role language plays in constructing, discussing, managing, or even experiencing emotions.

Thus, a central interest in the study of language and culture is to shed light on different languages and ways of communication as they have developed in their respective cultural contexts. The cross-linguistic perspective helps us to realize the extent of linguistic variation and the spread of certain forms and practices, while anthropological-linguistic in-depth studies provide an understanding of their cultural context, i.e., ideas, practices, ideologies, etc., in which languages have developed according to the communicative needs of their speakers.

4.2 Language and culture from an areal perspective

The areal perspectives presented in Part III of this volume allow us to shed light on the interplay of language and culture in particular regions around the globe. People may share social and linguistic features and characteristics in contrast to speakers located in other parts of the world. This focus on particular language families and larger cultural units, however, does not mean that we are dealing with a homogeneous group in each geographical setting. From a linguistic perspective, the languages of a larger area (or continent) such as Oceania or Africa, for instance, do not all belong to one and the same language phylum (e.g., Oceania is the home of Austronesian and Papuan languages; Afro-Asiatic, Nilo-Saharan, Niger-Congo, and "Khoisan" languages and even one Austronesian language are located on the African continent). The geographic contexts vary in their degree of diversity concerning phylogenetic range (i.e., the number of language families), and also language density (i.e., the number of languages or language varieties) and typological diversity (i.e., the range of linguistic structures). South America, for instance, is an area of extreme linguistic diversity in all three aspects. Here the focus on single subareas, such as the Amazon region, already includes multiple languages, language families, and diverse language structures. In some areas, we also find so-called "Sprachbünde" (or linguistic areas, e.g., in Southeast Asia, the Balkans, or Ethiopia) which are characterized by a high density of different language families that have been in close contact with each other over a long period of time and thus have structurally adapted to each other. Finally, the areas also differ in terms of our knowledge of languages, societies, and speakers' ways of life. Europe, with its Indo-European languages, is by far the best researched region. Some other well-grounded areal perspectives are provided in this book, including Africa (by Ameka and Amha, Chapter 13), Native North America (by Jim and Webster, Chapter 14), Amazonia in South America (by Aikhenvald, Chapter 15), Australia and Oceania (by Rumsey, Singer, and Tomlinson, Chapter 16), Mainland Southeast Asia (by Enfield and Sidnell, Chapter 17), and finally Europe (by Underhill and Głaz, Chapter 18).

Languages may share multiple features for several reasons: genetic relationship, language contact, or a shared cultural background. The societies of a (sub)area often share a joint history, both prior to colonialism and also since then. The colonial impact on local languages of one area is often similar, or at least shows certain shared traits (both structurally and ideologically). As a consequence, research topics of areal relevance can be identified, such as a strong focus on language endangerment, among other issues, in Native North and South America and Australia. Lately, globalization, the Internet, and social media have led to worldwide language and culture contact with new dynamics and processes of change.

Ameka and Amha (Chapter 13, this volume) focus on the ethnosemantic topics of sensory experiences and color, on the ethnosyntactic topics of possessive marking, third-party communication (logophoricity), and nominal classification, and on the ethnopragmatic topics of greetings and farewells in African contexts. Jim and Webster's work (Chapter 14, this volume) is on ethnopoetics: They argue for a dialogical approach between the (often) native poet and the (usually) foreign ethnographer to gain a more emic cultural understanding of verbal art and poetics. Aikhenvald (Chapter 15, this volume) describes shared Amazonian phenomena, namely a shared worldview (animism) including ideas on change of shape or appearance (trickster creator), and their expression by grammatical means (e.g., nominal classifiers, similative markers, or double marking of syntactic function on noun phrases). Rumsey, Singer, and Tomlinson (Chapter 16, this volume) focus on multilingualism (complex patterns of alternation and their significance for social and territorial identity), the management of intangible heritage (documentation and revitalization of language, music, and dance), kin classification, and language acquisition and socialization in indigenous Australia. The topics relating to Oceania include language ideology (with reference to translation and transformation, and the impact of new media), and language acquisition and socialization. Enfield and Sidnell (Chapter 16, this volume) discuss some cultural concepts (e.g., of material culture) encoded in language structure and also culture-specific ways of language use in two settings in mainland Southeast Asia, namely historical developments in Vietnam and contemporary life in central Laos. Finally, Underhill and Głaz (Chapter 18, this volume) address multiple topics and approaches in the research on language and culture in Europe. These include contributions of European scholars to the field, research on language and culture in Europe (e.g., studies in the field of cognitive sociolinguistic, translation and worldview, or intercultural pragmatics), the role of European languages as world languages, and the European Union and its internal diversity (including in terms of a multilingual and multicultural academia).

In analogy with the focus on geographically contiguous areas, it is also worth investigating places with a similar natural environment (e.g., the Arctic or the Tropics). The natural environment, i.e., factors such as climate, topography, and geography, undoubtedly has an impact on various aspects of speakers' ways of life. Historically, people came to adapt to the conditions and available resources of their habitat (e.g., with particular kinds of housing, clothing, food, etc.), and among other influences, environmental factors have influenced the socio-economic development of societies and their spread[13] (e.g., Diamond 2007). A question that arises is whether societies of a particular climate zone show similarities and whether these similarities are also reflected in linguistic forms and practices (e.g., regarding spatial description in dense rainforest areas). These perspectives leave room for future anthropological-linguistic research.

5 Outlook and expectations

The purpose of this volume is to provide insights into the broad range of research areas that currently comprise the AL/LA subdiscipline. While focusing on core topics in linguistics and cultural studies and encompassing various

---

13 Theories and hypotheses on the spread of social groups are investigated in multidisciplinary approaches, combining archeological findings, studies on human DNA, and the distribution of language families.

geographical areas that have played an important role in anthropological linguistic work, this volume does not necessarily serve as a handbook-like overview, but is intended to pave the way for the "Anthropological Linguistics" book series and invite promising exchanges. Contributions dealing with classical cultural inscriptions in the grammar of languages are expected, as well as more ethnographically oriented studies dealing with contemporary practice-oriented approaches and current ethnographies of communication. The areas of study represented in this volume, written by specialists in their respective topics and fields, aim in particular to inspire colleagues working in related aspects around language and culture to bridge methodological differences and come together to establish a new (and broader) understanding of the discipline, where alternative approaches are most welcome (allowing new directions to be pursued and innovative empirical terrain to be explored).

In future studies on language and culture (in our book series and beyond), we hope to stimulate a dialogue on AL/LA that reflects the "recognition of the complex interplay between language as a human resource and language as a historical product and process" (Duranti 1997: 83), produces new results, opens new debates, and "celebrates" the diversity in people's speech and thought, "awed by the power through which human beings construct an infinite variety of symbolic universes", as Hill and Hill (1986: 446) put it.

References

Agar, Michael. 1994. *Language shock. Understanding the culture of conversation*. New York: Morrow.

Ahearn, Laura. 2012. *Living language. An introduction to linguistic anthropology*. Chichester, UK: Wiley.

Austin, John L. 1962. *How to do things with words. The William James lectures delivered at Harvard University in 1955*. Oxford: Clarendon Press.

Barnard, Alan. 1987. Khoisan kinship. Regional comparison and underlying structures. In Ladislav Holý (ed.), *Comparative anthropology*, 189–209. Oxford: Blackwell.

Bender, Andrea. 2013. Kognitionsethnologie. In Bettina Beer & Hans Fischer (eds.), *Ethnologie. Einführung und Überblick*, 287–307. Berlin: Reimer.

Bickel, Balthasar. 2015. Distributional typology. Statistical inquiries into the dynamics of linguistic diversity. In Bernd Heine & Heiko Narrog (eds.), *The Oxford handbook of linguistic analysis*, 901–923. Oxford: Oxford University Press.

Bouquiaux, Luc. 2004. *Linguistique et ethnolinguistique. Anthologie d'articles parus entre 1961 et 2003*. Leuven-Paris-Dudley, MA: Peeters and SELAF.

Bouquiaux, Luc & Jacqueline M. C. Thomas (eds.). 2013. *L'ethnolinguistique – Haudricourt et nous, ses disciples*. Saint-Martin-au-Bosc: SELAF.

Brown, Penelope & Stephen C. Levinson. 1993. *Linguistic and non-linguistic coding of spatial arrays. Explorations in Mayan cognition*. Nijmegen: Max Planck Institute for Psycholinguistics.

Burling, Robbins. 1970. *Man's many voices. Language in its cultural context*. New York: Holt, Rinehart and Winston.

Butler, Judith. 1988. Performative acts and gender constitution. An essay in phenomenology and Feminist theory. *Theatre Journal* 40 (4). 519–531.

Casasanto, Daniel. 2017. Relationships between language and cognition. In Barbara Dancygier (ed.), *The Cambridge handbook of cognitive linguistics*, 19–37. Cambridge: Cambridge University Press.

Darnell, Regna. 1997. The anthropological concept of culture at the end of the Boasian century. *Social Analysis. The International Journal of Anthropology* 41 (3). 42–54.

Diamond, Jared. 2007. *Arm und Reich. Die Schicksale menschlicher Gesellschaften*. Frankfurt: Fischer.

Dimmendaal, Gerrit J. 2022. *Nurturing language. Anthropological linguistics in an African context*. Berlin & Boston: De Gruyter Mouton.

Dixon, R. M. W. 1980. *The languages of Australia*. Cambridge: Cambridge University Press.

Duranti, Alessandro. 1997. *Linguistic anthropology*. Cambridge: Cambridge University Press.

Eckert, Penelope. 2012. Three waves of variation study. The emergence of meaning in the study of sociolinguistic variation. *Annual Review of Anthropology* 41. 87–100.

Enfield, N. J., Paul Kockelman & Jack Sidnell. 2014. Introduction. Directions in the anthropology of language. In N. J. Enfield, Paul Kockelman & Jack Sidnell (eds.), *The Cambridge handbook of linguistic anthropology*, 1–24. Cambridge: Cambridge University Press.

Evans, Nicholas & Stephen C. Levinson. 2009. The myth of language universals. Language diversity and its importance for cognitive science. *Behavioral and Brain Sciences* 32. 429–448.

Evans-Pritchard, Edward. 1940. *The Nuer. A description of the modes of livelihood and political institutions of a Nilotic people*. Oxford: Oxford University Press.

Foley, William. 1997. *Anthropological linguistics*. Malden, MA: Blackwell.

Gal, Susan & Judith Irvine. 2019. *Signs of difference. Language and ideology in social life*. Cambridge: Cambridge University Press.

Haviland, John. 1978. Guugu-Yimidhirr brother-in-law language. *Language in Society* 8. 365–393.

Heine, Bernd. 1997. *Possession. Cognitive sources, forces, and grammaticalization*. Cambridge: Cambridge University Press.

Henrich, Joseph, Steven Heine & Ara Norenzayan. 2010. The weirdest people in the world? *Behavioral and Brain Sciences* 33 (2–3). 61–83.

Herbert, Robert K. 1990. Hlonipha and the ambiguous woman. *Anthropos* 85 (4–6). 455–473.

Heringer, Hans Jürgen. 2004. *Interkulturelle Kommunikation*. Tübingen: Narr Francke.

Hill, Jane H. & Kenneth C. Hill. 1986. *Speaking Mexicano. Dynamics of syncretic language in Central Mexico*. Tucson: University of Arizona Press.

Hoenigman, Darja. 2012. A battle of languages. Spirit possession and changing linguistic ideologies in a Sepik society, Papua New Guinea. *The Australian Journal of Anthropology* 23. 290–317.

Hunn, Eugene. 2006. Ethnoscience. In Keith Brown (ed), *Encyclopedia of language and linguistics*, 2nd edition, 258–260. Amsterdam: Elsevier.

Hymes, Dell H. 1968. The ethnography of speaking. In Joshua A. Fishman (ed.), *Readings in the sociology of Language*, 99–138. The Hague: Mouton.

Hymes, Dell H. 1972. On communicative competence. In J. B. Pride & Janet Holmes (eds.). *Sociolinguistics. Selected readings*, 269–293. Harmondsworth: Penguin.

Hymes, Dell H. 1989. Ways of speaking. In Richard Bauman & Joel Sherzer (eds.), *Explorations in the ethnography of speaking*, 433–452. Cambridge: Cambridge University Press.

Kerswill, Paul & Heike Wiese (eds.). 2022. *Urban contact dialects and language change. Insights from the Global South and Global North*. New York: Routledge.

Labov, William. 1972. *Sociolinguistic patterns*. Philadelphia: University of Pennsylvania Press.

Lentz, Carola. 2017. Culture. The making, unmaking and remaking of an anthropological concept. *Zeitschrift für Ethnologie* 142 (2). 181–204.

Levinson, Stephen. 1996. Frames of reference and Molyneux's question. Cross-linguistic evidence. In Paul Bloom, Merrill Garrett, Lynn Nadel & Mary Peterson (eds), *Language and space*, 109–169. Cambridge, MA: MIT Press.

Lucy, John. 1992. *Grammatical categories and cognition. A case study of the linguistic relativity hypothesis*. Cambridge: Cambridge University Press.

Malotki, Ekkehart. 1983. *Hopi time. A linguistic analysis of the temporal concepts in the Hopi language*. Berlin: Walter de Gruyter.

Milroy, James & Lesley Milroy. 1978. Belfast. Change and variation in an urban vernacular. In Peter Trudgill (ed.), *Sociolinguistic patterns in British English*, 19–36. London: Arnold.

Milroy, James & Lesley Milroy. 1985. Linguistic change, social network and speaker innovation. *Linguistics* 21. 339–384.

Mitchell, Alice. 2015. *Linguistic avoidance and social relations in Datooga*. New York: The State University of New York at Buffalo dissertation.

Nassenstein, Nico & Andrea Hollington (eds.). 2015. *Youth languages in Africa and beyond*. Berlin & Boston: De Gruyter Mouton.

Nassenstein, Nico & Anne Storch (eds.). 2020. *Swearing and cursing. Contexts and practices in a critical linguistic perspective*. Berlin & Boston: De Gruyter Mouton.

Palmer, Gary. 1996. *Towards a theory of cultural linguistics*. Austin, TX: University of Texas Press.

Radcliffe-Brown, Alfred R. 1940. On joking relationships. *Africa. Journal of the International African Institute* 13 (3). 195–210.

Robinson, Douglas. 2003. *Performative linguistics. Speaking and translating as doing things with words*. London & New York: Routledge.

Senft, Gunter. 2010. *The Trobriand Islanders' ways of speaking*. Berlin & Boston: De Gruyter Mouton.

Senft, Gunter. 2013. Ethnolinguistik. In Bettina Beer & Hans Fischer (eds.), *Ethnologie. Einführung und Überblick*, 271–286. Berlin: Reimer.

Senft, Gunter & Ellen B. Basso (eds.). 2009. *Ritual communication*. Oxford & New York: Berg.

Sharifian, Farzad. 2011. *Cultural conceptualisations and language. Theoretical framework and applications*. Amsterdam & Philadelphia: John Benjamins.

Sharifian, Farzad (ed.). 2015. *The Routledge handbook of language and culture*. London: Routledge.

Sidnell, Jack & Tanya Stivers (eds.). 2012. *The handbook of conversation analysis*. Malden, MA: Wiley-Blackwell.

Silverstein, Michael. 1981. *The limits of awareness* (Working papers in sociolinguistics 84). Austin, TX: Southwest Educational Development Laboratory.

Tambiah, Stanley. 1979. A performative approach to ritual. *Proceedings of the British Academy* 65. 113–166.

Tavárez, David. 2014. Ritual language. In N. J. Enfield, Paul Kockelman & Jack Sidnell (eds.), *The Cambridge handbook of linguistic anthropology*, 496–516. Cambridge: Cambridge University Press.

Treis, Yvonne. 2005. Avoiding their names, avoiding their eyes. How Kambaata womenrespect their in-laws. *Anthropological Linguistics* 47 (3). 292–320.

Völkel, Svenja. 2010. *Social structure, space and possession in Tongan culture and language. An ethnolinguistic research*. Amsterdam & Philadelphia: John Benjamins.

Völkel, Svenja. 2016. Tongan-English language contact and kinship terminology. *World Englishes* 35 (2). 242–258.

Völkel, Svenja. 2021. Tongan honorifics and their underlying concepts of *mana* and *tapu*. A verbal taboo in its emic sense. *Pragmatics & Cognition* 28 (1). 26–57.

Walsh, Michael. 1994. Interactional styles in the courtroom. An example from Northern Australia. In John Gibbons (ed.), *Language and the law*, 217–233. London: Longman.

Wolff, Phillip & Kevin Holmes. 2011. Linguistic relativity. *Cognitive Science* 2 (3). 253–265.

Widlok, Thomas. 2020. Zur Bedeutung der Sprache für die ethnologische Feldforschung. In Bettina Beer & Anika König (eds.). *Methoden ethnologischer Feldforschung*, 77–89. Berlin: Reimer.

Wierzbicka, Anna. 1992. *Semantics, culture, and cognition. Universal human concepts in culture-specific configurations*. Oxford: Oxford University Press.

Part II: **Fields of research**

Birgit Hellwig

2 Language acquisition and language socialization

Theories of linguistic and cognitive development tend to be grounded in data that is biased towards the major European languages and cultures, with language acquisition and socialization data being available for only 1–2% of the world's languages (Kidd and Garcia 2022). The empirical bias continues to exist despite important early efforts that contributed cross-linguistic and cross-cultural perspectives, such as, e.g., the classic series "The crosslinguistic study of language acquisition" (Slobin 1985–1997), or the language socialization paradigm within linguistic anthropology (e.g., Schieffelin and Ochs 1986). Recent years have seen a renewed interest in this topic, and a growing number of language acquisition and socialization studies emerged that focus on underresearched languages around the world. This contribution gives an overview of three salient lines of research (investigations into the learning environment of the child, the ideologies of language development and the properties of the input), illustrating the phenomena with the help of examples from Qaqet (a Baining language of Papua New Guinea), and identifying desiderata for future research.

1 Introduction

Research into children's developing knowledge of language and culture finds itself at the intersection of two disciplines. On the one hand, language acquisition

Acknowledgements: I thank David Bradley, Nico Nassenstein, Svenja Völkel and two anonymous reviewers for their support and helpful comments on earlier versions of this chapter, and I am indebted to Brown and Gaskins (2014) and San Roque and Schieffelin (forthcoming) for inspiration. The chapter originated within a project on the acquisition of Qaqet, and I sincerely thank the communities of Raunsepna, Lamarain and Kamanakam, as well as all the Qaqet adults and children who participated and contributed to the project. Special thanks go to the two families of Paul Alin and Lucy Nguingi, and of Henry Lingisaqa and Marcella Tangil. I gratefully acknowledge funding from the Australian Research Council (2011–2014), the Endangered Languages Documentation Programme (2012–2013) and the Volkswagen Foundation's Lichtenberg program (2014–2022), as well as the support from the National Research Institute of Papua New Guinea.

Birgit Hellwig, University of Cologne/Germany, e-mail: bhellwig@uni-koeln.de

https://doi.org/10.1515/9783110726626-002

research, which is centrally concerned with language, and only marginally with culture. And on the other hand, child socialization research, which adopts cultural and social perspectives, not linguistic perspectives. While this division continues to dominate the field, there are approaches to bridge the gap. The most important and influential one dates back to the 1980s, when linguistic anthropologists Elinor Ochs, Bambi Schieffelin and colleagues developed the field of language socialization with its central tenet of "socialization through the use of language and socialization to use language" (Schieffelin and Ochs 1986: 163). Around the same time, Dan Slobin and colleagues, coming from linguistic and psycholinguistic backgrounds, promoted the cross-linguistic study of language acquisition (Slobin 1985–1997). Their own focus was on language, but they were amenable to including cultural perspectives, encouraging the "collection of comparable cross-linguistic and cross-cultural data on the acquisition of communicative competence" (Slobin et al. 1967: ix). For a while, converging interests across disciplines generated exciting synergy effects, and a large number of relevant studies emerged during the 1980s and 1990s.

Subsequently, research into language socialization slowed down, but is currently reviving again within the context of language documentation. The field of language documentation emerged in the 1990s in response to the endangerment of the world's languages and with the purpose of creating "a comprehensive record of the linguistic practices characteristic of a given speech community" (Himmelmann 1998: 166; see also Hale et al. 1992; see Bradley, this volume). Initially, language documentation focused exclusively on adult language, and only recently extended its scope to include child language. Over the past decade, a number of projects emerged in this context, striving to integrate perspectives from language documentation, anthropology and psycholinguistics. The framework for this interdisciplinary approach is currently the subject of an intense, and highly inspiring, debate. Much of the debate revolves around the multitude of methodological and ethical challenges that "often make it difficult to follow the best-practice approaches to data collection which are commonly assumed in lab-based FLA [First Language Acquisition] research" (Kelly et al. 2015: 287; see also Hellwig 2019, Kelly and Nordlinger 2014). But the more fundamental debate concerns the integration of the various perspectives and goals: given the difficulties of constructing language acquisition corpora under fieldwork conditions, such corpora should ideally serve multiple purposes and meet the needs of different research fields as well as those of the participating communities.

From a psycholinguistic perspective, the goal is to broaden the empirical database that underlies theories of learning: since languages and learning environments differ widely, a larger and more representative sample is needed in order to be able to understand how children learn language. Currently, however, acquisition data is available for at most 1–2% of the world's languages, with a heavy bias towards the major European languages and cultures (e.g., Kidd and Garcia 2022; Lieven and Stoll 2009). This psycholinguistic perspective constitutes an important impetus for cross-linguistic research into language learning, but it is not the only perspective. From an anthropological perspective, the goal continues to be an understanding of the interplay of language and culture in socialization. From a language documentation perspective, the goal is to create a record of all the linguistic practices of a community, including the linguistic practices that children engage in (Hellwig and Jung 2020). And from a community perspective, one important goal of language documentation (amongst others) is to understand processes of language learning and transmission in contexts of endangerment, with a view to supporting the maintenance and revitalization of a language (Child Language Research and Revitalization Working Group 2017).

The different perspectives come with different views on the relative importance of qualitative and quantitative approaches, impacting in turn on the types of data needed and the methods of data collection, but also on the role of culture. From its beginnings, language documentation has had a strong affinity to anthropology; see, e.g., Franchetto (2006) and Hill (2006) who both contributed anthropological perspectives to the standard reference work on language documentation. Both disciplines emphasize qualitative approaches and share a common interest in the relationship between language and culture, including in language ideologies and attitudes. Psycholinguistics and mainstream language acquisition research, on the other hand, emphasize quantitative approaches, with cultural factors being of interest in as far as they shape the learning environment (e.g., the type of input that children encounter). Ideally, these different perspectives are integrated, thereby allowing us "to disentangle properties of children's early language that are universal – hence, plausibly determined by the basic capacity for language acquisition – from properties that are shaped by the learning environment, and especially by exposure to a language with a specific structure" (Bowerman 2010: 594). The development of such an integrated approach is not a trivial matter, though, and it will continue to be a topic of debate for still some time.

Against this background, this chapter now turns to three central topics in the study of language acquisition and socialization: the learning environments of children and the types of interactions that children engage in (Section 2); ideologies of language development and their role in shaping interactions with children (Section 3); and properties of the input, such as child-directed language and language routines that scaffold language learning (Section 4). While language learning is a life-long process that continues well beyond childhood, the focus of this chapter is on early childhood. The aim is to give an overview of current discussions in the field and to illustrate the issues by means of a case study. The case study is on Qaqet, a Papuan language of the Baining family (Glottolog code: qaqe1238), which is spoken by around 15,000 people in East New Britain Province of Papua New Guinea. The data for this illustration originated in the context of an on-going language documentation project on the language used by and with children (Hellwig et al. 2014). The focus is on children aged 2 to 4 years, but the documentation also includes their younger and older siblings and cousins, thus covering a broader age range. The currently available data comes from the remote mountainous village of Raunsepna where children grow up with Qaqet as their dominant language. For now, the national lingua franca Tok Pisin only plays a minor role in this remote setting.

2 Learning environment

Language learning takes place in the interaction between children and their environment and interlocutors, whereby different socio-cultural environments and interlocutors provide children with different opportunities and challenges for learning. In this process, children are involved as active participants who contribute to the exchange, reproducing linguistic practices, but also shaping and modifying them. Throughout their day, they engage in various types of interaction, but one type of engagement has assumed special status within language acquisition research: the dyadic interaction between an adult carer (often the mother) and a child over an object (often a toy), whereby both maintain joint attention on the object, and the carer uses a special register labeled child-directed language. There is considerable research available that shows convincingly how this setting fosters language learning. Joint attention helps the child to develop an understanding of her interlocutor's intentions and to form associations between the language she hears and the surrounding context (e.g., Tomasello 1995, 1999; for cross-cultural perspectives, see e.g., Brown 2011, Callaghan et al. 2011). And child-directed language tends to be characterized by lexical and structural properties that are tied to the context and/or facilitate the segmentation of the speech stream: short utterances, few hesitations and errors, exaggerated prosody (large pitch ranges, high F0, long duration, more pauses), numerous repetitions and varied repetitions, a restricted vocabulary including nursery lexemes, reference to the present time and context, and many questions and imperatives (see Saint-Georges et al. 2013 for a review; see also the early standard volumes by Snow and Ferguson 1977 and Gallaway and Richards 1994).

As discussed below, such dyadic interactions with children over toys are un-common in many parts of the world. However, comparable settings often exist, as illustrated with the help of Example (1) from Qaqet. It is an extract from a re-cording of two children helping their mother prepare food. In Lines i–iv, the mother interacts with her older child (aged 3;2);[1] and in Lines v–xi, she enlists this child to draw the attention of her younger child (aged 1;11). The extract shows joint attention over an object (the greens), and it exhibits some of the typi-cal structural features of child-directed language: short utterances, repetitions, reference to the here and now, and questions and imperatives; exaggerated pros-ody is present, too, but not indicated in the transcript. This extract comes close to the setting described in much of the literature, albeit with two caveats: the in-teraction is not over a toy object, and more than one child is involved. In particu-lar, the last point is relevant for the Qaqet learning environment, as it is common for adults to address the oldest child present and/or to communicate through older children with younger children.

(1) Participants: Mother, YRA (3;2), YDS (1;11) (LongYDS20150506_1 1578.153 1597.746)

    i.   Mother to YRA: *nyilamakumuiara* 'see the greens here'
    ii.   YRA to mother: *ah? ah?* 'huh? huh?'
    iii.   Mother to YRA: *kumu* 'greens'
    iv.   YRA to mother: *lungria kumu?* 'these greens?'
    v.   Mother to YRA: *nyi, YDS, nyinyim sagelamakumuiara* '(say to her) you, YDS, look at the greens here'
    vi.   YRA to YDS: *nyinyim amakumuiara* 'look (at) the greens here'
    vii. YDS does not look at the greens
    viii. Mother to YDS: *oi, akumu, lungeriara* 'hey, the greens, these ones'
    ix.   YRA to YDS: *oi, akumuiara* 'hey, the greens here'
    x.   YDS to YRA: *da?* 'right?'
    xi.   YRA to YDS: *ee* 'yes'

Of course, children also participate in other types of interaction, but it is gener-ally assumed that directed interaction with its joint attentional focus consti-tutes a typical experience for them. Much of our research is thus predicated on data collected in such settings, including both naturalistic data (recorded in the child's home) and experimental data (where this setting is recreated in a lab

---

[1] Ages of children are given in the format YEAR;MONTH, e.g., 3;2 means an age of 3 years and 2 months.

environment). This focus has had the unfortunate side-effect of neglecting other types of interactions, a few notable exceptions notwithstanding, e.g., an early contribution beautifully entitled "the rest of the family: the role of fathers and siblings in early language development" (Barton and Tomasello 1994). To be clear, variability in the input was and is researched, especially in relation to socio-economic factors, showing that socio-economic status (SES) impacts on how parents communicate with their children. But the focus is on the amount and quality of directed interaction and its concomitant consequences for children's development – it is not on the availability of other types of interaction. Anthropological studies, by contrast, have early on highlighted the extent of diversity across the world, casting doubt on the universal predominance of directed interaction (see Lieven 1994 for a summary of early literature). These studies often used interview and observational techniques, which made it difficult to appraise the amount of time a child spends in different types of interaction and the kinds of language she is exposed to. As a result, even though these anthropological reports were registered within language acquisition research, their relevance for language learning was underestimated for a long time.

In more recent times, we observe a re-orientation of the field, and a growing body of research investigates more closely the types of input that children receive in different communities, both qualitatively and quantitatively. There is considerable variation, both across communities and across children of different ages, but a recurring pattern is emerging: the important role of multiparty interaction within a mixed group of interlocutors or within a group of peers of different ages, where children overhear language that is not directed at them and that is produced by a variety of adult and child interlocutors (see, e.g., Casillas, Brown and Levinson 2020a for Tseltal Mayan, Casillas, Brown and Levinson 2020b for Yélî Dnye, Cristia et al. 2019 for Tsimane; Shneidman and Goldin-Meadow 2012 for Yucatec Mayan, Mastin and Vogt 2016 and Vogt, Mastin and Schots 2015 for Changana). This line of research has been considerably aided by the development of devices such as LENA that facilitate day-long recordings, providing automatized speaker identification and word counts (Casillas and Cristia 2019).

Example (2) illustrates a multiparty interaction from Qaqet. It features three adults and three children sitting together over a meal. Most of the hour-long recording consists of the adults talking amongst themselves. The children sometimes listen in, sometimes interact amongst themselves, and sometimes interact with the adults. The extract in (2) comes from a longer discussion about an incident where someone bought a chicken, and opinions in the community are divided as to whether or not he should have been given it as a present. The discussion is fairly animated, and the two older children initially paid attention, but then started playing with their baby brother. When their brother falls down, the oldest child tries very hard to gain the adults' attention (Lines ii, iii and vii), albeit unsuccessfully.

(2)   Participants: Mother, Father, Uncle, ZJS (4;6), YJL (2;11), ZDL (0;10) (Long-YJL20141127_1 1954.234 1984.371)
  i.   Father: 'they will have to find money for a chicken, a small chicken'
  ii.   ZJS tries to scare away his baby brother ZDL, who falls down
  iii.   ZJS to uncle: 'look over there, at the baby's head' [tugs at uncle, points at ZDL]
  iv.   Father: 'like this'
  v.   Uncle: 'the chickens used to be here'
  vi.   Mother: 'those ones there'
  vii.   ZJS to uncle: 'uncle, he fell down' [turns into uncle's field of vision]
  viii. Father: 'is that our custom, or what?'
  ix.   Uncle: 'it isn't'
  x.   Father: 'it's really not our custom'
  xi.   Uncle: 'the custom won't kill you, last time I simply gave away a chicken (as a present)'

And Example (3) is an illustration of peer interaction. In this extract, two children narrate an event in the past (when they saw a chainsaw) and challenge each other's accounts. The younger child (aged 2;11) hears fairly complex narrative structures from her older brother (aged 4;7). The extract shows that the younger child not only understands these structures, but is also capable of producing a complex narrative herself.

(3)   Participants: ZJS (4;7), YJL (2;11) (LongYJL20141210_1 1630.280 1670.782)
  i.   YJL: *kua medu luqia, nyitluqiamuk, pemaqavel? pemaqavel?*
              'that one [the chainsaw] in the past, you saw it over there, in the bush? in the bush?'
  ii.   ZJS: *ee, i.. imu.. murl nguamit ngunemapupu, dema S., dema N., duretluqi*
              'yes, in.. in.. in the past I went together with grandmother, and with S., and with N., and we were seeing it'
  iii.   YJL: *dap ngua?* 'what about me?'
  iv.   ZJS: *dap ngua de saksakmetngua ingutlama.. amasensoqi, de saksakmetngua ingutlamasensoqi*
              'and I was surprised to see the.. the chainsaw, and I was surprised to see the chainsaw'

v. YJL: *murl, nguatiramanu deip ngua dungutluqi, lu amanep, pemahausik*
'in the past, I went over there and then I saw it, down there, at the hospital'

vi. ZJS: *hoi, nyi de quas nyitluqi* 'hey, you didn't see it'

vii. YJL: *deqerl* 'I did'

viii. ZJS: *oi, nyi de quas nyikak* 'hey, don't lie'

ix. YJL: *medu qurlinguaamek, medu qurlinguaamek*
'in the past I stayed down there, in the past I stayed down there'

x. ZJS: *gel nema?* 'with who?'

xi. YJL: *medu qurlinguaira, medu qurlinguaira*
'in the past I stayed here, in the past I stayed here'

xii. ZJS: *denyitluqi?* 'and you saw it?'

xiii. YJL: *ee* 'yes'

The three settings illustrated above feature very different kinds of interaction and language. Research has advanced to the point where we can be certain that the settings illustrated in (2) and (3) constitute a significant part of children's day-to-day interaction in many parts of the world, and are probably more common than the setting illustrated in (1). But there remain two important desiderata for future research.

First, to map out the extent of the variation. We know that children from different communities participate to varying degrees in different types of interaction, and while dyadic directed interaction is very common in some communities, it is much rarer in others. There are proposals for typologizing communities along this dimension, linking the observed differences to cultural ideologies, expectations and lifestyle. This topic is taken up in Section 3.

And second, to understand the impact of the different settings on language learning. The available research presents us with puzzling findings. Mastin and Vogt (2016) show for rural Changana children that joint attention on objects is often silent, and they report a negative correlation with vocabulary learning: the more time children spend in this type of setting, the smaller their vocabulary size. I.e., joint attention does not always seem to facilitate language learning. Conversely, Shneidman and Woodward (2016) discuss studies that suggest that children who experience little directed interaction are better at learning from observation than children who experience much directed interaction. I.e., children seem to be able to learn language from observation. Both kinds of findings are unexpected and their interpretation is not straightforward – largely because only little data is available and research has only just begun. Given that children everywhere learn language without any obvious signs of delays in their language development, it is clear that we need to intensify our research efforts into how learning takes place in these different settings. See also Section 4 for further discussion.

Answers to the above questions will not only impact on our theories of learning, but also carry over into applied contexts. As pointed out by the Child Language Research and Revitalization Working Group (2017), a better understanding of the contexts of language learning and transmission will be able to inform community-based efforts to maintain and preserve their languages.

3 Ideologies of language development

Different groups entertain different ideas of children's development and the requirements of child-rearing. An important goal of anthropological research is thus to identify shared cultural beliefs that shape individual attitudes and impact on the ways interlocutors interact with children (e.g., Gaskins 2006, Harkness and Super 1996, Lieven 1994, Lieven and Stoll 2009, Ochs and Schieffelin 1984; see also Kroskrity, this volume, on language ideologies). Of particular interest are views on children as conversational partners and on the role and responsibilities of carers for language acquisition. In some cultures, babies are seen as conversational partners long before they produce or understand language. However, as shown by numerous anthropological studies, this view is not universal. Some cultures only recognize children as conversational partners once they start talking themselves (e.g., among the Kaluli in Papua New Guinea; see Schieffelin 1990), or believe that children cannot be taught and have to learn language independently for themselves (e.g., among the rural African-American Trackton community; see Heath 1983). It should be noted, though, that such ideologies do not mean that children are ignored. For example, while Kaluli adults only rarely address a pre-verbal child, they frequently talk about her in her presence. Furthermore, children participate in various interactional routines in all socio-cultural contexts (see Section 4).

For Qaqet, Frye (2019: 23–65) has conducted a detailed study of ideologies, identifying the following set of beliefs surrounding children's development. Young children, including babies, are seen as conversational partners, and talking to them is considered crucial for their language development. It is the parents' responsibility to teach them language, but the important role of siblings is recognized as well. People are generally aware that at least some interlocutors adapt their language when talking to children, although many are worried that this kind of language will cause children to acquire incorrect Qaqet. At the same time, the independence of children is recognized and highly valued: children are seen as their own agents, learning at their own pace, but with an intrinsic motivation to learn. It is assumed that they learn through participation in the interactions and activities surrounding them, not so much through explicit instruction. Adults and older siblings assume the role of guides in this process; this also includes correcting inappropriate language or behavior.

Different ideologies are hypothesized to promote different kinds of interaction with the child, and while some are assumed to foster dyadic child-directed interaction from an early age on, others are said to encourage types of interactions that are not centered on the child, in particular multiparty and peer interaction (see Section 2). The relationship between ideology and interactional practice has been most extensively studied for various Mayan communities of Mexico and Guatemala. For example, Casillas, Brown and Levinson (2020a) found that Tseltal Mayan children hear only 3.6 minutes of child-directed language per hour on average – much less than, e.g., US American middle-class children (see also the overview in Shneidman and Woodward 2016). Such a result is in line with expectations, given the non-child-centered ideology of many Mayan communities. However, a follow-up study by Casillas, Brown and Levinson (2020b) on Rossel Island (Papua New Guinea) shows similar results (3.13 minutes per hour), despite a predominantly child-centered ideology. They conclude that the actual language input is shaped more by the similar lifestyle of Tseltal Mayan and Rossel Island communities (i.e., subsistence economy, multiple generation households) than by their very different ideologies about children's development and child-rearing. There exists only little research, though, and more studies are needed on the extent to which ideologies are reflected in the interactional patterns adopted with children.[2]

The possible links between ideology and practice are debated in the literature. An early proposal from language socialization recognizes two ideal types of orientation towards the child: "adapting situations to the child and adapting the child to situations" (Ochs and Schieffelin 1984: 304). In the first type, the communication is assumed to be structured so as to adapt to the needs of the child, revolving around a preference for dyadic interaction and child-directed language. In the second type, it is assumed that children are being socialized to act appropriately in a given situation, with communication revolving around multiparty interaction and the modelling of utterances for the child to repeat. Another proposal from cross-cultural psychology identifies three types, which are based on

---

2 For Qaqet, a comparable study is still pending, but initial findings suggest a similar pattern to that on Rossel Island: while there are clear elements of a child-centered ideology, children tend to participate more frequently in multiparty and peer interactions than in child-directed interactions.

differences in lifestyle and corresponding cultural expectations (Keller 2012): urban industrial (fostering the development of cognitive skills, expecting children to successfully participate in school), rural non-industrial (fostering the development of communal responsibilities, expecting children to successfully participate in a subsistence-based lifestyle) and urban non-industrial (a mix of the other two). Again, the different expectations are assumed to be reflected in the structure of communication, with dyadic directed interaction being prevalent in the urban industrial type, and multiparty non-directed interaction, in the rural non-industrial type. Under all approaches, it is clear that the identified types constitute ideal types, and that there is considerable variation – with a corresponding need to document and describe the variation that exists within and across communities.

A further research focus is on cultural notions about what children need to learn. Throughout the anthropological literature, a recurring topic is the need for children to learn about their place in the social network (see also Fleming, this volume, on social indexicality). This includes not only learning about kinship relations, but also about the places connected with relatives and neighbors, as illustrated in Example (4) for Qaqet. It is taken from a recording where two children play a game listing various place names. They are overheard by their mother who intervenes at some point and prompts them for further place names, sometimes providing the name (Line iii), and sometimes encouraging the children to provide the name by linking the place to persons (Lines v and viii) or other places (Line x) known to the children. This preoccupation with places is also reflected in a noticeably large number of 'where' questions used with and by children. Many studies remark on similar patterns, noting the importance of interactions about kinship relations and social spaces, as well as a prevalence of 'where' questions.

(4) Participants: Mother, ZJS (5;0), YJL (3;4) (LongYJL20150516_1 305.650 346.415)
    i.   Mother: *de nema?* 'and what else?'
    ii.   ZJS: *kuas nguadrlem* 'I don't know'
    iii. Mother: *Kedel* 'Kedel'
    [. . .]
    iv. ZJS: *de nema? kuasik nguadrlem, mama, nyiris*
               'and what else? I don't know, mama, say it'
    v.   Mother: *dap kui ma.. D., de qurliqi qua?*
               'what about.. D., where does she stay?'
    vi. ZJS: *D.? kuasik, de quas nguadrlem, Madreh?*
               'D.? no, I don't know, is it Madres?'

vi. Mother: *Ladrit* 'Ladrit'

[. . .]

vii. Mother: *dap ma S., de qurliqa qua?* 'what about S., where does he stay?'

ix. ZJS: *kuas nguadrlem* 'I don't know'

x. Mother: *amakainaqiamit nemgi?* 'which water is over there?

xi. ZJS: *Bilangarl, ulungeravit, ma Bilangarl?*
'Bilangarl? is it up there, Bilangarl?'

xii. Mother: *mh* 'yes'

Learning about their place in the social network also includes learning about the behavior expected of them. A central expectation of Qaqet children of all ages, for example, is to run errands and convey messages or small items (Frye 2019: 34–39). Older children are sent over longer distances to other households, while younger children fetch items from within the vicinity. Even babies participate in this task: adults give them small items to hold, often betelnuts, and orient them bodily towards the recipient who takes the item and thanks the baby, using the interjection *ta* 'thank you' (borrowed from Australian English, presumably via Tok Pisin), with a marked rising pitch contour. Example (5) illustrates the joint efforts of a mother and her older daughter (aged 3;6) to socialize her younger son (aged 1;5) into this role. The mother asks her son to get her a blanket (Lines i and iii), but he does not carry out the request. She then turns to his elder sister (Line v) who gets the blanket. Following that, the boy thanks his sister (Line vii), thus demonstrating some awareness of the expectations and the appropriate verbal behavior. At the same time, the mother turns to her son – not her daughter – and thanks him (Line viii), thereby conveying that he was the intended addressee all along. This kind of triadic interaction is very common among the Qaqet, with older siblings acting on behalf of younger siblings, modelling the appropriate behavior and/or language for them. Other behaviors expected of Qaqet children include, e.g., learning to share food, or older children learning to accommodate to the needs and wishes of younger children. Again, studies remark on similar expectations in different communities around the world.

(5) Participants: Mother, YJL (3;6), ZDL (1;5) (LongYJL20150701_1 1217.050 1229.910)

i. Mother to ZDL: *nyiramablankerem* 'get the blanket'

ii. ZDL looks up, but does not get the blanket

iii. Mother to ZDL: *nyiramablankerem inamuk* 'get the blanket from over there'
iv. ZDL looks up, but does not get the blanket
v. Mother to YJL: *de nyiramablankerem inavuk* 'get the blanket from up there'
vi. YJL gets the blanket
vii. ZDL to YJL: *ta* 'thank you'
viii. Mother to ZDL: *ta* 'thank you'

A different type of activity is the interaction over objects, where interlocutors label objects for the child and/or elicit labels from the child. For example, the Qaqet mother in (6) asks her younger daughter for an object label (Line i). The daughter is still busy attending to a previous conversation, and her older brother supplies the label instead (Line iii), with the daughter asking for confirmation (Line iv). The mother then makes another attempt (Line v), and this time succeeds in eliciting the label from her daughter (Line vi) and confirms the correctness of the label (Line vii).

(6) Participants: Mother, YRA (3;2), YDS (1;11) (LongYDS20150506_1 512.839 519.777)
   i. Mother to YDS: *dap magiqi mara?* 'what is this here?'
   ii. YDS attends to a previous conversation
   iii. YRA to YDS: *atulki* 'salt'
   iv. YDS to Mother: *da?* 'right?'
   v. Mother to YDS: *nyaris* 'say it'
   vi. YDS to Mother: *atulki* 'salt'
   vii. Mother to YDS: *ee* 'yes'

Again, we observe that the relative importance of these activities differs across cultures. In particular, activities that center on object labeling (as in 6) tend to be common in North American and European environments, while activities that center on learning about social roles (as in 4) and responsibilities (as in 5) tend to play a more important role in other parts of the world. For example, Vogt, Mastin and Schots (2015) find that adults use a larger proportion of utterances with a cognitive intention (such as labeling or eliciting object names) in a Dutch environment than in a Mozambican environment. Conversely, rural Mozambican children hear proportionally more utterances directing them to perform their responsibilities, while urban Mozambican children hear more utterances on social roles. But yet again, there is a need for more such studies to understand the extent of variation within and across communities.

4 Properties of the input

Children encounter different kinds of language during the different interactions and activities they participate in, and a major task of language acquisition research is to investigate the structures that appear in the input. This investigation is important from two perspectives. First, it is central to studying the acquisition of any given phenomenon, because factors such as the frequency and the saliency of a phenomenon in the input impact on its acquisition. A famous example comes from the late acquisition of the ergative in Samoan. Ochs (1985: 826–832) identifies a number of structural properties that complicate its acquisition (e.g., the ergative marker is not obligatory and it is prosodically not salient), but mainly attributes its late acquisition to the social norms of its use: it is common in formal contexts, but rare in informal conversations within the family. I.e., children not only encounter very few ergatives in their input, but they also have little reason to use the ergative themselves. Given the crucial importance of the input, language acquisition studies thus always strive to investigate the distribution of a phenomenon in the input.

And second, such an investigation is central to identifying those properties of the input that facilitate language learning and that can give insights into how children learn language. As outlined in Section 2, this line of research has focused on child-directed language, both on identifying its characteristic properties and on investigating their impact on learning. Specifically, the typical prosodic features of child-directed language are known to facilitate the segmentation of speech and the identification of boundaries; the reference to the here and now facilitates the learning of word meaning; and the use of repetitions and varied repetitions facilitates the acquisition of morphosyntax. Evidence for their facilitating effect comes from a variety of sources (see Saint-Georges et al. 2013 for a systematic review). This includes studies of naturalistic data that examine how the use of a property in child-directed language relates to, or predicts, children's lexical or syntactic development (e.g., Waterfall 2006 on repetition and variation), as well as experimental studies on artificial language learning (e.g., Onnis, Waterfall and Edelman 2008 on repetition and variation). While these properties are known to facilitate acquisition, it is important to stress that they are not consciously employed to teach language, but emerge as a by-product in the interaction with young children, i.e., with immature interlocutors. As Ervin-Tripp (1980: 394) phrases it, "[i]t now appears that many of the structural peculiarities of baby talk [child-directed language] are a result of the different interactional goals of adults interacting with children." See also Ferguson (1977) on clarifying processes in communicative interaction with children, or Saxton (2009: 80) who argues that "it is difficult to imagine how communication could be at all successful without resorting to at least some of the characteristic features of Child Directed Speech."

While the facilitating role of the properties of child-directed language is thus well researched, we still know little about the universality of this register. There are studies on languages that lack a child-directed speech register altogether (e.g., Kaluli; see Schieffelin 1990), or that exhibit different structural properties (e.g., a normal-to-faster speech rate and a low F0 in K'iche' Mayan; see Pye 1986). But there are also studies of languages whose child-directed language register shares many of the properties identified in the literature (e.g., Qaqet; see Frye 2019; see also the discussion of Example 1 in Section 2). In particular, the prevalence of repetitions and varied repetitions seems to be a very common phenomenon across the world's languages (see also Slobin et al. 2010). As more such studies emerge, we will get a better understanding of the extent of variation with regard to the presence/absence of the register, its characteristic features, and the contexts of its use (i.e., who uses it to children of which ages and in which contexts).

In any case, the investigation of child-directed language is only part of a more comprehensive investigation into the kinds of language that children encounter. Anthropological studies were the first to show the existence of interactional routines that very likely provide children with learning opportunities equivalent to those offered by child-directed language. The most famous such routine is the *a:la:ma* (also known as *elema*) 'say like that' routine among the Kaluli (Schieffelin 1990), which was subsequently reported to exist in other languages as well (see, e.g., Rumsey 2015 for the Papuan language Ku Waru, or Watson-Gegeo and Gegeo 1986 for the Oceanic language Kwara'ae). It is a prompting routine that models an utterance for the child and requests the child to repeat the prompt. As such, it socializes children into using the appropriate response in a given context. Example (7) illustrates this routine among the Qaqet. The mother prompts her younger child to use the tag question *da?* 'right' (Lines i and iii), and enlists the help of her older child (Lines v and vii), who enthusiastically joins in with her efforts to prompt the younger child (Lines iv, vi and viii).

(7)   Participants: Mother, YRA (3;2), YDS (2;0) (LongYDS20150516_2 70.807 82. 372)
    i.   Mother to YDS: *ma: "da?"* 'like this: "right?"'
    ii. Mother to YDS: *ee* 'yes'
    iii. Mother to YDS: *nyitaqen ma: "da?"* 'say it like this: "right?"'

    iv. YRA to YDS: *da!* 'right!'
    v.   Mother to YRA: *nyiruqun ma YDS ikitaqen* 'tell YDS to say it'
    vi. YRA to YDS: *nyitan* 'say it'
    vii. Mother to YRA: *[. . .] nyiruqun naqip kitaqen ma: "da"?*
                      '[. . .] tell her to say it like this: "right?"'
    viii. YRA to YDS: *da!* 'right!'

The mother and older child use the prompting routine in (7) to model yet another typical routine among the Qaqet, the tag-question routine. The tag-question routine constitutes one of the earliest and most frequent utterances among Qaqet children. As hypothesized by Frye (2019: 140–141), children use it to signal their attention and participation in a conversation (see 1x and 6iv for examples of this function). It also constitutes an important context for word learning, as illustrated in (8). Here, the older child introduces a presumably new word, *qulavaska* 'a kind of taro' (Line i), and the younger sister first responds with the tag-question routine (Line ii), and then turns to her mother and attempts more or less successfully to pronounce the new word (Lines iv–viii).

(8)   Participants: Mother, YRA (3;9), YDS (2;6) (LongYDS20151204_1 483.705 495. 365)
    i.   YRA to YDS: *giavaqaira amala.. amaqulaviska* 'your.. *qulavas* taro here'
    ii.   YDS to YRA: *da?* 'right?'
    iii. YRA to YDS: *ee* 'yes'
    iv. YDS to mother: *aqulaquis ka*
    v.   *avu.. avullai ka*
    vi.   *aquista*
    vii.   *avulaquistka*
    viii.   *alu qavas*
        [target: *aqulavaska* '*qulavas* taro']

Examples (7) and (8) illustrate but two of the language routines used among the Qaqet. Further routines and discourse practices include the teasing of children for their errors, as well as taking the perspective of the child and speaking for the child by imitating the perceived properties of child language. Similar routines are attested across different languages, and while their functions and properties differ from those of child-directed language, they are probably nevertheless effective for language learning. Currently, our research is at a stage where we know of the existence of a number of recurring routines, but it is very likely that the study of further languages will unearth additional relevant routines. Furthermore, the effect of these routines on language learning remains to be investigated: intuitively, it is very likely that they are at least equivalent to the properties of child-directed language, but to my knowledge, the necessary research is still pending.

5 Conclusion

This chapter has outlined three salient lines of investigation in language acquisition and socialization: investigations into the learning environment of the child (Section 2), the ideologies of language development (Section 3) and the properties of the input (Section 4). Mainstream acquisition research has adopted a focus on a child-centered ideology, with a prevalence for dyadic child-directed interactions over objects as well as child-directed language. Conversely, the anthropological literature has early on highlighted the importance of ideologies not centered on the child, with a prevalence for multiparty and peer interaction as well as language routines that do not necessarily have their basis in child-directed language. Research undertaken since the 1980s has identified considerable diversity across the world's languages and cultures, but there is room for many more such studies – with the goal of more comprehensively mapping out the existing variation.

Beyond this descriptive focus, the challenge is to investigate the impact of the diverse contexts on learning. Since children everywhere learn their communities' language(s), it is clear that learning must be possible across all these contexts. However, while the facilitating role of child-directed interaction and language is well understood, research into the effects of other contexts on learning has only just begun.

The aim of this contribution was to give an overview of the above lines of investigation, indicating both the main research questions as well as desiderata for future research. Much of current research is situated at the intersection of three disciplines (psycholinguistics, anthropology, language documentation), and strives to include community perspectives. Within this context, the cross-linguistic and cross-cultural investigation of language acquisition has received a new impetus, and research has intensified over the past 10 years or so. The expansion of the field promises new insights into the diversity of acquisition and socialization processes around the world, with a view towards developing a more adequate understanding of how children learn language in the diverse socio-cultural environments they grow up in.

References

Barton, Michelle E. & Michael Tomasello. 1994. The rest of the family. The role of fathers and siblings in early language development. In Clare Gallaway & Brian J. Richards (eds.), *Input and interaction in language acquisition*, 109–134. Cambridge: Cambridge University Press.

Bowerman, Melissa. 2010. Linguistic typology and first language acquisition. In Jae Jung Song (ed.), *The Oxford handbook of linguistic typology*, 591–617. Oxford: Oxford University Press.

Brown, Penelope. 2011. The cultural organization of attention. In Alessandro Duranti, Elinor Ochs & Bambi B. Schieffelin (eds.), *Handbook of language socialization*, 29–55. Oxford: Blackwell.

Brown, Penelope & Suzanne Gaskins. 2014. Language acquisition and language socialization. In N. J. Enfield, Paul Kockelman & Jack Sidnell (eds.), *The Cambridge handbook of linguistic anthropology*, 187–226. Cambridge: Cambridge University Press.

Callaghan, Tara, Henrike Moll, Hannes Rakoczy, Felix Warneken, Ulf Liszkowski, Tanya Behne & Michael Tomasello. 2011. Early social cognition in three cultural contexts. *Monographs of the Society for Research in Child Development* 76 (2). 1–142.

Casillas, Marisa, Penelope Brown & Stephen C. Levinson. 2020a. Early language experience in a Tseltal Mayan village. *Child Development* 91 (5). 1819–1835.

Casillas, Marisa, Penelope Brown & Stephen C. Levinson. 2020b. Early language experience in a Papuan community. *Journal of Child Language* 48 (4). 1–23.

Casillas, Marisa & Alejandrina Cristia. 2019. A step-by-step guide to collecting and analyzing long-format speech environment (LFSE) recordings. *Collabra: Psychology* 5 (1). 24.

Child Language Research and Revitalization Working Group. 2017. *Language documentation, revitalization, and reclamation. Supporting young learners and their communities.* Waltham, MA: EDC.

Cristia, Alejandrina, Emmanuel Dupoux, Michael Gurven & Jonathan Stieglitz. 2019. Child-directed speech is infrequent in a forager-farmer population. A time allocation study. *Child Development* 90 (3). 759–773.

Ervin-Tripp, Susan M. 1980. Speech acts, social meaning and social learning. In Howard Giles (ed.), *Language: Social psychological perspectives*, 389–396. Oxford and New York: Pergamon Press.

Ferguson, Charles A. 1977. Baby talk as a simplified register. In Catherine E. Snow & Charles A. Ferguson (eds.), *Talking to children. Language input and acquisition*, 209–235. Cambridge: Cambridge University Press.

Franchetto, Bruna. 2006. Ethnography in language documentation. In Jost Gippert, Nikolaus P. Himmelmann & Ulrike Mosel (eds.), *Essentials of language documentation*, 183–211. Berlin: De Gruyter Mouton.

Frye, Henrike. 2019. *Child-directed speech in Qaqet. A Baining language of East New Britain, Papua New Guinea.* Cologne: University of Cologne dissertation.

Gallaway, Clare & Brian J. Richards (eds.). 1994. *Input and interaction in language acquisition.* Cambridge: Cambridge University Press.

Gaskins, Suzanne. 2006. Cultural perspectives on infant–caregiver interaction. In N. J. Enfield & Stephen C. Levinson (eds.), *Roots of human sociality. Culture, cognition and interaction*, 279–298. Oxford: Berg.

Harkness, Sara & Charles M. Super. 1996. *Parents' cultural belief systems. Their origins, expressions, and consequence.* New York: Guilford Press.

Hale, Ken, Michael Krauss, Lucille J. Watahomigie, Akira Y. Yamamoto, Colette Craig, LaVerne Masayesva Jeanne & Nora C. England. 1992. Endangered languages. *Language* 68 (1). 1–42.

Heath, Shirley B. 1983. *Ways with words. Language, life, and work in communities and classrooms.* Cambridge: Cambridge University Press.

Hellwig, Birgit. 2019. Linguistic diversity, language documentation and psycholinguistics. The role of stimuli. *Language Documentation and Conservation* SP 16. 5–30.

Hellwig, Birgit, Carmen Dawuda, Henrike Frye & Steffen Reetz. 2014. *Qaqet child language corpus 2014–2022.* Language Archive Cologne.

Hellwig, Birgit & Dagmar Jung. 2020. Child-directed language – and how it informs the documentation and description of the adult language. *Language Documentation and Conservation* 14. 188–214.

Hill, Jane H. 2006. The ethnography of language and language documentation. In Jost Gippert, Nikolaus P. Himmelmann & Ulrike Mosel (eds.), *Essentials of language documentation*, 113–128. Berlin: De Gruyter Mouton.

Himmelmann, Nikolaus P. 1998. Documentary and descriptive linguistics. *Linguistics* 36 (1). 161–195.

Keller, Heidi. 2012. Autonomy and relatedness revisited. Cultural manifestations of universal human needs. *Child Development Perspectives* 6. 12–18.

Kelly, Barbara, William Forshaw, Rachel Nordlinger & Gillian Wiggelsworth. 2015. Linguistic diversity in first language acquisition research. Moving beyond the challenges. *First Language* 35 (4–5). 286–304.

Kelly, Barbara & Rachel Nordlinger. 2014. Fieldwork and first language acquisition. In Lauren Gawne & Jill Vaughan (eds.), *Selected papers from the 44th Conference of the Australian Linguistic Society*, 2013, 178–192.

Kidd, Evan & Rowena Garcia. 2022. How diverse is child language acquisition research? *First Language.* Advance online publication.

Lieven, Elena V. 1994. Crosslinguistic and crosscultural aspects of language addressed to children. In Clare Gallaway & Brian J. Richards (eds.), *Input and interaction in language acquisition*, 56–73. Cambridge: Cambridge University Press.

Lieven, Elena V. & Sabine Stoll. 2009. Language. In Marc H. Bornstein (ed.), *The handbook of cross-cultural developmental science*, 543–555. Mahwah, NJ: Erlbaum.

Mastin, J. Douglas & Paul Vogt. 2016. Infant engagement and early vocabulary development. A naturalistic observation study of Mozambican infants from 1;1 to 2;1. *Journal of Child Language* 43 (2). 235–264.

Ochs, Elinor. 1985. Variation and error. A sociolinguistic approach to language acquisition in Samoa. In Dan I. Slobin (ed.), *The crosslinguistic study of language acquisition*, Vol. 1, 783–838. Mahwah, NJ: Erlbaum.

Ochs, Elinor & Bambi B. Schieffelin. 1984. Language acquisition and socialization. Three developmental stories and their implications. In Richard A. Shweder & Robert A. Levine (eds.), *Culture theory. Essays on mind, self and emotion*, 276–319. Cambridge: Cambridge University Press.

Onnis, Luca, Heidi R. Waterfall & Shimon Edelman. 2008. Learn locally, act globally. Learning language from variation set cues. *Cognition* 109 (3). 423–430.

Pye, Clifton. 1986. Quiché Mayan speech to children. *Journal of Child Language* 13 (1). 85–100.

Rumsey, Alan. 2015. Language, affect and the inculcation of social norms in the New Guinea Highlands and beyond. *The Australian Journal of Anthropology* 26. 349–364.

Saint-Georges, Catherine, Mohamed Chetouani, Raquel Cassel, Fabio Apicella, Ammar Mahdhaoui, Filippo Muratori, Marie-Christine Laznik & David Cohen. 2013. Motherese in interaction. At the cross-road of emotion and cognition? (A systematic review). *PLoS ONE* 8 (10). e78103.

San Roque, Lila & Bambi B. Schieffelin. Forthcoming. Language socialisation in the Papuan context. In Nicholas Evans & Sebastian Fedden (eds.), *The Oxford guide to the Papuan languages*. Oxford: Oxford University Press.

Saxton, Matthew. 2009. The inevitability of child directed speech. In Susan Foster-Cohen (ed.), *Language acquisition*, 62–86. Basingstoke: Palgrave Macmillan.

Schieffelin, Bambi B. 1990. *The give and take of everyday life. Language socialization of Kaluli children*. New York: Cambridge University Press.

Schieffelin, Bambi B. & Elinor Ochs. 1986. Language socialization. *Annual Review of Anthropology* 15. 163–191.

Shneidman, Laura A. & Susan J. Goldin-Meadow. 2012. Language input and acquisition in a Mayan village. How important is directed speech? *Developmental Science* 15 (5). 659–673.

Shneidman, Laura & Amanda L. Woodward. 2016. Are child-directed interactions the cradle of social learning? *Psychological Bulletin* 142 (1). 1–17.

Slobin, Dan I. (ed.). 1985–1997. *The crosslinguistic study of language acquisition*, Vol. 1–5. Mahwah, NJ: Erlbaum.

Slobin, Dan I., Melissa Bowerman, Penelope Brown, Sonja Eisenbeiß & Bhuvana Narasimhan. 2010. Putting things in places. Developmental consequences of linguistic typology. In Jürgen Bohnemeyer & Eric Pederson (eds.), *Event representation in language and cognition*, 134–165. New York: Cambridge University Press.

Slobin, Dan I., Susan M. Ervin-Tripp, John J. Gumperz, Jan Brukman, Keith Kernan, Claudia Mitchell & Brian Stross. 1967. *A field manual for cross-cultural study of the acquisition of communicative competence*, second draft. Berkeley: University of Berkeley.

Snow, Catherine E. & Charles A. Ferguson (eds.). 1977. *Talking to children. Language input and acquisition*. Cambridge: Cambridge University Press.

Tomasello, Michael. 1995. Joint attention as social learning. In Chris Moore & Philip J. Dunham (eds.), *Joint attention. Its origins and role in development*, 103–130. Hillsdale, NJ: Erlbaum.

Tomasello, Michael. 1999. *The cultural origins of human cognition*. Cambridge, MA: Harvard University Press.

Vogt, Paul, J. Douglas Mastin & Diede M. A. Schots. 2015. Communicative intentions of child-directed speech in three different learning environments. Observations from the Netherlands, and rural and urban Mozambique. *First Language* 35. 341–358.

Watson-Gegeo, Karen A. & David Gegeo 1986. Calling out and repeating routines in Kwara'ae children's language socialization. In Bambi B. Schieffelin & Elinor Ochs (eds.), *Language socialization across cultures*, 17 –50. Cambridge: Cambridge University Press.

Waterfall, Heidi R. 2006. *A little change is a good thing. Feature theory, language acquisition and variation sets*. Chicago: University of Chicago dissertation.

David Bradley

3 Language endangerment and reclamation

One of the key issues confronting scholars in linguistics and anthropology this century is the loss of a large part of humanity's linguistic heritage. It is thus essential both to understand what is driving this process, and to make the maximum effective effort to resist the loss of traditional linguistic and cultural diversity. This chapter sets out some of the main causes and outlines various possible strategies for maintaining or reclaiming languages which are losing their vitality. The range of situations is highly diverse, and each community may wish to respond in different ways.

1 Introduction

Language endangerment is a critical issue for human societies and for our disciplines. Predictions differ, but it has been suggested that up to 90 per cent of the world's currently spoken languages may cease to be spoken this century, if nothing is done to reverse the current trends in language shift (Krauss 1992). Fortunately, since that estimate, some progress is being made, and more is possible. This loss of linguistic and cultural diversity would be a major tragedy likely to lead to weakening of group identity, negative attitudes both within and outside many communities, loss of crucial ecological and other knowledge and major gaps in our understanding of the full range of human linguistic and cultural diversity. This is very serious: the proportion of endangered languages is much higher than the proportion of endangered species, and language is a key component of and means to express the diversity of our humanity.

Over many years, linguists doing research in and with communities have developed strategies to reclaim their languages, strengthening and expanding the use of these languages. These include the language nest model, the master and apprentice model, the cultural immersion model, a variety of models for use in educational settings such as the two ways model, and so on. Linguists and anthropologists often assist communities to develop and disseminate writing systems, to produce relevant materials, to train, motivate and support ingroup language workers and to help to maintain positive community attitudes. However, it is essential that the community be in control of such activities.

David Bradley, La Trobe University, Melbourne/Australia, e-mail: D.Bradley@latrobe.edu.au

https://doi.org/10.1515/9783110726626-003

Language reclamation is a complex process; the appropriate strategies and methods differ greatly depending on the degree of endangerment which the language has reached. We have developed a model which recognizes the many factors involved in endangerment and the various different stages of endangerment which require different approaches. In North America over the last ten years, most scholars have come to use the overall term reclamation for these approaches, as the more widely-used general term revitalization suggests that the process and methods are unitary, that the target languages do not currently have full vitality and that the goal is to bring every language back to some putative earlier conservative state, all of which are often not the case. The alternative term maintenance suggests entirely conservative goals, with no innovations. Revitalization or maintenance in these senses is not always appropriate or possible. Not all communities actually want to aim for this, and unclear or unrealistic goals may lead to failure, which can be worse than doing nothing. It is essential to recognize local needs and desires, work within local capabilities and use a resilience thinking approach, accepting realistic and achievable goals and work in stages toward reclaiming language use.

The chapter presents a number of examples chosen from personal experience from various areas of the world illustrating the issues involved in language endangerment and showing various different types of language reclamation responses.

2 What is language endangerment?

Language endangerment is the loss of mother-tongue language skills within a community. It is usually a gradual process resulting from social changes which lead to the shift to another language or languages. It is also often associated with changes in attitudes about the group's language and weakening of positive group identity, as well as many other factors discussed in Section 3 below.

Until relatively recently, scholars used a variety of metaphors related to death to describe this phenomenon: language death; dying or moribund language; and dead or extinct language. In the last thirty years, the more neutral terms language endangerment, endangered language and sleeping language have gradually come into use. This is an example of the general tendency to create new euphemisms to replace negative terms, which is widespread across all human languages. The process of resisting or reversing language endangerment has been called language maintenance (which suggests keeping something as it is) or language revitalization (which suggests bringing something back to life);

both are rather oversimplified and misleading views of the processes involved, which are very diverse depending on the stage of endangerment which has been reached. The various main subtypes of this process, now often called reclamation, are discussed in Section 4 below.

The term extinct has mainly been replaced with sleeping as used here to refer to languages where there is still a community which identifies with that language but does not speak it, also known as dormant in the EGIDS scale discussed below. UNESCO even prefers to avoid the term endangered and instead uses in danger of disappearing, but still uses the term extinct. The terms extinct and dead are particularly offensive in the context of formerly sleeping languages which are undergoing reclamation, as Leonard (2020) indicates. Perhaps we can never expect Hittite, Etruscan or Tangut to be reclaimed, but as long as there is a community which identifies with the language, there is always hope.

There are two widely-used scales for endangerment. One is the partly nonlinear 8-level Fishman Graded Intergenerational Disruption Scale (GIDS, Fishman 1991: 81–111). This has been further developed into the Extended GIDS scale with 11 levels (Lewis and Simons 2010), two of which have two subcategories giving a total of 13 levels (though five levels on the GIDS scale from 1 to 5 and seven levels on the EGIDS scale from 0 to 6a are assessed by criteria of status and use in education and are not endangered). The other is the linear six-point Wurm/UNESCO scale (Wurm 1998); this was also developed into the Krauss scale (Kraus 2007) from a (safe) to e (extinct), potentially with + and – for most of the five points on the scale. Other proposed scales include the ElCat Language Endangerment Index (LEI) from 0% to 100% based on four unequally weighted subscales (Lee and Van Way 2016), the multiscalar European Language Vitality Barometer (EuLaViBar, Åckermark et al. 2011) and the OLSI index of vitality (Moretti, Pandolfi and Casoni 2011: 20–22) with 26 components in 11 categories, some mainly focussed on languages spoken in developed countries, among others. For an extended comparison and discussion of these scales, see Bradley and Bradley (2019: 14–23). For all of these scales other than levels 1 to 5 in GIDS, levels 0 to 6a in EGIDS and a in Krauss which are not currently endangered, the major criterion is the current intergenerational transmission and vitality of the language within the community; for the Wurm/UNESCO scale, Levels 6 to 8 of the GIDS scale and 6b to 10 of the EGIDS scale, this is the only criterion; for the ElCat LEI this has an 80% weighting in the overall index, with three subcomponents: 40% intergenerational transmission, 20% number of speakers and 20% trend in number of speakers.

The two most widely used scales of language endangerment are EGIDS and the Wurm/UNESCO scale. These are compared in Table 3.1. In the original

Wurm (1998) version of the scale, the term Severely Endangered was used instead of Seriously Endangered, and Moribund was used instead of Critically Endangered. The table shows the terms used in UNESCO (2003); more recent materials from UNESCO such as Moseley (2010) use the term Vulnerable instead of Potentially Endangered, and Definitely Endangered instead of Endangered.

Table 3.1: EGIDS and Wurm/UNESCO scales of endangerment compared.

EGIDS	Wurm/UNESCO
0 International	–
1 National	–
2 Regional	–
3 Trade	–
4 Educational	–
5 Written	–
6a Vigorous	–
6b Threatened	Potentially Endangered
7 Shifting	Endangered
8a Moribund	Seriously Endangered
8b Nearly extinct	Critically Endangered
9 Dormant	Extinct
10 Extinct	Extinct

At the Potentially Endangered, Vulnerable or EGIDS Level 6b stage only some children are learning the language. At the Endangered, Definitely Endangered or EGIDS Level 7 stage, no children are learning the language. At the Seriously Endangered or EGIDS Level 8a stage, only grandparents still speak the language; and at the Critically Endangered and EGIDS Level 8b stage, only a few very old speakers remain. These are somewhat artificial divisions. Of course all of these scales oversimplify a multitude of diverse sociolinguistic situations; and languages are often at very different stages of endangerment in different parts of the community. Some of the relevant factors are discussed below in Section 3.

As Walsh (2009) and others since have pointed out, for all these endangerment scales there are difficulties in the classification of languages which move from a greater degree of endangerment to a lesser degree due to reclamation efforts. Lewis and Simons (2010) briefly discuss a separate revitalization EGIDS for Level 6b to 10. When a formerly sleeping language is undergoing revival, and this is using written materials in educational settings with some members of the community, it automatically moves up to Level 4 of GIDS and EGIDS even though it may not yet meet the criteria for any of the intermediate levels 5 to 8b based on current transmission and use. In general, when a new orthography is created and put into use in the community, a language at any stage beyond GIDS Level 4 moves to that level; GIDS Levels 1 to 5 and EGIDS Levels 0 to 6a are based on criteria of status, education and literacy, regardless of actual transmission and use. However, a language can be the language of a recognized indigenous group, have official status and a long-established writing system, but nevertheless become a sleeping language, like Manchu in China. Writing is of course important, as discussed in Section 5.4 below, but it does not outweigh everything else.

The linguistic consequences of endangerment often include rapid change in the structure of the language, including loss of patterns not present in the replacing language. For a number of examples, see Bradley and Bradley (2019: 146–173). For a more extended overview of the long-term structural impact, which can lead to a less diverse range of patterns across the languages of the world, see Evans (2010).

3 Factors in endangerment

The key factor in language endangerment is the attitudes of the members of the group to their language (Bradley 2002, Bradley and Bradley 2019: 64–83) and whether they view language as a key component of group identity (Bradley 1983, Kroskrity this volume). This is also referred to as voice (McCarty et al. 2018), indigenous ways of knowing, cultural continuance, responsibility, belonging, and agency. Self-determination, empowerment and control over aspects of group identity and life are usually a key desire, often disrespected by outsiders. Endangerment is often promoted by negative outgroup and in-group attitudes about the value of the indigenous language and mistaken views that ongoing bilingualism is bad; such negative attitudes can be reversed. One major outcome of positive identity and attitudes is happiness and well-being (Bradley and Bradley 2019: 73–74); some countries like Bhutan have made happiness a crucial national goal.

One important component of identity is names; sometimes even the name of a group and its language is contested, with an autonym (the group's own name for itself), which can sometimes change, in competition with one or more exonyms (outsiders' names for them) which can be pejorative and may be rejected by the group, or used as an alternative when communicating with outsiders; for example Myaamia versus Miami (Leonard 2020). Personal and place names are another important expression of a group's identity and connection to their traditional families and land.

Another characteristic of identity is group membership, usually determined by descent. Sometimes this is an official category: the identity registration of almost every person in China is as a member of one of the 56 recognized nationalities, as determined by family background. Sometimes membership is controlled by the group itself, as by tribal councils in North America. Often where status as a member of an indigenous group is not valued, many individuals do not choose to identify as part of that group; this is particularly so for people whose family background is mixed. When reclamation leads to greater self-esteem within the community, some of these individuals may re-identify and return to the group.

Apart from attitudes and identity, another crucial issue is language transmission and use; this is discussed further below (Section 5.2) and in Bradley and Bradley (2019: 84–119). Often an endangered language gradually disappears from use in more and more domains (situations of use), retreating eventually into the home and family and then from lower generations even there. Thus, to reclaim a language, it is essential to reintroduce and use it in as many domains as possible, preferably starting in the family. McCarty et al. (2018) note for example the value of traditional storylines and personal narratives to reinforce links across generations and provide cultural continuity. New technology has also created various new domains and made their use more convenient.

Other factors include internal and external demographic, geographical, economic, historical and sociocultural ones, as discussed in Bradley and Bradley (2019: 120–145); as well as political and educational issues discussed in Bradley and Bradley (2019: 174–207).

Demographic factors relate to group population and the distribution of language knowledge within this population; sometimes these are difficult to determine, and estimates of group population size and distribution of fluency may differ greatly depending on how the group is categorized and by whom. These intersect with geographic factors such as population distribution, concentration and degree of control of traditional land, accessibililty and presence of outsiders in these areas, and whether bi- or mutilingualism is normal in the area or there is a tendency to spread the use of a dominant language.

Economic activities which detract from ongoing group cohesion and increase contact with the wider society also promote language endangerment. While it is possible to have economic success within a small indigenous society if local resources are sufficient and outsiders do not take over local production, it is not reasonable to expect that indigenous societies must continue their traditional subsistence lifestyle if this does not provide the economic benefits that they desire. It is important for groups to maintain as much control as possible over their land and resources, and not fall into exploitative relationships in the sale of their outputs or loss of land. Governments as well as outsiders who wish to exploit local resources, such as minerals, timber, fish and so on, should be required or at least encouraged to provide both respect and support for the community and its language and culture, and training and jobs. This often does not happen.

All human societies have their own indigenous history and traditions which deserve respect; sometimes these are entirely oral. One valuable contribution that an outsider researcher can make is to document such oral materials and make them available to the community. If scholars had not done this and other research in the past, most of the languages around the world which are currently sleeping would have to remain so, and much of this precious knowledge would be gone. Where there are written traditions which persist inside the community, these should also be documented and preserved for posterity, when the current custodians of this knowledge are no longer available to read and explain them. For example, the traditional manuscripts of the four distinct literary traditions for languages within the Yi national minority in China, Nosu, Nasu, Nisu and Sani, can now only be read by traditional priests, usually called *bimo* in the relevant literature from the Nosu term for these priests. Various local governments, research institutes and publishers in China have combined to produce a massive corpus of this literature. I have also located copies of many manuscripts which were taken by colonialists to England and France during the 19th and early 20th century and are now reposing unused in various libraries and archives, some since the 1880s and all before 1950. I am also working with remaining local *bimo* and other Yi experts to transcribe, translate, annotate and disseminate them. A similar Nosu example is Bender and Aku (2019); there are also parallel oral versions from societies speaking closely-related languages, such as Lahu (Walker 1995). This kind of historicity is a valuable support for the persistence of indigenous knowledge, and helps to maintain positive attitudes and identity. Members of many indigenous communities themselves also collect and translate this kind of work, but some may need assistance to disseminate it.

Many aspects of society can support the preservation of the language used to express it. These include family and other human relationships; social roles;

material culture and activities; knowledge of the natural environment and so on. Human relationships crucially include marriage and the links which it reinforces or creates; endogamy and in-group kinship connections of all kinds promote ongoing transmission of language and culture. Similarly, strong leaders and specialists such as traditional priests, medical experts and other experts such as blacksmiths and boatbuilders reinforce and transmit cultural knowledge, and lead the community in ongoing calendrical, religious and life cycle events. Expertise in productive work such as hunting and gathering, agriculture, animal husbandry, fishing as well as the making of traditional clothing, utensils, tools and other artefacts and food preparation is also important. The focus on some of these found in many societies is reflected and maintained in complex taxonomies which also reveal deep knowledge of the natural environment and the plants, animals and other natural features in it. All of this risks being lost forever due to adoption of outside technologies and lifestyles, language shift and the disappearance of traditional experts. It is important to document sociocultural information, and to disseminate this where useful. For example, a traditional antimalarial based on artemisia used by various indigenous groups such as the Lisu in southwestern China has recently become the most effective antimalarial available to modern medicine. It is also possible to reclaim aspects of culture, such as the recent Bisu revival of traditional women's clothing as seen in the oldest photographs from a century or so ago. Such revived cultural practices can be important in reinforcing a group's identity, though there may be some issues with their authenticity. The revived Bisu clothing is black and white, as in the old black and white photographs, while most groups in the area who speak closely-related languages wear dark blue clothing, traditionally dyed with indigo. Various kinds of community reclamation actions which revolve around cultural activities are discussed further in Section 5.2 below.

Political factors promoting language endangerment usually originate from the nation state and the wider society. Most nation states have a national policy on language which supports one or a few major languages, implemented by a range of planning measures through the education system and across national institutions and the media. There is usually little policy directed at the preservation of linguistic and cultural diversity, and if there is, it is often not implemented in reality. The 2008 constitution of Burma guaranteed to support the languages and cultures of all of the 135 ethnic groups in the country, and the subsequent ethnic and education laws were designed to implement this through initial mother-tongue education. We tried to assist many groups in various parts of the country through a UNICEF project between 2013 and 2018; however, in reality

Burmese continues to be the sole language of education and national life in areas under government control.

Even a positive national policy and strong and well-intentioned government support for a language may not be sufficient to overcome other negative factors; Rumantsch in Switzerland is one of four national languages, strongly supported by one cantonal government, with five long-established distinct literary varieties three of which are endangered, one severely. See further discussion below in Section 5.1 on how education can be deployed to support the preservation of linguistic diversity, and Section 5.4 on how to develop and implement mother-tongue literacy; also Bradley and Bradley (2019: 174–207) on these and other relevant aspects of language policy and language planning.

A variety of external factors also affect language vitality; for example colonization, conquest or other types of aggression, with or without population movement; religious proselytisation and other types of externally-induced cultural change; language exogamy without ongoing bilingualism; changes in accessibility due to new roads, bridges, transport systems and so on, and the resulting increased contact with and in-migration of outsiders; economic changes due to loss of land or shifts to other modes of subsistence such as producing cash crops or wage labor; and environmental issues – land degradation and so on. Many traditional societies are known for their greater concern and care for the environment, but with loss of control of land and shifts in language and culture this is becoming less effective. Environmental issues which have led to language shift, such as inundation or environmental degradation of traditional land, is very widespread already and will increase this century. For example, Gong ceased to be spoken in its traditional area in western Thailand when this was inundated by two large dams in the 1980s (Bradley 1989), and one of the last two remaining communities has also been displaced by a smaller dam in recent years. So environmental progress for the wider society in the form of clean hydroelectric power and better control of water flow to minimize seasonal flooding and increase irrigation can be at the expense of an indigenous community and its land, and so a negative for its endangered language.

The impact of all these types of factors on persistence and change in traditional societies and their languages is extremely complex and does not lend itself to simple quantification or scales. Some small groups keep their languages despite the presence of a variety of negative factors; others lose them despite a more favorable situation.

4 Types of reclamation

In Bradley and Bradley (2019: 208–224) we have separated reclamation into six subtypes, depending on the stage of endangerment reached and the response. Table 3.2 shows these six subtypes.

Table 3.2: Subtypes of Reclamation.

SUBTYPE	CURRENT USERS	AIM	TARGET
Revitalization	yes but decreasing	increase use	existing language
Revival	no	recreate wide use	former language
Heritage	no	limited use	symbolic
Renativization	yes but literary only	expand domains	existing language expanded
Nativization	contact situation with L2 speakers	stabilize	new standard
Denativization	yes, various distinctive varieties	create new standard	new compromise standard

The first is Revitalization, where the endangered language still has mother-tongue speakers who can act as an authentic resource for reclaiming the language more widely. The appropriate actions differ greatly depending on how endangered the language is. The second type is Revival, where a language is sleeping but the community wishes to reawaken it. The third type is Heritage, where the community wishes to maintain its identity and may use some of its sleeping language symbolically but not reawaken it for widespread spoken use. A fourth type is Renativization, where the language is still used within the community, but only in restricted domains, and is brought back into full use, as for Hebrew. A fifth type is Nativization, in which a contact language definitively separates from its main lexical source languages, is recognized as an independent speech form and may cease to decreolize even if it is in ongoing contact with the prestige lexical source language, becoming an independent, more stable and widely-used language; for example, Tok Pisin in Papua New Guinea; or Nativisation can be accompanied by increasing endangerment, as for Patuà in Macau; see also the chapter in this volume by Dimmendaal for further discussion. Denativization, the final type, involves the creation and implementation of an artificial compromise variety, one without mother-tongue speakers, often as a policy response to a desire for unity; some examples include Rumantsch in

Switzerland (Bradley and Bradley 2019: 198–207), Irish in Ireland and Lisu in China and South-East Asia (Bradley 2010). This is a somewhat risky strategy, and may lead to problems, as seen with Rumantsch, or can be successful, as for Lisu and Irish.

Of course these six types of reclamation are not mutually exclusive. A community with a sleeping language may wish to move from Heritage to Revival, and where Revival succeeds, then to Revitalization; or they may decide that Revitalization or Revival are not being achieved, and opt for Heritage instead. Denativisation is also involved where one of these first three types of reclamation is implementing a compromise variety. Renativization, Nativization and Denativization can be problematic where speaker attitudes to the newly expanded, newly stabilized or newly-created variety are negative.

One problem in many reclamation efforts is unrealistically ambitious goals which lead to disappointment. It is extremely important to have achievable goals and work in stages. If the goal of a reclamation is an immediate and complete return to some maximally conservative earlier variety of the target language, this may prove disastrous. Resilience thinking (Gunderson, Allen and Holling 2010) has shown us that once an ecological situation has reached a tipping point, it may be possible to reach a new stable situation, but not to return to the original state; this is also true for languages.

In resilience linguistics, we strive to understand the many issues threatening the language (Section 3 above), work to overcome them using proven methods (Section 5 below) and achieve a new stability for the language, one in which bilingualism is normal and the in-group language continues and possibly expands in use in a form which speakers feel positive about. This may be different from the traditional language, but is still a focus of identity and pride.

5 Reclamation processes

5.1 Learning in educational contexts

As language reclamation is such a diverse process depending on the degree of ongoing language knowledge and use in the community, it is difficult to generalize, but schools and other similar formal pedagogical settings are one of the main places where such activities take place, especially where home and family transmission is no longer widespread.

The Language Nest model, first developed in New Zealand and now widely implemented around the developed world, with particular success in New Zealand,

Hawaii and elsewhere, puts preschool-age children in a setting where elders who speak the language use it with them in their first introduction to formal education. This has been shown to be highly effective, even where the children have not previously been socialized in the language and where their parents do not speak it. Programs of this type go under many names; some Head Start programs in the US, which were intended to provide a transition for groups with a distinct language and culture to join the mainstream education system, are also effectively like language nests. The main problem for students who progress from language nests is to provide an ongoing continuation of language reclamation and use through the rest of the school system and back into the community.

Programs based in mainstream schools are extremely diverse. One type is heritage support, providing positive exposure to traditional culture with some limited symbolic language use. This can be implemented in a community for all students, including those who are not of indigenous background, as it is in some remote communities in Australia. There are also various approaches to more intensive use of languages in schools: as a language subject of various sizes and durations, or as medium of instruction for some or all learning. Though UNICEF currently recommends that all children have access to initial education in the medium of the mother tongue of the students, this is not often implemented for indigenous or immigrant minority groups. There may be transitional support, with the intention that students who are currently dominant in their indigenous or non-mainstream language should shift to the mainstream school language within a specified period. For example, three years of transitional mother-tongue medium education in some subjects has long been the official policy in China, but the support for and duration of this transition has been greatly reduced in recent years, with the closure of most village schools in remote indigenous areas and a widespread move to boarding schools where Chinese is the dominant language, even for beginning primary school.

Where children arrive at primary school with indigenous language skills, there are various ways that ongoing bilingualism can be supported. Alongside transitional efforts to improve students' knowledge of the dominant language and medium of most education, one approach is to have ongoing study of the local indigenous mother tongue as a substantial continuing subject in the curriculum, as in Australian two-way or both ways education, and sometimes also to have other subject material delivered in this language. This requires very extensive preparation of materials and training of teachers for these language and other subjects. Most of the endangered languages around the world have not achieved the level of official recognition that provides for formal education in their languages, and relatively few of them have officially-recognized materials and trained teachers for this kind of ongoing mother-tongue learning.

In China, there are nominally two streams in areas where recognized national minorities have been officially granted autonomy. One has an ongoing minority language subject with limited class time but otherwise follows the normal national curriculum in Mandarin Chinese. The other is a blended system with some subjects taught in the minority language and others taught in Chinese, continuing up to separate tertiary institutions; this is only available for some of the largest national minorities, and these streams are not very popular as they do not lead to jobs providing social mobility. Local officials in officially recognized autonomous areas, including members of the national minorities themselves, often prefer to promote standard Chinese and to offer only limited mother-tongue education, sometimes not even an ongoing single subject; outside the autonomous areas, minority languages receive almost no support. Also, the official national minority categories are similar to the Chinese majority category, which includes a very wide range of mutually unintelligible 'dialects' sharing the same official ethnic category. Some national minorities include numerous distinct languages with separate literary traditions. Members of the Yi nationality speak about eighty languages, four of which have quite distinct orthographies which are used to a limited degree in education, all in newly-standardized forms (Bradley 2001, 2009); many of the other languages spoken by members of the Yi nationality are endangered and there has been no educational or other provision for their languages, apart from some failed attempts in the 1990s (Bradley 2005, 2011a). In reality, very few children from national minorities in China have access to ongoing mother-tongue education, even though this is guaranteed in the current 1982 constitution and other laws.

Unfortunately most education systems around the world do not cater for ongoing learning and use of indigenous or immigrant mother tongues at all, and many provide no transition to the language of the school, normally a national language which may be unfamiliar to children. This provides a very strong motivation for parents to socialize their children in the language which they know will be used in school, to help their children to succeed there.

Boarding schools and other even more extreme ways of removing children from their communities have an unacceptable and shocking history in many countries; unacceptable assaults on non-mainstream language use in them were one of the main reasons that many indigenous languages ceased intergenerational transmission. This destruction of indigenous languages and rights continues in some places, but has fortunately stopped in others. It is also possible to have a positive approach to education outside the community; for example, in Thailand public education beyond basic primary takes place only in towns and cities, not in remote villages, and only in Thai medium. There are many privately-run hostels for individual indigenous groups in many small towns across the north of the country which allow students to attend main-stream Thai-medium schools but which also provide mother-tongue literacy classes after hours, in an environment where the mother tongue is also in nor-mal everyday use and there is ongoing connection with children's families; these are mainly supported by payments from parents (Bradley 1985).

Another widespread learning strategy is effectively like learning a second language in a school: as a subject during or after normal class hours, or in sep-arate school-based programs such as the widespread Saturday schools in Aus-tralia. Many such programs cater for children who do not speak the endangered language of their community; languages in immigrant settings tend to be more endangered than they are in the country of origin, though there are counterex-amples, such as some of the languages of eastern Indonesia now better pre-served in the Netherlands (van Engelenhoven 2002). In many countries, the national curriculum and language policy do not allow for non-majority mother-tongue medium or subject language learning in schools, so it is up to the com-munity; delivery can be outside school hours in community organizations, often including religious ones. Where an established local indigenous organiza-tion such as a North American tribal council exists, such classes often take place under the auspices of these organizations.

Apart from school-type settings for children, there are various other ways that language reclamation can be carried out through formal education. Adult education classes can take various approaches. Where the language is in use in the community but literacy in the mother tongue is a goal, adult literacy classes may be implemented. There may be classes and events for a variety of tradi-tional activities, including traditional oral or written literature. Where the lan-guage is sleeping or less widely spoken but there is demand for reclamation, adult second language learning classes can be widespread, as for Ainu in Japan. Where adults who did not acquire their community's traditional mother tongue in childhood wish to progress beyond the level of proficiency reached in such classes, there are also more intensive programs such as those outlined in Olthuis, Kivelä and Skuttnab-Kangas (2013) for Saami in Finland.

In settings where language transmission has been broken for so long that only a few elders are fluent, the master and apprentice approach developed and implemented by Hinton can be highly valuable; see Hinton (2001) and Hinton, Vera and Steele (2002). In this process, a single younger apprentice learns lan-guage and cultural knowledge very intensively from a single master, a fluent elder speaker. The apprentices can later become community leaders in language reclamation, with the necessary skills to spread the language further as teachers themselves.

In some communities, language is viewed as an in-group code and out-siders, including outside scholars, are not welcomed or have restricted access; this is often in reaction to bad experiences in the past. Thus language classes and activities may be restricted to in-group members; traditional texts may be considered sacred and private; and even a dictionary can be a contested re-source. Other communities welcome outsiders to learn their language and par-ticipate, though some family connection and ongoing commitment may still be preferred.

5.2 Community action

The ideal for language acquisition is during early childhood in the home from parents and other carers; for further discussion and a case study see Hellwig (this volume). Often the grandparents are the secret weapon, especially if they are monolingual or more fluent in the in-group language. Parents and grand-parents who try to use the language as a secret code may transmit the language effectively, even if they do not intend to do so. One type of reclamation strategy is for parents who did not grow up as speakers but who have subsequently learned the language to socialize their children in the language which is being reclaimed, as for Kaurna in Australia (Bradley and Bradley 2019: 224–226) or for Hebrew in Israel early last century.

One of the most effective strategies for language reclamation is in-group community activities; sometimes these are also open to outsiders, as a means of raising the community's profile and increasing its mainstream prominence. They often include attractive folkloristic elements, and are sometimes also used to attract mainstream tourists. Even where language is not a core cultural value and language reclamation is not a community goal, sometimes museumified festivals and other activities may still persist as an expression of identity.

There are long-established festivals which support reclaiming indigenous culture such as the Irish Féis, the Welsh Eisteddfod, the Jinghpaw Kachin Manau and other similar events, which feature dance, music, clothing, craft, food and other cultural activities. These are often not focused on language use and welcome participation by outsiders, though sometimes they do crucially in-clude language reclamation activities, such as various Cornish festivals which include competitions for Cornish bards, like the biennial Kernewek Lowender festival in Australia since 1973. Some such activities transcend former indige-nous group boundaries, such as the North American plains-style drumming and smoking ceremonies which build overall indigenous identity and link dif-ferent groups.

Some festivals are based on a traditional calendar and may also include traditional religious activities; sometimes non-traditional religious festivals such as Christmas or Easter may also become a focus for displays of culture and language use. New calendar-based festivals such as the Lahu gourd festival in China may be created or existing local festivals may be more widely implemented across composite groups, such as the Yi torch festival in China which was originally mainly Nosu; these are a means of expressing and celebrating group identity. Such festivals usually include displays of written language where an orthography exists, and many also include displays of linguistic virtuosity – for example the traditional oral Lisu New Year song (Bradley, Bya and Ngwaza 2007).

Sometimes public events express majority recognition of indigenous rights, such as the welcome to country which is now normal at the beginning of nearly every public event in Australia. These welcomes to country can be delivered by a non-indigenous person in English expressing respect for the local group by name and their rights to the land, but are often delivered at more major events by a local indigenous person from that group. Where possible, they are increasingly being given in the local language, such as Kaurna in Adelaide (Bradley and Bradley 2019: 208).

The cultural immersion model, also known by the more recent term Learning and Observing by Pitching In or LOPI (Henne-Ochoa et al. 2020, Leonard 2020), refers to community activities, often mainly directed at younger group members, which include a strong language and culture reclamation focus and are in-group only. These may include excursions into traditional lands to observe and practice traditional activities under the guidance of expert elders; organized camps and workshops over an entire summer, shorter holidays, weekends, days or part days which bring groups of young people together to reclaim language and culture, often together with elders; traditional but often revived and expanded festivals which involve large community gatherings; ongoing collective use of social media and other internet resources (Saxena and Borin 2006, Wyman 2012) and so on.

The most effective language reclamation in human history has been the Renativization of Hebrew in Israel since the 1880s. Initially implemented by Jewish nationalists during Turkish rule and continuing during British rule, this expanded and developed the use of what had been for over two millennia a literary language of religion and scholarship into a modern spoken and written language which since 1948 is the official language of a nation state used in all domains by many millions of mother-tongue speakers, supported by a highly-successful *ulpan* immersion school model for rapid adult second language learning by immigrants (Bradley and Bradley 2019: 162–172). Some other languages have also made great progress in the last fifty or more years, such as Irish in Ireland, Welsh in Wales and so on, and many more are on the reclamation path.

5.3 Authenticity

Linguists know that all languages change, and that sociolinguistic attitudes of adults to innovative speech by younger people are generally negative. We also know that being bilingual is a cognitive as well as a social advantage. However, widespread community views that young people speak badly and that being bilingual is a disadvantage have often combined to speed language shift and reduce the motivation for and effectiveness of reclamation.

As Dorian and many others have shown, the structure of languages which are endangered often changes very rapidly (Dorian 2010). For examples of the types of change which have recently taken place in all areas of the structure of Gong in Thailand, see Bradley and Bradley (2019: 147–160). During language endangerment, there are usually semi-speakers (Dorian 1977) whose speech production is quite different from that of older traditional speakers, sometimes with a great deal of variation and interspeaker differences.

Where young people speak a radically different variety of the language, or where the language shows the effects of substantial contact with some dominant language, negative attitudes among elders may be particularly strong. In the case of many contact languages traditionally viewed as creoles, the low prestige of the contact language and the tendency to ongoing decreolization due to the pull of the main lexical source language may lead to endangerment, as in the case of Patuà in Macau and its main lexical source language Portuguese (Bradley and Bradley 2019: 241–245). However, in some communities, elders do accept and value the speech of younger people and a norm based on it, as in the case of Bisu in Thailand (Bradley and Bradley 2019: 32–36); they think that some version of the language is better than none (Bradley and Bradley 2019: 14).

Where a sleeping language is being reclaimed, the reclaimed variety is based on available materials previously produced by linguists and others, which may be incomplete. It is therefore often the case that parts of the reclaimed variety need to be reinforced with material from other languages or created anew. Loanwords can be contested; both by the source community as really being their words, and by some of the reclaiming community as to how authentic they are. Also, the overall authenticity of a reclaimed language may be contested, particularly by outsiders and sometimes by insiders as well.

There may also be disagreement as to whether the speech of a participant in a reclamation process is a valid expression of community norms; acceptance by the community is the key here. In particular, do elders accept the speech of semi-speakers or younger learners?

Another question which affects views about the authenticity of a language is the historicity of the normative variety of a reclaimed language: is it a valid expression of a historical version of the language? Views on this differ greatly; speakers of Hebrew regard Biblical Hebrew as the direct precursor of modern spoken Hebrew, despite very substantial differences. Sometimes the normative variety is a composite of various regional varieties, as for Irish, so it achieves historicity through these compromises. However, one cannot go to a *Gaeltacht* (an area where Irish is still officially a mother tongue) in Ireland and hear standard literary Irish spoken, other than in the local school. Sometimes the normative literary variety is based on one language or variety; this can be based mainly on one particular regional variety with a strong literary tradition and high prestige, as in the case of German Hochdeutsch, or it can be one among several languages spoken in the area of a particular mission which was selected by missionaries for wider written use, such as Tumbuka in northern Malawi, or some other locally-developed lingua franca. Tumbuka has a mother-tongue speech community; this is not the case for literary Lisu, which is a simplified composite created in the 1920s for Bible translation, but now also used as a lingua franca between speakers of very distinct subvarieties of Lisu and as a literary language, and influencing the spoken varieties to varying degrees (Bradley 2010).

Sociolinguistic attitudes about loanwords are also relevant; the variety of Chamorro spoken in Guam has more Spanish loanwords than the variety spoken in the Northern Marianas, and speakers from the Northern Marianas regard Guam Chamorro as mixed, less authentic and less prestigious. Note that if the proportion of loanwords in a language is a criterion for authenticity and historicity, English fails the test.

5.4 Writing

From a strictly linguistic perspective, the existence of one or more orthographies to represent a language is relevant only insofar as these may allow us to access written information in the language, modern and from earlier periods. However, from the perspective of a community, a writing system is often an important symbol of modernity and component of identity, authenticity and historicity, very useful for reclamation and other purposes and very highly valued, though there are exceptions. For some languages, there is one orthography but it does not represent the phonology of the language well; and for some languages there is already more than one competing orthography. In the case of many languages which are being reclaimed, there was no traditional orthography, and so one may need to be created. In all these cases, the views of the community must be paramount. If no orthography is desired, none is necessary and the reclamation can proceed orally, perhaps reinforced by some linguistic transcription where necessary.

Even if an existing orthography has problems, outsiders are not entitled to change it; that is up to the community. In South-East Asia, a failed attempt to add marking of tones to the Jinghpaw Kachin orthography and a separation of the Lahu and Lahu Si orthographies both led to very painful controversies. If the community cannot compromise on one orthography, reclamation materials need to be produced in all those required; we have produced Lisu dictionaries in the orthography based on Chinese *pinyin* used in China from 1958 (Bradley 2004) and in the Christian orthography widely used by Christians in China and elsewhere since 1917 (Bradley et al. 2006).

Creating or reforming orthographies should be undertaken with the full cooperation of the community, preferably in an interactive process which has lately come to be called an alphabet design workshop (Easton and Wroge 2012). It should use a writing system which provides maximum transfer to the local dominant language or languages; hence when the Bisu in Thailand created their script with me in 1977, we used the Thai script, not a romanization. For numerous other examples of the same process in Thailand, now known as the Mahidol model from the name of the university where it was further developed, see Premsrirat and Hirsh (2018). Decisions made when creating an orthography may later cause problems, as when speakers of Bisu from Burma and China who could not use this Thai-based script unexpectedly appeared many years later. Now there is also a Bisu romanisation used in Burma, based on the Lahu Baptist romanization, as the Bisu in Burma were converted to Christianity by Lahu Baptist missionaries and were familiar with Lahu printed materials. It would have been much better to use only one orthography, but it is now too late for Bisu. Unfortunately, in some societies choices about orthography remain a matter of contention, a complication which is counterproductive for successful reclamation.

Some communities have successfully unified competing orthographies, like the Kayan in Burma who formerly had two romanizations, a Catholic one and a Baptist one, but have recently successfully combined them; they have also subsumed a number of quite distinctive spoken varieties into the use of one literary variety, Pekon Kayan. The Iu Mien from China, Laos and Thailand met in China in 1984 and unified their orthography into one romanization based mainly on a 1982 romanization discussed and adopted at a conference in the US, with some revisions to make it more similar to Chinese *pinyin*. In the process, they replaced three earlier versions using Thai script and two other earlier romanizations from Thailand and China (Purnell 1987); this has since become very widely used.

Written materials which we produce should be in forms that are accessible to community members and useful for reclamation; for example, our 2006 Lisu dictionary has a Lisu introduction and all entries use Lisu script in Lisu alphabetical order. It is important also to disseminate and archive them in suitable ways: not behind paywalls or hard copy only with academic publishers and full of our disciplines' jargon. The Boasian trilogy, now expanded to four, grammar, texts, dictionary and archiving, may also need to be carried out in a different sequence to meet the needs of reclamation: firstly choices concerning the orthography to be used, a very early focus on pedagogical materials and simple reading materials if these are lacking, then the dictionary, texts, archiving and eventually a grammar. Given current technology, it is now also possible to share oral materials and interact either in writing or orally on the internet or by phone; however, we need to bear in mind that some societies, particularly those in remote areas, have limited access to these technologies.

6 Conclusion

We must strive for linguistic resilience (Bradley 2010, 2011b, Bradley and Bradley 2019: 75–78), using available resources to re-develop a new stable linguistic ecology. This can also strengthen group identity and help to develop positive attitudes about the group and its language and culture (Bradley 1983, 2002). It may also be necessary to work for change in national language and education policies, providing for the recognition of linguistic human rights of minority groups (Bradley 2007) including initial mother-tongue education. The goal of language reclamation is usually not use of the language for all purposes at all times; it must be what the community wants and can achieve (Thieberger 2002), alongside full knowledge of the dominant language of the wider society. It is also of course possible that a community may now not be motivated to undertake the effort to reclaim their language; in such cases, we should do the maximum possible to document the language and its cultural context, so that if and when the community changes its views, the information to assist in any kind of reclamation effort is available. Many of the reclamation efforts in North

America and Australia are now based on and supported by old linguistic and anthropological research materials.

There are major ethical and methodological issues involved in any field research by outsiders in a community; this is particularly so for communities whose language is endangered. For discussion of some of these issues, see Bradley and Bradley (2019: 38–63, 228–246). Often the endangerment is an outcome of earlier negative experiences, and often there is considerable resentment of and hostility to outsider researchers as representatives of the dominant society. Previous extractive linguistics and ethnography, outsiders coming in to collect data according to their own priorities and then using it without giving anything back to the community, have created bad feelings in many places.

There is a worldwide movement, particularly prominent in some Anglophone countries and their former colonies, toward decolonizing knowledge; see for example Msila (2017). Among other things, this means respect for indigenous languages and the knowledge of the world which they embody, and empowering indigenous communities to make their own decisions.

Groups themselves and their own leaders should be making the decisions about language reclamation. Where possible, they should be assisted by in-group linguistic experts; see for example Perley for Maliseet in Canada (Perley 2011), Sallabank for Guernésiais in Guernsey (Sallabank 2018), Leonard for Miami in the US (Leonard 2020) and many others. This is why it is also extremely important to motivate, train and help such in-group experts. The reclamation should have realistic goals and use appropriate methods to lead and support the community and strive to replace existing negative attitudes that have been a factor in endangerment, decolonize indigenous knowledge and use the language in the way that the community wishes to.

References

Åckermark, Sia Spilopoulou, Johanna Laako, Anneli Sarhimaa & Reeta Toivanen. 2011. ELDIA EuLaViBar toolkit. [https://phaidra.univie.ac.at/view/o:301101] (accessed 16 April 2021).
Bender, Mark & Aku Wuwu. 2019. *The Nuosu book of origins. A creation epic from southwest China*. Seattle: University of Washington Press.
Bradley, David. 1983. Identity. The persistence of minority groups. In John McKinnon & Wanat Bhruksasri (eds.), *Highlanders of Thailand*, 46–53. Kuala Lumpur: Oxford University Press.
Bradley, David. 1985. Traditional minorities and language education in Thailand. In David Bradley (ed.), *Language policy, language planning and sociolinguistics in South-East Asia* (Pacific Linguistics A-67), 87–102. Canberra: Department of Linguistics, Research School of Pacific Studies, Australian National University.

Bradley, David. 1989. The disappearance of the Ugong in Thailand. In Nancy C. Dorian (ed.), *Investigating obsolescence. Studies in language contraction and death*, 33–40. Cambridge: Cambridge University Press.

Bradley, David. 2001. Language policy for the Yi. In Stevan Harrell (ed.), *Perspectives on the Yi of Southwestern China*, 195–214. Berkeley: University of California Press.

Bradley, David. 2002. Language attitudes. The key factor in language maintenance. In David Bradley & Maya Bradley (eds.), *Language endangerment and language maintenance*, 1–10. London: Routledge Curzon.

Bradley, David. 2004. Chinese as a pluricentric language. In Michael G. Clyne (ed.), *Pluricentric languages,* 305–324. Berlin: De Gruyter Mouton.

Bradley, David. 2005. Sanie and language loss in China. *International Journal of the Sociology of Language* 163. 159–176.

Bradley, David. 2007. Language policy and language rights. In Osahito Miyoka, Osamu Sakiyama & Michael E. Krauss (eds.), *The vanishing languages of the Pacific Rim*, 77–90. Oxford: Oxford University Press.

Bradley, David. 2009. Language policy for China's minorities. Language policy for the Yi. *Written Languages and Literacy* 12 (2). 170–187.

Bradley, David. 2010. Language endangerment and resilience linguistics. Case studies of Gong and Lisu. *Anthropological Linguistics* 52 (2). 123–140.

Bradley, David. 2011a. Success and failure in Yi orthography reform. In Joshua A. Fishman & Ofelia García (eds.), *Handbook of language and ethnicity*, Vol. 2, 180–191. Oxford: Oxford University Press.

Bradley, David. 2011b. Resilience thinking and language endangerment. In Bai Bibo & David Bradley (eds.), *Extinction and retention of mother tongues in China*, 1–43. Beijing: Nationalities Press [in English and Chinese].

Bradley, David & Maya Bradley. 2019. *Language endangerment*. Cambridge: Cambridge University Press.

Bradley, David, Bya Beloto & David Ngwaza. 2007. *Lisu new year song*. Chiang Mai: Actsco.

Bradley, David, with Edward R. Hope, Maya Bradley & James Fish. 2006. *Southern Lisu dictionary* (STEDT Monograph Series 4). Berkeley: STEDT Project, University of California Berkeley.

Dorian, Nancy C. 1977. The problem of the semi-speaker in language death. *International Journal of the Sociology of Language* 12. 23–32.

Dorian, Nancy C. 2010. *Investigating variation. The effects of social organization and social setting*. New York: Oxford University Press.

Easton, Catherine & Diane Wroge. 2012. *Manual for alphabet design through community interaction for Papua New Guinea elementary teacher trainers*, 2nd edition. Ukarumpa, PNG: Summer Institute of Linguistics.

van Engelenhoven, Aone. 2002. Concealment, maintenance and renaissance. Language and ethnicity in the Moluccan community in the Netherlands. In David Bradley & Maya Bradley (eds.), *Language endangerment and language maintenance*, 272–309. London: Routledge Curzon.

Evans, Nicholas. 2010. *Dying words. Endangered languages and what they have to tell us*. Chichester & Malden MA: Wiley Blackwell.

Fishman, Joshua A. 1991. Reversing language shift: *Theoretical and empirical foundations of assistance to threatened languages*. Clevedon: Multilingual Matters.

Gunderson, Lance H., Craig R. Allen & Crawford H. Holling. 2010. *Foundations of ecological resilience*. Washington DC: Island Press.

Henne-Ochoa, Richard, Emma Elliott-Groves, Barbra A. Meek & Barbara Rogoff. 2020. Pathways forward for indigenous language reclamation. Engaging indigenous epistemology and learning by observing and pitching in to family and community endeavors. *Modern Language Journal* 104 (2). 481–493.

Hinton, Leanne. 2001. The master-apprentice language learning program. In Leanne Hinton & Ken Hale (eds.), *The green book of language revitalization*, 51–59. Cambridge, MA: Academic Press.

Hinton, Leanne, with Matt Vera & Nancy Steele. 2002. *How to keep your language alive. A commonsense approach to one-on-one language learning*. Berkeley: Heyday Books.

Krauss, Michael E. 1992. The world's languages in crisis. *Language* 68 (1). 4–10.

Krauss. Michael E. 2007. Classification and terminology for degrees of endangerment. In Matthias Brenzinger (ed.), *Language diversity endangered*, 1–8. Berlin: De Gruyter Mouton.

Lee, Nala Huiying & John Van Way. 2016. Assessing levels of endangerment in the Catalogue of Endangered Languages (ElCat) using the Language Endangerment Index (LEI). *Language in Society* 45. 271–292.

Leonard, Wesley J. 2020. Musings on Native American language reclamation and sociolinguistics. *International Journal of the Sociology of Language* 263. 85–90.

Lewis, M. Paul & Gary F. Simons. 2010. Assessing endangerment. Expanding Fishman's GIDS. *Revue Roumane de Linguistique* 55 (2). 103–120.

McCarty, Teresa L., Sheilah E. Nichols, Kari E. B. Chew, Natalie G. Diaz, Wesley J. Leonard & Louellyn White. 2018. Hear our languages, hear our voices. Storywork as theory and praxis in indigenous-language reclamation. *Daedalus* 147 (2). 160–172.

Moretti, Bruno, Elene Maria Pandolfi & Matteo Casoni. 2011. *Vitalità de una lingua minoritaria. Aspetti e proposte metodologiche*. Ticino: Osservatorio Linguistico della Svizzera Italiana.

Moseley, Christopher (ed.). 2010. *Atlas of the world's languages in danger*, 3rd edition. Paris: UNESCO. [http://www.unesco.org/languages-atlas/] (accessed 16 April 2021).

Msila, Vuvusile (ed.). 2017. *Decolonizing knowledge for Africa's renewal. Examining African perspectives and philosophies*. Randburg, RSA: KR Publishing.

Olthuis, Maria-Liisa, Suvi Kivelä & Tove Skutnabb-Kangas. 2013. *Revitalizing indigenous languages. How to recreate a lost generation*. Bristol: Multilingual Matters.

Perley, Bernard C. 2011. *Defying Maliseet language death*. Lincoln, NB: University of Nebraska Press.

Premsrirat, Suwilai & David Hirsh (eds.). 2018. *Language revitalization. Insights from Thailand*. Bern: Peter Lang.

Purnell, Herbert C. 1987. Developing practical orthographies for the Iu Mien (Yao). *Linguistics of the Tibeto-Burman Area* 10 (2). 128–141.

Sallabank, Julia. 2018. Language planning and ideologies in Guernsey. *Multilingua* 38 (1). 93–111.

Saxena, Anju & Lars Borin (eds.). 2006. *Lesser-known languages of South Asia. Status and policies. Case studies and applications of information technology*. Berlin: De Gruyter Mouton.

Thieberger, Nicholas. 2002. Extinction in whose terms? Which parts of a language constitute a target for language maintenance programmes? In David Bradley & Maya Bradley (eds.),

Language endangerment and language maintenance, 310–328. London: RoutledgeCurzon.

UNESCO. 2003. *Language vitality and endangerment.* International Expert Meeting on the UNESCO Programme Safeguarding Languages, 12 March 2003. [http://www.unesco.org/new/en/culture/themes/endangered-languages/dynamic-content-single-view-meeting/news/expert_meeting_on_safeguarding_endangered_languages/] (accessed 16 April 2021).

Walker, Anthony R. 1995. *Mvuh hpa mi hpa. Creating heaven, creating earth.* Chiang Mai: Silkworm Books.

Walsh, Michael. 2009. The rise and fall of GIDS in accounts of language endangerment. In Hakim Elnazarov & Nicholas Ostler (eds.), *Endangered languages and history. Proceedings of the 13th FEL conference, 24–26 September 2009, Khorog, Tajikistan*, 134–141. Bath: Foundation for Endangered Languages.

Wurm, Stephen A. 1998. Methods of language maintenance and revival. In Kazuto Matsumura (ed.), *Studies in endangered languages. Papers from the International Symposium on Endangered Languages, Tokyo 19–20 November 1995*, 191–211. Tokyo: Hituzii Syobo.

Wyman, Leisy Thornton. 2012. *Youth culture, language endangerment and linguistic survivance.* Bristol: Multilingual Matters.

Gerrit J. Dimmendaal

4 Emerging languages and the creation of new communicative styles

New language varieties and co-developing new communicative styles come about as the result of language shift, but these also develop through the copying of communicative styles while maintaining one's primary language. The present contribution aims to investigate these two socio-linguistic situations with a special focus on Africa. We may define "speech style" as the meaningful deployment of language in order to achieve particular communicative effects or social meanings. As a concept it usually refers to degrees of formality, or to variation according to audience or context of speech; "communicative style" as a concept focuses on the interactional dimension of speech styles. This chapter describes some of these interactional features, which are sometimes transferred from one language to another when new varieties emerge from new types of social interaction.

As a result of colonialism and urbanization, different varieties of New Englishes, for example, as well as new varieties of French, Portuguese and Spanish, have come about in different parts of the world over the past centuries, and several of these have also been described to some extent in the literature, as discussed in Section 1. But on closer inspection it turns out that such dynamic processes are – and have been – part and parcel of language ecology in other types of socio-political circumstances which have nothing to do with European colonialism, as discussed in Section 2.

For the description and analysis of these new varieties (or "language birth", as this phenomenon has also been called) in terms of speech styles, concepts derived from anthropological linguistics, interactional sociolinguistics, conversation(al) analysis and cognitive linguistics, as well as speech act theory, need to be investigated. Discussing this vast area is beyond the scope of the present article and therefore it can only be summarized and briefly elaborated upon in Section 3.

Acknowledgments: The present author would like to express his gratitude to two anonymous referees as well as to the editors for their constructive criticism and detailed comments on an earlier draft, and to Mary Chambers for her corrections and important editorial comments.

Gerrit J. Dimmendaal, University of Cologne/Germany, e-mail: gerrit.dimmendaal@uni-koeln.de

https://doi.org/10.1515/9783110726626-004

1 The creation of new communicative styles in expanding Indo-European languages

Understanding language ecology from a historical point of view involves the investigation of environmental factors such as climate (change), socio-economic and technological developments, political structures and language ideologies. Research on language obsolescence and the fate of endangered languages, as one potential language-ecological outcome of language contact, has been high on the priority list of linguists over the past decades. An alternative historical outcome of language contact, the emergence of new languages and corresponding new communicative styles, has received somewhat less scholarly attention so far.

Language loss and language shift have presumably been part and parcel of the history of mankind for perhaps 200,000 years now, i.e., for as long as educated guesses on the existence of modern humans and their languages allow us to date back this phenomenon, which makes modern humans unique as a species. Different factors appear to be responsible for the dynamics behind these adaptive processes. The current skewed spread of Afroasiatic languages (see Figure 4.1) across the Middle East and the area surrounding the Sahara on the African continent, to

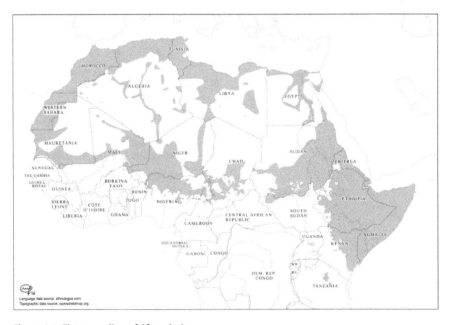

Figure 4.1: The spreading of Afroasiatic.

take just one example, already strongly suggests that climate changes were one factor determining where people could (or could no longer) survive. Paleographical research shows that the last glacial period came to an end around 11,000 years ago; wetter periods set in subsequently, which in turn led to the spreading of humans away from riverine zones and mountains to new areas suitable for humans in Africa and other parts of the world; desertification set in again some 6,000 years ago, as argued by, for example, Kuper and Kröpelin (2006). The investigation of genetically related languages, combined with archaeological research (including osteology) and research on the DNA structure of speakers, allows us to some extent to formulate plausible hypotheses on the historical spreading of languages and speech communities, for example for the Afroasiatic family (see Ehret 2000, Dimmendaal 2019), or for Nilo-Saharan (Dimmendaal and Babiker forthcoming).

Another factor affecting the degree of genetic and typological diversity across the planet is what is known in biology as Rapoport's rule. The higher degree of variation in ecozones allows for the development of more biological diversity in tropical than in arctic zones.

This corresponds to a much higher degree of linguistic diversity in the former than in the latter; in arctic regions, people are traditionally forced to move with the seasons in order to survive; in tropical zones much smaller ecozones usually suffice for people to be able to survive. Isolation from neighboring groups speaking the same language leads to dialect variation and, in due course, to new languages. The large number of Chadic languages (compared to other sub-branches of Afroasiatic) shows that there is another factor affecting language ecology, namely wetter rather than dryer (sub)tropical ecozones.

Of course, these are not the only factors determining diversity. Technological developments, such as the introduction of agriculture or pastoralism, clearly lead to an increase in populations and thereby to an expansion of humans, primarily along an east to west axis, as shown for example by Diamond (1997). Political factors play a role as well, again as suggested by the linguistic picture regarding genetic and typological diversity between languages. The vast area where only Ancient Egyptian was spoken, for example, shows that centralization of power and the extinction of other languages tend to co-evolve. Where centralized states existed or still exist in Europe, the degree of linguistic diversity is usually much smaller than in areas without such power relations, and of course similar tendencies can be observed in other parts of the world where states emerged, either due to an active policy of language unification (as in various European states), or because people belonging to minorities gave up their language in favor of dominant (majority) languages.

All of these factors also play a role in how and why new varieties of languages came about. The appearance of colonial actors speaking Indo-European languages and searching for new trade routes from the 15th century onwards was also made possible because their exploratory travels were financed to a large extent by powerful centralized states. At the time of the European expansion, states like Great Britain, the Netherlands, Portugal and Spain were already characterized by the dominance of one national language, sometimes combined with the active suppression of minority languages. Consequently, the expansion of these states into new territories tended to be largely isomorphic with the expansion of their national languages, although dialectical variation within the latter is sometimes reflected in the new languages, as with Australian English or varieties of French in the Americas.

New varieties of colonial languages as a result of these historical processes between the 15th and the 20th centuries resulted in a list of more than fifty new varieties of Indo-European languages (Holm 1988). These new languages were classified as "pidgins" when they constituted emergency languages not (yet) used by speakers as a first language, and as "creoles" once they became the primary language of a specific community. These definitions are somewhat problematic, because such contact languages may reach a certain degree of conventionalization (or "standardization") before becoming the primary language, as with Tok Pisin in Papua New Guinea or Nigerian Pidgin English in Nigeria (see Dimmendaal 2011: 230–236, and literature discussed therein).

For decades, several specialists of these new varieties of Indo-European languages elsewhere in the world have claimed that these newly emerging languages are not related to their source (or "lexifier") language, i.e., not part of Indo-European; see, for example, Thomason and Kaufman (1988), or earlier versions of the *Ethnologue*. They have also been claimed again and again to possess unique properties not found in other types of languages affected by language contact; see Bakker et al. (2017). But as argued by authors like DeGraff (2005) and as discussed in Dimmendaal (2011: 213–236), such claims about "exceptionalism" for these newly created languages are more about language ideologies than about useful taxonomic criteria; see also the chapter on language ideology by Paul Kroskrity (this volume).

Languages may "pidginize" or "creolize" to different degrees, depending on such factors as the degree of isolation from primary language speakers, the degree of contact with the latter, or typological differences between the languages in contact. Hence, English-based contact varieties such as Saramaccan in Suriname and Jamaican English differ quite strongly in the degree of substrate they manifest, although both show influences from the original language(s) of the new speakers, who came mainly from West Africa.

Because Indo-European languages like English, or other languages belonging to the same family, are well-studied (particularly in comparison to many languages in other parts of the world), they have also become the subject of investigation concerning the question of how new dialect varieties, or distinct languages (once mutual intelligibility was no longer given) came about. Since, from a phenomenological point of view, such processes can be observed most easily in the case of expanding Indo-European languages, these serve to arrive at a first structural analysis of emerging languages and corresponding restyling by new speakers. This, however, should not lead to the – erroneous – conclusion that we are observing a new and unique phenomenon, as argued below.

We acquire and become aware of preferred speech styles in our primary language, or in different languages in the case of individuals growing up in multilingual communities, during early childhood, in tandem with the grammar of the language(s) we acquire while growing up, as shown first in the pioneering studies published in Schieffelin and Ochs (1987). Language-specific features prime children to pay special attention to phonological or morphosyntactic features during primary language acquisition. But at the same time, they also acquire knowledge about preferred and dispreferred speech styles. Cross-cultural differences in language socialization were probably first shown in the collection of studies edited by Schieffelin and Ochs (1987), which contains contributions on speech communities in such different parts of the world as Japan, Lesotho, New Guinea and the United States. See the chapter by Birgit Hellwig (this volume) for the current state of the art in this respect.

Analyses of speech styles revolve around the totality of linguistic forms employed by speakers in the course of conversational interaction and involve ways of organizing social interaction. In order to make this latter dimension more concrete, let us have a look at some concrete phenomena first.

In a pioneering contribution on the replication or transfer of features from regional languages in West Africa into French, the language of the (former) colonizer which became the official language in several countries in the area, Bird and Shopen (1979: 105) point out:

> When Maninka people speak other languages in the West African context, they behave in similar ways, or as nearly so as they are able given the limitations they find in speaking other languages. A Maninka person expressing himself in French will typically display many of the same cultural values that he does when he speaks Maninka [a major lingua franca of Burkina Faso, Gambia, Guinea, the Ivory Coast, Mali and Senegal; GJD]: there will be extensive greetings and leave-takings, respect for the bonds of friendship and marriage, and a similar concern for the principles of badenya.

The concept of *badenya* may be translated as 'mother-child-ness' or 'comity', which "includes such notions as politeness, modesty, and unselfishness; conflict is to be avoided at all costs, but if there has to be conflict, every attempt should be made to avoid direct confrontation" (Bird and Shopen 1979: 93). The new style described by these authors shows that speakers may belong to the same speech community (in that mutual intelligibility is involved for speakers of French in West African countries and France), but different communities of practice and corresponding communicative styles can be identified between for example France and West Africa, or France and Central Africa.[1]

The notion "speech community" was one of the four key concepts of the "ethnography of communication" model developed by Hymes (1968) in his pioneering contribution in anthropological linguistics; in addition, speech events, constituent factors of speech events and functions of speech play a central role in his etic framework. Greeting strategies of the type discussed for Maninka and West African French as spoken in the region constitute just one type of speech event one finds cross-culturally. Here Hymes (1968) lists seven constituent factors which are relevant from a cross-cultural perspective: Sender (Addresser), Receiver (Addressee), Message Form, Channel, Code, Topic and Setting (Scene, Situation). Furthermore, seven types of speech functions are listed by him, one of which is the contact (phatic) dimension.

Scholars from the West have tended to interpret greetings as instances of "small talk" without any purpose of communicating ideas. Scholars from Africa, such as the prolific anthropological linguist Felix K. Ameka (e.g., Ameka 2009: 129, this volume, and many other publications) on Ewe in Ghana as well as on other languages across West Africa, have argued that phatic communion (or communication) is also about displaying cultural values such as inclusiveness and harmony, and about genuine inquiries about the well-being of others.

Polzenhagen (2007) presents the reader with a detailed analysis of cultural conceptualizations in West African English. These are particularly prominent in Nigerian Pidgin English, which has replaced a range of languages as the primary language of communication for many people in southern Nigeria. Polzenhagen (2007: 176–178) presents a range of new style figures in West African English (involving "codes" as a constituent factor in Hymes' descriptive model), from domains such as corruption and fraud, as in the following sentence from a short story by the Nigerian author Adimora-Ezeigbo (1999):

(1)   *she never chop money belle full*
      'she never consumes money till satiety'

---

1 Anchimbe (2008) describes stylistic varieties of French as spoken in another former colony, Cameroon, where the use of kinship terms plays an important role in politeness strategies when addressing others. Kießling and Mous (2006) is a further informative source.

Similar metaphorical extensions related to 'eating' are identified by Polzenhagen (2007: 154–167) in the domains of leadership, witchcraft and material wealth in his observations on an extensive survey of media in new varieties of English. Thus, in Cameroonian English the following statement may be made when a new government official is appointed (Polzenhagen 2007: 156):

(2)   *they have given him plenty to eat*

Parallel to Anchimbe (2008) for French, Polzenhagen (2007: 96, 122) also mentions the "non-literal" use of kinship terms such as *cousin, father, mother, brother/sister,* or *son,* in West African English, for a friend or a member of the same (local) community, as in the following example from an online source (cited in Polzenhagen 2007: 123); representation with italics retained as in the quoted source:

(3)   *Sons, Daughters* or any other legal resident *of The Land* of Liberia

Based on such examples from the media, Phillipson (1992: 244) states: "What is at stake when English spreads is not merely the substitution or displacement of one language by another but the imposition of new 'mental structures' through English." As the examples above should help to illustrate, these affect lexical and morphosyntactic as well as pragmatic domains, the latter also reflected in communicative styles, as further illustrated by the following examples from East Africa.

Nassenstein (2016) interprets Ugandan English as an example of the transfer of speech styles, particularly from two dominant languages in the country, Luganda and Acholi, onto this official language of the country. Apart from lexical borrowing (including interjections), modifications in the sound structure, morphological influence (such as the use of the Luganda diminutive *ka-*, e.g., *ka-child* 'small child'), "Luganda-like" politeness strategies can be observed in the southern part of the country, as with the discourse (attitude) marker *-ko*, which forms a phonological word with the preceding constituent (and from a linguistic point of view would therefore be characterized as an enclitic). An example from Nassenstein (2016: 404):

(4)   Luganda:
      linda-ko
      wait.IMP-ENCL
      'wait, please/would you mind making an effort of waiting?'

(5)   Ugandan English:
      wait-ko for me!' but please, wait for me!'

In her conversation analysis of Acholi, Rüsch (2021: 193–199) discusses interesting instances of "re-framing" or the transfer of frames into English in Northern Uganda from the regional language Acholi.[2] These include the transfer of a repair strategy, as it is called in conversation analysis, namely the insertion of question words in declarative sentences in Northern Uganda English as a rhetorical style figure. She mentions a sign in the city of Gulu, hanging from a rope around a plot of land near a café where newly sown grass was starting to grow, saying: '*Don't walk on the what? The grass*', thereby transferring a conversation strategy from the regional language Acholi (Rüsch 2021: 197–198).

According to Mesthrie (2019), a total of four types of Englishes exist in Africa, identifiable in terms of their history, functions and linguistic characteristics, of which two are discussed in the present study. Creolized varieties of English in West Africa, as in Example (1), have a history going back to the repatriation of slaves from the Caribbean and the United States in the 19th century. Second language varieties, which are the most widespread on the continent, are prototypically associated with British colonization and its education systems; Ugandan English as used in (4) and (5) above is an example of this type.

Scholars like Deborah Tannen have analyzed new varieties of English among immigrant communities in the United States. As argued by Tannen (1982) in her comparison of conversational styles among Greek, American and Greek-American couples in the United States, people may lose knowledge of Greek, but keep the speech style of the parents' and grandparents' language (p. 230), due presumably to the existence of separate social networks and corresponding communities of practice. In a further contribution, Tannen (1985: 102) lists nine features assumed to be characteristic of New York Jewish conversational style: fast rate of speech; fast rate of turn-taking; if a turn is not acknowledged, try again; marked shifts in pitch; marked shifts in amplitude; preference for storytelling; preference for personal stories; tolerance of and preference for simultaneous speech; abrupt topic shifting.

During colonial times new varieties of Portuguese also developed among colonizers and local communities in so-called "hybrid (third) spaces", as they are called by Bhabha (2004), for example in Brazil. Novinger (2003) discusses differences in politeness strategies between Brazilian Portuguese and North American English, although her observations would also seem to apply to differences from

---

2 Brown (2011: 88) conveniently refers to this phenomenon as "re-framing".

Portuguese as spoken in Portugal. According to Novinger (2003: 198–199), "Brazilians are more emotionally open and direct with their peers than are North Americans, and they do not feel they have really communicated with someone if they do not know what that person's feelings and personal opinions are . . . and Brazilians complain that North Americans are not direct in revealing what they 'really think', that is, their emotions, the mutual perception of indirectness is a two-way communication problem between Brazilians and North Americans." Moreover, interrupting the speaker tends to be interpreted as a sign of enthusiasm and interest, rather than disrespect (or impoliteness).

As shown by Alexandra Y. Aikhenvald (this volume), there are differences in language ideologies also within a country like Brazil. But even if Novinger (2003) may be talking about stereotypes to some extent, it is still interesting to investigate to what extent there has been influence from West African languages in the habitus of speakers when using the national language, Portuguese, not only in its grammar but also with respect to speech styles (or stylects) as part of a more general transfer of frames and corresponding scenarios or sequencing schemas for conversational interaction by enslaved people from West Africa (and from what is now the Democratic Republic of the Congo) to this area in South America. Scenarios as sequences of acts represent speakers' generalized knowledge about the sequence of speech events in specific contexts. Concepts like frame and scenario (or scene) were developed within the field of cognitive linguistics, for example by Fillmore (1975, 1976). Their relevance can already be observed in the greeting strategies in Maninka above and are discussed extensively in Dimmendaal (2022).

Transferring speech styles onto the dominant official language of a country inherited from the former colonizer, be it English, French, or Portuguese, can thus be observed in different parts of the world. L1 (first language) English predominates in Southern and East Africa and is best represented in South Africa. The latter shows significant similarities with the other major Southern Hemisphere varieties of English in Australia and New Zealand, according to Mesthrie (2019). But there is also clear evidence of influence from regional languages in South Africa. With respect to the use of English in interpersonal interaction in one speech community in the country, Gough (1996) formulated this as "thinking in Xhosa and speaking in English". In her study on Zulu, de Kadt (1992) points out that here direct requests are associated with a high degree of politeness; in English as spoken by white first language speakers in South Africa, indirect politeness and off-record strategies (in the sense of Brown and Levinson 1987) are preferred. Also, directives in Zulu are often subject to negotiation and debate, and therefore to going beyond a single turn. This may also lead to intercultural misunderstandings when such strategies are transferred into South African English (de Kadt 1995).

As the examples above should also help to show, very different cultural patterning can be expressed in one and the same language, so that different communities of practice within the same speech community may experience consistent miscommunication in spite of the fact that they are employing the same lexico-grammatical material. This of course also applies to other expanding languages of wider communication, such as the newly created varieties of Arabic in northern Africa and the Sahel region, or Swahili in Central Africa.

Apart from verbal communication, non-verbal communication may be involved in the development of new speech styles. When enslaved people from West Africa and their descendants acquired varieties of English, French, or Spanish in the Caribbean, they not only developed new speech styles, but they also transferred some of the gestures from their former languages. The best known migrating conceptualizations are probably "suck teeth" (or "kiss teeth") and "cut eye", as gestures of disapproval, which are described in a number of sources, for example Hollington (2016).

It is a well-known fact these days that speakers may be multilingual and that they may switch between different registers; this also applies to non-verbal communication. In an early source, Birdwhistell (1968: 381) pointed out that "biculturalism" may extend into kinesics, as shown by his comparison of gestural and expressional patterning among Kutenai (Ktunaxa) First Nation communities living in the border area between Canada and the United States, and (white Anglo-Saxon) American "body language". The recognition that a bilingual Kutenai moved in a consistently and regularly different manner when speaking Kutenai than when speaking English could not be understood until systematic analysis of the structure of American kinesics was undertaken.

Colonialism and urbanization have clearly played an important role in the creation of new language varieties and new speech styles over the past centuries. But on closer inspection, one finds (sometimes indirect) evidence that such transfer also occurs and has occurred in the past in other sociolinguistic situations, though along similar structural lines, as shown in the next section.

2 The creation of new speech styles outside colonial realms: Minority groups in Eastern and Central Africa

Whereas a range of studies are available on new speech styles in Indo-European languages, similar phenomena outside these colonial contexts are much less well documented. Nevertheless, direct and sometimes conjectural (indirect) evidence suggests that such modifications must have been part and parcel of the linguistic history of other speech communities as well. In the discussion below we will focus on minorities in Central and Eastern Africa, as the literature on these often stigmatized communities also appears to be less well known to the scholarly world at large.

The two areas discussed below are Eastern Africa, where communities are found which were often referred to in the older scientific literature by the derogatory term "Ndorobo", and Central Africa, where tropical forest foragers are found who are frequently referred to as "pygmies".

We will focus on these two regions in Africa because case studies on contrasting communicative styles are available, either within one and the same speech community, or between neighboring communities speaking closely related languages. These studies describe communities which can be assumed to have shifted from their former language as part of an adaptation strategy. However, as further argued, there are reasons to believe that this shift also involved a transfer of former communicative styles into their new primary languages. Such (partly stigmatized) minorities are also found in other parts of the world, for example in India and Malaysia. Given what appear to be comparable socio-economic conditions for these often stigmatized groups, it would be interesting to compare the socio-historical research findings on conversational styles from the two areas in Africa discussed here with those in Asia in the future.

Ever since the earliest studies on pastoralists in Eastern Africa appeared at the beginning of the 20th century, there has also been the occasional reference to submerged hunter-gatherer communities. Among the Maa in Kenya and Tanzania, such communities, sometimes also practicing agriculture, were referred to as *ol-torróbònì* (singular), *il-tóróbò* (plural) 'people without cattle' in one of the Maa dialects, Maasai. Groups living among the pastoral Maa or in adjacent areas in Kenya and Tanzania, such as the Akie, Aásax, Okiek, Omotik and Yaaku, and other communities in neighboring countries such as Uganda or Ethiopia, subsequently came to be referred to in the anthropological literature by the derogatory term *Dorobo* (also *Ndorobo*) as well. More recently, the Ethiopian linguist Moges Yigezu identified another such group, calling themselves

Ngaalam and living as hunter-gatherers in the forest zones of southwestern Ethiopia (Yigezu 2018).

Typically, such minorities either speak a dialect or a sociolect of the language spoken by their dominant neighbors, or a language closely related to the language of neighboring pastoral or agricultural people. Thus, Ngaalam is most closely related to the Didinga-Murle cluster in South Sudan, whose speakers are agricultural pastoralists, and to Baale, who are agriculturalists. Only rarely do such submerged groups speak a language constituting a linguistic isolate, as with Hadza in Tanzania, or Ongota (Biraile) and Shabo (Mikeyir) in Ethiopia. Whereas the sociolinguistic situation for the small Hadza community appears to be fairly stable, Ongota speakers, for example, are gradually shifting towards a major language in the area, Tsamakko (Savà and Tosco 2000).

These communities are not necessarily the modern descendants of prehistorical hunter-gatherers (although some of them may be); they may also have become impoverished, losing cattle or fertile agricultural land due to climate change or other ecological disasters. Characteristically, however, they live in a kind of symbiotic relationship with demographically more numerous and socio-economically dominant agricultural or pastoral neighbors. Speaking the language(s) of these latter groups may thus be seen as part of an adaptive strategy.

Due to the extensive study by Leikola (2014). information is available on differences in speech styles for one such submerged speech community, that of the Manjo and the dominating community of the Gomar. Both communities speak the same language, Kafa (which belongs to the Omotic branch of Afroasiatic), but they maintain their own separate social network, thereby constituting two communities of practice each with its own type of language ideology, as discussed in Dimmendaal (2022).

As a result primarily of extensive research by Japanese anthropologists and linguists, case studies are now available on speech styles among tropical forest foragers in Central Africa, often referred to by the derogatory term "pygmies" (with their tall neighbors being referred to as "grands noirs" in countries like the Democratic Republic of the Congo). Typically, these communities of forest foragers speak either the same language as their dominant neighbors, or a language closely related to the language of the latter. Table 4.1 summarizes information on the language affiliation of these various communities. As suggested already by the fact that these communities speak languages belonging to two distinct language phyla, or even three, if one takes Ubangian to constitute an independent language family (as the present author does), these communities most likely adapted linguistically to neighboring groups. Of the communities listed in Table 4.1, "the Aka, Baka, and Asua speak a language that cannot be understood by the speakers of languages belonging to the same family. Otherwise, all other Pygmy groups speak variants of the languages spoken by surrounding farmers" (Bahuchet 2012: 7).

Table 4.1: Tropical forest foragers in Central Africa and some of their languages.

Community	Country	Genetic classification of their language
Aka (Yaka, Beka)	Central African Republic, Democratic Republic of the Congo	Bantu (Niger-Congo)
Asua	Democratic Republic of the Congo	Central Sudanic (Nilo-Saharan)
Baka	Cameroon, Gabon	Ubangi (isolated family/ Niger-Congo)
Bagyeli/Bakola	Cameroon	Bantu (Niger-Congo)
Efe	Democratic Republic of the Congo	Central Sudanic (Nilo-Saharan)
Mamvu	Democratic Republic of the Congo	Central Sudanic (Nilo-Saharan)
Sua, Kango	Democratic Republic of the Congo	Bantu (Niger-Congo)
Twa	Uganda, Democratic Republic of the Congo, Rwanda/Burundi	Bantu (Niger-Congo)

The Central Sudanic family is spread over a large area stretching from the Nigerian borders across Chad to Sudan and South Sudan with a southward extension into the Central African Republic, the Democratic Republic of the Congo and Uganda. Most of the speech communities speaking Central Sudanic languages have no or few pygmoid features in their DNA structure, as far as present knowledge goes. Similarly, Bantu is spread from southeastern Nigeria towards Eastern and Southern Africa, again by communities with no or few traits showing pygmoid affiliation genetically, except in the Central African area.[3] We can therefore be fairly certain that communities of forest foragers in the area switched (from some unknown language) to these languages spoken by agricultural groups migrating into the traditional home area inhabited by these forest foragers; for further details, also on

---

3 The term "pygmoid" is sometimes used for people with mixed ancestry in Central Africa, as well as for so-called Negritos in Asia.

population genetics, the interested reader is referred to a contribution by a leading specialist in the field, Bahuchet (2012).

Speech styles of these communities described so far in the literature suggest that the language shift involved primarily an acquisition of grammar, whereas at least some of the speech styles reflected in their language use apparently originated from some other source, the most likely one, of course, being the former languages of these foraging communities. What we know about these diverging speech styles we owe primarily to publications by Japanese scholars, some of which were published primarily in Japanese; this is unfortunate, as it makes these sources less accessible to the community of anthropological linguists at large. Those published in English include Kimura (1990, 2003, 2014) and Sawada (1987, 1990).

The Efe, in the northeastern corner of the Democratic Republic of the Congo, constitute one such community, consisting of forest foragers speaking the Central Sudanic language Lese, who live in close association with farmers who call themselves Lese and who also speak Lese.[4] While the main means of subsistence of the semi-nomadic Efe consists of hunting and collecting honey and wild plants, they also practice some farming. However, they also depend on agricultural products from the neighboring farmers, on whose farms Efe men engage in clearing work (Terashima 1986). Members from the dominant Lese community are often in a patron-client relationship with an Efe and may refer to their client as *Efe-maia* 'my Efe', a relationship which is inherited from father to son on both sides. There is also intermarriage between Efe women and Lese men, whose offspring are considered to be Lese (Terashima 1986, 1987).

The distinction between the speech styles of Efe people speaking Lese and those of ethnic Lese is described by Sawada (1990). Characteristics indexical of Efe ethnicity as defined by speakers themselves mainly concern their songs, but also their conversations. Morning conversations in the Efe camp (as types of performance) may take place while sitting 10 meters apart at the edges of the camp, thereby requiring loud voices, in terms of the key used, and with only few overlaps (Sawada 1990: 166). After the evening meal from about 7 p.m., Efe men gather around the fire outside their huts and start speaking loudly. The conversations from this hour onward are accompanied by marked excitement that differs from the conversations at other hours. Characteristically, the exchanges and turn-takings occur with overlaps between turns, as the Efe men become increasingly more excited. Since the Efe men speak loudly, rhythmically and with other

---

4 The name Mbuti is used by different communities in the Ituri Forest speaking Asua, Efe, Sua and Kango, and a subgroup speaking a dialect of Sua (Bahuchet 2012: 20).

musical effects in the evening conversations, they can be considered as group performances (Sawada 1990: 166).

One of the characteristics of the Efe's singing is that it contains only a few words. A nursing Efe girl may sing a wordless, sad-tuned lullaby to a crying baby. "The song continues for about 15 seconds and has no words. The Efe baby begins to hear such a lullaby without words from right after birth" (Sawada 1990: 166). Another interesting observation made by the same author during his fieldwork is the call and answer between a parent and child, the former calling the child's name, ". . . and with little interval the child answers, 'uo', even from the other side of the camp" (p. 166).

One characteristic of Hymes' (1968) descriptive ethnography of communication, and part of the proposed emic approach towards the investigation of speech events, is the search for words which name these speech events. Efe distinguish between three types of songs: the first are *owa*, songs which are sung without dancing; when accompanied by dancing (or certain body movements) they are called *emu*; and those for adolescents, adults and old people are called *obe*. Community members apparently know whether the song originated from their own community or not. There is also little mutual appreciation of "the other's" music between Lese and Efe (Sawada 1990: 173). Consequently, these songs are indexical of these groups' distinct ethnic identities.

Evening conversations after dinner among the Efe sometimes reach a climax characterized by loud voices, short intervals and frequent turn-taking, as well as repetition of what the other said. In terms of Brown and Levinson's (1987) politeness model, this speech style may be interpreted as a positive face strategy (a concept not used by Sawada 1990), as speakers share common ground and support each other's opinions in this way. Moreover, a speaker often produces musical effects such as repeating the refrains of the preceding utterance's intonation contour, and also by clapping his hands to the rhythm of his utterance; see Sawada (1990: 187–188) for further details, who also describes parallels between the structure of turn-taking in evening conversations and singing songs in terms of a solo and response phase followed by a dense polyphonic chorus phase (which parallels with overlaps in conversations).

In his exemplary conversation analysis of Baka, an Ubangian language spoken in Cameroon and Gabon, Kimura (2001) compares the speech styles of this community of forest foragers with those of the neighboring community speaking the Bantu language Bakwele (as well as with a community speaking Japanese, based on the investigation of interactions between Japanese students in a cafeteria at a university). The interactions between Baka and Bakwele are less characterized by patron-client relationships than between the Efe and Lese and therefore serve the purpose here of showing significant differences in speech styles between neighboring communities living in close interaction without their languages being related genetically. Kimura (2001: 119) points out the following in this respect:

> When I asked a Baka informant about the conversation style of the Bakwele, he answered in [the] Lingala language 'Bazalí makelélé', meaning 'They are noisy'. I think this phrase was not only expressing the phonetic loudness of the Bakwele utterance, but also having an interactional implication. Figuratively speaking, the Bakwele conversation is filled with utterance akin to a path paved with flagstones . . . Probably the Baka informant used the term 'makelélé (noisy)' to represent this solidity of Bakwele's utterance in contrast to the softness or flexibility of their own.

Kimura (2001) also argues that in Baka conversations both utterance overlap and long silences are more frequent than in Bakwele. Moreover, the observed overlaps in Baka conversations are cooperative rather than confrontational. Kimura (2003: 33) claims that this synchronization or parallel distributed interaction is also observable in the polyphonic singing and dancing of Baka people.

The ultimate aim of describing differences in speech styles between distinct speech communities interacting with each other should of course be to explain what social conditions (historically or synchronically) motivate such differences. To date, there are still very few in-depth documentations using modern language documentation technology for the Central African area; the data archived for the Bakola speech community in Cameroon (see Table 4.2) still awaits an in-depth analysis of speech styles.[5] Here a dominant group of farmers lives in a symbiotic relationship with a small community of forest foragers speaking the same language.

The case study by Hoymann (2010) on ǂĀkhoe Haiǁom shows what such a sociolinguistic and psycholinguistic analysis may look like. This endangered language, spoken in Northern Namibia by a San community of less than 200 people traditionally living as hunter-gatherers, was investigated in a multidisciplinary language-documentation project by the anthropologist Thomas Widlok and two linguists, Gertie Hoymann and Christian Rapold.[6] Hoymann (2010) is the first detailed analysis of speech styles in ǂĀkhoe Haiǁom, based on video recordings of natural conversations and using conversation analysis as a method. The author compares data on questions and answers among speakers of ǂĀkhoe Haiǁom with data from nine other languages spoken in different parts of the world. The following two examples illustrate the two question types

---

5 See [https://dobes.mpi.nl/projects/bakola/project/] (accessed 17 February 2022).
6 See [https://archive.mpi.nl/tla/islandora/search/%2A%3A%2A?f%5B0%5D=cmd.Language%3A%22Hai//om%22] (accessed 17 February 2022).

in this language, polar (or yes-no) questions and content (or question-word) questions, respectively.

(6) *uri   ra   /gôa-e*
     jump PROG child-SN.A
     'does the child jump?'

(7) *tae-e   nē   e*
     what-3SN.A DEM 3SN.A
     'what is this?'

Interestingly, ǂĀkhoe Haillom has a markedly different distribution from the other languages in that it has a majority of content questions, whereas the other languages all have a majority of polar questions. One further conclusion to be drawn from the database investigated by Gertie Hoymann is that ǂĀkhoe speakers virtually never request confirmation, while in the other languages requests for confirmation make up between 20% and 50% of all questions.

Moreover, ǂĀkhoe Haillom silences between questions and answers are relatively long compared to those of the other languages. Based on the audio-visual recordings, it was also concluded that ǂĀkhoe Haillom speakers select a next speaker relatively less often than speakers of the other languages in the comparative study do.

What could be the reason(s) for such diverging speech styles? The frequent reliance on open questions, i.e., content questions ('where', 'what' etc.), provides the answerer with greater "freedom" in choosing a type of answer than polar questions would provide, as the latter constrain the recipient to 'yes' or 'no' answers. The culture of ǂĀkhoe speakers leads them to pose questions in a way that is less coercive and less restrictive of the answerer than with speakers of other languages. Hoymann (2010) relates these differences from other speech communities investigated in the question-answer project to the social constellation of ǂĀkhoe Haillom speakers, which may be characterized as a society of intimates.

Presumably related to this latter property of this speech community, the ǂĀkhoe Haillom data show a high number of questions that get no response or uptake, around 23% (Hoymann 2010: 2734). This puts ǂĀkhoe at the highest end of the "no response" scale for the ten languages compared in the project, together with Lao (in Laos). This frequent lack of responses in ǂĀkhoe can be explained, according to Hoymann (2010), by a cultural difference in turn-taking that causes speakers not to select a next speaker, which would have pressured someone for an answer. This habitus in turn reflects a mutual concern for individual independence or privacy.

For the Central African foraging communities discussed above, a shift in primary language towards that of their dominant neighbors is the most plausible explanation for the fact that they speak genetically related but partly diverging languages. Of course, this may have happened several times in the past, sometimes several generations ago, as a result of which these communities speak closely related but now distinct languages (Bahuchet 2012).

It should also be kept in mind that multilingual speakers may copy speech styles from their neighbors without shifting from their primary language. This appears to be the case for speakers of the Nilotic language Alur in the border area between northwestern Uganda and the northeastern corner of the Democratic Republic of the Congo. Southall (1953) shows how speakers borrowed numerous ideophonic words from their western neighbors speaking Central Sudanic languages. These tended to be adverbs expressing sensations related to physical qualities of their environment, i.e., things one smells, feels, or sees, which one wants to share with others. As a result, the number of phonemes in Alur almost doubled (Dimmendaal 2011: 182–184). Similarly, in speech communities speaking Southern Bantu languages like Xhosa or Zulu, extensive borrowing of clicks from Khoisan languages resulted in extremely complex phoneme inventories. The motivation for these borrowings was primarily a conversational style known as "hlonipha", which involved a taboo on the use of certain words or words that sounded similar to these, primarily in interactions with in-laws; the interested reader is referred to Dimmendaal (2022, Chapter 5) for a survey of the literature on this phenomenon.

3 Linguistic and non-linguistic manifestations of language creation: A brief synopsis

In the discussion above, concepts were used from such different fields as anthropological linguistics, interactional sociolinguistics and cognitive linguistics, all of which provided important insights into the creation of new speech styles over the past decades. The various relevant concepts and their linguistic manifestations in social interactions are summarized in Table 4.2. With all of these descriptive and analytical models and the concepts they use, it is crucial, in the present author's view, to compare the etic framework of the scholar interested in these issues and the emic perspective of speakers. Language ideologies of speakers and their metalinguistic reflections on these may be "imagined", without necessarily corresponding to the observations of outsiders.

Table 4.2: Methodologies contributing to the analysis of speech styles.

Ethnography of communication

- speech community
- speech events
- constituent factors of speech events
- functions of speech

Cognitive linguistics and speech act theory

- frames
- scenarios (or schemas)
- conversational maxims

(Im)politeness research

- Bald-on statements
- Positive face (im)politeness strategies
- Negative face (im)politeness strategies
- Off-record (im)politeness strategies

Conversation analysis

- Structure of turn-taking (pause, overlap, number of turns)
- Act sequences and concepts like schisming

Interactional sociolinguistics

- Community of practice
- Identity
- Language ideology
- Indexicality
- Performance

Non-verbal communication

- Facial expressions
- Gestures

At different points in the above sections, the term "politeness" has been used. This domain falls under the domain of "constituent factors" in Hymes' model. Of course, research on this topic is primarily associated with the classical contribution by Brown and Levinson (1987). In their seminal contribution these authors refer to the rational "model person" (regardless of the community in which this person grows up) with his or her positive face and negative face as a speaker or hearer. The model proposed by Brown and Levinson (1987) has been criticized by authors from Asia or Africa in various accounts, for example for its focus on the individual rather than on social groups. Kasanga (2011: 47), for example, argues that "group face" is crucial and that this concept should be linked to social indexing, "involving rights and obligations of individuals within the parameters of socio-cultural norms".

A further point of criticism concerns the decontextualized classification of speech acts by Brown and Levinson (1987), as they claim that specific locutionary acts inherently affect either positive or negative face needs. The present author however subscribes to the basic correctness of the Brown-and-Levinson taxonomy (Dimmendaal 2022, Chapter 10). At the same time important criticisms, for example by Watts (2003), need to be taken into account. This author propagates a discursive or contextualized approach towards the interpretation of speech acts. Indeed, these are particularly important in order to understand culture-specific elaborations of specific speech styles. For example, negative face strategies may be combined with a direct style, as in Korean, where social hierarchies and corresponding respect and social distance need to be reflected in the use of proper pronominal registers, as features associated with negative face strategies. But once such registers are properly used, speakers may be direct in their speech style (Song 2014).

The discursive (contextualized) dimension is also crucial in order to understand how the intended meaning of some utterance may be the opposite of the primary interpretation (thereby flouting Grice's maxim of quality; Grice 1975). Such speech styles can be observed, for example, with joking relationships, where individuals who are close may call each other names and "insult" each other. These, however, are to be interpreted, it is claimed in Dimmendaal (2022, Chapter 10.3), as *culture-specific* elaborations upon discourse strategies which speakers learn during language acquisition when they learn about specific frames (contexts) and corresponding scenarios (or act sequences) through communicative experiences.

The present author shares the view expressed in Kádár and Haugh (2013: 104) that the nature of specific speech acts and their impact on the positive face and negative face needs of speakers and hearers can only be understood if we assume there is a universal basis to their *inherent* character. This also applies to impoliteness strategies, an area where authors like Culpeper (2005) should be mentioned. Dimmendaal (2022) mentions the example of the common German farewell greeting *Schönen Tag noch!* 'have a nice day'. In its primary meaning (following Grice's maxim of quality) its use is a positive politeness strategy. But in a conflict situation, the same utterance may be a (positive) impoliteness strategy, as the speaker means exactly the opposite of what (s)he is saying, namely that the other person can "go to hell". Apart from the context, the distinct (falling) intonation as a prosodic signal provides the crucial contextualization cue for the interpretation of such a turn-constructional unit.

Research on speech styles also received an important impetus from conversation analysis, as developed by sociologists in the 1960s. Among the huge bulk of literature subsequently produced using this model, the pioneering contribution by Sacks, Schegloff and Jefferson (1974) needs to be mentioned, as it opened the floor for a range of interesting contributions on intercultural commonalities as well as differences. Agar (1994) is one of the first contributions on intercultural differences in communicative styles, based on experiences in Austria, India, Mexico and the United States. The examples discussed in this monograph reflect differential proposition schemas as abstractions acting as models of proper verbal behavior for communities of practice or speech communities. Such different patterns of verbal and non-verbal interaction across groups, as instantiations of differences in scenarios or proposition schemas (as well as other schemas, such as event schemas or role schemas, as proposed in cognitive linguistics), allow one to come to grips with intercultural misunderstandings in a more systematic manner when combined with two further analytical approaches, namely (im)politeness strategies and conversation analysis.

The investigation of performance as one of the "pillars" of interactional sociolinguistics is also relevant for anthropological linguistics, since different speech styles also play a role in the creation of distinct social identities from an intercultural perspective, as illustrated for Central African forest forager communities above. The indexical value of songs as channels (as one of the constituent factors in Hymes' model) can be transferred ideologically in the process. This is what appears to have happened in the case of Efe speakers in the Democratic Republic of the Congo. This habitual social activity, as well as other semiotic acts of identification, produces social identities. We should be grateful to the late Michael Silverstein (for example Silverstein 1979) for his quintessential observations in this respect.

The brief discussion of shifting communicative styles in language contact situations in the present chapter only allowed for the introduction of some of the relevant parameters in the investigation of speech styles (which are summarized in Table 4.2). Ameka and Terkourafi (2019) argue, quite rightly, that research themes such as the analysis of speech acts and corresponding conversational implicatures, (im)politeness theories and conversation analysis have been dominated by studies on Western languages. It is hoped that the present chapter helps to compensate to some extent for this unfortunate domination.

References

Adimora-Ezeigbo, Akachi. 1999. *Rituals & departures*. London: Karnak House.

Agar, Michael. 1994. *Language shock. Understanding the language of conversation*. New York: Morrow.

Ameka, Felix K. 2009. Access rituals in West African communities. An ethnopragmatic perspective. In Gunter Senft & Ellen B. Basso (eds.), *Ritual communication*, 127–152. Oxford: Berg.

Ameka, Felix K. & Marina Terkourafi. 2019. What if . . .? Imagining non-Western perspectives on pragmatic theory and practice. *Journal of Pragmatics* 145. 72–82.

Anchimbe, Eric A. 2008. 'Come greet Uncle Eric'. Politeness through kinship terms. In Bernard Mulo Farenkia (ed.), *De la politesse linguistique au Cameroun/Linguistic politeness in Cameroon*, 109–119. Frankfurt am Main: Peter Lang.

Bahuchet, Serge, 2012. Changing language, remaining pygmy. *Human Biology* 84 (1). 11–43.

Bakker, Peter, Finn Borchsenius, Carsten Levisen & Eeva Sippola. (eds.). 2017. *Creole Studies – phylogenetic approaches*. Amsterdam & Philadelphia: John Benjamins.

Bhabha, Homi K. 2004. *The location of culture*. Abingdon: Routledge.

Bird, Charles & Timothy Shopen. 1979. Maninka. In Timothy Shopen (ed.), *Languages and their speakers*, 59–111. Cambridge, MA: Winthrop Publishers.

Birdwhistell, Ray L. 1968. Kinesics. *International Encyclopedia of the Social Sciences* 8. 379–385.

Brown, Lucien. 2011. *Korean honorifics and politeness in second language learning*. Amsterdam & Philadelphia: John Benjamins.

Brown, Penelope & Stephen C. Levinson. 1987. *Politeness. Some universals in language usage*. Cambridge: Cambridge University Press.

Culpeper, Jonathan. 2005. Impoliteness and entertainment in the television quiz show. The weakest link. *Journal of Politeness Research* 1 (1). 35–72.

DeGraff, Michel F. 2005. Linguists' most dangerous myth. The fallacy of Creole exceptionalism. *Language in Society* 34 (4). 533–591.

de Kadt, Elizabeth. 1992. Politeness phenomena in South African Black English. In Laurence F. Bouton & Yamuna Kachru (eds.), *Pragmatics and language learning*, Vol. 3, 103–116. Urbana-Champaign, IL: University of Illinois at Urbana-Champaign.

de Kadt, Elizabeth. 1995. The cross-cultural study of directives. Zulu as a non-typical language. *South African Journal of Linguistics/Suid-Afrikaanse Tydskrif vir Taalkunde, Supplement* 27. 45–72.

Diamond, Jared M. 1997. *Guns, germs, and steel – the fates of human societies*. New York & London: W. W. Norton & Company.

Dimmendaal, Gerrit J. 2011. *Historical linguistics and the comparative study of African languages*. Amsterdam & Philadelphia: John Benjamins.

Dimmendaal, Gerrit J. 2019. A note on the spreading of Afroasiatic. In Rainer Voigt (ed.), *5000 Jahre semitohamitische Sprachen in Asien und Afrika*, 29–39. Cologne: Rüdiger Köppe.

Dimmendaal, Gerrit J. 2022. *Nurturing language. Anthropological linguistics in an African context*. Berlin & New York: De Gruyter Mouton.

Dimmendaal, Gerrit J. & Hiba Babiker. Forthcoming. Nilo-Saharan. The merits and limits of inter-disciplinary approaches. In Martine Robbeets and Mark Hudson (eds.), *Oxford handbook of archaeology and language*. Oxford: Oxford University Press.

Ehret, Christopher. 2000. Language and history. In Bernd Heine & Derek Nurse (eds.), *African languages – an introduction*, 272–297. Cambridge: Cambridge University Press.

Fillmore, Charles J. 1975. An alternative to checklist theories of meaning. In Cathy Cogen (ed.), *Proceedings of the First Annual Meeting of the Berkeley Linguistics Society, February 15–17*, 123–131. Berkeley, CA: Berkeley Linguistics Society.

Fillmore, Charles J. 1976. Frame semantics and the nature of language. *Annals of the New York Academy of Sciences* 280. 20–32.

Gough, David H. 1996. Thinking in Xhosa and speaking in English. The theory and practice of contrastive analysis. *South African Journal of Applied Language Studies* 4. 2–19.

Grice, H. Paul. 1975. Logic and conversation. In Peter Cole & Jerry L. Morgan (eds.), *Syntax and semantics*, Vol. 3: *Speech acts*, 41–58. New York: Academic Press.

Hollington, Andrea. 2016. Emotions in Jamaican. African conceptualizations, emblematicity and multimodality in discourse and public spaces. In Anne Storch (ed.), *Consensus and dissent. Negotiating emotion in the public space*, 81–104. Amsterdam & Philadelphia: John Benjamins.

Holm, John. 1988. *Pidgins and creoles*, Vol. 1. Cambridge: Cambridge University Press.

Hoymann, Gertie. 2010. Questions and responses in ǂÃkhoe Haillom. *Journal of Pragmatics* 42. 2726–2740.

Hymes, Dell H. 1968. The ethnography of speaking. In Joshua A. Fishman (ed.), *Readings in the sociology of language*, 99–138. The Hague: Mouton.

Kádár, Dániel Z. & Michael Haugh. 2013. *Understanding politeness*. Cambridge: Cambridge University Press.

Kasanga, Luanga A. 2011. Face, politeness, and speech acts. Reflecting on intercultural interaction in African languages and varieties of English. In Gabriele Sommer & Clarissa Vierke (eds.), *Speech acts and speech events in African languages*, 41–64. Cologne: Rüdiger Köppe.

Kießling, Roland and Maarten Mous. 2006. "Vous nous avez donné le français, mais nous sommes pas obliges de l'utiliser comme vous le voulez". Youth languages in Africa. In Christa Dürscheid & Jürgen Spitzmüller (eds.), *Perspektiven der Jugendsprachforschung*, 385–402. Frankfurt am Main: Peter Lang.

Kimura, Daiji. 1990. Verbal interaction of the Bongando in central Zaire. With special reference to their addressee-unspecified loud speech. *African Study Monographs* 11 (1). 1–26.

Kimura, Daiji, 2001. Utterance overlap and long silence among the Baka Pygmies. Comparison with Bantu farmers and Japanese university students. *African Study Monographs* 26. 103–121.

Kimura, Daiji. 2003. Bakas' mode of co-presence. *African Study Monographs Supplementary Issue* 28. 25–35.

Kimura, Daiji. 2014. Everyday conversations of the Baka pygmies. *African Study Monographs Supplementary issue* 47. 75–79.

Kuper, Rudolph & Stefan Kröpelin. 2006. Climate-controlled Holocene occupation in the Sahara. Motor of Africa's evolution. *Science* 313. 803–807.

Leikola, Kirsi. 2014. *Talking Manjo. Repertoires as means of negotiating marginalization*. Helsinki: University of Helsinki dissertation.

Mesthrie, Rajend. 2019. African Englishes from a sociolinguistic perspective. *Oxford Research Encyclopedia of Linguistics*. [https://oxfordre.com/linguistics/view/10.1093/acrefore/9780199384655.001.0001/acrefore-9780199384655-e-225] (accessed 27 April 2022).

Nassenstein, Nico. 2016. A preliminary description of Ugandan English. *World Englishes* 35 (3). 396–420.

Novinger, Tracy. 2003. *Communicating with Brazilians. When "yes" means "no"*. Austin: University of Texas Press.

Phillipson, Robert. 1992. *Linguistic imperialism*. Oxford: Oxford University Press.

Polzenhagen, Frank. 2007. *Cultural conceptualisations in West African English – a cognitive-linguistic approach*. Frankfurt a. M. & Berlin: Peter Lang.

Rüsch, Maren. 2021. *A conversational analysis of Acholi. Structure and socio-pragmatics of a Nilotic language of Uganda*. Leiden & Boston: Brill.

Sacks, Harvey, Emanuel A. Schegloff & Gail Jefferson. 1974. Simplest systematics for organization of turn-taking for conversation. *Language* 50 (4). 696–735.

Savà, Graziano & Mauro Tosco. 2000. A sketch of Ongota, a dying language of southwest Ethiopia. *Studies in African Linguistics* 29 (2). 59–136.

Sawada, Masato. 1987. The evening conversation of the Efe Pygmy men and its social implication. A men's display to women. *African Study Monographs, Supplementary Issue* 6. 85–96.

Sawada, Masato. 1990. Two patterns of chorus among the Efe, forest hunter-gatherers in northeastern Zaire – why do they love to sing? *African Study Monographs* 10 (4). 159–195.

Schieffelin, Bambi B. & Elinor Ochs (eds.). 1987. *Language socialization across cultures*. Cambridge & New York: Cambridge University Press.

Silverstein, Michael. 1979. Language structure and linguistic ideology. In Paul R. Clyne, William F. Hanks & Carol L. Hofbauer (eds.), *The elements. A parasession on linguistic units and levels*, 193–247. Chicago: Chicago Linguistic Society.

Song, Sooho. 2014. Politeness in Korea and America. A comparative analysis of request strategy in English communication. *Korea Journal* 54 (1). 60–84.

Southall, Aidan W. 1953. *Alur society. A study in processes and types of domination*. London: Oxford University Press.

Tannen, Deborah. 1982. Ethnic style in male-female conversation. In John J. Gumperz (ed.), *Language and social identity*, 217–231. Cambridge: Cambridge University Press.

Tannen, Deborah. 1985. Silence: Anything but. In Deborah Tannen & Muriel Saville Troike (eds.), *Perspectives on silence*, 93–111. Norwood, NJ: Ablex.

Terashima, Hideaki. 1986. Economic exchange and the symbiotic relationship between the Mbuti (Efe) Pygmies and the neighboring farmers. *Sprache und Geschichte in Afrika* 7 (l). 391–405.

Terashima, Hideaki. 1987. Why Efe girls marry farmers? Socio-ecological backgrounds of inter-ethnic marriage in the Ituri forest of central Africa. *African Study Monographs Supplementary Issue* 6. 65–83.

Thomason, Sarah Grey & Terrence Kaufman. 1988. *Language contact, creolization, and genetic linguistics*. Berkeley: University of California Press.

Watts, Richard J. 2003. *Politeness*. Cambridge: Cambridge University Press.

Yigezu, Moges. 2018. Ngaalam: An endangered Nilo-Saharan language of southwest Ethiopia – a sociolinguistic survey on language vitality and endangerment. In Helga Schröder & Prisca Jerono (eds.), *Nilo-Saharan issues and perspectives*, 25–42. Cologne: Rüdiger Köppe.

Paul V. Kroskrity
5 Language ideologies and social identities

Language ideologies, funderstood as the beliefs, feelings, and emergent conceptions about language structure and use that often index the political economic interests of individual speakers, ethnic or other interest groups, and nation-states (Kroskrity 2000, 2010), provide crucial resources for projects involving the construction of social identities of varying scale. Drawing on detailed case studies of two very different Native American communities, Village of Tewa (N. Arizona) and Western Mono (Central California) and a broad survey of many other language communities, this chapter examines the vital role of language ideologies in processes of language contact and multilingualism, language shift or maintenance, and language revitalization/reclamation. While explicit language ideologies as well as those that emerge in the practical consciousness of everyday language activity help speakers construct a myriad of identities, this survey will focus on three types of *ideologically informed identifications* distinguished by relative ideological source. One, *Indigenous language ideologies* provide ontological resources for communities that view themselves as consubstantial with their cultural ideologies and language practices. These can take the form of explicit discourses of identity or tacit understandings that emerge from everyday and/or ceremonial activities. Two, *contact-related language ideologies* are community understandings of multilingualism and language contact phenomena and how these map onto identification processes. These may include identities associated with multilingual practice such as egalitarian multilingualism, compartmentalization, shift, and diglossia. Three, *imposed language ideologies* are also used by nation-states in an attempt to erase Indigenous identities and other sub-national identities and to racialize linguistic minorities by imposing stigmatized identities.

Acknowledgments: I want to thank the editors for inviting me to write this chapter. In addition I would also like to thank two anonymous reviewers for their useful comments and suggestions.

Paul V. Kroskrity, University of California, Los Angeles/United States,
e-mail: paulvk@anthro.ucla.edu

https://doi.org/10.1515/9783110726626-005

1 Introduction

Shared language structures and patterns of use have long served as criterial attributes of group identities. But this very notion of shared language is just one of many language ideological resources that speakers and their communities everywhere use to nucleate these groups and to endow individuals with social identities. Language ideologies, understood as "the beliefs, feelings, and conceptions about language structure and use that often index the political economic interests of individual speakers, ethnic or other interest groups, and nation-states" (Kroskrity 2010: 192), provide crucial resources for projects involving the construction and construal of social identities of varying scale. My goal in this chapter is to better understand projects of social identity as "sites of ideological work" (Gal and Irvine 2019: 167) and to explicate the resources that language ideologies provide to speakers and communities for these projects. Social identities are those which people derive from their participation in, and association with, various social groups; social identities may be analytically distinguished from personal identities that are more uniquely biographical in origin.[1]

This chapter will build on the well-recognized observation that language ideologies perform an important role in social identity construction (Kroskrity 2000: 23–31, 2004: 509–511, 2010: 203–205). First, I will briefly explore the analytical resources provided by language ideological approaches that make them especially appropriate for understanding projects of language and identity. To exemplify some of these properties I will rely on data and observations of my two long-term research projects on the Village of Tewa (aka Arizona Tewa) and the Western Mono (of Central California) (Kroskrity 1993, 1998, 2000, 2009, 2017). In three sections that follow that introduction of ideological resources, I will provide further case studies by surveying several productive patterns of identity projects in which language ideological work provides critical resources. One, *indigenous language ideologies* provide ontological resources for communities that view themselves as consubstantial with their cultural ideologies and language practices.[2] Such ideologies arise from within social groups that can be identified as either

---

1 For more on personal and other types of identities that will not be treated here, readers should consult such sources as Bauman (2004), Coulmas (2019), Giddens (1991), and Taylor (1989).
2 In this first mention of "indigenous", I want to briefly explicate the rationale for use of it with initial upper/lower case. When the word is used primarily as a descriptive term for "local" or "native to a place", I will use lower case and reserve the upper for those instances when Indigenous could be replaced by such designations as Native American, or First Nations.

language or speech communities (Gumperz 1968, Silverstein 1996) and are typically related to their indigenous economies, ceremonial organizations, and forms of social organization. Two, *contact-related language ideologies* are community understandings of multilingualism and language contact phenomena and how these map onto identification processes. These may include identities associated with multilingual practice such as egalitarian multilingualism (Sankoff 1980: 8–9), compartmentalization, shift, and diglossia (Gumperz 1968). For the third I will briefly conclude by examining *imposed language ideologies* used by nation-states and powerful elites in an attempt to erase indigenous identities and other sub-national identities and to racialize linguistic minorities by imposing stigmatized identities within the hierarchies they seek to produce. Unlike the first two identity project types, this third type is externally imposed and only rarely, if ever, represents the targeted group's own sense of identity. While these are three productive patterns, they are not offered as a comprehensive typology but more as an introduction to an important but neglected topic. These patterns thus only sample a broader range of identity work for which languages and their language ideological foundations are regularly deployed.

2 Language ideological resources

Basic language ideological theory and more recent scholarship provide useful tools and strategies that complement other linguistic anthropological approaches, such as Bucholtz and Hall's (2004) "tactics of intersubjectivity", for the analysis of language and identity. I have described language ideological theory as a cluster concept consisting of five inter-related dimensions which can be briefly identified as 1) positionality, 2) mediation, 3) multiplicity, 4) awareness, and, 5) identity. Since the last of these is inextricably tied to the subject of this chapter, only the first four require explication here. Interested readers may wish to consult a more elaborate treatment of these definitional attributes (e.g., Kroskrity 2000, 2010) and a more complete account of the impact of their different language ideologies (2018) on the Tewa and Mono communities than the summary treatment provided here.

The first, *positionality*, locates language ideologies – including those relating language and identity – within the larger political-economic systems of the societies from which they emerge. The second, *mediation*, is a recognition of how beliefs and feelings about language structures connect those structures to features of the sociocultural worlds of their speakers. Third, *multiplicity*, is the recognition that language ideologies are most meaningfully studied – as they are experienced by language speakers – as one of many beliefs and feelings about language that circulate within or between social groups. The most recognizable form of multiplicity is overt contestation and debate because this is when taken-for-granted ideologies may emerge in discursive consciousness, sparking greater *awareness* and the possibility of agentive change. Though some scholars have treated the concept of language ideologies as if it were most useful in labeling the more out-of-awareness, practical consciousness, habitus-like notions about language structure and use (e.g., Sallabank 2013: 72), I would contend that language ideologies must involve the entire spectrum of awareness ranging from practical to discursive consciousness (Kroskrity 1998). Language users are indeed folk-theorists of their languages but their ethnotheories may be very divergently expressed, ranging from solely through the practice of actual linguistic conduct all the way to explicit metapragmatic commentary emerging in conversational discourses where speakers articulate claims about language and identity. This is one of the main reasons why the study of language ideologies must be an ethnographic enterprise as well as one that involves ethnographic interviewing.

2.1 Positionality

Regarding positionality, it matters that the Village of Tewa, with its long history of sedentary farming and theocratic governance, distributes power and authority unequally whereas the Western Mono, with their traditional practice of hunting and gathering, their relatively decentralized social organization, and their former pattern of seasonal movement are highly egalitarian. For the Tewa, heritage speakers of a Kiowa-Tanoan language and a Pueblo community of about 700, this fusing of political power and religious authority in ceremonial leaders and the sacred register of *te'e hiili* ('kiva speech') created both a "shared language" capable of becoming an emblem of identity, in a process of *adequation* (Bucholtz and Hall 2004: 382) but also a register that could be used to stratify people and thereby produce *distinction* (Bucholtz and Hall 2004: 384), elevating the ceremonial elite and lowering those with limited knowledge of that register or no authority to use it. In addition to its cultural prominence in the ceremonial system, the Tewa language plays a special and distinctive role as an "ethnic boundary" marker that distinguishes the Tewa from the otherwise culturally similar Hopi majority (Kroskrity 1993). This identity differentiating role is entextualized in Tewa oral histories about the "language curse" their leaders placed on Hopi clan leaders more than

300 years ago for failure to reward Tewa military service for them.[3] According to this curse as a form of cultural revenge, Hopis would be unable to learn Tewa but the Tewa would speak the majority Hopi languages "and will ridicule you [Hopis] in both your language and our own" (Dozier 1954: 292).

In contrast to the details of positionality that make the Tewa language an exceptionally available sign of group identity, the decentralized society of the Western Mono former hunter-gatherers, coupled with their close identification with neighboring Indigenous groups like the Foothill Yokuts and the Southern Sierra Miwok did not provide a basis for making Mono available as a sign of tribal identity. Today the Western Mono number about 2,000 and live in Central California towns located on the Western slopes of the Sierra Nevada Mountains in Central California. Multilingualism, intermarriage, and shared patterns of land usage actually tended to promote linkages between a regional identity and a trilingual linguistic repertoire of Mono, Yokuts, and Miwok. Ceremonial activity, for these Central California groups, was focused more on individual health, life crises, and healing than on an agricultural cycle and cosmic order maintenance. Though highly valued for their knowledge and abilities, healers in Indigenous Central California did not create a distinctive linguistic register.

2.2 Mediation and multiplicity

Given its sociocultural prominence, Tewa kiva speech practices became a cultural model worthy of emulation in analogous everyday practices involving indigenous linguistic purism, strict compartmentalization, and displays of linguistically encoded identities (Kroskrity 1998). Just as ceremonial practitioners needed to observe norms outlawing the use of other languages, code-switching to other languages, and other forms of language mixing that would deviate from the kiva speech register, everyday speakers in more mundane activities would practice purism and reject loanwords from other languages. The Tewa were multilingual but they did not syncretize their linguistic knowledge, observing instead the norm of using the appropriate language for particular speech events. Thus, linguistic purism was closely tied to compartmentalization and these were both ideologies of proper and effective language use that were indexical signs of the influence of kiva speech. The ceremonial identities, iconized (or rhematized) (Irvine and Gal

---

3 The language curse was a form of revenge not just for the lack of payment to the Tewa warriors but also for the insulting ways they were treated according to folk histories still told in the Village of Tewa today.

2000) by role-specific kiva-speech, provided the basis for the Tewa language to serve as emblem of group identity.[4]

Much as the positionality of kiva speech can be related to a set of derivative ideologies that display connections between the larger social worlds of speakers and their languages, so can we see ideologies of an egalitarian multilingualism, syncretism, variationism, referentialism, and utilitarianism as emerging from the social world of the Western Mono. Borrowing freely from neighboring languages and displaying a range of unranked individual variation that did not need to be evaluated against a well-demarcated set of cultural norms, the multiple beliefs and practices of the Western Mono can all be related to the macro-features of their economic adaptation. In accord with their hunting and gathering economy and adaptive, utilitarian ideology it spawned, languages were associated with the functional vocabulary that underlay technologies for producing food and shelter more than with the individuation of particular linguistic identities.

2.3 Awareness

Given the cultural salience of language as a valorized emblem of identity, it is no wonder that awareness levels regarding discourses of language and identity would be elevated. Nowhere is this made more apparent, than in the Tewa saying, *Naavi hiili, naavi woowatsi na-mu* ('My language is my life.') Less common is a discourse of identity that draws an analogy between local agricultural practices and language use. This is expressed in the following translation of a Tewa man's attempt to compare the growing of different colors of corn in separate fields with linguistic purism and compartmentalization (Kroskrity 2000: 338–339):

> You know those different colors of corn just don't happen. If you want blue corn, if you want red corn, you must plant your whole field only in that color. If you plant two colors together you get mixed corn. But we need to keep our colors different for the different ceremonies and social dances which require that color. . . . Same way our languages. If you mix them they are no longer as good and useful. The corn is a lot like our languages – we work to keep them separate.

The ideological work of separating languages is here quite explicitly tied to agricultural practices analogous to linguistic purism and strict compartmentalization;

---

4 Though the semiotic process of iconization, in which a linguistic sign comes to "stand for" a group was introduced in Irvine and Gal (2000), these authors later found the process to be more accurately labeled as rhematization (Gal and Irvine 2019: 42–43). Torn between fidelity to theoretical nuance and a pre-existing tradition of using the earlier term, I will use both interchangeably.

both are also explicitly linked to the ceremonial system and its requirement for differentiated colors. This may be considered a deliberate cultivation of difference and a recognition of the way specific linguistic practices maximize the difference between languages and minimize or eliminate their co-occurrence in the same domains of usage. Tewa people are both aware of and proud of their linguistic purism which they regularly discuss as an attribute of their linguistic superiority over Tewa as spoken in various New Mexican pueblos. Their language, from the perspective of the Village of Tewa, is to be looked down on as "mixed" with Spanish.[5]

In contrast to the explicit Tewa discourse of language and identity and the recognition of linguistic purism as a means for maintaining their heritage language as a "pure" and effective emblem of their identity, Western Mono developed no metalanguage or metacommentary about language(s) and linguistic practice, including the role of language in constructing any type of social identity. In the Mono world, linguistic syncretism displayed a culturally approved adaptability and a regional cosmopolitanism. If a social identity was to be displayed it could be most effectively done so by speaking useful languages or borrowing useful words from neighboring languages in order to project a regional identity. Using the tactic of distinction, Monos were more like to ideologically differentiate other groups not by what they spoke but by what they ate.[6] For the Mono, specific languages played more of a bridge-building function than a boundary marking one and they were to be valued for their practical merit rather than as valorized emblems of identity. In this contrast of groups and their language ideologies, it is plain to see how sociocultural experience saturates the way language is used, understood, and valued.

This contrastive analysis of Tewa and Mono language ideologies provides a basis for viewing how different language ideologies inform their distinctive social identities and provide a basis for better understanding how language ideologies provide critical resources for social projects and their related tactics of intersubjectivity (Bucholtz and Hall 2004). The following sections continue to

---

5 Actually both language communities show a robust resistance to loanwords. Dozier (1956) estimated Rio Grande Tewa as having no more than 5% loanwords from Spanish in spite of more than a century of domination by Spanish colonists. Still residents of the Village of Tewa do have a reason to feel superior to their New Mexican linguistic kin since their total number of loanwords from any language is about 1% (Kroskrity 1993). So at least insofar as lexical measures are concerned, the Village of Tewa's informal regime of linguistic purism is very effective.

6 Examples of groups identified by Monos were "acorn eaters", brine-fly larvae eaters (*kwi-zabi-tɨka'*), and later for those more fully incorporated into the cash economy and its commerce – bread eaters (*kumasa-tɨka'*).

explore the language ideological contribution to various social projects in a wider range of social groups and will use conceptual tools that have been developed by scholars to better understand the semiotic processes involved in their production (e.g., indexicality, iconization/rhematization, fractal recursivity, and erasure (Irvine and Gal 2000, Gal and Irvine 2019)).[7]

3 Indigenous language ideologies

In the social transformations of contemporary language communities (Silverstein 1998) the inevitable contact of indigenous, national, and even global language ideologies is omnipresent. It is nevertheless often possible to distinguish beliefs and feelings about language that have originated earlier in the historic development of specific groups often as a result of long-term adaptation to a particular environment, or in association with enduring social institutions or cultural practices. Why bother distinguishing indigenous language ideologies from those of more recent contact? I think there are at least two reasons for wanting to analytically distinguish them. One important reason is that beliefs and feelings about language that have emerged over hundreds of years and that are closely tied to long-standing economic adaptations, indigenous religious beliefs and practices, and the group's indigenous social organization are likely to be enduring forces that are especially impactful. Similar to the way Whorf (1956: 156) saw "linguistic lag" as a dialectic of reciprocal influence in which cultural change would lead linguistic, I would say that indigenous linguistic ideologies more tied to specific languages persist, possibly resist, and otherwise influence the novel language ideologies brought by culture contact and cultural change.

This observation is closely related to my conclusions in an earlier comparison of the language ideological assemblages of the Tewa and Mono communities (Kroskrity 2018). For each of these groups, many contemporary language ideologies are traceable to indigenous cultural institutions and practices. For the

---

7 I would like to offer what I hope is a user-friendly gloss of some of the metalanguage of language ideological theory. Indexes are types of signs that through use have an association with some person or object. Iconization (later rhematization) is when a particular sign comes to emblematically "stand for" a particular group. Fractal recursivity is a replication of nested relationships (like Russian dolls). Ideological erasure happens when users ignore or background unruly information in order to simplify a complex field of experience and highlight some basic pattern. Readers who have a serious interest in language ideologies should consult the originals.

Western Mono, indigenous language ideologies of egalitarian multilingualism, utilitarianism, and variationism are directly traceable to their band-level non-hierarchical society, to their seasonal movement and regional distribution, and to their experience as hunter-gatherers. None of these ideologies provide significant support for making Mono an emblem of group identity. In contrast, the Tewa have multiple language ideologies that do so. These include their chartered multilingualism in which the Tewa language is conspicuously rhematized as the emblem of Tewa identity. But this identification is also supported by Tewa ceremony and the practices of compartmentalization and purism as well as by explicit discourses of language and identity.

But even with these very significant differences attributable to indigenous language ideologies, the vast majority of members in *both* groups, in the late 20th and early 21st century would affirm the importance of their heritage languages to their tribal identities. This apparent ideological convergence is the product of culture change spurred by two somewhat distinct causes. Both groups have been exposed to the linguistic nationalism of the nation state with its use of English as an icon of national identity (Kroskrity 2009). Both groups have also been unusually reflective about their heritage languages in the more recent context of seeing them as "endangered languages" with uncertain futures (Avineri and Kroskrity 2014). But while contact-related culture change has fostered a discourse of language and tribal identity in both groups, the Mono case is the result of the hegemonic influence of the state both in undermining indigenous multilingualism and replacing all other Indigenous languages in the Mono linguistic repertoire with English. The emergence of Mono as an emblem of tribal identity during the last fifty years contrasts with the long-standing Tewa pattern of Indigenous emblematization of the heritage language. Significantly, only in the Tewa community is a current discourse of language and identity accompanied by enduring community-based efforts to revitalize the language and to teach youth in after-school classes.[8] So the older and indigenous ideologies that support language and identity appear to provide more robust and persistent resources for their speakers than do ideologies acquired through contact in these cases.

Another reason why distinguishing indigenous ideologies from those of contact is highly significant is that groups like the North Siberian Sakha (aka Yakut),

---

8 As I am writing this in April 2021, classes have now been suspended because of the COVID-19 pandemic for slightly more than a year but they are scheduled to resume when the Village of Tewa community, like the larger Hopi Reservation that includes it, is able to safely resume the operation of indoor activity. It is also relevant to note that the teaching of Tewa, while supported by the majority, is not without its village-internal critics. See Kroskrity (2012).

as represented by Jenanne Ferguson (2019) in her ethnographic monograph, explicitly view some language ideologies as "their own" and as important parts of their culture to be propagated in public discourse; "these 'local' or indigenous ideologies of language are also an intrinsic part of what it means to be Sakha, in terms of identity, but also as a human subject acting in the world" (Ferguson 2019: 83).

Numbering approximately 450,000, these speakers of a Turkic language that was once exclusively spoken in rural areas now include many successful urban migrants. Many language ideologies appear to be linguistic versions of indigenous religion-based ontologies of language that connect it to spirit beings, the land, and subsistence activities in the natural world. The Sakha language is animate, powerful, and capable of agency and endowed with a moral efficacy as means of connecting with the protection of one's guardian spirit and of offering sacrifices to a natural world full of spiritual life. These were not just the beliefs of Sakha religious practitioners; many in the community understood these beliefs as their own. But now during a period of cultural revalorization of groups once regarded as backward and locked in the past, Sakha themselves have codified some of these beliefs which are taught in Siberian schools that have become more open to the inclusion of minority cultures. Similarly, for urban Sakha, ceremonies in the Sakha language that were once suppressed are now celebrated publicly as Sakha language cultural events. On the personal level, Sakha believe that if an individual does not speak the language, their guardian spirit will leave them. Relatively purist forms of Sakha are viewed as necessary to show respect for one's guardian spirit, other people one interacts with, and a natural world populated with animate beings. Thus, Sakha identity is to a significant degree realized through showing proper respect to the living language by both speaking it well (in terms of phonology and grammar) and following the language ideologies that were once an implicit part of religious practice but now an explicit part of Sakha linguistic culture (Ferguson 2019: 103).

Examples of indigenous language ideologies that derive from religious beliefs and or spiritual understandings are too plentiful to make a comprehensive survey feasible here so I will limit my treatment to three additional cases. Hawaiian is a Polynesian language of the Austronesian language family and it is spoken by about 18,000 speakers. One of the most potent Hawaiian language ideologies is that the heritage language is crucial to maintaining *mauli* ('life, heart, spirit'): in this view, the Hawaiian language is the key to "strengthening of the Hawaiian *mauli* or life force which allows for the continued existence of a Hawaiian people" (Wilson and Kamana 2001: 148). For the indigenous Guarani of Paraguay, the sacred word-soul, *ayvu* or *ñe'e* is:

of divine origin and it is the task of the shaman to determine which kind of word-soul is instantiated in the child during the naming ceremony. . . . The Guaraní is not "called" this or that way but "is" this or that . . . as each person's name indexes his or her divine origin. Being Guaraní is thus intimately connected, via the soul, to language or speech.

(Hauck 2018: 79)

Guarani is a rare case in the Americas of an Indigenous language having a co-official status. The benefits of Paraguayan state support are very much responsible for the 6.5 million speakers of this member of the Tupian-Guarani language family. Lacking similar state support, the Yo'eme (aka Yaqui) of Southern Arizona and Northern Mexico, also display a belief about their language that emanates from their traditional religion. In the myth of origin for their heritage language is divinely created, conferring an authority to the language and a responsibility to its speakers:

The Yaqui language is a gift from *Itom Achai*, the Creator, to our people and therefore shall be treated with respect. Our ancient language is the foundation of our cultural and spiritual heritage without which we could not exist in the manner that our Creator intended. (Pascua Yaqui Tribe Language Policy (Trujillo 1997: 15))

Speakers of a heritage language from the Uto-Aztecan family, the Yo'eme number about 20,000 and live in southern Arizona (USA) and the Sonoran state of northern Mexico. These examples suggest that the many indigenous language ideologies – both those that can be scientifically proven to be indigenous as well as those defined by members as such – are likely to be ontological, in Ferguson's (2019) sense, where they represent spiritual beliefs and worldviews about languages and the actions of speakers using them. If, as Ferguson has suggested, ontology has been missing from studies of language ideologies that may be because most studies do not focus on indigenous languages and have instead examined national languages in particular institutional contexts. Regardless of how "indigenous" indigenous ideologies may be, their power stems in part from their real or imagined temporalization of a traditional past with actions embodying those beliefs in the present and future.

4 Contact-related language ideologies and identities

As a segue to language contact, it is important to observe that the distinction of indigenous and contact-related ideologies while historically relevant, is clearly more of a cline than a binary especially when we consider how ideological differentiation, using both adequation and distinction, work to produce what Jaffe (1999) has called "the logic of oppositional identity." This logic shapes a presentist reading of tradition for many groups by emphasizing distinctive linguistic, discursive, and ideological differences between groups in contemporary contact. In situations of long-term contact between social groups, and especially so in hegemonic situations, these indexes of linguistic groups are ideologically differentiated and rhematized as emblems of group identity (Irvine and Gal 2000, Gal and Irvine 2019). These are what the anthropologist Fredrik Barth called *diacritica* of ethnic identity because even in situations of cultural and language contact that reduce the total inventory of differences, the persisting differences become semiotically transformed into badges of identity, moving from the dim awareness of practical consciousness to the "front and center" of speakers' discursive consciousness (Barth 1969). This, for example, is in operation when the Sakha emphasize the connection of their language to a spiritually inhabited natural world and view their language as a living being rather than just emphasize the intimate relationship of language and their personal "souls" – a belief that is partially convergent with that of the hegemonic Russian population. It is also why the Village of Tewa has so emphasized its distinctive Tewa language and its unique "linguistic curse" with its rhematizing narrative of identity differentiation since so many other features of cultural life and linguistic practice are shared with the Hopi majority with whom they have lived for almost 325 years.

Though the logic of oppositional identity prompts speakers to emblematize distinctive features, the process of rhematization itself is extremely productive although it can take many forms. The Aché speak a language of the Tupi-Guarani Family that does not enjoy Paraguayan state support. They are a heritage language community of less than 1,000 former hunter-gatherers which has experienced considerable language change under pressure from both co-official Spanish and indigenous Guarani. The hegemonic influence of Guarani, paired with little metalinguistic attention to Aché given by its own speakers and the practice of syncretism has resulted in a mixed language-Guaraché – that has become the default language of the group (Hauck 2018). In studies of peer interaction among Aché children, Hauck (2015) has observed a metalinguistic awareness of Aché as a distinct language activated when children and their families talk about or enter into forest activities that are still indexed to the indigenous subsistence practices of the group. This often comes in the form of what Hauck calls metalinguistic repair – where one speaker corrects the Guaraché form to its Aché equivalent, proving that the child both recognizes the linguistic difference and understands its indexical connection to Aché cultural practices.[9]

While the Aché case demonstrates how rhematization of language and identity can exist while co-occurring with the practice of linguistic syncretism, the secular U.S. Yiddish heritage language "metalinguistic" community, analyzed by Avineri (2014), reminds us that rhematization more often co-occurs with ideologies of linguistic purism. In contrast to the Yiddish metalinguistic community – one defined more by talk about a language than by talk in it – Avineri describes the Orthodox Hasidic Yiddish-speaking community, as many as 200,000 living mostly in urban areas of the northeastern U.S., which uses the language as its main form of everyday communication. Using ideologies that nostalgically source authentic Yiddish to historical, pre-World War II, Yiddish speaking communities in Europe, the metalinguistic community views itself as curating a pure, and therefore more authentic form of Yiddish and contrasts its practices with the linguistic hybridity of the Ultra-Orthodox. In doing so, the metalinguistic community displays a boundary-marking language ideological purism in its disapproval of the kind of linguistic adaptations that have allowed the ultra-Orthodox to add new words, including loanwords from English, and to speak a language that shows the influence of other languages. The metalinguistic community frequently rejects the linkage of Yiddish to ultra-Orthodox Judaism as well as other linguistic practices it views as impure or non-traditional. Thus while the Ultra-Orthodox rely on an iconization of Yiddish language use to express their distinctive identity, the metalinguistic Yiddish community has constructed a purist register and a nostalgic discourse of Yiddish with which to emblematize an identity that distinguishes them both from the dominant society as well as from the "other" Yiddish speaking community.

For some groups, like the Village of Tewa mentioned earlier, their purism is an indigenous one arising from their own cultural institutions and ceremonial practices. But for many groups, linguistic purism is more the result of culture contact with the purism of state-sponsored standardized languages. In some cases, the ideology of purism conflicts with the syncretic practices indexed to the hybrid identities emerging from contact situations. For the Siberian Buryat, a Mongolic language with about 250,000 speakers who are experiencing language shift to Russian, Buryat has been relegated to merely a "kitchen language".

---

9 Hauck (2015) indicates that the ideological differentiation of Aché from both Guarani and Guaraché is interactionally accomplished by a heightened awareness of Aché forms when thinking about the forest activities because of both the indexical connection of that language to the place where hunting and gathering are performed and the presence of Hauck himself as someone especially interested in that language.

But, even in the comfort of this relaxed, private space, Kathryn Graber (2017: 166) represents speakers telling jokes that deflect their guilt for not speaking a purer form of Buryat even in these private spaces but it is also a means for resisting a puristic ideal so difficult to achieve in the Russian saturated world they inhabit. Similar tensions exist for the "Nuyorican" community of Puerto Rican New Yorkers analyzed by Zentella (1997). Puerto Rican Americans in the U.S. number around 5 million though a significant number do not speak Spanish. Though younger members value hybridity and conspicuous code-switching as a means of expressing their hybrid identities and the syncretic linguistic practices that contribute to their construction, they also live in Spanish and English-speaking worlds where linguistic purism is conventionally observed. This double dose of linguistic purism is related to their occasionally pejorative view of code-switching. They view it not as an expression of their distinctive identities and skills in both languages, but rather as a limitation, as a "crutch" for their presumed disability – an inability to speak according to monolingual ideals. Their folk analysis contrasts with Zentella's own analysis of the vast majority of observed instances of code-switching. In her study, code-switching happens not when speakers lack the words in another language but, most often, when it is a rhetorically motivated choice.

Non-indigenous linguistic purism is recruited to a variety of identity projects in contemporary indigenous communities. In Northern Mexico, Nahuatl speakers who were subsistence farmers in the Malinche region, as described by Jane and Kenneth Hill (Hill and Hill 1980, Hill 1985) have been incorporated into the cash economy and often must leave their fields in the countryside for factory work in cities. Speakers of a Uto-Aztecan language, the Nahuatl community which numbers 1.7 million, has been exposed to Spanish for more than 400 years. During this time, they have not only been engaged in a syncretic project with considerable lexical borrowing and grammatical convergence, they have also been exposed to the linguistic purism associated with state-sponsored Spanish. In the larger context of what Dorian (1981) has called sociolinguistic tip and the struggle of speakers to maintain Nahuatl despite language shift and massive symbolic domination of Spanish, factory workers like Don Leobardo, retiring to their former home communities, import the purism associated with the Mexican Spanish standard to their rural home towns. Describing him as a "linguistic terrorist", Hill depicts Don Leobardo as someone who wields his discourse of Nahuatl purism like a club but not in defense of Nahuatl and its syncretic project but rather as a way of using his limited folk analysis of contact to advance his own interests and claim to local authority and position (Hill 1985). Even though Nahuatl represents a language which he can pidginize at best, Don Leobardo projects an imagined purer Nahuatl, challenging the conventional syncretic use as if his appeals to a Nahuatl purism make him a cultural authority. Probing further, we come to see Don Leobardo's apparent linguistic ruthlessness not as an expression of a self-serving malevolence but as evidence of his own pathetic brutalization via what Jane and Kenneth Hill call "internal colonialism through proletarianization" (Hill and Hill 1980: 41). Like other city-dwellers, many Nahuatl-community exiles develop a purism that condemns any effort to learn Malinche Mexicano because their importation of purism prompts a misrecognition of a syncretic project as a corruption of the heritage language. While linguistic purism can be used to fabricate an authoritative local identity in this Nahuatl community, it can also be used by indigenous communities to actually purify a register of their language for formal use.

Miki Makihara's (2007) study of the Eastern Polynesian language Rapa Nui spoken by less than a thousand people, on Easter Island belonging to Chile, where Spanish is the only official national language presents a different use of purism – as an ideological resource for creating a distinctive register of a politicized indigenous identity. Though Makihara describes the Indigenous people as typically speaking a highly syncretic Rapa Nui with significant lexical borrowing and grammatical convergence, she also observes the development of a more formal, purified register designed to be used at those times when Rapa Nui leaders are officially representing their indigenous community. The development of this formal register clearly shows an awareness of the linguistic purism of the national standard of Chilean Spanish as well as the rhematization of language and group identity that is displayed by the dominant society (2007). In a nation that refuses to recognize the Indigeneity of its largest native group – the Mapuche who number almost two million – the Rapa Nui are attempting to make their own linguistic difference more pronounced in public usage and at time when only about 10% of their people speak the language in order to preserve their status as the only Indigenous group recognized by the Chilean state. In the Southwestern U.S., the diminutive tribe of several hundred San Juan Southern Paiutes who reside on land that was part of the Navajo Reservation in Arizona and Utah fought for federal recognition as a distinct tribal nation. In order to do this, tribal leaders who were bilingual in Southern Paiute, a Uto-Aztecan language, and Navajo, an Athapaskan language, needed to represent themselves as Paiute speakers in order to substantiate their claim to being a distinct group entitled to recognition. In these performed testimonies, Southern Paiutes needed to ideologically erase their multilingualism in order to conform to the state's preferred ideology of language and identity that rhematized one to the other (Bunte 2009). These emblematic uses of language consistently involve some form of rhematization that links an identifying language to the group identity it naturalizes while ideologically erasing any potentially discrepant or disqualifying details. In this way, Southern Paiutes erase their multilingualism in Navajo and Rapa Nui erase their language attrition and hybridity even though these are conspicuous features of their speech communities. While truer of ideological erasure rather than of actual linguistic practice, since the majorities of these communities normally engage in bilingual speech and linguistic syncretism, these erasures do need to be performed in key sites of identity production such as in federal recognition hearings or in official public statements addressed by indigenous leaders to representatives of the nation states.

Jenny Davis (2016), a Chickasaw linguistic anthropologist, provides details that reveal the ideological work of creating ethnolinguistic identities and what she calls *language affiliation* in her heritage language community.[10] The Chickasaw have a heritage language that belongs to the Muskogean Family. As gaming revenue promotes a de-diasporization of community members returning to this Oklahoma community, the heritage language has enjoyed revalorized significance as an icon of tribal identity. Though the Chickasaw number around 50,000, only about 75 are fluent and about 1,000 more have some knowledge of the language. About 5,000 additional tribal citizens participate in language programs. Via the national model of iconization yet constrained by a massive language shift to English, Chickasaw has become such a touchstone of identity in this community that those who are not speakers locate themselves in relationship to relatives who were fluent speakers or who are currently learning the language. The Chickasaw language is a prominent part of the linguistic landscape of the Reservation and it is proudly worn on tee-shirts and other clothing by tribal members. Davis calls the supporters of the language, such as learners, less than fluent-speakers, and other supporters of Chickasaw language revitalization, "language affiliates". This alignment with an ancestral language is similar to the Yiddish metalinguistic community previously mentioned. In both cases a rhematization of language and identity is performed (for most) not through fluent speaking as much as by metalinguistic and metapragmatic discourses about the language. In both cases, displays of support may be performed in a dominant language and what is erased is the expectation that fluent language use is the only valued way to express an ethnolinguistic identity. Where the two heritage language communities differ is in their temporal orientation. Whereas the Yiddish metalinguistic community locates its authoritative model in a nostalgically represented past, the Chickasaw community continues to use its language on social media, to develop new apps

---

10 Davis (2016: 100) views language affiliation as a Chickasaw discourse of ethnolinguistic identity which allows non-fluent speakers to express their support and belonging. These non-fluent speakers may have "(1) a familial relationship to Speakers; (2) some level of Chickasaw learning or activism; and/or (3) a familial relationship to the language learners in the second category".

for it, and to place the heritage language into new contexts in the present and the imagined future (Davis 2016).

Indigenous, or local, language communities have adapted to incorporation by nation-states or to their colonizing influence often through an ideological interaction of iconization of language to group identity while simultaneously engaged in the "oppositional identity" (Jaffe 1999). For the Western Mono, as described above, contact with linguistic nationalism of the U.S. and its intolerance of linguistic diversity, resulted in a reduction of the trilingual indigenous linguistic repertoire, once typical of their Western Sierra Foothill region, to only the opposition of Mono and English, each iconized to group identities at a different scale. Though Western Mono linguistic variation across such existing communities as North Fork, Auberry, and Cold Springs is noticed by older speakers, the differences are ideologically erased, preserving a unified group identity naturalized by "shared" language. But this is not the case, for the Kumeeyay/Kumiai (a Yuman language) of Baja California and Northern Mexico where an intensely localist language ideology sharply differentiates the linguistic variation found in about a dozen communities with a combined population of several thousand and about 500 speakers in Mexico and 50 across the border in the USA. From Margaret Field's (2012) recent study of these Yuman Language Family communities, we see that this emphasis on tying very local social identities to distinctive language forms is responsible for why the language displays so many dialects that are distinguishable through distinctive lexical divergence. Since most speakers exhibit more awareness of the words of their language rather than its grammatical pattern, the lexicon is more of a linguistic site for language ideological intervention – new, local forms may emerge and be iconized to a specific community or puristic practices may develop to proscribe loanwords from outside it.

Analyzing a nation in which similar ideologies exist, Jaffe (1999, 2003) has described how Corsicans, numbering about 150,000 with at least some speaking ability in the Romance language, attempt to accommodate their own localist preferences while simultaneously seeking something like the authority of the French Standard which was imposed by colonial language policy. While Corsican language planners have consciously opposed the creation of Standard Corsican and instead embraced polynomic approaches that attempt to honor the regional variation represented in various Corsican communities without ranking them, teaching the language proves very difficult. It is impossible to create curricular materials that represent all the local varieties and any individual teacher will inevitably over-represent his or her local forms since they lack the knowledge required to properly display proper polynomic linguistic diversity in the classroom (Jaffe 2003). There is thus a mismatch between localist language ideologies and the actual practice of language instruction with the goal of authoritatively representing a more singular, prescriptive model of language use. The Corsican case demonstrates how even when minority language policy is carefully constructed with a high degree of awareness of local language ideologies, the task of translating this curated policy into effective pedagogical practice is at best very difficult especially when a competing Standardized French regime has conditioned popular conceptions of legitimacy and authority. It is also a case of intentional "oppositional" identity construction as Corsican language activists and planners seek alternative and distinctive language instruction according to localist ideologies that contrast with the standardist, globalist norms indexed to French.

Such "oppositional identities," made distinctive by contrastive and competing ideologies, typify the situation that prevails in many indigenous communities in the USA. In a study of metalinguistic commentary from some indigenous communities in the southwest, including Jicarilla Apache, Sandia Tiwa, and Tesuque Tewa communities, linguistic researchers from the University of New Mexico found a consistent pattern in how heritage language speakers verbally constructed the opposition of English as a "dead" language – lifeless, drab, and strictly transactional – with the vitality of their heritage languages as vital, colorful, and culturally meaningful ways of seeing and being in the world (Gomez de Garcia et al. 2009). Ironically all these language communities have experienced very significant language shift to English and the majority of their members are using English to accomplish most tasks in the practical world, reserving the heritage languages for indigenous special occasions such as ceremonies. While some speakers attributed their understanding of the cultural superiority of their languages to their being verb-centered and having the morphological complexity of polysynthetic languages, it seems also to be relevantly related to the need to bolster and valorize an oppositional identity that compensates for heritage language removal from practical and economic spheres by iconizing itself to an alternative group identity endowed with great cultural and spiritual value (Gomez de Garcia et al. 2009). But while this opposition of iconized languages to national and indigenous identities fills the need for revalorizing heritage languages and potentially bolstering revitalization efforts, it also promotes the ideological erasure of language shift and the declining number of contexts in which heritage languages are used.

In contemporary Catalan, as described by Kathryn Woolard (2016, 2020), we find a similar pairing of rhematization and oppositional identities, around not just the practice of bilingualism but around the very language ideologies indexed to it. In contrast to the situation of many minority languages elsewhere in the world, many advocates of Catalan reject "bilingualism" because of its local meaning in the Spanish national context. As Woolard (2020: 257) observes, advocacy for

bilingualism in Catalonia often has an inverse relationship to bilingual practice. Catalan advocates see in bilingualism "a condescending Spanish language
ideology" and their use of ideology is in the Marxist sense of a distorted false
consciousness rather than the more universalist sense of a perspective emerging from a positioned interest (as in language ideological research). In this
dominant ideology, bilingualism (as practice) is for "lesser" others. But advocacy for bilingualism in Catalonia emanates largely from opponents of Catalan
normalization who want to protect their ability to use Spanish exclusively
within a policy of bilingualism. Just as so-called policies of multiculturalism in
nations like Guatemala amount, in practice, to an asymmetry in who has to
learn the other's language and culture, bilingualism in Catalonia would really
only require the linguistic minority to learn the state's dominant language (Barrett 2016, Woolard 2020). By rejecting bilingualism, advocates of Catalan normalization reject the prospect of diglossia and the subordination of Catalan
that it would represent. Normalization follows an oppositional logic in which,
via fractal recursivity and adequation, Catalan would assume the functions for
Catalonia that Spanish performs in the nation-state. Though this semiotic principle captures the way ideologies can be used to rationalize new arrangements actual metalinguistic commentary is more likely to wax romantic and represent
Catalan as a "mother tongue" in opposition to the "divided spirit" represented by
bilingualism (Woolard 2020: 263). Even though most Catalan speakers, who number about 7.3 million, are bilingual, the rejection of the ideology of bilingualism
provides its own ideological support for a Catalan-language based identity.

I will conclude this section by briefly noting a language community that
embraces its bilingualism and uses an ideology of identity that ties contemporary Navajo identity to a linguistic repertoire of Navajo and English. With a population of 300,000 – one half of which are speakers – the Navajo Nation has
experienced a language shift and considerable language contact in the form of
linguistic convergence, language-mixing, and code-switching (Field 2009). Navajo poets, the contemporary wordsmiths who write poetry in both Navajo, a
Na-Dene language, and English and also use the mixed register "Navlish" may
suggest a partial alternative to oppositional identity. While they consciously
use Navajo and English to index and iconize distinct cultural resources, they
link their identities as contemporary Navajos not just to their heritage language
but to their linguistic repertoire containing both. By compartmentalizing the expressive use of Navajo to kinship, polite speech, sacred mountains, placenames
and other cultural domains, many Navajos use their poetry to preserve and
ideologically distinguish the indexical orders associated with each of their languages at the same time they embrace both as part of contemporary Navajo

identity (Webster 2012, Jim and Webster, this volume). Echoing the Navajo poet Esther Belin (2014: 40) who described English as a "tribal" language, linguistic anthropologist Anthony Webster concludes that "[i]t is time to understand Navajo English as a Navajo (Diné) language" (Webster 2011: 80).

5 Imposed language ideologies

Any account of how language ideologies are deployed in social identity production must recognize that not all social identities are products of a language group's self-determination. Though prominent theories of ethnic identity construction in contact situations, such as the important work of Barth (1969), have emphasized the role of self-ascription and the semiotic basis for maintaining ethnic group boundaries through the group's own interpretive acts, those same semiotic resources can be utilized by nation-states to racialize groups into social hierarchies, by constructing what Balibar (1991) has called a "spectrum of racisms". Racialized identities are at least as old as colonialism and they continue to be reproduced by contemporary nation states and the inequalities promoted by global capitalism (van Dijk 2003, Hill 2008, Rosa and Flores 2020). Linguistic racisms play a significant role in this process and I have elsewhere (Kroskrity 2020) reviewed how language ideological approaches have disclosed and analyzed their operation.

Rather than reproduce those observations in the limited space available here or begin to sample what is becoming a significant and growing literature on linguistic racism and raciolinguistics (e.g., Alim, Reyes, and Kroskrity 2020), I want to end this section, and this chapter, by making several concluding observations related to the preceding sections.

The first, and my motivation for ending this chapter on the topic of linguistic racism, is to emphasize that there are some linguistic identities that language community members are less able to control because they are the products of systems of oppression. Unlike identities produced by indigenous ideologies or by those that reflect adaptations to language contact, racialized identities are spawned by powerful groups and elites with privileged positions in political economic systems. It is from their perspective that racial slurs like the *n-word* (for African Americans), *digger* (for California's Indigenous), or *fisher* (for Scottish Gaelic fisherfolk) are reproduced and circulated as stigmatized categories of people in overt linguistic racist acts that recreate hierarchies of social identity (Dorian 1981: 61, Hinton 1994, Hill 2008). But since the late 20th century, overt linguistic racism and the use of explicit slurs have given way to more indirect expressions of what may be termed "covert linguistic racism" which is usually not read as racist by those in the dominant society and therefore reproduced more openly and circulated more widely (van Dijk 2003). Such covertly racist forms as Mock Spanish (Hill 2008) or Hollywood Injun English (Meek 2006) do not involve taboo racial slurs; they instead rely on indexical orders constructed by dominant groups in parodic registers in order to regiment popular belief and practice. Stereotypes of denigrated identities emerge from these indexical orders and project images of denigrated others that may be constructed as violent, corrupt, immoral, backward, unintelligent, forever foreign, doomed, or inevitably disappearing depending upon the racial formation or point on the spectrum of racisms.[11] As Barbra Meek and I, in separate contributions, have noted settler colonial societies have a special need to erase Indigenous others as part of their own national narrative (Meek 2006, 2020, Kroskrity 2020). This can be accomplished, in the USA context, by representing Native American characters in popular mass media as only capable of a register of English that ironically resembles "foreigner talk" (Meek 2006) or by decontextualizing Native American traditional narratives and finding all features that do not conform to Eurocentric literary expectations to be signs of an inferior identity (Kroskrity 2015), or by internet circulation of anonymously authored "Indian jokes" that represent Native Americans as infantilized, primitive, and ignorant others who are out of place in the modern world (Meek 2013, Kroskrity 2021). These racializing representations rhematize contrastive images of dominant and stigmatized identities, demonstrating the amoral productivity of these language ideological resources. As a powerful force in guiding identity projects, they can serve the interests of both dominant and minority groups. Since identity production is a crucial site of language ideological work, deliberations about linguistic sovereignty, language documentation and revitalization, and language policy must include language ideologies. They perform a critical mediating role between the levels of linguistic organization – language structures and cultural patterns of use – and the language communities that find in them ongoing resources for the construction of various social identities.

---

11 The stereotypes mentioned here represent a collection of features associated with the collected and sometimes interchangeable stereotypes of Native Americans, African Americans, Asian Americans, and Latinos. See various chapters in Alim, Reyes, and Kroskrity (2020) for further details.

References

Avineri, Netta. 2014. Yiddish endangerment as phenomenological reality and discursive strategy. Crossing into the past and crossing out the present. *Language & Communication* 38. 18–32.

Avineri, Netta & Paul V. Kroskrity. 2014. On the (re-)production and representation of endangered language communities. Social boundaries and temporal borders. *Language & Communication* 38. 1–7.

Balibar, Étienne. 1991. Racism and nationalism. In Étienne Balibar & Immanuel Wallerstein (eds.), *Race, nation, class. Ambiguous identities*, 37–67. London: Verso.

Barrett, Rusty. 2016. Mayan language revitalization, hip-hop, and ethnic identity in Guatemala. *Language & Communication* 47. 144–153.

Barth, Fredrik. 1969. *Ethnic groups and boundaries. The social organization of cultural difference*. Boston: Little, Brown & Company.

Bauman, Zygmunt. 2004. *Identity*. Cambridge: Polity.

Belin, Esther. 2014. Morning offerings, like salt. In Lloyd L. Lee (ed.), *Dine perspectives: Revitalizing and reclaiming Navajo thought,* 39–43. Tucson: University of Arizona Press.

Bucholtz, Mary & Kira Hall. 2004. Language and Identity. In Alessandro Duranti (ed.), *A companion to linguistic anthropology*, 369–394. Malden, MA: Blackwell.

Bunte, Pamela A. 2009. *"You keep not listening with your ears!" Language ideologies, language socialization, and Paiute identity*. In Paul V. Kroskrity & Margaret C. Field (eds.), *Native American language ideologies*, 172–189. Tucson: University of Arizona Press.

Coulmas, Florian. 2019. *Identity. A very short introduction*. Oxford: Oxford University Press.

Davis, Jenny L. 2016. Language affiliation and ethnolinguistic identity in Chickasaw language revitalization. *Language and Communication* 47 (3). 100–111.

Dorian, Nancy C. 1981. *Language death. The life cycle of a Scottish Gaelic dialect*. Philadelphia: University of Pennsylvania Press.

Dozier, Edward P. 1954. *The Hopi-Tewa of Arizona* (University of California Publications in Archeology and Ethnology 44/3), 257–376. Berkeley: University of California Press.

Dozier, Edward P. 1956. Two examples of linguistic acculturation. The Yaqui of Sonora, Arizona, and the Tewa of New Mexico. *Language* 32 (1). 146–157.

Field, Margaret C. 2009. Changing Navajo language ideologies and changing language Uuse. In Paul V. Kroskrity & Margaret C. Field (eds.), *Native American language ideologies: Beliefs, practices and struggles in Indian country*, 31–47. Tucson: University of Arizona Press.

Field, Margaret C. 2012. Kumiai stories. Bridges between the oral tradition and classroom practice. In Paul V. Kroskrity (ed.), *Telling stories in the face of danger*, 115–126. Norman, OK: University of Oklahoma Press.

Ferguson, Jenanne. 2019. *Words like birds. Sakha language discourses and practices in the city*. Lincoln, NE: University of Nebraska Press.

Gal, Susan & Judith Irvine. 2019. *Signs of difference. Language and ideology in social life*. Cambridge: Cambridge University Press.

Giddens, Anthony. 1991. *Modernity and self-identity*. Cambridge: Polity.

Gomez de Garcia, Jule, Melissa Axelrod & Jordan Lachler. 2009. English is the dead language. Native perspectives on bilingualism. In Paul V. Kroskrity & Margaret C. Field (eds.), *Native American language ideologies*, 99–122. Tucson: University of Arizona Press.

Graber, Kathryn E. 2017. The kitchen, the cat, and the table. Domestic affairs in minority-language politics. *Journal of Linguistic Anthropology* 27 (2). 151–170.

Gumperz, John J. 1968. The speech community. In David L. Sills & Robert K. Merton (eds.), *International Encyclopedia of the Social Sciences*, 381–386. New York: Macmillan.

Hauck, Jan David. 2015. Language mixing and the metalinguistic awareness of Aché children. *Texas Linguistic Forum* 58. 40–49.

Hauck, Jan David. 2018. The origin of language among the Aché. *Language & Communication* 63. 76–88.

Hill. Jane H. 1985. The grammar of consciousness and the consciousness of grammar. *American Ethnologist* 12 (4). 725–737.

Hill, Jane H. 2008. *The everyday language of White racism*. Malden, MA: Wiley-Blackwell.

Hill, Jane H. & Kenneth C. Hill. 1980. *Speaking Mexicano. The dynamics of syncretic language in Central Mexico*. Tucson: University of Arizona Press.

Hinton, Leanne. 1994. *Flutes of fire. Essays on California Indian languages*. Berkeley, CA: Heyday Press.

Irvine, Judith & Susan Gal. 2000. Language ideology and linguistic differentiation. In Paul V. Kroskrity (ed.), *Regimes of language*, 35–83. Santa Fe, NM: School of Advanced Research.

Jaffe, Alexandra. 1999. *Ideologies in action. Language politics on Corsica*. Berlin: De Gruyter.

Jaffe, Alexandra. 2003. Misrecognition unmasked? "Polynomic" language, expert statuses and orthographic practices in Corsican Schools. *Pragmatics* 13. 515–537.

Kroskrity, Paul V. 1993. *Language, history, and identity. Ethnolinguistic studies of the Arizona Tewa*. Tucson: University of Arizona Press.

Kroskrity, Paul V. 1998. Arizona Tewa kiva speech as a manifestation of a dominant language ideology. In Bambi B. Schieffelin, Kathryn A. Woolard & Paul V. Kroskrity (eds.), *Language ideologies, practice and theory*, 103–122. New York: Oxford University Press.

Kroskrity, Paul V. 2000. Regimenting languages. Language ideological perspectives. In Paul V. Kroskrity (ed.), *Regimes of language. Ideologies, polities, and identities*, 1–34. Santa Fe, NM: School of Advanced Research.

Kroskrity, Paul V. 2004. Language ideologies. In Alessandro Duranti (ed.), *Companion to linguistic anthropology*, 496–517. Malden, Massachusetts: Basil Blackwell.

Kroskrity, Paul V. 2009. Embodying the reversal of language shift. Agency, incorporation, and language ideological change in the Western Mono communities of central California. In Paul V. Kroskrity & Margaret C. Field (eds.), *Native American language ideologies*, 190–210. Tucson: University of Arizona Press.

Kroskrity, Paul V. 2010. Language ideologies – evolving perspectives. In Jürgen Jaspers (ed.), *Language use and society* (Handbook of pragmatics highlights 7), 192–211. Amsterdam: John Benjamins.

Kroskrity, Paul V. 2012. "Growing with stories". Ideologies of storytelling and the narrative reproduction of Arizona Tewa identities. In Paul V. Kroskrity (ed.), *Telling stories in the face of danger. Narratives and language renewal in Native American communities*, 151–183. Norman, OK: University of Oklahoma Press.

Kroskrity, Paul V. 2015. Discursive discriminations in the representation of Western Mono and Yokuts stories. Confronting narrative inequality and listening to Indigenous voices in Central California. In Paul V. Kroskrity & Anthony K. Webster (eds.), *The legacy of Dell Hymes*, 135–163. Bloomington, IN: Indiana University Press.

Kroskrity, Paul V. 2017. To "we" (+inclusive) or not to "we" (-inclusive). The cd-rom Taitaduhaan (our language) and Western Mono future publics. In Paul V. Kroskrity & Barbra A. Meek (eds.), *Engaging Native American publics*, 82–103. New York: Routledge.

Kroskrity, Paul V. 2018. On recognizing persistence in the indigenous language ideologies of multilingualism in two Native American communities. *Language & Communication* 62. 133–144.

Kroskrity, Paul V. 2020. Theorizing linguistic racisms from a language ideological perspective. In H. Samy Alim, Angela Reyes and Paul V. Kroskrity (eds.), *The Oxford handbook of language and race*, 68–89. New York: Oxford University Press.

Kroskrity, Paul V. 2021. Covert linguistic racisms and the (re-)production of white supremacy. *Journal of Linguistic Anthropology* 31 (3). 180–193.

Makihara, Miki. 2007. Linguistic purism in Rapa Nui political discourse. In Miki Makihara & Bambi Schieffelin (eds.), *Consequences of contact. Language ideologies and sociocultural transformation in the Pacific*, 49–69. New York: Oxford University Press.

Meek, Barbra A. 2006. And the Injun goes how! Representations of American Indian English in (white) public space. *Language in Society* 35 (1). 93–128.

Meek, Barbra A. 2013. The voice of (white) reason. Enunciations of difference, authorship, interpellation, and jokes. In Shannon T. Bischoff, Deborah Cole, Amy V. Fountain & Mizuki Miyashita (eds.), *The persistence of language*, 339–363. Amsterdam: John Benjamins.

Meek, Barbra. 2020. Racing Indian language, languaging an Indian race. Linguistic racism and the representation of indigeneity. In H. Samy Alim, Angela Reyes & Paul V. Kroskrity (eds.), *The Oxford handbook of language and race*, 369–397. New York: Oxford University Press.

Rosa, Jonathan & Nelson Flores. 2020. Reimagining race and language: From raciolinguistic ideologies to a raciolinguistic perspective. In H. Samy Alim, Angela Reyes & Paul V. Kroskrity (eds.), *The Oxford handbook of language and race,* 90–107. New York: Oxford University Press.

Sallabank, Julia. 2013. *Attitudes to endangered languages. Identities and policies.* Cambridge: Cambridge University Press.

Sankoff, Gillian. 1980. *The social life of language.* Philadelphia: University of Pennsylvania Press.

Silverstein, Michael. 1996. Encountering language and the languages of encounter in North American ethnohistory. *Journal of Linguistic Anthropology* 6 (1). 126–144.

Silverstein, Michael. 1998. Contemporary transformations of local linguistic communities. *Annual Review of Anthropology* 27. 401–426.

Taylor, Charles. 1989. *Sources of the self. The making of modern identity.* Cambridge, MA: Harvard University Press.

Trujillo, Octaviana B. 1997. A tribal approach to language and literacy in development in a trilingual setting. In John Reyhner (ed.), *Teaching Indigenous languages*, 10–21. Flagstaff, AZ: Northern Arizona University.

Van Dijk, Teun A. 2003. *Elite discourse and racism.* Newbury Park, CA: SAGE Publications.

Whorf, Benjamin Lee. 1956. *Language, thought, and reality. Selected writings of Benjamin Lee Whorf*, edited by John B. Carroll. Cambridge, MA: MIT Press.

Webster, Anthony K. 2011. "Please read loose". Intimate grammars and unexpected languages in contemporary Navajo literature. *American Indian Culture and Research Journal* 35 (4). 61–86.

Webster, Anthony K. 2012. To give an imagination to the listener. Replicating proper ways of speaking in and through contemporary Navajo poetry. In Paul V. Kroskrity (ed.), *Telling stories in the face of danger*, 205–227. Norman, OK: University of Oklahoma Press.

Wilson, William H. & Kauanoe Kamana. 2001. "Mai loko mai o ka'j'ini: Proceeding from a dream". The 'Aha Punana Leo connection in Hawaiian language revitalization. In Leanne Hinton & Ken Hale (eds.), *The green book of language revitalization in practice*, 147–175. San Diego: Academic Press.

Woolard, Kathryn A. 2016. *Singular and plural. Ideologies of linguistic authority in 21st century Catalonia*. New York: Oxford University Press.

Woolard, Kathryn A. 2020. "You have to be against bilingualism!" Sociolinguistic theory and controversies over bilingualism in Catalonia. *WORD* 66 (4). 255–281.

Zentella, Ana Celia. 1997. *Growing up bilingual. Puerto Rican children in New York*: Malden, MS: Blackwell.

Christian Meyer & Benjamin Quasinowski

6 Conversational organization and genre

Large parts of spoken and written language are organized in and as genres. Genres serve as contextures of reference for the interpretation and production of discourse. Since they are accomplishments of cultural practices and thus provide a vantage point on culture, they are an important research field for linguistic anthropologists. However, as conversation analysts have shown, all speech is organized by a set of principles that can be claimed to be universal. Our goal in this chapter is to connect genre analysis to the analysis of conversational organization. The structure of the chapter is as follows. First, we review conversation analytical findings on fundamental principles of conversational organization. We focus on the organization of turn-taking. Turn-taking has been claimed to be a "candidate universal" of conversational organization, but this assumption has also been critiqued by some linguistic anthropologists. However, there is now a substantial base of comparative research which allows a more nuanced assessment. The second part of the chapter provides an overview of linguistic anthropology's engagement with genres and introduces a range of methods for their analysis. We sketch important developments after Boas' descriptive studies of Native American languages, such as positioning genres in relation to speech events in the ethnography of communication and the concept of generic intertextuality, influenced by the rediscovery of Bakhtin's work on genre and dialogism. We also discuss the impact on genre analysis of approaches outside of anthropology, such as developments in the sociology of knowledge and institutional conversation analysis. Finally, by using an example from a workplace meeting in a Kazakh hospital, we consider how genre analysis can be fruitfully combined with a conversation analytical perspective.

1 Introduction

In contrast to conversational organization, genres have long been a topic of considerable interest in linguistic anthropology. They have been studied from a wide and diverse spectrum of approaches and disciplines. While this interdisciplinary

Christian Meyer, University of Constance/Germany, e-mail: christian.meyer@uni-konstanz.de
Benjamin Quasinowski, University of Bremen/Germany,
e-mail: bquasinowski@uni-bremen.de

https://doi.org/10.1515/9783110726626-006

research field addressed a wide array of cultures, languages, and historical epochs, in a diverse range of media and modalities, the purview of our chapter is to discuss a research perspective that approaches genres in the lived forms in which they are encountered in social interaction. From such a perspective, genres are not examined as disembodied structures of textual constituents, but as embodied performances of communicative patterns that are revealed through participants' use of linguistic and other means in the affairs of their daily lives.

Genres are important for many formal and ritualistic uses of language, but they are also embedded in the ordinary course of conversation, such as when someone weaves a joke into a convivial conversation, when two neighbors chatting over the fence start gossiping about a mutual acquaintance, or when kids use puns in their disputes. As we will see, conversational organization and genre can be considered as two different analytical levels, each drawing attention to different aspects of sociocultural life. At the same time, however, the principles that organize ordinary conversation are not absent from speech in generic forms. Accordingly, an analysis of the matrix of interactional practices and resources that provide for the emergence of genres must precede analyses of the latter. For a discipline like linguistic anthropology, which embraces the linguistic and cultural diversity of humanity, this may seem challenging, as it implies that research in a foreign language or speech community demands a holistic analysis of language use in interaction. However, this challenge is already met halfway by the fact that there are a number of rules and principles of assumedly universal applicability. If social interaction, as the "primordial site of human sociality" (Schegloff 2006), is indeed amenable to formal description independent of cultural and linguistic particularities, this can be used as a foundation from which to embark on the project of studying genres-in-interaction comparatively. The foundations for this endeavor were laid by work in the discipline of Conversation Analysis (CA).

The initial task in this chapter is thus to give an overview of the claims made by CA about "candidate universals" of social interaction, focusing on conversational organization. Section 2 reviews the discussion on the phenomenon that is most central for the organization of conversation, namely the turn-taking system first described by Sacks et al. (1974). Although claims of universality were initially put forward by researchers working mainly in English and a small number of mostly related languages, throughout the years these claims have been examined, refined, and elaborated by scholars working with data from diverse languages and cultures.

Section 3 then gives an overview of linguistic anthropology's engagement with genre and the attempt to locate genres in relation to speech events in the ethnography of communication and the concept of generic intertextuality.

Another important approach to the study of genre was developed by bringing CA together with the sociology of knowledge. The resulting variant of genre analysis has been applied to different fields. Work in CA that discloses the particularities of interaction under institutional conditions suggests that there are merits in combining a genre perspective with the perspective of institutional talk. The latter brings into focus the specific systems of turn-taking, language registers, activity types, and overarching interactional structures characteristic of institutional settings. It thus has an elective affinity to genre analysis. The different approaches to genre analysis have each focused on different aspects of genre as an interactional and linguistic phenomenon. Accordingly, the concepts and definitions of genres used by these approaches also differ slightly. Section 3 condenses selected findings from the various works about the relationship between genre and speech community and the relationships between different genres (i.e., intertextuality). We also deal with genres and their communicative functions and with the relationship of genres to their institutional context. At the end of Section 3, we provide an example of how an institutional CA perspective can be combined with an analysis of genre as embodied talk in interaction.

2 Conversational organization

Conversation analysis, as a sociological and anthropological endeavor, emerged in the 1960s in close interaction with Harold Garfinkel's ethnomethodology. Its basic assumption, that interaction is essentially and intrinsically orderly, immediately challenged some of the fundamental beliefs of linguistic anthropology, re-orienting its focus from structural interests to the performative dimensions of speech. CA's notion of order has become famous in Sacks' expression that in conversation there is "order at all points" (1984: 22). This order, however, is not a result of social structure or internalized norms, but methodically produced *in situ* by the participants in social situations. Because interactants themselves are constantly confronted with the problem of understanding the actions of others and reacting to them in appropriate ways, they apply methods which render their actions recognizable. Allowing for joint action and intersubjectivity, orderliness is thus a necessary feature of the social, and thus must be universal for human societies and languages.

Consequently, CA's goal is to empirically identify the procedures by which the participants, in the course of a conversation, produce and display its orderliness to one another, analyze the behavior of their co-participants in regard to the orderliness expressed in it, and make the results of these analyses manifest in subsequent utterances (see Schegloff and Sacks 1973: 291). Hence, orderliness does not constitute an end in itself, but is rather an implicit means to solve the structural and procedural problems of interaction. Without turn-taking, social coordination and joint action are impossible (Schegloff 1988: 98, Heritage 2008: 305).

Since conversations can be conducted in all kinds of specific contexts and local settings, however, Sacks et al. (1974: 699) conclude that there must be "some formal apparatus which is itself context-free" that can be applied to context specific circumstances and yet be recognizable and, as this entails, manageable. As an "enabling institution" (Schegloff 1987: 208) it must be "extremely general" (Wilson 1991: 23), so that it can be used for the accomplishment of any social event. Correspondingly, each interaction sequence exhibits both *context sensitive elements* and *context free principles*. Context sensitivity (read: culture specificity) and context independence (universality) do not exclude but complement one another (Sacks et al. 1974: 699).

2.1 Organization of turn-taking

Ordinary conversations are internally organized in such a way that neither the speakership nor the length of a turn or topic is pre-assigned, and yet usually only one person speaks at a time, "with minimization of gap and overlap" (Schegloff 1988: 98). The analysis of turn-taking in conversation is concerned with the question of how the implicit organizational work is performed by the co-participants in such way that it remains unnoticed and the topic of the speech event that is relevant from the actors' point of view can be pursued (i.e., a talk about the joint trip to the lake yesterday, an argument about the forthcoming presidential election).

The turn-taking system is viewed as a practical, methodical solution to the problem of how to ascertain that co-interactants do not talk at once all the time during interaction. Instead, it manages the orderly succession of contributions by determining at which points in the course of an utterance a subsequent speaker can, or must, act (Schegloff 1988: 134, n. 10).

The concrete formal properties of turn-taking identified in the canonical model of turn-taking (Sacks et al. 1974) comprise two resources and a rule set operating on them. The two resources are (1) "turn constructional resources" (TCUs), i.e., the elements of a contribution to a conversation that construct a turn as being recognizable for the participants as such and that allow the hearers to project its possible end (1974: 701–702); and (2) "turn allocation resources", i.e., elements of a contribution to a conversation that signal the attribution of the next turn to a specific speaker.

The projectability of turn ends through TCUs allows hearers to anticipate possible "transition relevance places" (TRPs), i.e., the points in a sequence where turns end and speaker changes become possible without creating procedural problems such as overlaps or longer gaps. It allows hearers to schedule the exact moment when they might take over the turn. The projectability of turn ends and, consequently, of TRPs has the effect of minimizing gaps between turns in conversations.

Sacks et al. (1974: 704) have identified a rule set that organizes the allocation of turns at TRPs. The rules are hierarchically ordered and apply at each TRP:

1. If, within an ongoing turn, the current speaker selects another participant as next speaker (e.g., through a question), then this participant has the right and duty to become next speaker at the first TRP. The prior speaker is obliged to stop speaking.
2. If, within an ongoing turn, the current speaker does not apply rule 1, then any participant of the conversation may self-select and claim the turn by beginning to speak at the first TRP. The first starter acquires the right to speak and the prior speaker is obliged to stop speaking.
3. If, within an ongoing turn, the current speaker does not select another participant as next speaker and no other participant of the conversation self-selects, then the current speaker may, but does not need to, continue speaking at the TRP.

This rule set is locally administered by the participants. This means, for example, that when an overlap occurs at a TRP because two former listeners in a conversation simultaneously start speaking, one of them usually withdraws shortly after.

Overlaps at TRPs ("transitional overlaps") are common, and the fact that they are solved *in situ* through the withdrawal of one of the overlapping parties shows the normative orientation and self-organizing work of the participants. If none of them withdraws, the overlap is managed by the co-participants in units of talk smaller than turns such as syllables. "Overlap resolution devices" are then employed which mainly consist of "hitches and perturbations", i.e., momentary arrests in the continuity of the talk production (hitches) or marked departures from the prosodic character of the talk articulation (perturbations) (Schegloff 2000: 11). The latter may consist of a louder volume, a higher pitch, a faster or slower pace, sudden cut-offs accompanied by the articulation of phonetic stops, and prolonged or stretched next sounds (Schegloff 2000: 12). When these devices are employed during overlapping talk, the overlap situation usually gets ended shortly afterwards and the "only one party talks at a time" situation is reinstalled.

Schegloff (2000: 5–6) has identified other, non-competitive forms of overlap such as dialogical feedback signals from the hearers, who ratify and display understanding, conditional hearer support in word searching or "choral" formats such as joint laughter, collective greetings, leave-takings, and congratulations.

Turn-taking is a phenomenon emerging moment-by-moment. It is "a local system, distributing just a next turn over the course of any given turn, growing incrementally through a series of such 'nexts'" (Schegloff 2007: 250). The temporal sequencing of interactional moves is ordered insofar as later moves refer to earlier ones as their context (Schegloff 2007: 1–3). CA has coined the concept of "adjacency" to denominate this phenomenon. Adjacency pairs are constituted in their basic form by two turns placed one after the other by different speakers. The two turns are "relatively ordered" (Schegloff 2007: 13), i.e., they are composed by "adjacency pair first parts" and "adjacency pair second parts". Second parts, such as replies, answers, acceptances of invitations, or greeting responses, when uttered, always follow and do not make any sense without first parts such as questions, summonses, invitations, or greeting addresses. Moreover, second parts are also normatively expected to follow first parts as active responses and signals of understanding. The realization of a first part communicates a normative expectation, a social pressure on the co-interactant to realize a second part. This powerful constraint set by a first pair part has been termed "conditional relevance" (Schegloff 1968: 1085).

Sequentiality provides the means to constantly and mutually affirm and reaffirm the progression of interaction and to adjust interpretations of the exchange. With this general principle, human communication intrinsically exhibits means of securing communication and mutual understanding. These means can be directed in two ways. First, they are "precautionary" in that utterances right from the start are designed for the specific recipients in a specific context. Sacks et al. (1974: 727) call this preventive means of securing mutual understanding "recipient design". A speaker has to anticipate the knowledge and perspective of the hearer in order to successfully communicate. Well-known examples are practices of referring to persons or places (Sacks and Schegloff 1979, Schegloff 1972).

Secondly, mutual understanding is secured by means of post-treatment, i.e., by practices which reinstall understanding once a misunderstanding or a communicative error (mispronunciation, semantic or syntactic lapse, etc.) on the part of the speaker or hearer has occurred (Schegloff 1992). These practices are dealt with by conversation analysis under the label of "repair" (Schegloff et al. 1977). When a communicative problem occurs, the participants temporarily suspend their conversational topic until the problem is solved. When remedying the communicative problem, co-interactants tend to prefer procedures of self-correction over other-initiated corrections, so that recipients who have noticed the error on the part of the speaker tend to generously provide opportunities for them to self-repair.

While this simplest systematics of conversational organization was based on auditory data, it was subsequently found that gaze plays a crucial role in the establishment of a participation framework with regard to the roles of speaker, hearer, and addressee as well as for the organization of turn transition. As Goodwin (1981: 55–94) discovered, when a speaker does not obtain the gaze of his recipient during the course of a turn, this leads to troubles in the progressivity of the conversation. Investigations into other modalities such as gesture (Streeck 2009) and touch (Nishizaka 2007) have since been intensified and multimodal CA (cf. Mondada 2018) has become a standard that now draws an encompassing picture of the function and interplay of different modalities in conversational organization.

2.2 The universality of turn-taking organization

Conversational organization, from the CA perspective, represents a pure and pre-conventional sociality (Wilson 1991: 26), transcending "both culture and personal volition" (Hilbert 1990: 798), and adopting "the status of species-specific social behavior". To the question of whether conversational turn-taking is "a function of species (i.e., an adaptation to the contingencies of interaction between sighted, language-using bipeds) or [. . .] a function of 'culture'", Sidnell (2001: 1265, 1285, 1287) takes the universal model of turn-taking to be "probable if not proven", since it is grounded on a "species-specific adaptation to the contingencies of human interaction".

Schegloff (e.g., 1992, 2006) insists that interaction constitutes, in close relation to its status as the "primordial site of sociality", a universal human phenomenon of order. For him, the turn-taking system is an existential and fundamental principle of social life, allowing for the existence of human cooperation. For him, the "features of the organization of human interaction that provide the flexibility and robustness that allow it to supply the infrastructure that supports the overall or macrostructure of societies" include the way that people "talk in turns, which compose orderly sequences through which courses of action are developed; they deal with transient problems of speaking, hearing or understanding the talk and reset the interaction on its course; they organize themselves so as to allow stories to be told; they fill out occasions of interaction from approaches and greetings through to closure, and part in an orderly way" (Schegloff 2006: 70–71).

Sidnell (2007: 241) claims that "participation in conversation poses similar tasks and problems everywhere quite independently of the particular language used or the particular sociocultural setting in which the interaction takes place". The CA account of conversational organization provides a "robust base" that reflects "the specifically human 'form of life'" but also involves "local resources" so that it results in a "local inflection of essentially generic organizations of practice" (ibid.). These local resources consist of semiotic systems (grammar, social categorization) and factors such as scale and population distribution. Heritage (2008: 314), likewise, advocates a universal interaction order for all of humankind, even in the minutiae of interaction.

From an anthropological perspective, these universalist claims, says Moerman (1990/91: 175–176), "are so audacious that I am surprised that so few anthropologists have tried to test and challenge them in 'exotic' languages and cultures". Large theoretical claims are made, while the comparative empirical basis on which they are grounded is still scarce.

2.3 Ethnographic critiques of the universality thesis

Accordingly, early ethnographers of speaking have accused CA of ethnocentric presuppositions and over-generalizations. Bauman and Sherzer (1975: 110) say that not all societies share the rules CA proposes, advancing Reisman's (1974a) report on Antiguan peasants who conduct "contrapuntal conversations", in which all voices participate simultaneously and try to hold their turn even if interrupting others. Reisman (1974a: 115) says that in Antigua, "there is no sense of interruption, or need to fit carefully into an ongoing pattern of conversation, or need to stop if somebody else speaks". The scarce material he presents (1974b: 69–71) does indeed suggest a conversational dynamic in which numerous competitive overlaps occur without being terminated, accompanied by hitches and perturbations.

Ethnographers have described the occurrence of overlap and simultaneous speech as being frequent in many different societies. However, when examining these reports, the reasons for this situation are often in accordance with the basic CA principles, for example, when reported overlaps are part of a joint social activity ("choral") and therefore non-competitive (Hayden 1987, Sawada 1987), or when they consist of expanded hearer signals that appear uncommon in the CA standard model due to their greater length (Tannen 1985).

More complex situations refer to embodied social practices, norms, and concepts. For example:

(1) A greater occurrence of overlaps can emerge through a dissimilar participation framework and the indeterminacy of addressing and listener roles. This difference of footing is sometimes derived from a different usage of the

senses in conversation, especially of gaze, and a resultant lack of signals of attention and participation (Walsh 1991, Kimura 2001). Philips (1976: 83–84) therefore criticizes early CA for being overly speaker centered and not capturing listeners' nonverbal contributions.

(2) In some of the communities observed, the type of speech situation that CA assumes to be primordial is less prevalent, i.e., a social situation in which neither speaker succession nor thematic focus is pre-structured. In presumably all societies, age, sex, and other hierarchies can influence even ordinary conversations. A non-default occurrence of simultaneous speech or lengthy gaps can also be explained by a high degree of social intimacy. When people know each other extremely well and have ubiquitous opportunities for interpersonal exchange, they have no need to thoroughly secure intersubjectivity methodically (Kimura 2003). Ervin-Tripp (1987: 50), therefore, criticizes in CA a "parliamentary view of the floor as a scarce resource".

(3) Some egalitarian communities accomplish an active decentering of authorship. Through their conversational organization, they prevent individuals from gaining prominence in political and other situations. In the public debates of the Xavante of the Brazilian upper Xingú region, discourses are held by a plurality of voices through which, at the end, a co-constructed utterance emerges (Graham 1995: 142). This is achieved by hearers who constantly utter discursive fragments and repair devices, which become successively integrated into the main speech by the dominant speaker. Though these hearer reactions occur in overlap with the main turn, they are not competitive, so that this evidence again does not challenge the CA model of conversational organization.

2.4 Comparative CA findings

While the aforementioned studies were not carried out within the CA paradigm and by the deployment of CA methods, in recent years, a number of data-based studies in comparative CA have been conducted that now allow for a more thorough inspection of cross-cultural differences in conversational organization.

The first studies from a CA or an ethnomethodological perspective were conducted by Moerman (1972, 1977, 1988) on the Lue, and Bilmes (1975, 1976, 1985) on a Kammyang-speaking community, both in Northern Thailand, and Liberman (1980, 1985) on a linguistically diverse Aboriginal community in Central Australia. Moerman partly confirmed the CA position (e.g., on repair) and Bilmes partly expanded them from a pragmatist as well as an ethnomethodological position (e.g., on preference), while Liberman partly rejected them as valid only for "Western" societies (e.g., on conditional relevance). They thus also laid the theoretical and methodological grounds for working in non-native language settings.

Subsequent work in comparative CA turned researchers' interest to the importance of fundamentally diverse grammatical structures for the arrangement of TCUs and, as this entails, for the projectability of TRPs. Some of this work showed that different grammatical structures, such as those of Japanese (Fox et al. 1996), also occasion dissimilar action opportunities on the level of turn-construction and turn-taking (e.g., repair). Other work detected the importance of prosody and intonation in the construction of turns (Selting 1996). This work on syntax, prosody and turn-taking is still continuing today (e.g., Park 2016).

Shortly after this, the first linguistically detailed conversation analytic studies about remote communities were published. Sidnell found that Reisman's impression of "contrapuntal conversations" in Antigua stems from the fact that "prefaces or pre's which indicate that more talk is forthcoming, and rush-throughs which pre-empt self selection by another participant at a point of possible completion" are ubiquitous (2001: 1284). In a quantitative study, Stivers et al. (2009) have confirmed that, in ten fundamentally different languages, turn-taking after polar questions is universally organized so as to minimize gap.

Gardner and Mushin (2007), however, found that among the Garrwa of Northern Australia "talk was not built to be a relevant next" (2007: 13) as it is described for Anglo-Americans. The principles of "adjacency" and "nextness" appear to be endowed with less conditional relevance. Overlaps emerge "when the speakers are being disattentive to the content and action of each other's talk, though there is evidence that they are still being attentive and sensitive to the rhythms of the talk and to TRPs" (Gardner and Mushin 2007: 12–13). Similarly, "long silences appear 'ordinary'" (Mushin and Gardner 2009: 2043) and are even viewed as "comfortable silence" (ibid.: 2049). The reason the authors give for this situation is that the co-interactants live closely together and have "the expectation that there are open ended opportunities to continue a conversation" (ibid.). A recent study on Italian confirms that conditional relevance is loosened when familiarity is high and turns are multi-addressed (Bassetti and Liberman 2021). In multi-party conversations, only the emphatic establishment of a dyad through several semiotic means might trigger the canonical turn-taking system (Blythe et al. 2018).

The ensuing research presented encompassing perspectives on culture and conversational organization (e.g., D'hondt 2019: 505–511) and intensified cross-cultural comparison (Dingemanse et al. 2017, Dingemanse and Enfield 2015), and addressed further modalities (gesture, gaze, touch) in the study of conversational organization (on gaze: Rossano et al. 2009; on gesture: Haviland 2003; on the interplay of several modalities: Meyer 2017, Mihas 2017). Li (2014) showed, for example, how, in Mandarin syntax, prosody and body movements diverge in projecting possible turn completions. Specifically, it was shown how the different temporal and semiotic properties of the individual modalities affect the establishment of participation frameworks for interaction. The canonical CA model presupposes that social situations are organized based on the way that the co-participants are aware with whom they are engaged in turn-taking. When gaze is not used for signaling recipiency or addressing, and audio-signals or touch do not or only selectively fill that gap, the interaction system remains unclear. The participants can then build on this vagueness and produce an uncommon amount of overlap that remains ambiguous for the co-participants with regard to the interaction system to which it is attributable (Meyer 2018, Rüsch 2021). In conversations among the Wolof of Northwestern Senegal, this is exploited for the performance of the ideal of the self-assertive person who will not withdraw (Meyer 2018).

Thus, generally, the CA patterns of conversational organization were confirmed, even though a range of "notably different cultural exploitations of the patterns" was observed (Kendrick et al. 2020). While it was documented that "overlaps and gaps occur constantly", these exceptions were found to have "functional effects, arising from the very fact that people perceive them as exceptions", ultimately supporting the universal basic model (Enfield and Sidnell 2014: 98). The functional effects of speech events and the situated exploitation of expected patterns by social actors are concerns that CA shares with genre analysis.

3 Genre

It was Franz Boas who first investigated genres as part of his larger endeavor of studying non-European languages. Boas focused on the native communities of North America, where he was concerned with the emergence, development, and diffusion of genres such as folktales and myths. The methodology he advocated encompasses a number of principles that have since remained important cornerstones of linguistic anthropology and its work on genre (Boas 1911). At a time when automatic recording devices were rarely available during fieldwork, Boas collaborated with native speakers to create written records of the oral genres he considered characteristic of the communities he was studying (Boas 1940: 199–210). All records of linguistic phenomena were produced in the original language and not merely in the form of translations (cf. Darnell 1990: 247–252). This required the researchers themselves to develop a good command of the language spoken in the field (Boas 1911: 60). Although there are further methodological

principles to which linguistic anthropologists adhere today (ranging from technical issues such as the use of audio and video recordings to a more thorough reflection on ethical considerations), the principles outlined by Boas and characteristic
of his work – doing collaborative research, learning and documenting the source
language – are still important for students of genres in foreign language contexts
(cf. Duranti 1997: 52–56).

3.1 Genre and the ethnography of communication

In hindsight, further problems in the way Boas and his students conceptualized
research on languages and genres can be identified. Boas not only held up a
reifying model of language, which allowed language and linguistic phenomena
to be treated as entities separate from culture and society (Bauman and Briggs
2003: 263–265), but his understanding of language also downplayed the fact
that language is always part of a particular socio-cultural and interactive setting. Language does not manifest itself primarily in the form of texts and grammars, nor in monological ways of speaking, as collections of dictated narratives
and interviews might suggest.

   In contrast to such an understanding of language, as something to be studied in isolation, later researchers advocated the idea that the use of language in
naturally occurring occasions must take center stage, since the primary manifestation of language is rather the variety of lived and embodied forms of ordinary
speech. Within linguistic anthropology, the ethnography of speaking (Hymes
1962, Bauman and Sherzer 1974), later referred to as the ethnography of communication (Hymes 1974a), turned this idea into an empirical research program (see
Keating 2001 for an overview). Although envisaged as a comparative endeavor
with the aim of arriving at generalizations and a theory of language use, or communication, Hymes and others studied linguistic diversity and difference through
particularistic ethnographies that documented language use as a central activity
in human life. Rather than starting from an abstract notion of language, the ethnographers of communication saw the notion of speech community as "the unit
of description as a social, rather than linguistic, entity" (Hymes 1974a: 47). This
entailed the view that members of a particular community share distinct knowledge about the rules of appropriate language use, with regard not only to the
production of forms of speech but also to their interpretation. Besides the notion
of speech community, Hymes distinguished other important units of analysis:
speech situations, speech events, and speech acts. Speech situations provide
contexts for speech events (the speech activities of a community's communicative repertoire, e.g., having a conversation), which in turn are constituted by

speech acts (e.g., a directive, a joke), which Hymes considers the minimal unit of analysis (Hymes 1974a: 51–53). Ethnographic descriptions had to elucidate the specific "ways of speaking" of a community, including the communicative competencies required to participate in the speech events of a community (as opposed to a narrowly defined competency to use grammar correctly).

Hymes proposed 16 components of speech that ethnographers of communication could use as a heuristic schema for studying speech communities. Empirical studies do not necessarily have to cover all of these components, but the components could be used to direct attention to phenomena that have already proven to be relevant in previous studies. Hymes famously combined these components into the mnemonic SPEAKING, where G stands for genre.[1] By genre, Hymes writes, "[is] meant categories such as poem, myth, tale, proverb, riddle, curse, prayer, oration, lecture, commercial, form letter, editorial, etc." (Hymes 1974a: 61). It seems easy to continue this non-exhaustive list of instances of genres, though Hymes did not give a definition of his concept of genre. He suggested, however, that, heuristically, all speech could be examined for formal characteristics that make it a "manifestation of genres" (Hymes 1974a: 61, Hymes 1974b: 443), implying that speech communities could be investigated as to their repertoires, distribution, and amount of, as he calls it in reference to genre, "generic" speech (Hymes 1974b: 443–444), ultimately allowing empirically based general evidence about these communities (cf. Mayes 2005). This advice has been followed by many researchers, with the result that today there is a large stock of ethnographic descriptions of genres in various speech communities.

Studies such as Sherzer's (1974, 1983) description of the ways of speaking among the Panamanian Kuna, while grounded in an analysis of metalinguistic ethno-concepts and distinctions of linguistic varieties and genres, applied the heuristic schema proposed by Hymes. Sherzer was thus able to distinguish several more or less formal genres from "everyday speech" and describe the unique features of each genre according to parameters such as formality, linguistic resources, participants, social roles and relations, and setting. However, Sherzer's research also showed that dimensions such as the formality of speech events is rarely categorical, so that neither clear boundaries between generic and non-generic speech nor strict definitions of generic taxonomies can easily be arrived at (see also Ferguson 1994). Other studies have similarly relied on the dimension of formality versus informality in their analysis of genres, e.g., Duranti's (1983, 1994) research on *lāuga*, a Samoan oratory genre, in ceremonial and in political

---

1 The others are Scene/Setting, Participants, Ends, Act sequence, Keys, Instrumentalities, and Norms (Hymes 1974: 54–62).

settings, or more recently Dubuisson's (2017) investigation of *bata*, a Kazakh form of blessing, in everyday and ceremonial settings. These studies show the continuing relevance of the central concepts laid out in the foundational works of Hymes.

However, although the ethnography of communication engendered much research on genres across different languages and cultures, the resulting studies have largely been descriptive and particularistic in kind. Serious efforts to generalize from individual findings a theory of genre, a motif that seems consistent with Hymes' vision of a theory of communication, have not been made. This may in part be due to the quite vague definition of central analytic concepts in the ethnography of communication, such as speech event and genre. Intuitively, for example, the telling of a joke may seem a prototypical case of a genre. But then, isn't joking an activity "directly governed by rules or norms for the use of speech", and therefore a speech event according to Hymes' definition (Hymes 1974a: 52)? Hymes himself seems to have recognized the danger of such definitional questions, arguing for the analytical separation of speech events and genres. With the example of sermons, he wrote that a "sermon as a genre is typically identical with a certain place in a church service, but its properties may be invoked, for serious or humorous effect, in other situations. Often enough a genre recurs in several events" (1974: 61). This remark implies that genres, as communicatively embodied phenomena, are not bound to particular circumstances such as speech situations and speech events, but can be transposed into contexts other than those of their "normal" or conventional occurrence. However, if the properties of a sermon are being invoked through the telling of a joke, where does the sermon genre end and where does the joke genre begin? In such cases, one could arguably speak of a blending of genres, as evidenced in Sacks' analysis of a joke (1974), when he observes that the telling of a joke takes the form of a story. Moreover, another issue comes up with Hymes' remark: who is ultimately the arbiter of whether or not an utterance is an instance (or part) of a particular genre? In other words, is this question to be decided by the ethnographer's interpretative authority, or, alternatively, by the members of a speech community (Ben-Amos 1969) as they themselves "identify different kinds of speaking and writing" (Maxwell 2020: 1)? And finally, as Irvine (1979) has argued, the formality-informality polarity is also too rough-grained, since the very same speech event can be formal in some aspects and informal in others, and formality thus has to be conceptualized in a multidimensional manner.

3.2 Intertextuality of genres

The question of the delineation and interplay of genres has been taken up by linguistic anthropologists influenced by the work of the literary critic Mikhail Bakhtin, particularly by his essay on speech genres (Bakhtin 1986). Bakhtin did not provide a simple solution to this problem. Not unlike Hymes, he held that all utterances are in one way or another instances of generic speech and that there is an "extreme heterogeneity of speech genres" (Bakhtin 1986: 60, 77). Generic speech, he suggested, is learned in the same practical way children learn their native language and the correct use of grammar. And just as grammar provides orientation for speakers to produce and parse sentences, speech genres provide orientation for the production and understanding of speech at large: "We learn to cast our speech in generic forms and, when hearing others' speech, we guess its genres from the very first words (. . .). [F]rom the very beginning we have a sense of the speech whole, which is only later differentiated during the speech process" (Bakhtin 1986: 79). Bakhtin distinguished between primary speech genres, which are mostly associated with everyday speech, and secondary speech genres, such as novels and scientific research. In accordance with his dialogic conception of language, which implied that "[e]ach utterance is filled with echoes and reverberations of other utterances to which it is related" (1986: 91), Bakhtin drew attention to the interplay of speech genres, such as when more complex genres "digest" primary genres and alter their form (Bakthin 1986: 62).

Bakhtin's conceptualization of genre inspired several linguistic anthropologists, including, among others, Hanks (1987), who complemented the notion of genre as an orientation framework with Bourdieu's theory of habitus, thus viewing generic knowledge as enabling and constraining resources for social practice. However, Bahktin's understanding of the interaction between genres, covered under the notion of intertextuality, was taken up by Briggs and Bauman (1992), in particular, who viewed intertextuality as the performative creation of relationships between texts and genres. They suggest "that the creation of intertextual relationships through genre simultaneously renders texts ordered, unified, and bounded, on the one hand, and fragmented, heterogeneous, and open-ended, on the other" (ibid.: 147). Through formulaic expressions and decontextualized phrases like "once upon a time", utterances construct expectations for hearers and speakers about what will follow and how it will follow. In this way, the invocation of a genre may provide speakers and hearers with a sense of order. Moreover, when a well-known traditional fairy tale follows after the phrase "once upon a time", the "intertextual gap" between an abstract text or textual fragment and its embodied performance can be minimized (Briggs and Bauman 1992: 150). On the other hand, expectations need not necessarily be met, and the phrase "once upon a time" may be recontextualized as part of a humorous performance, creating a wider gap between an abstract genre (participants' expectations) and its embodied manifestation.

3.3 Genres as solutions to communicative problems

Another approach that has developed in response to the ethnography of communication is the kind of communicative genre analysis that was pioneered by the sociologist Thomas Luckmann and his students (Luckmann 1995, Luckmann and Bergmann 1995, Günthner and Knoblauch 1995). Luckmann also held that genres serve as orientation frameworks, but he amended this concept with his theory of knowledge and analytical procedures from CA. Therefore, similarly to the understanding of social interaction in CA, he conceptualized communicative genres as stabilized and conventionalized patterns that provide solutions to communicative problems. He assumed that communication is channeled through the requirements of the institutionalized dimension of social situations (Luckmann 1995: 178). By perpetuating certain communicative patterns within specific social contexts, communicative genres contribute to the solution of a basic problem of human sociality, namely, the co-ordination of action and the maintenance of intersubjectivity. Through prefabricated communicative patterns and practices tailored to specific social situations, communicative genres help interactants to achieve mutual alignment, projection of each other's perspectives, and the certainty that they need in order to act (Luckmann 1995: 183).

Unlike Hymes and Bakhtin, Luckmann is very clear about the possibility of the occurrence of non-generic speech. He took from conversation analysis the notion of ordinary conversation, which he understands as the default mode of (largely) non-generic speech. Communicative genres, for him, are thus isles in a sea of conversation. Luckmann's communicative genre analysis has engendered many empirical studies, e.g., on gossip (Bergmann 1993), reproaches (Günthner 1997), Georgian toasts (Kotthoff 1995), and job interviews (Birkner 2004).

3.4 Genre analysis and institutional CA

The connection between CA and genre analysis can be exploited even further when one realizes the elective affinity between CA's understanding of institutions and the concepts of genre of the more recent approaches (see Blum-Kulka 2005). Institutional CA studies (Drew and Heritage 1992) have shown how the parameters of the turn-taking system differ when interaction is organized under institutional conditions. It has been shown that participants orient to the specifics of institutional interaction, in settings such as schools, courtrooms, doctor-patient interaction, news interviews, talk shows, and many more. Conversation analysts sometimes refer to the communicative forms found in these settings as genres (Heritage and Clayman 2010: 215). They assume, for one thing, that interaction in these institutional contexts is built on the principles and rules of ordinary conversation, but at the same time systematically diverges from the "default" system of turn-taking. Accordingly, Heritage and Clayman distinguish between various turn-taking systems. In some conditions, such as in court, news interviews, or in the class room, participation is much more strictly regulated than in ordinary conversation. Moreover, the types of turns used in these settings are largely defined in advance and assigned to participants based on the respective institutional roles that they have. For example, a typical feature of interaction in courts, class rooms, and news interviews is that one party (judge / lawyer, teacher, reporter) has the right – and obligation – to ask questions to which another party (witness in a hearing, student, interviewee) is expected to respond (Heritage and Clayman 2010: 38). Participants regularly display their orientation to the kind of normative expectations associated with such predefined rules and principles. Moreover, if these normative expectations are disregarded by participants, others are often ready to sanction them, demonstrating their orientation to the institutional context. Other forms of institutional interaction are characterized by less rigid systems of turn-taking. For example, in meeting talk, one typically finds the institutional role of a chair, who is responsible for managing turn transition and allocating turns to speakers. By the very fact that talk is mediated by this institutional role, meeting chairs are invested with a certain amount of authority (Heritage and Clayman 2010: 38). Of course, in reality, turn-taking systems rarely fit one of these two models completely. There are hybrid types that incorporate both pre-allocated and mediated components of turn-taking.

While genre research in the ethnography of speaking tradition was an explicit endeavor to do research on non-Western communities, cross-cultural research in the institutional talk approach of CA is emerging only now.

3.5 An empirical example

In this last section, we demonstrate the empirical application of an approach that combines the CA perspective with genre analysis in a non-Western setting. We also connect our analysis to studies that deliberately set out to study genres as genres-in-interaction. Our analysis shows how genres exploit the turn-taking system when providing solutions to specific interactive and social problems and exigencies. It also demonstrates the intertextuality of different written and oral genres, the interplay of these genres, and the ways in which they are interactively constructed. Consistent with Luckmann's understanding of communicative genres as sedimented forms providing solutions for recurrent communicative problems, we will see that in the course of the embodied interaction analyzed here, genres shift from one to another, permanently solving and creating social problems, while exhibiting universal patterns.

The data presented below are from a staff meeting in a village hospital in Kazakhstan. This meeting regularly consists of a series of institutional activities and phases, including the discussion of a system for monitoring infant health.

Figure 6.1: A record card.

Figure 6.1 shows a copy of an index card used within this system. At the top it indicates the period for which it is representative. Directly below are the addresses of the population being monitored and the name of the nurse accountable. The table contains various data about the part of the village population represented. Important for us is line 9: the number of "paperless people". This refers to migrants who have neither a Kazakhstani passport nor a valid residence permit. Often these are migrants born in neighboring countries, such as Uzbekistan or China (Muratbayeva and Quasinowski 2021). Although the hospital provides primary health care services for them, their unclear legal status frequently leads to administrative problems. As a result, paperless people are perceived as troublesome patients, a perception reinforced by discourses of cultural alterity. Paperless Kazakh migrants from China and other countries are sometimes attributed with a way of life that is "incompatible with the local culture".

The following analysis[2] shows how the written genre of index cards is interactively re-contextualized and how it serves as a starting point for a series of genres and activity types unfolding in the subsequent interaction sequences, including directive, mockery, reproach, and gossip. At the beginning of the episode, KU, the director of the hospital, is examining the index cards that the nurses have completed over the previous week. When he spots the surname of nurse AY on the card, KU speaks her name aloud, thus establishing a public association between her and the card. As a result, his directive, uttered in line 6, needs no further mention of the addressee: AY immediately heads toward KU, who is sitting at the desk at the other end of the room. The directive uttered in this institutional context and in the context of KU's examination of the index cards is a generic device that raises the expectation that trouble is on the way.

```
(1)  001  KU   tak=kto u nas.
                So, who do we have here?
     002        ayBEkova;
                Aybekova.
     003        (3.1)
     004  KU   tak,
                So
     005        (0.8)
     006  KU   BEri kel;
                Come here.
```

There are several generic *activities* that typically occur after this kind of situation, one of which is the reproach. Reproaches are characterized by a specific participation framework with two obligatory roles: a producer who finds fault with the violation of a rule and an addressee who is attributed responsibility for the rule violation (Günthner 2000: 75–76). Part of the reason for KU's discontent is that

---

2 The transcription follows the conventions of GAT2 (Selting et al. 2011). The languages spoken are Kazakh and Russian. Russian sentences and phrases, as well as Russian parts of the translation, are underlined.

AY failed to fill in the blanks at the top of the index card, which specify the period to which the card relates. In lines 19 and 24, KU asks two questions. The use of interrogatives like "why" or "what" is an important resource for constructing reproaches (Günthner 2000: 90), as they put a supposedly shared basis of reasoning into doubt and implicitly negate the interlocutor's capacities to reason normally.

```
(2) 007      ((CK laughs for 1.5s, AY approaching CK))
    008  KU  žoq (0.2) siğïrayğan köziñmen ešteñe körMEYsiñ ba?=
             No, (0.2) can't you see with your squinting eyes?
    009      =MEN siyyaqtï;
             Like me.
    010      (0.7)
    011  KU  MIne;=
             Look here.
    012      S: (.) PO: (.) žoq;=mïna žaqta ŽAzu kerek;
             from, to is missing, it must be written here.
    013      (2.9)
    014  KU  sen byustGAL'ter artïna kiymeysiñ (ğoy)?
             You don't put your bra on the back!
    015      ALdïña kiyesiñ ğoy?
             You put it on the chest!
    016      ((several participants laughing))
    017  KU  von ŽAZïlğan ğoy mïna žerde;
             It is written here.
    018      (0.7)
    019  KU  al nege so al nege isTEYsiñder,
             And why do you why do you do that?
    020      čtoby aliev (0.2) butïna siysïn dep
             So that Aliev (0.2) Curbashevic will be pissed off?
    021      ((several laughing))
    022      (1.2)
    023  KU  (bul)<<t>nege soLAYsïñ?
             Why are you like this?
    024      äDEYi žasaysïñ?>
             Do you do it on purpose?
    025      (0.5)
    026  AY  <<p>žoq>
             No.
```

Günthner (2000: 90–110) mentions a range of other means that speakers use to construct reproaches, including an "accusatory voice", affect markers, swearing, extreme case formulations, contrast formulations, modal verbs, and modal particles. KU uses some of these means in this episode, but it is mockery that most conspicuously constructs his reproach. By mocking AY, KU puts the reproach in a particularly affect laden frame. Before stating the reason for his discontent with AY's flawed completion of the index card, KU mocks her by putting into question her very ability to see clearly (8–9). Then he points to the empty blanks on the index card and explicitly states that they must be filled in (12).

A long pause follows where AY gives no response (13). Reproaches make responses, such as accounts, rejections of the premises, or counter-reproaches, conditionally relevant (Günthner 2000: 79). Nothing of this ensues, however, and it may be the lack of a response that pushes KU to upgrade his reproach. He uses a degrading sexualized allegory to create the contrast between doing something right or wrong (14–15). Only when AY denies KU's rhetorical question about whether she filled the index cards erroneously on purpose (24–26) does he give up mocking her.

KU shifts his attention to the paperless migrants living in AY's street by asking her to identify those "without documents" (50–51). AY uses a relational reference term (53) to identify the three paperless persons indicated on the index card. *Täte*, a kinship term, attached to a first name, works as an honorific to address and refer to women older than the speaker, but is not necessarily indicative of a kin relationship between speaker and referent. However, AY's use of the first name in connection with the honorific indicates that Clara, a cleaning lady at the hospital, is a mutual acquaintance of the speaker and the addressee. KU displays his inability to identify her (55) and only after other participants (SA, MI, GK) specify the cleaning lady's surname does KU display his understanding with an overtly negative assessment about paperless migrants (61).

(3) 050 KU BEZ dokumentov;=
          Without papers,
     051   =KIMder osï žerde;
          who are they at that place?
     052   (0.5)
     053 AY klara täteniñ: eki nemereciMEN (0.3) kelini.
          Clara täte's two grandchildren and (0.3) her
          daughter-in-law.
     054   (0.7)

```
055  KU    QAY klara;
            Which Clara?
056  AY    [(        )
057  SA    [tïnišbaeva
             Tynyshbaeva.
058  MI    [tïniš[baeva
             Tynyshbaeva.
059  GK          [tïnišbaeva
                   Tynyshbaeva.
060        (0.2)
061  KU    užas (kakoy)
            That's terrible!
```

Mentioning Clara and her relatives opens the gates for another genre: gossip. As in the case of reproaches, there is a specific participation framework for gossip. Bergmann (1993: chap. 3) identifies a triadic configuration consisting of a producer, a recipient, and an object (or target) of gossip. The three participants in this configuration are usually close to each other (e.g., friends, relatives, neighbors). Similar to reproaches, gossip concerns the moral order of a community, against the backdrop of which misconduct or rule violations are made the topic of the conversation. The person responsible for, or connected with, a moral breach, is made the target of the gossip. Since this is often a person close to the gossipers, they face a dilemma (Bergmann 1993: 208–210). For one thing, there is a preference to make absent person the topics of criticism, especially if they are found to be guilty of a moral breach; at the same time, there is an obligation to handle information about persons close to oneself with care. It is precisely gossip that allows for a sufficiently "discrete indiscretion" that provides a communicative solution to this structural problem.

In our episode, the participants orient to this delicate nature of gossip. Even though staff members with non-medical occupations do not regularly participate, the cleaning ladies are sometimes present in the meetings. Thus, when responding to KU's question (53), AY first assures herself that Clara is not among the participating members this morning. Once assured, she is free to mention the cleaning lady's name as a proxy for her paperless relatives. More importantly, the cleaning lady's absence provides the grounds for the subsequent gossip that targets her and her family.

In gossip, the use of social categories (e.g., drunkard, loafer, adulterer) is an important means to express moral judgments about individuals, allowing the generalization of a particular misbehavior that a person has committed (Bergmann 1993: 177–178). From the perspective of sequential organization, this presupposes that the individual has already been introduced to the conversation and an example of his or her misbehavior has been reported. A single instance is thus blown up into a social category that reinforces the individual's misbehavior as a general feature of his or her kind. In our case, however, the order of gossip is somewhat reversed, since the name of the target (the daughter-in-law) is never mentioned. Instead, right from the start, references to her are established through generalizing and implication-rich social categories and descriptors. After her introduction as Clara's daughter-in-law, internist GA categorizes her as Kalpak, a member of an ethnic group of neighboring Uzbekistan.

In the subsequent discussion of the woman's legal status, it turns out that although she is married to Clara's son, she has not yet obtained Kazakh citizenship. One of the participants reveals that the daughter-in-law's Uzbek passport will be invalid in a few weeks and that she has gone to Karakalpakstan to renew her passport, leaving her baby with Clara. KU then shifts the conversation to more general complaints about paperless migrants in the village. Throughout the conversation, Clara's daughter-in-law resurfaces as a personification of the social category complained about. Eventually, GA recounts, in a multi-unit turn accompanied by non-competitively overlapping hearer assessments that momentarily suspend the institutionally pre-structured turn-taking system, a series of events that corroborate the representation of the daughter-in-law built up so far.

```
(4)  172  GA  KLA:ra eki qaytara onï žiber[di qaraqalpaqïstanğa:--
                Clara sent her two times to Karakalpakstan
     173  SA                               [žiBERdi (iyä) žiberdi;
                                           [she sent her, yes, she sent her
     174  GA  °h bir ret öziniñ äkesiMEN žiberdi;
                Once she sent her together with her own father.
     175      äkesi aparMAdï;
                (But) The father didn't bring her there.
     176      bir ret öziniñ ↑KÜYEUWIN ertip–
                Once she took her own husband with her.
     177      aqšasïn bärin berip [žiberDI,
                She gave all the money and sent her.
     178  MI                     [(        )
     179  GA  žasaMAY qaytïp keldi;
                She returned without accomplishment.
     180      (0.4)
     181  GA  kaKAYA ta tam aferistka;
                (She is) some fraud there.
```

182		ya ne ZNAyu;
		I don't know (what to say).
183		èto sem* èto ŽENščina;=sama;
		this fam this woman, herself.*
184		(0.6)
185	?	mhm
186	GA	ona DAže: è:
		She even uh:
187		[klaru daze ŽAL'ko inogda;
		sometimes one even feels sorry for Clara.

At the end of her account, GA categorizes Clara's daughter-in-law as a fraud (181), a descriptor with outright negative connotations. As Bergmann (1993: 132) observed, gossipers are "never merely prosecutors and judges", but regularly display compassion and tolerance for the target of the gossip. In our episode, the gossipers do display their understanding and compassion, not for the moral culprit, but for Clara, who is the only character in the gossip referred to by name, and who is an employee of the hospital.

In the context of the village community, where there is a cleft between an ethnically mixed but predominantly Kazakh population and those with a recent migrant background (including "people without documents"), Clara's family embodies double membership. Since, in the rural communities of Kazakhstan, an individual person of a certain age is also a representative of his or her family, gossip about individuals is gossip about families. Therefore, even though Clara herself is not the violator of any moral rules here, the misconduct and reprehensible character of her daughter-in-law inevitably reflect upon her and her family. GA's expressions of pity for Clara can therefore be understood as an effort to mitigate between saving the social face of her family, which is a morally integral part of the village community, and condemning individually reprehensible behavior that is attached to particular social categories ("people without documents", "in-laws"). This is reflected in the final sequence in our episode (220–231), when participants give a summarizing evaluation and KU puts it all in the nutshell of a Russian proverb, thus providing a final example of the interactive intertextuality of genre-in-interaction.

(5) 220 GA enDI: (.) <u>vot tak bot;</u>
              Now that's what it is
     221   ey TOže trudno;
              She's having a hard time, too.
     222   (0.2)
     223   KLAre tože trudno ey;
              Clara is having a hard time.
     224 SA <<p>takaya vot ženščina (xxxx)>
              Such a woman
     225   (1.3)
     226 KU <u>nu</u>
              So what!
     227 MA <u>taKIX polno,</u>
              There's a lot of this sort.
     228 ?   mhm
     229   (1.9)
     230 KU <u>malen'kie deti govoryat !SPAT'! ne dayut;</u>
              They say little children don't let you sleep,
     231   <u>bol'šie deti !ŽIT'! ne dayut</u> degen sol ğoy;
              grown up children don't let you live it is said.

4 Conclusion

We reviewed CA's findings on fundamental principles of conversational organization and various (anthropological) traditions of studies of genre-in-interaction. By
using an example from a workplace meeting in a Kazakh hospital, we considered
how genre analysis can be fruitfully complemented by the CA perspective. The
example shows that CA of ordinary and institutionally adapted talk that exhibits
a typical pre-structured turn-taking system, and creates specific expectations as
to "nexts", can be brought together with a genre perspective that considers the
institutionality and interactive embodiment of genres. The institutional activities
are therefore permanently traversed by generic ones. The genres, in turn, can be
explicated through thorough analysis of their linguistic and turn-taking patterns.
Moreover, as we have seen, one genre intertextually develops out of, is enabled,
and draws on the resources established by its predecessor and there are multiple
transitions and overlappings between them. Mockery is incorporated in and gossip emerges from reproach, and the proverb at the end is the concluding evaluation and "formulation" of the gossip stories.

Based on the premise that the turn-taking system is an intrinsic part of human conversational interaction, it could be demonstrated that this system articulates with communicative genres, e.g., when, in the course of gossip, co-participants redefine the participation framework by uttering assessments, agreements, and individual contributions, thus abandoning their institutional roles as passive listeners who only talk when given the turn by the hospital director. Furthermore, time and again, the dissolution of institutional talk through genres of non-institutional talk stops and the institutional order is re-installed. Arguably, the meeting chair has an important role in initiating genre-specific talk and thus also in adjusting the parameters of turn-taking organization in the institutional context. The organization of turn-taking within genre-specific talk thereby overrules the principles of institutional conversational organization. Thus, the situated exploitation of expectable patterns by social actors not only refers to both conversational organization and genre, but also to the interplay between them and their effects in producing a participation framework and defining the situation.

Speech events have functional effects in a broad range of dimensions. Reproaches, for example, can serve to render visible norms in relation to good work and ultimately to socialize members into membership roles. Mockery upgrades a reproach, thus sharing its function while solving a situational interactional problem. Gossip is only loosely bound to the institutional context. It demonstrates that the boundaries between village community and institutional relationships can be fuzzy. In our case, the staff of the hospital know many of their patients not only from within the hospital, but from convivial contexts in the village community. Their relationships "intrude" into the institutional context and create space for village gossip. The structural solution that gossip provides is also that of showcasing inappropriate conduct and thereby supporting the moral order. The proverb finishes the extra-institutional episode, so that the interaction can transition to institutional topics gain.

References

Bakhtin, Mikhail. 1986. *Speech genres and other late essays*. Austin: University of Texas Press.

Bassetti, Chiara & Kenneth Liberman. 2021. Making talk together. Simultaneity and rhythm in mundane Italian conversation. *Language & Communication* 80. 95–113.

Bauman, Richard & Joel Sherzer. 1975. The ethnography of speaking. *Annual Review of Anthropology* 4 (1). 95–119.

Ben-Amos, Dan. 1969. Analytical categories and ethnic genres. *Genre* 2 (3). 275–301.

Bergmann, Jörg. 1993. *Discreet indiscretions. The social organization of gossip*. London: Taylor & Francis.

Bergmann, Jörg & Thomas Luckmann. 1995. Reconstructive genres of everyday communication. In Uta M. Quasthoff (ed.), *Aspects of oral communication*, 289–304. Berlin: Walter de Gruyter.

Bilmes, Jack. 1975. Misinformation and ambiguity in verbal interaction. A Northern Thai example. *International Journal of the Sociology of Language* 5. 63–75.

Bilmes, Jack. 1976. Rules and rhetoric. Negotiating the social order in a Thai village. *Journal of Anthropological Research* 32 (1). 44–57.

Bilmes, Jack. 1985. "Why that now?" two kinds of conversational meaning. *Discourse Processes* 8 (3). 319–355.

Birkner, Karin. 2004. Hegemonic struggles or transfer of knowledge? East and West Germans in job interviews. *Journal of Language and Politics* 3 (2). 293–322.

Blum-Kulka, Shoshana. 2005. Rethinking genre. Communicative genres as social interactive phenomenon. In Kristine Fitch & Robert Sanders (eds.), *Handbook of language and social interaction*, 275–231. Mahwah: Lawrence Erlbaum.

Blythe, Joe, Rod Gardner, Ilana Mushin & Lesley Stirling. 2018. Tools of engagement. Selecting a next speaker in Australian Aboriginal multiparty conversations. *Research on Language and Social Interaction* 51 (2). 145–170.

Boas, Franz. 1940. *Race, language and culture*. New York: The Macmillan Company.

Boas, Franz. (ed.) 2013 (1911). *Handbook of American Indian languages*, Vol.1. Cambridge: Cambridge University Press.

Briggs, Charles L. & Richard Bauman. 1992. Genre, intertextuality, and social power. *Journal of Linguistic Anthropology* 2 (2). 131–172.

Briggs, Charles L. & Richard Bauman. 2003. *Voices of modernity. Language ideologies and the politics of inequality*. Cambridge: Cambridge University Press.

D'hondt, Sigurd. 2019. Situated language use in Africa. In H. Ekkehard Wolff (ed.), *The Cambridge Handbook of African Linguistics*, 491–512. Cambridge: Cambridge University Press.

Darnell, Regna. 1990. *Edward Sapir. Linguist, anthropologist, humanist*. Berkeley: University of California Press.

Dingemanse, Mark & N. J. Enfield. 2015. Other-initiated repair across languages. Towards a typology of conversational structures. *Open Linguistics* 1 (1). 96–118.

Dingemanse, Mark, Giovanni Rossi & Simeon Floyd. 2017. Place reference in story beginnings. A cross-linguistic study of narrative and interactional affordances. *Language in Society* 46 (2). 129–158.

Drew, Paul & John Heritage. 1992. Analyzing talk at work. An introduction. In Paul Drew & John Heritage (eds.), *Talk at work*, 3–65. Cambridge: Cambridge University Press.

Dubuisson, Eva-Marie. 2017. *Living language in Kazakhstan. The dialogic emergence of an ancestral worldview*. Pittsburgh: University of Pittsburgh Press.

Duranti, Alessandro 1983. Samoan speechmaking across social events: One genre in and out of a fono. *Language in Society* 12. 1–22.

Duranti, Alessandro. 1994. *From grammar to politics. Linguistic anthropology in a Western Samoan village*. Berkeley: University of California Press.

Duranti, Alessandro. 1997. *Linguistic anthropology*. Cambridge: Cambridge University Press.

Enfield, N. J. & Jack Sidnell. 2014. Language presupposes an enchronic infrastructure for social interaction. In Daniel Dor, Chris Knight & Jerome Lewis (eds.), *The social origins of language*, 92–104. Oxford: Oxford University Press.

Ervin-Tripp, Susan M. 1987. Cross-cultural and developmental sources of pragmatic generalizations. In Jef Verschueren & Marcella Bertuccelli-Papi (eds.), *The pragmatic perspective*, 47–60. Amsterdam: John Benjamins.

Ferguson, Charles. 1994. Dialect, register, and genre. Working assumptions about conventionalization. In Douglas Biber & Edward Finegan (eds.), *Sociolinguistic perspectives on register*, 15–30. Oxford: Oxford University Press.

Fox, Barbara, Makoto Hayashi & Robert Jasperson. 1996. Resources and repair. A cross-linguistic study of syntax and repair. In Elinor Ochs & Emanuel A. Schegloff (eds.), *Interaction and grammar*, 185–237. Cambridge: Cambridge University Press.

Gardner, Rod & Ilana Mushin. 2007. Post-start-up overlap and disattentiveness in talk in a Garrwa community. *Australian Review of Applied Linguistics* 30 (3). 35.1–35.14.

Goodwin, Charles. 1981. *Conversational organization. Interaction between speakers and hearers*. New York: Academic Press.

Graham, Laura. 1995. *Performing dreams. Discourses of immortality among the Xavante of Central Brazil*. Austin: University of Texas Press.

Günthner, Susanne 1997. Complaint stories. Constructing emotional reciprocity among women. In Helga Kotthoff & Ruth Wodak (eds.), *Communicating gender in context*, 179–218. Amsterdam: John Benjamins.

Günthner, Susanne. 2000. *Vorwurfsaktivitäten in der Alltagsinteraktion. Grammatische, prosodische, rhetorisch-stilistische und interaktive Verfahren bei der Konstitution kommunikativer Muster und Gattungen*. Tübingen: Max Niemeyer Verlag.

Günthner, Susanne & Hubert Knoblauch. 1995. Culturally patterned speaking practices. The analysis of communicative genres. *Pragmatics* 5 (1). 1–32.

Hanks, William F. 1987. Discourse genres in a theory of practice. *American Ethnologist* 14 (4). 668–692.

Haviland, John B. 2003. How to point in Zinacantán. In Sotaro Kita (ed.), *Pointing. Where language, culture, and cognition meet*, 139–170. Mahwah: Lawrence Erlbaum.

Hayden, Robert M. 1987. Turn-taking, overlap, and the task at hand. Ordering speaking turns in legal settings. *American Ethnologist* 14 (2). 251–270.

Heritage, John 2008. Conversation analysis as social theory. In Bryan Turner (ed.), *The New Blackwell Companion to social theory*, 300–320. Oxford: Blackwell.

Heritage, John & Steven Clayman. 2010. *Talk in action. Interactions, identities, and institutions*. Oxford: Wiley-Blackwell.

Hilbert, Richard A. 1990. Ethnomethodology and the micro-macro order. *American Sociological Review* 55 (6). 794–808.

Hymes, Dell H. 1962. The ethnography of speaking. In Thomas Gladwin & William Sturtevant (eds.), *Anthropology and human behavior*, 13–53. Washington, DC: Anthropological Society of Washington.

Hymes, Dell H. 1974a. *Foundations in sociolinguistics. An ethnographic approach*. Philadelphia: University of Pennsylvania Press.

Hymes, Dell H. 1974b. Ways of speaking. In Richard Bauman & Joel Sherzer (eds.), *Explorations in the ethnography of speaking*, 433–451. Cambridge: Cambridge University Press.

Irvine, Judith T. 1979. Formality and informality in communicative events. *American Anthropologist* 81 (4). 773–790.

Keating, Elizabeth. 2001. The ethnography of communication. In Paul Atkinson, Amanda Coffey, Sara Delamont, John Lofland & Lyn Lofland (eds.), *Handbook of ethnography*, 285–301. London: SAGE Publications.

Kendrick, Kobin H., Penelope Brown, Mark Dingemanse, Simeon Floyd, Sonja Gipper, Kaoru Hayano, Elliott Hoey, Gertie Hoymann, Elizabeth Manrique, Giovanni Rossi & Stephen C. Levinson. 2020. Sequence organization. A universal infrastructure for social action. *Journal of Pragmatics* 168. 119–138.

Kimura, Daiji. 2001. Utterance overlap and long silence among the Baka Pygmies. Comparison with Bantu farmers and Japanese university students. *African Study Monographs*, Supplementary Issue 26. 103–121.

Kimura, Daiji. 2003. Bakas' mode of co-presence. *African Study Monographs*, Supplementary Issue 28. 25–35.

Kotthoff, Helga. 1995. The social semiotics of Georgian toast performances. Oral genre as cultural activity. *Journal of Pragmatics* 24 (4). 353–380.

Li, Xiaoting. 2014. *Multimodality, interaction and turn-taking in Mandarin conversation*. Amsterdam: John Benjamins.

Liberman, Kenneth. 1980. The organization of talk in aboriginal community decision-making. *Anthropological Forum* 5 (1). 38–53.

Liberman, Kenneth. 1985. *Understanding interaction in central Australia. An ethnomethodological study of Australian Aboriginal people*. Boston: Routledge & Kegan Paul.

Luckmann, Thomas. 1995. Interaction planning and intersubjective adjustment of perspectives by communicative genres. In Esther N. Goody (ed.), *Social intelligence and interaction*, 175–188. Cambridge: Cambridge University Press.

Maxwell, J. M. 2020. Genre. In James Stanlaw (ed.), *The international encyclopedia of linguistic anthropology*, 1–5. Oxford: Wiley-Blackwell.

Mayes, Patricia. 2005. Linking micro and macro social structure through genre analysis. *Research on Language and Social Interaction* 38 (3). 331–70.

Meyer, Christian. 2017. The cultural organization of intercorporeality. Interaction, emotion, and the senses among the Wolof of Northwestern Senegal. In Christian Meyer, Jürgen Streeck & J. Scott Jordan (eds.), *Intercorporeality. Emerging socialities in interaction*, 143–171. New York: Oxford University Press.

Meyer, Christian. 2018. *Culture, practice, and the body. Conversational organization and embodied culture in Northwestern Senegal*. Stuttgart: Metzler.

Mihas, Elena. 2017. *Conversational structures of Alto Perené (Arawak) of Peru*. Amsterdam: John Benjamins.

Moerman, Michael. 1972. Analysis of Lue conversation. Providing accounts, finding breaches, and taking sides. In David N. Sudnow (ed.), *Studies in social interaction*, 170–228. New York: MacMillan & Free Press.

Moerman, Michael. 1977. The preference for self-correction in a Tai conversational corpus. *Language* 53 (4). 872–882.

Moerman, Michael. 1988. *Talking culture. Ethnography and conversation analysis*. Philadelphia: University of Pennsylvania Press.

Moerman, Michael. 1990/1991. Exploring talk and interaction. *Research on Language and Social Interaction* 24. 173–187.

Mondada, Lorenza. 2018. Multiple temporalities of language and body in interaction. Challenges for transcribing multimodality. *Research on Language and Social Interaction* 51 (1). 85–106.

Muratbayeva, Bakyt & Benjamin Quasinowski. 2021. 'Ask us decently and then we will not reject anyone!' Providing informal healthcare in a Kazakh medical space. In Rano Turaeva & Rustamjon Urinboyev (eds.), *Labour, mobility and informal practices in Russia, Central Asia and Eastern Europe. Power, institutions and mobile actors in transnational space*, 214–231. London & New York: Routledge.

Mushin, Ilana & Rod Gardner. 2009. Silence is talk. Conversational silence in Australian Aboriginal talk-in-interaction. *Journal of Pragmatics* 41 (10). 2033–2052.

Nishizaka, Aug. 2007. Hand touching hand. Referential practice at a Japanese midwife house. *Human Studies* 30 (3). 199–217.

Park, Jae-Eun 2016. Turn-taking in Korean conversation. *Journal of Pragmatics* 99. 62–77.

Philips, Susan U. 1976. Some sources of cultural variability in the regulation of talk. *Language in Society* 5 (1). 81–95.

Reisman, Karl. 1974a. Contrapuntal conversations in an Antiguan village. In Richard Bauman & Joel Sherzer (eds.), *Explorations in the ethnography of speaking*, 110–124. Cambridge: Cambridge University Press.

Reisman, Karl. 1974b. Noise and order. In William W. Gage (ed.), *Language in its social setting*, 56–73. Washington: The Anthropological Society of Washington.

Rossano, Federico, Penelope Brown & Stephen C. Levinson. 2009. Gaze, questioning and culture. In Jack Sidnell (ed.), *Conversation analysis. Comparative perspectives*, 187–249. Cambridge: Cambridge University Press.

Rüsch, Maren. 2021. *A conversational analysis of Acholi. Structure and socio-pragmatics of a Nilotic language of Uganda*. Leiden: Brill.

Sacks, Harvey. 1974. An analysis of the course of a joke's telling in conversation. In Richard Bauman & Joel Sherzer (eds.), *Explorations in the ethnography of speaking*, 337–353. Cambridge: Cambridge University Press.

Sacks, Harvey. 1984. Notes on methodology. In J. Maxwell Atkinson & John Heritage (eds.), *Structures of social action*, 21–27. Cambridge: Cambridge University Press.

Sacks, Harvey & Emanuel A. Schegloff. 1979. Two preferences in the organization of reference to persons in conversation and their interaction. In George Psathas (ed.), *Everyday language. Studies in ethnomethodology*, 15–21. New York: Irvington.

Sacks, Harvey, Emanuel A. Schegloff & Gail Jefferson. 1974. A simplest systematics for the organization of turn-taking for conversation. *Language* 50 (4). 696–735.

Sawada, Masato. 1987. The evening conversation of the Efe Pygmy men and its social implication. A men's display to women. *African Study Monographs*, Supplementary Issue 6. 85–96.

Schegloff, Emanuel A. 1968. Sequencing in conversational openings. *American Anthropologist* 70 (6). 1075–1095.

Schegloff, Emanuel A. 1972. Notes on a conversational practice. Formulating place. In David N. Sudnow (ed.), *Studies in social interaction*, 75–119. New York: MacMillan & Free Press.

Schegloff, Emanuel A. 1987. Between micro and macro. Contexts and other connections. In Jeffrey C. Alexander, Bernhard Giesen, Richard Munch & Neil Smelser (eds.), *The micro-macro link*, 207–234. Berkeley: University of California Press.

Schegloff, Emanuel A. 1988. Goffman and the analysis of conversation. In Paul Drew & Antony J. Wooton (eds.), *Erving Goffman. Exploring the interaction order*, 89–135. Cambridge: Polity Press.

Schegloff, Emanuel A. 1992. Repair after next turn. The last structurally provided defense of intersubjectivity in conversation. *American Journal of Sociology* 97 (5). 1295–1345.

Schegloff, Emanuel A. 2000. Overlapping talk and the organization of turn-taking for conversation. *Language in Society* 29 (1). 1–63.

Schegloff, Emanuel A. 2006. Interaction. The infrastructure for social institutions, the natural ecological niche for language, and the arena in which culture is enacted. In N. J. Enfield & Stephen C. Levinson (eds.), *Roots of human sociality. Culture, cognition, and interaction*, 70–96. Oxford, New York: Berg.

Schegloff, Emanuel A. 2007. *A primer in conversation analysis, 1: Sequence organization in interaction*. Cambridge: Cambridge University Press.

Schegloff, Emanuel A., Gail Jefferson & Harvey Sacks. 1977. The preference for self-correction in the organization of repair in conversation. *Language* 53 (2). 361–382.

Schegloff, Emanuel A. & Harvey Sacks. 1973. Opening up closings. *Semiotica* 8 (4). 289–327.

Selting, Margret. 1996. On the interplay of syntax and prosody in the constitution of turn-constructional units and turns in conversation. *Pragmatics* 6 (3). 371–338.

Selting, Margret et al. 2011. A system for transcribing talk-in-interaction: GAT 2. *Gesprächsforschung – Online-Zeitschrift zur verbalen Interaktion* 12. 1–41. [http://www.gespraechsforschung-ozs.de/heft2011/px-gat2-englisch.pdf] (accessed 30 April 2022).

Sherzer, Joel. 1974. Namakke, Sunmakke, Kornmakke. Three types of Cuna speech event. In Richard Bauman & Joel Sherzer (eds.), *Explorations in the ethnography of speaking*, 263–282. Cambridge: Cambridge University Press.

Sherzer, Joel. 1983. *Kuna ways of speaking*. Austin: University of Texas Press.

Sidnell, Jack. 2001. Conversational turn-taking in a Caribbean English creole. *Journal of Pragmatics* 33 (8). 1263–1290.

Sidnell, Jack. 2007. Comparative studies in conversation analysis. *Annual Review of Anthropology* 36. 229–244.

Stivers, Tanya, N. J. Enfield, Penelope Brown, Christina Englert, Makoto Hayashi, Trine Heinemann, Gertie Hoymann, Federico Rossano, Jan de Ruiter, Kyung-Eun Yoon & Stephen C. Levinson. 2009. Universals and cultural variation in turn-taking in conversation. *Proceedings of the National Academy of Sciences* 106 (26). 10587–10592.

Streeck, Jürgen. 2009. *Gesturecraft. The manu-facture of meaning*. Amsterdam: John Benjamins.

Tannen, Deborah. 1985. Silence. Anything but. In Deborah Tannen & Muriel Saville-Troike (eds.), *Perspectives on silence*, 93–111. Norwood: Ablex.

Walsh, Michael. 1991. Conversational styles and intercultural communication. An example from Northern Australia. *Australian Journal of Communication* 18 (1). 1–12.

Wilson, Thomas P. 1991. Social structure and the sequential organization of interaction. In Deirdre Boden & Don H. Zimmerman (eds.), *Talk and social structure. Studies in ethnomethodology and conversation analysis*, 22–43. Berkeley: University of California Press.

Susanne Mohr & Anastasia Bauer

7 Gesture, sign languages and multimodality

Language is inherently multimodal, drawing not only on acoustic cues but also on manual signals like gestures or manual signs in sign languages, as well as a multitude of semiotic resources available via different semiotic channels. This chapter considers some dimensions of spoken and signed communication within a broader view of multimodal communicative practices. Thus, we take a multidimensional rather than a binary approach to the gesture-sign continua (Kendon 1988, 2004, McNeill 1992, 2000) and review them against the background of recent theories in sign language and gesture studies. We maintain that the multimodal, multichanneled, and multisemiotic nature of language should be acknowledged beyond the field of gesture and sign language studies and be included in general theories

Acknowledgments: We extend our thanks to the many signers who have participated in our sign language documentation projects in Australia, Botswana, Ireland, Russia, and South Africa over the years. We would like to thank Svetlana Burkova (Novosibirsk, Russian Federation) for allowing access to the RSL corpus video and ELAN files for further annotation. We also thank Roman Poryadin for his assistance with the annotation of mouthings in the RSL project and with the translation of the abstract of this chapter into International Sign. Szilard Racz-Engelhardt and Tatjana Schnellinger, as well as the anonymous reviewer, have our gratitude for their comments and valuable feedback on this paper. We are also indebted to Helena Sommer for drawing a map of our data collection sites.

The data on Ts'ixa and *tshaukak'ui* discussed in this paper was collected under a research permit issued by the Ministry of Youth, Sports and Culture of the Government of Botswana for the project "The Kalahari Basin area: a 'Sprachbund' on the verge of extinction" within the European Science Foundation EUROCORES program EUROBABEL led by Tom Güldemann (Humboldt University of Berlin); we thank Anne-Maria Fehn for permission to use the data for this publication. The Yolngu data was collected for the project "Village Sign Languages" within the European Science Foundation EUROCORES program EUROBABEL led by Ulrike Zeshan (University of Central Lancashire, UK). The RSL research was funded by a German Research Foundation grant received by the second author. The project title is "A corpus study of mouthing and fingerspelling in Russian Sign Language: description and implications for cross-modal contact" (BA 4311/1-1).

In accordance with the requirements of the Vancouver Declaration, both authors have contributed to the conceptualization, data collection, analysis, writing, and editing of this paper. Both authors have read and agreed to the published version of the manuscript.

Susanne Mohr, Norwegian University of Science and Technology/Norway,
e-mail: susanne.mohr@ntnu.no
Anastasia Bauer, University of Cologne/Germany, e-mail: anastasia.bauer@uni-koeln.de

https://doi.org/10.1515/9783110726626-007

of language. We consider multimodal communicative practices by looking into different types of gestures such as co-speech gestures and emblems, as well as signs in different types of sign languages, i.e., primary, alternate, emerging, and village sign languages. Our data stem from previous and ongoing research on Irish, South African and Russian Sign Languages, as well as indigenous alternate sign languages in Australia, and visual hunting signals and gestures among several hunter-gatherer groups in Botswana (see Bauer 2014, Mohr 2014, Mohr, Fehn, and De Voogt 2019). Altogether, we show that the visual-gestural and oral-aural modalities are closely intertwined not only with regard to sign languages but also in contemporary communication in general.

1 Introduction

Anthropological linguistics is, at its core, concerned with language in its cultural and social contexts. This extends to communication and the meaning-making process[1] at large. While more linear models of communication (e.g., Shannon and Weaver 1949) were mostly concerned with individual senders and receivers of messages, interactional approaches (Hymes 1972, Goffman 1974) recognize the importance of the situational context and cultural conventions, for instance as *frames* and *scripts*. However, they do not adequately acknowledge the importance of multimodality for the meaning-making process, and this issue has only been brought forth more recently in accounts such as Kress' (2010) *social semiotic approach*. He argues that "communication is always multimodal" (Kress 2010: 36) and suggests that language is only one part of a diverse repertoire of semiotic resources available in the meaning-making process (see also Kusters et al. 2017). Thus, various modes such as writing, speech, images and color, but also, and most importantly for this chapter, gestures, gaze, posture, drawings, etc., contribute to making meaning in different situations. While these means were traditionally distinguished into "verbal" and "non-verbal" forms of meaning-making, it has recently been argued that rather than trying to keep these different means apart, linguistics should investigate how they are interrelated (Kendon 2014). Thus, communication should be conceived of as a social process, which involves making and remaking signs in different situations rather than merely sending them to an addressee.

---

[1] We use "meaning-making" here in a social semiotic sense, referring to various practices used to design and interpret meanings.

While gesture and sign language researchers have increasingly been advocating for a multimodal concept of language, multimodal meaning-making is still often overlooked in theoretical models of communication and in mainstream linguistics (McNeill 1985, Kendon 2004, Ferrara and Hodge 2018, Perniss 2018). Sign language and gesture studies of the last decades have successfully highlighted the inherent multimodality and semiotic diversity of language (Enfield 2009, Kibrik 2010, 2018, Kendon 2004, Vigliocco, Perniss, and Vinson. 2014, Bressem and Müller 2017, Cooperrider 2019). The multimodal, multichanneled, and multisemiotic nature of language should, however, be adopted beyond the field of gesture and sign language studies and should be accounted for and included in general theories of language. But what is considered a multimodal communicative practice anyway? Do gestures and signs automatically make up multimodal expressions, while spoken language alone does not?

This chapter is intended as a contribution to the efforts of "re-orienting language theory to account for the varied communicative practices and to reflect multimodal language" (Ferrara and Hodge 2018: 12). We report on the ongoing discussion of multimodality in language by bringing together various examples emerging from sign language studies and gesture research in the last decades. Thus, we consider some dimensions of face-to-face interaction within a broader view of multimodal communicative practices. We are particularly interested in how gesture and sign language have been studied from a multimodal perspective and follow a multidimensional rather than a binary approach to the gesture-sign continua (Kendon 1988, 2004, McNeill 1992, 2000, Coppola and Senghas 2017).

We look into different types of gestures such as co-speech gestures and emblems, as well as signs in different types of sign languages, i.e., primary, alternate or village sign languages. We also discuss language contact across modalities, elaborating on contact between sign and speech and sign and other modes. The overview of these topics is provided with reference to our own previous and ongoing work on Irish, South African, and Russian Sign Languages, as well as Indigenous alternate sign languages in Australia (such as Yolngu Sign Language, used in the Northern Territory), and visual hunting signals and gestures among several hunter-gatherer groups in Botswana (Ts'ixa and ‖Ani-Khwe) (see also Bauer 2014, 2019, 2020, Mohr 2012, 2014, 2015, 2021, Green et al. 2018, Mohr, Fehn, and De Voogt 2019, Jorgensen, Green, and Bauer 2021). A map providing an overview of the different locations where our data is taken from is provided in Figure 7.1.

We first outline a few basic concepts related to multimodality (Section 2), then discuss gesture (Section 3) and different types of gesture, such as pointing gestures (Section 3.1) and emblems (Section 3.2). In Section 4, we provide a brief introduction to different sign language types, including Deaf community sign languages (Section 4.1), alternate sign languages (Section 4.2), and village

Figure 7.1: Regions of data collection.

sign languages (Section 4.3), and unpack some considerations about the relationship between gesture and sign (Section 4.4). In Section 5, we present examples of multimodal expressions demonstrating the interplay of modalities, channels, and modes. We discuss signs with co-occurring speech (Section 5.1), signs with mouthings (Section 5.1), and sign blends with other modes (Section 5.3), such as signs in multimodal social media spaces (Section 5.3.1) and signs with sand drawings (Section 5.3.2).

2 Multimodality

Sign language research since the 1960s has shown that natural language exists in at least two modalities. Signed languages are produced in the manual-visual modality, spoken languages are transmitted in the oral-auditory modality. Thus, the term *modality* is used to refer to the physical and sensory modality in which language is processed, such as the auditory, visual or tactile modalities. Multimodality thus refers to communication involving more than one perceptual modality. Speech without any body or hand movements is therefore unimodal, as would be gestures which are produced without speech. While theoretically possible, unimodal communication is extremely unlikely, as most human communication does make use of several modalities in the meaning-making process.

While language modality greatly influences the form of linguistic representation, we agree with Goldin-Meadow and Brentari (2017) that the classical division of language only by its modality is not ideal. When talking about gesture and sign, it is important to consider not only modality, but also channels. The term "channel"[2] is reserved for the means of language production, such as the vocal tract, mouth, hands, eyes, eyebrows, head, pen, sand, smartphone, etc. Speakers, signers, and gesturers draw on a wide variety of channels and can simultaneously employ different ones for communication. Thus, language is also multichanneled.

Striving for "a modality-free understanding" of language, Ferrara and Hodge (2018: 2) build upon Clark's (1996) theory of language use and propose that three "methods of signaling" (describing, indicating, and depicting) create multimodal "composite utterances" in human language (see also Kendon 2004, Enfield 2009). This draws on the Peircean notions of symbols, indices, and icons. In this vein, conventionalized and arbitrary symbols, such as words or emblematic gestures, usually *describe* meaning and have traditionally been the focus of linguistics. Both indices and icons can be either conventionalized or non-conventionalized. Indices, such as pointing gestures or demonstrative pronouns, are usually physically connected to their referents and *indicate* meaning in this way. Icons, on the other hand, partially *depict* meaning through perceptual resemblances with their referent, as is exemplified by referential gestures or ideophones. Importantly, linguistic signs may have features of all of these categories, which are hence not mutually exclusive (Ferrara and Hodge 2018). Ideophones are a case in point, as they have both symbolic and iconic properties: they are fully conventionalized signs of the language they form part of and describe or mimic a sensory perception (for a more extensive overview, see Dingemanse 2011). "[F]ace-to-face interaction allows for the [. . .] use of all three methods of signaling, but particularly promotes the use of methods for indicating and depicting" (Ferrara and Hodge 2018: 9). Composite utterances thus need to be interpreted holistically rather than componentially (Enfield 2009) in order for us to really understand multimodal meaning-making.

As Ferrara and Hodge (2018: 1) further indicate, "[s]igners and speakers coordinate a broad range of intentionally expressive actions within the spatiotemporal context of their face-to-face interactions". These expressive actions are carried out drawing on a diverse semiotic repertoire consisting of resources in different modalities and utilizing different channels. Unfortunately, there is as

---

2 Note that the term "channel" is used in various ways in the multimodality literature. Very often it is equated with the term "modality" (Coppola and Senghas 2017). Kibrik (2010: 135) differentiates three information channels: segmental (verbal), prosodic and visual.

yet no comprehensive theory of language that captures the "semiotic plurality of human communication" (Ferrara and Hodge 2018: 2). An anthropological linguistic approach can be conducive to such a theory, as it considers language and communicative practices in their physical and cultural environments (see for example Duranti and Goodwin 1992). Ferrara and Hodge (2018: 8–10) illustrate the compositionality of utterances based on examples from deaf-deaf[3] and hearing-hearing interactions. They show how language users, independently of the modality they choose, describe, depict, and indicate meaning during their interactions. With this semiotic approach in mind, we also consider communication to be multisemiotic.

Since speakers and signers live in "highly dynamic communicative ecologies" (Ferrara and Hodge 2018: 2), language presents just one of many available "modes" of meaning-making. A mode can be defined as "semiotic resources used for making meaning, both verbal (writing, speech) and non-verbal (image, gesture, gaze, posture, music, color, signs and so on)" (Bock 2019: 42). This emphasizes that language is only one of several options among a variety of resources used for meaning-making and it might in fact not be the most powerful one. As outlined later in this chapter, gesture (a non-verbal and visual mode) plays an important role in meaning-making and may create composite utterances consisting of several modes of communication. Other visual modes are just as important as language in contemporary communication, especially online (Bock 2019). This is shown by research into the use of emojis, for instance (e.g., Thurlow and Jaroski 2020). However, semiotic ideologies, especially among laypeople, are often biased towards language, valuing it higher than other semiotic means (Thurlow 2017).

When people communicate – independent of the modality, i.e., speaking or signing – they use a variety of channels, methods, and modes. We believe that the term "multimodality" strongly relates to these dimensions mentioned above and recognizes language as multimodal, multichanneled, and multisemiotic, helping us to understand the "complexity and heterogeneity of human communication" (Cooperrider, Abner, and Goldin-Meadow 2021: 2). Multimodality challenges the narrow view of language as belonging to the oral-auditory modality; it questions the boundaries between "language" and "gesture", "linguistic" and "non-linguistic", "verbal" and "non-verbal" (Kendon 2014: 3) and reveals a multiplicity of communicative practices. Having shown that communicative channels,

---

3 We use the convention "Deaf" to refer to signed language users who are also part of a cultural minority. The non-capitalized "deaf" is used to refer solely to audiological status or in cases where linguistic and cultural status is not being highlighted.

semiotic methods of signaling, and modes of meaning-making are interrelated and connected to the notion of multimodality, we employ the term "multimodal" for communicative utterances that include more than one sensory modality (vocal and visual), rather than instances where many channels (e.g., eyes and eyebrows) or modes are employed in a communicative event (see also Green 2014 for a similar understanding of multimodality).

3 Gesture

As Lempert (2019) argues, diachronic and synchronic variation, an insistence on naturalistic research designs and a focus on situating human behavior in an expansive sociocultural context are at the heart of the anthropological method. All of these are similarly present in gesture studies as well (Brookes and Le Guen 2019: 120), even though "the impact of social organization, culture and environment has had somewhat less attention" in this field. Thus, most studies on gesture have focused on the speaker as the unit of analysis and do not take the potential influence of the interaction or the wider context adequately into account. Interactional studies on gesture do show the importance of social interaction on gesture usage, however (e.g., Goodwin 2000, Sweetser 2006). This, as well as the fact that the first studies on gesture were in fact conducted from an anthropological point of view (Kendon 2019), emphasizes the interrelationship between anthropology and gesture (studies). Today, it is very much desirable to study gesture across different cultures and as used in different circumstances, including comparisons of when gesture is used with when it is *not* used (see Kendon 2019).[4] This can help us study the duality of gesture systems, i.e., their unmistakable similarities but at the same time broad worldwide diversity (Cooperrider 2019).

In line with Kendon (2019: 142), "gesture" is understood here as "any sort of visible bodily action that plays a role in an utterance". The emphasis here is on *any* visible bodily action, not limited to the hands (Lempert 2019), but which has to have some communicative intention (Kendon 2004). The term "gesture" has often been criticized because it is "muddied with ambiguity, theoretical and ideological baggage" (Kendon 2017: 31), and for its limitation to the visual modality (Okrent 2002). Okrent (2002) illustrates this with examples of spoken

---

4 Note that not everyone would necessarily agree. Lempert (2019: 176) argues that "comparison is not what most sociocultural anthropologists today aspire to do".

language elements being used in a gestural manner, such as the meaningful manipulation of the vowel length in (1):

(1)   *It was a loooooooooong time.*   (Okrent 2002: 187)

We support a modality-free understanding of gesture, as research has convincingly shown that gesture can be oral (e.g., vocal lengthening as in Example (1) or the discussion on ideophones by Dingemanse 2011) as well as visual (see the discussion on mouth actions by Sandler 2003 and Fontana 2008, as well as Section 5.2). Endorsing these terminological considerations, we are not able to ignore a long-standing tradition of using the term "gesture" for movements of the hands. Similar to Le Guen, Petatillo, and Kinil Caché (2020: 328), we refer to either manual or oral gestures in the following.

Early anthropologists and linguists, among them Boas and Sapir, already considered gesture and bodily movements to be an important part of human behavior (Brookes and Le Guen 2019: 127). The development of the kinesics framework by Birdwhistell (e.g., 1955), as well as work on gesture use in everyday communication and signing, for instance in Australian Aboriginal groups among recently widowed women (Kendon 1988, Haviland 1993), has been equally significant for the development of an anthropological linguistic study of gesture. Brookes and Le Guen (2019) further make the point that early work on symbolic and social interaction, as well as the development of conversation analysis (e.g., Goffman 1969, Schegloff and Sacks 1973), have contributed importantly to the methodological study of gestures in an anthropological framework. Thus, studying different types of gestures is revealing in terms of interactional practices and their social norms, and concerning the influence of social ideologies on the use and form of gestures. Lempert's (2011) work on Obama's use of gestures and their different functions is an interesting example. Ultimately, Brookes and Le Guen (2019: 129) claim that "gesture can inform understanding of current concerns in anthropology around identity, race, gender and power".

In the following sections, we provide an overview of linguistic anthropological analyses of gesture in relation to interactional practices and in various modalities and social contexts. This will further an understanding of how the universal capacity to gesture and the diverse form-meaning mappings of gestures go together (Cooperrider 2019). Before doing so, a few words on general distinctions between different types of gestures and functions are in order. Gestures have been classified in a variety of ways by a number of researchers (e.g., Ekman and Friesen 1969, 1972, McNeill 1992, 2015, Müller 1998, Özyürek 2012).

Kendon's (2004) famous continuum ranges from "co-speech gestures" to "pantomime" to "emblems" to "sign languages" (see Figure 7.2), with the possibility of communicative practices being located in between the individual points of the continuum.

Co-speech gestures ---- pantomime ---- emblems ---- sign languages

Figure 7.2: Kendon's (2004) continuum of gestural practices.

Co-speech gestures are spontaneous movements produced when people speak (e.g., deictic gestures, iconic gestures, metaphoric gestures; see McNeill 1992). Emblems are hand movements with conventional forms and meanings within particular communicative ecologies – for example, the thumbs up or the "okay" gesture in the European countries; snap on the throat (in relation to alcohol) or twisting an index finger at one's temple (to mean 'fool, idiot') in Russia and some other East European countries.

In this section, we are concerned with communicative practices located to the left of the sign languages end of the continuum; the latter are discussed in Section 4 of this chapter. Since Kendon's and McNeill's work, researchers have made a number of refinements in the definitions of those types of gestures located on the continuum. It has been shown, for example, that the same gestures can be used both as a co-speech gesture and as emblems (e.g., the palm-up gesture). McNeill's idea about gestures being idiosyncratic has been critically rethought. A research team led by Müller has been actively developing the concept of recurring gestures in recent years (Ladewig and Bressem 2013). The difference between recurring gestures (i.e., negation gestures like "moving things aside" or "holding away gesture"), as opposed to emblems, is apparent in Ladewig's (2014: 1559) definition of recurring gestures, which are "conventionalized to a certain degree, are culturally shared, and thus can be identified clearly within the stream of manual movements. [. . .] [They] often work on the level of speech, fulfilling pragmatic functions". Ladewig (2014) also argues for a more flexible transition from singular gestures (iconic and metaphoric gestures) to recurrent gestures and from recurrent gestures to emblems. Emblems, on the other hand, are fully conventionalized and can substitute speech.

Cooperrider (2019) mentions *gestural practices* as another class of gestures that is often overlooked. These map a conventionalized gradable parameter of form onto a gradable parameter of meaning (Cooperrider 2019: 216), such as pointing with exaggerated height to indicate distant entities in Mesoamerica (Mesh 2017), or among speakers and signers of Australian Aboriginal (sign) languages such as Arrernte (ISO 639-3 aer[5]) (Wilkins 1999, 2003: 187), Warlpiri (ISO 639-3 wbp), and Warumungu (ISO 639-3 wrm) (Kendon 1988: 24), Yolngu (ISO 639-3 dhg) (Bauer 2014: 185), or among speakers and signers of Yucatec Maya (ISO 639-3 yua) (Le Guen 2011). With respect to function, Müller (1998) maintains that gestures can generally express feelings, attitudes, and illocutionary acts, refer to concrete and abstract entities, support searching for words or verbal repair and emphasize the semantics of verbal language (see also McNeill 1992, Kendon 2004, Goldin-Meadow 2003).

In the following we discuss two different types of co-speech gestures, namely pointing gestures and emblems, as well as the ways in which they possibly overlap, in more detail.

3.1 Pointing gestures

Co-speech gestures, i.e., the manual movements that speakers produce when they talk, have become the most popular gesture type in the gesture research literature in the last decades (Kelly, Özyürek, and Maris 2010). McNeill's (1992) groundbreaking study of co-speech gesture showed that gesture forms a single and unified system with speech. Further research revealed that co-speech gesture plays a role in processing and learning language and other cognitive skills (Goldin-Meadow and Singer 2003, Özyürek 2018, Holler and Levinson 2019). Gestures that co-occur with speech are "co-expressive but not redundant" (McNeill 1992: 22) and gesture and speech are temporally aligned (Kita 1993). Finally, gesture supports learning and is viewed as a precursor to language in younger and older children (Rohlfing 2019).

Co-speech gestures manifest themselves in different types, including representational gestures (iconical and metaphorical), deictic gestures (points), and beat gestures (rhythmic movements closely coordinated with speech). Iconic gestures are semantically related to speech and can also add information which is not present in the spoken utterance, e.g., information about shape, height, size or spatial orientation.

While co-speech gestures and their frequency might differ considerably across language communities, recent research shows that there are some commonly shared gestural forms (e.g., Ladewig 2014). In their overview, Brookes and

---

5 The ISO codes indicated here refer to the spoken languages mentioned. The sign languages referred to are not registered in the *Ethnologue* (Eberhardt, Simons, and Fennig 2021), except for Yolngu Sign Language (ISO 639-3 ygs).

Le Guen (2019: 122) cite several examples of such shared forms, such as the holding upwards of the palm towards the interlocutor when asking a question or giving information. This gesture seems to have a pragmatic function. However, there seem to be variants of what Cooperrider, Abner, and Goldin-Meadow (2018) call the "palm-up epistemic" gesture, as, for instance, in the Nepali language Syuba (ISO 639-2 syw): it involves a hand shape with the fingers partly curled in (Gawne 2018).

As Cooperrider (2019: 220) claims, "pointing in one form or another is, by all accounts, universal". It refers to moving some part of the body towards a referent via an imagined vector (Kendon 2004) and is a sub-technique of indicating, as one form of (multimodal) meaning-making outlined earlier in this chapter. Pointing can consist of certain gestural practices and might be subject to cultural conventions, such as pointing to the wrist to refer to the time of day in Anglo-European cultures (Cooperrider 2019). Types of pointing are multifarious across cultures, given that humans are opportunistic and flexible pointers (Cooperrider 2019: 220) and might point with various parts of the body or other auxiliary means, depending on practicality. Some conventional ways of pointing seem rather restricted geographically, such as lip-pointing (outlined by Enfield 2001 for Laos). Certain cultures seem to prefer certain ways of pointing, e.g., Anglo-European cultures show a strong preference for manual pointing as compared to what Cooperrider, Slotta, and Núñez (2018) describe for the Yupno (ISO 639-3 yut) in Papua New Guinea, who show equal measures of manual and non-manual pointing.

Size indications can be considered to be a specific type of pointing gesture. While size gestures can in fact be formed ad hoc and have certain non-conventional elements, i.e., for indicating a specific height, many cultures have conventionalized size gestures or gesture practices (Cooperrider 2019). This might include reference to the class of an entity, as documented by Nyst (2016) for a village sign language in Ghana, or Fox Tree (2009) for sign languages in Mesoamerica. The type of entity referred to is also indicated in size gestures among the Ts'ixa[6] in Botswana. This is shown in Figure 7.3, in which a Ts'ixa woman indicates the size of a child.

As also outlined in Mohr (2015: 940) and Fehn (2012), the direction of the palm is crucial in this case, as it must be turned upwards when indicating the size of a person (child) who would otherwise be prevented from growing further. The size of inanimate objects can be indicated with the palm facing downwards (Fehn 2012). Interestingly, the size gestures seem to be emblematic, and are used

---

6 Ts'ixa is classified as a dialect of the Shua cluster (ISO 639-3 shg).

Figure 7.3: Height indication (people) among the Ts'ixa, reprinted with permission from Mohr (2015: 940).

in both spoken language as co-speech gestures and in *tshaukak'ui*,[7] the manual hunting sign system used by the Ts'ixa. Fehn (2012: 152) also points out that pointing gestures are usually obligatory and do not require or have a spoken language equivalent. This is not the case for gestures indicating size among the Ts'ixa but might have been at some point, similar to the obligatory gestures used for counting among the neighboring Khwe (Khwedam, ISO 639-3 xuu) (see also Fehn 2012).

Among the Ts'ixa and particularly in *tshaukak'ui*, manual pointing is very common, although other body parts do play a role in the gesture inventory. This is illustrated in Figures 7.4–7.6, showing pointing gestures directed at entities located at different distances from the speaker. Another feature that is encoded in these gestures is the visibility of the referent, indicated by the height of the

---

7 *Tshaukak'ui* means 'talk with hands' in Ts'ixa.

Figure 7.4: Pointing gesture for visible distal entities among the Ts'ixa, modified and reprinted with permission from Mohr (2015: 949).

Figure 7.5: Pointing gesture for non-visible distal entities among the Ts'ixa.

Figure 7.6: Pointing gesture for (visible) proximal entities among the Ts'ixa, modified and reprinted with permission from Mohr (2015: 949).

outstretched arm and eye gaze (see also Mohr 2015: 949), with visible distal entities requiring an arm outstretched at shoulder height and the gaze directed at the entity (Figure 7.4) and non-visible entities requiring the outstretched arm extended above shoulder height and the gaze directed upward towards the fingers (Figure 7.5). Proximal pointing gestures are directed downwards with the gaze directed at the entity referred to (Figure 7.6).

Finally, pointing gestures also play an important role in indicating the time of day among the Ts'ixa (see also Le Guen 2012 on Yucatec Maya time gestures). They refer to the course of the sun, as shown in the gestures for 'morning', 'afternoon', and 'evening' in the accompanying video (and Figure 7.7), which have been reported to be used frequently by all Ts'ixa above the age of 30 in Mababe (Fehn 2012: 160). They are used during hunting but also in everyday conversation.

Figure 7.7: Times of day gestures among the Ts'ixa.

This is similar to an absolute referencing system which is used among several groups (among them the Ts'ixa) to indicate locations in pointing to the exact location of a certain place, for instance a city, relative to the location of the speaker.

As mentioned above, many of the pointing gestures shown here are conventionalized to a certain extent and thus share some properties with emblems, which are fully conventionalized and can substitute for speech. They are discussed in more detail in the next section.

3.2 Emblems

The notion of "emblems" goes back to Ekman and Friesen (1969) and has been widely used in gesture research ever since. Emblems are also sometimes called quotable gestures and have an established and conventionalized form-meaning relation (e.g., Kendon 2004, Müller 2010, Ladewig 2014, Brookes and Le Guen 2019). Kendon (2019) suggests that one of the earliest and most thorough studies of this type of gesture is De Jorio's (1832) work on gestures in Naples. Similarly noteworthy is Morris et al.'s (1979) comparative study on emblematic gestures in forty different locations in Europe, for instance on the "ring gesture" and its meanings. While comparative studies like these show that emblems differ cross-linguistically, some gestural forms, such as negation and affirmation, can be shared across different cultures (see Kendon 2004, Brookes and Le Guen 2019, Cooperrider 2019). Darwin's (1872) study on negation gestures and Jakobson's (1972) discussion of negation and affirmation are early, partly anthropologically inspired, examples. This might hint at the idea that "there are kinesic expressions that are common to all human communities" (Kendon 2019: 157).

With regard to function, Kendon (1981) shows that most emblems cover similar domains, for instance interpersonal regulation, expressions of current states of affairs, and comments about others. This includes the following categories (Kendon 2019: 157–158):
1) gestures as commands or requests, serving for interpersonal control
2) gestures as announcements about a given state or attitude of the actor
3) gestures that comment on the personality or state of another

As outlined in the previous section, some gestures may in fact replace words and fill constituent slots in spoken utterances ("obligatory gestures", as mentioned above), leading to "mixed [multimodal] syntax" or composite utterances (Ferrara and Hodge 2018). Examples of this are the aforementioned number or size gestures among the Khwe and the Ts'ixa respectively.

Interestingly, some gestures are shared across the hearing and signing communities within one cultural space (a country, for instance) (see for instance Brookes and Nyst (2014) on gestures in the Sub-Saharan region). This is the case for the size and number gestures among the Ts'ixa and Khwe, except that in these cases, the signing community is not deaf, as *tshaukak'ui* rather seems to be an alternate sign language or gesture system (see Mohr 2015, Mohr, Fehn, and De Voogt 2019).

Mohr (2007) also reports that the emblematic gestures in her study on the semantic transparency of different signs in German Sign Language (Deutsche Gebärdensprache, DGS), such as the gesture for 'drink' (one hand clasps an imaginary round container, which is tilted backwards as if drinking the liquid contained), and the one for 'phone/make a phone call' (the extended thumb and pinky on one hand is moved towards one ear and the mouth in order to mimic a phone), were easily comprehensible to German non-signers as the gestures are shared across these two communities. The same applied to "indicative signs", i.e., pointing gestures indicating the speaker or the addressee (Mohr 2007: 83). Given that her stimuli were taken from American Sign Language (ASL) material, this implies that these gestures might indeed be shared in Western circles in general. However, as mentioned at the beginning of this section, it is likely that there will be (slightly) different gestures in different cultures.

4 Sign languages

In this section we briefly introduce the major sign language types described in the literature so far and report on how they differ from each other. The classification presented here is non-exhaustive. We leave out such communication systems as International Sign, homesign or tactile sign languages and refer the reader to Pfau (2012) and Bauer (2014) for a detailed discussion of sign language types, sign language typology and manual communication systems in general.

4.1 Deaf community sign languages

The existing classifications of natural sign languages (Zeshan 2008) reflect the developments in the field of sign language linguistics to some extent. In the 1960s, sign language research started with descriptions of some Deaf community sign languages (also called "urban" or "established" sign languages) such as ASL (American Sign Language), NGT (Sign Language of the Netherlands), and SSL (Swedish Sign Language). Most linguistic theories in the field are still largely based on the data from these urban sign languages of developed countries. While some of these sign languages, such as ASL, BSL (British Sign Language), Auslan (Australian Sign Languages), and DGS, are now fairly well investigated, other Deaf community sign languages (such as Russian, Polish or Greek Sign Languages) are still under-explored and require more research.

Deaf community sign languages usually occur in large, urban areas and may have a number of dialects. Deaf communities are formed by Deaf people from different backgrounds who are brought together from different areas, regions or even countries (as in case of Israeli Sign Language) in locations such as a school for the deaf or a deaf association. According to the *Ethnologue* (Eberhard, Simons, and Fennig 2021), there are 128 Deaf community sign languages, among them two sign languages (Israeli and Nicaraguan Sign Languages) which have also been termed "emerging" sign languages due to their comparatively young age (Meir et al. 2010).

4.2 Alternate sign languages

The sign languages under the label "alternate sign languages" (Kendon 1988) (sometimes referred to as "secondary" or "auxiliary" sign languages) differ greatly from Deaf community sign languages in their origin and use. While the latter type of sign language is mainly used as a primary means of communication by Deaf persons, alternate sign languages are often developed in hearing communities as a replacement for speech in certain cultural contexts when speech is either impractical or inappropriate. Alternate sign languages exist in various parts of the world and vary greatly in the degree of their complexity (Pfau 2012). They are used, for example, when silence is required or speaking is impractical: in monastic Benedictine orders maintaining a vow of silence, in noisy workplace environments such as sawmills in British Columbia, during hunting or diving or as military signs (Meissner and Philpott 1975, Pfau 2012, Mohr 2015). They can also serve as a lingua franca between groups that do not share the same spoken language, as with Plains Indian Sign Language(s) by Native Americans or Keresan Pueblo Indian Sign Language by hearing and deaf Native Americans (Kelley and McGregor 2003, Davis 2010). Some of these rather seem to be clusters of dialects that share common linguistic and social properties, as has been shown by Mohr, Fehn, and De Voogt's (2019) analysis of several hunting sign systems among hunter-gatherer groups in Botswana and Namibia. These are indicative of a *Sprachbund* in the Kalahari Basin area. This concept was first proposed by Güldemann (1998), challenging the traditional classification of indigenous non-Bantu languages as the "Khoisan" family. In light of contemporary research on language practices in Southern Africa, today three lineages are proposed instead, i.e., Tuu, K'xa, and Khoe(-Kwadi) (see also Güldemann 2014). The hunting-sign systems found in the Kalahari Basin linguistic area further emphasize the existence of a *Sprachbund*.

In Aboriginal Australia, alternate sign languages are embedded in the communicative ecology, as they are used for particular "cultural and pragmatic reasons" (Jorgensen, Green and Bauer 2021). The use of these sign languages is primarily associated, in the literature, with the widespread practice of speech taboos, usually imposed on particular kin in the context of bereavement, where sign is used instead of speech during extended periods of mourning (Kendon 1988). The use of elaborate sign languages by Indigenous Australians may also have other communicative reasons. Bauer (2014) shows that Yolngu signing is used in the communities of North East Arnhem Land, although there are no extensive speech taboos, in which spoken language is banned for extended periods of mourning such as those found in Central Australia. The alternate sign language is used by Yolngu when giving directions, for communication between interlocutors who are visible to each other yet out of earshot, in contexts of certain types of gender-restricted ceremonies, while hunting, and for communication with deaf and hard-of-hearing persons (Bauer 2014). This sign language is thus a secondary language for many hearing Yolngu and a primary language for some deaf Yolngu. Sign languages which are shared between hearing and deaf individuals are also referred to as shared sign languages (Nyst 2012) (see more on shared sign languages in Section 4.3).

Linguistic research on these languages started with Kendon's (1988) seminal work on alternate sign languages in the North Central Desert communities of Australia. Apart from Kendon's publications, Australian indigenous sign languages have sadly received rather little scholarly attention from sign language linguists until recently (see Bauer 2014, Carew and Green 2015, Green et al. 2018 for recent investigations into some of these sign languages).

4.3 Village sign languages

The latest addition to the sign language typological grouping is so-called "village or rural sign languages", that is, sign languages used in rural communities with a high incidence of (often hereditary) deafness (De Vos and Zeshan 2012). Due to the shared use of sign language by hearing and deaf signers, almost all village sign languages are shared sign languages. There are currently at least two dozen reported cases of such shared sign languages, according to the

Ethnologue (Eberhard, Simons, and Fennig 2021), with two well documented languages being Kata Kolok, used in the Bengkala and Bila villages of North Bali (De Vos and Zeshan 2012), and Adamorobe Sign Language, in the village of Adamorobe in Ghana (Nyst 2012).

Besides a greater rate of incidence of deafness, rural signing communities are usually characterized by social homogeneity, which is witnessed in the dense social networks and the large amount of communally shared information between the community members. Village sign languages develop in small-scale geographically isolated rural communities where cross-modal multilingualism is often the norm. The hearing members of the community are usually fluent in the local spoken language(s) as well as the local sign language and the use of village sign language is never restricted to deaf members in such communities.

4.4 Gesture in sign languages

The relationship between gesture and sign has attracted much scholarly attention in the last few decades (see Goldin-Meadow and Brentari 2017 for the latest discussion). Researchers have recently recognized that signers gesture just as speakers do, but that the distinction between sign and gesture is blurred, because they occur within a single modality. Consider, for example, the case of palm-up, a manual activity taking the form of rotating one's forearms so that the palms of the hands face upward. Speakers very often rotate their forearms during communication. Palm-up form is widely used by speakers and signers with the same set of meanings (Cooperrider, Slotta, and Núñez 2018). Thus, both signers and speakers make frequent use of this form for a variety of functions and researchers differentiate between the gestural and signed uses of this form (Zeshan 2004, Van Loon, Pfau, and Steinbach 2014). While palm-ups may fulfil various linguistic functions in signed conversation (e.g., interrogative or negation signs in Yolngu (Bauer 2014)) in sign language research, it is also an example of a co-sign gesture.

Gestures from surrounding speaking communities are essential for sign languages as they may draw on gestures for lexicalization and grammaticalization purposes (see Pfau and Steinbach 2006 for an overview). This process has been described, for example, for Yucatec Maya Sign Language. A widespread emblematic one-handed gesture with curved thumb and an index finger meaning 'money' is used by the Yucatec Maya and has been transformed to Yucatec Maya Sign Language to become the noun MONEY (Le Guen, Petatillo, and Kinil Canché 2020: 303).

Some researchers have also claimed that sign and gesture form an integrated system in the same way as speech and gesture do. Certain types of verbs or pointing signs in sign languages have been reported to combine both sign and gestural elements (Liddell 2000: 354). For example, a study by Schembri, Jones, and Burnham (2005) highlights a surprising degree of similarity in the forms produced by native signers, home-signers, and gesturers.

While some scholars make a clear cut distinction between gesture and sign (Goldin-Meadow and Brentari 2017), others rather conceptualize the boundary along a number of dimensions, reminiscent of Kendon's (2004) continuum, i.e., (1) whether a form is categorical or gradient, and (2) whether it participates in a combinatorial system or is holistic and non-combining (Coppola and Senghas 2017).

Apart from producing idiosyncratic hand gestures concurrently with the signs, sign languages may also use other channels or even another modality in addition to gesture. Emmorey (1999) has shown that signers produce gestures with their face or other parts of the body that co-occur with their signs. Similarly, Sandler (2003, 2009) has argued that while speakers gesture with their hands, signers may use another channel to gesture, namely their mouth. She compares mouth gestures in sign languages with iconic co-speech gestures (see more on mouth gestures in Section 5.2). These mouth gestures express a meaning/constitute a part of the meaning of the sign, e.g., a depiction of the referent's size and/ or shape. An example of such mouth gestures from Russian Sign Language (henceforth RSL) is provided in Figure 7.8.

The mouth gesture 'puffed cheeks' in Figure 7.8 denotes a round three-dimensional object, a ball, while the mouth gesture 'cheeks sucked-in' is used with the manual sign to mean 'through a very thin pipe'. Sandler (2003) states that sign language differs from spoken language in that the gesture co-occurring with the sign is transmitted within the same modality. Fontana (2008), however, puts forward a hypothesis that sign language may also use the oral modality to gesture. She parallels mouthing accompanying signs with beat co-speech gestures in spoken language (see Section 5.2 for more information on mouthings). Because mouthings are considered to be remnants of spoken language, signs accompanied by mouthings are considered multimodal according to the definition.

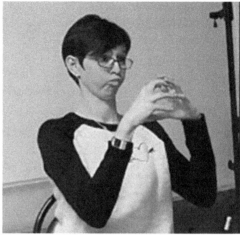

Figure 7.8: a. RSL mouth gesture 'cheeks sucked-in' b. RSL mouth gesture 'puffed cheeks'.[8]

5 The interplay of modalities, channels, and modes

We do not discuss spoken language per se in this section, but it should be kept in mind that spoken language is usually part of a multimodal utterance. Any occurrence of any co-speech gesture is by definition multimodal. Consider for example the Russian verbal deictics *von/vot* 'there/here', which are almost always accompanied by (a finger) pointing (Grišina 2017). In Yucatec Maya, words such as *beytak/buka'aj* 'of this particular height/size' are also (almost always) accompanied by a gesture (Le Guen, Petatillo, and Kinil Canché 2020: 300). Speech accompanied by gesture (co-speech gestures or emblems) is thus only one component of a "composite signal" or "composite utterance" (Enfield 2009) which includes speech and gesture.

In this section we focus on sign languages and provide some examples of language contact and multimodal interactions. Sign languages are socially and linguistically unique in that most sign languages are minority languages and their users are always in contact with speakers of the majority language, i.e., a/

---

8 The screenshot in Figure 7.8a, showing a RSL mouth gesture 'cheeks sucked-in', is taken from the online RSL Corpus (Burkova 2015). Figure 7.8b is taken with the author's permission from the elicitation corpus gathered by Kyuseva (2020: 177).

several spoken language(s). Further, due to their visual nature and non-concatenative morphology, sign languages can combine material from different modalities and via different channels simultaneously in order to express lexical and grammatical categories. Language contact phenomena in sign languages are hence multifarious. In the following, we describe the co-occurrence of signs with speech (Section 5.1), signs with mouthings (Section 5.2), and signs with other modes (Section 5.3).

5.1 Sign with speech

When sign language occurs with gesture (i.e., any manual gesture or mouth gesture), they share the same visual modality and therefore do not form a multimodal ensemble. However, sign language may co-occur with speech or mouthings. In this case we are dealing with multimodal interactions involving verbal and visual elements. In the following we give some examples of signs co-occurring with speech and afterwards turn to the discussion of a cross-modal contact phenomenon, i.e., mouthings.

Alternate sign languages present an especially fruitful arena in which to look for instances of signs co-occurring with speech. In Australian indigenous sign languages signs are known to completely replace speech, especially during so-called "sorry business", periods of mourning (Kendon 1988). What is less known is that signs also frequently co-occur with speech to form multimodal utterances. Green and Wilkins (2014) show how in cases where a spoken language combines with sign, both modalities contribute semantically to the utterance. Consider the following examples of such composite utterances given by Green and Wilkins (2014: 239). Speakers of Arandic can say *kwatye-ke* (water-DAT) and then produce a manual sign NOTHING/NO/NEGATION, formed by a rapid "flip" of a flat hand with the fingers spread, to convey the meaning '(there's) no water'. Arandic signs are also used to disambiguate polysemous terms in speech. Thus, the Arandic word *ngkwarle* is polysemous with regard to the meanings 'sweet honey-like/nectar-like food(s)' and 'grog, booze, alcohol', but the sign DRINK co-occurring with this spoken element can disambiguate the meaning towards the alcoholic sense.

In Yolngu Sign Language, speech is seldom used with kin signs (Bauer 2014: 51). Rather, signers usually pronounce a Yolngu spoken word like *balanya* 'something like/this kind' instead of articulating the spoken kin term, as presented in (2). In this example, the signer produces the Yolngu sign SIBLING by slapping the calf of the leg (Figure 7.9) and simultaneously pronounces the word *balanya*, as if attracting the attention of the interlocutor to the sign.

(2) *balanya   rraku   wahna*
this kind   1SG.POSS   where
SIBLING   IX   PALM-UP?
'Where is my sister?'

(Bauer 2014: 51)

Figure 7.9: Yolngu sign SIBLING.

In this Yolngu example speech does not disambiguate or specify the meaning of the polysemous kin sign. Speech is rather used here to underline the meaning of the sign that is to emphasize the use of a particular body part.

Please note that the case of signs with co-occurring speech demonstrated here differs from the behavior referred to as "sign-speaking" (Zeshan and Panda 2018). Sign-speaking is a communicative practice of bilinguals who know both a signed and a spoken language and use spoken words co-occurring with manual signs simultaneously in particular settings. While, in the case of alternate sign languages, signs with co-occurring speech are an important social and cultural communicative practice used by hearing people, sign-speaking is a bimodal-bilingual behavior driven by the communicative needs of participants in deaf-hearing groups in the absence of a separate sign language interpreter (Zeshan and Panda 2018).

5.2 Sign with mouthings

Generally, there are two types of mouth movements in sign languages (Boyes Braem and Sutton-Spence 2001). The first type, mouth gestures, is language inherent and does not stem from contact between spoken and sign languages. These are movements of the mouth such as the RSL example of 'cheeks sucked-in' in Figure 7.8a, which add meaning either to the individual sign or to the whole utterance.

The second type, mouthings, appears to originate in spoken-sign language contact as it refers to spoken language words that are mouthed (usually un-voiced) while producing a manual sign or sign sequence (Boyes Braem and Sutton-Spence 2001). An example is a mouthed "apple" accompanying the manual Irish Sign Language (ISL) sign APPLE or an articulated word "three" accompanying the sign THREE. There are also minimal pairs distinguished by mouthings alone, such as the RSL signs SPEED and IMPOSSIBLE.

The use of mouthings in native signing is omnipresent. Earlier studies report that mouthing is the largest mouth action category. A DGS corpus analysis showed that more than 80% of all utterances feature at least one mouthing (Ebbinghaus and Heßmann 1995). That is to say, every second manual element in a typical signed utterance is accompanied by a mouthing in DGS (Ebbinghaus and Heßmann 1995). In Australian Sign Language and Irish Sign Language data more than 70% of all mouth actions are mouthings and in Dutch Sign Language data 80% of all mouth actions with manual signs are mouthings (see Johnston, van Roekel, and Schembri 2016, Mohr 2014, and Bank 2014 respectively). The newest RSL corpus study reveals that sign languages vary with regard to the frequency of mouthing. Russian signers use significantly fewer mouthings in natural deaf-deaf interactions than reported for other Deaf community sign languages investigated to date (Bauer and Kyuseva 2022).

Various categorizations of mouthings have been suggested, for instance by Bank, Crasborn and van Hout (2011), with a more fine-grained distinction by Mohr (2014). They are based on the formal, functional, and semantic relations between mouthings and signs. In Mohr and Leeson (forthcoming), Mohr's (2014) distinction into six categories with various subcategories is summarized according to three larger types: one-to-one matches of mouthings and signs, mouthings and signs that do not match completely but are formally or semantically related, and mouthings and signs that do not seem to be related in any way. These are illustrated in Table 7.1 below. It needs to be kept in mind that this categorization is based on ISL/English and that other categorizations are possible, and indeed probable, in other sign-spoken language pairings, depending on their particular linguistic structures and cultural factors.

Table 7.1: Mouthing categories (based on Mohr and Leeson forthcoming: 16).

One-to-one matches of mouthings and signs	Mouthings and signs that do not match completely but are formally and semantically related	Mouthings and signs that are not related
Subcategories	Subcategories	Subcategories
1) one-to-one matches of mouthings and the manual sign	2) mouthings semantically related to the manual sign	6) mouthings that do not directly correspond to the meaning expressed by the manual sign a) simultaneous compounds or modifier mouthings b) spread mouthings c) relating to overall discourse/conversation
	3) verb mouthings with particularities a) accompanying what would be prepositional verbs in English b) accompanying classifier constructions	
	4) inflected verb/noun mouthings	
	5) reduced mouthings	

It is beyond the scope of this chapter to elaborate on all of these types in detail, hence only a few are commented on in the following. The first category, shown in the leftmost column of Table 7.1, comprises examples such as "apple" accompanying APPLE, as mentioned above. The second category, shown in the middle column, includes examples where the mouthing slightly deviates from the manual sign, as in "cappuccino" accompanying CUP-OF-TEA, i.e., 2) in Table 7.1. It also includes inflected mouthings, such as "photos" accompanying PHOTOGRAPH or "went" accompanying GO, i.e., 4) in Table 7.1 (Mohr 2014). These account for the fact that in sign languages, some grammatical categories like tense are not expressed by inflection but by sentence adverbs. In spoken English, however, a verb needs to be inflected for tense and mouthings can reflect this. In sign languages surrounded by spoken languages with many inflections, mouthings tend to be inflected more often as a result (see also Racz-Engelhardt 2017). Spoken Russian, like most Slavic languages, is highly inflected. It has a rich case morphology. Russian nouns, pronouns, adjectives, numerals, and demonstratives bear *case* suffixes; Russian verbs are modified for tense, mood, voice, and aspect, and all categories for gender and number. An RSL corpus analysis reveals that the amount of inflected mouthing is higher in RSL than in English or Dutch. The RSL mouthings are mostly inflected for case, but instances of gender, person, number, and aspect inflections are also attested (Bauer 2019: 28). Consider the RSL example in (3):

(3)   [RSL]

	school.ACC.SG			_novosib........lea_	
	школу			_новосиб_	_учи_
IX	ШКОЛА	ЗАКОНЧИТЬ	ПОСТУПИТЬ	НОВОСИБИРСК	УЧИТЬСЯ
ix	school	graduate	enter	NOVOSIBIRSK	learn

'I graduated school and entered the university in Novosibirsk'

(Bauer 2020: 136, http://ukoeln.de/WXULY)

The accusative case marking from Russian is clearly visible in the articulation of the RSL mouthing /školu/ in (3). In 86% of the cases, the sign SCHOOL occurs in the RSL corpus with a non-inflected standard mouthing. Why deaf RSL users use the inflected mouthing in some cases and why the consistency of its appearance varies among signers is still unclear and requires further research. What is clear, however, is that the use of inflections in RSL and other sign languages reflects active knowledge of both languages and may play an important role in facilitating the understanding of signed communication.

Finally, the third category, shown in the rightmost column of Table 7.1, comprises simultaneous, cross-modal compounds. These have also been mentioned for other sign languages, such as Norwegian Sign Language (Vogt-Svendsen 2001), and are especially intriguing because they illustrate the potential of cross-modal meaning-making. An example from ISL (see also Mohr 2014) is the sign STRIPES-ON-TOP-OF-SHOES accompanied by a mouthed "brown, beige", i.e., 6a) in Table 7.1. This is a good example of a composite utterance, as both material from signed and spoken language *together* contributes to the meaning-making process.

An important issue to be mentioned concerning mouthings is that their use is often related to linguistic and social factors. Morphological complexity and word class do seem to play a role in the frequency and distribution of mouthings (see Mohr 2014, Bauer and Kyuseva 2022) but social factors like gender and age are possibly even more distinctive, at least with respect to ISL. Thus, Mohr (2012, 2014) showed that female signers in the *Signs of Ireland Corpus* generally use more mouthings than men and that younger signers (age group 18–35) in general use more mouthings than older signers (age groups 36–50 and 51+). This correlation was more pronounced among the men than among the women, showing the close interconnection between these two social factors. These findings seem to go back to the strict segregation of boys and girls for religious reasons at Irish deaf schools and different ways of teaching.[9] Given that deaf schools are usually the first place where deaf children are introduced to the Deaf community and where they learn sign language for the first time, schooling and educational policies play an important role for sign languages everywhere (e.g., Woll and Ladd 2003). In Ireland, boys and girls were even discouraged from mixing socially outside of school (Le Master and Dwyer 1991), resulting in two separate gendered varieties of ISL. This situation has been changing since the late 1980s/90s but gender differences at and beyond the lexical level are still visible in contemporary ISL (Leeson and Grehan 2004, Mohr and Leeson forthcoming). Interestingly, other social and cultural factors such as the onset of sign language acquisition and the language of communication used at home during childhood did not prove to have an impact on the use of mouthings in ISL (Mohr 2012).

Mouthing has always been understood as a spoken language contact phenomenon in sign language research (Boyes Braem and Sutton-Spence 2001, Johnston, Van Roekel, and Schembri 2016). Thus, Bank, Crasborn, and Van Hout (2011: 250) believe that casual spoken Dutch is an important source for NGT mouthings. Nadolske and Rosenstock (2007) describe ASL mouthings as "derived from spoken English" and Mesch and Schönström (2020) consider Swedish Sign Language mouthings to be "borrowed from the spoken Swedish language". According to this view, a mouthing construction (a manual sign co-occurring with a mouthing) presents a vivid example of a multimodal interaction involving different modalities and different channels. Bauer and Kyuseva (2022) show that mouthing might be an even more complex phenomenon. They argue that RSL mouthings can be viewed as one of the products of contact between a signed and a written language. Their study shows that RSL mouthings lack the visual phonetic characteristics of vowel reduction patterns which are present in spoken Russian but absent in the orthography. By putting forward a hypothesis that written language is a possible gateway to the occurrences of

---

9 This specifically refers to so-called "oralist" education policies, stipulating the exclusive use of English as the medium of instruction in Ireland. It was introduced 10 years earlier at the girls' than at the boys' school in Dublin.

mouthings in sign languages, Bauer and Kyuseva (2022) bring new insights into the origin of mouthings and reveal that the multimodal practices of deaf signers are comprised of a more complex interplay of signed, spoken, and written language modalities than previously thought.

5.3 Sign and other modes

5.3.1 Signs in multimodal social media spaces

Where the use of sign languages in the media is concerned, various modes of communication converge. Written language dominates computer-mediated communication (Herring 2013), making online spaces less deaf-friendly (Kurz and Cuculik 2015). *Deaf spaces* are spaces where Deaf people meet and share experiences through visual communication (Solvang and Haualand 2014). This requires the specific use of sign language (in videos, pictures, etc.), given that in some countries, illiteracy among the deaf and hard of hearing is high (see Magongwa 2010 on South Africa). Some initiatives aimed at supporting Deaf people and at breaking down communication barriers between deaf and hearing people also create deaf-friendly online spaces. In a study on the online representation of sign language and deafness by two companies from the hospitality industry in Cape Town, Mohr (2021) found that the internationally widespread I-LOVE-YOU sign 🤟 is frequently used by both institutions on social media. Specifically, the interviewed Deaf participants from South Africa felt that it is a strong, identity-providing sign, which expresses solidarity with the Deaf community in South Africa, and possibly beyond. Jennifer,[10] a Deaf member of staff at one of the companies, said she would use the sign on social media: "[. . .] to show solidarity of being deaf and having a common language and culture across diversity. On social media, it's important to use because it gives us visibility and confirms identity online."

Based on this, one company even used the sign as part of its branding and created its logo in clever ways so as to be able to trademark it (see Figure 7.10).

The commodification of language taking place in this way has been shown to be typical of the tourist industry (e.g., Nassenstein 2019), and seems to apply to the hospitality industry in a similar way. Linking the sign, sign language learning videos, and a social media campaign with the hashtag #signtember (run on Twitter and Instagram from 2016–2018), the companies created deaf-friendly, multimodal online spaces that at the same time signal their virtues as

---

10 The name is a pseudonym.

Figure 7.10: The I-LOVE-YOU sign as trademarked by a South African coffee house chain.

inclusive work spaces and promote a positive image. The campaign is intriguing because it emphasizes the use of sign language (South African Sign Language in this case) by exploiting the metadiscursive functions of hashtags such as enacting the ambient community, creating a thematic space via folksonomic topic marking, creating searchable talk, and expressing the author's attitude towards a post/topic (Zappavigna 2011, 2015, Zappavigna and Martin 2018). Besides #signtember, which created a thematic space related to deafness and sign language, associated hashtags like #DeafAwarenessMonth, #DeafEmpowerment, and #SouthAfricanSignLanguage fulfilled the aforementioned functions and contributed to creating deaf-friendly spaces online. In this vein, by combining pictures of the I-LOVE-YOU sign, sign language learning videos, and written language hashtags, this is a nice illustration of how communication draws on various modes, among which verbal, written communication is only one of various resources employed to make meaning.

5.3.2 Sand stories

Our final example presents a blend of modes, channels, and modalities and contributes to the analysis of multimodality. It is the fascinating case of Aboriginal sand drawings, which involve, among other things, oral-verbal and visual-manual elements. Arandic sand drawing practices are described by Green (2014) as multimodal events including speech, song, sign, gesture, and drawings on the ground.

As a part of Central Australian social and cultural practices, the sand drawing presents a traditional storytelling of Aboriginal art. These sophisticated narratives are drawn on the ground, while the narrator simultaneously uses a different hand for gesturing or signing. At the same time, the performance of the sand story may be interwoven with speaking or signing. The expressive potential of this semiotic practice is quite high. Full narratives can be told with or without spoken language by older women and also younger people (Green 2014). This ancient traditional narrative performance demonstrates a way of representing simultaneous multimodal phenomena, captured in the complexity of such storytelling forms. By analyzing Arandic sand drawing practices, Green (2014: 99) proposes a system which "breaks away from a strict demarcation between drawing and sign/gesture, and allows for better descriptions of the ways that expressive aims are achieved by using a combination of semiotic means".

6 Concluding remarks

As outlined in the introduction, social semiotic approaches to communication presuppose a multimodal account of language. With the examples presented in this chapter we intended to show that multimodality is very much part of any linguistic (inter)action. Speech, taken in its most natural form, is produced along with gesture, and signing in its most natural form is produced with mouthings or co-occurring speech.

We began this paper by asking what exactly is considered a multimodal communicative practice. Gestures and signs alone do not automatically make up multimodal expressions, but in co-occurrence with speech they become part of one. We prefer to use the term "multimodal" for communicative utterances that include more than one sensory modality, rather than instances where many channels or modes are employed in a communicative event.

In this brief sketch of recent gesture and sign language research, we have tried to capture some multimodal, multichanneled, and multisemiotic aspects of language. We have revealed a multiplicity of communicative practices by discussing a number of multimodal interaction examples from different parts of the world, such as Africa and Australia.

We have also tried to emphasize that contact between modalities is omnipresent in communication regardless of whether we are concerned with spoken or sign languages. One cross-modal contact phenomenon, namely mouthings, was discussed as a vivid example of multimodal utterances.

We believe that analyzing multimodal communicative systems in use – sign, gesture, and speech – opens up an illuminating window on how humans systematically deploy communicative resources in interaction to jointly create meaning.

References

Bank, Richard, Onno Crasborn & Roel van Hout. 2011. Variation in mouth actions with manual signs in sign language of the Netherlands (NGT). *Sign Language & Linguistics* 14 (2). 248–270.
Bank, Richard. 2014. *The ubiquity of mouthings in NGT. A corpus study*. Utrecht: LOT.
Bauer, Anastasia. 2014. *The use of signing space in a shared sign language of Australia*. Berlin: De Gruyter Mouton and Ishara Press.
Bauer, Anastasia. 2019. When words meet signs. A corpus-based study on variation of mouthing in Russian Sign Language. In Anastasia Bauer & Daniel Bunčić (eds.), *Linguistische Beiträge zur Slavistik*, 9–35. Frankfurt: Peter Lang.
Bauer, Anastasia. 2020. Das Konzept der multimodalen Sprache am Beispiel von der Russischen Gebärdensprache. *Bulletin der deutschen Slavistik* 26. 131–139.
Bauer, Anastasia & Maria Kyuseva. 2022. New insights into mouthings. Evidence from a corpus-based study of Russian Sign Language. *Frontiers in Psychology*. DOI:10.3389/fpsyg.2021.779958
Birdwhistell, Ray L. 1955. Background to kinesics. *ETC: A Review of General Semantics* 13 (1). 10–18.
Bock, Zannie. 2019. Approaches to communication. In Zannie Bock & Gift Mheta (eds.), *Language, society and communication. An introduction*, 35–53. Pretoria: Van Schaik.
Boyes Braem, Penny & Rachel Sutton-Spence (eds.). 2001. *The hands are the head of the mouth. The mouth as articulator in sign languages*. Hamburg: Signum.
Bressem, Jana & Cornelia Müller. 2017. The Negative-Assessment-Construction – a multimodal pattern based on a recurrent gesture? *Linguistics Vanguard* 3. 1–9.
Brookes, Heather & Victoria Nyst. 2014. Gestures in the Sub-Saharan region. In Cornelia Müller, Alan Cienki, Ellen Fricke, Silva H. Ladewig, David McNeill & Jana Bressem (eds.), *Body – language – communication. An international handbook on multimodality in human interaction* (HSK 38.2), 1154–1161. Berlin: De Gruyter Mouton.
Brookes, Heather & Olivier Le Guen. 2019. Gesture studies and anthropological linguistics. *Gesture* 18 (2/3). 119–141.
Burkova, Svetlana. 2015. *Russian Sign Language Corpus*. [http://rsl.nstu.ru/] (accessed 27 May 2021).
Carew, Margaret & Jennifer Green. 2015. Making an online dictionary for Central Australian sign languages. *Learning Communities* 16. 40–55.
Clark, Herbert H. 1996. *Using language*. Cambridge: Cambridge University Press.
Cooperrider, Kensy. 2019. Universals and diversity in gesture. *Gesture* 18 (2/3). 209–238.
Cooperrider, Kensy, Natasha Abner & Susan Goldin-Meadow. 2018. The palm-up puzzle. Meanings and origins of a widespread form in gesture and sign. *Frontiers in Communication* 3. 1–16.

Cooperrider, Kensy, Jordan Fenlon, Jonathan Keane, Diane Brentari & Susan Goldin-Meadow. 2021. How pointing is integrated into language. Evidence from speakers and signers. *Frontiers in Communication* 6. DOI:10.3389/fcomm.2021.567774

Cooperrider, Kensy, James Slotta & Rafael Núñez. 2018. The preference for pointing with the hand is not universal. *Cognitive Science* 42 (4). 1375–1390.

Coppola, Marie & Ann Senghas. 2017. Is it language (yet)? The allure of the gesture-language binary. *The Behavioral and Brain Sciences* 40. e50. DOI:10.1017/S0140525X1500285X

Darwin, Charles. 1872. *The expression of emotions in man and the animals*. London: John Murray.

Davis, Jeffrey. 2010. *Hand talk. Sign language among American Indian Nations*. Cambridge: Cambridge University.

De Jorio, Andrea. 1832. *La mimica degli antichi investigata nel gestire napoletano*. Napoli: Fibreno.

De Vos, Conny & Ulrike Zeshan. 2012. Introduction. Demographic, sociocultural, and linguistic variation across rural signing communities. In Ulrike Zeshan & Connie de Vos (eds.), *Sign languages in village communities. Anthropological and linguistic insights*, 2–26. Berlin: De Gruyter Mouton & Ishara Press.

Dingemanse, Mark. 2011. Ideophones and the aesthetics of everyday language in a West-African society. *The Senses and Society* 6 (1). 77–85.

Duranti, Alessandro & Charles Goodwin (eds.). 1992. *Rethinking context. Language as an interactive phenomenon*. Cambridge: Cambridge University Press.

Eberhard, David M., Gary F. Simons & Charles D. Fennig (eds.). 2021. Ethnologue. Languages of the world. Twenty-fourth edition. Dallas, Texas: SIL International. [http://www.ethnologue.com] (accessed 27 May 2021).

Ebbinghaus, Horst & Jens Heßmann. 1995. Form und Funktion von Ablesewörtern in gebärdensprachlichen Äußerungen. *Das Zeichen* 8 (30), 480–487; 9 (31), 50–61.

Ekman, Paul & Wallace Friesen. 1969. The repertoire of non-verbal behavior. Categories, origins, usage and coding. *Semiotica* 1 (1). 49–98.

Ekman, Paul & Wallace Friesen. 1972. Hand movements. *Journal of Communication* 22. 353–374.

Emmorey, Karen. 1999. Do signers gesture? In Lynn S. Messing & Ruth Campbell (eds.) *Gesture, speech, and sign*, 133–159. Oxford: Oxford University Press.

Enfield, N. J. 2001. Lip-pointing. A discussion of form and function with reference to data from Laos. *Gesture* 1 (2). 185–211.

Enfield, N. J. 2009. *The anatomy of meaning. Speech, gesture, and composite utterances*. Cambridge: Cambridge University Press.

Fehn, Anne-Maria. 2012. Some notes on traditional Ts'ixa gesture inventories. In Gabriele Sommer & Clarissa Vierke (eds.), *Speech acts and speech events in African languages*, 145–168. Cologne: Rüdiger Köppe.

Ferrara, Lindsay & Gabrielle Hodge. 2018. Language as description, indication and depiction. *Frontiers in Psychology* 9. 716.

Fox Tree, Erich. 2009. Meemul Tziij. An indigenous sign language complex of Mesoamerica. *Sign Language Studies* 9 (3). 324–366.

Fontana, Sabina. 2008. Mouth actions as gesture in sign language. *Gesture* 8, 104–123.

Gawne, Lauren. 2018. Contexts of use of a rotated palms gesture among Syuba (Kagate) speakers in Nepal. *Gesture* 17 (1). 37–64.

Goffman, Erving. 1969. *The presentation of self in everyday life*. London: Allen Lane.

Goffman, Erving. 1974. *Frame analysis. An essay on the organisation of experience*. London: Harper and Row.

Goldin-Meadow, Susan. 2003. *Hearing gesture. How our hands help us think*. Cambridge, MA: Harvard University Press.

Goldin-Meadow, Susan & Melissa Singer. 2003. From children's hands to adults' ears. Gesture's role in the learning process. *Developmental Psychology* 39 (3). 509–520.

Goldin-Meadow, Susan & Diane Brentari. 2017. Gesture, sign, and language. The coming of age of sign language and gesture studies. *Behavioral and Brain Sciences* 1. 1–82.

Goodwin, Charles. 2000. Action and embodiment within situated human interaction. *Journal of Pragmatics* 32 (10). 1489–1522.

Green, Jennifer. 2014. *Drawn from the ground. Sound, sign and inscription in Central Australian sand stories* (Language Culture & Cognition 13). Cambridge: Cambridge University Press.

Green, Jennifer & David Wilkins. 2014. With or without speech. Arandic Sign Language from Central Australia. *Australian Journal of Linguistics* 34. 234–261.

Green, Jennifer, Anastasia Bauer, Alice Gaby & Elizabeth Ellis. 2018. Pointing to the body. Kin signs in Australian indigenous sign languages. *Gesture* 17 (1). 1–36.

Grišina, Elena. 2017. *Russkaja žestikuljacija s lingvističeskoj točki zrenija.* (Russian gesticulation from a linguistic point of view). Moscow: Izdatel'skij dom JASK.

Güldemann, Tom. 1998. The Kalahari Basin as an object of areal typology. A first approach. In Mathias Schladt (ed.), *Language, identity and conceptualisation among the Khoisan*, 137–169. Cologne: Rüdiger Köppe.

Güldemann, Tom. 2014. 'Khoisan' linguistic classification today. In Tom Güldemann & Anne-Maria Fehn (eds.), *Beyond 'Khoisan' historical relations in the Kalahari Basin*, 1–40. Amsterdam & Philadelphia: John Benjamins.

Haviland, John B. 1993. Anchoring, iconicity, and orientation in Guugu Yimithirr pointing gestures. *Journal of Linguistic Anthropology* 3 (1). 3–45.

Herring, Susan C. 2013. Discourse in Web 2.0. Familiar, reconfigured, emergent. In Deborah Tannen & Anna Marie Trester (eds.), *Discourse 2.0. Language and new media*, 1–25. Washington, DC: Georgetown University Press.

Holler, Judith & Stephen C. Levinson. 2019. Multimodal language processing in human communication. *Trends in Cognitive Sciences*. 23 (8). 639–652.

Hymes, Dell. 1972. On communicative competence. In John B. Pride & Janet Holmes (eds.), *Sociolinguistics. Selected readings*, 269–293. Harmondsworth: Penguin.

Jakobson, Roman. 1972. Motor signs for 'yes' and 'no'. *Language in Society* 1 (1). 91–96.

Johnston, Trevor, Jane van Roekel & Adam Schembri. 2016. On the conventionalization of mouth actions in Australian Sign Language. *Language and Speech* 59 (1). 3–42.

Jorgensen, Eleanor, Jennifer Green & Anastasia Bauer. 2021. The phonology of alternate sign languages in Australia. *Languages* 6 (2). 81.

Kelly, Spencer, Asli Özyürek & Eric Maris. 2010. Two sides of the same coin. Speech and gesture mutually Interact to enhance comprehension. *Psychological Science* 21 (2). 260–267.

Kelley, Walter & Tony McGregor. 2003. Keresan Pueblo Indian Sign Language. In O. T. Jon Reyhner (ed.), *Nurturing native languages*, 141–148. Flagstaff, AZ: Northern Arizona University.

Kendon, Adam. 1981. Geography of gesture. *Semiotica* 37 (1/2). 129–163.

Kendon, Adam. 1988. How gestures can become like words. In F. Poyatos (ed.), *Cross-cultural perspectives in nonverbal communication*, 131–141. Toronto: Hogrefe.

Kendon, Adam. 2004. *Gesture. Visible action as utterance*. Cambridge: Cambridge University Press.

Kendon, Adam. 2014. Semiotic diversity in utterance production and the concept of 'language'. *Philosophical Transactions of the Royal Society B* 369. DOI:10.1098/rstb.2013.0293

Kendon, Adam. 2017. Reflections on the 'gesture-first' hypothesis of language origins. *Psychonomic Bulletin & Review* 24 (1). 163–170.

Kendon, Adam. 2019. Gesture and anthropology. *Gesture* 18 (2/3). 142–172.

Kibrik, Andrej A. 2010. Mul'timodal'naja lingvistika [Multimodal linguistics]. In Yuri I. Alexandrov & Valery D. Solovyev (eds.), *Kognitivnye issledovanija* – IV, 134–152. Moscow: IP RAN.

Kibrik, Andrej A. 2018. Russkij mul'tikanal'nyj diskurs. Čast' I: Postanovka problemy. *Psichologičeskij žurnal* 39 (1). 70–80.

Kita, Sotaro. 1993. *Language and thought interface. A study of spontaneous gestures and Japanese mimetics*. Chicago: University of Chicago dissertation.

Kress, Gunther. 2010. *Multimodality. A social semiotic approach to contemporary communication*. London: Routledge.

Kusters, Annelies, Massimiliano Spotti, Ruth Swanwick & Elina Tapio. 2017. Beyond languages, beyond modalities. Transforming the study of semiotic repertoires. *International Journal of Multilingualism* 14. 219–232.

Kurz, Christopher A. N. & Jess Cuculik. 2015. International deaf space in social media. The deaf experience in the US. In Michele Friedner & Annelies Kusters (eds.), *It's a small world. International deaf spaces and encounters*, 225–235. Washington, DC: Gallaudet University Press.

Kyuseva, Masha. 2020. *Size and shape specifiers in Russian sign language. A morphological analysis*. Melbourne: University of Melbourne & University of Birmingham dissertation.

Ladewig, Silva H. & Jana Bressem. 2013. New insights into the medium hand. Discovering structures in gestures on the basis of the four parameters of sign language, *Semiotica* 197. 203–231.

Ladewig, Silva H. 2014. Recurrent gestures. In Cornelia Müller, Alan Cienki, Ellen Fricke, Silva H. Ladewig, David McNeill & Jana Bressem (eds.), *Body – language – communication/Körper – Sprache – Kommunikation*, Vol. 2, 1558–1574. Berlin & New York: De Gruyter Mouton.

Leeson, Lorraine & Carmel Grehan. 2004. To the lexicon and beyond. The effect of gender variation on Irish Sign Language. In Mieke van Herreweghe & Myriam Vermeerbergen (eds.), *To the lexicon and beyond. Sociolinguistics in European deaf communities*, 39–73. Washington, DC: Gallaudet University Press.

Le Master, Barbara & John P. Dwyer. 1991. Knowing and using female and male signs in Dublin. *Sign Language Studies* 73. 361–396.

Le Guen, Olivier. 2011. Modes of pointing to existing spaces and the use of frames of reference. *Gesture* 11 (3), 271–307.

Le Guen, Oliver. 2012. An exploration in the domain of time. From Yucatec Maya time gestures to Yucatec Maya Sign Language time signs. In Ulrike Zeshan & Connie de Vos (eds.), *Sign languages in village communities. Anthropological and linguistic insights*, 209–250. Berlin: De Gruyter Mouton & Ishara Press.

Le Guen, Olivier, Rebecca Petatillo & Rita (Rossy) Kinil Canché. 2020. Yucatec Maya multimodal interaction as the basis for Yucatec Maya Sign Language. In Oliver Le Guen,

Josefina Safar & Marie Coppola (eds.), *Emerging sign languages of the Americas*, 290–349. Berlin & Boston: De Gruyter Mouton.

Lempert, Michael. 2011. Barack Obama, being sharp. Indexical order in the pragmatics of precision-grip gesture. *Gesture* 11 (3). 241–270.

Lempert, Michael. 2019. What is an anthropology of gesture? *Gesture* 18 (2/3). 173–208.

Liddell, Scott K. 2000. Blended spaces and deixis in sign language discourse. In David McNeill (ed.), *Language and gesture*, 331–357. Cambridge: Cambridge University Press.

Magongwa, Lucas. 2010. Deaf education in South Africa. *American Annals of the Deaf* 155 (4). 493–496.

McNeill, David. 1985. So you think gestures are nonverbal? *Psychological Review* 92. 350–371.

McNeill, David. 1992. *Hand and mind. What gestures reveal about thought.* Chicago, IL: University of Chicago Press.

McNeill, David. 2000. Introduction. In David McNeill (ed.), *Language and gesture*, 1–10. Cambridge: Cambridge University Press.

Meir, Irit, Mark Aronoff, Wendy Sandler & Carrol Padden. 2010. Sign languages and compounding. In Sergio Scalise & Irene Vogel (eds.), *Cross-disciplinary issues in compounding*, 301–322. Amsterdam: John Benjamins.

Meissner, Martin & Stuart Philpott. 1975. The sign language of sawmill workers in British Colombia. *Sign Language Studies* 9. 291–308.

Mesch, Johanna & Krister Schönström. 2020. Use and acquisition of mouth actions in L2 sign language learners. *Sign Language & Linguistics* 24 (1). 36–62.

Mesh, Kate. 2017. *Points of comparison. What indicating gestures tell us about the origins of signs in San Juan Quiahije Chatino Sign Language.* Austin, TX: The University of Texas at Austin dissertation.

Mohr, Susanne. 2007. *Sign languages as natural languages. The linguistic design features.* Aachen: RWTH Aachen University MA thesis.

Mohr, Susanne. 2012. The visual-gestural modality and beyond. Mouthings as a language contact phenomenon in Irish Sign Language. *Sign Language and Linguistics* 15 (2). 185–211.

Mohr, Susanne. 2014. *Mouth actions in sign languages. An empirical study of Irish Sign Language.* Berlin: De Gruyter Mouton and Ishara.

Mohr, Susanne. 2015. Tshaukak'ui – hunting signs of the Ts'ixa in Northern Botswana. In Julie Bakken Jepsen, Goedele de Clerck, Sam Lutalo-Kiingi & William McGregor (eds.), *Sign languages of the world. A comparative handbook*, 933–953. Berlin & Boston: De Gruyter Mouton.

Mohr, Susanne. 2021. The meaning of I love you. A multimodal analysis of South African Sign Language on social media. Paper presented at the *Institutskolloquium* of the Department of Anthropology and African Studies, 20 April 2021, University of Mainz.

Mohr, Susanne, Anne-Maria Fehn & Alex De Voogt. 2019. Hunting for signs. Exploring unspoken networks within the Kalahari Basin. *Journal of African Languages and Linguistics* 40 (1). 115–147.

Mohr, Susanne & Lorraine Leeson. Forthcoming. Ireland's third official language: Irish Sign Language. In Raymond Hickey (ed.), *The Oxford handbook of Irish English*. Oxford: Oxford University Press.

Morris, Desmond, Peter Collett, Peter Marsh & Maria O'Shaughnessy. 1979. *Gestures. Their origins and distribution.* London: Jonathan Cape.

Müller, Cornelia. 1998. *Redebegleitende Gesten. Kulturgeschichte – Theorie – Sprachvergleich*. Berlin: Azore Spitz.

Müller, Cornelia. 2010. Wie Gesten bedeuten. Eine kognitiv-linguistische und sequenzanalytische Perspektive. *Sprache und Literatur* 41 (1). 37–68.

Nadolske, Marie & Rachel Rosenstock. 2007. Occurrence of mouthings in American Sign Language. A preliminary study. In Pamela Perniss, Roland Pfau & Markus Steinbach (eds.), *Visible variation. Comparative studies on sign language structure*, 35–61. Berlin: De Gruyter.

Nassenstein, Nico. 2019. The Hakuna Matata Swahili. Linguistic souvenirs from the Kenyan coast. In Angelika Mietzner & Anne Storch (eds.), *Language and tourism in postcolonial settings*, 130–156. Bristol: Channel View.

Nyst, Victoria. 2012. Shared sign languages. In Roland Pfau, Markus Steinbach & Bencie Woll (eds.), *Sign language. An international handbook* (HSK 37), 552–574. Berlin: De Gruyter Mouton.

Nyst, Victoria. 2016. Size and shape depictions in the manual modality. A taxonomy of iconic devices in Adamorobe Sign Language. *Semiotica* 210. 75–104.

Okrent, Arika. 2002. A modality-free notion of gesture and how it can help us with the morpheme vs. gesture question in sign language linguistics (Or at least give us some criteria to work with). In Richard Meier, Kearsy Cormier & David Quinto-Pozos (eds.), *Modality and structure in signed and spoken languages*, 175–198. Cambridge: Cambridge University Press.

Özyürek, Asli. 2012. Sign Language. In Roland Pfau, Markus Steinbach & Bencie Woll (eds.), *Sign language. An international handbook* (HSK 37), 626–646. Berlin & Boston: De Gruyter Mouton.

Özyürek, Asli. 2018. Role of gesture in language processing. Toward a unified account for production and comprehension. In Shirley-Ann Rueschemeyer & M. Gareth Gaskell (eds.), The *Oxford handbook of psycholinguistics*, 592–607. Oxford: Oxford University Press.

Perniss, Pamela. 2018. Why we should study multimodal language. *Frontiers in Psychology* 9. 1–5.

Pfau, Roland & Markus Steinbach. 2006. Modality-independent and modality-specific aspects of grammaticalization in sign languages. *Linguistics in Potsdam* 24. 135–182.

Pfau, Roland. 2012. Manual communication systems. Evolution and variation. In Roland Pfau, Markus Steinbach & Bencie Woll (eds.), *Sign language. An international handbook* (HSK 37), 513–551. Berlin & Boston: De Gruyter Mouton.

Racz-Engelhardt, Szilard. 2017. *Morphological properties of mouthing in Hungarian Sign Language (MJNY)*. Hamburg: Universität Hamburg dissertation.

Rohlfing, Katharina. 2019. Learning language from the use of gestures. In Jessica S. Horst & Janne von Koss Torkildsen (eds.), *International handbook of language acquisition*, 213–233. Abingdon: Routledge.

Sandler, Wendy. 2003. On the complementarity of signed and spoken languages. In Yonata Levy & Jeannette Schaeffer (eds.), *Language competence across populations. Towards a definition of specific language impairment*, 383–409. Mahwah, NJ: Lawrence Erlbaum.

Sandler, Wendy. 2009. Symbiotic symbolization by hand and mouth in sign language. *Semiotica* 174. 241–75.

Schegloff, Emanuel A. & Harvey Sacks. 1973. Opening up closings. *Semiotica* 8 (4). 289–327.

Schembri, Adam, Caroline Jones & Denis Burnham. 2005. Comparing action gestures and classifier verbs of motion. Evidence from Australian Sign Language, Taiwan Sign

Language, and nonsigners' gestures without speech. *The Journal of Deaf Studies and Deaf Education* 10 (3). 272–290.

Shannon, Claude E. & Warren Weaver. 1949. *A mathematical model of communication.* Urbana: University of Illinois Press.

Solvang, Per Koren & Hilde Haualand. 2014. Accessibility and diversity. Deaf space in action. *Scandinavian Journal of Disability Research* 16 (1). 1–13.

Sweetser, Eve. 2006. Personal and interpersonal gesture spaces. Functional contrasts in language and gesture. In Andrea Tyler, Yiyoung Kim & Mari Takada (eds.), *Language in the context of use. Cognitive and discourse approaches to language and language learning*, 25–52. Berlin: De Gruyter Mouton.

Thurlow, Crispin. 2017. Forget about the words? Tracking the language, media and semiotic ideologies of digital discourse. The case of sexting. *Discourse, Context and Media* 20. 10–19.

Thurlow, Crispin & Vanessa Jaroski. 2020. Emoji invasion. The semiotic ideologies of language endangerment in multilingual news discourse. In Crispin Thurlow, Christa Dürscheid & Federica Diémoz (eds.), *Visualizing digital discourse. Interactional, institutional and ideological perspectives*, 45–64. Berlin: De Gruyter.

Van Loon, Esther, Roland Pfau & Markus Steinbach. 2014. The grammaticalization of gestures in sign languages. In Cornelia Müller, Alan Cienki, Ellen Fricke, Silva H. Ladewig, David McNeill & Jana Bressem (eds.), *Body – language – communication. An international handbook on multimodality in human interaction* (HSK 38.2), 720–730. New York: De Gruyter Mouton.

Vigliocco, Gabriella, Pamela Perniss & David Vinson. 2014. Language as a multimodal phenomenon. Implications for language learning, processing and evolution. *Philosophical transactions of the Royal Society of London. Series B, Biological sciences* 369 (1651). 20130292.

Vogt-Svendsen, Marit. 2001. A comparison of mouth gestures and mouthings in Norwegian Sign Language (NSL). In Penny Boyes Braem & Rachel Sutton-Spence (eds.), *The hands are the head of the mouth. The mouth as articulator in sign languages*, 9–40. Hamburg: Signum.

Wilkins, David. 1999. Spatial deixis in Arrernte speech and gesture. On the analysis of a species of composite signal as used by a Central Australian Aboriginal group. In Elisabeth André, Massimo Poesio & Hannes Rieser (eds.), *Proceedings of the workshop on deixis, demonstration and deictic belief in multimedia contexts, held on occasion of ESSLI XI*, 31–45. Utrecht, The Netherlands.

Wilkins, David. 2003. Why pointing with the index finger is not a universal (in sociocultural and semiotic terms). In Sotaro Kita (ed.), *Pointing. Where language, culture, and cognition meet*, 65–70. Mahwah, NJ: Lawrence Erlbaum Associates.

Woll, Bencie & Paddy Ladd. 2003. Deaf communities. In Marc Marschark & Patricia E. Spencer (eds.), *The Oxford handbook of deaf studies, language and education*, 151–163. Oxford: Oxford University Press.

Zappavigna, Michele. 2011. Ambient affiliation. A linguistic perspective on Twitter. *New Media and Society* 13. 788–806.

Zappavigna, Michele. 2015. Searchable tak. The linguistic functions of hashtags. *Social Semiotics* 25 (3). 274–291.

Zappavigna, Michele & James R. Martin. 2018. #Communing affiliation. Social tagging as a resource for aligning around values in social media. *Discourse, Context and Media* 22. 4–12.

Zeshan, Ulrike. 2004. Interrogative constructions in sign languages. Cross-linguistic perspectives. *Language* 80 (1). 7–39.

Zeshan, Ulrike. 2008. Roots, leaves and branches. The typology of sign languages. In R. M. de Quadros (ed.), *Sign Languages. Spinning and unraveling the past, present and future.* TISLR 9, 671–695. Petrópolis, Brazil: Editora Arara Azul.

Zeshan, Ulrike & Sibaji Panda. 2018. Sign-speaking. The structure of simultaneous bimodal utterances. *Applied Linguistics Review* 9 (1). 1–34.

David Tavárez

8 On ritual speech: Epistemologies, history, and the social order

This chapter investigates the nexus between authority and carefully calibrated and highly patterned actions accomplished through and alongside language. In the anthropological literature, many of these practices are described as belonging to ritual activities, as they instantiate, represent, or memorialize world-changing acts. This exploration focuses on a variety of representative examples drawn from Mesoamerica, Amazonia, the Andes, South Asia, and Africa. Through a survey of historical case studies, ethnographic research, and various theoretical approaches, the chapter outlines five important domains demarcated by ritual speech: language ideologies, epistemologies, and the construction of authoritative ontological models about the cosmos; performances that interdigitate speech and collective identities that actors perceive as customary; the diversity and precariousness of ritual language at the boundaries of intelligibility; ritual performance and the demarcation of social differences; and the relation between ritual speech and non-human forms of agency.

1 Introduction

On November 18, 1704, several town officials led by the nobleman don Juan Martín of the Northern Zapotec community of Lachirioag in the diocese of Oaxaca in colonial Mexico revealed to an ecclesiastical judge their most sacred possession: a box with "the root, or tree trunk, of their genealogy", kept at the sacred mountain of Yahuiz. The judge ordered the box opened. Inside it, besides lancets for self-sacrifice, were small effigies, "precious" stones and bundles stained with the blood of turkeys that contained sacred objects. The eldest member of each Zapotec lineage was charged with the custody of such sacred bundles. The one unveiled on that momentous occasion belonged to Martín's great-grandfather, don Cristóbal Martín, who was also known as Yaglaba, 1-Rabbit, a name assigned to him at birth, in keeping with the Zapotec version of the 260-day Mesoamerican divinatory count. In compliance with an amnesty offer made by the bishop of Oaxaca that yielded more than 100 calendrical manuals, the people of Lachirioag also turned in two songbooks (Tavárez 2022).

David Tavárez, Vassar College, New York/United States, e-mail: tavarez@vassar.edu

https://doi.org/10.1515/9783110726626-008

Like the better-known Nahua *Cantares Mexicanos*, these *dij dola* 'songs and chants', were organized in stanzas punctuated by sung syllables, and performed to the beat of wooden cylindrical drums. On behalf of the community, ritual specialists sang these songs to summon ancestors who possessed animal co-beings, and which descended from upper realms designated as *quina*, 'fields', and *quiya*, 'reed fields'. These seventeenth-century songs referenced specific ancestors who descended from Sky with gifts of *doo biga*, 'jewel strings', and who received *yaza*, 'broad leaves,' two items that were unambiguously depicted in Zapotec stone monuments carved more than a thousand years earlier between the 6th and 9th centuries CE, in the late Classic Period (Urcid 2005). The deep continuities that tied ancient and colonial Zapotec ritual protocols were preserved by political elites despite intense prosecution from colonial institutions and internal resistance from other Zapotec elites and commoners. They also constituted an epistemic front that sought to bracket and manage various forms of Christian hegemony (Tavárez 2022).

In spite of their apparent remoteness, these Zapotec observances shared a common ground with many practices deployed in contemporary ritual protocols. As is argued below, all of these protocols frequently depict claims about authority and the social order in the face of political tensions; are informed by language ideologies, or dominant epistemological stances and perceptions about language; and are executed through multiple forms of ritual labor, which incorporated a variety of speech genres, non-human actors, iconography, and implements. This chapter investigates the nexus between authority and ritual – understood here as a collection of carefully calibrated and highly patterned actions – which are accomplished through and alongside speech – a necessarily broad rubric that includes structured verbal and bodily performances, along with silences and omissions.

In the anthropological literature, many of these practices are described as belonging to ritual activities, as they instantiate, represent, or memorialize world-changing acts. This exploration focuses on a variety of representative analyses of ritual labor in North America, Mesoamerica, Amazonia, the Andes, South Asia, and Africa. Through a survey of case studies, ethnographic research, and various theoretical approaches, the chapter explores and outlines four important domains demarcated by ritual speech, which recur in colonial Zapotec ritual and across many other studies: language ideologies and local epistemologies; historical narratives and ritual authority; ritual practices and the social order; and ritual labor, non-human actors, and materiality. As an expansion of a previous survey of ritual speech (Tavárez 2014), this chapter focuses on recent proposals and analyses published in the past decade by linguistic anthropologists, ethnographers, and ethnohistorians.

2 Language ideologies and epistemological orientations

In an attempt to examine the relationships between three vast domains – language, ideology, and political economy – Paul Friedrich (1989) described their interdigitation as "linguacultural ideologies": a set of collective notional, pragmatic, and critical perspectives. From a different vantage point, an influential analysis by Irvine (1989) provides a more granular and historicized approach to the study of political economy and collective linguistic practices, and a second essay by Judith Irvine and Susan Gal (2000) examines fractal recursivity and other processes by which colonial and imperial states in Africa and Europe managed and regimented linguistic diversity. Another approach, which overlaps with Friedrich in terms of its emphasis on various forms of intentionality, is that of Katherine Woolard (1998), which corrals similarly unwieldy domains and presents a contrast between two poles in a broad continuum for language ideologies: one that rests on ideational or conceptual beliefs holding a claim to universal truth, and another focused on rationalizing beliefs that make possible, in part, the legitimation of particular social orders.

As these approaches focus on notions held by individuals in a collectivity, such beliefs require an account of intentionality. A foundational work (Austin 1975) proposes that speech acts draw their illocutionary force from appropriate social situations and authorized speakers, however minimally defined. A parsimonious definition of intentionality that is broadly compatible with a notional focus on language is found in the work of John Searle (1995: 25–26), who proposed that "collective intentionality" is composed from a "sense" of doing or engaging with the world together, so that individual intentions are related to commonly shared collective intentions. This vast definition of intentionality may hold up even if one takes into account that the code of conduct followed by social actors does not disclose, in and of itself, their full motivations or principal objectives (Goffman 1967). As a response to these and other intuitive accounts of actions, Nick Enfield and Jack Sidnell (2017), while assuming that social actions are inherently apprehended as having a purpose, contend that human conduct is deeply contoured by social accountability, and that the categorization and labeling of actions occurs primarily at the metapragmatic level, if and when human actors are held to account.

Beyond assumption and belief, other analytical paths focus on the extraordinary diversity of semiotic processes, which never exist singly or in isolation, but are always embedded in recursive ways. In a nod towards Friedrich's and Woolard's take on ideology as rationalization, Paul Kockelman (2015) argues that metasemiotic processes may constitute beliefs about the world, and thus, what we call "ideologies", even if they may become fetishized as notions and perceptions. As obvert beliefs, these ideologies, however, are one of several possible metasemiotic procedures for bracketing the world, as other material processes not rooted in mental representations may hold a greater sway.

While semiosis and metasemiosis may be recursive in endless ways, ritual performances are frequently based on a highly selective deployment of metasemiosis; hence, their epistemological framing is salient precisely because it foregrounds and simplifies certain processes, while excluding other forms of semiosis. A recurring axis of salience is formed by chronotopes, to use the term derived from the enormously influential work of Mikhail Bakhtin (1981), or by the concatenation of temporal and spatial domains in a variety of configurations, if the interdigitation of time and space is defined in other ways. Metasemiosis also plays a central role. As elegantly shown by Michael Silverstein (2009: 271–274), while various metasemiotic process may be at play in various social stances that are either performative or transformative, for a ritual to be effective, it must be reflexively calibrated in a way in which the bounded chronotope(s) in which protocols take place may be linked with their impact in the world as a "macrocosm". In particular, oratorial practices, as Rupert Stasch (2011) argued, summarize and encapsulate impossibly dense depictions of broad categories of time-space that model the entire cosmos through microcosmic action. From an opposite perspective, and with a focus on the Sinhalese Buddhist practices in Sri Lanka, Bruce Kapferer (1997) contends that the healing songs used in a ritual that combats sorcery effects is not a microcosmic portrayal of the world, but a separate domain with its own ontology.

3 Ritual authority and historical narratives

3.1 Specialized names and terms

In a variety of ritual traditions, practitioners carefully learn and archive specialized terms and proper names whose very possession and deployment enforces a hierarchy of knowledge (Briggs 1995). To return to a colonial example, Central Mexican public deity personification practices, which were the focus of large public pageants held every twenty days during the *xihuitl*, a 365-day cycle, were suppressed by civil and religious authorities after the 1520s. Nonetheless, a substantial corpus of Nahua prayers transcribed by the parish priest Hernando Ruiz de Alarcón in the early seventeenth century (Ruiz de Alarcón 1984) indicates that some ritual specialists continued to embody a select group of deities. This ritual oral genre was characterized by a highly sophisticated manner of designating entities with names: there was an astounding number of epithets for referring to oneself as a Nahua deity, calling forth propitiated entities, and designating a range of objects and entities. The native label for the genre was transparent: it was *nahualtocaitl*, or complex epithets with a parallel structure (*tocaitl*) that reflected the authoritative knowledge possessed by a shape-shifting specialist (*nahualli*). An important language ideology informed this genre: every entity in the world, including deities, animals, natural features, and objects, bore a unique name, personal or calendrical, whose significance was rooted in historical narratives. Uttering the appropriate names allowed practitioners to make demands of powerful beings who upheld the cosmological order. Nahua practitioners' emphasis on presenting these powerful names also embodies an "enactive" language ideology (Rumsey 1990), which, according to the analysis of contemporary Nahua ideologies about language use carried out by Jane Hill (1998), privileges performances that deploy idealized forms of speech.

These powerful names, which belonged in the broader category of proper names, have distinct referential properties. Saul Kripke's (1980) lucid analysis of naming and designation proposed a crucial distinction between "rigid" and "non-rigid" designators. While the latter might require descriptions or contextualization to establish a referent, rigid designators, a category that includes proper names, rested on an initial act of reference, a "baptismal act" (Kripke 1980: 35) that was successful only if a community of speakers shared the same association between proper name and referent. This account allows to fix the referents for both the powerful *nahualtocaitl*, and for the new names of wondrous Christian entities – such as "Jesus", "Mary", or "Holy Trinity" – that were introduced by missionaries in an attempt to bridge the significant gap between Indigenous and colonial language ideologies (Errington 2007, Keane 2006), and in a bid to erase the collective memory of preconquest deities and *nahualli* names.

From a different perspective, Carlo Severi (2012) focused on names and proper nouns to explore the structure of the Demon Chant in Kuna ritual discourse, which nests lists of proper nouns as it traverses the many underground villages in the eight underworld levels of Kuna cosmology. In a comparative approach that also includes Haida and Andean examples, Severi argues that an "art of memory" that was employed to store and recite lengthy ritual accounts is defined by the relationships among mnemonic, iconographic, and logical vectors, which feature the convergence of parallel phrases, pictographic representations, and symbols.

3.2 Ritual and tradition

While terms like "custom" and "tradition" seemingly denote unchanged beliefs and ritual protocols, the close scrutiny of their use often reveals that, even when used by practitioners, these terms serve as a shorthand for ideologies about the past that encompass changes through time, accretion, and elisions. In Latin America, and in Mesoamerican societies in particular, the post-colonial term *el costumbre* is widely used for practices of Indigenous origin, and stands in contrast with the article-noun grammatical gender agreement in standard Spanish, *la costumbre*, 'custom'. *El costumbre* thus refers to a wealth of local ritual and devotional practices that stand in contrast with practices legitimized and upheld by the Catholic Church and other institutions. In Nahua societies, these practices may be contemporary versions of elaborate protocols that focus on the importance accorded to maize, and on relations of reciprocity with sacred entities that bring rain and fertility (Sandstrom 1992, Stresser-Péan 2009). Even when particularly deep continuities appear to play a role, as in the renewal celebrations in the "fire-penance" complex in Preconquest Mexica and contemporary Tlapanec societies (Dehouve 2018), these celebrations have obvert political meanings tied to the yearly renewal of a new group of office holders.

Alternatively, *costumbre* may also have its center of gravity in the worship of Christian saints, and also have a deeply hybrid constitution, both in terms of how Christian entities are conceived, and in the deployment of parallel forms that form the core of Mesoamerican rhetorical practices (Lupo 1995). A reading of the legend of Judas Iscariot, based on the hagiographic tradition of the *Legenda aurea* and transposed into a Nahuatl manuscript by devout Indigenous Christians in the sixteenth century, focused on transgressive behaviors and on Iscariot's death by his own hand, an episode whose retelling echoed the demise of a powerful Mesoamerican sorcerer associated with the Central Mexican deity Tezcatlipoca (Olko 2017). In the early twenty-first century, the agency of Judas as a both transgressor and enforcer of public Christian morality is preserved in a Sakapultek Maya community in Guatemala, which, during Holy Week, unveils a "testament" putatively authored by the apostle that laments communal shortcomings and denounces the transgression of Christian mores (Shoaps 2009). The relationship between Catholic and Indigenous language ideologies in Mesoamerica stands in contrast with other colonial Christian ideologies: thus, in Papua New Guinea, the onus placed by Protestant Christianity on truthfulness clashes with Urapmin assumptions that speech is an unreliable site for referencing stable social meanings (Robbins 2007).

Hybrid ritual and devotional practices reside in a complex matrix that does not necessarily lead to the hegemonic dominance of orthodox Christian practices: as noted by Nahua anthropologist Abelardo de la Cruz (2017), the people of Chicontepec in Mexico's Huasteca region have grown to accept both *el costumbre*, which emphasizes a local cosmology, and the practices of Catholic catechists, who arrived in the aftermath of liberation theology movements and failed to redirect public ceremonies towards contemporary Catholic teachings. In Oaxaca, the historical undercurrents that structure a Christian celebration, the Day of the Dead, associated both with Mexican national culture and with highly localized Indigenous practices, have also yielded a celebration that focuses on singing contests that serve as a vehicle for Mazatec language preservation, Indigenous identity revival, and forms of belonging that are separate from nation-state projects (Faudree 2013).

As is the case in the case of Zapotec ancestor worship and the uttering of the *nahualli* names, the claims to authority made by ritual practitioners frequently rest on performances that reference historical narratives, but which are recapitulated through individualized ritual labor. Some analysts have focused on a diversity of semiotic practices that exactingly enact historical accounts. As shown by Michael Lambek (2002), certain specialists in Madagascar act as mediators between the general population and *tromba*, royal ancestors. Through these performances, mediums embody accounts that are linked to legendary narratives and important genealogical groups that may be traced, in some instances, to the seventeenth century. Following a narrative mediated by individual acts of revelation that bear a strong resemblance to colonial narratives of specialist empowerment (Tavárez 2022), Mapuche ritual specialists, or *machi*, are handed down objects essential to their practice that include a *kultrung* 'drum' and a *likankua* 'spiritual stone'; receive herbal remedies they will administer; and tie their existence to Ngünechen, a cardinal Mapuche deity (Bacigalupo 2016).

Hence, the important work of managing powerful entities rests often, but not always, on the knowledge and performative capabilities of ritual specialists. Whether a recitation, or as a dynamic concatenation of speech acts, specialists and non-specialists who interact with powerful beings or essences have to demonstrate their mastery in public or private contexts. In a noted examination of discourse structure, Joel Sherzer (1991) observed that a lengthy Kuna incantation, the "way of the snake", highlighted a ritual specialist's deep knowledge of the nature of a redoubtable snake entity – including its appearance, anatomy, and place in the world – which was demonstrated through punctual descriptions. This discourse-centered approach is deeply invested in the description of phrase segments, repetition, parallelism, and in the elucidation of a vocabulary that transforms common Kuna words into specialized terms deployed in specialists' chants. One counterpoint to this approach, and a complimentary one in some regards, is the analysis of the multiple semiotic resources deployed in a series of healing performances held by Wauja speakers in Amazonia (Ball 2018: 60–72). In contrast with other societies, Wauja community members place the burden of "bringing" and representing "spirit-monsters" on non-specialists, who are tasked with deploying indices for disease manifestations and maintaining iconic links between themselves and these redoubtable spirits, whose potential for damage must be tamed.

But "traditional" narratives are subject to dynamic recombinations and re-phrasings that may be linked to long-term transatlantic exchanges, as occurs in the case of Candomblé. As J. Lorand Matory (2005) established through innovative historical and ethnographic research, the spread of Candomblé from Africa's West Coast to Brazil was made possible by Afro-Brazilian elites who profited from their links to African authoritative knowledge in Brazil, and whose prestige grew in West Africa due to their role in transatlantic commercial exchanges. With a focus on current practice, Paul Johnson (2002) examined the performances of human vessels who embody *orixás*, African ancestral sacred beings, and who are placed in strategic relations within the *orixá* web of kinship. These embodiments, which serve as conduits for *axé*, or power, are performed in *terreiros*, places of worship closed to outsiders. But sometimes historical narratives in Candomblé fold onto themselves: some "natural" entities or hallowed sites that emerge as "unprecedented events" are not new; instead, they are reappearances of earlier narratives and sites that were deliberately pushed into oblivion (Sansi 2016).

3.3 Ritual speech at the boundaries of intelligibility

Another signature feature of ritual speech – an indifference towards, or the absence of, semantic or morphological transparence – is mediated by collective ideas regarding the boundaries of intelligibility. The study of fanciful or unintelligible "magical words" deployed in ritual speech appears in classical ethnographic analyses by Bronislaw Malinowski (1929, 1965), was reconsidered in a critical reassessment by Stanley Tambiah (1985), and has informed a number of critical responses to Malinowski's and Tambiah's stances (Senft 2010, Mosko 2014).

Some recent work in the field proposes that intelligibility ideologies are rooted in perceptions of hybridity that are linked to language hierarchies. Hence, the intricacy of the relationship between a hegemonic language in Morocco and North Africa, Modern Standard Arabic, and a Berber minority language, Tashel-hit, leads to discourses that project hegemonic language into the minority tongue through a series of calques. But spontaneous ritual performance employs hetero-glossia and multivocality, two far more flexible maneuvers that interdigitate Arabic singing and Tashelhit metadiscursive observations, yielding what Tashelhit female performers simply call *awal ngh* 'our talk' (Hoffman 2008: 222). In an analysis that follows Sherzer's discourse-centered approach, Laura Graham (2019) decodes *a'ãma mrémé*, a playful variant deployed by *a'ãma* ritual specialists, and which functions through lexical substitutions of nouns and verbs that figure exclusively in *a'ãma* speech. This variant, thus, centers *a'ãma* identity and ceremonial roles in A'uwẽ-Xavante society, and contributes to the density of this group's dualistic social ordering. Afro-Cuban Santería protocols, which have a considerable investment on broad epistemic claims (Holbraad 2012), provide another example of obliqueness. Lucumí, a ritual register employed by some practitioners, possesses a relative opaqueness and an unintelligibility that serves as audible proof of its authenticity, and supports claims about its historical origin in colonial transatlantic exchanges (Wirtz 2005).

Moreover, ritual performance may also transform a different boundary for comprehension: the one between social intelligibility and human subjectivity. A study of immigrant Syriac Orthodox liturgical practice in the Netherlands examines how dissonant singing and unharmonious performances provide vocal agency to a community of believers whose sensory experiences, as members of a diaspora, have been deeply molded by intricate interactions with Turkish, Dutch, and Syrian forms of secularism (Bakker Kellogg 2015). But some highly patterned and densely symbolic linguistic performances do not center the knowledge of practitioners, but instead evoke the very limits of language practices. Glossolalia, or the production of unintelligible speech that is publicly perceived as a specialized register, has been studied across a variety of ritual traditions (May 1956). Indeed, among South Korean Christian worshippers who follow this well-known practice, glossolalia and cacophonous group prayers demarcate the limits of customary and intelligible language practices, and glossolalia itself may be approached as a form of cultural semiosis that emerges at the very boundaries of linguistic production (Harkness 2017).

4 Ritual in society

4.1 Ritual practice and the social order

Social identities are often depicted and reconstituted through ritual language, which also may serve as a particularly obvert depiction of the social and cosmological order. Indeed, customary protocols in ritual oratory may be understood as a complex succession of interdiscursive events that legitimize the self-realization of a social group, or an entire society, as occurs in both the "Spirit Power" quest among speakers of Kiksht in the Pacific Northwest, and the granting of one of five "great names" by Worora specialists in Australia to announce future members of their social groups to those who will become to their parents (Silverstein 2009).

Some recent work explores the tensions among individual identities, collective identities, and social divisions. As Magnus Course (2011) noted in his work on Mapuche ritual, the emergence of a *che* 'true person', in Mapudungun, is inescapably at odds with the erosion of individual autonomy that may occur through social obligations, and this theme was explored by Mapuche educator and political leader Manuel Manquilef, who advocated for the self-realization of Indigenous individuals while maintaining a steady emphasis on Mapuche traditional protocols. In a very different setting – that of Lakota society – Daniel Posthumus (2019) examined the constitution of a ritual *thiyóšpaye*, a grouping of core and sub-core member families that participate frequently in ritual events. This flexible association of individuals is managed by a mediator and specialist who is linked by obligations of reciprocity and forms of equality to all participants through a dynamic relationship characterized by mutual influence and exchanges. More contingent uses for ritual speech in terms of marking social divides may include the mapping out of an indexical ground that metonymically construct a place of safety for a patient, as is the case for some Navajo prayer rituals (Field and Blackhorse 2002).

Going further into social links among and beyond family groups, Aaron Ansell (2017) examined a blessing ritual in the *sertão* backlands of northeastern Brazil, which is performed by individuals with transgenerational kinship links to the participants. These blessings present family obligations as an important part of the public sphere, and emerge as potential models for impartiality and civility beyond immediate kinship groups. Indeed, collective ceremonies may also be used to reimagine and reestablish how kinship groups and societies are perceived by powerful outsiders. Recent work in Kenya addresses a ceremony that represents contradictions between rural Samburu families and paradigms stemming from colonial domination that depicted Samburus as "radical Others" in terms of their sexuality (Meiu 2016). This protocol, called *lopiro*, calls for an end to quotidian adulterous relations, and attempts to reset "moral forms of collective belonging" to a nestled series of social divisions – clan membership, age ranking, and societies within and beyond Kenya. In the end, as shown by Juan Luis Rodríguez (2020), Venezuela and other nation-states rely on semiotic mediation and the quotidian use of speech genres in order to produce "revolutionary" subjects in self-proclaimed multi-ethnic societies.

4.2 Ritual practice and social difference

An interdiscursive approach to ritual has permitted some analysts to document and contextualize a multiplicity of ritual activities that bridge public and private domains. Timothy Knowlton (2015) has focused on the use of writing in votive text-artifacts in church sites for the worship of Christian saints in Guatemala as a metasemiotic resource in full public view that concretizes private communications with saints mediated by ritual, thus forming interdiscursive "chains of signification" that bridge intimate and public domains. Michael Wroblewski (2019) investigated interdiscursive narratives and staged representations of ritual in Amazonian Ecuador. By focusing on heterogeneously constituted urban and rural communities of practice that possess a diversity of knowledges, this researcher concluded that these Napo Kichwa discourses, which may be considered as forms of ritual activism, are inherently pluralistic, for they embrace multiple epistemologies, forms of expression and polivocalities.

Other researchers have examined the nexus between ritual and the representation of transnational and transmigrant collective identities. North American Coptic worshippers based in a Colorado congregation with a small number of fluent Arabic speakers or readers of Coptic texts established a cantillation school to adapt English content to Coptic hymnody and to reinterpret a variety of Egyptian, Coptic, and US-English forms of expression to fashion and disseminate a transcultural ritual protocol (Lozano 2015). For the diasporic African Guyanese community, *kweh-kweh* rituals, which articulate ancestral authority, address uncomfortable topics, and present advice to a couple before the celebration of their marriage, the patterned deployment of particular proverbs provide an opportunity for demarcating a difference between "authentic" Guyanese identity and those considered as "foreigners", based on proverb comprehension and a socially adequate demonstration of affect (Richards-Greaves 2016). Moreover, intensely sensory embodied experiences, partially mediated through language, may also play an important role in regimenting the experiences of audiences at ritual celebrations, which may include children and young adults who celebrate patriotic holidays in the United States in customary ways (Clark 2017).

Ritual participation also serves as a dynamic vehicle for demarcating the divide between communities united by core beliefs, and the public sphere at large. The compelling acoustic parameters of exemplary recitations of the Qur'an, distributed via low-cost recordings across a heterogeneous urban soundscape, are received as demonstrations of faith by interested audiences (Hirschkind 2006). An analysis of a neo-Pentecostal evangelist group (Elisha 2017) provides another example. This group of believers present a public depiction of their church in the New York Dance Parade by engaging in the performance of "spiritual warfare", a continuous struggle with the mores of the world historically rooted in the Pauline epistles. Such a participation in a public celebration requires that these Christians undergo "intensive ritualization" that allows them to preserve symbolic boundaries between their actions and the secular world, and these performances are impacted by "proximation", or a rapport of contiguity between distinct categories, such as religious practice and artistic performance.

Another commanding protocol for demarcating important historical, social and ethnic boundaries appears in some emergent forms of aboriginal public expression in Australia. These forms of Indigenous emplacement are entwined with more general projects of political reparation that embrace various modes for enunciating apologies and making public attempts at reconciliation. In particular, two concise rituals known as "Acknowledgments" and "Welcomes to Country" recognize the deep divide between Indigenous inhabitants and settlers, and rethink hegemonic relations between these two groups as a host-guest framework. Such rituals contribute to a recasting of forms of recognition that have been framed in recent years by multiple debates about authenticity and the origins of Australian Indigenous and settler communities (Merlan 2014). Other novel ritual forms emerged as a strategy for managing and attempting to control the interest of Westerners in traditional forms of ritual labor involving consciousness-altering cultigens that have been publicized and commodified extensively. In Iquitos, Peru, ritual specialists who cater to visitors and tourists seeking to ingest ayahuasca have developed lengthy edifying speeches that provide a ritual "frame", following the analysis of Gregory Bateson (1958), for the entire event as a liminal and transformative experience which surpasses a commodified interaction (Fotiou 2020).

5 Non-human agency in ritual practice

5.1 Animals

Animal species, and animal entities or presences, conform a vast category of important ritual participants, whether or not they are perceived as ontologically similar or distinct from practitioners and audiences. Besides the staggeringly abundant literature on animal iconography and non-human remains in archaeology, zooarchaeology, and biological anthropology, the influential work of Eduardo Viveiros de Castro on perspectivism (1998), followed by the ambitious classification of cosmological and cultural practices into four vast ontological models by Philippe Descola (2013), has generated several debates regarding the analytical advantages of models that employs pluralistic ontologies.

More recent work on ritual has focused primarily on semiotic and discursive practices that construct and manage human-animal relations. Antonella Tassinari (2015) posited that the Karipuna, who control territory that straddles the borders of French Guyana and Brazil, manage the presence of alterity in their society through the establishment of reciprocal networks. These configurations allow for exchanges with other Indigenous groups in the region, such as Palikurs, Galibi-Kaliñas, and Galibi-Marwornos, with Christian saints and sacred animals, and with powerful Others, including non-indigenous neighbors and state authorities at various levels. Also in Amazonia, in the Upper Xingu region, the Kamayurá (Apùap) epistemological accounting and classification of the acoustic-musical domain includes, besides human actors, the voices and sounds of animals, spirits, and inanimate entities. As Menezes Bastos (2013: 288) argued, this "world hearing" worldview places human and non-humans on the same ontological level, and constitutes a broad regime of perception that stands at a remove, and sometimes in opposition to, encroaching modernity.

Finally, in Bali, as noted by the presence of long-tailed macaques in temple spaces is regarded as a sacred phenomenon, due to the mediation of traditional knowledge about the depiction of monkeys and other primates in Hindu texts. Through an ethnoprimatological approach (Peterson, Riley, and Oka 2015), this apparently simple arrangement is complicated by the fact that it is only Balinese Hindus resident in Bali who associate macaques with sacredness, while their transmigrant counterparts in South Sulawesi, Indonesia, perceive these primates primarily as a destructive presence in and around sacred sites. It is also relevant to recall that some languages possess grammatical categories that codify references to animals on the same plane as humans. A salient case is that of Tunica, a Louisiana language isolate with a gender-number affix paradigm that marks gender, animacy, and number in complex ways, resulting in the assignment of feminine gender as the unmarked possibility for every nominal that refers to non-humans in this language (Heaton and Anderson 2017).

5.2 Materiality and ritual objects

Ritual speech is also deeply intertwined with material elements that are tied to practitioner agency, or which can possess agency and potency in their own right. The links between these can interact as simple patterns, such as the reiterative tapping of a bough bouquet on a patient's body during a Chol Maya healing ritual, a rhythmic movement in coordination with the sequences of a chant that aims to cure targets *kisiñ* 'embarrassment sickness' (Rodríguez and López 2019). Text-artifacts also figure among ritually significant material entities, as is the case in Vietnam, where texts in mortuary rituals regiment mourning and constrict moral personhood (Shohet 2018). The deliberate assemblage of spoken words with a variety of material exchanges, which may include gifts of pigs and buffaloes, also marks collective belonging in localities enmeshed in a center-periphery dynamic in multi-cultural states such as Indonesia (Donzelli 2020).

In other contexts, the meanings of artifacts are closely tied to precise display practices, as is the case among Chagga-speaking people in Tanzania's Kilimanjaro Region. This group's specialists embrace an elaborate protocol for "showing" a variety of items, such as beer, milk, entrails, and finger millet, which have revelatory practices that refer to both the past and the future. The practice of "showing" may not be fully conveyed by the analytical notions of symbol and signification (Myhre 2015), and both this procedure and the substances it highlights may be understood as an enunciation of rhizomatic, ever-changing world "events", to use Gilles Deleuze's influential characterization.

In a return to an anthropological terrain previously delimited by Claude Lévi-Strauss, Sylvia Caiuby Novaes (2016) contextualizes the deployment of an important set of objects in Bororo funerals – in particular, decorated jaguar skins, mortuary gourds, and plaits made of human hair – that index personhood and social categories and structure the sensory modalities that infuse end-of-life celebrations. Furthermore, in some instances, the inclusion of community members in a ceremony hinges on the distribution of objects that help constitute participation frameworks. In southeastern Senegal, the circulation of kola nuts handed out during naming celebrations held for young girls allow both attendees and non-attendees to participate and bear witness to the ceremony, and exclusion from these circuits may result in responses – such as disseminating a teasing denomination for the child – that are understood by community members as a piercing attempt at dissent (Sweet 2019).

6 Concluding remarks

With a focus on anthropological and ethnohistorical research on ritual speech published in the last decade, this essay has argued that successful ritual practice hinges on the construction of authoritative ontological models about the cosmos and its inhabitants, including humans. Ritual speech also orchestrates performances that articulate representations of collective identities, and rests on the diversity of a hierarchical forms of authoritative knowledge. Moreover, this chapter explored the epistemological and ideational terrain on which ritual speech is positioned; discussed several examples of the interdigitation of ritual speech with historical accounts and narratives; investigated the representation of social orders, social differences, and transnational identities in ritual speech; and examined the dynamic relations among ritual practice, materiality, and non-human actors. This essay also summarized several theoretical approaches to the study of ritual speech, which include language ideologies and various accounts of intentionality; discourse-centered analyses that privilege the examination of speech structure; a focus on semiotic chains, semiotic recursivity, and metasemiotic processes; and various emergent models that examine the nexus of social action and ritualized speech practice. In historical terms, this review encompasses ancestor worship in colonial societies and also contemporary rituals involving translocality and migration in a diversity of cultural contexts in the Americas, Asia, and Africa.

Lastly, ritual performances make ambitious epistemic claims about society and also about cosmological, epistemological, and/or natural realms by evoking, depicting, or representing sacred or powerful entities that are frequently perceived as being absent. These apparent absences, which are filled by the metasemiotically calibrated ritual labor of practitioners and audiences, provide a motivation for the summoning of sacred beings across a variety of social contexts. A particularly evocative model for the mapping of these absences in Christianity was developed by Michel de Certeau (1982: 110). This work proposed a "triangular schema" as the structure of mystical discourse: events, symbolic discourse, and social practices rotated around an absent body: that of Christ. Thus, "an initial deprival of the body continually creates institutions and discourses that are the effects and substitutes of this absence" (my translation). While the majority of the cases discussed in this essay go well beyond Certeau's paradigm of absence, they share, at a level that is both intimate and immediate, a cardinal motivation: in order to recreate the world microcosmically, or to welcome and embody powerful beings, or to demarcate a domain that makes salient epistemic contentions, practitioners must engage in demanding ritual labor that takes speech as its principal, but not its proprietary, axis of performance.

References

Ansell, Aaron. 2017. Democracy is a blessing. Phatic ritual and the public sphere in northeast Brazil. *Journal of Linguistic Anthropology* 27. 22–39.

Austin, John Langshaw. 1975. *How to do things with words*. Cambridge, MA: Harvard University Press.

Bacigalupo, Ana Mariella. 2016. *Thunder Shaman. Making history with Mapuche spirits in Chile and Patagonia*. Austin: University of Texas Press.

Bakhtin, Mikhail. 1981. *The dialogic imagination*, translated by Caryl Emerson & Michael Holquist. Austin: University of Texas Press.

Bakker Kellogg, Sarah. 2015. Ritual sounds, political echoes. Vocal agency and the sensory cultures of secularism in the Dutch Syriac diaspora. *American Ethnologist* 42. 431–445.

Ball, Christopher. 2018. *Exchanging words. Language, ritual, and relationality in Brazil's Xingu Indigenous Park*. Albuquerque: University of New Mexico Press.

Bateson, Gregory. 1958. *Naven. A survey of the problems suggested by a composite picture of the culture of a New Guinea tribe drawn from three points of view*, 2nd edition. Stanford: Stanford University Press.

Briggs, Charles L. 1995. The meaning of nonsense, the poetics of embodiment, and the production of power in Warao healing. In Carol Laderman & Marina Roseman (eds.), *The performance of healing*, 185–232. New York: Routledge.

Certeau, Michel de. 1982. *La fable mystique. XVIe – XVIIe siècle*. Paris: Gallimard.

Clark, Cindy D. 2017. Enculturation incarnate. Ritual sensoria in U.S. patriotic holidays. *Ethos* 45. 24–47.

Course, Magnus. 2011. *Becoming Mapuche. Person and ritual in Indigenous Chile*. Urbana: University of Illinois Press.

Cruz, Abelardo de la. 2017. The value of El Costumbre and Christianity in the discourse of Nahua catechists from the Huasteca region in Veracruz, Mexico, 1970's-2010's. In David Tavárez (ed.), *Words and worlds turned around. Indigenous Christianities in colonial Latin America*, 167–288. Boulder: University of Colorado Press.

Dehouve, Danièle. 2018. The New Fire and corporal penance. In Andrew Scherer & Vera Tiesler (eds.), *Smoke, flames and the human body in Mesoamerican ritual practice*, 411–434. Washington, D.C.: Dumbarton Oaks.

Descola, Philippe. 2013. *Beyond nature and culture*. Chicago: University of Chicago Press.

Donzelli, Aurora. 2020. *One or two words. Language and politics in the Toraja Highlands of Indonesia*. Singapore: NUS Press.

Elisha, Omri. 2017. Proximations of public religion. Worship, spiritual warfare, and the ritualization of Christian dance. *American Anthropologist* 119. 73–85.

Enfield, N. J. & Jack Sidnell. 2017. *The concept of action*. Cambridge: Cambridge University Press.

Errington, Joseph. 2007. *Linguistics in a colonial world. A story of language, meaning and power*. New York: Wiley, John and Sons.

Faudree, Paja. 2013. *Singing for the dead. The politics of Indigenous revival in Mexico*. Durham: Duke University Press.

Field, Margaret & Taft Blackhorse Jr. 2002. The dual role of metonymy in Navajo prayer. *Anthropological Linguistics* 44 (3). 217–230.

Fotiou, Evgenia. 2020. The importance of ritual discourse in framing Ayahuasca experiences in the context of Shamanic tourism. *Anthropology of Consciousness* 31. 223–244.

Friedrich, Paul. 1989. Language, ideology and political economy. *American Anthropologist* 91. 295–313.

Goffman, Erving. 1967. *Interaction ritual. Essays on face-to-face behavior*. New York: Doubleday.

Graham, Laura R. 2019. A'ãma Mrémé. A playful window into A'uwê-Xavante language, cognition, and social organization. *Journal of Linguistic Anthropology* 29. 213–220.

Harkness, Nicholas. 2017. Glossolalia and cacophony in South Korea. Cultural semiosis at the limits of language. *American Ethnologist* 44. 476–489.

Heaton, Raina & Patricia Anderson. 2017. When animals become humans. Grammatical gender in Tunica. *International Journal of American Linguistics* 83 (2). 341–363.

Hill, Jane. 1998. Today there is no respect. Nostalgia, respect, and oppositional discourse in Mexicano language ideology. In Bambi Schieffelin, Paul Kroskrity & Katherine Woolard (eds.), *Language Ideologies. Practice and theory*, 68–86. Oxford: Oxford University Press.

Hirschkind, Charles. 2006. *The ethical soundscape. Cassette sermons and Islamic counterpublics*. New York: Columbia University Press.

Hoffman, Katherine E. 2008. *We share walls. Language, land and gender in Berber Morocco.* Malden, MA: Blackwell.

Holbraad, Martin. 2012. *Truth in motion. The recursive anthropology of Cuban divination.* Chicago: University of Chicago Press.

Irvine, Judith. 1989. When talk isn't cheap. Language and political economy. *American Ethnologist* 16 (2). 248–267.

Irvine, Judith & Susan Gal. 2000. Language ideology and linguistic differentiation. In Paul Kroskrity (ed.), *Regimes of language. Ideologies, polities, and identities*, 35–84. Santa Fe: School of American Research.

Johnson, Paul. 2002. *Secrets, gossip, and Gods. The transformation of Brazilian Candomblé.* Oxford: Oxford University Press.

Kapferer, Bruce. 1997. *The feast of the sorcerer. Practices of consciousness and power.* Chicago: University of Chicago Press.

Keane, Webb. 2006. *Christian moderns. Freedom and fetish in the mission encounter.* Berkeley: University of California Press.

Knowlton, Timothy W. 2015. Inscribing the miraculous place. Writing and ritual communication in the chapel of a Guatemalan popular saint. *Journal of Linguistic Anthropology* 25. 239–255.

Kockelman, Paul. 2015. Four theories of things. Aristotle, Marx, Heidegger, and Peirce. *Signs and Society* 3 (1). 153–192.

Kripke, Saul. 1980. *Naming and necessity*. Cambridge: Harvard University Press.

Lambek, Michael. 2002. *The weight of the past. Living with history in Mahajanga, Madagascar.* New York: Palgrave Macmillan.

Lozano, Teresita D. 2015. 'It's a Coptic thing'. Music, liturgy, and religious identity in an American Coptic community. *World of Music* 4 (2). 37–56.

Lupo, Alessandro. 1995. *La tierra nos escucha: La cosmología de los nahuas a través de las súplicas rituales*. Mexico: Consejo Nacional para la Cultura y las Artes, Instituto Nacional Indigenista.

Malinowski, Bronislaw. 1929. *The sexual life of savages in Northwest Melanesia.* London: Routledge.

Malinowski, Bronislaw. 1965. *Coral gardens and their magic.* 2 vols. Bloomington: Indiana University Press.

Matory, J. Lorand. 2005. *Black Atlantic religion. Tradition, transnationalism, and matriarchy in the Afro-Brazilian Candomblé*. Princeton: Princeton University Press.

May, L. Carlyle. 1956. A survey of glossolalia and related phenomena in non-Christian religions. *American Anthropologist* 58 (1). 75–96.

Meiu, George Paul. 2016. Belonging in ethno-erotic economies. Adultery, alterity, and ritual in postcolonial Kenya. *American Ethnologist* 43. 215–229.

Menezes Bastos, Rafael José de. 2013. Apùap world hearing revisited. Talking with 'animals', 'spirits' and other beings, and listening to the apparently inaudible. *Ethnomusicology Forum* 22 (3). 287–305.

Merlan, Francesca. 2014. Recent rituals of Indigenous recognition in Australia. Welcome to country. *American Anthropologist* 116. 296–309.

Mosko, Mark. 2014. Malinowski's magical puzzles. Toward a new theory of magic and procreation in Trobriand society. *HAU: Journal of Ethnographic Theory* 4 (1). 1–47.

Myhre, Knut C. 2015. What the beer shows. Exploring ritual and ontology in Kilimanjaro. *American Ethnologist* 42. 97–115

Novaes, Sylvia Caiuby. 2016. Iconography and orality. On objects and the person among the Bororo. *Gesto, Imagem, e Som: Revista de Antropologia* 1 (1). 88–115.

Olko, Justyna. 2017. The Nahua story of Judas. Indigenous agency and loci of meaning. In David Tavárez (ed.), *Words and worlds turned around. Indigenous Christianities in Colonial Latin America*, 150–171. Boulder: University of Colorado Press.

Peterson, Jeffrey V., Erin P. Riley & Ngakan Putu Oka. 2015. Macaques and the ritual production of sacredness among Balinese transmigrants in South Sulawesi, Indonesia. *American Anthropologist* 117. 71–85.

Posthumus, David C. 2019. The ritual Thiyóšpaye and the social organization of contemporary Lakota ceremonial life. *Journal for the Anthropology of North America* 22 (1). 4–21.

Richards-Greaves, Gillian. 2016. 'Taalk Half, Lef Half'. Negotiating transnational identities through proverbial speech in African Guyanese Kweh-Kweh rituals. *Journal of American Folklore* 129 (514). 413–435.

Robbins, Joel. 2007. You can't talk behind the Holy Spirit's back. Christianity and changing language ideologies in a Papua New Guinea society. In Miki Makihara & Bambi Schieffelin (eds.), *Consequences of contact. Language ideologies and sociocultural transformations in Pacific societies*, 25–39. Oxford: Oxford University Press.

Rodríguez, Juan Luis. 2020. *Language and revolutionary magic in the Orinoco Delta*. New York: Bloomsbury.

Rodríguez, Lydia & Sergio D. López. 2019. Performing healing. Repetition, frequency, and meaning response in a Chol Maya ritual. *Anthropology of Consciousness* 30. 42–63.

Ruiz de Alarcón, Hernando. 1984. *Treatise on the heathen superstitions that today live among the Indians Native to this New Spain (1629)*, translated and edited by J. R. Andrews and R. Hassig. Norman: University of Oklahoma Press.

Rumsey, Alan. 1990. Wording, meaning, and linguistic ideology. *American Anthopologist* 92. 346–361.

Sandstrom, Alan. 1992. *Corn is our blood. Culture and ethnic identity in a contemporary Aztec Indian village*. Norman: University of Oklahoma Press.

Sansi, Roger. 2016. Miracles, rituals, heritage. The invention of nature in Candomblé. *Journal of Latin American and Caribbean Anthropology* 21 (1). 61–82.

Searle, John. 1995. *The construction of social reality*. New York: The Free Press.

Senft, Gunter. 2010. *The Trobriand Islanders' way of speaking*. Berlin: De Gruyter Mouton.

Severi, Carlo. 2012. The arts of memory. Comparative perspectives on a mental artifact. *HAU: Journal of Ethnographic Theory* 2 (2). 451–85.

Sherzer, Joel. 1991. *Verbal art in San Blas. Kuna culture through its discourse*. Cambridge: Cambridge University Press.

Shoaps, Robin. 2009. Ritual and (im)moral voices. Locating the testament of Judas in Sakapultek communicative ecology. *American Ethnologist* 36 (3). 459–477.

Shohet, Merav. 2018. Two deaths and a funeral. Ritual inscriptions' affordances for mourning and moral personhood in Vietnam. *American Ethnologist* 45. 60–73.

Silverstein, Michael. 2009. Private ritual encounters, public ritual indexes. In Gunter Senft & Ellen Basso (eds.), *Ritual communication*, 271–291. Oxford: Berg Publishers.

Stasch, Rupert. 2011. Ritual and oratory revisited. The semiotics of effective action. *Annual Review of Anthropology* 40. 159–74.

Stresser-Péan, Guy. 2009. *The Sun God and the Savior. The Christianization of the Nahua and Totonac in the Sierra Norte de Puebla, Mexico*. Boulder: University of Colorado Press.

Sweet, Nikolas. 2019. Ritual contingency. Teasing and the politics of participation. *Journal of Linguistic Anthropology* 30. 86–102.

Tambiah, Stanley J. 1985. *Culture, thought, and social action. An anthropological perspective*. Cambridge: Harvard University Press.

Tassinari, Antonella. 2015. Saints, animals and outsiders. Rituals and celebrations among the Karipuna from the Curipi River (Amapá, Brazil). *Études rurales* 196 (2). 73–88.

Tavárez, David. 2014. Ritual language. In N. J. Enfield, Paul Kockelman & Jack Sidnell (eds.), *The Cambridge handbook of linguistic anthropology*, 496–516. Cambridge: Cambridge University Press.

Tavárez, David. 2022. *Rethinking Zapotec time. Cosmology, ritual, and resistance in Colonial Mexico*. Austin: University of Texas Press.

Urcid, Javier. 2005. *Zapotec writing. Knowledge, power, and memory in Ancient Oaxaca*. Foundation for the Advancement of Mesoamerican Studies. [http://www.famsi.org/zapo tecwriting] (accessed 28 December 2021).

Viveiros de Castro, Eduardo. 1998. Cosmological deixis and Amerindian perspectivism. *Journal of the Royal Anthropological Institute* 4 (3). 469–488.

Wirtz, Kristina. 2005. "Where obscurity is a virtue". The mystique of unintelligibility in Santería ritual. *Language and Communication* 25 (4). 351–375.

Woolard, Kathryn. 1998. Language ideology as a field of inquiry. In Bambi Schieffelin, Paul Kroskrity & Kathryn Woolard (eds.), *Language ideologies. Practice and theory*, 3–47. Oxford: Oxford University Press.

Wroblewski, Michael. 2019. Performing pluralism. Language, indigeneity, and ritual activism in Amazonia. *Journal of Latin American and Caribbean Anthropology* 24. 181–202.

Alice Mitchell & Anne Storch
9 The unspoken

Let me tell you something, said the old woman.
We were sitting, facing each other,
in the park at _____, a city famous for its wooden toys.

Louise Glück, A sharply worded silence

Linguistic avoidance and taboo are topics of abiding interest for anthropological linguists. Classic anthropological concepts relating to shame, pollution, and danger, as well as sacredness and purity, can shape language use in dramatic ways. This chapter briefly reviews common subjects of taboo in languages – e.g., personal names, death, sex, disease, the supernatural, bodily effluvia, etc. – and discusses the kinds of linguistic creativity and change that such taboos bring about. Here we also highlight areas of verbal taboo which are less well studied, including communicative practices relating to menstruation and female sexuality. This point leads into a discussion of the role of censorship and self-censorship in linguistic research itself, in which we consider how cultural sensibilities and assumptions of researchers regarding what one should and should not talk about influence different stages of the research process. The final part of the chapter takes up the topic of "breaking the silence", emphasizing the ways in which verbal taboos are dynamic aspects of social life, always available for negotiation, resistance, and potential inversion.

1 What remains unspoken

The unspoken (or unsigned) is the name of a city not mentioned, the entire story not told. It is about not letting others know what we know, perhaps out of tactfulness, or embarrassment, or fear of causing offense. It is also the secret not unveiled, the secret words not said: PINs, codewords, the truth about something. Here it differs a bit from Walter Benjamin's public secret which needs to be revealed at certain times in order to unfold its power (Taussig 1999). Sometimes the unspoken is the name of the dead, so that they do not return, or the name of something terrible and powerful, like a bear or a lion. And then the

Alice Mitchell, University of Cologne/Germany, e-mail: alice.mitchell@uni-koeln.de
Anne Storch, University of Cologne/Germany, e-mail: astorch@uni-koeln.de

https://doi.org/10.1515/9783110726626-009

unspoken is part of the language of intimacy, signifying certainty, shared knowledge, and the safety of a long-standing relationship. Or the unspoken might simply result from boredom or disinterest. Here, it comes close to silence, which however differs, by being   instead of _____. The unspoken is also horror, like Kurtz's horror, or like that of grandfathers who had been to war. There were stories told, but the horror was unspoken. Trauma can be the unspoken. And then it is shame and embarrassment. The unspoken is sensual perception, like a particular smell for which there might be no word in a particular language, or an emotion not destined to be put into words, like envy. Also critique, like after sharing one's latest paper with a colleague who will not mention it afterwards. Unspoken is also guilt, as in crime, and anything that needs to be hidden, like undesirable desire. And then the unspoken are words that are forbidden, like *Führer* at a memorial site for the victims of fascism, where the guide may be called *Begleiter* instead, a companion. The unspoken can also be the unwritten. It can then be neglect: not speaking to someone and also not sending a card or a letter, for example to ask for forgiveness for all that unspokenness. The unwritten also concerns languages that are marginalized and thus not easily shared with others, such as Romani (Matras 2014) or Hone (Storch 2011).

Investigating "the unspoken" in linguistics might at a first glance seem absurd. Yet, it is a central part of contemporary anthropological linguistics, where diverse ways of making meaning are explored. Interestingly however, in anthropological linguistics, engagement with the unspoken mostly concerns taboo, although taboo words and language represent only a small part of the unspoken. But why is linguistic taboo, as just one of many diverse aspects of the unspoken, so interesting to anthropological linguists? A partial explanation has to do with linguists' focus on matters of structure and form: prohibited words and alternative vocabularies catch the attention of those attempting to document, describe, and compare languages. Another possible answer might be that such a focus emerges out of a particular genealogy of practice. Being concerned also, if not foremost so, with languages spoken in communities who were made objects of earlier ethnographic description, anthropological linguistics provided insights into what was of interest for European anthropologists: taboo and ritual, for example. In the early-twentieth-century beginnings of relevant disciplines such as African linguistics, the silences of others were often deemed mysterious and religious – in demand of expert knowledge, as they seemed to differ so much from the silences in the colonial center. A hundred years later, a change of perspective had taken place, which resulted in inspiring work with a much wider scope on taboo in language that also included profane practices and censoring, as in Keith Allan and Kate Burridge's seminal work "*Forbidden words*" (2006). Concluding their book, both authors suggest a different reason for linguists' interest in taboo, namely the dynamicity, creativity, and subversion that can be observed there:

> Linguistic prohibition, like other kinds of prohibition and censorship, is doomed to failure in the longer term. Like the worm in the bud, forbidden words feed on censoring imposed by hypocritical decorum. But when we look at the exuberance of expressions that proliferate around the forbidden, it is also clear that we are having a lot of fun. These expressions range from the exquisitely lyrical to the downright crass; yet many demonstrate an expressiveness and poetic ingenuity worthy of William Shakespeare.
>
> (Allan and Burridge 2006: 252–253)

Turning the gaze to the power of language in its constant potential as a norm-breaking device, there is much to learn here about how we not only achieve social coherence, but also challenge it in order to gain individual agency and spur on change. And in a world where language is conceptualized according to hegemonic ideologies of standardization and normed literacy, there is much to learn from decolonial and Indigenous language concepts and ideologies that attach much weight to the power of the secret and of creativity.

This chapter first briefly reviews common subjects of taboo in languages – e.g., personal names, death, sex, disease, the supernatural, bodily effluvia, etc. – and discusses the kinds of linguistic creativity and change that such taboos bring about. Here we also highlight areas of verbal taboo which are less well studied, including communicative practices relating to menstruation. Bleeding becomes a "red thread", to use the German expression, picked up elsewhere in the chapter. We also discuss censorship and self-censorship, including in linguistic work itself, where we consider how different research participants' cultural sensibilities and assumptions about what one should and should not talk about shape their interactions. The final part of the chapter takes up the topic of "breaking the silence", emphasizing the ways in which verbal taboos are dynamic aspects of social life, always available for negotiation, resistance, and potential inversion.

2 Taboo and avoidance in anthropological linguistics

As mentioned, work in anthropological linguistics on linguistic avoidance has paid most attention to taboo linguistic forms and how people work around them in speech, often by way of conventionalized euphemisms or avoidance registers. Subjects of linguistic taboo come from similar conceptual domains across languages: sex and genitalia, bodily effluvia, dangerous animals, supernatural beings, death, and so on (see Allan and Burridge 2006 for a detailed treatment of these areas of language use.) These taboo topics might be theorized in terms of classic anthropological concepts of shame, pollution, and danger, or sacredness and purity, though we need to be careful about making assumptions regarding what is shameful or polluting in a given community, as becomes clear at various points below. While the sources of linguistic taboos can look quite similar in different places, we of course also find cultural and historical particularity in what is considered linguistically out of bounds. Albert (1964: 43), for instance, commented that in 1950s Burundi it was "forbidden to tell what one has eaten for dinner". During Donald Trump's presidency, media commentators noted an unwillingness among his opponents to call Trump by his name, an avoidance behavior Fine (2020: 73–74) also observed among online activists. In addition to semantically motivated word tabooing, linguistic items can become taboo on account of their phonological resemblance to taboo forms, as in the "near-homophone" avoidance that accompanies in-law name avoidance in parts of Africa (see below). And in some cases, entire ways of speaking might be avoided in certain contexts and replaced with alternative linguistic varieties, as in the case of special registers used when hunting or gathering certain foods (see e.g., Franklin 1972), or when talking in the presence of certain in-laws (see e.g., Haviland 1979), or when recently widowed (see Fleming 2014 and references therein).

With respect to taboo and avoidance, Fleming (2011: 160) draws a useful distinction between "context-bound avoidance" and "true unmentionability", the latter reserved for linguistic forms whose performative effect of taboo-breaking – and the subsequent problems this brings about – cannot be undone. While someone might never address their mother with her first name, the name is unproblematic to utter in other contexts, such as when reporting the speech of people who freely use her name. In contrast, with true name taboos, uttering the name always produces the unwanted pragmatic effects of taboo-breaking, even in reported speech. True taboo is a much more restricted phenomenon than context-bound avoidance and has received more attention from linguists, though one can potentially develop into the other (as Fleming 2011 tentatively suggests for name taboos). Though taboo words, expressions, or gestures are difficult to interpret as anything other than "bad" language, regardless of speaker intention or participant framework, taboo forms are often still context-dependent in the sense that they may only apply to certain types of person or settings. Avoidance of the names of wild animals might only be necessary between dusk and dawn, for example, and it is only in certain environments that ordinary speech becomes dangerous (see examples in previous paragraph).

Many linguists have been drawn to taboo on account of its generative properties: the unspoken is a site of innovation and change. The quote in the introduction from Allan and Burridge (2006) describes the creativity and even pleasure that results from artfully sidestepping objectionable language. Fleming and Lempert (2011) also highlight the paradoxical productivity of the prohibited. People invent elaborate and sometimes comic work-arounds for taboo topics (e.g., *Auntie Flo has come to visit* for 'menstruation'), or draw on the resources of other languages (e.g., *derrière* for 'backside') or other modalities (e.g., South African gestures for 'fuck' and other potentially offensive words as documented by Brookes 2004: 202). Taboo concepts are also associated with linguistic instability and flux, since, as is well known, euphemistic forms can become rapidly "infected" themselves by the undesirable concepts they denote, necessitating the creation of new forms and strategies for avoidance. Word tabooing is therefore also of consequence for work in historical and comparative linguistics (Holzknecht 1988, Tuite and Schulze 1998).

In many parts of the world, systematic tabooing has led to the emergence of conventionalized avoidance registers, i.e., sets of linguistic items metapragmatically linked through their specialized linguistic function as substitutes for offending words. In rural Datooga communities, for instance, many married women take part in a respect-driven practice called *gíing'áwêakshòoda*, which involves avoiding the names of one's senior in-laws as well as lexically related and similar-sounding words (see Mitchell 2015 for details). Over time, women have developed a community-wide avoidance vocabulary of alternative expressions for almost all ordinary lexical items. The linguistic scope of some avoidance registers has been extensive enough to often invite the term 'language', e.g., "women's language of respect" (Finlayson 2002) or "brother-in-law language" (Haviland 1979), though these varieties are typically constructed from the materials of one or more 'ordinary' languages. The ways in which avoidance vocabularies map onto the patterns of ordinary speech and how they are related to and embedded in culture-specific ideas and practices of taboo have been one focus in anthropological linguistics (e.g., Dixon 1971, Treis 2005). For those more concerned with language in society, these practices have attracted interest because of their obvious role in mediating sociocultural differences and producing certain kinds of relationships (see e.g., Stasch 2003, Mitchell 2018). And for the study of language variation and change, specialized avoidance registers provide notable evidence of language engineering or "deliberate change" (Thomason 2007).

Avoidance vocabularies used to circumvent taboo linguistic forms have often been presented in the literature as static objects – an impression bolstered by their representation in word lists and tables (Mitchell forthcoming). Where time does enter the picture is typically in discussions of the disappearance of these special forms of speech, though the processes of change which lead to their devaluation and demise have rarely been closely studied. Processes of creation and spread make for an equally interesting topic, one which Hoenigman (2012) captures in her work on "hidden talk" among Awiakay of Papua New Guinea. This special speech variety, in which all Tok Pisin borrowings are replaced by alternative forms, has developed for use during trips to town as a protective strategy for what is perceived to be a high-risk context. Deflecting harm through speech disguise has a rich history in this community, as Hoenigman explains. Through her ethnographic work and attention to spontaneous interaction, we are able to see how Awiakay speakers explicitly link the dangers of travel with patterns of speech (e.g., line 20, p. 202) as well as how avoidance forms are actively negotiated among community members. Part of this negotiation involves policing other people's language: Hoenigman includes an example where one man rebukes another for using a non-disguised form. The metapragmatic policing of taboo language is an understudied dimension of the unspoken and one that may help us understand more about how linguistic taboos, and the sociocultural meanings associated with them, persist or change. For clues about unmentionable topics, outsider linguists might pay attention to metapragmatic reactions to their own communicative blunders. Mitchell was once rebuked by a nine-year-old girl for saying 'snake' at dusk, an episode which pointed to the continued relevance of animal naming taboos in Datooga communities. Such moments also provide a smooth point of entry into a metapragmatic discussion about taboo language.

In addition to the everyday discursive negotiation of prohibited language, avenues for fruitful inquiry might include overlooked or less well studied subjects of taboo. Much has been written about naming prohibitions, for instance, while the way people talk about menstruation and other aspects of sexuality – and even the extent to which these aspects of experience are hidden in the first place – has rarely been addressed in anthropological linguistics, despite the enormous literature on these topics in sociocultural anthropology. One notable exception is Agyekum's (2002) study of the language of menstruation among Akan people of Ghana. He reports that *kyima* 'menstruation' is unmentionable and documents a wide range of euphemisms drawing on domestic, horticultural, and spatial imagery. Central to his analysis is the idea that, although people speak obliquely about menstruation, this phenomenon is represented linguistically not only as polluting and dirty, but also as life-giving and beneficial, reminding us that even "classic" taboo concepts may be multivalent. (The very source for the term 'taboo', the Polynesian concept *tapu*, also bears a double meaning of both forbidden and sacred – see Völkel 2021 for details.) Agyekum's (2002) study also reminds us of the value of identifying emic terms for taboo and avoidance in a given community, as he does for Akan, rather than assuming that "taboo" constitutes a unified category everywhere.

Besides the more obvious topics relating to taboo in anthropological linguistics that we have presented here, there are still others, which often tend to be misunderstood or considered "private", and are therefore perceived as not relevant for understanding an entire community or its language(s). All kinds of topics go unspoken in families and friendship groups and such small-scale avoidance practices may tell us different stories about taboo. Thinking beyond the level of single words and utterances, we can also ask about the unspoken as it shapes our own discipline and understanding of other people's languages – topics to which we now turn.

3 Silence and euphemistic censorship

Not language, but its absence: what is so important about these absences? And what are they – silences, noise, omission, confusion? The unspoken takes on different shapes, and it seems as if it is as diverse as the languages that we tend to position in the void that the unspoken leaves behind. Where there is erasure, it seems, there could always be a word, just which remains to be determined. A Latin word, or a term that forms part of the offensive vocabulary in one's own language such as German or English, or something that stems from another language spoken in one's environment? The "unspoken" does not necessarily mean that no speaking or signing is involved – in fact, it can mean that more words and signs are involved in order to talk about a topic which is not to be mentioned implicitly. And therefore, things that are not said can potentially be expressed in numerous ways, using extensive avoidance language, as is the case with the expression of sexual organs and the bodily effluvia related to them. This is, of course, too simplistic to be sufficient.

"Because it is a taboo" has been a frequent and convenient explanation for not saying something, avoiding a term or keeping silent, when the topic was a language "from the margins", such as almost any African language. Even though highly present in contributions to the anthropological linguistics of these languages, the unspoken and taboo remains framed and presented as fundamentally ahistorical and static, as if it were just self-evident that genitals are not openly referred to and the secretions of the human body were potentially dangerous. Nassenstein (2021) offers a different perspective by illustrating the richness of historical connections and complexity of indexicalities with regards to that what is often simply claimed to be "unspeakable" and thus "taboo" (also Nassenstein and Storch 2020). The presence of rich terminologies for genitalia in youth languages, informal and often playful language spoken in the street or talk shared in bars does not necessarily result out of taboo and prohibition (such as in various cases in different European languages), but speaks of people's creative abilities to claim back sexual sovereignty and to negotiate colonially scripted and potentially harmful gender concepts (Figure 9.1).

Figure 9.1: Sanitary pad playfully arranged on a no-parking sign in El Arenal (Spain), a predominantly heteronormative, white male party destination (Storch 2018).

By bringing the intricate connections into play that form part of constructing and categorizing the "unspoken", our perspective changes: an interaction in which the unspoken is made the topic of linguistic research always also refers to how we negotiate concepts and theories of language and embodiment that are based on the shared experience of the colonial encounter and postcolonial entanglements. In a contribution to a panel on southern theory (Sociolinguistic Symposium 22, Auckland 2019), Nick Faraclas spoke on the taboo of gay sexual practices and queer lifestyles in much of Africa as a result of the introduction of European legislation and Christian missions. Whose taboo and whose unspoken words do explanations of forbidden topics here relate to?

More needs to be asked about the data and analyses we tend to work with. How many linguists working on languages of the Global South have elicited detailed terminology for female genitalia, and from whom? What kinds of cultural ideologies about politeness and taboo structured the course of such discussions? In Enfield's (2006) elicitation guide for studying the semantic typology of the human body, eight basic images of the body are presented: male, front and back, female, front and back, and then "modest" versions of the same with a fig leaf over the pubic area. More detailed representations of genitalia are not included. With what spoken or unspoken assumptions have linguists decided which version of these elicitation tools to use? And did some of their interlocutors feel reminded of the pictures taken of nude people in colonial contexts, meant to support ideologies of racialized inequality? And to what extent is linguistic research on body terminology structured by a "belief that the body comes primarily or exclusively in two types – female and male" (Zimman 2014: 17)? As Zimman explains, such a belief – along with our ideas about the "secret parts" of those bodies – is just as cultural and discursively constructed as gender.

An example of these discursive dynamics at work in intercultural knowledge production comes from Storch's (2011) account of Hone construction of the male body as potentially vulnerable and hence unspeakable, while women's bodies were not. In daily life practice, this meant that male bodies were constructed as non-secreting closed bodies, and men would be careful not to be seen urinating. Elder members of the community claimed that there was a connection with witchcraft and with the fear of women's power stemming from a formerly matriarchal society. As a result, folktales shared in storytelling afternoons were rich in expressions for female genitalia, something that conversation partners and people helping with the translation of these stories found extremely hard to convey, knowing that Storch's own social background was one in which female genitals were taboo and not spoken about. Mitchell had a similar experience while trying to capture everyday conversation in Datooga homesteads. One evening she set up her recording equipment and two teenage girls began singing comical made-up songs full of swear words such as 'your vagina' and 'your father' (see Mitchell 2020 on the offensive potential of kin terms in Datooga). One of the senior women scolded them mildly by saying, "say good words, girls, leave these silly words that someone's going to write down". The evaluation of the appropriateness of the girls' use of bad language was thus strongly linked to the researcher's presence and the fact that these words would be recorded and taken away somewhere. Perhaps the rude song, sung among close female relatives and children in the darkness, would otherwise have gone unremarked upon.

Another episode illustrates cross-cultural mediation of what should go unsaid. During a field trip spent in Pindiga, one of the formerly Hone-speaking villages in north-east Nigeria, Storch stayed in a house close to the market, facing a sandy road busy with passers-by. An old oil barrel in front of the house was to be used as rubbish bin. Easily accessible, the barrel was frequently searched by neighboring children, who one day managed to scatter used sanitary pads all over the little road. How unspoken the obvious could be became discernible immediately: nobody mentioned the incident or referred to the trash in any way. The reason for the neighbors' silence was not the taboo of menstruation in a society that feared the power of the female body. Not at all, as the secretions of the vagina were a frequent topic in stories and songs; it was the knowledge about the taboos of the Europeans and the attempt to help the guest keep face, a complex negotiation of politeness practices and translation. The very public display of the used sanitary pads not only made conceivable the work that is part of hospitality and communication practices in diverse and multilinguistic settings, but also the power of the unspoken. By creating a discursive void that basically belied that which was visible and open, the power of menstrual blood, and more precisely the words for it, were brought into a play which up to this moment had been played differently. The defacement that happened through the search and display of delicate trash was not remedied, but it also was not unfolding any powers that the public secret is supposed to hold in store (Taussig 1999).

In her study on menstrual taboos, Alma Gottlieb analyzes the euphemisms and avoidance terminologies used to refer to menstruation as communicative acts of shame, humiliation and removal of power directed to women, thereby also negating and erasing the "striking diversity of menstrual experiences, especially in the Global South" (Gottlieb 2020: 144). By turning the gaze to precisely these experiences, she comes to a different perspective on taboo: "[. . .] Western interpretations of *tapu* have emphasized an exclusively negative moral valuation of taboo, for reasons [. . .] related to the dominant philosophical orientation of dualism" (Gottlieb 2020: 151). But wouldn't the experience of taboo and the unspoken almost always be part of complex encounters in diverse environments and with diverse participants? And wouldn't therefore the totalitarian constructs based on precisely that dominant philosophical orientation of dualism make us miss the actual power of transgression and the unspoken, namely the capacity of people to find creative ways to deal with such an experience, to remedy the situation and offer healing?

These questions are of some meaning too for those who seek to answer them. The inability to accept diversity and to encounter one another as diverse persons who can connect produces different silences and avoidances. Moreover, these silences and avoidances touch on a very general issue of established publicly accepted perspectives in public and political discourse, reaching beyond the unspoken concerning female bodies but representing related power regimes. In certain contexts it is not only the abject female secretion organ, female voice and body that get silenced (Carson 1995), but also whatever is constructed as related to it – weakness, powerlessness, diminutiveness, and so forth (Aikhenvald 2016). And therefore, at the academic institutions that host research on the unspoken and the unspeakable in the languages of the Global South (and of language elsewhere), crisis can be equally met with silence. No public statement addressing students or teachers to acknowledge the anxieties of those whose academic career will be cut short by the pandemic, and no word of consolation is uttered to those who feel the burden harder than others. Depression and fear are not addressed in any of the sparse letters emailed to them. The crisis is not called by its name, but referred to as a "challenge", in a single story of success. Facing the state of emergency, there is much silence and nothing to give one another, no hospitality and no encounter of the other. The narratives of success at play here can be analysed as strategies to manage contingency; the tales of effectively having met the "challenge" could as well be seen as being related to taboo. Omission can be analyzed as ritual language, referring to the desire that something will not happen. The ritual is about order and power, and secrecy is at its basis. We know that something remains unsaid – must not be said, is unspeakable – but there is nothing to be gained from such knowledge. Silence here is defacing, ridiculing distress and disease. The diversity in experiences of the pandemic remains negated, as only one single story gets told, namely that of success, progress, and overcoming the "challenge". In other words, even though something is always being said – and at times extensively so – the unspoken is also present, as that which does not, and at times *cannot* be said. Denying other realities, silencing particular voices and avoiding people who do not seem to fit ideologically or politically, are manifestations of the unspoken too.

In her work on *"Linguistic diversity and social justice"* (2016), Ingrid Piller has argued that this contradictory discourse is fundamental for understanding how powerful language is that is constructed as bounded, singular and globally valid. It surfaces in various ways, Piller claims: in sociolinguistic research claiming immigration to Europe has become excitingly diverse (or "super-diverse") but at the same time revealing a Eurocentric view on what immigration is and how it typically happens (2016: 22–23), in urban language policy highlighting the brilliance of truly multilingual cities (and counting the numbers of languages spoken there), while speakers of languages other than English or the respective official language face considerable exclusion and marginalization (2016: 1–3), and the celebration of linguistic diversity in a linguistics that hardly takes note of contributions written in any language other than English (2016: 179–180). Linguistic injustice concerns not only the barriers of not being offered hospitality and translation, but also a fundamental exclusion of worldviews and ways of expressing individual experiences.

In other words, the silence imposed on marginalized languages representing linguistic diversity, has two sides: the actual erasure, and the avoidance language hiding erasure. The euphemistic terminologies in which the pandemic is addressed and the euphemistic language in which diversity is referred to seem to have similar functions: hide the very silence into which those who are "diverse" and unsuccessful in meeting the "challenge" are thrown. And as long as the unspoken remains unquestioned, order and power remain intact. The leak, in communication, of the female body, offers other possibilities (MacDonald 2007).

But once the void is addressed, it becomes a game changer. Speaking about the failure to offer hospitality and connections between different people and different social groups, and about the inability to offer solidarity, makes euphemistic avoidance language lose its stigmatizing power over marginalized people. Exposing the stigma thereby means moving words into wrong places. Anette Hoffmann (2021) shows in her essay on scandalous speech how calling the unspoken not by its avoidance name ("challenge") but by what it actually is ("disaster") sets free an enormous power. As she writes about colonial practices of collecting data, she describes the act of collecting what has often been called "data" as cutting a man's face from his skull. And this is exactly what had happened: in 1806, Hinrich Lichtenstein cut off the facial skin of a man whom he had before met and spoken to.

Cutting off his face from his skull: words out of place. Putting them there tends to not remain without punishment, such as referring to a female scholar as having PMS. Quite unsettling, this game. But language out of place is readily there, its potential to change the game just is switched off as long as the power game is on.

4 Breaking silences, filling the void

Anthropologists have long cautioned against understanding taboos as "rules" that are automatically adhered to. Avoidance practices can be scaled up or down and taboos can of course be broken, either spontaneously or in culturally agreed upon circumstances, like during carnivals or rituals, when taboo breaking becomes more powerful than the taboo itself. Datooga women who carefully avoid uttering the names of their senior in-laws in their everyday lives are encouraged to break this taboo when they are in the late stages of labor – a liminal, life-or-death situation in which it becomes acceptable to call on the ancestral spirits of the household. These kinds of exceptional inversions of the forbidden have been the subject of interpretation in symbolic anthropology and folklore. But how does less "controlled" breaking of taboos occur, and with what effects? Can the relaxation (or alternatively, the tightening) of word tabooing help us chart shifts in moral ideologies, perhaps brought about by missionization, formal schooling, or political movements?

Online debates about how to refer to genitalia when addressing children illustrate the conscious deliberation – and Googling – that guides people's word choices regarding taboo subjects. Some people link the use of the "proper" or most direct term for something (in this case Latin-derived terms like "vagina" and "penis", once euphemisms themselves) with increased knowledge of sexuality that might even play a role in promoting consensual sex. Figure 9.2 is taken from the blog of a fertility app which attempts to 'bust misconceptions' about female genitalia – among adults, rather than children – that arise through not talking enough about them.[1] One of their goals is to teach women the difference between the term "vulva" and "vagina", the latter having undergone semantic extension in lay speech to denote the former, as Burridge and Benczes (2018: 186) explain. Others argue that the labels themselves don't matter, only that that they are used openly enough for people to recognize and not feel shame about different parts of their own body. The ways caregivers talk about or studiously ignore sexual topics may provide insights into how the unspoken is reproduced or upturned. In some communities, uninhibited talk about genitals and sex perhaps occurs in reference to animals, rather than humans. (Mitchell recalls a three-year-old Datooga boy pointing to the testicles of a goat that was being skinned and butchered and saying "it's a boy!", an assessment which his mother happily confirmed.)

In the same way that teetering around the edge of the unspoken leads to innovative language use, breaking silences often inspires acts of creativity. A Datooga-speaking nurse who once gave a talk to a group of women about HIV decided to use avoidance words as euphemisms for sex and genitalia. The comical effect of a man (i.e., a non-stereotypical user) using avoidance language presumably lightened the tone of the discussion. For our purposes, this example shows how a single individual creatively and spontaneously adapted the function of avoidance language from words that solve the problem of name tabooing to words that address a different kind of unspoken. Speaking about the unspoken is often the courageous work of activists and artists. Gottlieb (2020) provides multiple examples of creative attempts to break the menstrual taboo in different parts of the world, including the "free bleeding" of women who run marathons while menstruating.

---

1 [https://www.naturalcycles.com/cyclematters/what-is-the-vulva] (accessed 8 June 2021).

5 Vulva Facts You Should Know

Get ready to learn all about the vulva as we answer the question 'what is the vulva?', bust misconceptions and uncover the truths about the vulva we wish everyone knew. Whether you're a verified vulva expert or a knowledge-thirsty novice, grab a coffee, get comfy and join us on this voyage of learning all things vulva.

FEB 4, 2020   4 MIN READ   ✓ Scientifically Reviewed

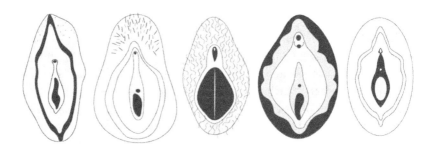

Figure 9.2: Educating women about their genitalia.

Yet, these practices, like the taboo they put into question, have their genealogy. Bleeding in public, putting the menstruating female body "out of place", is not only a strong statement in the framework of current activisms. It also is highly performative and dynamically scripted along pre-existing performances. Third-wave feminism hereby offers a possibility for a creative play with previous feminist movements that have already resulted in a critical debate on the politicization of the discarded, such as the menstruating female body (Bobel 2010, Bobel and Kissling 2011). The work of feminist artists such as Judy Chicago, Kiki Smith and others has focused strongly on menstruation, showing not only menstrual blood, but its emergence, dripping on clothes and furniture, leaving traces. The strong images of the abject and discarded created and exhibited by female artists since the 1960s and 1970s have not only helped to offer different perspectives on female bodies and the diverse experiences of menstruating (and thus abject) women, but also a new way of expressing protest (e.g., Gutiérrez-Albilla 2008, Ross 1997). Bleeding in public could be performed in highly ritualized ways and as an artful performance, instead of being treated as a shameful mistake.

The creative representations of women sharing moments in menstruating, like in Zanele Muholi's photographic work, often also make violence against female bodies visible and thereby show how empowerment through protest and vulnerability remain brutally entangled with one another. In other words, the postcolonial setting of Muholi's photography (among many other African feminist artists and their work) cannot be looked at without having to consider the contradictory discourse they also hint at, which is on continuing imperial formations, where individual sovereignty must be reclaimed over and over again against colonial duress. This experience appears to be central to anthropology and linguistics, Roque (2022) suggests. Because blood has been made matter out of place much more often than in these contributions within the field of abject art. Blood on paper cards, hundreds if not thousands of them, collected during the second part of the twentieth century, in order to create a language map that would make sense of the linguistic diversity of East Timor. Bleeding because one has to, not because one can, Roque argues, is one of the key differences between the players in anthropological linguistic fieldwork in colonial and postcolonial contexts. The "informant" and "speaker" *has to* bleed, the anthropologist or linguist *can* bleed.

5 Some concluding thoughts

The paradoxical nature of the unspoken has resulted in the production of strange, othering texts. While that which is truly unspoken cannot easily be imagined, empirical studies on the unspoken of the Other suggest that it can, as long as it is located in a different place and context. Such simplification of the unspoken resulted, it seems, in often violent methodology and research practice, as well as in a poor understanding of what lies at the base of the description on offer. In the past century, anthropological linguists have mostly encountered the censored in the lexicons of the languages they study but the links between words, discourse, and ideology remain underexplored.

Strands of our discussion here could be conceptualized by future anthropological linguists as an encouragement to seek for a better understanding of this topic, enhance their methodological and theoretical approaches and become more reflexive and sensitive towards Indigenous theory. But there are other possibilities and other dynamics that also come into play. The experience of the pandemic, the failure of populist politicians and neoliberal governments to handle it, and the related increasing competition in an academic environment where resources are dwindling and the brutality of authoritarianism increases have resulted in different perspectives. The gaze is no longer simply on the postcolonial Other but as reflection turned to anthropological linguists' own

This page is intentionally left blank

Figure 9.3: Discursive space intentionally left blank

contexts and positionalities. Silences are broken and debates about institution-alized racism, continuation of colonial and imperial formations in knowledge production as well as gender inequalities in academia fill a void that has long been ignored. The inability of the bureaucratic university to mourn the losses of victims of the pandemic, and to address the human failures that lead to so much death, to deal effectively with institutionalized inequality that has made particular people extremely vulnerable during the crisis, made female scientists and southern scholars lose out in many cases, leads to a change in how we want to play the academic game (Figure 9.3).

References

Aikhenvald, Alexandra Y. 2016. *How gender shapes the world*. Oxford: Oxford University Press.

Agyekum, Kofi. 2002. Menstruation as a verbal taboo among the Akan of Ghana. *Journal of Anthropological Research* 58 (3). 367–387.

Albert, Ethel M. 1964. "Rhetoric," "logic," and "poetics" in Burundi. Culture patterning of speech behavior. *American Anthropologist* 66 (6). 35–54.

Allan, Keith & Kate Burridge. 2006. *Forbidden words. Taboo and the censoring of language*. Cambridge: Cambridge University Press.

Bobel, Chris. 2010. *New blood. Third-wave feminism and the politics of menstruation*. New Brunswick: Rutgers University Press.

Bobel, Chris & Elizabeth Arveda Kissling. 2011 Menstruation matters. Introduction to representations of the menstrual cycle. *Women's Studies* 40 (2). 121–126.

Brookes, Heather. 2004. A repertoire of South African quotable gestures. *Journal of Linguistic Anthropology* 14 (2). 186–224.

Burridge, Kate & Réka Benczes. 2018. Taboo as a driver of language change. In Keith Allan (ed.), *The Oxford handbook of taboo words and language*, 179–198. Oxford: Oxford University Press.

Carson, Anne. 1995. The gender of sound. In *Glass, irony and God*, 119–142. New York: New Directions.

Dixon, R.M.W. 1971. A method of semantic description. In Danny D. Steinberg & Leon A. Jakobovits (eds.), *Semantics. An interdisciplinary reader in philosophy, linguistics, and psychology*, 436–471. Cambridge: Cambridge University Press.

Enfield, N. J. 2006. Elicitation guide on parts of the body. *Language Sciences* 28 (2). 148–157.

Faraclas, Nicholas. 2019. A critical analysis of neo-colonial discourse promoting homophobia in the Anglophone countries of the Caribbean and the Afro-Atlantic. Paper presented at the *Sociolinguistics Symposium* 22, 27–30 June 2018, University of Auckland.

Fine, Julia C. 2020. #MagicResistance. Anti-Trump witchcraft as register circulation. *Journal of Linguistic Anthropology* 30 (1). 68–85.

Finlayson, Rosalie. 2002. Women's language of respect: isihlonipho sabafazi. In Rajend Mesthrie (ed.), *Language in South Africa*, 279–296. Cambridge: Cambridge University Press.

Fleming, Luke. 2011. Name taboos and rigid performativity. *Anthropological Quarterly* 84 (1). 141–164.

Fleming, Luke. 2014. Negating speech. Medium and modality in the development of alternate sign languages. *Gesture* 14 (3). 263–296.

Fleming, Luke & Michael Lempert. 2011. Introduction. Beyond bad words. *Anthropological Quarterly* 84 (1). 5–13.

Franklin, Karl J. 1972. A ritual Pandanus language of New Guinea. *Oceania* 43 (1). 66–76.

Glück, Louise. 2014. *Faithful and virtuous night.* New York: Farrar, Straus & Giroux.

Gottlieb, Alma. 2020. Menstrual taboos. Moving beyond the curse. In Chris Bobel, Inga Winkler, Breanne Fahs, Katie Ann Hasson, Elizabeth Arveda Kissling & Tomi-Ann Roberts (eds.), *The Palgrave handbook of critical menstruation studies*, 143–162. London: Palgrave Macmillan.

Gutiérrez-Albilla, Julián Daniel. 2008. Desublimating the body. Abjection and the politics of feminist and queer subjectivities in contemporary art. *Journal of the Theoretical Humanities* 13 (1). 65–84.

Haviland, John B. 1979. Guugu Yimidhirr brother-in-law language. *Language in Society* 8 (3). 365–393.

Hoenigman, Darja. 2012. From mountain talk to hidden talk. Continuity and change in Awiakay registers. In Nicholas Evans & Marian Klamer (eds.), *Melanesian languages on the edge of Asia. Challenges for the 21st century* (LD&C Special Publication 5), 191–218. Honolulu: University of Hawai'i Press.

Hoffmann, Anette. 2021. Skandalträchtig drauflosreden. Vorschlag zur Entsachlichung des Sprechens von der Erbeutung von Körpern, Objekten, und von Praktiken der kolonialen Linguistik in vier Stücken. *The Mouth* 9. 11–30.

Holzknecht, Susanne. 1988. Word taboo and its implications for language change in the Markham family of languages, PNG. *Language and linguistics in Melanesia* 18. 43–69.

MacDonald, Shauna M. 2007. Leaky performances. The transformative potential of menstrual leaks. *Women's Studies in Communication* 30 (3). 340–357.

Matras, Yaron. 2014. *I met lucky people. The story of the Romani Gypsies.* London: Penguin.

Mitchell, Alice. 2015. Words that smell like Father-in-Law. A linguistic description of the Datooga avoidance register. *Anthropological Linguistics* 57 (2). 195–217.

Mitchell, Alice. 2018. Allusive references and other-oriented stance in an affinal avoidance register. *Journal of Linguistic Anthropology* 28 (1). 4–21.

Mitchell, Alice. 2020. "Oh, bald father!" Kinship and swearing among Datooga of Tanzania. In Nico Nassenstein & Anne Storch (eds.), *Swearing and cursing. Contexts and practices in a critical linguistic perspective*, 79–101. Berlin: De Gruyter Mouton.

Mitchell, Alice. Forthcoming. Documenting difference. Interactional approaches to the documentation of special registers. In Richard Sandoval & Nicholas Williams (eds.), *Interactional approaches to language documentation* (Language Documentation and Conservation SP). Honolulu, Hawai'i: University of Hawai'i Press.

Nassenstein, Nico. 2021. On metaphor and taboo. Labeling sex organs in African youth language practices. Paper presented at *WOCAL* 10, 7–12 June 2021, University of Leiden.

Nassenstein, Nico & Anne Storch. 2020. *Metasex – The discourse of intimacy and transgression.* Amsterdam: John Benjamins.

Piller, Ingrid. 2016. *Linguistic diversity and social justice.* Oxford: Oxford University Press.

Roque, Ricardo. 2022. Bleeding languages. Blood types and linguistic groups in the Timor Anthropological Mission. *Current Anthropology*. [https://www.journals.uchicago.edu/doi/10.1086/719788] (accessed 26 May 2022).

Ross, Christine. 1997. Redefinitions of abjection in contemporary performances of the female body. *RES: Anthropology and Aesthetics* 31. 149–156.

Stasch, Rupert. 2003. Separateness as a relation. The iconicity, univocality and creativity of Korowai mother-in-law avoidance. *The Journal of the Royal Anthropological Institute* 9 (2). 317–337.

Storch, Anne. 2011. *Secret manipulations. Language and context in Africa.* New York: Oxford University Press.

Taussig, Michael. 1999. *Defacement.* Stanford: Stanford University Press.

Thomason, Sarah G. 2007. Language contact and deliberate change. *Journal of Language Contact* 1. 41–62.

Treis, Yvonne. 2005. Avoiding their names, avoiding their eyes. How Kambaata women respect their in-laws. *Anthropological Linguistics* 47 (3). 292–320.

Tuite, Kevin & Wolfgang Schulze. 1998. A case of taboo-motivated lexical replacement in the indigenous languages of the Caucasus. *Anthropological Linguistics* 40 (3). 363–383.

Völkel, Svenja. 2021. Tongan honorifics and their underlying concepts of mana and tapu. A verbal taboo in its emic sense. *Pragmatics & Cognition* 28 (1). 26–57.

Zimman, Lal. 2014. The discursive construction of sex. Remaking and reclaiming the gendered body in talk about genitals among trans men. In Lal Zimman, Jenny L. Davis & Joshua Raclaw (eds.), *Queer excursions. Retheorizing binaries in language, gender, and sexuality*, 13–34. Oxford: Oxford University Press.

Luke Fleming
10 Social indexicality

This chapter offers a dedicated treatment of social indexicals: patterned phonological, morphological, or lexical alternations that stereotypically, but nonreferentially, index particular social identities, relationships, or worlds. Drawing
on a wide range of empirical examples involving the indexing of social gender, I
argue that in modeling social indexicality we must distinguish and track the interaction between three distinct dimensions of the sociolinguistic sign: indexical
features, indexical functions, and indexical focus. The features of a social index
are the social attributes or cultural qualities which tokens of the index recur-
rently reflect or make manifest in interaction. By the function of the social index
we distinguish between indexicals which merely provide social information
about the person indexed versus those which performatively enact qualities of
relationship, like respect or disdain. Finally, the focus of the index is how the
person or persons indexed are picked out. Relying upon the coordinate systems
of interactions roles, indexical focus provides the instructions for determining
who is the origo (or source) and who is the target of the index. The paper explores the interaction between these parameters, finishing by highlighting the
way in which a particular indexical functional modality – indefeasible performativity – causes the "denaturalization" of the interactional role primitives of
Speaker, Addressee, and Referent upon which the indexical focus system is
scaffolded.

1 Introduction

The goal of this chapter is to provide a scaffold for the comparative study of
type-level *social indexicality* in language: socially patterned phonological, morphological, or lexical alternations that stereotypically, but nonreferentially,
index particular social identities, relationships, or worlds. Efferent linguistic
signs – whatever their propositional content – always also additionally invoke
supplementary social significations. The nonreferential invocation of social
meanings by linguistic forms implies that those forms are interpreted as indexical
signs; that is, linguistic signs are here understood to point to, or make manifest,
sociocultural meanings in the contexts of their occurrence (Silverstein 1976).

Luke Fleming, University of Montreal/Canada, e-mail: luke.fleming@umontreal.ca

https://doi.org/10.1515/9783110726626-010

Social meanings may be interactionally emergent; significations produced by the intratextual patterning of sign-tokens, as in "poetic parallelism" (Jakobson 1960), or by intertextual relations between them, as in "voicing" (Bakhtin 1981), are often emergent effects (Agha 2007: 16).

In this chapter we will not focus on emergent social indexicality. Rather, we will dedicate our discussion to type-level or stereotyped social indexicality. "Slang" vocabularies or phonolexical "accents" are linguistic repertoires whose social meanings are not wholly emergent in interaction, but rather have some constancy across social space and time. These are linguistic alternations which are associated with particular social meanings for a network of individuals socialized to those stereotypes across some relevant historical horizon – the "social domain" of the register (Agha 2007: 15). Such type-level social indexicality may be grounded in a statistical or frequency-based relationship between the occurrence of sign-types and contextual-variables (Silverstein 1985). The relationship which Labov (1966 [2006]) discovered between post-vocalic /r/ and the social class of the speech animator in 1960s New York City was a statistical relationship of this sort. But there are some social indexicals for which the relationship between sign-vehicle and pragmatic act or social attribute approaches being a categorical one. It is social indexical types of this last sort – honorific vocabularies, baby talk registers, categorical gender indexical alternations, etc. – which constitute the core concern of this chapter.

This empirical domain has been subject to important investigation and theorization in the work of Stephen Levinson (1983) under the label of "social deixis", a term intended to pick out "those aspects of language structure that encode the social identities of participants (properly, incumbents of participant-roles), or the social relationship between them, or between one of them and persons and entities referred to" (ibid.: 89). Although Levinson's approach has been productive, pushing field workers to observe and document social indexical phenomena in more granular detail, there are some shortcomings with that approach (see also Footnote 7 for further critical engagement). For one thing, the use of "deixis" (after Fillmore 1975) obscures more than it elucidates. There are good reasons to reserve the term "deixis" for those hybrid signs which involve both a symbolic/ semantic component and an indexical/pragmatic one – that is, for Jakobsonian shifters (Hanks 1992: 96, Manning 2001: 55). By using "deixis" to cover both referential indexicals, like pronouns, and purely pragmatic indexicals, like accents, the important distinction between the functionally uniform phenomenon of denotational indexicality, on the one hand, and the heterogeneous and variegated domain of purely pragmatic (social) indexicality, on the other, is papered over. As Manning (2001) has shown, even if we do restricted the term "deixis" in this manner, "social deixis" continues to pick out a salient class of sociolinguistic phenomena: formal alternations that *referentially* index social distinctions (for instance, pronouns referentially indexical of segmentary lineages in Ku Waru; Merlan and Rumsey 1991).

A more substantive problem with Levinson's approach is the notion that "socially deictic" alternations "encode" social categorical distinctions. This effectively collapses a multi-tiered relationship between sociopragmatic norms and discursive practices (cf. Agha 1993a: 133). That is, it misrecognizes the complex and typologically variable relationship between (metapragmatic) stereotypes about social indexicals, on the one hand, and their actual pragmatic effects in interaction, on the other, as something akin to a morphosemantic coding relationship. Once again, denotational indexicality or deixis is inappropriately being drawn upon to model the space of (social) indexical phenomena which, because they are freed from the constraints of referential function, can be home to a much more heterogeneous and open-ended range of semiotic processes.

My goal in this chapter will be to provide an analytic framework that will be heuristic for those studying type-level social indexicality and for evaluating cross-linguistic comparability, or not, of social indexical formations. Through a range of examples loosely strung together by the theme of gender indexicality, I argue that we must *minimally* consider three distinct parameters if we are to ground social indexicality as an empirical domain of comparative or typological investigation. We must attend to indexical features, indexical foci, and indexical functions.

(1.) By "features" of the index I mean the social attributes or social differences that are invoked by occurrences of the index. As I will show, these indexical features may be structured in a manner equivalent to semantic features in grammar or by means of social stereotypes of a quite different kind. (2.) By the "function" of the index, I mean the kind of social activity that is accomplished in and through the deployment of tokens of the index, and the relative indefeasibility of such accomplishments. Some social indexicals merely characterize a particular social attribute or difference independent of the propositional content of the utterance (e.g., characterize speaker gender [Garifuna] or characterize the relative ["even" or "odd"] generation membership of the speaker-referent dyad [Adnyamathanha]). For lack of a better term, I will characterize indexes of this kind as having an *informative function*. Other social indexicals, like honorifics and anti-honorifics, are resources drawn upon to accomplish culturally specific performative acts, like enacting respect and disdain. We will characterize these as having a *performative function*. (3.) By the "focus" of the index I mean the interactional roles like "speaker of the index" or "addressee of the index" that are occupied by the individuals whose social characteristics and differences relative to one another are presupposed or entailed in and through the deployment of tokens of the social indexical (Agha 1993a). As we will show, indexical focus may be sensitive to (really, *denatured by*) indexical function. Closely paralleling the tripartite structure of grammatical person, social indexicals in "informative function" relate the interactional role primitives of Speaker [= S], Addressee [= A], and Referent [=R]. Social indexicals in "performative function" often index inhabitants of these same roles. However, where the performative functions of anti-honorific or taboo variants are indefeasible, honorifics may index a parallel but more absorptive set of interactional roles (i.e., Animator [=An.], Recipient [=Rec.], and Nonparticipant [=N]).

Taken together, then, we are concerned to understand social indexicality as a phenomenon wherein linguistic signals employed to accomplish particular social acts [functions] presume a particular sociocultural sketch or characterization [features] of the social identities of (or relations between) the individuals occupying particular interactional roles [foci] with respect to those signals.

As already intimated, these three parameters are complexly interrelated. As with any typological study, in elucidating the range of variation within any one of these dimensions we must try and control for variation in the other dimensions. My method of exposition will be to proceed from cases of nonreferential indexicality most formally and functionally parallel to referential indexicality and move, by degrees, into a semiotic field that is less recognizable from the standpoint of structural linguistics. As we will see, there are two broad classes of nonreferential person indexicals; those that are distinguished from referential indexicals (or deictics) in terms of speech act *function* and those that are distinguished only in terms of their indexical *focus* properties. We begin with the second kind first.

2 Pragmatic gender and indexical focus

As a point of departure, we look at the categorical indexing of social gender. In most languages-in-culture, the use of "gendered" language is entangled with other sociocultural projects (Ochs 1992), like the expression of affect and emotion (Kulick 1992), and is an important semiotic resource for the performative constitution of sexual or gendered identities. The variable deployment of creaky voice in American English, for instance, is a resource that language users draw upon to accomplish an analog or gradient indexing of gender, among other qualities of social identity. Ways of speaking which we readily understand as "gendering" (typically, but not exclusively, the speaker of the utterance) contrast markedly with the ways in which semantic gender features encoded in linguistic form are employed to reflect and reproduce the social genders of discourse referents. In the latter instance, language users are faced with a set of symbolic and discrete (even digital) categorical distinctions from which they must choose (e.g., MASCU-LINE, MIXED, FEMININE, NEUTER, etc. genders). In all languages (even in those lacking "grammatical gender") social gender is symbolically encoded in this manner. So, for instance, social gender is a distinctive feature in all kinship terminologies (e.g., English G^{+1} ['mother': 'father']:: G^0 ['sister': 'brother']:: G^{-1} ['daughter': 'son'], where 'G' = generation). Within this domain, relevant local cultural ontologies of gender, and the associated rites and procedures by which gender is 'attributed' to individuals (e.g., Putnamian denotational stereotypes, Austinian rites of gender baptism, etc.), establish the authority (or its opposite) for the 'extension' of semantic genders in reference to particular individuals.[1]

---

1 Even the most structural of semantic gender features as these are extended in human reference routinely involve backing from social stereotypes, and in some languages-in-culture those stereotypes presume upon "criteria" (Putnam 1996:230) which cultures of science have drawn upon in defining biological sexes as natural kinds (see Aikhenvald 2016 and McConnell-Ginet 2014 for contrasting perspectives on how biological sex, social gender, and grammatical gender are linked up to one another). Notably, contemporary language politics concerning gendered pronominal reference in Standard Average European language communities involve the emergence of new ideologies of person reference which have the effect of destabilizing publically observable signs (or "gender performance" in the sense of Butler 1988) as the sufficient grounds for 'appropriate' gendered reference. Thus, for instance, the solicitation that one provide one's preferred 3rd person pronouns (e.g., *they/them/their*) enacts an ideology of language where semantic gender "extended" in human reference depends not upon the language structural backing of the grammatical gender of the head noun (e.g., French *la sentinelle* 'the guard' as feminine regardless the social gender of the referent; after Wechsler 2009) nor upon denotational stereotypes (in the sense of Putnam 1996) which draw upon emblems of gender (e.g., dress, comportment, sexed bodies, etc.) to determine the "appropriate" semantic gender to be employed in "correct" reference, but rather upon "explicitly" performative auto-baptism. That is, this linguistic ideology (which is simultaneously an ideology of gender) privileges self-ascription by means of discrete, symbolic, gender categorical distinctions as *the* overriding determinant of gender ascription. Within this ideological framework, the auto-baptism is not performative of gender identity itself, which may be conceptualized as timeless. Rather, it discloses this aspect of identity to others. Gender disclosing acts in this way appear to be structured in an analogous manner to rites of "coming out" within gay communities, rites that similarly do not change sexual identities but only their social facticity (Chirrey 2003). Gendered reference under these conditions becomes equivalent to rigid designation in the mode of personal names (Kripke 1980). That is, semantic gender is rigidly indexical of particular individuals rather than of natural kinds. Just as with a name, a semantic gender is assigned to a social person through an explicit baptismal act of gender disclosure and reproduced through a speech chain linking any given act of felicitous gender-characterizing reference to that individual to an originating and sanctioning auto-baptismal event. Note that the formulaic presentation of "one's pronouns" in

So we have gender in two modes. On the one hand, we have an iconic-indexical and necessarily performative "gender*ing*" through the deployment of gender stereotyped (or *engendered*) linguistic and non-linguistic signs. These signs may be deployed in complex ways that involve transposable voicing effects that thus "gender" not the speaker but a distinct indexical focus, like speech recipient (Harvey 2002). On the other hand, we have a symbolic and necessarily categorical division into distinct classes, categories or (grammatical) genders. Crucially, gender in this second, symbolic mode of semantic categorization is incorporated into the propositional form of utterances such that social gender itself becomes an object of reflexive conceptual engagement and reflection.

On the influential account of Butler (1988), it would appear that the stability and discreteness of gender categories manifest in the second, symbolic mode is forever doomed to fail to capture the much more complex iconic-indexical enactment of social gender in the first mode. In actual social life, the explicit and denotational categorization of social gender in linguistic symbolism can only at best be approximated by a relentless and endless discursive praxis whereby the cumulative co-textual cohesion and coherence of gender shibboleths across different signaling media and across text-segments is precisely the "iterative" semiotic substance out of which one "does gender" in its normative mode (cf. Agha 2007: 337 on "degrees of [register] cohesion"). Such praxis in turn requires entrained techniques of repression and suppression or, alternatively, of reflexivity and hyper-vigilance, making this an important site of subject formation in those societies where this kind of mirroring relationship between the enactment of gender and the symbolic classification of genders is attested. "Discrete genders are part of what 'humanizes' individuals within contemporary culture; indeed, those who fail to do their gender right are regularly punished" (Butler 1988: 522).

Though rare, in some languages there are repertoires of linguistic forms that nonreferentially index social gender in a manner continuous with the denotation of social gender in the symbolic mode. We can call these "*categorical*

---

the ordering nominative/accusative/genitive tropically invokes the ordered oral recitation of Latin declensions, the emblematic top-and-center of institutionalized prescriptive grammar. This trope involves a "citational reversal" (Butler 1997) of canons of "correct usage". In the high-modern mode, the idea of "correct" language made appeal alternatively to aesthetics, tradition or reason under the framework of grammaticality. In this post-modern mode, prescriptive grammar is transposed into a moral register concerned with the ethical disclosure and withholding of social gender as a proprietary substance of the self.

gender indexicals" (after Silverstein 1985, Fleming 2012, Rose 2015, Bakker 2019). To exemplify this phenomenon we draw upon Mary Haas' (1944) foundational treatment of her own fieldwork data from Koasati (Muskogean; historically American Southeast). In Koasati, morphophonological alternations in verbal suffixes in the indicative and imperative moods can only be accounted for by making appeal to the social gender of the speaker (whether the actual speaker in the here-and-now <u>signaling event</u> $[S/E^s]$ or the represented <u>speaker</u> in a <u>narrated event</u> $[S/E^n]$) of the utterance. Importantly, these alternations are not limited to 1st person reference but also occur in 3rd person reference. Thus, for instance, *lakáw* and *lakáws* both mean 'He is lifting it'; *mól* and *móls* both mean 'He is peeling it.' These paired variants have the same propositional content. So what is the difference in signification? The forms ending in /-s/ nonreferentially index the masculine social gender of the occupant of the speaker role. The forms ending in /-Ø/ nonreferentially index the feminine social gender of the speaker. These are thus speaker-focal gender indexical alternations.[2]

Information gleaned from the use of categorical gender indexicals does not constitute part of the propositional content of the utterances in which these signals occur. Nevertheless, and importantly, the "characterizing properties" (Hanks 1992) of categorical gender indexicals are not different in kind from those of semantic gender markers as these are extended in indexical reference to persons. Just as with semantic genders, they characterize the indexical focus as either of masculine or feminine gender. The sole difference between categorical gender indexicals and semantic gender as employed in indexical reference (e.g., 3rd person singular pronominal reference to a particular individual in American English) is in the indexical focus to which the gender feature is applied (see Rose 2013 for a demonstration of this complementarity for pronominal paradigms). It is not the kind of social information that is communicated, but whom it is communicated about, that

---

2 Following the convention fashioned by Ribeiro's (2006) in his treatment of Karajá data, we will denote this pragmatic gender distinction with the "male" and "female" symbols, i.e., *lakáw*$_{S♀}$ and *lakáws*$_{S♂}$. (The subscript letter denotes the indexical focus to which the gender feature is applied, where S = Speaker, A = Addressee and R = Referent.) The use of these symbols implies no differential commitment to biological sex as the basis for distinguishing social gender in the pragmatic as opposed to semantic mode. Gender ideologies and stereotypes are equally important in determining semantic and pragmatic gender assignation to persons (see Note 1 above). Rather, the distinctive ways of denoting the gender feature – either as MASCULINE versus FEMININE or as ♂ versus ♀ is meant to highlight the different domain of application (semantic versus pragmatic, respectively) of the gender feature. In Karajá (Macro-Gê), morphophonological variants – like the alternation between /k/ and /Ø/ – presuppose the masculine or feminine social gender of the speaker irrespective the gender of addressee or referent (see Fortune and Fortune 1975 for a dedicated description).

distinguishes gender as it is incorporated into person deixis and categorical nonreferential gender indexicality. What linguists readily recognize as sex-based semantic gender "extended" in indexical reference – henceforth *gender deixis* – is the special case where gender features are exclusively applied to a set of interactional roles consisting solely of discourse referents. Where the gender feature is indexically attributed to a set of individuals not equivalent to the referential set, we have *pragmatic gender*.

We exemplify this complementarity between semantic gender (as instantiated in reference to specific persons) and pragmatic gender (as instantiated in the nonreferential indexing of the occupants of particular interactional roles) in Figure 10.1. The figure is schematic, providing only exemplification of representative formal alternations in which social gender is indexed rather than providing any systematic inventory and description. In the top half of Figure 10.1 (labeled "Absolute Focus") we have schematized systems where a gender feature is applied to only one interactional role primitive. Gender indexical systems of this sort have an *absolute* (or one-place) *indexical focus* (adapting terminology from Levinson 1983 and Agha 1993a). Paralleling the tripartite (1st, 2nd, and 3rd) structure of grammatical person for the domain of referential person indexicality, gender features may be applied to one of the following three interactional roles: (1.) the speaker [S] of the indexical token, (2.) the addressee [A] of the indexical token, or (3.) the referent [R] of the indexical token. We have already seen that Koasati (top right) is a case of speaker-focal gender indexicality: the social gender of the speaker is presupposed independent of the social gender of the addressee or the referent. Contrastingly, Basque represents an addressee-focal system – verb-final particles presuppose the social gender of addressee irrespective the gender of the speaker or the referent. For instance, *diagok*$_{A\male}$ 'he/she/it stays' [addressed to a man] contrasts with *diagon*$_{A\female}$ 'he/she/it stays' [addressed to a woman] (Alberdi 1995). Finally, there are gender deictic alternations like those between the English anaphors *he* and *she*, where the alternation presupposes the social gender of the referent regardless the gender of the speaker or the addressee. (On the selection of appropriate semantic gender as a function of the social gender of the discourse referent see Wechsler 2009 and Corbett 1991 on "hybrid nouns".)

In the bottom half of Figure 10.1 (labeled "Relational Focus") we have presented languages where gender features apply to the union of more than one interactional role primitive. These are languages where gender indexicality has a **relational** (or minimally two-place) **indexical focus**. In these cases a gender feature is quantified over a set produced by summing the genders of two or more interactional role atoms. For the case of the Speaker-Addressee dyad we have the

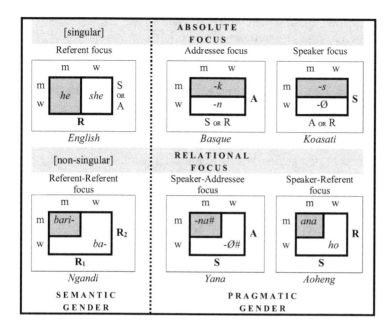

Figure 10.1: The difference between semantic gender and pragmatic gender is a matter of indexical focus.[3]

well-known case of Yana (Sapir 1985: 206–207). Word-final morphophonological alternations in Yana distinguished Speaker-Addressee dyads that were exclusively masculine from all other possible dyads. (Though Sapir's article was entitled "*Male and female forms of speech in Yana*" he makes the perspicacious remark that "[t]he terms 'male' and 'female' are not entirely adequate, for the male forms are used only by males in speaking to males, while the female forms are used by females in speaking to males or females and by males in speaking to females" Sapir 1985: 206.) For the case of the Speaker-Referent dyad we have provided the case of Aoheng, a language of Borneo (after Sellato 1981). Aoheng has two 3rd person singular anaphors, one employed by men in referring to men (*ana*) and another (*ho*) employed in all other configurations (i.e., S_m-R_w or S_w-R_w or S_w-R_m). For the case of Referent-Referent dyads we have the case of Ngandi, an Australian language. In Ngandi, the dual prefix *bari-* is only employed where

---

3 Abbreviations: S = Speaker; A = Addressee; R = Referent; m = man; w = woman. The marks "w" and "m" characterize the social gender of the occupant of the interactional role indicated on the opposite side of the box.

both referents are men, in all other configurations (i.e., $R1_m$-$R2_w$ or $R1_w$-$R2_w$ or $R1_w$-$R2_m$) the form *ba-* is employed (Heath 1978: 35).[4]

As we can see, what distinguishes semantic gender from pragmatic gender is not the character of the characterizing property or feature but rather the indexical focus to which that feature is applied. Semantic gender deixis sensu stricto is the special case where gender features exclusively characterize the social gender of discourse referents. When gender features are applied to any other interactional role or combinations of them we have pragmatic gender. For social indexicals in "informative function", pragmatic feature application can be provisionally defined in the following manner: *For a feature to have a pragmatic application it must be applied to an indexical focus at least one of whose components is not contained in the denotation of the expression in question.*[5]

From this perspective, sex-based semantic gender (Corbett 1991) comes to be seen as only one possible way of articulating social gender (qua "characterizing property" of linguistic form) with interactional role. To be sure, the anchoring of social gender to the occupant of the "referent of" role is the most common and generative type cross-linguistically, yielding the diachronic emergence of elaborate noun class systems which are by no means limited to human nouns (Corbett 2013). Nevertheless, from a strictly typological viewpoint such referent focal gender indexicality is a special case.

---

4 Fleming (2015) provides a more sustained defense of the analysis of Speaker-Referent cases like Aoheng as cases of pragmatic gender rather than as semantic gender. Let me quickly review that argument. On a feature account, there are two ways to analyze a language like Aoheng. We can interpret *ana* as involving the instantiation of a [+/- masculine] feature both to an absolute referent-focus (in the semantic domain) and to an absolute speaker-focus (in the pragmatic domain). Alternatively, and more parsimoniously, we can interpret *ana* as instantiating the feature [+/- masculine] to a relational Speaker-Referent focus. This second treatment is not only more parsimonious, it also brings cases where monadic gender features are applied to Speaker-Referent pairs into line with the treatment of Speaker-Addressee gender indexicality in Yana (Sapir 1985: 206–207) and Kurux (Ekka 1972).

5 For a case that poses problems for this analysis, see Uranw 2009 on Nepalese Kurux. Indian Kurux exhibits Speaker♀-Addressee♀ focal categorical gender indexicality in its pronominal paradigm (Ekka 1972). Nepalese Kurux (also called Uranw-Kurux) has a slightly different system. Here, the same forms which instantiate the S♀-A♀ in Indian Kurux function as speaker-focal gender indexicals, but only in 1st person forms. Though these forms do characterize the gender of one of the referents (i.e., the speaker), in the 1st inclusive and exclusive plural forms they do not characterize the gender of occupants of any role other than that of speaker. This appears to represent a system truly intermediate between pragmatic and semantic gender. Perhaps this is a historically transitional form as the system of pragmatic gender is re-analyzed as gender deixis.

All of the cases discussed thus far are ones where social gender is encoded as a *monadic feature*. That is, the indexical features [+/- masculine] and [+/- feminine] can be applied to one and only one interactional role (i.e., a monad). Categorical social indexicals with absolute focus always apply monadic features. But monadic features may also be applied to an unordered but non-singular set. This can be seen in the examples from Yana and Aoheng where [+ masculine] specification for the gender feature is universally quantified over the Speaker-Addressee dyad and the Speaker-Referent dyad, respectively. Though the monadic encoding of gender is far and away more common, there are also semantic and pragmatic domains where gender is encoded by means of dyadic features. Many Austronesian sibling term sets, for instance, encode gender as a *dyadic feature* [+/- cross-sex]. Dyadic features necessarily apply to relational foci, since they encode inherently relational attributes (e.g., older than/younger than, even/odd generations, in-group/out-group, etc.).

Rather than in the coding of gender, the most fecund site for the elaboration of dyadic features in categorical social indexicality is undoubtedly kinship relationality. Many Aboriginal Australian languages encode a [+/- different moiety] feature – that is, a dyadic feature which stipulates whether the members of a non-singular set are all of the same marriage group or not. Even more widespread is a [+/- disharmonic generation] feature – that is, a dyadic feature which stipulates whether the members of a non-singular set are of "even" (i.e., ... G^{-4}, G^{-2}, G^0, G^{+2}, G^{+4} ...) or "odd" generations (i.e., ... G^{-5}, G^{-3}, G^{+1}, G^{+3}, G^{+5} ...) with respect to one another. These features are extended into pragmatic domains in languages of south Australia, in particular Adnyamathanha, where they non-referentially index speaker's relative marriage group membership and relative generation with respect to pronominal referents (Schebeck 1973, Scheffler 1977: 878–879). This appears also to be the case in Onya Darat, an Austronesian language of Borneo (Tadmor 2015). I mention these cases in passing to underscore that the phenomenon of categorical social indexicality is not limited to sex-based gender.

3 Social indexicals in performative function

As we have seen, the categorical indexing of social gender is distinguished from the referential indexing of gender (or gender deixis) by one parameter alone – indexical focus. Both gender deixis and categorical gender indexicality merely "characterize" the social gender of a given person. In the case of referential indexing, this characterization of social gender is itself incorporated into the propositional content of the utterance, while in the case of nonreferential indexicals it is not. Nevertheless, other than informing discourse recipients of the social gender of discourse participants, categorical gender indexicals cross-linguistically do not necessarily accomplish any other salient sort of social action. This is reflected in the ubiquity of their use. Rather than variably gendering speech or speakers through different frequencies or intensities of use within and across contexts of interaction, they occur – much as with semantic distinctions – with a law-like regularity. Their use reflects and reproduces independently constituted gender identities and statuses rather than performatively bringing them into being. This is most apparent in the way in which gender indexical contrasts are employed in reported speech constructions. In languages with categorical gender indexicals, gender alternants index speaker-gender as opposed to animator-gender. That is, alternants appropriate to the gender of the represented speaker of a reported speech construction override the use of alternants appropriate to the gender of the actual speech animator (see Fleming 2012: 311–315 for numerous examples and corresponding references). The use of "male" forms by women or of "female" forms by men is not fraught with the kind of anxieties of performance characteristic of voicing gendered speech which does not cohere with other aspects of speech animator's gender presentation in Standard Average European language communities.[6]

In this section, we turn to social indexicals that do differ from referential indexicals in terms of the social acts that they accomplish. Rather than social indexical contrasts that merely characterize the social attributes of particular persons, we will be interested in social indexicals that accomplish performative acts. For empirical examples, we will draw upon honorific registers, and in particular, alternations between non-honorific and honorific pronouns. (After Brown and Gilman 1960, we will call these T-V systems, where "T" serves as a shorthand for a non-honorific pronoun and "V" the shorthand for an honorific pronoun.)

---

6 The use of gender variants as a function interactional role occupancy in the *narrated event* (rather than in the *event of signaling*) helps to analytically distinguish these alternations from dialect differences. Here is Haas' characterization for Koasati: "Members of each sex are quite familiar with both types of speech and can use either as occasion demands. Thus if a man is telling a tale he will use women's forms when quoting a female character; similarly, if a woman is telling a tale she will use men's forms when quoting a male character. Moreover, parents were formerly accustomed to correct the speech of children of either sex, since each child was trained to use the forms appropriate to his or her sex" (Haas 1944: 145). For these reasons the term "genderlect" or "gender dialect" should be dispreferred for denoting these highly grammaticalized gender indexical alternations (cf. Dunn 2014). But see Bakker (2019) for important historical reconstructions suggesting that categorical gender indexicals have in some cases diachronically developed out of genderlects, sensu stricto.

Here I will work through a number of examples where social gender becomes entangled with acts of honorification. As we will see, where social indexicals have performative functions, the articulation of linguistic form with social gender is more complex, rather than being isomorphic with the symbolic and categorical distinction between masculine and feminine.

3.1 Honorifics and indexical focus

Honorifics can and have been analyzed in terms of their indexical focus properties (Comrie 1976, Silverstein 1976, Levinson 1983, Agha 1993a, Fleming 2017). Unlike categorical gender indexicals, all honorifics have a minimally two-place or relational indexical focus. This reflects their mediating role in the constitution and definition of social relationships. Honorifics accomplish relational acts – whether of humble respect or social exclusion – and thus instantiate a two-place relationship between an origo of deference indexicality (the person who does the deferring) and the target of deference indexicality (the person who is deferred to). Following Agha 1998 we will call the indexical focus of an honorific its *deference focus*. In this sub-section I discuss deference focus linked to the interactional role primitives of speaker [S], addressee [A], and referent [R]. (I do not discuss humiliatives in this paper; see Fleming 2016 for further discussion of those.) In the concluding section of this chapter, I discuss other kinds of deference focus that involve interactional role denaturing conditioned by the performative indefeasibility of anti-honorific variants.

Speaker$_{origo}$-Referent$_{target}$ [S-R] focus is the most common deference focus cross-linguistically (Agha 2007: 318). This likely reflects referentialist biasing in speaker metalinguistic awareness (Silverstein [1981] 2001); language users tend to conflate the act of deferring towards another and the act of making reference to them, their possessions, actions, etc. Nevertheless, Speaker$_{origo}$-Addressee$_{target}$ [S-A] honorifics are also attested. Indeed, in some languages, honorific repertoires are differentiated by deference focus type. In Javanese, the distinction between vocabulary sets labeled in local metapragmatic terminology as *ngoko* [non-honorific], *madya* [mid-honorific], and *krama* [high honorific] are interpreted as enacting speaker's respect towards the addressee (i.e., S-A focus). Contrastingly, the vocabulary set labeled *krama inggil* expresses speaker's estimation of referent's deference entitlements (i.e., S-R focus). Finally, most (but not all) of the vocabulary items labeled *krama andhap* index the deference-entitlements of one discourse referent with respect to another discourse referent. For instance, the verb *caos* 'to give' signals that the referent of the subject of the verb owes deference towards the referent of the recipient (see Errington 1988 on verbs of transfer and supplication).

This last honorific type – the ones with Referent$_1$-Referent$_2$ [R1-R2] deference focus – represent a maximal regimentation of nonreferential indexicality by the semantico-referential properties of co-occurring linguistic form; in this case, and this case alone, both the origo and the target of the index are themselves discourse referents. Lexical honorifics of this kind are particularly well attested in Southeast and East Asian languages; e.g., Javanese (Errington 1988), Tibetan (Agha 1993b), Dzongkha (van Driem 1998), Japanese and Korean (Uehara 2011). Such R1-R2 honorifics index speaker's estimation of the relative deference entitlements owed to the (referent of the) dative benefactee or goal of the predicate by the (referent of the) predicate subject (Agha 1993b: 97). (Common predicates with R1-R2 honorific alternants include 'give', 'petition', 'speak to', etc.) Though these verbs index a deference relationship between referents, it is clear that their privileged use occurs where the exalted referent is the addressee of the utterance and the humbled referent is the speaker. The emic designators for such forms reflect these speaker-humbling functions; in Japanese these forms are labeled as *kenjigoo* 'self-humbling' honorifics; in Javanese, verbs of this type are typically classed as part of the *krama andhap* or 'low' [i.e., speaker/referent-lowering] *krama* vocabulary (Errington 1988: 99).

Within the context of the typological framework that is sketched here, such R1-R2 have a special significance. For gender indexicality, we argued that any gender feature that is applied exclusively to the interactional role of referent (i.e., an absolute R focus [like English *he/she*] or a relational R1-R2 focus [like Ngandi *bari-/ba-*]) constituted a semantic gender category rather than a pragmatic one. How, then, can we argue that R1-R2 honorifics are nonreferential indexicals? It is the dimension of indexical function which importantly distinguishes Ngandi gendered plurals and Javanese *krama andhap* verbs. Categorical gender indexicals have a merely informative function. No act other than the characterization of social gender need be accomplished by the occurrence of tokens of the social indexical. If this characterization were to be exclusively applied to discourse referent(s), we would simply have a system of semantic gender. Honorifics, however, clearly have a speech act function (prototypically, the enactment of respect) that is not reducible to the "neutral" characterization of identities and relationships. Honorifics do not (symbolically) encode a categorical social relationship between the origo and the target of the indexical. They (indexically) enact respect. Thus R1-R2 honorifics, even if they have an exclusively referent-keyed focus, are not referential indexicals because they accomplish social acts saliently distinct from reference and predication. To recap: Categorical gender indexicals (qua nonreferential indexicals) are distinguished from referential indexicals in terms of indexical focus but not by indexical function. Constrastingly, honorifics (qua nonreferential indexicals) are always already distinguished from referential indexicals in terms of their indexical functions (whatever their indexical focus description).

3.2 Metapragmatic stereotypes and social information in honorification

Even if honorifics do not encode categorical social information as "characterizing properties", they can and do become entangled with social distinctions of diverse kinds. Keeping with the theme of social gender, and focusing in particular on honorific pronouns, we here discuss some ways in which social attributes and distinctions become sutured to social indexicals which have performative functions.

In the well-studied European T-V systems, multiple, overlapping, and complexly interacting factors condition pronominal usage. Summarizing Paul Friedrich's work on the T-V distinction in 19th century Russian, Susan Ervin-Tripp (1969: 100) cites the following parameters conditioning variation in pronominal usage:

> *Status marked settings* mentioned by Friedrich were the court, parliament, public occasions, duels, and examinations [i.e., V-use]. *Rank* inferiors might be lower in social class, army rank, or ethnic group, or be servants [i.e., T-use]. *Familiarity* applied to classmates, fellow students, fellow revolutionaries, lovers, and intimate friends [i.e., T-use].
>
> (Ervin-Tripp 1969:100)

Tokens of *ty* or *vy* may invoke a varied range of contextual frames, social relationships and identities.

We call honorific alternations – like Russian *ty/vy* – which are productively employed in an indefinitely wide range of role relationships *generalized honorifics*. In languages-in-culture of this sort, the social dimensions "at play" in the occurrence of an honorific token cannot be determined without attending to a range of co(n)textual cues. In European languages like French and German, it may not even be type-level social statuses or roles, but inherently event-specific factors concerning the interactional history of the pair of interlocutors which are the most important considerations in determining whether it is T or V which is reciprocally employed. V is typically exchanged in first encounters between strangers and then again over an intertextual series of interactions until interlocutors negotiate – through a more or less explicit rite of "dispensation" (Agha 2007: 33–37) – a shift to reciprocal T, enacting the mutual incorporation of the interacting pair into a sphere of greater intersubjective accessibility and "intimacy" (e.g., Clyne et al. 2009: 53, 55, Halmøy 2009: 102). To be sure, such shifts have so-cial meanings, but these meanings are as motivated by the history of encounters between the interactants as they are by widely circulating metapragmatic stereo-types. Janet Morford's (1997) study of Parisian French, for instance, offers cases where ethnic group membership, political party affiliation, age-difference, role re-lationships within the work place, social class, among other more evanescent and contingent social differences condition the continued use of reciprocal *vous* or a shift to reciprocal *tu*. The important takeaway for our purposes: In languages-in-culture of this kind, the social significances of T-V usage are always emergent in interaction.

We can contrast T-V systems of this sort with honorific pronouns that are ex-clusively stereotyped as appropriate for use *by*, *for*, or *with* particular social cate-gories of person. These we call *restricted honorifics* (terminological distinction after Choksi 2010). So, for instance, in Geoffrey O'Grady's (1963: 79) Nyangumarta grammar, we are informed that dual number is used as an honorific, but only in addressing a mother's brother. In this case, V form pronouns are stereotypically employed in a highly circumscribed set of discursive contexts. Indeed, knowing only that a token of the dual honorific has occurred, socialized Nyangumarta speakers can infer the social relationship between the "speaker of" and the "ad-dressee of" the token as a relation between a sister's child and a mother's brother. In restricted honorific systems, some social categorical information (ei-ther about the origo of the index, the target of the index, or the relationship be-tween them) is *decontextualizably deducible* given an occurrence of a pragmatic token of V (Silverstein 1981 [2001]). That is to say, restricted honorifics (but not generalized ones) are pragmatic signs for which a specific statement about the social identities and relationships of the origo and target of the index "formu-lable in the language, is entailed (follows as true) by the effective occurrence of [the] pragmatic form" (ibid.: 391).

Because the literature on so-called "address systems" is so overwhelmingly biased towards the study of European languages, the existence of restricted hon-orifics has not been sufficiently appreciated (but see Davies 1991 and King 2001). Nevertheless, the distinction between "generalized" and "restricted" honorifics should not be overly reified; it is meant to underline the striking range in the so-cial specificity of honorific practices cross-linguistically. But there is also rich so-cial structuring of honorific practice intermediate between these extremes. In many hierarchical societies norms of non-reciprocal honorification are analo-gously structured across multiple domains. In some dialects of Kannada (Dravid-ian), for instance, lower caste individuals are expected to address upper caste individuals with the honorific plural though they receive the singular in return, "the wife normally addresses the husband with the plural pronoun but the husband does not return the courtesy . . . [and] children address their mother in the singular but their father in the plural" (Sridhar 1990: 207). Here analogies between role relationships – low-caste : high-caste :: wife: husband :: child: father – are mutually figurating. Keeping with our thematic focus, analogies between normative contexts of non-reciprocal T-V usage in Kannada can be seen to simultaneously *hierarchize* social genders and *gender* inter-caste relations. An ideology of status-differentiation materialized through non-reciprocal pronominal address is instantiated across multiple social levels and frames (i.e., between castes but also within the family) in a fractally recursive manner (Gal and Irvine 2019). Correspondingly, these systems – intermediate between the generalized and the restricted – might be called *fractal hierarchical T-V systems*.

Returning to restricted honorifics, these are sometimes conceptually keyed to some social attribute of the target of deference focus. Recall, here, honorific repertoires in the languages of Polynesia. So, for instance, in Tongan, distinct [S-R] honorific vocabularies are employed depending upon the social rank – commoner versus chief versus king – of the associated discourse referent (Völkel 2010). Most common of all, however, restricted honorifics are keyed to the social relationship between the origo and the target of deference indexicality.[7]

---

7 Let me interject a word on my use of "absolute" and "relational" to denote indexical focus valence of social indexicals. This terminology is adapted from Levinson (1983), but by using it only to denote indexical focus valence it deviates from that earlier usage. In his influential treatment of "social deixis", Levinson proposes that there "are two basic kinds of socially deictic information that seem to be encoded in languages around the world: **relational** and **absolute**" (Levinson 1983: 90). He extensionally defines the relational type by listing different two-place indexical focus types which characterize honorifics: "speaker and referent", "speaker and addressee", "speaker and bystander", and "speaker and setting" (ibid.). We conserve this meaning here; a relational social indexical is one with a (minimally) two-place indexical focus. He continues: "The other main kind of socially deictic information that is often encoded is *absolute* rather than relational. There are, for example, forms reserved for certain speakers, in which case we may talk (after Fillmore 1975) of **authorized speakers**. For example, in Thai the morpheme *khráb* is a polite particle that can only be used by male speakers, the corresponding form reserved for female speakers being *khá* [. . .] There are also in many languages forms reserved for **authorized recipients**, including restrictions on most titles of address (*Your Honour, Mr President*, etc.) [. . .]" (ibid.: 91). On my reading, Levinson's distinction between "absolute social deixis" and "relational social deixis" conflates the dimension of indexical focus valence (one-place or two-place) with the dimension of indexical features (or stereotypes). So while his exemplification of "relational social deixis" emphasizes the two-place or relational character of the social indexical, the definition of 'absolute' social deixis does not center on indexical focus properties but rather on indexical features (e.g., social gender of speaker, social rank of referent). The problem is that "relational (social deixis)" and "absolute (social deixis)", as defined, are not mutually exclusive or even opposed categories. Both of the Thai honorific particles, *khráb* and *khá*, enact speaker's respect towards the addressee – that is,

Metapragmatic stereotypes that restrictively characterize the origo-target pair
are particularly well-attested in societies where kinship provides an enveloping
institutional framework for social relationality. In such societies, the comportments
characteristic of particular kin relationships may be differentiated such that some
relationships are characterized by an extreme of permissive interpersonal license
(so-called "joking relationships") while others are associated with extreme reticence and respectful non-engagement (so-called "avoidance relationships").
Honorific pronouns (among many other enregistered signs of respect) are often
stereotypically restricted in their use to such respect-laden avoidance relationships (Kruspe and Burenhult 2019).

Table 10.1: Pronominal reference to cross-cousins and affines in Kobon
(Papuan) (Davies 1981: 153, 166).

SEMANTIC CATEGORY	VERBAL SUFFIXES	KIN RELATION OF PRONOMINAL REFERENT$_{target}$ TO SPEAKER$_{origo}$
plural	-öl	Cross-sex affine/cross-cousin
dual	-il	Same-sex affine/cross-cousin
singular	-∅	Others

---

they are both two-place social indexicals. The difference between the two involves metapragmatic stereotypes, which themselves draw upon social distinctions, that frame the appropriateness of the use of the forms as a function of the social gender of the origo of the deference
focus. The analytic of "authorized speaker" is here trying to get at the same kind of thing
that we capture with the analytic of "restricted" honorification. The problem, however, is
that restricted stereotypes do not always typify only the origo or only the target of an honorific (i.e., "authorized speakers" and "authorized recipients", respectively). More commonly,
metapragmatic stereotypes model "authority" to use an honorific as contingent upon the social relationship between the origo and the target. So, for example, honorific dual pronouns
in Santali are stereotyped as appropriate where a speaker addresses his or her parent-in-law
or vice versa [Speaker$_{G+/-1.in-law}$-Addressee$_{G+/-1.in-law}$]. Clearly here we must speak of an "authorized" Speaker$_{origo}$-Addressee$_{target}$ dyad. But then to employ "absolute" (which itself is
contrasted to "relational") to denote this quintessentially relational kind of "social information" is contradictory. Unfortunately, this conflation of indexical focus and indexical features in the paired terms "absolute"/"relational" has affected literatures building upon
Levinson (1983). For instance, Chandralal (2010) describes Sinhala lexical honorifics –
which are normatively restricted for use in referring to the person, possessions, or actions of
Buddhist monks – as "absolute social deictics". In the terminology proposed here, we would
describe them as Speaker$_{origo}$-Referent$_{target}$ relational honorifics [axis of indexical focus]
with a socially restricted deference target [axis of indexical features].

In the Papuan language, Kobon, both the dual and the plural are skewed in honorific reference. Because number skewing occurs in both 2nd and 3rd person reference, but not in 1st person reference, we can be sure that the indexical focus of the honorific is S-R – honorific forms are used when the honored target is the referent of the pronoun, regardless the identity of the addressee (Fleming 2018). Importantly, as we can see in Table 10.1, the use of these honorifics is restricted to individuals who are in an avoidance relationship with one another – that is, they are normatively only employed with one's in-laws or with cross-cousins.

The distinction between the use of the dual and plural is determined by an inherently relational or dyadic gender distinction – same- versus different-sex. Same-sex in-laws and cross-cousins are normatively expected to employ the dual in reference to one another while cross-sex in-laws and cross-cousins are expected to use the plural. This is not an arbitrary or merely diacritic difference. In Kobon society, cross-sex avoidance pairings are supposed to be more respectfully avoidant of one another than are same-sex dyads. For instance, cross-sex avoidance relations, but not same-sex ones, employ different house entrances, "cannot share their fire, cooking or eating utensil, food or water, or eat any part of an animal raised by" the other (Davies 1991: 401). Use of the plural thus enacts a trope of heightened honorification with respect to the dual (see Benjamin 1999: 13 on Temiar for a parallel scaling of honorification over number categories). Just as plural number is "bigger than" dual number on the plane of referential function, so too is the respect which cross-sex avoidance relations enact towards one another "greater than" that expressed by same-sex relations on the plane of non-referential function.

3.3 Iconic figuration in social indexicality: Gender features and features of gender

As the Kobon case suggests, the links between indexical forms (i.e., plural versus dual) and gender stereotypes (i.e., the distinction between, and grading of, same-sex versus cross-sex avoidance relationships) are more complex in honorification that in categorical gender indexicality. Here, the skewing of a given semantic feature is not simply diacritic of a particular social relationship. Rather, the semantic meanings of the forms that are skewed in honorific reference appear to additionally offer an iconic sketch or portrait of some dimension of the social relationships that they index. One can hear a *semantic echo* in the non-referential signification of Kobon honorific pronouns (i.e., plural > dual > singular: most respectful > respectful > least respectful). This non-arbitrary fitting of indexical form to sociopragmatic function suggests that speakers' own reflexive engagements have channeled the diachronic development of the honorific system.

Iconic readings of indexical form may mean that particular semantic features are more fitting for achieving particular social indexical functions. So, for instance, in some Khoekhoe dialects, the 2nd person mixed gender plural pronoun (*saátù*) is employed in honorific address to "a person of either sex who is entitled to a high degree of respect from the speaker" (Hagman 1977: 45). (Khoekhoe has an exceptionally rich system of gender deixis, with masculine, feminine and mixed gender dual and plural 1st, 2nd, and 3rd person pronouns.) In addition to this canonical V form plural, the 2nd person masculine plural pronoun (*saáko*) is sometimes used by men in addressing "a male equal with whom the speaker has an especially close personal relationship; this use of *saáko* may be called the 'familiar' second person masculine singular pronoun; *saáts* [2nd person masculine singular], however, may always be used in its stead" (ibid.). Clearly, the skewing of the plural and masculine feature values – when structurally opposed to the use of the mixed gender plural in honorific address – is felicitous for iconically figuring the homosocial intimacy which the use of this social indexical performatively enacts. The erstwhile plural masculine semantic value of *saáko*, on the denotational plane, iconizes the plural masculinity of the speaker-addressee dyad, on the interactional plane.

But iconic readings of indexical form may also mean that particular social categories of person are seen as more fittingly indexed by the features that are skewed in achieving honorification. Take here the closely related Munda languages, Mundari, Santali, and Kharia. In all of these languages, dual number is skewed in honorification (Hoffmann 1903, Choksi 2010, Peterson 2014). Furthermore, in all three, the 1st person dual exclusive is employed as an honorific. The three languages thus share a typologically highly marked honorific paradigm (Fleming 2018; see Cysouw 2005). Nevertheless, despite these formal-functional parallels, the social stereotypes governing honorification vary dramatically between these languages. In Kharia, the dual appears to function as a generalized honorific; Peterson (2014: 88) simply states that the honorific dual is used, both in speaker- and addressee-reference, in addressing "someone to whom respect must be shown." In Santali, the use of the dual is a restricted honorific stereotyped for use – again, in both speaker- and addressee-reference – between children-in-law and parents-in-law (Choksi 2010, MacPhail 1983). (Skewing of dual number in pronominal honorification is similarly linked to in-law relationality in the distantly related Aslian languages, see Kruspe and Burenhult 2019, as well as in the Vietic language, Kri, see Enfield 2022.) Most remarkable, however, is the Mundari pattern as recounted by Hoffmann (1903, cited in Peterson 2014):

Married women always use the Exclusive Dual form of the personal Pronoun when speaking of themselves. [. . .] [A]nyone speaking to a married woman is supposed to use the Dual form of the Personal Pronoun [. . .] It would be considered both rude and indecent were any one to address a married woman with the Singular form of the second person. Husbands may use the Singular form, but even they generally observe the above rule. The Dual form of the Pronoun is also very frequently used when speaking of married women in the third person. [. . .] This peculiarity is the more striking, because the Mundas not only have none of the ceremonial or polite forms which abound in some other Agglutinative languages, but they never even use any honorific Plural or Dual of address. *Am, thou* is used to address superiors as well as equals and inferiors.

(Hoffmann 1903: 8–9)

The Mundari dual is readily felt to be fitting as a sign of the gender status of the married woman: "The reason of this peculiar use of the Dual lies in the manner in which the Munda conceives the family, viz., as a moral unity. Hence the wife always includes her husband in the Pronoun of the first person. *Aling* [1st dual exclusive] in fact means literally *he* and *I*" (ibid.). There is a semantic echo of the marital pair always audible in the speech of a married woman (cf. Mitchell 2018 on "allusive reference" in Datooga avoidance register). It is *as if* reference to the husband and wife dyad were made each time a married woman speaks of herself – even though, strictly speaking, the husband is not part of the propositional content of utterances employing the form. Reading between the lines, the use of the 1st person dual exclusive by a married woman can be interpreted as a demeanor indexical of sexual reserve and modesty. Like a wedding ring, or the double peaked *iqhiya* 'head cloth' donned by married Xhosa women (Rice 2015), the use of the 1st person dual exclusive by a woman serves as a badge of marital status. The *exclusive* (i.e., not you) dual serves as a broadcast signal that the woman who speaks has already been paired off (double entendre intended). The sexualized connotation of the singular (and thus the modesty of the dual) is underscored by Hoffmann's observations (a.) that it would "rude and indecent" to address a married woman in the singular and (b.) that the husband can facultatively employ the singular in addressing his own wife.

If the Khoekhoe example shows that particular semantic features may be recruited to the indexing of certain relationships because of their iconic fit to them (i.e., the use of [+masculine] and [+plural] feature values to index solidary homosociality), the Mundari example shows that pre-existing honorific forms (here the honorific dual shared by a number of Munda languages) may become restricted in their use to certain social kinds because they appear to iconically represent those kinds in a particularly fitting manner. Notably the canalization of the iconic reading of the honorific dual as [woman$_{Referent}$ + husband] appears to have restructured the indexical focus of the Mundari honorific register of person deixis. In both Kharia and Santali the use of the 1st person exclusive dual functions as a Speaker$_{origo}$-Addressee$_{target}$ honorific. That is, the speaker defers to addressee through the use of the dual not only in addressee-reference but also in speaker-reference. In Mundari however, the dual always has a married woman as its referentially anchored focus. Thus the form is honorific in 2nd and 3rd person reference. In the 1st person, meanwhile, is operates as a speaker-focal demeanor indexical of modest propriety and of marital status.

4 Indefeasible performativity and interactional role denaturing

As we have seen, social indexicals in performative function do not encode social information. Rather, metapragmatic stereotypes frame – with varying degrees of restrictiveness and exclusivity – the social statuses of, or social relationships between, the origo and target of the index. The social information that the index communicates is generated in a totally different way in categorical gender indexicality than it is in performative indexicality. In the former, indexical features are a structural aspect of the pragmatic grammar and their signification the only function of the index. In the latter, social information is deducible (or not) from token occurrences by virtue of metapragmatic stereotypes of honorification that identify (or fail to identify) the activity of deploying the index with particular social identities or relations. Further, this social signification is always ancillary to performative functions (of respecting, insulting, etc.).

Switching our attention to the dimension of indexical focus, thus far the same interactional role primitives of speaker [S], addressee [A], and referent [R] have been sufficient to model the focus of social indexes in both performative and informative function. In this section we look at some honorific alternations drawn from studies of avoidance registers, and for which our triad of interactional role primitives cannot capture attested indexical focus types (for more in-depth coverage of "avoidance registers" see Mitchell and Storch's chapter in this volume).

As mentioned in the discussion of Kobon honorific pronouns, in-law (or affinal) avoidance is common cross-culturally. Such relationships are negotiated by a range of linguistic and nonlinguistic comportments that are enregistered as emblems of intersubjective respect and restraint. The lexical repertoires of such kinship-keyed avoidance registers are composed of words and expressions that substitute for everyday (i.e., non-avoidance or non-honorific) words and expressions in terms of their denotational functions in contexts where those words are tabooed. To say that everyday words are tabooed is to say that there are contexts in which the negatively valued performative functions of everyday words – as those occur in the speech of certain kinship-related individuals or in particular kinship-defined social settings – is not canceled out or *defeased* by a range of language-structural, discursive and interactional parameters that commonly do defease pragmatic (and semantic) functions. Restricting myself only to those parameters that are pertinent to our discussion of indexical focus, I look at how speakerhood may fail to defease animator$_{origo}$ focus, how addressivity may fail to defease recipient$_{target}$ focus, and how discourse reference may fail to defease nonparticipant$_{target}$ focus. Under these conditions, the interactional role primitives of Speaker, Addressee, and Referent are *denatured* into their simpler correlates conforming to the "roles" or nodes of signal producer (or Animator), signal receiver (or Recipient) and indexable person in the world (or Nonparticipant). I offer an empirical exposition of each of these transitions before explicating the concept of denaturation in more depth.

4.1 Denaturation of the origo of deference focus: Speaker > Animator

Perhaps the best known affinal avoidance registers are the "mother-in-law languages" historically and contemporaneously employed in many Aboriginal Australian speech communities. These consist of large lexical repertoires which substitute for everyday vocabulary in speaking to or about persons who can, thereby, be construed as related to the utterance producer through a particular kinship or other role relationship (e.g., a circumciser with his initiand [Lardil], a widow with her deceased husband's kin [Winda Winda]). At first glance, mother-in-law languages appear to pattern in a manner parallel to the lexical honorific registers and categorical gender indexicals that we have already looked at. Take, for example, the mother-in-law vocabulary employed in addressing or in reference to *ganji* (a man's mother-in-law and her siblings and their kin reciprocals) by Mangarayi speakers and described by Francesca Merlan (1982). At the time of Merlan's fieldwork on Mangarayi, "older people still (sometimes) use[d] proper avoidance style with reference to or in speaking to in-laws" (ibid.: 132). What is more, "correct avoidance style [was] often used by both middle-aged and older speakers in narrating texts that tell of interactions between *ganji*" (ibid.). This parallels the Koasati gender indexicals discussed above (see the quotation from Haas 1944 in footnote 6); the affinal register was routinely employed in reported speech constructions where its use presupposed that the "represented" speaker in the narrated event (E^n) and the "represented" addressee in that same narrated event stood in a particular affinal relationship

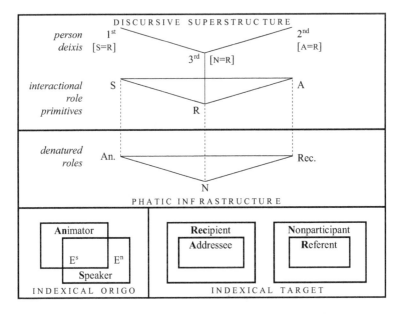

Figure 10.2: Relationship between interactional role primitives (S, A, R) and their denatured analogs (An., Rec., N).

to one another. Indeed, much of what is known about mother-in-law languages comes from elicitation carried out in contexts where speech animators were not co-present with in-laws or other avoidance relations. Aboriginal Australian avoidance registers, like Guugu-Yimidhirr *guugu dhabul* 'forbidden words' and Dyirbal *jalnguy* (glossed in English, by R. M. W. Dixon's chief informant as 'mother-in-law language'), were documented largely by linguistic elicitation where informants represented the speech of avoidance relations (Haviland 1979, Dixon 1990).

And yet, there is an important sociopragmatic asymmetry that can be observed when we contrast the "mention" of avoidance speech in non-avoidance contexts to its "use" in contexts of actual affinal co-presence. When the speech animator (the person who physically produces the linguistic signal) is co-present with his or her own avoidance relation, heteroglossic register shifts between everyday and avoidance registers in representing the speech of others may themselves be suspended. Where the speech animator in the event signaling (E^s) actually does stand in a relevant avoidance relationship either to a speech recipient or discourse referent, everyday words and expressions may be unmentionable. That is, the occurrence of everyday vocabulary – even when cited as the speech of another – risks causing insult, injury, shame or embarrassment to the

speech animator (qua deference origo) and the relevant affinal alter (qua deference target). Here the negatively evaluated performative effects of everyday
speech for affinal relationality appear to spill over the quotation marks, to "leak"
from the (then-and-there) narrated event into the (here-and-now) event of signaling (cf. Irvine 2011). In the most focal avoidance contexts, *monoglossic* production of the avoidance register is the norm – "a man in his mother-in-law's
presence finds it difficult to behave towards her in any way other than as her
son-in-law; and further, his conduct towards everyone else on the scene is very
strongly shaped by their co-presence, and the social emphasis placed on it" (Merlan 1997: 108).

In these focal avoidance contexts, then, the origo of deference focus is not associated with the role of speaker (which varies across narrating and narrated
events) but with the denatured interactional role of speech animator. The occupant
of the animator role is identified with the source of a physical linguistic signal capable of reaching – through a medium, contact or channel – the ears, eyes or
other relevant sensory organ of a signal receiver or recipient (Goffman 1981). This
role forms part of the simplex phatic infrastructure of communication upon which
the interactional role of speaker is emergent. The speaker role is more functionally
complex, for it involves a metapragmatic model of *speakerhood* which may be
keyed either to the event of signaling (E^s) or to the narrated event (E^n), as a function of the reflexive or reportive regimentation of interactional role inhabitancy
(whether that is achieved implicitly through voicing effects and play acting or
more explicitly through the machinery of verbs of speaking and logophoric pronouns). The animator role is more simplex, for it is pinned to the event of signaling
(E^s): the role of animator is assigned to whoever is engaged in the production of
the very signal that constitutes the event of signaling in the first place.[8]

The indefeasibility of performative functions under reportive calibration (i.e.,
where $E^n{\neq}E^s$) is a classic feature of verbal taboos. In English, this is evinced in
special delocutive forms like *the F-word* used to cite taboo expressions without

---

[8] The invocation of the reflexive ($E^n{=}E^s$) versus reportive ($E^n{\neq}E^s$) calibration of interactional
roles across narrated and narrating events of semiosis draws upon Silverstein's (1993) reappro-
priation of Jakobson's (1957) notation for describing shifters. See Kockelman 2004 and Nakassis
2020 for further developments. The terminological distinction between "speaker" and "animator",
and the association of the latter with the phatic facticity of speech production, follows Erving Goffman's formulation: "In canonical talk, one of the two participants moves his lips up and down to
the accompaniment of his own facial (and sometimes bodily) gesticulations, and words can be
heard issuing from the locus of his mouth. [. . .] [H]e is [. . .] an individual active in the role of
utterance production. He is functioning as an 'animator.' Animator and recipient are part of the
same level of and mode of analysis, two terms cut from the same cloth, not social roles in the full
sense so much as functional nodes in a communication system" (Goffman 1981: 144).

producing replicas of them. In written language, it is manifest in the use of hyphens or punctuation marks (*What the $%*&?*) to serve as orthographic noise masking the spelling of curse words. Here speakerhood – re-presenting the taboo replica as the speech of another – does not defease the pragmatic entailments of taboo tokens within the here-and-now event of signaling. In a wholly analogous manner, speakerhood does not defease the entailments of everyday language for Mangarayi speech animators who find themselves in the co-presence of avoidance relations.

4.2 Denaturation of the target of deference focus: Addressee > Recipient

Another way in which avoidance speech may overrun the constraints that routinely hedge in more canonical honorific speech involves the dynamics of *addressivity*. We will use addressivity as a cover term for all of the ways that ratified addressees are distinguished from nonratified bystanders in ongoing discursive interaction. These ways may be relatively explicit, as when a 2nd person singular pronoun is used to refer to a particular discourse recipient, or relatively implicit, as when fleeting glances or subtle shifts of body posture help to constitute the addressee of an utterance. In honorific registers that have a Speaker$_{origo}$-Addressee$_{target}$ deference focus, like the *krama/madya/ngoko* speech levels of Javanese, addressivity serves to defease the social pragmatics of speech level choice vis-à-vis unratified bystanders. A parent may address his or her child with *ngoko* forms without risk of offending co-present members of his or her own parents' generation, for whom *madya* or *krama* forms would be the norm in address (example adapted from Geertz 1989: 20–21).

In Aboriginal Australia, mother-in-law vocabulary is often used in speech addressed to avoidance kin. And sometimes, as in Mangarayi, its context-conditioned use is limited to actual discourse address. However, in a number of communities for which mother-in-law vocabularies are attested, the avoidance register is not only employed in address but is also supposed to be used when one is merely in the co-presence of one's most focal avoidance relations. In Gooniyandi (Kimberley), the avoidance "style was used [. . .] when speaking to a classificatory *maddiyali* [mother-in-law]" but also when merely "in the presence of (within earshot of) a close *maddiyali*" (McGregor 1989: 641). (Because Gooniyandi practice universal kinship and have a prescriptive rule of marriage, *maddiyali* corresponds to a class of individuals. A "close" *maddiyali* is either one that is genealogically close to ego or the actual mother of ego's wife.) Note that in the most focal avoidance relationship – the one between a man and his close mother-in-law – the negative pragmatic effects of using everyday speech (i.e., disrespecting an in-law and, correspondingly, shaming oneself) are not defeased by addressivity. Even if the speech animator is not speaking *to* his mother-in-law, her presence as a speech recipient is sufficient to condition a switch to the affinal respect vocabulary.[9]

In secondary literatures, mother-in-law language has been treated as having a "speaker-bystander" deference focus (e.g., Comrie 1976, Levinson 1983, Agha 1993a). If by "bystander" we understand a speech recipient who is not the addressee, this description may be technically correct for certain cases, like Dyirbal and Umpila. But in these languages, the avoidance register has this specificity of indexing a recipient who is *not* addressed precisely because direct address between a mother-in-law and son-in-law is itself subject to sanction. (Similar proscriptions on the constitution of a phatic channel of communication are characteristic of avoidance relationships cross-culturally; they are certainly not limited to Indigenous Australia and are not inherently linked to avoidance vocabularies.) Notably, there are instances where direct address is not proscribed, as between Guugu Yimidhirr brothers-in-law, and yet where the avoidance register is still employed whether or not alter is a ratified addressee or a non-addressed bystander (Haviland 1979). For these reasons, we employ the simplex and *absorptive* role of "Recipient" (rather than the more specific "Bystander") to characterize this deference target type.[10]

---

9 Similar recipient targeting was attested for Dyirbal and Guugu Yimidhirr avoidance registers. R. M. W. Dixon's chief language consultant in the 1960s, Chloe Grant, who helped him develop his seminal work on Dyirbal mother-in-law language, reported that "[t]here was never any choice involved [. . .] A man would talk with his wife in Guwal, the everyday language style, but if a mother-in-law was within hearing, he had immediately to switch to Jalnguy" (Dixon 1984: 91). Similarly for Guugu Yimidhirr, a "man would use [avoidance register] words if his mother-in-law was within earshot, even if she was on the other side of an obstruction or otherwise out of view" (Haviland 1979: 370).

10 By "absorptive" I allude to the asymmetry between Recipient and Addressee roles (on analogy to Agha's 1996: 647–648 treatment of Tibetan demonstratives). The role of discourse addressee is more specific than, and englobed within, the category of speech recipient; addressees are always recipients, but recipients aren't always addressees. This asymmetry is visually represented by placing the Addressee box within the Recipient box at the bottom of Figure 10.2.

4.3 Denaturation of the target of deference focus: Referent > Nonparticipant

The most prevalent lexical avoidance registers employed in the mediation of kin relations cross-culturally are organized around the avoidance of the personal names and (near) homophones of the names of avoided kin. Name and homophone avoidance registers – or *name registers*, for short – are found all over the world (see Simons 1982 for Oceania; see Fleming 2014 for a global survey). As we just saw for the social pragmatics of mother-in-law registers, the Speaker$_{origo}$-Addressee$_{target}$ deference focus can be denatured into an Animator$_{origo}$-Recipient$_{target}$ focus type. In name registers, we are confronted with the denaturing of the other major "politeness axis" (Comrie 1976), the Speaker$_{origo}$-Referent$_{target}$ focus type.

Names and naming are sites of particularly intense sociopragmatic elaboration cross-culturally. In Brown and Ford's (1961) classic study of naming in American English, the reciprocal use of the First Name was associated with a solidary or equalitarian relationship between the speaker and the referent while the reciprocal use of Title + Last Name was seen as indexical of a more restrained and respectful role relationship. Bracketing the question of the sufficiency of this characterization of the social acts accomplished through the use of the alternation, it is clear that names, inasmuch as they function as social indexicals, signify something about the character and quality of the relationship between the speaker of the name token and the referent of the name token. Indeed, because names function as "rigid" designators (or referential indexicals) of particular persons (Kripke 1980), they are particularly well-suited for signaling speaker-referent relations.

At first glance, then, the enregistered avoidance of the personal names of in-laws as a sign of respect might be thought to operate along the Speaker$_{origo}$-Referent$_{target}$ "politeness axis". However, just as mother-in-law speech may target an interactional role that exceeds and englobes that of the addressee, name registers may enact deference that emanates out from, but is not ultimately limited by, the discourse reference of the name. For in name registers, a range of form types which englobe the personal name are avoided and subject to lexical substitution in the respectful speech of kin of the relevant social category. Characteristically, not only the personal name, but the proper noun from which it is drawn and of which the name is but one referentially-bound instantiation, is also tabooed (on the distinction between proper name and proper noun see Schlücker and Ackermann 2017). For instance, in many Caucasus societies, patrilocal post-marital residence is or was the rule, and in-marrying women were not supposed to use the names of male affines (nor they hers). The bride's linguistic avoidances applied not only to the name as used in reference but to the proper noun. Thus, we read in Tuite and Schulze (1998: 378, n. 18) of an Abkhaz sister-in-law who is proscribed from uttering the name of her brother-in-law, Kiasou. It is not just his name but the proper noun itself that is subject to avoidance. She must, for instance, also avoid ever referring to her own brother by name, since he also happens to bear the same name as that of her brother-in-law. This latter avoidance is respectful, not towards the discourse referent of the name – the speaker's brother – but rather towards his unnamed and unreferred to namesake, the woman's brother-in-law. More elaborate name registers do not stop at the proper noun but may affect homophones of other lexical types and even words which share only a syllable in common with the name (e.g., Zulu after Raum 1973).

Given that name registers are treated at length in the chapter by Mitchell and Storch in this volume, I will not delve into greater detail here. Our purpose in drawing attention to social indexicals of this sort is simply to illustrate the denaturation of referent focus that occurs in these cases. Where the Mehinaku son-in-law of a man named *Yapu* avoids using the term *yapu* 'stingray' in speaking about this species of cartilaginous fish, he enacts deference towards his father-in-law despite the fact that his father-in-law is not the referent or even the oblique topic of discourse (example after Gregor 1977). Here the deference focus of the social indexical is maximally unmarked. It is neither a discourse referent nor is it a discourse recipient. For this reason, I refer to name registers as having a "*nonparticipant focus*" (cf. Irvine 2009 on "remote focus"). Once again, the nonparticipant role is an absorptive role with respect to the referent role. If by a nonparticipant we mean an indexicable social person, a referent is always a nonparticipant, but a nonparticipant is not always a discourse referent. This absorptive role rises to relevance where discourse reference fails to defease the anti-honorific function of phonological forms similar or identical to the name of an avoidance relation.

4.4 Denaturation and register asymmetries

We have argued that interactional role denaturation occurs as a result of the performative indefeasibility of normatively negatively valued social indexicals (i.e., verbal taboos). At first glance, this circumstance ("normatively negatively valued social indexicals") may appear to represent a very special case, with limited generalizability. But interactional role denaturation is certainly not limited to kinship-keyed avoidance registers. A set of cases where an analogously asymmetric (in)defeasibility with respect to interactional role may be discerned involve those practices of register shifting which we call "code-switching". So, for instance, code-switching is often conditioned by the linguistic attachments of the addressee – as in situations where bilinguals employ their "heritage" language in addressing their parents but a local national standard language in addressing their own children. However, sometimes the mere presence of a speech recipient (who need not be the addressee) may condition a switch of this sort. In contexts of progressive language shift in Indigenous speech communities, it is typically the stigmatized source code that is avoided in this recipient-focal manner and not the target, colonial or national standard language (see, for example, McEwan-Fujita 2010 on speech recipient conditioned Gaelic-to-English code-switching). To be sure, code-switching may be sensitive to bystanders in a range of ways (see examples in Rijkhoff 1998). Nevertheless, alternations between "prestige" and "stigmatized" varieties can exhibit the same sort of denaturing of interactional role primitives. Just as with the avoidance register examples, the performativity of the stigmatized variety may exhibit an asymmetric indefeasibility with respect to the prestige variety. (Just as we define "taboo" functionally in terms of performative indefeasibility, "stigma" similarly appears to be tractable to such a line of analysis.)

I have employed the term "denaturation" in allusion to thermal denaturation of proteins in biological systems: As the temperature of a protein is raised a melting point is reached at which the protein loses vital structural properties leading to its "inactivation" or loss of function in the complex cellular processes in which it participates. As we have seen for avoidance registers, as the performative "temperature" of taboo or stigmatized social indexicals is raised, the indexical focus properties of the index may lose structure and associated function, becoming stuck to the phatic substrate upon which discursive interaction is scaffolded. That is, performative effects become stuck to speech animators and recipients, and even to spectral nonparticipants never actually referred to in discourse. This "falling" out of discursively represented worlds of denotational textuality into the surround of the here-and-now interaction appears to be a general property of indefeasibly performative social indexicals. And it suggests something of the limits of linguistic and discursive structure for the calibration, transposition, and framing of social indexical effects.

5 Conclusion

Through schematic exemplification, this chapter has sought to provide a framework for thinking about how social identities and differences, attributes and relationships, become relevant to the type-level pragmatics of social indexicals. I have distinguished indexical function, indexical focus, and indexical features as three distinct parameters that we can attend to in locating social indexical phenomena within a comparative or typological frame. Some of the variation within, and interconnections between, these dimensions are illustrated in Figure 10.3.

An overarching claim of this chapter is that we can distinguish person deixis from nonreferential person indexicality in two ways (see top box, Figure 10.3). First, some social indexicals are distinguished from referential indexicals only in terms of the indexical focus to which the "characterizing property" or indexical feature is applied. So, in the first sections of the chapter, I was at pains to show that so-called "categorical gender indexicality" (type 2) is distinguished from "gender deixis" (type 1) in terms of the indexical focus to which gender features are applied. In gender deixis, gender features are attributed exclusively to discourse referent(s) (i.e., R or R1-R2). In categorical gender indexicality, gender features are attributed to all other possible indexical focus configurations that can be built up out of the tripartite set of interactional role primitives of speaker, addressee, and referent (i.e., S, A, S-A, S-R, and A-R). The phenomenon of categorical social indexicality is not limited to social gender. Although not exemplified here, in some languages, kinship features pattern in a parallel manner over semantic and pragmatic domains, only there for dyadic features (like relative kinship generation or relative marriage group membership) as opposed to monadic features (like masculine or feminine) (see Schebeck 1973 on Adnyamathanha; Tadmor 2015 on Onya Darat).

But social indexicals are also distinguished from person deictics in a second manner. Some classes of social indexicals accomplish performative functions that are quite clearly distinct from the informative function of merely characterizing the social attributes of particular persons. An assertion employing honorific speech or baby talk, in addition to making an assertion, additionally involves enactments of, for instance, respect or affection. Here social indexicality is distinguished from person deixis in terms of the social activity that it subtends. In formal pragmatics, it is precisely in terms of this functional dimension that "expressive meanings" have been distinguished from "on the record" ones (Potts 2005). The term *jerk* not only refers to an individual but additionally involves the speaker's expression of a negative affective stance towards that referent. In this sense, *jerk* can be understood as a S-R nonreferential indexical. Such performative indexicals (types 3 and 4) necessarily put into play different kinds of signification than reference and predication.

Drawing on honorifics for empirical examples, we have shown that social information does not attach to performative indexicals in the same way as its does to categorical indexicals. That is, performative indexicals do not encode

REFERENTIAL INDEXICALITY			NONREFERENTIAL/SOCIAL INDEXICALITY						
ABS.	REL.	*INDEXICAL FOCUS*	ABS.	REL.	*INFORMATIVE FUNCTION / PERFORMATIVE FUNCTION*	ABS.	REL.	*INDEFEASIBLE PERFORMATIVITY*	ABS.	REL.

ABS.	REL.		ABS.	REL.		ABS.	REL.		ABS.	REL.
-	-		S	S-A		-	S-A		-	AN.-REC.
-	-		A	S-R		-	S-R		-	AN.-N
R	R-R		-	-		-	R-R		-	-
(1) gender deixis			*(2) categorical gender indexicality*			*(3) honorific pronouns*			*(4) avoidance registers*	

Vertical labels (left→right between groups): INDEXICAL FOCUS · INFORMATIVE FUNCTION / PERFORMATIVE FUNCTION · INDEFEASIBLE PERFORMATIVITY

INDEXICAL FEATURES			
monadic	*dyadic*	*restricted*	*fractal*
[± masculine]	[± cross-sex]	e.g., Mundari	e.g., Kannada
[± feminine]	[± same-sex]	married woman	wife: husband :: low-
(ABS. or REL.)	(only REL.)	honorific dual	caste: high-caste :: T: V
categorical features		metapragmatic stereotypes	

INDEXICAL FOCUS ROLE ATOMS		
R = S [1ST PERSON]	S [SPEAKER]	An. [ANIMATOR]
R = A [2ND PERSON]	A [ADDRESSEE]	Rec. [RECIPIENT]
R = N [3RD PERSON]	R [REFERENT]	N [NONPARTICIPANT]
grammatical persons	interactional roles	denatured roles

Figure 10.3: Foci, features, and functions in person indexicality.[11]

social information. Rather, metapragmatic stereotypes may restrict – to varying degrees – socially appropriate or normatively expected origos, targets or origo-target pairings of particular honorific alternants (cf. Levinson 1983 on "authorized speakers" and "authorized recipients"). In restricted honorification (e.g., Tongan speech levels, Mundari dual honorific pronouns, etc.), language users are able to recover decontextualizably deducible social information concerning the social attributes of the origo or the target of the index. But again, these are structured inferences scaffolded by metapragmatic stereotypes, not categorial interpretations "read off" indexical form. Indeed, the relationship between pragmatic functions and semantic features is quite different in the case of honorific pronouns (type 3) as compared to pragmatic genders (type 2). Here, pragmatic functions are often

---

11 The four types of person indexicals discussed in this chapter and how they are distinguished by indexical function (top box), by different kinds of indexical features (middle box), and by interactional roles as these are realized in referential (left), nonreferential (middle), and denatured (right) indexical focus types (bottom box). Abbreviations: ABS. = Absolute (or one-place) focus; REL. = Relational (or two-place) focus; S = Speaker; A = Addressee; R = Referent; An. = Animator; Rec. = Recipient; N = Nonparticipant.

rationalized by the mediation of what I have called semantic echoes. That is, metapragmatic stereotypes informing honorific practice come to be interpreted as iconic with the notional meanings of the semantic feature values of the forms employed as honorifics. Our most conspicuous example was the Mundari dual employed by and for married women. Here we argued that because marriage implies a duality, the social category of the married woman served as a conceptual anchor (and sociolinguistic attractor) for secondary-rationalizations of the honorific dual.

Finally, we discussed how the interactional role atoms [S, A, R] that fill the origo and target of the deference focus of an honorific may be denatured by performative function. Here, the anti-honorific forms which alternate with honorific repertoire items may have performative functions that are not defeased where the origo-of-deference indexicality is the Animator but not the Speaker, where the target-of-deference indexicality is a speech Recipient but not the Addressee, or where the target-of-deference indexicality is a Nonparticipant but not the Referent. Drawing examples from kinship-keyed avoidance registers, we showed how the two canonical kinds of relational deference focus – Speaker$_{origo}$-Addressee$_{focus}$ [e.g., Javanese *krama/madya/ngoko*] and Speaker$_{origo}$-Referent$_{focus}$ [e.g., Javanese *krama inggil/ngoko*] – can undergo interactional role denaturing when anti-honorific functions are indefeasible. It was in this context that we located phenomena like 'bystander' indexicality in Aboriginal Australian mother-in-law registers, or nonparticipant indexicality in Afro-Eurasian daughter-in-law registers.

In sum total, social indexicality represents a vast and heterogeneous borderland between the built environment of symbolism-supporting language structure and the iconic and indexical pathways of purely pragmatic cultural semiosis that surround and spread out from it. Nearer the symbolic center, those interactional roles which are reflected in the "duplex" (or denotationally-indexical) category of grammatical person (i.e., the 1st [S=R], 2nd [A=R], and 3rd [N=R] persons) are sufficient to model nonreferential indexicality. And the machinery of explicit metapragmatic discourse (i.e., Peircean symbols like verbs of speaking, logophoric devices, etc.) has regimenting authority, determining whether efferent social indexicals should be interpreted with respect to the actual event of signaling within which they occur (E^s) or with respect to a represented event of speaking (E^n [$\neq$E^s]). However, as social indexicals take on distinct modes of signification, like respect and disdain, their functions are less neatly channeled and circumscribed by the explicit framing of speech in speech. Although a special case of a wider phenomenon, the indefeasible performativity of tabooed and stigmatized linguistic varieties illustrates this functional spillover into the phatic order of interaction. Here we are faced with a phenomenon "in language" wholly continuous with the broader, purely pragmatic semiotics of culture.

References

Agha, Asif. 1993a. Grammatical and indexical convention in honorific discourse. *Journal of Linguistic Anthropology* 3 (2). 131–163.

Agha, Asif. 1993b *Structural form and utterance context in Lhasa Tibetan. Grammar and indexicality in a non-configurational language*. New York: Peter Lang.

Agha, Asif. 1996. Schema and superposition in spatial deixis. *Anthropological Linguistics* 38 (4). 643–682.

Agha, Asif. 1998. Stereotypes and registers of honorific language. *Language in Society* 27 (2). 151–193.

Agha, Asif. 2007. *Language and social relations*. New York: Cambridge University Press.

Aikhenvald, Alexandra. 2016. *How gender shapes the world*. Oxford: Oxford University Press.

Alberdi, Jabier. 1995. The development of the Basque system of terms of address and the allocutive conjugation. In José Ignacio Hualde, Joseba A. Lakarra and R. L. Trask (eds.), *Towards a history of the Basque language*, 279–293. Amsterdam: John Benjamins.

Bakhtin, Mikhail M. 1981. Discourse in the novel. In Michael Holquist (ed.), *The dialogic imagination*, 259–422. Austin: University of Texas Press.

Bakker, Peter. 2019. Intentional language change and the connection between mixed languages and genderlects. *Language Dynamics and Change* 9 (2). 135–161.

Benjamin, Geoffrey 1999. *Temiar kinship terminology. A linguistic and formal analysis*. Pulau Pinang: Academy of Social Sciences (AKASS).

Brown, Roger & Albert Gilman. 1960. The pronouns of power and solidarity. In Thomas A. Sebeok (ed.), *Style in language*, 253–276. Cambridge, MA: MIT Press.

Brown, Roger & Marguerite Ford. 1961. Address in American English. *Journal of Abnormal and Social Psychology* 62. 375–385.

Butler, Judith. 1988. Performative acts and gender constitution. An essay in phenomenology and feminist theory. *Theatre Journal* 40 (4). 519–531.

Butler, Judith. 1997. *Excitable speech. A politics of the performative*. New York: Routledge.

Chandralal, Dileep. 2010. *Sinhala*. Amsterdam & Philadelphia: John Benjamins.

Chirrey, Deborah A. 2003. "I hereby come out". What sort of speech act is coming out? *Journal of Sociolinguistics* 7 (1). 24–37.

Choksi, Nishaant. 2010. The dual as honorific in Santali. In *Proceedings of the 32nd all India Conference of Linguists*, 125–130.

Clyne, Michael, Catrin Norrby & Jane Warren. 2009 *Language and human relations. Styles of address in contemporary language*. Cambridge: Cambridge University Press.

Comrie, Bernard. 1976. Linguistic politeness axes. Speaker-addressee, speaker-referent, speaker-bystander. *Pragmatics Microfiche* 1 (7). 1–12.

Corbett, Greville. 1991. *Gender*. New York: Cambridge University Press.

Corbett, Greville. 2013. Sex-based and non-sex-based gender systems. In Matthew S. Dryer & Martin Haspelmath (eds.), *The world atlas of language structures online*. Leipzig: Max Planck Institute for Evolutionary Anthropology.

Cysouw, Michael. 2005. A typology of honorific uses of clusivity. In Elena Filimonova (ed.), *Clusivity. Typology and case studies of the inclusive-exclusive distinction*, 213–230. Amsterdam & Philadelphia: John Benjamins.

Davies, John. 1981. *Kobon*. Amsterdam: North-Holland.

Davies, John. 1991. Marked pronouns and verbs for marked social relationships in a Chadic and a Papuan language. In Andrew Pawley (ed.), *Man and a half. Essays in Pacific Anthropology and Ethnobiology in honour of Ralph Bulmer*, 397–405. Auckland: Polynesian Society.

Dixon, R.M.W. 1984. *Searching for Aboriginal languages*. New York: University of Queensland Press.

Dixon, R.M.W. 1990. The origin of "mother-in-law vocabulary" in two Australian languages. *Anthropological Linguistics* 32 (1/2). 1–56.

Dunn, Michael. 2014. Gender determined dialect variation. In Greville G. Corbett (ed.), *The expression of gender*, 39–68. Berlin & Boston: De Gruyter Mouton.

Ekka, Francis. 1972. Men's and women's speech in Kurux. *Linguistics* 81. 25–31.

Enfield, N. J. 2022. Asymmetries in the system of person reference in Kri, a language of upland Laos. In Dwi Djenar & Jack Sidnell (eds.), *Signs of deference, signs of demeanour. Interlocutor reference and Self-Other relations across Southeast Asian speech communities*, Singapore: NUS Press.

Errington, Joseph. 1988. *Structure and style in Javanese. A semiotic view of linguistic etiquette*. Philadelphia: University of Pennsylvania Press.

Ervin-Tripp, Susan. 1969. In Leonard Berkowitz (ed.), *Advances in experimental social psychology*, Vol. 4, 91–165. New York: Academic Press.

Fillmore, Charles J. 1975. *Santa Cruz lectures on deixis*. Bloomington: Indiana University Linguistics Club.

Fleming, Luke. 2012. Gender indexicality in the Native Americas. Contributions to the typology of social indexicality. *Language in Society* 41. 295–320.

Fleming, Luke 2014. Australian Exceptionalism in the Typology of Affinal Avoidance Registers. *Anthropological Linguistics* 56 (2). 115–158.

Fleming, Luke. 2015. Speaker-referent gender indexicality. *Language in Society* 44 (3). 425–434.

Fleming, Luke. 2017. Honorific alignment and pronominal paradigm: Evidence from Mixtec, Santali, and Dhimal. *Proceedings of the Annual Meeting of the Berkeley Linguistics Society* 43. 95–120.

Fleming, Luke. 2018. Undecontextualizable. Performativity and the conditions of possibility of linguistic symbolism. *Signs and Society* 6 (3). 558–606.

Fortune, David L. & Gretchen Fortune. 1975. Karajá men's-women's speech differences with social correlates. *Arquivos de Anatomia e Antropologie* 1. 109–124.

Gal, Susan & Judith Irvine. 2019. *Signs of difference. Language and ideology in social life*. New York: Cambridge University Press.

Geertz, Hildred. 1989. *The Javanese family. A study of kinship and socialization*. Prospect Heights, IL: Waveland Press.

Goffman, Erving. 1981. *Forms of talk*. Philadelphia: University of Pennsylvania Press.

Gregor, Thomas. 1977. *Mehinaku. The drama of daily life in a Brazilian Indian village*. Chicago: University of Chicago Press.

Haas, Mary R. 1944. Men's and women's speech in Koasati. *Language* 20 (3). 142–149.

Hagman, Roy S. 1977. *Nama Hottentot grammar*. Bloomington: Indiana University.

Halmøy, Odile. 2009. La concurrence *tu/vous* en français contemporain. Paramètres, polarités et paradoxes. In Bert Peeters & Nathalie Ramière (eds.), *Tu ou Vous. L'embarras du choix*, 99–113. Limoges: Lambert-Lucas.

Hanks, William F. 1992. The indexical ground of deictic reference. In Charles Goodwin & Alessandro Duranti (eds.), *Rethinking context. Language as an interactive phenomenon*, 43–76. Cambridge: Cambridge University Press.

Harvey, Keith. 2002. Camp talk and citationality. A queer take on 'authentic' and 'represented' utterance. *Journal of Pragmatics* 34. 1145–1165.

Haviland, John B. 1979. Guugu Yimidhirr brother-in-law language. *Language in Society* 8 (3). 365–393.

Heath, Jeffrey. 1978. *Ngandi grammar, texts, and dictionary*. Canberra: Australian Institute of Aboriginal Studies.

Hoffmann, Johann. 1903. *Mundari grammar*. Calcutta: Bengal Secretariat Press.

Irvine, Judith T. 2009. Honorifics. In Gunter Senft, Jan-Ola Östam & Jef Verschueren (eds.), *Culture and language use*, 156–172. Amsterdam & Philadelphia: John Benjamins.

Irvine, Judith T. 2011. Leaky registers and eight-hundred-pound gorillas. *Anthropological Quarterly* 84 (1). 15–40.

Jakobson, Roman. 1957. Shifters, verbal categories, and the Russian verb. In *Selected Writings*, Vol. 2, 16–22. Cambridge: Harvard.

Jakobson, Roman. 1960. Concluding statement. Linguistics and poetics. In Thomas A. Sebeok (ed.), *Style in language*, 350–377. Cambridge: MIT Press.

King, John T. 2001. The affinal kin register in Dhimal. *Linguistics of the Tibeto-Burman Area* 24 (1). 163–182.

Kockelman, Paul. 2004. Stance and subjectivity. *Journal of Linguistic Anthropology* 14 (2). 127–150.

Kripke, Saul A. 1980. *Naming and necessity*. Cambridge: Harvard University Press.

Kulick, Don. 1992. Anger, gender, language shift and hate politics of revelation in a Papua New Guinean village. *Pragmatics* 2 (3). 281–296.

Kruspe, Nicole & Niclas Burenhult. 2019. Pronouns in affinal avoidance registers. Evidence from the Aslian languages (Austroasiatic, Malay Peninsula). In Paul Bouissac (ed.), *The social dynamics of pronominal systems. A comparative approach*, 289–317. Amsterdam & Philadelphia: John Benjamins.

Labov, William. 2006. *The social stratification of English in New York City*, 2nd edition. Cambridge: Cambridge University Press.

Levinson, Stephen. 1983. *Pragmatics*. New York: Cambridge University Press.

MacPhail, R. M. 1983. *Introduction to Santali*. Calcutta: Firma KLM Private Ltd.

Manning, H. Paul. 2001. On social deixis. *Anthropological Linguistics* 43 (1). 54–100.

McConnell-Ginet, Sally. 2014. Gender and its relation to sex. The myth of 'natural' gender. In Greville G. Corbett (ed.), *The expression of gender*, 3–38. Berlin & Boston: De Gruyter Mouton.

McEwan-Fujita, Emily. 2010. Ideology, affect, and socialization in language shift and revitalization. The experiences of adults learning Gaelic in the Western Isles of Scotland. *Language in Society* 39. 27–64.

McGregor, William. 1989. Gooniyandi mother-in-law "language":Dialect, register, and/or code? In Ulrich Ammon (ed.), *Status and function of language and language varieties*, 630–656. Berlin: De Gruyter Mouton.

Merlan, Francesca. 1982. 'Egocentric' and 'altercentric' usage of kin terms in Mangarrayi. In Jeffrey Heath, Francesca Merlan & Alan Rumsey (eds.), *The languages of kinship in Aboriginal Australia*, 125–140. Sydney: Oceania Publications.

Merlan, Francesca. 1997. The mother-in-law taboo. Avoidance and obligation in Aboriginal Australian society. In Francesca Merlan, John A. Morton & Alan Rumsey (eds.), *Scholar and sceptic. Australian Aboriginal studies in honour of L. R. Hiatt*, 95–122. Canberra: Aboriginal Studies Press.

Merlan, Francesca & Alan Rumsey. 1991. *Ku Waru. Language and segmentary politics in the western Nebilyer Valley, Papua New Guinea*. New York: Cambridge University Press.

Mitchell, Alice. 2018. Allusive references and other-oriented stance in an affinal avoidance register. *Journal of Linguistic Anthropology* 28 (1). 4–21.

Morford, Janet 1997. Social indexicality in French pronominal address. *Journal of Linguistic Anthropology* 7 (1). 3–37.

Nakassis, Constantine V. 2020. Deixis and the linguistic anthropology of cinema. *Semiotic Review* 9. [https://www.semioticreview.com/ojs/index.php/sr/article/view/65] (accessed 20 April 2022).

Ochs, Elinor. 1992. Indexing gender. In A. Duranti & C. Goodwin (eds.), *Rethinking context*, 335–358. Cambridge: Cambridge University Press.

O'Grady, Geoffrey N. 1963. *Nyangumata grammar*. Bloomington: Indiana University dissertation.

Peterson, John. 2014. Figuratively speaking – number in Kharia. In Anne Storch & Gerrit J. Dimmendaal (eds.), *Number – constructions and semantics. Case studies from Africa, Amazonia, India and Oceania*, 77–110. Amsterdam & Philadelphia: John Benjamins.

Potts, Christopher. 2005. *The logic of conventional implicatures*. Oxford: Oxford University Press.

Putnam, Hilary. 1996. The meaning of 'meaning'. In Andrew Pessin & Sanford Goldberg (eds.), *The twin earth chronicles. Twenty years of reflection on Hilary Putnam's "The meaning of meaning"*, 3–52. New York: M. E. Sharpe.

Raum, O. F. 1973. *The social functions of avoidances and taboos among the Zulu*. New York: Walter de Gruyter.

Ribeiro, Eduardo. 2006. Subordinate clauses in Karajá. *Boletim du Museu Paraense Emílio Goeldi Ciências Humanas* 1 (1). 17–47.

Rice, Kathleen. 2015. *"Most of them, they just want someone to under them". Gender, generation, and personhood among the Xhosa*. Toronto: University of Toronto dissertation.

Rijkhoff, Jan. 1998. Bystander deixis. In Yaron Matras (ed.), The Romani element in non-standard speech, 51–67. Wiesbaden: Harrassowitz.

Rose, Françoise. 2013. Le genre du locuteur et de l'allocutaire dans les systèmes pronominaux. Genre grammatical et indexicalité du genre. *Bulletin de la Société de linguistique de Paris* 108. 381–417.

Rose, Françoise. 2015. On male and female speech and more. Categorical gender indexicality in indigenous South American languages. *International Journal of American Linguistics* 81 (4). 495–537.

Schebeck, Bernhard. 1973. The Adnjamathanha personal pronoun and the "Wailpi kinship system". *Papers in Australian Linguistics* 6 [A-36]. 1–46.

Scheffler, Harold W. 1977. Kinship and alliance in South India and Australia. *American Anthropologist* 79 (4). 869–882.

Schlücker, Barabara & Tanja Ackermann. 2017. The morphosyntax of proper names. An Overview. *Folia Linguistica* 51 (2). 309–339.

Sellato, B. J. L. 1981. Three-gender personal pronouns in some languages of Central Borneo. *Borneo Research Bulletin* 13. 48–49.

Sapir, Edward. 1985. *Selected writings of Edward Sapir in language, culture and personality.* Berkeley: University of California Press.

Silverstein, Michael. 1976. Shifters, linguistics categories, and cultural description. In Keith H. Basso & Henry A. Selby (eds.), *Meaning in anthropology*, 11–55. Albuquerque: University of New Mexico Press.

Silverstein, Michael. 1985. Language and the culture of gender: At the intersection of structure, usage, and ideology. In Elizabeth Mertz & Richard J. Parmentier (eds.), *Semiotic mediation: Sociocultural and psychological perspectives*, 219–259. Orlando, FL: Academic Press.

Silverstein, Michael. 1993. Metapragmatic discourse and metapragmatic function. In John Lucy (ed.), *Reflexive language: Reported speech and metapragmatics*, 33–58. Cambridge: Cambridge University Press.

Silverstein, Michael. 2001. The limits of awareness. In Alessandro Duranti (ed.), *Linguistic anthropology. A reader*, 382–401. Malden: Blackwell.

Simons, Gary F. 1982. Word taboo and comparative Austronesian linguistics. In Amran Halim, Lois Carrington & S. A. Wurm (eds.), *Papers from the third international conference on Austronesian linguistics*, Vol. 3, 157–226. Canberra: Pacific Linguistics.

Sridhar, S. N. 1990. *Kannada*. New York: Routledge.

Tadmor, Uri. 2015. When culture grammaticalizes. The pronominal system of Onya Darat. In Rik de Busser & Randy LaPolla (eds.), *Language structure and environment. Social, cultural, and natural factors*, 77–98. Amsterdam: John Benjamins.

Tuite, Kevin & Wolfgang Schulze. 1998. A case of taboo-motivated lexical replacement in the indigenous languages of the Caucasus. *Anthropological Linguistics* 40 (3). 363–383.

Uehara, Satoshi. 2011. The socio-cultural motivation of referent honorifics in Korean and Japanese. In Klaus-Uwe Panther & Günter Radden (eds.), *Motivation in grammar and the lexicon*, 191–212. Amsterdam & Philadelphia: John Benjamins.

Uranw, Ram Kisun. 2009. Pronominalization in Uranw-Kudux. *Nepalese Linguistics* 24. 369–378.

van Driem, George. 1998. *Dzongkha*. Leiden: Research School CNWS.

Völkel, Svenja. 2010. *Social structure, space and possession in Tongan culture and language. An ethnolinguistic study.* Amsterdam & Philadelphia: John Benjamins.

Wechsler, Stephen. 2009. 'Elsewhere' in gender resolution. In Kristin Hanson & Sharon Inkelas (eds.), *The Nature of the word – Essays in honor of Paul Kiparsky*, 567–586. Cambridge: MIT Press.

Vera da Silva Sinha

11 Time: Sociocultural structuring beyond the spatialization paradigm

Ways of thinking and communicating about time and space manifest differences that can be observed cross-culturally and cross-linguistically. Space is widely viewed as the principal source domain for the linguistic and conceptual structuring through metaphoric mapping of time. The spatialization of time in thought, language, and familiar cultural artefacts has been in recent years a key topic in cognitive science and anthropology. Cultural artefacts for marking and planning time (e.g., calendars) are intrinsically numerical, and are spatially organized in terms of numbered timelines or cycles. However, a limitation of research to date is that many empirical studies have been based on evidence from "WEIRD" (Western, Educated, Industrialized, Rich, Democratic) populations. It is known that calendars are historical inventions that measure "time" in terms of intervals of duration; therefore, calendar and clock time are embedded within systems of METRIC TIME. Calendar and clock time may, in many cultural settings, be non-existent, absent, vague or subordinated to event-based time (which has also been called "ecological time"). Event-based time intervals are organized as complex systems of lexicalized indices. This chapter will provide an overview of research in linguistics and other disciplines that explores the relations between space and time, including metaphor, timelines, and event-based time, as well as studies that focus on spatial concepts and spatial frames of reference. This chapter will conclude by providing an account of key studies that focus on cultural-linguistic analysis of event-based time concepts.

Acknowledgments: I would like to thank the Awetý, Kamaiurá, Amondawa and Huni Kuĩ communities, and especially Dr. Wary Kamaiura Sabino, Dr. Joaquim Kaxinawa and Dr. Tataiya Kokama, speakers and expert knowledge-holders of their respective languages and cultures. Without their sharing of their knowledge and expertise with me, this research would not have been possible. I am grateful to the reviewers and editors and to Peter Austin, Chris Sinha and Anaïs Augé for their critical comments on earlier versions of this manuscript.

Vera da Silva Sinha, University of Oxford/United Kingdom, e-mail: vera.sinha@gmail.com

https://doi.org/10.1515/9783110726626-011

1 Introduction

How humans conceptualize time is a question that has provoked extensive debate through different disciplines, from philosophy (McTaggart 1908, Davis 1976) and anthropology (Evans-Pritchard 1939, Bourdieu 1977, Bloch 1977, Whitrow 1989, Wright 1991, Gell 1992, Munn 1992, Adam 1994, Ingold 1995, Pinxten 1995, Hubert 1999, Postill 2002, Schieffelin 2002, Birth 2012) to cognitive science and linguistics (Whorf 1950, Lucy 1992, Gumperz and Levison 1996, Levine 1998, Brown 2012, Bowerman, Bowerman and Choi 2003, Gentner and Goldin-Meadow 2003, Levinson 2003, Moore 2006, 2014, Núñez and Sweetser 2006, Bohnemeyer 2009, Jaszczolt 2012, 2018, 2019, Sinha et al. 2011, Tenbrink 2011, Núñez and Cornejo 2012, Silva Sinha et al. 2012, Núñez and Cooperrider 2013, Majid et al. 2013, Sinha and Gärdenfors 2014). In this debate, the relationship between time and space has occupied the core of the discussion and has been a key topic of research, not only in the humanities and social sciences but also in physics, cosmology, biology, and neuroscience (Bender et al. 2009, Buzsáki and Tingley 2018, Gontier 2018).

All cultures and languages have ways of encoding and thinking about time and space. People move through space, and in so doing they also move through time (Casasanto and Boroditsky 2008), although in some cultures, people do not think about time in terms of movement (Silva Sinha 2018, 2019, Rodríguez 2019). In space, people give directions, locate things in space, and conceptualize location in space. People perceive objects as being "in space", either statically or dynamically, and events as being related to each other "in time". Speakers in many languages may conceptualize events metaphorically in terms of the motion of objects in space. These ways of perceiving and conceptualizing are motivated by meanings embedded in the practices, both linguistic and non-linguistic, that enable people to co-ordinate their situatedness in time and space, and are reflected in the lexicon and grammar of specific languages.

Before proceeding further, it is important to clarify what is at stake in an exploration of time and space in culture, and culture in time and space. First, cultures are conceived here as being both "webs of meaning" (Geertz 1973) and ensembles of practices. People in diverse settings have ways of doing things, ways of thinking, ways of feeling, and employ a variety of discourses to express them. Concepts of time and space cannot be understood independently of these constituents of cultural settings.

Second, this chapter does not start from the assumption of an a-priori universal conceptual category or domain of "time", to be distinguished from an equally universal domain of "space". On the contrary, current developments in neuroscience (Buzsáki and Tingley 2018) question such a neat, biologically-given packaging of cognition, as well as the Kantian claim that concepts in each of these domains are essentially the same for all humans (Levinson 2003). When we use, as analysts, terms such as "temporal concepts" or "time reckoning", we are imposing a categorization that is theoretically and pragmatically appropriate for our own purposes, but does not necessarily align with the way that speakers think about their concepts and their practices. Third, neither languages nor cultures are uniform. Speakers (who are also actors in cultural practices) may command different repertoires in different contexts, some of which imply and draw upon culturally hybrid concepts, practices, and artefacts (Silva Sinha 2019). Language, culture, and mind may be said to be interdependent (Sinha 2017), but this should be interpreted as referring not to distinct entities in interaction, but to interwoven aspects of human activities in context. The use of the term "culture" in what follows should be read as a shorthand for, or a point of access to, this nexus of continuity and variation.

This chapter reviews arguments and evidence about ways people talk about time and space. It will provide an overview of research in linguistics and other disciplines that emphasizes the relations between space and time, including metaphor, timelines, and event-based time, and studies that focus on spatial concepts and spatial frames of reference. It will emphasize critical studies that focus on non-metric, event-based time concepts, providing an account for understanding time concepts across languages and cultures.

2 Time in culture

2.1 Time is socially embedded

Time, in particular social representations of time, has been a key topic in anthropology and sociology (Durkheim 1912, Evans-Pritchard 1939, Mauss 1966, Adam 1994, Hubert 1999 [1905]). Temporal concepts are culturally and linguistically widely variable (Gell 1992, Munn 1992, Thapar 1996). Time is embedded in culture and society, and it cannot be understood independently of social structure categories such as clan, moiety, phratry, residential or kinship group, and of the rituals that structure social life (Durkheim 1912, Mauss 1966, Hubert 1999 [1905]). Already in Durkheim's discussion, time has a duration, it underlies rhythms in people's collective and individual lives and it "has a particular local shape in particular local ways of life and representations" (Miller 2000: 16). For example, temporal divisions (days, weeks, months, and years) correspond to periodical recurrences of rites, feasts, and ceremonies. The time-environment involves both everyday, profane time and sacred time, which brings together concepts of time that involve infinitude, immutability, and indivisibility. Anthropological and linguistic studies have focused on time-reckoning – social and communicative practices that employ time interval concepts – in different cultures and languages (Evans-Pritchard 1939, Ingold 1995, Thapar 1996). Calendrical time expresses the rhythm of the collective activities, and simultaneously, it has the function of assuring their regularities. In this sense, Durkheim

> portrayed the social form of the transaction as extended in time (and as against overarching and abstract structural features) and as held together through a confluence of shared sentiments, beliefs, and values. Thus, the complex organic transactions are temporal not only because specifications of time are printed in contracts, but because faith in time is internalized and etched into the collective consciousness. (Katovich 1987: 379)

Temporality is also a controversial issue in the epistemology of social sciences, especially anthropology. As Fabian (1983, 2014) has pointed out, the denial in classical anthropological studies of "coevalness" (or a shared present) between researcher and the researched society brings about a discrepancy between the "here and now" of reality in the fieldwork and the conceptual standpoint from which anthropologists write and think about their "subjects" and their supposedly "timeless" social and cultural forms (see also Adam 1994, McElwain 1987, Ingold 1986). This leads to the representation of researched societies as "Other", standing frozen "outside" time and its flow. Fabian also refers to the history of temporizing rhetoric in anthropology, rooted in the sacred Judeo-Christian notion of time (calendrical and numerical time). This became secularized in European intellectual history, leading to the influential evolutionary frame in the 19th century, which inherited a spatialized time from the medieval notion of the "great chain of being", and recast this as an evolutionary sequence (Figure 11.1).

Figure 11.1: Human evolution silhouettes by *Vector Open Stock* (reproduced under CC BY 2.0 license, via Flickr).

This heritage of the spatialization of time had unfortunate consequences for the human sciences, such as anthropology, in that non-European subjects were naturalized as "primitive" and denied historical agency. In this context, throughout the 19th century the cultural-evolutionary approach provided the lens through which researchers and scholars looked at different cultures in terms of a universal scale of complexity and sophistication. Lewis Henry Morgan's (1877) theory of social and cultural evolution from savagery, through barbarism to civilization was one very popular and influential example. Many such theories were rooted in a Eurocentric, "implicitly (and its Social Darwinist variants, explicitly) racist *phylocultural complex*" (Sinha 2021: 388; see also Sinha 1988), which viewed non-European cultures as less evolved, and included the assumption that primitive languages lacked the complexity and clarity of the languages of "civilized" groups. Even today, it is common to encounter comments that reveal assumptions that indigenous languages lack sophistication and complexity, when compared with European languages, nurturing a still-existing social representation of "civilized" versus "uncivilized" society.

Munn (1992) discusses her ethnographic work among the Gawa people in the Trobriand Islands looking at *kula*, an exchange system between communities (see Munn 1983, 1986). She argues that temporality is a symbolic process produced in everyday social activities. Objects, space, and people constitute the dimensions of a past-present-future relation. This perception is constructed in the way people experience and give meaning to their everyday world.

> People are "in" a sociocultural time of multiple dimensions (sequencing, timing, past-present-future relations, etc.) that they are forming in their "projects". In any given instance, particular temporal dimensions may be the *foci* of attention or only tacitly known. Either way, these dimensions are lived or apprehended concretely via the various meaningful connectivities among persons, objects, and space continually being made in and through the everyday world. (Munn 1992: 116)

Time is not only an abstract principle in which we live as biological organisms, but it is also a local cultural construct governing our social interactions. Time is shaped, punctuated, organized, and endured in complex ways by people negotiating their lives and relations with others and with their environments.

2.2 The spatialization and linearization of time

Time reckoning and time concepts may be materially anchored (Hutchins 2005) in cognitive artefacts such as calendars and clocks. Calendars traditionally work as timekeepers in relation to the lunar and/or solar year, culturally shaping cognition by imposing the view that "all events, including future events, have their dates, which are unqualified temporal attributes of events. The date of an event does not change with the passage of time [. . .] If an event occurs at all, it must do so at a definite date" (Gell 1992: 157). Clocks and calendars are inventions that were created to measure time in terms of intervals of duration (Postil 2002). The main function of these artefacts is to keep track of time precisely measured, that is of *metric time* (Sinha and Gärdenfors 2014). These cognitive artefacts play a very important role in modern cultural time-keeping (ensuring punctuality, setting deadlines). Metric time is segmented and measured in terms of the duration of intervals (hours, minutes, seconds, days) and is conventionalized as "clock time" and "calendar time" (Levine 1998, Postil 2002, Sinha et al. 2011, Sinha and Bernárdez 2015).

However, not only do not all cultures use calendars (Austin 1998, Levinson and Majid 2013, Silva Sinha 2019), there are many other ways of indexing events to a time of occurrence or a time interval and communicating about temporal relations. We need to consider other material anchors in the built and natural environment, e. g., architecture, village and city layout, and landscape. In many cultures, temporal landmarks are intrinsically linked with cosmology and with environmental indexes (e.g., bird songs), celestial bodies (the sun, moon, and stars) and social activities (working time, lunchtime, teatime). For example, the Diyari people of South Australia say that "the sun 'enters' at sunset and 'comes out' at sunrise, spending the night at a place called *dityi mingka* 'sun hole'" (Peter K. Austin, personal communication, January 2022) while the Yupno people of Papua New Guinea refer to the time of events by mapping them to the topographic environment: the past is construed as downhill and the future as uphill (Cooperrider et al. 2022). Both of these examples involve a kind of spatialization of time, but not all metaphoric construals of time are spatial.

In the Amazonian languages Huni Kuĩ, Awetý and Kamaiurá the future is located in the head: THE FUTURE IS IN THE MIND. The future is what you see 'in the mind's eye' or imagination. In Huni Kuĩ, the past is located IN THE HEART, and never behind the speaker. Similarly, in Awetý and Kamaiurá the past is located *in the eyes*. The past in this sense, is linked with memories, and the memories can be *seen in the mind's eye* – REMEMBERING IS SEEING. The future is located *in front of the eyes*. This should not, however, be understood as a "reversal" of a timeline. *In front of the eyes* should *not* be understood as meaning 'future is ahead on a timeline' in Awetý and Kamaiurá. For Huni Kuĩ, Awetý and Kamaiurá speakers, the future is marked in the language as a *possibility of completion*, or *desire for completion*, of an anticipated or intended event. The evidence suggests that in these cultures, past and future are not conceptualized in terms of spatial orientation but in terms of the embodiment of mental representational capacities: *memory, anticipation, intention,* and *imagination* (Silva Sinha 2018, 2019).

Accustomed as we are to thinking in terms of clock and calendar time, researchers have often attempted to "translate" indigenous time concepts to metric time to make it more comprehensible. As Adam (1994: 516) points out,

> we build models to render our subject matter intelligible. We construct representations so that Nuer time-reckoning and Hopi cosmology, for example, become meaningful in the context of our own understanding [. . .] It is not the practice of model-building [. . .] but the nature of the models and of the assumptions underpinning them, that is at issue here.

Given the substantial body of knowledge about ancient civilisations' calendric systems, much research has been devoted to the search for precursors of metric time systems and cognitive artefacts that integrate time and number in spatial arrays. This introduces a further bias, namely an assumption that the spatialization of time is a human cognitive universal manifested in a mental timeline (MT), either rectilinear (a straight line along which events or points in time are ordered) or cyclical (a circle with recurring points, such as a clock face). Many everyday utterances in English depend for their interpretation upon the imaginary construction of past, present and future as extended on the mental timeline. Consider the following expressions:

(1) My birthday is *coming up*
     My past is *behind*
     My time *is gone*
     I am looking *forward* to my restirement

These expressions conceptualize the past and future of events in terms of their movement on a mental timeline, with an imaginary orientation of the speaker's point of view facing forwards towards the future. This orientation of the timeline appears to be true of many, but not all, languages. For example, in the Aymara language of the Andes[1] (Núñez and Sweetser 2006), in the Sasak language of Lombok, Indonesia (Austin 2012), in Vietnamese (Sullivan and Bui 2016) and Malagasy (Dahl 1995) the timeline's orientation is the reverse of this, so that the future is located behind the speaker, with the past in front. In Chinese, the past may be conceptualized as above, and the future below (Yu 1998, 2012, Gu et al. 2019).

---

[1] Spoken by the Aymara people in the Bolivian Andes, around the Lake Titicaca region of southern Peru and by some communities in northern Chile and some parts of Argentina. Aymara is an official language of Bolivia and Peru.

The linearization of time is not, however, universal. We have seen that the Huni Kuĩ, Awetý and Kamaiurá languages of Amazonia do not metaphorically represent time in terms of a line; many other languages have also been documented that do not have a mental timeline manifested in speech, gesture or sign (Le Guen and Pool Balam 2012, Le Guen 2017, Silva Sinha 2019, Rodríguez 2019). One motivation that is often invoked for the frequency across many languages of spatial metaphors for time is that time is in perceptual terms more abstract than space, and the conceptual metaphor follows a general rule in which an abstract target domain is conceptualized in terms of a more concrete source domain (Lakoff and Johnson 1999). The temporal metaphors used by speakers of the Huni Kuĩ, Awetý and Kamaiurá languages do indeed follow such a logic, by referring to what we would be tempted in English to call temporal "locations" in terms of the embodiment of thought and feeling. They are not, however, spatial metaphors. The preponderance in the literature of spatial metaphors for time, and the frequent assumption that the "mental timeline" is a transcultural cognitive universal (Hoerl and McCormack 2019), may be due to the way in which colonial expansion imposed a linear concept of time on colonized peoples. Non-linear temporalities were thereby effectively erased, while at the same time situating colonized peoples as "backward", non-coeval with the colonizer:

> The efficacy of linear time consisted in justifying the idea that the past of the colonized had no future except the one offered by the colonizer. Once dispossessed of any future-making function, such past was deemed irrelevant and should vanish into oblivion . . . By the monoculture of linear time, the colonial subject was de-specified as backward, primitive.
> (Sousa Santos 2021: 18–21)

2.3 Measuring time

Linear time is also time that can be *quantified* in terms of units of measurement analogous to the units of two-dimensional spatial distance. Metric time is defined in terms of ordered, countable, recursively structured units. The cognitive artefacts that anchor the measurement of metric time are the clock and the calendar and these are ubiquitous in the lives of most people around the world – on computers and phones, as well as watches. The word *chronos* meaning 'time measured', and the word *horologium*, meaning 'the pendulum clock', refer to devices that measure the elapse of time objectively. For example, clocks can be found everywhere in our lives – such as computers, digital watches and phones, where one can find a clock measuring the seconds, minutes, and hours, and it is ticking, counting time precisely. In the same way, calendars schedule our lives precisely in days, weeks, months, and years. Clock and calendar time are chronological, measurable time.

Although the history of timekeeping is usually told as one of increasing accuracy of measurement, it is also a history of changing social norms. In post-revolutionary France, for example, the Republican Calendar year began at midnight on the autumnal equinox as observed in Paris. The calendar had twelve months of 30 days each, each month being composed of three ten-day weeks (*decades*), and the month's names were based on seasonal characteristics in nature. The calendar used Roman numerals, and for this reason, it used the numeral "I" to indicate the first year of the republic. The *decades* scheduled work, rest, and festivities. Interestingly, this was very similar to the Ancient Egyptian calendar. Every four years, a leap day (*franciade*) was inserted into a leap year called *Sextile*. During this time, another calendar, the Rural calendar, was also in use. This was designed to represent familiar aspects of rural life while breaking with the traditional saint's day calendar. The days of the year were indexed or associated with rural life. For example, the *décadi* were named after agricultural tools used at the time. The *quintidi* 'fifth day' (*quinti* 'five' and *di* 'day') was named after a common animal of the region. The many other weekdays and months were named after features of the environment and agricultural products, e.g., trees, roots, flowers, fruits, *nivôse* (winter, snowing), while other names were derived from minerals (Renouard 1822, Ozouf 1989, Shaw 2011).

> Our starting point was the idea of celebrating, through the calendar, the agricultural system, and of leading the nation back to it, marking the times and the fractions of the year by intelligible or visible signs taken from agriculture and the rural economy. [. . .] As the calendar is something that we use so often, we must take advantage of this frequency of use to put elementary notions of agriculture before the people – to show the richness of nature, to make them love the fields, and to methodically show them the order of the influences of the heavens and of the products of the earth.

> [. . .] So we have arranged in the column of each month, the names of the real treasures of the rural economy. The grains, the pastures, the trees, the roots, the flowers, the fruits, the plants are arranged in the calendar, in such a way that the place and the day of the month that each product occupies is precisely the season and the day that nature presents it to us.
> (Fabre d'Églantine, 1793)

The French revolutionary metric time system also changed the clock. Each day was divided into 10 decimal hours, each hour into 100 decimal minutes, and each minute into 100 decimal seconds. In the "new" time, an hour was 144 minutes, a minute was 86.4 seconds, and a second was 0.864 seconds in the "old" time (that is, in the sexagesimal metric time system developed in Babylon in the second millennium BCE, and which remains in use as the conventional system until today). Clock time was not, however, fully imposed as a means to regulate social activities, especially work time, until the industrial revolution (Ingold 1995); and the national standardization of previously geographically disparate clock times occurred only with the introduction of railway timetables (Bartky 1989).

Not all societies employ (or have traditionally employed) either metric time intervals or large number systems. This does not mean that such societies, in which calendars and/or clocks were introduced only after encounters with other cultures (usually those that came to be dominant in the society) that did employ them, lacked concepts of time. Non-metric, event-based concepts of time are addressed below in detail. Given the importance that has been accorded to the conceptualization of time in terms of space (the spatialization of time), we turn now to research on spatial frames of reference, and on space and time, in language and cognition.

3 Space and time: Interweavings in culture and language

3.1 Spatial frames of reference

We, see, feel, and talk about objects and do things with them, and when we do, we are at the same time conceptualizing locations, directions, and movements of things in space. In human cognition, these forms provide support for concrete thinking about objects and events. As drivers, hikers, hunters, we move on different terrains, whether in urban life or on paths within the Amazon rainforest or in the cold air of the mountains in the Andes. These diverse environments affect our ways of moving and acting, and it would not be surprising to find that these factors also influence our spatial thinking. Levinson (2003), among others, has argued that "spatial cognition is at the heart of our thinking, and it plays a role in the abstract conceptualization of time and human social relations" (p. xvii). Researchers at the Max-Planck Institute for Psycholinguistics, under Levinson's leadership, developed large-scale cross-linguistic studies of spatial frames of reference (FoR) that have greatly influenced the cognitive science of space and spatial relations. A frame of reference is a coordinate system that refers to the way the speaker/observer understands the location of a given object in space, and the research by Levinson and his colleagues investigated how frames of reference vary between languages, and how this influences speakers' conceptualizations of spatial relations.

Figure 11.2: Drawing (© Tataiya Kokama and Geraldir Bernardino, reproduced by permission).

For example, if you look at the drawing in Figure 11.2, you will see that there is a river, a boat, and people, with three people on the river bank and one person standing at the stern (back end) of the boat facing the bow (front end) of the boat. If we asked a person on the riverbank to describe their own and the boat's location, this might be conceptualized in different ways dependent on the frame of reference that the speaker uses. If the speaker says that the boat is "in front of me" they are using a *relative FoR*; if they say "the boat is downriver from me", the speaker is using an *absolute FoR*; and if the speaker says "I am behind the boat" they are using an *intrinsic FoR*. When I describe the man in the boat as being at the stern of the boat, I am also using the intrinsic frame of reference, but he is also behind the woman and children at the bow of the boat, within both the relative and the intrinsic FoR.

To take another example, involving a dog and car – if the dog is described as being in front of a car, viewed from the point of view of an observer to one side of the car, there are two positions in which the dog could be, either at the front of the car or at its side between the car and the observer. In the first case, we say that an intrinsic frame of reference is being used because the car (ground or landmark) has an *intrinsic* front based on its direction of motion. In the second case, we say that a *relative* FoR is being used because "front" refers not to an intrinsic part of the car, but to the side facing the observer; the location is relative to the observer's position. The third possible FoR is *absolute*, which is based on a set of fixed coordinates or directions, such as cardinal directions or the position of a geographical landmark such as a mountain or a river. If we say: "the dog is to the south of the car", we are using an *absolute* FoR. Linguistic variation in frames of reference is related to the diversity of human cultural settings. While variations in spatial frames of reference and their culturally-dependent conceptualizations seem to be consonant with the classification postulated by Levinson and his team, even within a category (e.g., absolute FoR) a great deal of variation may be observed, related to environmental conditions.

In the last decade, the study of topographical landmarks, how the landscape and the environment are used for spatial conceptualization, e.g., "towards the mountains" or "upriver" (Brown 2012) has gained a great deal of attention. As was emphasized in our introduction, cultures should not be thought of as determining thought and language across all situations and for all speakers. The lexicalization of spatial relations in such topographical FoRs may be context-dependent within the same linguistic community, including variations dependent on physical scale (see Senft 2017, Pappas and Mawyer 2021). For example, in many Pacific communities, including the Solomon Islands, upwind-downwind applies at the island level of granularity, while towards mountains-towards sea applies at a more local level, including, e.g., on a table top (Peter K. Austin personal communication, January 2022). Absolute FoRs may also be anchored in relation both to topographic landmark and to cardinal direction. For example, in Lombok (Bali) the absolute FoR lexical opposition "towards mountain-towards sea" rotates around the compass, depending on the speaker's position in relation to the volcanic mountain range: north of the mountain, "towards sea" means north, while south of the mountain the same term means south (Peter K. Austin personal communication, January 2022).

3.2 Topography, space and time

An intriguing question is whether spatial frames of reference are commonly translated into temporal frames of reference (Bender and Beller 2014, Bender and Bennardo 2010). Research reviewed above shows that topography is an important factor in spatial concepts. Studies have also demonstrated how topographical features can influence concepts of time as well as space (Magga 2006, Brown 2012, Gaby 2012, Levinson and Majid 2013, Núñez et al. 2012). An example is

Yupno (one of the Finisterre languages of Papua New Guinea). Speakers use to-pographic (up/hill/downhill) terms for describing both spatial and temporal rela-tions. Núñez et al. (2012: 25) argue that "the Yupno construal [of time] is not linear but exhibits a particular geometry that appears to reflect the local terrain. The findings shed light on how, our universal human embodiment notwithstand-ing, linguistic, cultural, and environmental pressures come to shape abstract concepts". Their conclusion endorses the argument that language and culture in-teract, but refutes the argument that time and space concepts are universal schemes: "Abstract concepts are commonly grounded in spatial concepts. How-ever, as the present case study demonstrates, exactly which spatial concepts are recruited is culturally shaped, not universally given" (Núñez et al. 2012: 34, see also Cooperrider et al. 2022). Similarly, Aymara speakers use an absolute FoR em-bedded in the mountainous topography of the Andes and in their cosmology, in which people and objects "are conceived as having an implicit canonical orienta-tion facing east, a primary landmark determined by the sunrise" (Núñez et al. 2012: 965). The lexical items *nayra* 'front' and *qhipa* 'back' are employed in Ay-mara to refer to both space and time; which is viewed by Núñez et al. (2012) as a manifestation of "a broader macro-cultural worldview and its psycho-cognitive reality".

Just as has been shown for spatial concepts, the use of topographical FoRs for temporal reference is context-dependent and influenced by variations in social practices in communities. The Mianmin of Papua New Guinea also use rivers and surrounding landscape for orientation and direction. Their spatial reference is based upon the axis of the sun's motion and their two rivers orientation (Fedden and Boroditsky 2012: 1). They also use their body as a point of reference. People arrange events in time in relation to their bodies (left to right or toward the body). They also conceptualize time in relation to the landscape. People from this com-munity use more left to right temporal representations if they have experienced years of formal education. The increased use of left to right temporal representa-tions is linked with increasing formal education years, but the reverse is true for the pattern for absolute spatial representations for time (Fedden and Boroditsky 2012: 6–7). Looking further at the importance of formal education in the use of spatial language for temporal construal, Gaby (2012) compared two populations of ethnic Thaayorre from Pormpuraaw (an Australian community of the south-west of the Cape York Peninsula, Queensland): one group of Kuuk Thaayorre/En-glish bilinguals, and the other English monolinguals. Her conclusion was as follows:

> [D]espite their common physical, social, and cultural context, the two groups differ in their representations of time in ways that are congruent with the language of space in

Kuuk Thaayorre and English, respectively. Kuuk Thaayorre/English bilinguals represent time along an absolute east-to-west axis, in alignment with the high frequency of absolute frame of reference terms in Kuuk Thaayorre spatial description. The English-monolinguals, in contrast, represent time from left-to-right, aligning with the dominant relative frame of reference in English spatial description. This occurs in the absence of any east-to-west metaphors in Kuuk Thaayorre, or left-to-right metaphors in English. Thus, the way these two groups think about time appears to reflect the language of space and not the language of time.[2]   (Gaby 2012:1)

Although the recruitment of topographic features for *both* spatial and temporal absolute FoRs is widespread, it is not the case that the use of a topographic spatial FoR always implies that the same FoR will be used for temporal concepts. Speakers of the Mayan language Tzeltal employ a topographic absolute spatial FoR utilizing uphill/downhill (south vs. north) and sunrise and sunset (crossways directions). This frame of reference does not appear to be transferred to the domain of time. Brown (2012) found that there was no corresponding uphill/downhill FoR for time when speakers carried out tasks involving temporal reference. Brown (2012: 10) concluded that the "systematic and consistent use of spatial language in an absolute frame of reference does not necessarily transfer to consistent absolute time conceptualization in non-linguistic tasks; time appears to be more open to alternative construal". The representation of time in terms of space is widespread, in languages that conceptualize spatial relationships in absolute frames of reference, but it is not universal. Absolute spatial frames of reference are common among Australian languages, but these are not mapped to temporal conceptualizations (Austin 1998).

3.3 Spatial metaphors for time: A language universal?

Space-time metaphorical mappings are not restricted to absolute FoRs, and spatial meanings have been claimed to be a universal source domain for structuring time concepts (Lakoff and Johnson 1980, 1999, Fauconnier and Turner 2008). According to this theory, the human conceptual system is structured by a limited set of experientially-based concepts, which include: (1) a set of basic spatial relations such as front vs. back; up vs. down, (2) a set of basic ontological concepts, e.g., entity, container, and (3) a set of basic actions, e.g., eating, moving. The concepts that are not directly based on experience must, it is claimed, be metaphorical in nature, understood and structured

---

2 It should be noted that there is nonetheless a conventionalized, non-metaphoric left-to-right orientation in both text and calendar in English.

through mappings from this fundamental and limited set of experientially-based concepts (Boroditsky 2000). Therefore, it is claimed that it is only possible to talk about time through metaphorical mapping from the spatial source domain; "metaphorical mappings indeed shape abstract domains such as time from more concrete and experiential domains such as space" (Boroditsky 2000: 1).

The experience of "time passing" is one in which the observer experiences continuity and unidirectional change. Time is generally conceived in this way as a one-dimensional directional entity, and it has been claimed that this motivates the use of directional spatial terms as ahead vs. behind, up vs. down for temporal conceptualization (Boroditsky 2000: 4). If we accept that the domains of time and space domains share conceptual structure, this accounts for the frequency of space-time metaphorical mappings in many languages. It is undeniable that in the English language, time is conceptualized through the space domain and moves along a line, as illustrated in the examples below:

(2)   We are coming up to New Year
      New Year is coming up

In the first expression of Example (2), the deictic center or speaker "ego" moves towards the future along the timeline, towards the event/temporal landmark "New Year". This metaphoric construction exemplifies what is called the "Moving Ego schema" (ME). When time itself is considered to "flow" along a timeline as in the second expression of Example (2), moving from the future through the present, to the past, carrying events with it, the schema is called "Moving Time" (MT). In this schema, time moves towards ego along the timeline, from the future to the present. Both these constructional metaphors presuppose a direction of the timeline in which the "future is ahead of ego" and the "past is behind ego" (Clark 1973). However, it has been shown that such metaphorical constructions are not conventional or acceptable for speakers in all languages (Sinha et al. 2011); and as we saw in Section 2.2 above, in the Huni Kuĩ, Awetý and Kamaiurá languages of Amazonia, past and future are indeed conceptualized metaphorically, but in terms of embodied perception and cognition. In summary, while there is a great deal of evidence that people talk and think about temporal passage in terms of space in diverse languages and cultural settings, this is not the case for all of them,

What we call (metaphorically) the "passage" of time has, as well as the temporal relations between events, another experiental aspect, namely its *duration*. Subjectively, people can make duration judgments based on their experience. For example, if a person is asked whether a song was long or short after they have listened to the song, or if we ask a songwriter whether the duration of writing was longer or shorter when they were listening to a piece of music. The answer to these questions will be evaluated according to their subjective perception. It seems, however, that it is possible for speakers of many, perhaps all, languages to represent duration in terms of spatial extension. The nature of the number system used by the cultural community has been shown to impact the specific way in which the mapping of temporal duration to spatial extension (linear length) is made in experimental settings.

Many languages, including Amazonian languages, have five or fewer numeral words (Sinha Silva et al. 2017). A study carried out by Dehaene et al. (2008) compared French speakers with speakers of Mundurucu (a Tupian language of Brazil with four number terms), finding that Mundurucu speakers mapped numbers onto a logarithmic scale, whereas the French adults used a linear mapping in which the distance between any two adjacent numbers is invariant:

> at all ages, the Mundurucu mapped symbolic and non-symbolic numbers onto a logarithmic scale, whereas Western adults used linear mapping with small or symbolic numbers and logarithmic mapping when numbers were presented non symbolically under conditions that discouraged counting. This indicates that the mapping of numbers onto space is a universal intuition and that this initial intuition of number is logarithmic. The concept of a linear number line appears to be a cultural invention that fails to develop in the absence of formal education. (Dehaene et al. 2008: 1)

The Mundurucu system of number words is a cultural device that does not require measurement of invariance by addition and numerical subtraction system, as used in Western numeral systems (Dehaene et al. 2008: 4). The implication of this study is that the supposed "abstractness" of time is not so straightforward as is often assumed. We can directly perceive two objects and their spatial relationship. We can also directly experience two events and their temporal relationship in terms of their sequential relationship. We can only directly perceive what happens "in the now". However, through episodic memory, we can recall past events, and through imagination, we can anticipate future events. Future events may also be projective, based on experience, e.g., the sun will come up tomorrow, just as it has done every day of my life (Austin 2012). Therefore, through memory and imagination, we create past and future, and a sequence of events. The passage of time, the ever-changing "now", is based in experience, and so deictic time is not really abstract, except insofar as future events are imaginary, which is a philosophical issue (see McTaggart 1908, Price 1996).

Space, as we have seen, is not the only domain recruited to metaphorically conceptualize time, and we should also consider the notion of *change*. The epistemology of change perception is important because "from earliest infancy human beings orient primarily to changes in the surrounding world, learning to anticipate the regularities of events, to realize their intentions and desires through actions and to read the intention manifested in the actions of other" (Sinha and Gärdenfors 2014: 72). Additionally, change is essential for event classification (see Filipović 2007) and language typology seems to be sensitive to the relevant distinctions related to change. For example, different languages use different means to ensure that change in spatial configuration is signaled (Aske 1989), or to express the difference concerning the point within a motion event at which change was witnessed (e.g., when it already occurred or while it was occurring; see Filipović 2007, Filipović and Jaszczolt 2012).

In summary, although in the English language it is difficult, if not impossible, to think of and talk about time without employing metaphors that have as their source domain space and motion (Sinha and Gärdenfors 2014: 73), a considerable body of research has shown that the claim that time is always metaphorically structured from space in all languages and cultures in the world is not sustainable. Our own research (Sinha et al. 2011, Silva Sinha 2018, 2019) showed that in the Amondawa, Awetý, Kamaiurá and Huni Kuĩ languages and cultures of Brazil, speakers do not utilize spatial language to metaphorically express temporal relations. Similar results have been reported for the Yélî Dnye language, spoken in Rossel Island, Papua New Guinea (Levinson and Majid 2013). The notion of a "timeline" is also not universally applicable. It has been found that in Amondawa, Awetý, Kamaiurá, Huni Kui, there is no timeline (Sinha et al. 2011, Silva Sinha 2019); and Le Guen and Pool Balam (2012) have also claimed that there is "to some extent, non-linear, non-directional conception of time in Yucatec Maya" (see also Brown 2012 for the absence of a timeline in Yucatec Maya spoken in Mexico).

4 Event-based time

4.1 What is event-based time?

Time concepts, as we have already seen, are embedded in the natural environment and social practices. In many cases, time intervals are thought about in terms of events and happenings, in nature and in the social world. For example, we can say in English *Let's meet at lunchtime* or *See you in the autumn*. I have defined this way of conceptualizing time as *event-based* (Silva Sinha et al. 2012, Silva Sinha 2018, 2019). Event-based time units are defined by the events that index them and from which their names usually derive (e.g., *the sun is gone* [sunset]). Event-based time intervals may be based upon natural processes, such as the diurnal and seasonal cycles, or social norms and conventions. As noted above, not every culture employs metric time concepts. Event-based time concepts, in contrast, can be found in all languages and cultures: In this section, I mainly focus on how event-based time is expressed and used in cultural settings in which metric time is not conventionally lexicalized. The following examples intend to give an insight into understanding how concepts of time are constructed and motivated by cultural patterns and the relationship between language and culture, and how environment and cultural practices are used to index time in different cultural settings.

The term "event-based time", which refers to the events that index them and their names usually derived from them, was formulated during our research on certain Amazonian languages: Amondawa, Awetý, Kamaiurá, Hãtxa Kuĩ (Sinha et al. 2011, Silva Sinha et al. 2012, Silva Sinha 2018, 2019). In our ethnographic studies, we have found that in the Amondawa, Awetý, Kamaiurá and Hãtxa Kuĩ languages, time is not measured in terms of calendar or clock systems either. There are no translation equivalents (words) for "time" in these languages, and no names for days of the week or months of the year, in any of them.

Time is thought about in terms of events and happenings, in nature and the social world. The event-based time intervals are indicated (indexed) by environmental happenings (water level and animal songs), celestial bodies (sun, moon, and stars) and activities. Parts of the day, for example, are indexed either by activities, for example, *return from the field time* means before lunchtime; or by the sun's position: *the sun is on top of the head* means midday (Silva Sinha 2018, 2019, Silva Sinha et al. 2011, 2012). The sun's position in the sky, and the appearance of constellations, indicate the period or "right time" for social activities that people in the communities conventionally might do or can do. The sun's position is an indexical marker for a named time interval, whose name is defined either by the sun's position, the presence of light, or by a conventionally associated activity. Traditionally, these intervals imply that people would habitually engage in certain activities at the sun's position. However, these are true time intervals, distinct from the actual activity because the interval's name does not imply that the activity is actually taking place. Moreover, even the temporal labels that refer to the sun's position do not mark exact points in time but are also intervals. The boundaries between the intervals are not exact since they are event-based, not metric. The day and night intervals are also indexed and named by sun, light, dark, moon, and social activity. Environmental indexical markers include not only the sunlight but also the light of the day, the absence of light, shadows and the dark. The movement, the shape, color and size of the moon, the appearance and position of constellations are used to index time as well the level of water in the river, the breeze off the water, birdsong, monkey calls, the sound of the cicadas, the ripening of forest fruits, and the movements of animals. These indices make up the temporal fabric of life in these communities.

All the examples here described attest that Amondawa, Awetý, Kamaiurá, and Hãtxa Kuĩ conceptualize time through metonymic and fusional constructions, indexed by environmental happenings and celestial bodies (sun, moon, and stars). Event-based time concepts are more widespread in traditional cultural settings than has hitherto been recognized. Their occurrence is specific to particular cultural settings, depending on ecological niches intertwined with social structure, activities, and value systems. Event-based time has in fact been described in anthropological and linguistic studies of non-western cultures and languages for quite a long time. For example, Deborah Rose (2013, 2005, 2000) has described time in the Victoria River district in Australia, which she called "ecological time", comprising basic schemas that involve rain, sun, wet and dry seasons. These environment "forces", she said, coordinated activities and social lives. She noticed that some events are organized by a range of sequenced connections that co-occur simultaneously in this scheme: "when the march flies start biting, the crocodiles are laying their eggs. When the *jangarla* tree flowers, the barramundi are biting" (Rose 2000: 291). She argues that "Aboriginal people's time concepts do not fit the simplistic model of time's circle (or arrow)". Time is considered as consisting of "generations of living things, ecological time, synchronicities, interval, patterns and rhythms" and the comprehension of complex time concepts is necessary for the understanding of ecological processes (Salleh 2017 [1997]: 137 cited in Rose 2000: 288; see also Adam 1994).

In Diyari, a year is *kilpa waldra*, literally 'cold hot', that being the only two seasons in their location (Austin 2012). For the Bayungu (Australian people of the Gascoyne region of Western Australia) and many other Australian communities also reported using environmental indexes e.g., animals, birds, tides, fishes and plants, to build their hybrid calendars.[3]

In Bunun, an Austronesian language spoken in the central and southern mountainous areas of Taiwan, speakers do not talk about time in terms of calendars and clocks. Their time is linked or indexed to daily chores and traditional rituals. The Bunun language does not have a word for "time", and neither does it have concepts of the hour, minute, or second. They borrowed the term *zikan* (meaning 'year') from Japanese and use it when required. Traditionally, they

---

3 See [https://www.csiro.au/en/research/natural-environment/land/About-the-calendars] (accessed 20 January 2022).

have used seasons to represent a year, so *hamisan* ('winter') is used to express the notion of year. They have two seasons: *hamisan* ('winter') and *talapal* ('dry season'). The *buan* ('moon') represents ('counts') 12 months of the year. The moon has an important role in temporal events, since Bunun festivals and rituals are planned in accordance with the lunar cycle. The words *hanian* and *dihanin* are used to designate day, and the *dihanin* not only refer to 'day' but to 'sky', meaning 'day time', in opposition to the 'night'. Even though they refer to 'calendrical units' such as 'month', Huang (2016) explained that it is "unusual to refer to a time point by its order in a year or a month" (p. 6). Bunun time concepts are derived from the event process "the starting of TIME coincides with the beginning of an activity and its ending with activity's completion" (Huang 2016: 18). Time in this system is not a separate category but is fused with the event, in the same way as for the Amondawa (Silva Sinha et al. 2012).

Tamazight (formerly known as Berber), a Tarifit language of North Africa, also does not have a word that designates the full cycle of day and night. Speakers use the Arabic loan word *yawm* to express this concept, together with the Tamazight terms *swass* (daylight) and *djirth* (absence of the light) meaning night. Human activity is governed in the first of these by the sun and in the second by the constellations. Event indexes are the sun's position and heat, meal times, light and dark, breezes, and the length of shadows. There is a more negative connotation to 'day' than the night because "the light of the sun at *t'haa'* (noon) is dreaded; basically it hurts the bodies but mainly for it is an obstacle for all human activities" (El-Arbaoui Jelouli 2013: 223).

In Setswana, a Bantu language spoken in Southern Africa, the movements of the sun, moon, and stars and their positions indicate intervals in the day, and the change of seasons indexes when some activities take places, e.g., agricultural ploughing, harvesting. The term for 'day' is *letsatsi* (sun) and for 'month' *kgwedi* (moon). Many temporal references in Setswana are event-based and indexed in the natural environment. It appears that the term *letsatsi* (sun) is essential for temporal expressions in Setswana.

4.2 "Time reckoning" with event-based time

What implications does the prevalence of non-metric, event-based time in many cultural settings have for the way we should understand practices such as "time-reckoning" – a terminology that seems to imply the notion of counting units of time? Returning to my own ethnographic research in Amondawa, Kamaiurá, Awetý, and Huni Kuĩ, I have conjectured that in these cultures the completion of events and activities is the way time is reckoned. However, this practice does not mean that "counting" is absent from cultural practices. On the contrary, there is even a Kamaiurá word for it, *paparawaw* ('counting'). The number system in these languages consists of distinct terms for "one" and "two" and these words can be combined, allowing for counting to "three", "four", "five" or more, based on a compounding process, such as by juxtaposition, agglutination, or reduplication (Silva Sinha et al. 2017). The "basic" constituent words for number expressions (one and two) can also be combined with words for hand and foot, fingers/toes. These quantificational expressions are employed across contexts, and may be combined with other words (e.g., verbs of motion) and meaningful gestures (e.g., showing fingers) in ways which are specific to particular contexts. Time intervals can be counted, using hands, fingers, and toes, but as in the situation of a fishing expedition, one finger can represent one day (or another entity, such as a basket of fish). Finger counting sequences seems to appear in many cultures, but there is a variability of composition depending upon the cultural practices (Crump 1990, Bender and Beller 2011). For Kamaiurá and many other communities which use event-based time, what is most significant about the time interval and the event is that its conceptual basis is its "happening", particularly its completion. An event-based time interval for them is not a segment of "Time as Such" (Sinha et al. 2011), but something that occurs or should be done or accomplished.

Not only body parts, but also symbolic cognitive artefacts may be used for "reckoning" time. Traditionally in Awetý and Kamaiurá, the duration of a fishing or hunting expedition is "measured" by untying knots on a string (Figure 11.3). The activities for each day are planned and organized beforehand by the expedition leader, and then the information is communicated to his family and to the community. The leader estimates the length of string that will be necessary to complete the expedition in terms of the expected catch of game or fish, and ties a knot in the string for each day. Each knot on the string represents the completion of one day's activities and a night spent on the hunting or fishing expedition. During the expedition, every day a knot will be untied. Each knot untied is an index of both the overnight stay and the completion of one day's activities. However, it is important to note that the knots are *never* counted before the expedition sets out. Therefore, the knotted string is a representation of the expected duration of the expedition that will take place, but it is not a count or tally of the number of days. In fact, the number of knots tied at the beginning is just an estimate. The knots on the string do not enumerate an exact number of days planned for the expedition. Rather, there should be enough knots for the string to be used during the expedition. The knotted string is not a general instrument for counting days in all contexts but an artefact for use only in certain contexts. It is not a kind of calendar.

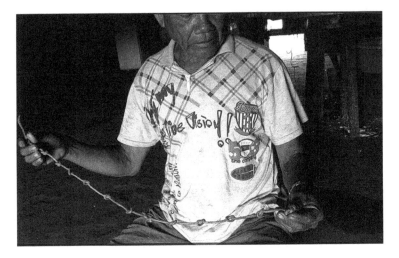

Figure 11.3: Tamahet Kamaiura demonstrates the use of knotted strings for time reckoning in 2016 (image © Silva Sinha).

4.3 Life stages in event-based time

Many communities worldwide do not use calendars to "reckon" their dates of birth. In Setswana, speakers mark their birth time in terms of a social or environmental event that indexes it. For example, "*o tshotswe ka ngwaga wa mabele a mantsho* (He/she was born in the year of black sorghum yield) or social events such as a tribal victory at war e.g., *kapuso ya ga Ntlatsang* 'at the time of *Ntlatsang's* rule')" (Kgolo 2018: 27).

Amondawa, Kamaiurá, Awetý, and Huni Kũĩ do not count ages in terms of years or months. Speakers of these languages consider life as being a process of learning punctuated by different stages of life. The life stages should be thought of as social status categories, not as points on a lifeline. The time of human life is "shaped" not by a timeline but by performative, epistemic, and social-relational categories. There are certain kinds of skilled activities, certain kinds of knowledge, and certain social responsibilities that are appropriate and necessary for each life stage. The transitions between these stages can involve rites of passage and organized learning. It is important to point out that the knowledge associated with one life stage category is not strictly restricted. The knowledge of each stage can be acquired during previous stages. For example, a young person, if they have acquired "adult" knowledge and responsibility (such as being a skilled fisherman or taking on household responsibilities, with a level of knowledge recognized by the entire community) will be regarded and respected as a fully-grown person, at least in that respect.

Physical and biological changes also index the stages. For example, the girl will be considered a fully responsible adult after her first period, when she will pass through the rite of passage in which she will acquire the knowledge and skills of a woman in their respective community. After the first puberty signs (voice changing), boys will pass through the rite of passage in these communities. In the stages of life, a very "young" (in "our" terms) girl who is married is an adult, but an older woman who has never married or had children will still be considered and treated as a youth unless the biological signs of ageing are very evident. The life stages focus on the skill and abilities but not a point in a timeline, with the numerical measurement as employed by teenagerhood in western culture (Silva Sinha 2018, 2019).

Life stages can also be indexed by onomastic (naming) systems. For example, individuals in the Amondawa community change their names during their lives. The rules governing the changes of name are based upon the cross-cutting category systems of life stage, gender, and moiety. It is obligatory for each individual to change his or her name when "moving" from one life stage to another, and each name is selected from a finite archive of names, each of which has a semantic value indicating moiety, gender and life stage. The principal event that can cause a change of names is the birth of a new family member. The new baby will be given a "newborn" name and may even assume a name previously held by the youngest existing family member, who then takes a new name. The "newborn" name given in the family can initiate a chain of name changes, in which all the existing children will acquire a new name. Transitions in an individual's social status also provoke a name change, e.g., an individual will change their name when she/he assumes a new role in the family or group. When the eldest son changes his name, his father changes his name too. A woman will change her name when getting married, and her previous name will go to her youngest sister. The name first given to a child in Amondawa is not used beyond a certain life stage. Changes of names imply that the individual has grown up and has new responsibilities in the family.

A comparable but slightly different onomastic system is found in Awetý and Kamaiurá cultures. When a child is born, if it is a boy, when the umbilical cord drops off, the child will receive the first set of names from both their grandfathers and an earring. If it is a girl, she will receive her grandmothers' first set of names. They receive their second set of names after the rite of passage from child to adult. When the boy becomes an adult, he will have a second pair of names from his (great-)grandfather's names from both father's and mother's sides. Girls become young adults and receive their (great-)grandmother's names from both sides. Only the second pair of names will be used for both men and women during adulthood (see Silva Sinha 2018). The life stages and related onomastic systems in Amondawa, Awetý and Kamaiurá are examples of symbolically represented and organized event-based time.

5 Conclusion

Concepts of time vary between and within languages because these concepts are strongly linked to worldviews and cultural practices. Social practices and cognitive artefacts are influential in determining the source domains that underlie cultural metaphors for time. Among the Amondawa, Kamaiurá, Awetý, and Huni Kuĩ, metaphors for time are not derived by mapping from the spatial domain, but by mapping from the domains of embodied perception and cognition. Conceptually, speakers of these languages locate past and future events in embodied cognitive and perceptual processes, rather than locating them along an oriented timeline. For Awetý and Kamaiurá the past is *in their eyes*. Their past consists of memories, and memories can be "seen" in "the mind's eye". Therefore, in Kamaiurá and Awetý, REMEMBERING IS SEEING. The future for Awetý and Kamaiurá, is in front of the speaker's eyes, but not far away; it is located in the immediate visual field. Past is not located behind the speaker for these cultures. In Huni Kuĩ, past events are located in the *heart* and future events and plans are located in the *head* (which is thought of as the location of the mind and thinking). This suggests that in these cultures past and future are conceptualized in terms not of spatial direction, but of embodied mental capacities: *memory, anticipation, intention*, and *imagination*.

In these Amazonian communities, the light of the day and the absence of the light, the shadows of the dark, the intensity of sunlight, the position, movement, shape, color and size of the sun and moon, and constellations of its positions and appearances, as well as the level of the water, the breeze off the water, birdsong, animals movements calls and sounds and the ripening of forest fruits, are all indices used to index time. These environmental happenings motivate the names of event-based time intervals that make up these communities' temporal fabric of life. Physiological changes due to ageing are also part of the conceptual repertoire that defines life stages for these communities. For example, to become a young woman or to become a young man involves physical and biological changes. However, these biological indices are situated in a conception of life stages that is organized around a performative, social understanding of lifespan.

Event-based time concepts can be found across human cultures, and almost certainly antedate the emergence of non-universal metric time systems. The invention of metric time brings with it changes in language and cognition, most importantly, the construction of a mental timeline and the spatialization of time in conceptual metaphors (Sinha 2015, Sinha and Bernárdez 2015). Events, and event structure, are the fundamental building blocks of human conceptualization (Sinha and Gärdenfors 2014). Temporal concepts are also, in all societies, embedded in practices supported by artefacts. These can include familiar and historically evolved artefacts such as compasses, clocks, calendars, and other time interval measurement systems based on language.

Further research on this field and subject is needed to continue to be able to better understand the fascinating variation in ways of thinking and talking about space and time across cultures. It is important to consider that "each of these languages expresses the unique knowledge, history and worldview of their speaker communities and each language is a specially evolved variation of the human capacity for language" (Endangered Languages Documentation Project, SOAS). Research on "non-WEIRD" (Western, Educated, Industrialized, Rich, Democratic) cultures and languages (Henrich et al. 2010), and especially in traditional cultures with lesser-known and endangered languages, will engender new understanding of transcultural commonalities and cross-cultural diversity in cognition and language. More research on the time and number relation, for example, will yield insights into how number and time are understood in terms of embodied mental processes (memory and perception). Research with endangered languages in this area not only brings scientific benefit, but also provides the foundation for developing and implementing practical programs of language and culture preservation and revitalization in these communities.

References

Adam, Barbara. 1994. Perceptions of time. In Tim Ingold (ed.), *Companion encyclopedia of anthropology. Humanity, culture and social life*, 503–526. London: Routledge.

Aske, Jon. 1989. Path predicates in English and Spanish: A closer look. *Annual Meeting of the Berkeley Linguistics Society* 15. 1–14.

Austin, Peter. K. 2012. Tense, aspect, mood and evidentiality in Sasak, eastern Indonesia. In Stuart McGill & Peter K. Austin (eds.), *Language documentation and description* 11, 231–251.

Austin, Peter. K. 2012. Tense, aspect, mood and evidentiality in Sasak, eastern Indonesia. In Stuart McGill & Peter K. Austin (eds.), *Language documentation and description* 11, 231–251. London: SOAS.

Bartky, Ian R. 1989. The adoption of standard time. *Technology and Culture* 30 (1). 25–56.

Bender, Andrea & Sieghard Beller. 2014. Mapping spatial frames of reference onto time. A review of theoretical accounts and empirical findings. *Cognition* 132 (3). 342–382.

Bender, Andrea & Sieghard Beller. 2011. Fingers as a tool for counting – naturally fixed or culturally flexible? *Frontiers in Psychology: Cognition* 2 (256). 1–3.

Bender, Andrea, Sieghard Beller & Giovanni Bennardo. 2010. Temporal frames of reference. Conceptual analysis and empirical evidence from German, English, Mandarin Chinese, and Tongan. *Journal of Cognition and Culture* 10. 283–307.

Bender, Andrea, Sieghard Beller, Giovanni Bennardo, Niclas Burenhult, Lisa Hüther, Kirill V. Istomin, Olivier Le Guen & Thora Tenbrink. 2011. Space (and time) for culture. *Cognitive Science* 33. 1338–1339.

Birth, Kevin. 2012. *Objects of time. How things shape temporality*. New York: Palgrave Macmillan.

Bloch, Maurice. 1977. The past and the present in the present. *Man* 12 (2). 278–292.

Bohnemeyer, Jürgen. 2009. Temporal anaphora in a tenseless language. In Wolfgang Klein & Ping Li (eds.), *The expression of time*, 83–128. Berlin & Boston: De Gruyter Mouton.

Boroditsky, Lera. 2000. Metaphoric structuring. understanding time through spatial metaphors. *Cognition* 75 (1). 1–28.

Boroditsky, Lera. 2001. Does language shape thought? Mandarin and English speakers' conceptions of time. *Cognitive Psychology* 43 (1). 1–22.

Bourdieu, Pierre. 1977. *Outline of a theory of practice*, translated by R. Nice. Cambridge: Cambridge University Press.

Bowerman, Melissa & Soonja Choi. 2003. Space under construction. Language-specific spatial categorization in first language acquisition. In Dedre Gentner & Susan Goldin-Meadow (eds.), *Language in mind. Advances in the study of language and thought*, 387–427. Cambridge: MIT Press.

Brown, Penelope. 2012. Time and space in Tzeltal. Is the future uphill? *Frontiers in Psychology* 3 (212). DOI:10.3389/fpsyg.2012.00212.

Brown, Penelope. 2015a. Language, culture, and spatial cognition. In Farzad Sharifian (ed.), *Routledge handbook on language and culture*, 294–309. London: Routledge.

Brown, Penelope. 2015b. Space, linguistic expression of. In J. D. Wright (ed.), *International encyclopedia of the social and behavioral sciences*, 2nd edition, Vol. 23, 89–93. Amsterdam: Elsevier.

Buzsáki, Györgi & David Tingley. 2018. Space and time. The hippocampus as a sequence generator. *Trends in Cognitive Sciences* 22 (10). 853–869.

Casasanto, Daniel & Lera Boroditsky. 2008. Time in the mind. Using space to think about time. *Cognition* 106 (2). 579–593.

Clark, Herbert H. 1973. Space, time, semantics and the child. In Timothy E. Moore (ed.), *Cognitive development and the acquisition of language*, 27–63. New York: Academic Press.

Cooperrider, Kensy, James Slotta & Rafael E. Núñez. 2022. The ups and downs of space and time. Topography in Yupno language, culture, and cognition. *Language and Cognition*. DOI:10.31234/osf.io/5x8zb

Crump, Thomas. 1990. *The anthropology of numbers*. Cambridge: Cambridge University Press.

Dahl, Øyvind. 1995. When the future comes from behind. Malagasy and other time concepts and some consequences for communication. *International Journal of Intercultural Relations* 19 (2). 197–209.

Davis, Richard. 1976. The Northern Thai calendar and its uses. *Anthropos* 71 (1–2). 3–32.

Dehaene, Stanislas & Elizabeth Brannon (eds.). 2011. *Space, time and number in the brain. Searching for the foundations of mathematical thought*. Cambridge: Academic Press.

Dehaene, Stanislas, Véronique Izard, Elizabeth Spelke & Pierre Pica. 2008. Log or linear? Distinct intuitions of the number scale in western and Amazonian Indigene cultures. *Science* 320 (5880). 1217–1220.

Durkheim, Émile. 1912. *The elementary forms of religious life*. Oxford: Oxford University Press.

D'Eglantine, Philippe François Nazaire Fabre. 1793. *Rapport fait à la Convention nationale, dans la séance du 3 du second mois de la seconde année de la République Francaise*. Paris: Imprimerie Nationale.

El-Arbaoui Jelouli, Amar. 2013. *A cognitive approach to Berber-Tamazight sociocultural reality. The bioconceptual organization of* Izri *poetics by Tarifit-speaking Riffian women*. Las Palmas: Universidad de Las Palmas de Gran Canaria dissertation.

Evans-Pritchard, Edward Evan. 1939. Nuer time-reckoning. *Africa: Journal of the International African Institute* 12 (2). 189–216.

Everett, Daniel. 2012. *Language. The cultural tool*. London: Profile Books.

Fabian, Johannes. 1983. *Time and the Other. How anthropology makes its object*. New York: Columbia University Press.

Fabian, Johannes. 2014. Ethnography and intersubjectivity: Loose ends. *HAU: Journal of Ethnographic Theory* 4 (1). 199–209.

Fauconnier, Gilles & Mark B. Turner. 2008. Rethinking metaphor. In Raymond Gibbs (ed.), *The Cambridge handbook of metaphor and thought*, 53–66. Cambridge: Cambridge University Press.

Fedden, Sebastian & Lera Boroditsky. 2012. Spatialization of time in Mian. *Frontiers in Psychology* 3 (485). DOI:10.3389/fpsyg.2012.00485

Filipović, Luna. 2007. *Talking about motion. A crosslingual investigation of lexicalization patterns*. Amsterdam: John Benjamins.

Filipović, Luna & Katarzyna M. Jaszczolt (eds.) 2012. *Space and time in languages and cultures. Linguistic diversity*. Amsterdam: John Benjamins.

Furet, François & Mona Ozouf. 1989. *A critical dictionary of the French revolution*. Cambridge: Harvard University Press.

Gaby, Alice. 2012. The Thaayorre think of time like they talk of space. *Frontiers in Psychology* 3 (300). DOI:10.3389/fpsyg.2012.00300

Geertz, Clifford. 1973. *The interpretation of cultures*. New York: Basic Books.

Gell, Alfred. 1992. *The anthropology of time. Cultural constructions of temporal maps and images*. Oxford: Berg.

Gentner, Dedre & Susan Goldin-Meadow (eds.). 2003. *Language in mind. Advances in the study of language and thought*. Cambridge: MIT Press.

Gontier, Nathalie. 2018. Cosmological and phenomenological transitions into how humans conceptualize and experience time. *Time and Mind* 11 (3). 325–335.

Gu, Yan, Yenqiu Zheng & Marc Swerts. 2019. Which is in front of Chinese people, past or future? The effect of language and culture on temporal gestures and spatial conceptions of time. *Cognitive Science* 43 (12). DOI:10.1111/cogs.12804

Gumperz, John J. & Stephen C. Levinson (eds.). 1996. *Rethinking linguistic relativity*. Cambridge: Cambridge University Press.

Henrich, Joseph, Steven J. Heine & Ara Norenzayan. 2010. The weirdest people in the world? *Behavioral and Brain Sciences* 33. 61–83.

Hoerl, Christoph & Teresa McCormack. 2019. Thinking in and about time. A dual systems perspective on temporal cognition. *Behavioral and Brain Sciences* 42. DOI:10.1017/S0140525X18002157

Huang, Shuping. 2016. Time as space metaphor in Isbukun Bunun. A semantic analysis. *Oceanic Linguistics* 55 (1). 1–24.

Hubert, Henri. 1999[1905]. *Essay on time. A brief study of the representation of time in religion and magic.* Oxford: Durkheim Press.

Hutchins, Edwin. 2005. Material anchors for conceptual blends. *Journal of Pragmatics* 37 (10). 1555–1577.

Ingold, Tim. 1986. *Evolution and social life,* Cambridge: Cambridge University Press.

Ingold, Tim. 1995. Work, time and industry. *Time and Society* 4 (1). 5–28.

Jaszczolt, Katarzyna M. 2012. Cross-linguistic differences in expressing time and universal principles of utterance interpretation. In Luna Filipović & Katarzyna M. Jaszczolt (eds.), *Space and time in languages and cultures. Linguistic diversity*, 95–121. Amsterdam: John Benjamins.

Jaszczolt, Katarzyna M. 2016. Temporal reference without the concept of time? In Barbara Lewandowska-Tomaszczyk (ed.), *Conceptualizations of time*, 3–24. Amsterdam: John Benjamins.

Jaszczolt, Katarzyna M. 2018. Time, perspective and semantic representation. *Language and Cognition* 10. 26–55.

Jaszczolt, Katarzyna M. 2019. *Human imprints of real time. From semantics to metaphysics.* University of Cambridge unpublished manuscript.

Katovich, Michael A. 1987. Durkheim's macrofoundations of time. An assessment and critique. *The Sociological Quarterly* 28 (3). 367–385.

Kgolo, Naledi N. 2018. Setswana lexical expressions of time. *Marang. Journal of Language and Literature* 30. [https://journals.ub.bw/index.php/marang/article/view/1311].

Lakoff, George & Mark Johnson. 1980. *Metaphors we live by.* Chicago: The University of Chicago Press.

Lakoff, George & Mark Johnson. 1999. *Philosophy in the flesh. The embodied mind and its challenge to western thought.* New York: Basic Books.

Le Guen, Olivier. 2017. Una concepción del tiempo no-lineal en dos lenguas: el maya yucateco colonial y actual y la lengua de señas maya yucateca, *Journal de la société des américanistes* [http://journals.openedition.org/jsa/15327] (accessed 20 April 2022). DOI:10.4000/jsa.15327

Le Guen, Olivier & Lorena Ildefonsa Pool Balam. 2012. No metaphorical timeline in gesture and cognition among Yucatec Mayas. *Frontiers Psychology* 3 (271). DOI:10.3389/fpsyg.2012.00271

Levine, Robert N. 1998. *A geography of time. The temporal misadventures of a social psychologist*, revised edition. New York: Basic Books.

Levinson, Stephen C. & Asifa Majid. 2013. The island of time. Yélî Dnye, the language of Rossel Island. *Frontiers in Psychology* 4 (61). DOI:10.3389/fpsyg.2013.00061

Levinson, Stephen C. & David P. Wilkins (eds.). 2006. *Grammars of space. Explorations in cognitive diversity*. Cambridge: Cambridge University Press.

Levinson, Stephen C. 2003. *Space in language and cognition. Explorations in cognitive diversity. Cambridge:* Cambridge University Press.

Lucy, John A. 1992. *Language diversity and thought. A reformulation of the linguistic relativity hypothesis.* Cambridge: Cambridge University Press.

Magga, Ole Henrik. 2006. Diversity in Saami terminology for reindeer, snow, and ice. *International Social Science Journal* 58 (187). 25–34.

Majid, Asifa, Alice Gaby & Lera Boroditsky. 2013. Time in terms of space. *Frontiers in Psychology* 4 (554). DOI:10.3389/fpsyg.2013.00554

Mauss, Marcel. 1966. *The Gift. Forms and functions of exchange in archaic societies.* London: Cohen and West Ltd.

McElwain, Thomas. 1987. Seneca Iroquois concepts of time. *The Canadian Journal of Native Studies* 7 (2). 267–277.

McTaggart, J. M. E. 1908. The unreality of time. *Mind* XVII (4). 457–474.

Miller, William Watts. 2000. Durkheimian time. *Time and Society* 9 (1). 5–20.

Moore, Kevin Ezra. 2006. Space-to-time mappings and temporal concepts. *Cognitive Linguistics* 17 (2). 199–244.

Morgan, Lewis Henry. 1877. *Ancient society; or, Researches in the Lines of Human Progress from Savagery, Through Barbarism to Civilization.* New York: H. Holt.

Munn, Nancy D. 1983. Gawan kula. Spatiotemporal control and the symbolism of influence. In Jerry W. Leach & Edmund Leach (eds.), *The Kula. New perspectives on Massim exchange,* 277–308. Cambridge: Cambridge University Press.

Munn, Nancy D. 1986. *The fame of Gawa. A symbolic study of value transformation in a Massim society.* Cambridge: Cambridge University Press.

Munn, Nancy D. 1992. The cultural anthropology of time. A critical essay. *Annual Review of Anthropology* 21. 93–123.

Núñez, Rafael E. & Carlos Cornejo. 2012. Facing the sunrise. Cultural worldview underlying intrinsic-based encoding of absolute frames of reference in Aymara. *Cognitive Science* 36 (6). 965–991.

Núñez, Rafael E. & Eve Sweetser. 2006. With the future behind them. Convergent evidence from Aymara language and gesture in the crosslinguistic comparison of spatial construals of time. *Cognitive Science* 30 (3). 401–450.

Núñez, Rafael E. & Kensy Cooperrider. 2013. The tangle of space and time in human cognition. *Trends in Cognitive Sciences* 17 (5), 220–229.

Núñez, Rafael E., Kensy Cooperrider, D. Doan & Jürg Wassmann. 2012. Contours of time. Topographic construals of past, present, and future in the Yupno valley of Papua New Guinea. *Cognition* 124 (1). 25–35.

Pappas, Leah & Alexander Mawyer. 2021. The place of space in Oceanic Linguistics. *Oceanic Linguistics* 61 (6). DOI:10.1353/ol.2021.0027

Pinxten, Rik. 1995. Comparing time and temporality in cultures. *Cultural Dynamics* 7 (2). 233–252.

Postill, John. 2002. Clock and calendar time. A missing anthropological problem. *Time and Society* 11 (2–3). 251–270.

Price, Huw. 1996. *Time's Arrow and Archimedes' Point. New Directions for the Physics of Time.* Oxford: Oxford University Press.

Renouard, Antoine-Augustin. 1822. *Manuel pour la concordance des calendriers républicain et grégorien,* 2nd edition. Paris: Antoine-Augustin Renouard.

Rodríguez, Lydia. 2019. "Time is *not* a line." Temporal gestures in Chol Mayan. *Journal of Pragmatics* 151. 1–17.

Rose, Deborah B. 2000. To dance with time. A Victoria River Aboriginal study. *The Australian Journal of Anthropology* 11 (2). 287–296.

Rose, Deborah B. 2005. Rhythms, patterns, connectivities. Indigenous concepts of seasons and change, Victoria River District, NT. In Tim Sherratt, Tom Griffiths & Libby Robin (eds.), *A change in the weather. Climate and culture in Australia,* 32–41. Canberra: National Museum of Australia.

Rose, Deborah B. 2013. *Anthropocene noir.* Arena Journal 41–42. 206–219.

Salleh, Ariel. 2017 [1997]. *Ecofeminism as politics: Nature, Marx and the postmodern*. New York: Zed Books.

Schieffelin, Bambi B. 2002. Marking time. The dichotomizing discourse of multiple temporalities. *Current Anthropology* 43 (S4). S5–S17.

Senft, Gunter. 2017. Absolute frames of spatial reference in Austronesian languages. *Russian Journal of Linguistics* 21. 686–705.

Shaw, Matthew. 2011. *Time and the French revolution. The Republican calendar, 1789–Year XIV*. Rochester, NY: Boydell Press, Royal Historical Society.

Silva Sinha, Vera da. 2018. *Linguistic and cultural conceptualisations of time in Huni Kuĩ, Awetý and Kamaiurá indigenous communities of Brazil*. Norwich: University of East Anglia dissertation.

Silva Sinha, Vera da. 2019. Event-based time in three indigenous Amazonian and Xinguan cultures and languages. *Frontiers in Psychology* 10 (454). DOI:10.3389/fpsyg.2019.00454

Silva Sinha, Vera da, Wany Bernardete de Araujo Sampaio & Chris Sinha. 2017. The many ways to count the world. Counting terms in indigenous languages and cultures of Rondônia, Brazil. *Brief Encounters* 1 (1). 1–18.

Silva Sinha, Vera da, Chris Sinha, Wany Bernardete de Araujo Sampaio & Jörg Zinken. 2012. Event-based time intervals in an Amazonian culture. In Filipović, Luna and Katarzyna M. Jaszczolt (eds.), *Space and time in languages and cultures II: Language, culture and cognition*, 15–35. Amsterdam: John Benjamins.

Sinha, Chris & Kristine Jensen de López. 2006. Language, culture, and the embodiment of spatial cognition. *Cognitive Linguistics* 11 (1–2). 17–41.

Sinha, Chris. 1988. *Language and representation. A socio-naturalistic approach to human Ddevelopment*. Hemel Hempstead: Harvester-Wheatsheaf.

Sinha, Chris. 2017. Getting the measure of meaning. In Barbara Dancygier (ed.), *The Cambridge handbook of cognitive linguistics*, 493–497. Cambridge: Cambridge University Press.

Sinha, Chris. 2021. Culture in language and cognition. In Xu Wen & John R. Taylor (eds.), *The Routledge handbook of cognitive linguistics*, 387–407. New York: Routledge.

Sinha, Chris & Enrique Bernárdez. 2015. Space, time, and space-time. Metaphors, maps, and fusions. In Farzad Sharifian (ed.), *The Routledge handbook of language and culture*, 309–324. New York: Routledge.

Sinha, Chris & Peter Gärdenfors. 2014. Time, space, and events in language and cognition. A comparative view. *Annals of the New York Academy of Sciences* 1326 (1). 72–81.

Sinha, Chris, Vera da Silva Sinha, Jörg Zinken, J. & Wany Bernardete de Araujo Sampaio. 2011. When time is not space. The social and linguistic construction of time intervals and temporal event relations in an Amazonian culture. *Language and Cognition* 3 (1). 137–169.

Sousa Santos, Boaventura de. 2021. Some theses on decolonizing history. *Seminar* 743 (07–2021). 16–24.

Sullivan, Karen A. & Linh Thuy Bui. 2016. With the future coming up behind them. Evidence that Time approaches from behind in Vietnamese. *Cognitive Linguistics* 27 (2). 205–233.

Tenbrink, Thora. 2011. Reference frames of space and time in language. *Journal of Pragmatics* 43 (3). 704–722.

Thapar, Romila. 1996. *Time as a metaphor of history. Early India: The Krishna Bharadwaj memorial lecture*. Oxford India: Oxford University Press.

Whitrow, G. J. 1989. *Time in history. Views of time from prehistory to the present day*. Oxford: Oxford University Press.

Whorf, Benjamin Lee. 1950. An American Indian model of the universe. *International Journal of American Linguistics* 16 (2). 67–72.

Wright, Ronald. 1991. *Time among the Maya. Travels in Beliza, Guatemala and Mexico.* New York: Grove Press.

Yu, Ning. 1998. *The contemporary theory of metaphor. A perspective from Chinese.* Amsterdam: John Benjamins.

Yu, Ning. 2012. The metaphorical orientation of time in chinese. *Journal of Pragmatics* 44 (10). 1335–1354.

Maïa Ponsonnet

12 Emotional language: A brief history of recent research

The world's languages offer myriads of different ways to talk about emotions, and this variation has been an object of study in anthropological linguistics for a long time. This chapter begins by recounting how this interest in the language of emotions emerged in the 1970s and 1980s, initially led by anthropologists who did not study language in and of itself. As presented in the second section, their work nevertheless led them to articulate a core question about language per se: how does it produce or transform emotions? In the last section, I review the multiple perspectives adopted by linguists – other than anthropological linguists – to examine emotional language, ranging from the description of words in individual languages to comparisons across languages, and the holistic study of speech and conversation. Along the way, I will highlight the strengths and weaknesses of research on emotional language, suggesting ways forward where possible. Overall, after five decades of remarkable progress in empirical description, the most salient challenge seems to be synthesis and the articulation and structuring of research questions.

1 Introduction

1.1 What and why?

Emotion is a fundamental aspect of human experience that colors all aspects of our lives and most of our interactions. Many researchers have acknowledged that emotion also pervades all dimensions of language and most stretches of discourse (Ochs and Schieffelin 1989: 9, Besnier 1990: 421–422). Therefore, the scientific study of emotional language is central to our understanding of human behavior and social organization. This chapter will recount the development of interest in emotional language in anthropology, linguistics, and anthropological linguistics, all disciplines for which it is a naturally central theme.

Before I explore the importance of research on emotional language further, I will briefly discuss definitions of "emotion". As pointed out by Izard (2010),

Maïa Ponsonnet, Centre National de la Recherche Scientifique in Lyon/France,
e-mail: maia.ponsonnet@cnrs.fr

https://doi.org/10.1515/9783110726626-012

Widen and Russell (2010), and Wierzbicka (2010), among others, there is no strong consensus about the nature of "emotion" as an object of scientific study. Apart from the term "emotion", authors from various disciplines also use a range of other labels to differentiate between subtly distinct adjacent notions. As summarized by Alba-Juez and Mackenzie (2019), some authors distinguish "emotion" and "feelings" (Damasio 1999, Wierzbicka 1999, Scherer 2013) and others prefer the term "affect" (Massumi 1995), while some choose to ignore the nuances between these terms (Besnier 1990: 421, Ponsonnet 2014a: 16). Given that this chapter considers the study of emotional language across authors and theoretical frameworks, it is better to adopt a broader definition, and I will therefore ignore these nuances.

In my own research, I define emotions as internal states that have a cognitive dimension (in contrast to sensations such as hunger or cold, for instance), as well as a subjective appraisal dimension (distinguishing them from purely intellectual evaluations such as belief or agreement). While emotions often pair up with physical or physiological responses, the above definition leaves them out (e.g., Ponsonnet 2020: 21), which leads to the inclusion of long-lasting states such as moods, attitudes, or dispositional inclinations within the scope of emotions (Besnier 1990: 421). This definition of "emotion" is not intended to overrule those chosen by other authors. Indeed, many anthropologists and anthropological linguists prefer definitions of emotions that include some aspects of the social context – such as interactions, behaviors, triggering events, and so on – as part of what they call "emotion" or "affect" (see Section 3 for further discussion). I find this approach less specific, and perhaps also further removed from the day-to-day use of the English word *emotion*, but it can certainly be useful in some fields of research. The discussions in the present chapter can be understood either within a narrower or a broader definition of emotion.

There are many reasons why anthropologists, and anthropological linguists in particular, want to study emotional language. As pointed out above, since emotions are everywhere in our lives and everywhere in our language, understanding how humans use emotional language is crucial to any "anthropological study", broadly understood as "the study of human life". Likewise, emotional language is relevant to anthropological linguists by definition, since the object of study of this field can be characterized as "how humans use language to organize their lives and define their selves". In addition, because emotions are not directly observable, and language is an important way in which humans manifest their emotions, it is tempting to hope that studying emotional language may also help us understand emotional experience itself. While this is a genuine possibility, it also opens up the risk of overconfidently and unreflectively using language as a "window on emotion". This temptation probably underpins a significant proportion of the research on emotional language, as will be discussed in several places throughout this chapter.

Apart from its evident relevance to anthropology and anthropological linguistics, emotional language also occupies a special space in the study of language, due to the range of semiotic statuses it recruits from. Many linguists have posited a key conceptual difference between *expressive* linguistic resources and *descriptive* linguistic resources (Irvine 1982, Besnier 1990: 419, Bednarek 2008, Foolen 2012: 350, Majid 2012a: 432, Ponsonnet 2014b: 21–22, Alba-Juez and Mackenzie 2019). Expressive emotional resources, for instance an interjection like *wow*, are those that linguists tend to interpret as causal effects of a state experienced by the speaker at the time of utterance: someone is supposed to say "*wow!*" because they feel impressed. Semiotically, such expressive resources are defined as those that convey meaning by *indexing* speakers' states, in Peirce's (1955) sense of the term "index". Descriptive emotional resources, on the other hand – for instance "she is impressed" – are not semiotically bound to the speaker's emotional state in this way. They can therefore refer to states experienced at any point in time, by the speaker or by others – just like most other utterances in any semantic domain. Of course, the simplistic dichotomy between expressive and descriptive resources does not do justice to the complex communicative nature of emotional language (Ponsonnet et al. forthcoming). Precisely for this reason, the co-presence and intimate interplay between expressive and descriptive linguistic resources in the semantic domain of emotions allows us to study expressive semiosis and how it combines with other types of semiosis to produce meaning in human life (Goffman 1978, Levy 1984: 230–231). In this respect, emotional language represents a privileged field of study for linguists seeking to examine the semiotic organization of human language.

1.2 State of the art

While the above paragraphs make it obvious why the study of emotional language is relevant to a number of disciplines interested in human life and communication, they also give a good indication that this is not an easy task. If emotions are ubiquitous and diffuse, they can only be hard to pin down and analyze. In spite of early interests of philosophers in the topic (Descartes 1649, Spinoza 1677, Hume 1740, James 1884), modern scientists have kept away from emotion for a long time, perhaps because it seemed to fall outside of the realm of systematization (Lüdtke 2015a). In the last half century, however, many life and human sciences – including biology, psychology, social sciences, and the humanities, among others – have taken an "affective turn", developing interests in emotion as an identified topic (see for instance Lemmings and Brooks 2014). Since then, a relative profusion of studies, stemming from a broad array of disciplines and frameworks, has taught us a lot about the nature and role of emotions in human life.

Following this trend, studies with a specific focus on the language of emotion started to appear in the late 1980s and 1990s, with a range of theoretical orientations, including, in particular, anthropological linguistics, lexico-semantic studies, cognitive linguistics, soon followed by others. As this chapter will attest, a lot more knowledge on how humans talk about emotions is available now than was the case even just 30 years ago. Much of this knowledge relies upon solid firsthand data and innovative methodologies, providing reliable, in-depth analyses of a broad range of linguistic phenomena. At the same time, notwithstanding some fields and authors who have achieved significant coherence and decisive results, the scientific production on emotional language remains somewhat disparate for the moment. This is perhaps unsurprising, with such a sizeable aspect of reality to cover – entire linguistic systems, and virtually all linguistic interactions. Perhaps the most revealing symptom of researchers' collective difficulty to create unity on this topic is the number of edited volumes (or handbooks) around the broad theme of "language and emotion". Between 1990 and today, at least a dozen such collective volumes have appeared, all presenting substantial numbers of very valuable, yet extremely diverse studies (often case studies).[1] They provide many useful insights, but we have yet to bring these insights together, in one way or probably several ways, before we can articulate overarching insights about emotional language. This observation is not intended as a criticism of these volumes and their contributors,[2] but as a diagnostic note suggesting that the science of emotional language now needs to work towards producing more syntheses.

The present chapter certainly does not aim to bring about definite coherence in emotional-language studies. This will more likely be a gradual process involving a number of parallel reflections from a range of subfields where

---

1 To cite just the ones I am familiar with: Lutz and Abu-Lughod (1990), with an anthropological linguistic orientation (see Section 2); Niemeier and Dirven (1997), including a range of linguistic approaches; Athanasiadou and Tabatowska (1998), with a cognitive linguistic orientation; Harkins and Wierzbicka (2001), adopting Natural Semantic Metalanguage methodology; Blumenthal, Novakova, and Siepmann (2014), with an emphasis on quantitative methods; Lüdtke (2015b), with a cognitive linguistics and psycholinguistics orientation; Tersis and Boyeldieu (2017), including miscellaneous descriptive approaches; Mackenzie and Alba-Juez (2019), with a Systemic Functional Linguistic angle; Pritzker, Fenigsen, and Wilce (2020), with an anthropological linguistic orientation; and Schiewer, Altarriba, and Chin (forthcoming).
2 Of which I am one myself.

studies of emotional language have emerged. With this long-term goal in mind, this chapter offers a brief history of the developments and avatars of scientific interest in emotional language, focusing (for the sake of feasibility, and given the theme of this book) on the segments that speak to anthropological linguistics. I will highlight the most cohesive research trends while at the same time identifying some areas that remain loose, in the hope that this might support those who are currently pursuing structured research programs around emotional language. I have tried to be as inclusive as possible; however, given the richness of the field, it is nearly impossible to be entirely exhaustive.

The narrative will start, in Section 2, with the early anthropological interest in emotions, emerging in the 1960s, and how emotional language was operationalized in these studies. Section 3 explains how, in the 1980s, this anthropological interest in emotions shaped up into an attention to emotional language itself. Instead of treating language as a means to find out about emotional states, anthropological linguists began to approach emotional language, and more specifically the emotional *use* of language, as a scientific object in itself. Section 4 shows how studies of emotional language from other linguistic subfields complement the anthropological linguistic approach, investigating comparable questions with a different set of methods and assumptions.

2 The role of language in anthropological works on emotion

Apart from some early insights from the work of major anthropologists (e.g., Mead 1928), the anthropological study of emotions for their own sake began in the last third of the 20th century. The 1970s saw the publication of the first anthropological monographs paying substantial attention to emotions, such as Briggs (1970) on the Utkuhikhalingmiut in Canada, and Levy (1973) on Tahiti. This was followed in the 1980s by works that set the foundations of anthropological approaches – and even more specifically, anthropological linguistic approaches – to emotions. Rosaldo's (1980) account of how the Ilongots' emotional inclinations explain their eagerness to "take heads" (i.e., kill people), and Lutz's (1988) discussion of the Ifaluks' "emotional landscape", have been the most influential, among a larger number of publications that developed similar perspectives around the same time (e.g., Myers 1979, Heelas and Locke 1981, Schweder and LeVine 1984, and Lutz and White 1986 for a review).

All these works offer thorough ethnographic accounts of behaviors, concepts, beliefs, and moral etiquettes related to emotions among the groups under consideration. As I will show below, language played an important role in these works. However, emotions in their social dimension usually remained their first and foremost object of investigation and theoretical reflection. Beyond specific descriptions of emotions, the main theoretical contribution of the works cited above – as expressed very explicitly by Rosaldo (1980) and Lutz (1988) for instance – has been to present emotions as culturally constructed social phenomena (Harré 1986). This emerged as an answer to psychologists who, in the same decades when these "anthropologies of emotions" flourished, were developing notions of emotions as universal adaptive functions (culminating with Ekman's 1992 theory of "primary" or "basic" emotions). Such views confine emotions to the domain of "nature". In response, anthropological accounts demonstrated how emotions depend upon the social contexts in which humans live, which in turn drew emotions back into the "cultural" domain.

2.1 Words and cultural representations

The vast majority of the anthropological accounts of emotions published throughout the 1970s and 1980s recruit language as an essential tool in ethnographic description. These descriptions typically take as their starting point one or two local words that do not find straightforward translations in English. The author then proceeds to explain this/these word/s based on a rich combination of observations, citations, or direct metalinguistic discussions with informants. This results in remarkably refined cultural translations that not only render the meaning of the pivot word(s), but present and analyze a wealth of ethnographic material. In this process, it is assumed that "untranslatable" words point to culturally salient concepts, which in turn guide and organize anthropological accounts. Famous words/concepts are, for instance, the Ifaluk words *song* and *fago*, which Lutz (1988) glosses as 'justifiable anger' and (approximatively) 'compassion, love and sadness' respectively; or the Ilongot *liget*, combining 'anger, energy, passion' (Rosaldo 1980: 247), which according to Rosaldo underpins the desire to "take heads".

While this approach results in maximally insightful translations, it also relies upon somewhat naïve conceptions of language. Firstly, throughout these texts, words are generally equated with concepts (e.g., Lutz 1988: 210), without much consideration for the distance between the two notions. The existence of a given word in a language is implicitly treated as unquestionable evidence that the concept it encodes is culturally prevalent. Of course, words do often encode culturally salient concepts. Levy (1984), drawing on Levy's (1973: 305) observations among the Tahitians and the absence of clear words for sadness in the Tahitian language, famously coined the term *hypercognition*. It encapsulates the idea that the presence of words to talk about certain emotions in a language correlates with a higher degree of cultural attention for this emotion. Emotions for which there are few words, on the other hand, are *hypocognized*.[3] Although this is not demonstrated, it may be reasonable to assume that a proliferation of words comes hand-in-hand with cultural salience. However, the existence of *some* word(s) for an emotion does not necessarily warrant the same conclusion (Malt, Gennari, and Imai 2010, Malt et al. 2011). In addition, not all important concepts are encoded by salient lexemes. This is illustrated, for instance, by the concepts of compassion and love in the Dalabon language (Australia). While Dalabon speakers do operate with these concepts to understand and explain their and others' emotional experience in conversations, words encapsulating just these concepts are scarce or dispersed in the Dalabon language (Ponsonnet 2014c: 196–199, 209–217). The general lack of attention to such nuances in the "anthropology of emotions" produced in the 1970s and 1980s results in a somewhat incautious use of vocabulary as a "window onto culture".

This overly confident reliance upon words as signposts for salient shared representations is often rendered more problematic by the tendency to focus on a relatively small number of lexemes (as recognized by Lutz and White 1986: 423), and particularly on nouns – as opposed to verbs, adjectives, etc.[4] Nouns tend to be salient in speakers' metalinguistic representations,[5] and therefore lend themselves naturally to anthropological explorations. However, in many languages of the world, nouns only represent a small fraction of the emotional lexicon (Ponsonnet 2016, Yacopetti and Ponsonnet forthcoming), and there is no evidence that they necessarily encode the concepts of emotion that play the strongest role in the local emotional etiquette. While vocabulary is never an ideal "window onto emotions" in any case, the focus on nouns imposes an additional limitation to a small set of presumed "key words".

2.2 The use of language

As noted by Rosenberg (1990), this reliance on language as a window on concepts of emotion is strangely at odds with the authors' own theoretical considerations

---

3 Levy does not specify whether hypercognition *results* from the availability of words, or whether a large number of words simply *reflects* hypercognition (without causing it).
4 With some exceptions; see, for instance, Briggs (1970).
5 Perhaps due to their referential status, and as evidenced by speakers' tendency to borrow nouns from other languages; see, for instance, Matras (2009: 166–168).

on language and how anthropologists should approach it. Both Rosaldo (1980) and Lutz (1988) explicitly condemn "referential conceptions of language" (Wittgenstein 1953), i.e., the naïve assumption that humans use language primarily to point at things in the world. Instead, Rosaldo and Lutz call for more attention to language use, i.e., to what people *do* with language, and in particular how they *use* language to enact, express, shape, and in a sense "produce" emotions in a social context. Indeed, Rosaldo's and Lutz's (and other authors') discussions of the meaning of presumed "key words" do include some quotes from speakers and provide rich context. Yet the purpose remains to describe the concepts these words are assumed to represent – or "point at". Rosaldo's premature passing sadly prevented her from pursuing further research on emotions in language use herself.[6] As discussed in Section 3, Lutz, on the other hand, went on to develop, produce, and channel significant works in this direction, essentially initiating what may be regarded today as the "linguistic anthropology of emotions" proper.

3 Emotions in anthropological linguistics

3.1 Emotions in discourse

As a direct response to Rosaldo's (1980) and Lutz's (1988) encouragements to examine language in use, in the late 1980s and 1990s anthropologists started to effectively study the way emotions are "created in, rather than shaped by, speech" (Abu-Lughod and Lutz 1990: 12). This goal aligns straightforwardly with the core tenets of anthropological linguistics, which essentially aims to study how human languages contribute to define, structure, and produce social identities, groups, and interactions. In 1990, Catherine Lutz and Lila Abu-Lughod co-edited a collective volume entitled *"Language and the politics of emotions"*. Their introduction to this volume (Abu-Lughod and Lutz 1990) articulate these goals very explicitly, and can easily be read as a "manifesto" for the study of emotional language in anthropological linguistics. The contributions in the volume offer foundational studies in this spirit.

In opposition to the "universalist" view of emotions, Abu-Lughod and Lutz (1990) reaffirm their view that emotions are a cultural phenomenon, and that "emotions and discourse are not separate variables, one belonging to the private

---

6 Michelle Rosaldo died in an accident in the field in 1981. She did contribute indirectly to later anthropological linguistics study of emotions via her husband Renato Rosaldo's writings on the experience of loss and bereavement (Rosaldo 1996).

world, the other to the public social world". As mentioned above, in their view discourse defines and produces emotion as much as it expresses it, which again supports the study of language *in use*, i.e., as a mode of social interaction rather than as a strictly referential tool (Wittgenstein 1953). This clear move away from the instrumentalization of language as a "window on emotions" represents a re-alignment of theory with practices, compared to the hiatus observed in Section 2.

Abo-Lughod and Lutz (1990) explicitly narrow down their definition of "discourse" to the most formal, elaborate, or artistic contexts, to the exclusion of everyday conversations. While this may seem restrictive to anthropological linguists broadly interested in language as a social tool, this focus renders the task more approachable, given the ubiquity of affect in language (see Section 3.2 on Besnier 1990). In line with this focus, the chapters in the edited volume "*Language and the politics of emotions*" analyze moral discourse (White 1990), Bedouin love poetry (Abu-Lughod 1990), griot talk in Wolof (Irvine 1990), and Tamil songs (Trawick 1990), among other topics. The interest of anthropological linguists in emotion and affects in well-identified, formal genres and perform-ances has remained prevalent through time (see Section 3.3, on Wilce 2009). On the other hand, attention to emotion in day-to-day speech has so far been more prevalent only in (relatively recent) linguistic research (see Section 4 below).

3.2 Research agenda

In the same year when Lutz and Abu-Lughod's edited volume appeared, Besnier (1990) published another foundational article entitled "*Language and affect*", based on comparable premises. Besnier's piece offers a substantial review of ex-isting publications on the topic, mostly from the preceding two decades. At the same time, it effectively articulates a working program for the on-going linguistic anthropology of emotions, identifying a number of research questions and ave-nues for future research.

Besnier partitions the task of studying what he calls "affect"[7] in language into two different organizing principles. The first principle, corresponding to the first part of Besnier's text (1990: 421–428), takes linguistic forms as its starting point. The author examines the range of possible loci of affect in language, i.e., types of linguistic resources that are more likely to encode emotions, and that

---

7 Besnier (1990: 421) does not differentiate between "affects", "feelings", or "emotions", and also includes "moods" and "attitudes" under the same grouping.

have been/should be investigated as part of the study of the relationship between language and emotions. The list is long given that "affect permeates all levels of linguistic and communicative structures" (ibid.: 437), including resources as diverse as metaphors, address terms, syntactic constructions, intonation, and laughter. So far, this language-oriented research program has mostly been fulfilled by linguists, and will be further discussed in Section 4.

In the rest of the article, Besnier reviews where the question of the emotional dimension of language has so far surfaced in anthropological linguistics publications. This defines a research agenda aiming to explore the interactions between "language and affect" to the extent that they overlap with the then established research questions of anthropological linguistics itself. Amongst areas of interest, Besnier mentions the semiotic status of emotional language and its relationship with indexicality (Besnier 1990: 428), i.e., the semiotic nature of emotional language discussed in the above introduction (Section 1.1); registers and genres, particularly in social contexts where emotional language plays a key role (e.g., psychological therapy or ritual, ibid.: 431–434); the role of emotional language in acquisition and socialization (ibid.: 420); and the interplay between language, emotion, and gender (ibid.: 434–436), as well as between language, emotion, and class (ibid.: 436–438). All these themes align neatly with the pivotal questions and methods of anthropological linguistics, around indexicality, identity, power, and social structures.

The majority of the literature cited by Besnier remains relevant today. Many major works that touch upon emotional language in the context of language acquisition and socialization (Ochs 1986, Ochs and Schieffelin 1989, Schieffelin 1990), language and gender (Lutz 1986, Smith 1985), or registers and style, for instance, all containing fundamental insights on emotional language, were published earlier than 1990. Naturally, a large amount of additional work on comparable topics has appeared since, and fortunately several published syntheses are available that help keep track of these rich investigations of emotional language. The most exhaustive are probably Wilce's (2009) monograph on "*Language and emotion*", along with the more recent handbook edited by Pritzker, Fenigsen, and Wilce (2020). Like Besnier's (1990) review, Wilce's (2009) comprehensive account structures the field of research on language and emotion around the broader questions tackled in anthropological linguistics, including, in particular, identity and identification, and language and power, as well as giving thorough attention to language in performance and in ritualized contexts. Wilce also considers how language informs the historicization and medicalization of emotions, as well as the question of emotions triggered *by* language. Pritzker, Fenigsen, and Wilce's

(2020) collection also includes further discussions on language acquisition, performance genres, and embodiment, with themed chapters for each of those. Wilce (2009) and Pritzker, Fenigsen, and Wilce (2020) offer comprehensive reviews of the vast literature on the topic, and I refer the reader to these volumes for references as well as syntheses on the above questions.

3.3 Embracing emotions?

The syntheses cited above demonstrate the richness of the anthropological linguistics literature on how emotions surface in discourse. Yet they also reveal that emotions are in fact relatively rarely treated as primary objects of study by anthropological linguists. Some publications do demonstrate an interest in emotional experience as such. However, with a few exceptions, the content on emotions in discourse is typically embedded within publications that address a broader topic of anthropological linguistics – for instance registers, rituals, language and gender, language and power, etc. This mirrors the organization of the syntheses cited above around these key disciplinary questions. In other words, emotional language tends to be approached as a piece of a larger jigsaw puzzle of anthropological linguistics.

A consequence of this less direct approach to emotions is that, to my knowledge, no synthesis exists that organizes the abundant literature on emotional discourse "by emotion". In other words, a reader interested in how humans around the world use language with respect to, say, the experience of grief, would have to harvest a large number of relevant works from a massive amount of text. The task would be arduous, since many of the publications in which the relevant information is included may be flagged (e.g., by their titles and abstracts) as literature on poetry or songs, for instance. Of course, an approach "by emotion" runs against the core theoretical views of anthropologists and anthropological linguists about emotions. We saw in the previous sections that researchers in these disciplines fundamentally regard emotional experience as a product of the cultural context in which it takes place, which rules out the existence of a universal set of biologically defined basic emotions (Ekman 1992). In this perspective, focusing on a specific emotion as a theme of enquiry or synthesis is not only artificial, but also stands at odds with the theoretical underpinnings of the discipline. Further, and presumably in reaction to more biological conceptions of emotions, some anthropological linguists have denied their "internal" (private) dimension altogether, instead approaching them as exclusively social, interactional phenomena. Wilce (2009: 8), for instance, following Haviland (2003: 481) and Kockelman (2003), prefers to define emotions as "[. . .] shared **intersubjective**[8] states, performed in complex multimodal contexts [. . .]". This contributes to the justification that emotions should be studied through the lenses of research questions on social interactions.

Over the years and decades, some anthropological linguists have nevertheless adopted one or two emotions as their explicit object of study. Amongst the emotions that have received the most dedicated attention are anger, which also attracts a lot of attention in cross-cultural studies in other subfields of linguistics (see Section 4); shame, which is an eminently social emotion with implications around empowerment; and grief, often embedded in specific ritualized contexts and genres. Emotions with lesser social or linguistic inscriptions, such as fear, for instance, have naturally attracted less attention in the anthropological linguistics literature. Lutz and White (1986: 427) offer a review structured around "problems with which the person is impelled to deal". This allows for cross-cultural comparison between similar emotional experiences without having to postulate any universal concept of emotion. For instance, contexts involving interpersonal conflict capture situations where anger-like emotions can be experienced and expressed; the loss of significant others triggers grief-like emotions, etc. Unfortunately, to my knowledge, Lutz and White's (1986) early synthesis has not been updated in recent years (and no comparable synthesis exists for other linguistic studies either; see Section 4 below). Organizing the vast literature produced by anthropological linguists on emotional discourse around emotional concepts/contexts would be a very worthwhile task to undertake. It would render a considerable amount of literature more readily accessible to a broader range of scientists, including historians, sociologists, political scientists, psychologists, and many more.

4 Emotions in other fields of linguistics

While anthropological linguists are interested in language *use*, and how it contributes to shaping human identities and social structures, most linguists prefer to study linguistic *codes*. That is, linguistic structures are the primary object of investigation in general linguistics. Understanding linguistic structures may include exploring how these structures are used, but the focus tends to remain on the properties of the tool, rather than on what speakers achieve with it. In line

---

8 Emphasis from the original text.

with this interest in structure, the methods of linguistics generally start from observable forms, i.e., words and constructions. Semantics (the study of meaning) is often implicitly treated as an addendum to the study of forms, and linguists sometimes express defiance about its vagaries. Emotional meanings, with their not-directly-observable denotata, have long been considered to lie entirely outside the realm of the empirically approachable dimensions of language. As a consequence, the "emotional turn" took place even later in linguistics than in anthropology. Linguists effectively began to pay some attention to emotions in the early 1990s, i.e., shortly after the emergence of a sustained interest in emotional language among anthropological linguists.

In line with these different goals, general linguists' theoretical stances regarding the nature of emotions, and the relationships of emotions with language, differ significantly from those observed in anthropological linguistics. Perhaps due to the focus on languages as codes rather than on social structures, linguists other than anthropological linguists are not particularly preoccupied with the question of the social or psychological nature of emotions. Many of them embrace (more or less explicitly) constructivist views of emotions as internal states (e.g., Scherer, Shorr, and Johnstone 2001, Feldman Barrett 2009, Boiger and Mesquita 2012, Lindquist and Gendron 2013). Linguists from several different subfields do treat emotional language as a "window onto cultural conceptions of emotions", as did early emotion anthropologists. Some linguistic subfields make this an explicit method and articulate theories to support this approach. Many linguists regard their scientific contributions to the understanding of emotional language as potentially useful to the investigation of emotional experience itself (Wierzbicka and Harkins 2001: 1, Majid 2012b).

Given their interest in languages as codes, linguists have generally put more effort into describing the types of linguistic resources available across languages to talk about emotions – i.e., what sort of "tools" (words, inflections, grammatical constructions, etc.) different languages offer to their speakers in this semantic domain. This complements the research program set by anthropological linguists in several ways. Firstly, examining emotional linguistic resources is a necessary preamble to the study of their use. Indeed, linguists (e.g., Foolen 2012) follow some of Besnier's (1990) recommendations, effectively mapping the shape and diversity of Besnier's "loci of affect in language" (see Section 3.2 above). This will be discussed in Sections 4.1 to 4.3 below. In addition, as mentioned earlier, many linguists also study how linguistic codes function in use, i.e., they investigate how emotional meanings unfold in speech, narratives, conversations, etc. In this vein, linguists from a range of methodological traditions attend to the same data as anthropological linguists – albeit with different questions in mind. These trends are presented in Section 4.4 below.

Another feature shared across linguists' approaches to emotional language, whether from anthropological linguists or from other subfields, is their diversity (in terms of data, methods, and research questions) – and, consequently, a relative lack of synthesis, already alluded to in the introduction to this chapter. Notwithstanding this dispersion, the following section highlights some of the areas where sustained research in one direction has brought decisive results on one question or another, and attempts to present the rest in a way that suggests pathways for further synthesis. Given the ubiquitous nature of emotional language, the field is so diverse that I have had to leave some trends aside. I have chosen to omit those with less potential for dialogue with anthropological linguistics, such as Potts' (2007) semantic formalization of expressive features, or the psycholinguistic research on bilingualism (Dewaele and Pavlenko 2004, Pavlenko 2005, 2006, 2014).

4.1 The lexicon

4.1.1 Natural Semantic Metalanguage

Anna Wierzbicka is probably the linguist whose name is most closely associated with the study of emotions. She had already worked on emotion for a number of years (Wierzbicka 1992a) when her seminal monograph "*Emotions across languages*" was published in 1999. Wierzbicka's (1999) work on emotion in language is grounded in the Natural Semantic Metalanguage framework, a method of semantic description based on "semantic primes", i.e., words/meanings that are believed to occur in every language in the world (Goddard and Wierzbicka 1994). These primes allow linguists to articulate non-circular definitions intended to be accessible to speakers of any language. Although the Natural Semantic Metalanguage framework can be applied in any semantic domain, it is particularly helpful with emotions, because it helps capture the subtle nuances of relatively abstract words. Natural Semantic Metalanguage definitions conveniently highlight differences between semantic "neighbors" across languages, such as the German word *angst* and the English word *fear*, for instance (Wierzbicka 1999: 134, Wierzbicka and Harkins 2001: 15).

This framework could be seen as a useful complement to anthropological discussions of emotions based on thorough translations of emotion words (see Section 2 above). Wierzbicka (1999) shares her primary goal with early emotion anthropologists such as Rosaldo (1980) and Lutz (1988) (whose works she cites); they all aim to demonstrate the non-universality of emotional concepts. In a sense, Wierzbicka's (1999) semantic discussions of German emotion words, for instance, richly contextualized against literary and historical references, are not too distant from Rosaldo's and Lutz's thorough "ethnographic translations" (see Section 2). In addition, Wierzbicka presents a systematic linguistic method (Natural Semantic Metalanguage) that provides some theoretical anchorage for such translations.

Like anthropologists of emotions, Wierzbicka uses emotion words as a window onto culture. She bases this approach upon the assumption that words, as the building blocks of communication, contribute to shaping social interactions (Wierzbicka 1999, chapter 6). Beyond defining and translating emotion words, she discusses what she calls "cultural scripts", i.e., patterns of interactions built around certain emotion words, and supposed to distinctively characterize different language communities. Wierzbicka's notion of cultural scripts pertains to a less anthropologically informed conception of "culture", and has been criticized for its essentialist overtones (Mondry and Taylor 1998).

Beyond her thorough analyses of emotion words in German, Russian, and Polish, Wierzbicka's (1999) monograph tackles major questions such as the relationship between facial expressions and emotional language, and includes a systematic discussion of potential universals of emotional language (1999: 273–305). The legacy of Wierzbicka's work on the study of emotional language can hardly be overestimated. It inspired several foundational collective volumes that in turn set the tone for future developments. Some of these volumes focused on Natural Semantic Metalanguage (Athanasiadou and Tabakowska 1998,[9] Harkins and Wierzbicka 2001), and some are more broadly oriented towards cognitive linguistics (Niemeier and Dirven 1997). A significant portion of the descriptive research on the linguistic encoding of emotions across languages stems from the tradition of Natural Semantic Metalanguage. These works often focus on nouns (Kornacki 2001, Zhengdao 2001), but other parts of speech are also covered (Wierzbicka 2001, Levisen 2016), including interjections (Wierzbicka 1992b, Goddard 2014). Recent publications have shown the potential of this research for application in "positive psychology" (Lomas 2016), in particular around the language of well-being and pain (Goddard and Ye 2016).

---

9 Although published before Wierzbicka's monograph, this collection was the outcome of a symposium in honor of Anna Wierzbicka.

4.1.2 Other lexical studies

Linguistic diversity in emotion lexica (i.e., words used to describe emotions) has attracted a significant amount of attention beyond the work of Wierzbicka and other Natural Semantic Metalanguage semanticists. Some in-depth linguistic studies have attempted semantic and lexicographic generalizations (Novakova and Tutin 2009, Dziwirek and Lewandowska-Tomaszczyk 2010). Cross-linguistic comparisons (Ponsonnet 2016, Ponsonnet 2018a) and even broader typological studies (Ogarkova 2013, Yacopetti and Ponsonnet forthcoming) are facilitated by the extensive lexical data provided not only by focused linguistic publications, but also by dictionaries, as well as by anthropological studies such as those discussed in the first section of this chapter. On this basis, we are beginning to reach an understanding of what meanings tend to be encoded by a dedicated word in most languages, what meanings are much rarer, and what scope of variation we can expect across the world's languages (see Ogarkova 2013 for a comprehensive discussion). Apart from linguists, psychologists have also carried out broader-scope comparative studies on emotion words, where universal tendencies in lexical distinctions serve as clues to human cognition (Russell 1991, Hupka, Lenton, and Hutchison 1999, Jackson et al. 2019).

4.2 Figurative language

Another subfield of linguistics that developed an interest in emotions around the same decades (1980s/1990s) is cognitive linguistics. Cognitive linguistics, as theorized following George Lakoff (1987), explicitly seeks to reveal the isomorphisms between the structure of languages and the mental structures of those who speak them. In other words, cognitive linguists approach language as a window on shared cultural representations, and they actually explore possible justifications for the proposed isomorphisms.

Figurative language is one aspect of language with a strong potential to reflect speakers' conceptual representations. "Metaphors", as defined by Lakoff and Johnson (1980) or Kövecses (2002), for instance, typically use linguistic descriptions of concrete events (e.g., *he was about to explode*) to talk about more abstract events (e.g., *he was very angry*). According to the cognitive linguistics framework, such linguistic associations reveal speakers' conceptual associations between pairs of phenomena – i.e., in this case, they conceptually associate anger with a force leading to an explosion. The underlying assumption (which has naturally been challenged; see, for instance, Geeraerts and Grondelaers 1995, Goddard 1996, Enfield 2002), is that humans need to scaffold the conceptualization of more abstract aspects of the world based on what they know of more concrete aspects of the world. Figurative language is in turn assumed to reflect how this is achieved.

The semantic domain of emotions is very rich in metaphors. This is perhaps unsurprising, given that others' emotions are not directly observable, and are therefore more abstract; and one's own personal emotional experiences lend themselves very naturally to "embodiment", i.e., representations in terms of physical aspects of the person (Csordas 1990, Pritzker, Pederson, and DeCaro 2020). Reflecting the figurative wealth of the semantic domain, emotions are in focus in early discussions of figurative language by cognitive linguists (e.g., Lakoff 1987: 380–416 includes a case study on anger). Overall, emotion metaphors are probably the aspect of the linguistic encoding of emotions that has attracted the most systematic and conclusive studies. Kövecses (2000) offers a comprehensive analysis of the figurative language of emotions in English (see also Kövecses 1998), and Kövecses (2008) includes discussions of emotion metaphors across languages. Somewhat like Wierzbicka, Kövecses exploits linguistic metaphors to extract cultural models (Kövecses 1995) that summarize shared expectations about how emotions develop and are experienced. This is another instance of language being used as a window onto shared representations and habits around emotions (Kövecses 2002: 123–136).

Much research has derived from these foundational works on figurative language. Anger metaphors, in particular, have been studied cross-linguistically to the extent that one of the many metaphorical representations of anger, namely its association with heat, is now regarded as quasi-universal (Kövecses 1995, Mikolajczuk 1998, Ogarkova and Soriano 2014, Ogarkova, Soriano, and Gladkova 2016). The figurative mapping of emotions onto parts of the body (i.e., the cross-linguistic distribution of expressions like *broken hearted* or *cold feet*, which are prevalent across languages (Wierzbicka 1999: 256), has attracted a significant amount of attention as well, again showing considerable cross-linguistic coherence amid some variation (Sharifian et al. 2008, Maalej and Yu 2011, Ponsonnet and Laginha 2020). For those prepared to assume that figurative language does reflect conceptual structures, this suggests a background of shared conceptual patterns for emotions across languages and cultures, against which variation takes place. Some studies have interrogated the influence of grammar upon the figurative affordance of emotions, pointing to cases where the availability of a particular grammatical construction constrains the range of emotional metaphors available in this language (Ponsonnet, Hoffmann, and O'Keeffe 2020). This in turn raises interesting questions regarding how this relates to conceptualization.

4.3 The typology of emotional linguistic resources

Lexica and figurative language, as discussed in the above paragraphs, represent the two loci of linguistic encoding of emotions for which we currently have the best cross-linguistic knowledge. For both, some of the cross-linguistic variation and regularities have been effectively mapped, taking into account a number of languages beyond the handful of large, dominant ones (English and other European languages, Chinese, etc.). However, lexica and figurative language correspond to just two of the "loci of affect" identified by Besnier (1990: 421–428), from a much longer list that also includes the following:[10]

– Ideophones, interjections[11]
– Person reference (e.g., pronouns, address terms)
– Sound symbolism (pertaining to phonetics and phonology)
– Evidentiality (e.g., the encoding of surprise as part of evidentiality systems, a.k.a. "mirativity")
– Evaluative morphology (particularly diminutives, i.e., things like the -y of *kitty* in English)
– Syntax (e.g., valency, clefting)
– Intonation

Some of the above linguistic resources have been studied cross-linguistically to the extent that it has been possible to draw some conclusions on their overall typology. Descriptions of evaluative morphology (in particular diminutives) are available for a range of languages, and Ponsonnet (2018b) offers an early typology of their emotional values. More generally, Ponsonnet and Vuillermet (2018) examine the morphological expression of emotions, i.e., how they can be expressed by small linguistic elements merged into words, like prefixes or suffixes, for instance. Emotion interjections have also been described in a number of languages (e.g., Ameka 1992, Evans 1992, Eastman 1992, Wierzbicka 1992b, Wilkins 1992 and other authors in the same special issue of the *Journal of Pragmatics* (Enfield and Wierzbicka 1992), Drescher 1997, Kockelman 2003, Goddard 2014, Ponsonnet 2014b: 109–126), including a typology for the Australian continent (Ponsonnet forthcoming a). Majid (2012a) offers a review of the existing literature on emotional language locus by locus, with

---

10 Besnier also lists aspects of language that do not pertain to the code, strictly speaking, such as "ways of speaking" (e.g., registers, code-switching), performance styles, and genres, the organization of conversation, laughing, and weeping.
11 I.e., specific parts of the lexicon.

an organization comparable to Besnier's. Ponsonnet (forthcoming b) also summarizes the findings for some of the resources.

Resources regarded as expressive (as defined in Section 1.1) have overall attracted little coverage. Our typological knowledge of emotional interjections is still in its infancy, and the literature on emotional intonation remains extremely scarce (Bolinger 1986, Omondi 1997, Ponsonnet 2014b: 127–142, Ponsonnet 2018c). This is all the more notable in the light of the omnipresence of these resources in speech, and of the opportunity they represent to understand the semiotic complexity of human languages (see Section 1.1). Generally speaking, again, our current grasp of the cross-linguistic diversity of the linguistic encoding of emotions across languages remains somewhat fragmented. The number of publications is not insignificant, but studies have often focused on one particular aspect in one particular language, with few efforts towards comprehensive coverage or pathways towards generalization. Even for major languages such as English or French, the literature tends to offer glimpses into a range of aspects of emotional language, but rarely links them systematically. Our knowledge of minority languages is even more dispersed (with some exceptions, e.g., Ponsonnet (2014b) on Dalabon, Australia).

So far, most linguists have approached the typology of emotional language from a semasiological point of view: they organize their investigations based on linguistic forms, starting from types of emotional linguistic resources, as I did here. However, as suggested for anthropological studies, onomasiological approaches, starting from emotion categories, could constitute welcome additions. Celle and Lansari's (2017) work on the language of surprise illustrates a fruitful onomasiological alternative. While the difficulty of bringing order into the complexity of language remains, even within just one emotional category, this organization may offer a more convenient entry point for non-linguists wishing to understand emotional languages (e.g., psychologists or anthropologists). Compiling the results from existing linguistic publications on a range of major categories of emotion into structured syntheses may be a worthwhile endeavor in the future. This would be especially fruitful for an emotion like anger, for instance, which has already attracted a great deal of research attention over the last few decades.

4.4 Emotions in speech

Even with the aspects of the linguistic code for which we have decent cross-linguistic knowledge, merely understanding how the code is structured is far from sufficient to understand how language conveys emotions. Knowledge of

326 — Maïa Ponsonnet

the code can serve as a useful grid to develop further research, but it usually only records the most basic properties of the linguistic resources in question. With emotion words, for instance, the descriptive and typological literature tells us about their denotative properties, but rarely ventures into analyzing their connotations. Yet emotions are most commonly expressed not through the operation of denotative functions, but via speakers' choices to *use* linguistic resources in certain ways for stylistic effects. For instance, the expressive value of an utterance will depend on whether the speaker chooses to use *whinge* or *complain*, *broken-hearted* or *sad*, etc. Therefore, lexical distinctions in the emotional lexicon are less relevant for the expression of emotions than contrasts in register. Likewise, with metaphors, the question is not so much what they reveal about conceptual associations, but their evocative power (Foolen 2012). The linguists who tackle these dimensions share with anthropological linguists an interest in language *in use*, i.e., in "discourse". In this respect, general linguists are more interested in everyday language, i.e., ordinary speech, than in the higher genres and performances brought to the fore by anthropological linguists.

To disentangle the complex questions alluded to above, some linguists quantitatively examine linguistic resources across large corpora (Bednarek 2008). Blumenthal, Novakova, and Siepmann's (2014) edited collection gives a good idea of the range of methods that can be recruited and the range of questions that can be answered (see also Novakova and Tutin 2009, Dziwirek and Lewandowska-Tomaszczyk 2010). The studies in this volume analyze a range of linguistic phenomena from the fine semantic nuances between near-synonym sets of emotion words or verbal constructions, to the connotations arising from the interplay between emotion words and the discourse context in which they occur. Based on larger amounts of contextualized data, these methods provide more detailed analyses of how linguistic tools are mobilized to produce emotional meanings. Once again, however, studies in this style remain somewhat disparate for the moment, and more unitary approaches would be most welcome – either focusing on types of expressive resources, or on types of method, or perhaps around one category of emotion. Most of these methods can only be applied to dominant languages for which we already have large, automated corpora, as well as fine-grained grammatical descriptions, but this should not prevent researchers from pursuing them wherever possible.

There also exist linguistic frameworks that directly tackle discourse organization. Conversation analysts, who investigate the structure of human conversation (Sacks, Schegloff, and Jefferson 1974, Sidnell and Stivers 2012), have applied their concepts and methods to the investigation of "troubles talk", for instance Jefferson (2015). Peräkylä and Sorjonen (2012) offer a valuable collection of studies about emotion in spontaneous interactions. In a slightly different tradition, recent developments in cognitive linguistics have explored the notion of e-implicature, i.e., the principles according to which emotional states are implicitly inferred in linguistic communication (Schwarz-Friesel 2015).

The most significant contribution to the study of the emotional impact of discourse structure comes from Systemic Functional Linguistics theory, a branch of linguistics concerned with discourse organization and functions. Within this tradition, the framework called Appraisal (Martin and White 2005) caters for the analysis of emotional discourse to some extent. Appraisal offers a set of tools that can be applied systematically across languages and genres to extract "evaluative" effects. As pointed out by Alba-Juez and Mackenzie (2019), Appraisal was designed to cover evaluation more broadly, of which emotions are only a subsystem. Accordingly, with some exceptions (e.g., Mackenzie and Alba-Juez 2019), most publications based on Appraisal theory examine rhetoric and/or ideology in public-oriented contexts such as political discourse or the media, rather than the linguistic description or expression of intimate emotional experience. However, the Appraisal framework stands out as an all-encompassing analytical tool specifically tailored to a semantic domain endowed with subjectivity, and as such is a very welcome effort towards synthesis.

5 Concluding remarks

This chapter has summarized the development of the interest in, and scientific investigation of, emotional language from an anthropological and linguistic point of view. In the 1970s, attention to emotion words initially emerged in the margins of cultural anthropologists' interest in emotions as social phenomena, which prompted them to treat language as a "window on shared representations". By the late 1980s, the same anthropologists had revised their angle and placed language use at the center of their research. This defined the mode of investigation of emotional language in anthropological linguistics, where language is no longer treated as a window onto another reality, but as the very reality to be investigated. As a consequence, emotional experience itself tends to recede behind the scene. Meanwhile, linguists other than anthropological linguists also started actively studying emotional language from the 1990s, developing a myriad of approaches and methods. Some of them also propose to use language as a window on shared representations; most of them seek to deepen our understanding of how human linguistic codes convey emotional concepts and experience. Naturally, the angles described above are all part of one and the same jigsaw puzzle. Language use can only be understood based on thorough analyses of linguistic codes; and only a thorough assessment of the relationship between emotional concepts, emotional experience, and emotional language can tell us where and when emotional language may offer a window on the representations of emotion or even emotional experience.

Half a century after the publication of the first anthropological accounts attuned to emotions and emotion words, emotional language is a well-established object of study in both anthropological linguistics and linguistics in general. The field has produced a wealth of data and analyses offering insights into a broad range of linguistic phenomena involving emotional language. With this strong basis, the next decades may now welcome additional efforts towards synthesis, and this could take a range of different forms. So far, the numerous trends of research on emotional language identified in this chapter have often (although not always) progressed side-by-side rather than jointly. Improving the synergies between (sub-)disciplinary traditions may help in bringing the pieces of the puzzle together. Although some authors (especially anthropological linguists) have published summaries that compile the existing literature into ordered, digestible accounts, there is room for further publications organizing the material under more accessible keywords – for instance by emotional categories. This may in turn help communication across (sub-)disciplines. In terms of producing new research, in-depth investigation of a smaller number of topics may now be preferable to more cursory insights. This will require a focus on emotional language as a research topic in and of itself, rather than treating it as an aside, addendum, or instrument while carrying out research on other matters. This shift requires us to develop and fund dedicated research programs on emotional language, which in turn implies addressing clear research questions.

Which research questions about emotional language should be prioritized certainly remains a matter for individual researchers/teams to decide. Many of the research programs already explored by existing publications would be worth extending and systematizing. For instance, Celle and Lansari's (2017) onomasiological study of surprise could be applied to other categories of emotion; lexical typologies like Ogarkova (2013) could be expanded, etc. In addition, there is a need to clarify fundamental questions that underlie the study of emotional language. For instance, it would be worth investigating the relationship of emotional language to emotional experience, asking, in particular, to what extent the use of expressive linguistic resources is a response to emotional arousal, and whether this use can in turn modify emotional experience (Ponsonnet forthcoming a). This would help clarify the extent to which language is actually a window on emotional experience, and the particular semiotic status of expressive emotional language.

In conclusion, with many material and methodological insights accumulated over several decades, yet many important questions left to be answered or even raised, emotional language is a highly fertile field of study for linguists in general and anthropological linguists in particular. Given the central role of emotion and emotion talk in human life, we can only hope that the field will attract the attention it deserves.

References

Abu-Lughod, Lila. 1990. Shifting politics in Bedouin love poetry. In Catherine Lutz & Lila Abu-Lughod (eds.), *Language and the politics of emotion*, 24–45. Cambridge: Cambridge University Press.

Abu-Lughod, Lila & Catherine Lutz. 1990. Introduction. Emotion, discourse, and the politics of every day life. In Catherine Lutz & Lila Abu-Lughod (eds.), *Language and the politics of emotion*, 1–23. Cambridge: Cambridge University Press.

Alba-Juez, Laura & Lachlan J. Mackenzie. 2019. Emotion processes in discourse. In Lachlan J. Mackenzie & Laura Alba-Juez (eds.), *Emotion in discourse*, 3–26. Amsterdam: John Benjamins.

Ameka, Felix. 1992. Interjections. The universal yet neglected part of speech. *Journal of Pragmatics* 18 (2–3). 101–118.

Athanasiadou, Angeliki & Elzbieta Tabakowska. 1998. *Speaking of emotions. Conceptualisation and expression*. Berlin: De Gruyter Mouton.

Bednarek, Monika. 2008. *Emotion talk across corpora*. Houndsmill: Palgrave McMillan.

Besnier, Niko. 1990. Language and affect. *The Annual Review of Anthropology* 19. 419–451.

Blumenthal, Peter, Iva Novakova & Dirk Siepmann. 2014. *Les émotions dans le discours/ Emotions in discourse*. Frankfurt: Peter Lang.

Boiger, Michael & Batja Mesquita. 2012. The construction of emotion in interactions, relationships, and cultures. *Emotion Review* 4. 221–229.

Bolinger, Dwight. 1986. *Intonation and its part. Melody in spoken English*. Stanford: Stanford University Press.

Briggs, Jean. 1970. *Never in anger*. Cambridge: Cambridge University Press.

Celle, Agnès & Laure Lansari. 2017. *Expressing and describing surprise*. Amsterdam: John Benjamins.

Csordas, Thomas J. 1990. Embodiment as a paradigm for anthropology. *Ethos* 18 (1). 5–47.

Damasio, Antonio R. 1999. *The feeling of what happens: Body and emotion in the making of consciousness*. New York: Harcourt Brace.

Descartes, René. 1649. *Les passions de l'âme*, 1996th edition. Paris: Bokking International.

Dewaele, Jean-Marc & Aneta Pavlenko (eds.). 2004. Language & emotions. A cross linguistic perspective. Special issue of *Journal of Multilingual and Multicultural Development* 25 (2–3).

Drescher, Martina. 1997. French interjections and their use in discourse. Ah dis donc les vieux souvenirs. In Susanne Niemeier & René Dirven (eds.), *The language of emotions. Conceptualization, expression and theoretical foundation*, 233–246. Amsterdam: John Benjamins.

Dziwirek, Katarzyna & Barbara Lewandowska-Tomaszczyk. 2010. *Complex emotions and grammatical mismatches. A contrastive corpus-based study*. Berlin & New York: Walter de Gruyter.

Eastman, Carol M. 1992. Swahili interjections: Blurring language-use/gesture-use boundaries. *Journal of Pragmatics* 18 (2–3). 273–287.

Ekman, Paul. 1992. An argument for basic emotions. *Cognition and Emotion* 6 (3–4). 169–200.

Enfield, N. J. 2002. Semantic analysis of body parts in emotion terminology. Avoiding the exoticism of "obstinate monosemy" and "online extension". *Pragmatics and Cognition* 10 (1–2). 1–25.

Evans, Nicholas. 1992. "Wanjh! Bonj! Nja!" Sequential organization and social deixis in Mayali interjections. *Journal of Pragmatics* 18 (2–3). 101–118.

Feldman Barrett, Lisa. 2009. Variety is the spice of life. A psychological construction approach to understanding variability in emotion. *Cognition and Emotion* 23 (7). 1284–1306.

Foolen, Ad. 2012. The relevance of emotion for language and linguistics. In Ad Foolen, Ulrike M. Lüdtke, Timothy P. Racine & Jordan Zlatev (eds.), *Moving ourselves, moving others. Motion and emotion in intersubjectivity, concsiousness and language*, 349–368. Amsterdam: John Benjamins.

Geeraerts, Dirk & Stefan Grondelaers. 1995. Cultural traditions and metaphorical patterns. In John Taylor & Robert E. McLaury (eds.), *Language and the cognitive construal of the world*, 153–179. Berlin: De Gruyter Mouton.

Goddard, Clifford. 1996. Cross-linguistic research on metaphor. *Language and Communication* 16 (2). 145–151.

Goddard, Clifford. 2014. Interjection and emotion (with special reference to "surprise" and "digust". *Emotion Review* 6 (1). 53–63.

Goddard, Clifford & Anna Wierzbicka. 1994. *Semantics and lexical universals. Theory and empirical findings*. Amsterdam: John Benjamins.

Goddard, Clifford & Zhengdao Ye. 2016. "*Happiness*" *and* "*pain*" *across languages and cultures*. Amsterdam: John Benjamins.

Goffman, Erving. 1978. Response cries. *Language* 54 (4). 787–815.

Harkins, Jean & Anna Wierzbicka. 2001. *Emotions in crosslinguistic perspective*. Berlin: De Gruyter Mouton.

Harré, Rom. 1986. An outline of the social constructionist viewpoint. In Rom Harré (ed.), *The social construction of emotions*, 2–14. Oxford: Basil Backwell.

Haviland, John. 2003. Comments on "The meaning of interjections in Q'eqchi' Maya. From emotive reaction to social and discursive action". *Current Anthropology* 44 (4). 480–481.

Heelas, Paul & Andrew Locke. 1981. Indigenous psychologies. The anthropology of the self. London: Academic Press.

Hume, David. 1740 (1940). *A treatise on human nature*. London: Penguin.

Hupka, Ralph B., Alison P. Lenton & Keith A. Hutchison. 1999. Universal development of emotion categories in natural language. *Journal of Personality and Social Psychology* 77 (2). 247–278.

Irvine, Judith T. 1982. Language and affect. Some cross-cultural issues. In Heidi Byrnes (ed.), *Georgetown University roundtable on languages and linguistics*, 31–47. Washington: Georgetown University Press.

Irvine, Judith T. 1990. Registering affect. Heteroglossia in the linguistic expression of emotion. In Catherine Lutz & Lila Abu-Lughod (eds.), *Language and the politics of emotion*, 126–161. Cambridge: Cambridge University Press.

Izard, Carroll E. 2010. More meanings and more questions for the term "emotion". *Emotion Review* 2 (4). 383–385.

Jackson, Josua Conrad, Joseph Watts, Teague R. Henry, Mattis List, Robert Forkel, Peter J. Mucha, Simon J. Greenhill, Russel G. Gray & Kristen A. Lindquist. 2019. Emotion semantics show both cultural variation and universal structure. *Science* (366). 1517–1522.

James, William. 1884. What is an emotion. *Mind 9* (34). 188–205.

Jefferson, Gail. 2015. *Talking about troubles in conversations*. Oxford: Oxford University Press.

Kockelman, Paul. 2003. The meaning of interjections in Q'eqchi' Maya. From emotive reaction to social discursive action. *Current Anthropology* 44 (4). 467–490.

Kornacki, Pawel. 2001. Concepts of anger in Chinese. In Jean Harkins & Anna Wierzbicka (eds.), *Emotions in crosslinguistic perspective*, 255–289. Berlin: De Gruyter Mouton.

Kövecses, Zoltán. 1995. Anger. Its language, conceptualization and physiology in the light of cross-cultural evidence. In John Taylor & Robert E. McLaury (eds.), *Language and the cognitive construal of the world*, 181–196. Berlin: De Gruyter Mouton.

Kövecses, Zoltán. 1998. Are there any emotion-specific metaphors? In Angeliki Athanasiadou & Elzbieta Tabakowska (eds.), *Speaking of emotions. Conceptualisation and expression*, 127–152. Berlin: De Gruyter Mouton.

Kövecses, Zoltán. 2000. *Metaphor and emotion. Language, culture and body in human feeling*. New York: Cambridge University Press.

Kövecses, Zoltán. 2002. *Metaphor. A practical introduction*. New York: Oxford University Press.

Kövecses, Zoltán. 2008. Metaphor and emotion. In Raymond W. Gibbs (ed.), *The Cambridge handbook of metaphor and thought*, 247–261. New York: Cambridge University Press.

Lakoff, George. 1987. *Women, fire, and dangerous things. What categories reveal about the mind*. Chicago: University of Chicago Press.

Lakoff, George & Mark Johnson. 1980. *Metaphors we live by*. Chicago: University of Chicago Press.

Lemmings, David & Ann Brooks. 2014. The emotional turn in the humanities and social sciences. In *Emotions and social change. Historical and sociological perspective*, 1–62. London: Routledge.

Levisen, Carsten. 2016. Postcolonial lexicography. Defining creole emotion words with the Natural Semantic Metalanguage. *Cahiers de lexicologie* 109. 35–60.

Levy, Robert I. 1973. *Tahitians. Mind and experience in the Society Islands*. Chicago: University of Chicago Press.

Levy, Robert I. 1984. Emotion, knowing and culture. In Richard A. Shweder & Robert Alan LeVine (eds.), *Culture theory. Essays on mind, self and emotion*, 214–237. Cambridge: Cambridge University Press.

Lindquist, Kristen A. & Maria Gendron. 2013. What's in a word? Language constructs emotion perception. *Emotion Review* 5 (1). 66–71.

Lomas, Tim. 2016. Towards a positive cross-cultural lexicography. Enriching or emotional landscape through 216 "untranslatable" words pertaining to well-being. *The Journal of Positive Psychology* 11 (5). 546–558.

Lüdtke, Ulrike M. 2015a. Introduction. From logos to dialogue. In Ulrike M. Lüdtke (ed.), *Emotion in language. Theory – research – application*, vii–xi. Amsterdam: John Benjamins.

Lüdtke, Ulrike M. 2015b. *Emotion in language. Theory – research – application*. Amsterdam: John Benjamins.

Lutz, Catherine. 1986. Emotion, thought, and estrangement. Emotion as a cultural category. *Cultural Anthropology* 1 (3). 287–309.

Lutz, Catherine. 1988. *Unnatural emotions. Everyday sentiments on a Micronesian atoll and their challenge to Western theory.* Chicago: Chicago University Press.

Lutz, Catherine & Lila Abu-Lughod. 1990. *Language and the politics of emotion.* Cambridge: Cambridge University Press.

Lutz, Catherine & Geoffrey M. White. 1986. The anthropology of emotions. *Annual Review of Anthropology* 15. 405–436.

Maalej, Zouheir & Ning Yu. 2011. *Embodiment via body parts. Studies from various languages and cultures.* Amsterdam: John Benjamins.

Mackenzie, J. Lachlan & Laura Alba-Juez (eds.). 2019. *Emotion in discourse.* Amsterdam: John Benjamins.

Majid, Asifa. 2012a. Current emotion research in language sciences. *Emotion Review* 4 (4). 432–443.

Majid, Asifa. 2012b. The role of language in a science of emotions. *Emotion Review* 4 (4). 380–381.

Malt, Barbara C., Eef Ameel, Silvia Gennari, Mutsumi Imai & Asifa Majid. 2011. Do words reveal concepts? In *Proceedings of the 33th Annual Conference of the Cognitive Science Society*, 519–524. Austin: Cognitive Science Society.

Malt, Barbara C., Silvia Gennari & Mutsumi Imai. 2010. Lexicalization patterns and the world-to-words mapping. In Barbara C. Malt & Phillip Wolff (eds.), *Words and the mind. How words capture human experience*, 29–57. Oxford: Oxford University Press.

Martin, James & Peter R. R. White. 2005. *The language of evaluation. Appraisal in English.* London & New York: Palgrave McMillan.

Massumi, Brian. 1995. The autonomy of affect. *Cultural Critique* 31. 83–109.

Matras, Yaron. 2009. *Language contact.* Cambridge: Cambridge University Press.

Mead, Margaret. 1928. *Coming of age in Samoa. A psychological study of primitive youth for Western civilisation.* New York: Morrow & Co.

Mikolajczuk, Agnieszka. 1998. The metonymic and metaphoric conceptualization of anger in Polish. In Angeliki Athanasiadou & Elzbieta Tabakowska (eds.), *Speaking of emotions. Conceptualisation and expression*, 153–191. Berlin: De Gruyter Mouton.

Mondry, Henrietta & John R. Taylor. 1998. The cultural dynamics of "national character". The case of the new Russians. In Angeliki Athanasiadou & Elzbieta Tabakowska (eds.), *Speaking of emotions. Conceptualisation and expression*, 29–48. Berlin: De Gruyter Mouton.

Myers, Fred R. 1979. Emotions and the self. A theory of personhood and political order among Pintupi Aborigines. *Ethos* 7 (4). 343–370.

Niemeier, Susanne & René Dirven. 1997. *The Language of emotions. Conceptualization, expression and theoretical foundation.* Amsterdam: John Benjamins.

Novakova, Iva & Agnès Tutin. 2009. *Le lexique des émotions.* Grenoble: ELLUG.

Ochs, Elinor. 1986. From feelings to grammar. A Samoan case study. In Bambi B. Schieffelin & Elinor Ochs (eds.), *Language socialization across cultures*, 252–272. Cambridge: Cambridge University Press.

Ochs, Elinor & Bambi B. Schieffelin. 1989. Language has a heart. *Text* 9. 7–25.

Ogarkova, Anna. 2013. Folk emotion concepts. Lexicalization of emotional experiences across languages and cultures. In JohnnyR. J. Fontaine, Klaus R. Scherer & Cristiana Soriano (eds.), *Components of emotional meanings. A sourcebook*, 46–62. Oxford: Oxford University Press.

Ogarkova, Anna & Cristina Soriano. 2014. Variation within universals. The metaphorical profile approach and ANGER concepts in English, Russian and Spanish. In Andreas Mussolf & Fiona MacArthur (eds.), *Metaphors in intercultural communication*, 93–116. London: Continuum.

Ogarkova, Anna, Cristina Soriano & Anna Gladkova. 2016. Methodological triangulation in the study of emotion. The case of "anger" in three language groups. *Review of Cognitive Linguistics* 14 (1). 73–101.

Omondi, Lucia N. 1997. Dholuo emotional language: An overview. In Susanne Niemeier & René Dirven (eds.), *The language of emotions. Conceptualization, expression and theoretical foundation*, 109–887. Amsterdam: John Benjamins.

Pavlenko, Aneta. 2005. *Emotions and multilingualism*. Cambridge: Cambridge University Press.

Pavlenko, Aneta. 2006. *Bilingual minds. Emotional experience, expression, and representation*. Clevedon: Multilingual Matters.

Pavlenko, Aneta. 2014. *The bilingual mind and what it tells us about language and thought*. Cambridge: Cambridge University Press.

Peirce, Charles Sanders. 1955. Logic as semiotics. The theory of signs. In Justus Buchler (ed.), *Philosophical writings of Peirce*, 98–119. New York: Dover Publications.

Peräkylä, Anssi & Marja-Leena Sorjonen. 2012. *Emotion in interaction*. Oxford: Oxford University Press.

Ponsonnet, Maïa. 2014a. Figurative and non-figurative use of body-part words in descriptions of emotions in Dalabon. *International Journal of Language and Culture* 1 (1). 98–130.

Ponsonnet, Maïa. 2014b. *The language of emotions. The case of Dalabon (Australia)*. Amsterdam: John Benjamins.

Ponsonnet, Maïa. 2014c. Les rôles de kangu «ventre» dans les composés émotionnels du dalabon (Australie du Nord). Entre figuratif et littéral. *Bulletin de la Société de linguistique de Paris* 109 (1). 327–373.

Ponsonnet, Maïa. 2016. Emotion nouns in Australian languages. In Peter K. Austin, Harold Koch & Jane H. Simpson (eds.), *Language, land and story in Australia*, 228–243. London: EL Publishing.

Ponsonnet, Maïa. 2018a. Lexical semantics in language shift. Comparing emotion lexica in Dalabon and Barunga Kriol (northern Australia). *Journal of Pidgin and Creole Languages* 33 (1). 226–255.

Ponsonnet, Maïa. 2018b. A preliminary typology of emotional connotations in morphological diminutives and augmentatives. *Studies in Language* 42 (1). 17–50.

Ponsonnet, Maïa. 2018c. Expressivity and performance. Expressing compassion and grief with a prosodic contour in Gunwinyguan languages (northern Australia). *Journal of Pragmatics* 136. 79–96.

Ponsonnet, Maïa. 2020. *Difference and repetition in language shift to a creole. The expression of emotions*. London: Routledge.

Ponsonnet, Maïa. Forthcoming a. Interjections. In Claire Bowern (ed.), *The Oxford guide to Australian languages*. Oxford: Oxford University Press.

Ponsonnet, Maïa. Forthcoming b. Emotional linguistic relativity and cross-cultural research on emotions. In Gesine Lenore Schiewer, Jeanette Altarriba & Bee Chin Ng (eds.), *Language and emotion. An international handbook*. Berlin: De Gruyter Mouton.

Ponsonnet, Maïa, Dorothea Hoffmann & Isabel O'Keeffe. 2020. Introduction. Grammar, culture, and emotion tropes. *Pragmatics and Cognition* 27 (1). 1–19.

Ponsonnet, Maïa, Robert Knox, Casey Lister, Bradley Walker & Nicolas Fay. Forthcoming. Are emotional signals communicative or expressive? An experimental test. *Emotion Review*.

Ponsonnet, Maïa & Kitty Laginha. 2020. The role of the body in descriptions of emotions. A typology of the Australian continent. *Pragmatics and Cognition* 27 (1). 20–83.

Ponsonnet, Maïa & Marine Vuillermet. 2018. Introduction. Morphology and emotions: a preliminary typology. *Studies in Language* 42 (1). 1–16.

Potts, Christopher. 2007. The expressive dimension. *Theoretical Linguistics* 33 (2). 165–198.

Pritzker, Sonya E., Janina Fenigsen & James M. Wilce. 2020. *The Routledge handbook of language and emotion*. New York: Routledge.

Pritzker, Sonya E., Joshua R. Pederson & Jason A. DeCaro. 2020. Language, emotion and the body. Combining linguistic and biological approaches to interactions between romantic partners. In Sonya E. Pritzker, Janina Fenigsen & James M. Wilce (eds.), *The Routledge handbook of language and emotion*, 307–324. New York: Routledge.

Rosaldo, Michelle Z. 1980. *Knowledge and passion. Ilongot notions of self and social life*. Cambridge: Cambridge University Press.

Rosaldo, Renato. 1996. Grief and a headhunter's rage. In Jon R. McGee & Richard Warms (eds.), *Anthropological theory*, 167–178. Mayfield: Mountain View.

Rosenberg, Daniel V. 1990. Language in the discourse of emotions. In Catherine Lutz & Lila Abu-Lughod (eds.), *Language and the politics of emotion*, 162–185. Cambridge: Cambridge University Press.

Russell, James A. 1991. Culture and the categorization of emotions. *Psychological Bulletin* 110 (3). 426–450.

Sacks, Harvey, Emmanuel A. Schegloff & Gail Jefferson. 1974. A simplest systematics for the organization of turn-taking for conversation. *Language* 50 (4). 696–735.

Scherer, Klaus R. 2013. Measuring the meaning of emotion words. A domain-specific componential approach. In JohnR. J. Fontraine, Klaus R. Scherer & Cristina Soriano (eds.), *Components of emotional meanings. A sourcebook*, 7–30. Oxford: Oxford University Press.

Scherer, Klaus R., Angela Shorr & Tom Johnstone. 2001. *Appraisal processes. Theory, methods, research*. Canary, NC: Oxford University Press.

Schieffelin, Bambi B. 1990. *The give and take of everyday life. Language and socialization of Kaluli children*. Cambridge: Cambridge University Press.

Schwarz-Friesel, Monika. 2015. Language and emotion. The cognitive linguistic perspective. In Ulrike M. Lüdtke (ed.), *Emotion in language. Theory – research – application*, 157–173. Amsterdam: John Benjamins.

Schweder, Richard A. & Robert Alan LeVine. 1984. *Culture theory. Essays on mind, self and emotion*. Cambridge: Cambridge University Press.

Schwiewer, Lenore, Jeanette Altarriba & Bee Chin Ng. Forthcoming. *Language and emotion. An international handbook*. Berlin: De Gruyter Mouton.

Sharifian, Farzad, René Dirven, Ning Yu & Susanne Niemeier. 2008. Culture and language. Looking for the "mind" inside de body. In Farzad Sharifian, René Dirven, Ning Yu & Susanne Niemeier (eds.), *Culture, body and language. Conceptualizations of internal body organs across cultures and languages*, 3–23. Berlin: De Gruyter Mouton.

Sidnell, Jack & Tanya Stivers. 2012. *The handbook of conversation analysis*. London: Wiley-Blackwell.

Smith, Philip M. 1985. *The female world of love and ritual*. Oxford: Basil Blackwell.

Spinoza, Baruch. 1677 (1992). *The ethics*, translated by Samuel Shirley. Indianapolis: Hackett Publishing Company.

Tersis, Nicole & Pascal Boyeldieu. 2017. *Le langage de l'émotion. Variations linguistiques et culturelles*. Paris: ENS Editions.

Trawick, Margaret. 1990. Untouchability and the fear of death in a Tamil song. In Catherine Lutz & Lila Abu-Lughod (eds.), *Language and the politics of emotion*, 186–206. Cambridge: Cambridge University Press.

White, Geoffrey M. 1990. Moral discourse and the rhetoric of emotions. In Catherine Lutz & Lila Abu-Lughod (eds.), *Language and the politics of emotion*, 46–68. Cambridge: Cambridge University Press.

Widen, Sherri C. & James A. Russell. 2010. Descriptive and prescriptive definitions of emotion. *Emotion Review* 2 (4). 377–378.

Wierzbicka, Anna. 1992a. Defining emotion concepts. *Cognitive Science* 16. 539–581.

Wierzbicka, Anna. 1992b. The semantics of interjections. *Journal of Pragmatics* 18 (2–3). 159–192.

Wierzbicka, Anna. 1999. *Emotions across languages and cultures. Diversity and universals*. Cambridge: Cambridge University Press.

Wierzbicka, Anna. 2001. A culturally salient Polish emotions. Przykro (pron. pshickro). In Jean Harkins & Anna Wierzbicka (eds.), *Emotions in crosslinguistic perspective*, 337–357. Berlin: De Gruyter Mouton.

Wierzbicka, Anna. 2010. On emotions and on definitions. A response to Izard. *Emotion Review* 2 (4). 379–380.

Wierzbicka, Anna & Jean Harkins. 2001. Introduction. In Jean Harkins & Anna Wierzbicka (eds.), *Emotions in crosslinguistic perspective,* 1–34. Berlin: De Gruyter Mouton.

Wilce, James M. 2009. *Language and emotions*. Cambridge: Cambridge University Press.

Wilkins, David. 1992. Interjections and deictics. *Journal of Pragmatics* 18 (2–3). 119–158.

Wittgenstein, Ludwig. 1953. *Philosophische Untersuchungen/Philosophical Investigations*, translated by G. E. M. Anscombe, P. M. S. Hacker, and J. Schulte. Malden: Wiley-Blackwell.

Yacopetti, Eleonor & Maïa Ponsonnet. Forthcoming. A semantic typology of emotion nouns in Australia. *Anthropological Linguistics*.

Ye, Zhengdao. 2001. An inquiry into "sadness" in Chinese. In Jean Harkins & Anna Wierzbicka (eds.), *Emotions in crosslinguistic perspective*, 359–404. Berlin: De Gruyter Mouton.

Part III: **Areal perspectives**

Felix K. Ameka & Azeb Amha

13 Research on language and culture in Africa

The chapter surveys research into the relations among language, culture, and cognition in Africa. A leitmotif is linguistic relativity; the hypothesis that our habitual linguistic practices influence the way we categorize and express the perceptual flow of daily experiences. The chapter is organized around how cultural meanings are encoded and are inferable from forms at all levels of language: syntactic, semantic and pragmatic. These are manifested in various domains including *categorization*. the cultural bases of nominal classification; the *sensorium*, linguistic and cultural evidence for the importance of seeing (colors and patterns), and of *balance*. Manifestations of oblique communication and its impact on grammar, in particular, the link between triadic communication and the use of logophoric and interpretive markers are part of our prime examples of the language-culture symbiosis. Trends in research into the cultural and conceptual bases of social interaction in African communities in particular ideologies of greetings and partings and the related practices of naming and addressing are discussed. An urgent direction in this research is multilingual socialization. We highlight the empirical knowledge African languages have contributed as well as the challenges they pose to existing models and frameworks in the study of the language-culture interface.

1 Introduction

Research on the language-culture nexus with respect to Africa has been conducted in various disciplines, especially philosophy; see, e.g., contributions in the *African Philosophy Reader* (Coetzee and Roux 1998), social and cultural anthropology (e.g., Fabian 1991), history (e.g., Vansina 1985), religion (e.g., Idowu 1973, Mbiti 2015), psychology (e.g., Scribner and Cole 1981), oral literature (e.g., Barber 1991, Okpewho 1992, Finnegan 2012), and, of course, linguistics (e.g., Calame-Griaule 1987, Dimmendaal 2022). The literature is vast and myriad themes have been discussed in the anthropological linguistics of Africa

Felix K. Ameka, Leiden University/The Netherlands, e-mail: f.k.ameka@hum.leidenuniv.nl
Azeb Amha, Leiden University/The Netherlands, e-mail: a.amha@asc.leidenuinv.nl

https://doi.org/10.1515/9783110726626-013

(see, e.g., Dimmendaal 2022). In this chapter we focus on two kinds of themes: (i) those topics that relate to salient knowledge systems in Africa which challenge claims about the universality and the elaboration of certain semantic domains in human language, and have remained unexplored or understudied in the field, for instance the sense of balance; (ii) topics related to distinct African ways of doing things with people but which have not impacted linguistic theorizing about pragmatics and social interaction, for instance triadic communication, greetings, salutations, and their ideologies. A reviewer questions whether one can essentialize ways of doing things with people and being with people as distinctly African. We recognize the plurality and diversity of African linguacultures;[1] however, we would argue that there are certain conceptual schemas, interactional norms, values, and ideologies that are common to African linguacultures, some of which we touch upon in this chapter (see, e.g., Gyekye 1996). Others can be gleaned from the literature. One such phenomenon is "social face" or "group face", as argued for by Nwoye (1992) and de Kadt (1998) for African linguacultures, as opposed to "individual face" in cultures where imposition is avoided in order to save face. We can add that the conceptual schema for the implementation of "respect" in African cultures is "avoidance behavior". The implementation of this varies from linguaculture to linguaculture, yet the underlying patterns are very similar. Moreover, these avoidance behaviors have labels in many of the cultures across Africa. The most famous label is *hlonipha* 'respect' in Zulu, with its cognate forms in southern African Bantu languages (Finlayson 2002). The Hausa call it *kunya* 'restraint' (Chamo 2011, Will 2017). In varieties of Fulfulde, it is called *yaage* or *semteende* 'self-restraint' (Ameka and Breedveld 2004). The Baatombu of Benin call it *sekuru* 'shame' (Schotman 1993). In Eastern Africa, the Datooga, Nilotic-speaking people in Tanzania, call their avoidance system *gíing'áwêak-shòoda*; among the Cushitic languages of Ethiopia it is called *baliʃʃa* in Sidama (Teferra 1987) and Kambaata (Treis 2005), while it is *laguu* in Oromo (Tesfaye 2007). Despite the particulars, these diverse linguacultures and others share a common conceptual schema that can be viewed as an Africanism.

The themes discussed in this chapter are a selection from the diverse topics and domains that have been investigated in the Africanist literature on anthropological linguistics and reflect the interests and concerns of the authors.

---

[1] The term "linguaculture" was first introduced by Paul Friedrich, who sees "language" and "culture" as constituting "a single universe of its own kind, not only in terms of analysis but also in terms of the point of view that is implied by the discourse and actions of the participants" Friedrich (1989: 306). Later, Michael Agar (1995) suggested "languageculture", since the form language is more used in English. We use the form linguaculture in this chapter.

Similarly, the illustrations are drawn predominantly, but not exclusively, from the linguacultures of which the authors have first-hand knowledge as native speakers and those which belong to their area of expertise. The first author's primary socialization is in the Ewe language and culture and his area specialization is West Africa. The second author has been primarily socialized simultaneously in Amharic (Ethio-Semitic) and Wolaitta (Omotic) and she is an expert on Ethiopian linguacultures. Several examples are given from these languages. We have drawn on cases from elsewhere to supplement our coverage.

The chapter is organized around the three domains of language-culture research or ethnolinguistics: ethnosemantics, ethnosyntax, and ethnopragmatics (Sharifian 2014, Goddard 2002). Each of these perspectives centers on a level of language structure and use and explores its relationships to cultural knowledge and practice. Ethnosemantics approaches the question from the vocabulary or lexicon; ethnosyntax delves into how culture is reflected in grammar; and ethnopragmatics relates to the cultural norms and frames that guide the use of language. These perspectives are interrelated and for a holistic understanding of the themes in anthropological linguistics each theme should be explored from the three perspectives. For instance, in relation to the senses and in particular the sense of balance that we discuss under ethnosemantics, there are morphosyntactic structures that are influenced by the cultural practice of headloading. In Ik, for example, there is a verbal derivation for describing the making of the cultural artefact of headpad (Schrock 2017). We also draw attention to socialization practices which fall under ethnopragmatics. Thus, the division is for organizational purposes and for highlighting the different perspectives of ethnolinguistics. Historically, ethnolinguistics was equated with ethnosemantics and ethnoscience. By organizing the chapter around the three related perspectives we intend to show the developments in the field as well. In Section 2, we focus on research on lexical semantic domains within perception, especially the visual in relation to color; importantly, we draw attention to balance as a sense and motivate this from cultural practices. In Section 3, we discuss the encoding of cultural meaning in grammar in possessive, logophoric, and nominal categorization constructions. Section 4 deals with topics of social interaction and its ideologies.

2 Ethnosemantics

Ethnosemantics, also called ethnoscience, originated in cognitive anthropology (see, e.g., D'Andrade 1995, Brown 2006 for an overview). Its interest is in thought (cognition) as revealed in the structure of linguistic categories. It approaches this question mainly through the study of vocabulary, identifying semantic features of lexical items and investigating taxonomic relations within vocabulary domains. Ethnosemantic studies construct models of how speakers of different linguacultures classify the world around them. This generates studies in kinship, ethnobiology, skin diseases, and interpersonal relations. Ethnosemantic studies, especially as practiced in cognitive and psychological anthropology, has moved beyond folk taxonomies to the study of cultural models to account for the cultural knowledge that is embodied in the meaning of elements in a domain. This knowledge is organized in schemas. Information for the construction of these models comes from a study of how people talk about a domain (e.g., marriage) and through these models one can get a glimpse of how cultural knowledge is organized in the mind (see, e.g., Holland and Quin 1987, Strauss and Quin 1998).

2.1 Language and the cultural sensorium

The anthropologist Kathryn Linn Geurts (2002a, b) gives an account of the sensory orders of the Anlo-Ewe (Gbe, Kwa, Niger-Congo)[2] which represents ways of knowing in an African community. She argues, first, that cultural variation in the sensory orders gives evidence of differentiation and elaboration of the various senses. This can be discovered through an investigation of the way (everyday) sensorial experiences are linguistically encoded in the local lexicon and performatively elaborated in cultural practices. From this, one can identify the culture-specific categories of the sensorium. She persuasively demonstrates that the cultural sensorium of the Anlo-Ewe and of many other African cultures is different from the Euro-American sensory orders (see e.g., Stoller 1989a, b on the Songhay). One of the differences is that Euro-American models treat states of perception, affect, and disposition as independent categories. In many African cultures, however, these are subsumed under one category. In Ewe, the category is *seselelãme* 'feeling inside the body' (Ameka 2002), which is a nominalization of the verbal expression in (1) by the reduplication of the verb and the adjunction of a locative phrase:

(1) se   náné   le   lã.me
     hear   something   at   flesh.containing.region
     'feel something in the body' (interlinear glosses added, FKA and AA)

---

2 The Anlo are a subgroup of Ewe who live on the coast in southeastern Ghana, bordering on and into Togo. They speak a distinct variety of Ewe, a Gbe, Kwa, Niger-Congo language.

Geurts (2002a: 45) indicates that "(. . .) it is difficult to make a direct translation into English of the term *seselelãme,* for it refers to various kinds of sensory embodiment which do not fit neatly into Anglo-American categories or words". Similar categories occur in Dagbani (Gur/Mabia, Niger-Congo) of northern Ghana that "lack a label for the western category of emotion – the word that best serves as a collective label for affective experiences also doubles as a label for nonemotive internal states of the body" (Dzokoto 2010: 69). Similarly, Fante, an Akan (Kwa) language (of Ghana) also lacks an equivalent for the English word *emotion*; rather, the term used, like the Ewe and Dagbani expressions, "covers both emotional experiences (such as *happy* and *sad*) and physiological states (such as *hunger* and *thirst*). An English translation of *atsinka* suggested by the Fante-English translators is 'what one feels or senses inside'" (Dzokoto and Okazaki 2006: 127).

Another dimension of difference is in the content of the sensorium. Geurts asserts that the "five senses model is *not* a scientific fact" (Geurts 2002a: 7, emphasis added), but rather that it is a folk or cultural model originating in Greek philosophy and spreading through European cultures into the rest of the world. Geurts (2002a: 44–69) argues that in the (Anlo)-Ewe sensorium there are at least nine terms, as shown in Table 13.1, some of which may strike some readers as mind-boggling. The labels Geurts (2002a: 46–47) gives (Column 1) are from her Anlo consultants and are represented in the traditional Ewe orthography, which sparingly marks tones. They are nominalizations based on the verb phrases that language users deploy when talking about scenarios characterizing the senses. We provide these in Column 3 with their glosses. We have added, in Column 3, some alternatives for "tasting" and "smelling".

Table 13.1: (Anlo-)Ewe cultural sensorium.

Senses	Description	Underlying form (FKA and AA)
nusese	Aural perception or hearing	< *se nú* 'hear thing'
agbagbaɖoɖo	A vestibular sense, balancing, equilibrium from the inner ear	< *ɖó agbagbá* 'set suspension (literally)' i.e., to balance (see below)
azɔlizɔzɔ / azɔlime	Kinesthesia, walking or a movement sense	< *zɔ azɔlĩ* 'move walk(ing), gait', i.e., walk, march < *azɔlĩ me* 'gait, walking, containing region', i.e., manner of moving, e.g., walking, or in life
nulele	A complex of tactility, contact, touch	< *lé nú* 'hold thing'

Table 13.1 (continued)

Senses	Description	Underlying form (FKA and AA)
nukpɔkpɔ	Visuality or sight	<*kpɔ́ nú* 'see thing'
nud̪ɔd̪ɔ and *nud̪ɔd̪ɔkpɔ*	Terms used to describe the experience of tasting	< *d̪ɔ́ nú kpɔ́* 'put.on thing see' / <*d̪ɔ́ nú se* 'put.on thing hear'
nuʋeʋese	Olfactory action or smell	< *ʋẽ́ nú se* 'sniff.at thing hear'/ < *ʋẽ́ nú kpɔ́* 'sniff.at thing see'
nufofo	Orality, vocality, and talking	< *fo nǔ* 'strike mouth'
seselelame	Feeling in the body; also synaesthesia and a specific skin sense	< *se le lã.me* 'hear at flesh/body inside'

The underlying forms given in Column 3 reflect a salient typological feature in the genius of Ewe which does not have verb derivational means. The majority of verbs in the language are transitive and combine with obligatory complements to express predicate meanings (e.g., Essegbey 1999, Ameka 2002). Because of this, predicative expressions tend to be given with either specific complements such as *fo nǔ* 'talk' (strike mouth), with cognate-like complements as in *zɔ azɔlĩ* 'walk (a walk)', or with generic place-holding complements such as *nú* 'thing', as exemplified by many of the terms (see Column 3).

Throughout, Geurts provides evidence from lexical encoding and from elaboration in ritual and cultural practices to support the contents of the Anlo-Ewe sensorium, especially for the ones that are "different" from the Euro-American sensory order. She reports that "a corresponding organ – the vestibular organ, on the labyrinth of the inner ear", has been identified for a sense of balance like for the other five senses (Geurts 2002a: 4). However, students throughout the world in schools based on the Western model of knowledge continue "learning that hearing, touch, taste, smell, and sight are senses, but they do not learn to categorise *balance* as a sensation or a sense. Yet balance is clearly treated as a sense in contemporary textbooks from such disciplines as biology, psychology and medicine" (Geurts 2002a: 3).

"Anlo-Ewe people consider (. . .) balancing (in a physical and psychological sense, as well as in literal and metaphorical ways) to be an essential component of what it means to be human" (Geurts 2002a: 4). Two cultural activity types that support balance as a sense among the (Anlo-)Ewe and many other African cultures are (i) children learning to sit up and take their first steps by themselves; (ii) headloading. Balance may have offered affordances in human evolution to habitual bipedalism (see Hurford 2014). In the rest of this section we motivate the idea that balance is a sense in Ewe and other African linguacultures.

It appears that in all human cultures, children are socialized into ways of being and moving by letting them experience and sense balance. Think of how children are helped in taking their first steps by wheeled walking aids, and how the Dutch, for example, introduce their children to cycling: from sitting on adult bicycles to push tricycles to bicycles. In Ewe, the expression used to characterize a child trying to support themselves in sitting up and in taking the first steps on their two feet instead of crawling is *ɖó agbagbá* 'set suspension'. Westermann (1973) provides two related senses of this expression: [a] to carry something on the head without touching it with the hands; to balance; and [b] to make the first attempts in walking (of a child).

(2) nyɔ́nu=a   ɖó   agbagbá
     woman=DEF set suspension
     'The woman is carrying a load on the head without holding it.'

Headloading, the act of carrying loads on the head to transport them, is a domain where balance is practiced in many cultures. The headloading activity has several phases, some of which have lexical expression in the linguacultures that practice it:

Phase 1: Put items on the head (load): This can be done with the help of someone else or by yourself. In Ewe, the verb for this (as well as for Phase 3) is *dró* 'put load up/down from head' (Ameka 2017). The participants involved could use a platform, called *agba* in Ewe. This word is polysemous and is also used for the load that is being carried.

Phase 2: involves maintaining and balancing the load on the head, moving from one place to another. During the movement, one can support the load with one's hands, or not. If you do not support the load with your hands, the Ewe describe the scenario with the expression *ɖó agbagbá* 'balance', discussed above and exemplified in (2). It seems that headloading was also more prevalent formerly in European cultures than it is today. There are clues from the lexicons of some of the languages. In German dialects one can find verbs such as *gaagele* 'balancing', which relates to the difficulty of carrying and balancing and is a bit pejorative. While moving along and carrying a load, one can put the load down halfway and rest before continuing. In parts of Germany today, one can still see the stone benches on which the load was placed in old market places and on the edge of old country roads. Such rest stops are called *Ruhen* (Anne Storch personal communication, August 2019). In Ewe such rest stops are called *agba-dró-fé* (lit.: 'load-put.up/down-place'), which has come to mean 'milestone' and the measure of 'mile'.

Phase 3: Put items down from the head. Like the putting up event, this can be done with the help of someone else or by oneself and could involve the use of a platform.

In the practice of headloading, an essential artefact provides affordances for carrying things on the head and balancing them. The thing on which the load rests is called a headpad in African Englishes. It is a kind of pillow or cushion used to protect the head, as well as to help balance the load on the head. There are words for such artefacts in some of the European languages too. In some German dialects it is called *krenge*. In Galician, where headloading was also practiced, this artefact is called *mulido* (Maria del Carmen Parafita Couto personal communication, December 2021). In African linguacultures where headloading is practiced there are words for the headpad and also verbs to *describe* how to make it. In Ewe the headpad is called *tsihé*. In Ik (Kuliak, Nilo-Saharan), it is *ikɨta* (Shrock 2017). Several Bantu languages have cognate forms for this cultural item, headpad, as shown by the respondents to Martin Benjamin's Facebook query on February 1, 2016, asking for the term for the fabric head ring that a woman in a photo accompanying the query is wearing to cushion her basket.[3] Some of the Bantu language terms provided include: *inkhatsa* (Siswati); *kata* (Swahili); *ngata* (Kinyarwanda), *ngata* (Chaga); *nkatha* (Xhosa) *nkatha* (isiNdebele); *ngata* (Kikuyu); and *inkatha* (Zulu).

Given these pieces of evidence, the widespread nature of cultural activities including child socialization to develop the sense of balance, and the identification of a vestibular organ that supports balance as a sense, it would be good if the models of the senses that we transmit to generations of learners were to be updated. Balance fits the mould of the other reified senses in that it is a human universal; there is a physio-biological organ linked to it. Like the other senses, different linguacultures have different values and give it different degrees of elaboration in their language use and cultural practices. It has been shown that in some cultures, e.g., Western European ones, the eyes (i.e., vision) are more

---

3 See [https://www.facebook.com/photo.php?fbid=10153250810717056&set=gm.10153943469200513&type=3&theater] (accessed 7 January 2022).

One of the respondents, Prof. Thomas Hinnebusch, gives a characterization of the material from which such artefacts are made: "Martin, as I'm sure you know, these head rings are not just made of cloth; in 'my day', 50 years ago, people used many sorts of material they had at hand: grass, papyrus and other reeds, banana leaves, virtually anything that could easily be shaped into a ring. Human inventiveness!!!! . . . ".

prominent. In other cultures, such as indigenous Australian ones, hearing and the ears are more important (see Sweetser 1990, Evans and Wilkins 2000). More recently it has been argued that the sense of smell, for example, which has been considered unimportant among the Western five senses, has high value in several cultures, including African linguacultures (see, e.g., Burenhult and Majid 2011, Storch 2014 and Viberg 2021).

2.2 Color

Color is arguably the most contested topic in linguistic relativity. The physical and natural environment offers a plethora of colors that we perceive and categorize in terms that our languages provide. Color is related to visual perception. Consider the colors we see in the sky, the sun, different colors of sand, and clay, e.g., black soil, red sand, etc. People also create and use different dyes and paints for the adornment of their bodies and for other artefacts in their environment such as floors, earthen stoves, fabrics, etc. It seemed as if each linguaculture had divided the color spectrum arbitrarily and that there were no commonalities to color nomenclature (Ray 1952). This sparked the research tradition of color naming as a testing ground for the relationship between language and thought (see Brown and Lenneberg (1954) and the color naming across languages, a tradition initiated by Berlin and Kay (1969) and the World Color Survey (see Kay et al. 2009)).

However, color naming research dates back even further, to the 19th century, and involved Africans, as noted by Dimmendaal (1995, 2015). Dimmendaal cites the work of Geiger (1871, 1872), who proposed a cross-cultural evolutionary theory of progressive emergence of color: first, 'black' and 'red'; second, 'black' vs. 'red'; third, 'yellow' appeared; fourth, 'white' was distinguished from 'red'; fifth, 'green' developed from 'yellow', and sixth, 'blue' developed. Geiger linked the elaboration of the color lexicon in a language to the physiological development of the speakers: "primitive" people had fewer color terms. He suggested, poignantly, that if one did not have a word for a color, it meant that one could not see such a color. Anyone familiar with the later work of Berlin and Kay (1969) can see the resonances.

Research among African language speakers in Berlin at the time was used to challenge Geiger's views. Virchow, a physical anthropologist contemporary with Geiger, tested speakers of Nubian languages (Nilo-Saharan) using color naming elicitation techniques and concluded that "although displaying anomalies of color vocabulary, [they] were quite able to discriminate colors in all parts of the spectrum, demonstrating this by sorting and matching colored papers and wools" (cited in Dimmendaal 1995: 2).

Color perception (in humans) depends on a number of interacting factors such as the physics of light, the physiology of the human eye, environmental conditions, object properties, and brain activity. Colors are usually thought of as having hue, which depends on wavelength and frequency. Many English color terms, such as red, blue, and yellow, refer to hues. Colors also have brightness, which refers to how pure or otherwise a hue is. This can distinguish the range of colors from vivid/bright red (no mixture with grey) to dull red/grey red on a dark-light scale. Colors also have saturation, which relates to the amount of light reaching the eye.

There is a diversity of terms for colors across languages and the question is whether there are universal constraints or commonalities in this domain. In the 1960s, Berlin and Kay investigated this question for 98 languages, with an in-depth study of 20 of them. They concentrated on basic color terms (BCTs). (a) A BCT is a monolexemic word, which eliminated English terms like *lemon-colored*, or *bluish*. (b) The significance of a BCT is that it is not included within the range of any other color term. Because the denotations of *crimson* and *scarlet* in English are included in red, these terms are not BCTs. (c) A BCT must have a wide range of application. Its application must not be restricted to a narrow class of objects. In this respect, *blonde* in English is not a BCT as it applies mainly to hair. (d) A BCT must be psychologically salient. That is, it must be near the top of the list of terms elicited in free listings of the domain. It must be generally known by speakers and have a generally agreed upon meaning. Terms such as *scarlet* and *crimson* are not very salient. BCTs were also defined using secondary criteria: the term (a) has the same grammatical properties as other BCTs; (b) is not derived from the name of an object; and (c) is not recently borrowed. The English term *orange*, although borrowed, qualifies as a BCT because it is not recent, even though the same term also names a plant and its fruit.

Two major findings from the investigation, which argued for the non-arbitrariness in color nomenclature, were (i) that there are 11 color categories from which languages draw, and (ii) that there is a universal hierarchy which constrains which terms languages have depending on the number of the categories they have a name for. The authors suggested that this hierarchy corresponded to the way in which color category terms evolved in languages. The 11 basic color terms are: WHITE, BLACK, RED, GREEN, YELLOW, BLUE, BROWN, ORANGE, PINK, PURPLE, and GREY. The seven implicational universals which correspond to seven stages in the evolution of color lexica can be represented as in Figure 13.1.

This hierarchy is to be understood along the lines: if a language has three basic color terms, then they would be words for BLACK, WHITE and RED. Several African languages have been described as having such a system, e.g., Tiv (Tivoid,

BLACK		GREEN <	YELLOW			PINK
	< RED <			< BLUE	<BROWN <	PURPLE
WHITE		YELLOW <	GREEN			ORANGE
						GREY
I	II	III	IV	V	VI	VII

Figure 13.1: Implicational universal relations among BCTs (Berlin and Kay 1969: 5).

Benue-Congo, Nigeria/Cameroon) and Mampruli (Gur, Ghana, Naden 2005). Some African languages, which have four basic terms, following the predictions, either have BLACK, WHITE, RED and YELLOW, e.g., Igbo (Igboid, Atlantic Congo, Nigeria); or BLACK, WHITE, RED and GREEN, e.g., Ibibio (Ibibio-Efik, Cross River, Nigeria) and Chumburung (Guang, Kwa, Ghana) – see Hansford (2010) for an evaluation of this conclusion.

Various investigations carried out on African languages contributed to the challenges to the paradigm. For instance, the category GREY appears already at stage III in Tsonga (Bantu) when it is supposed to appear only at stage VII. There are many languages that do not have separate terms for GREEN and BLUE, although they do have terms for categories lower in the hierarchy. Thus, Mursi (Nilotic, Sudan; see Turton 1980) does not separate these colors but it seems to have terms corresponding to 'grey' and 'pink'. Similarly, Zulu and other Bantu languages such as Setswana have a term for BROWN but no separate terms for GREEN and BLUE. These terms are being developed (see Davies et al. 1994, Davies and Corbett 1997). Then there is the problem of YELLOW, as pointed out for Kapsiki (Chadic, Cameroon) by van Beek (1977).

Such challenges led to various refinements of the original Berlin and Kay system. One of these is the recognition of different layers of colors. First, there are six primary colors corresponding to perceptual landmarks based on fundamental neural responses (instead of the 11 foci): black, white, red, yellow, green, and blue, which individually or in combination form the basis of the denotation of most of the major color terms of most of the languages of the world. Besides these six primary basic color categories, there are derived basic categories (based on fuzzy intersections), e.g., ORANGE = YELLOW & RED, and composite basic categories (based on fuzzy union), e.g., WARM = RED OR YELLOW. A more sophisticated partitioning of the color space has also developed. Evolutionary sequences are assumed to move from coarser to finer partitions (see Kay and McDaniel 1978, Kay, Berlin, Maffi, and Merrifield 1997, Kay and Maffi 1999 for the revisions and see also Kay et al. 2009 for the World Colour Survey).

Despite the revisions and attempts to address the issues with the paradigm, major criticisms persist. A major methodological critique concerns the use of Munsell color chips for the elicitation of color terms (Sanders and van Brakel 1997). In the African context, this problem was brought to the fore by Turton's report on the investigation of Mursi color terms where the consultants responded to one of the stimulus chips with the retort: "There is no such beast" (Turton 1980, see also Eczet 2019). The issue is whether one would not get different results if more natural elements and culturally embedded stimuli were used. The challenge for cross-cultural and cross-linguistic comparative semantic studies of semantic domains is to ensure that the same stimuli are used and the same things are being compared.

Another criticism is that the category of color may be a cognitive category but not a linguistic category. For one thing, there are several languages that do not have a word for 'color'. Moreover, such a category may be subsumed under a more general visual domain. Furthermore, the terms that are elicited do not constitute a morpho syntactic or a coherent semantic domain in some of the languages. Lucy (1997) remarks that color naming does reveal something but asks what it is:

> Well, I agree that something is there, but exactly what? I would argue that *what is there is a view of the world's languages through the lens of our own category*, namely, a systematic sorting of each language's vocabulary by reference to how, and how well, it matches our own.
> (Lucy 1997: 331, italics in original)

Wierzbicka's (e.g., 2008) charge is that the color naming paradigm is "deeply Anglocentric" (Wierzbicka 2005: 218; see also Wierzbicka 2014). Similarly, Dimmendaal (1995: 11), summing up some of the challenges from African languages for color research, notes that "ethnocentricism has (. . .) had its effects on the so-called objective investigation of colour". Kay (2006) is a spirited response to the criticisms put forward by Lucy and Wierzbicka, in particular.

The variations across languages in the color domain include the fact that many languages, including African ones, do not have a term that matches 'color'. Chumburung, a Guang language, for example, does not have an overall term for color and they do not seem to have borrowed the English term either (Hansford 2010). For some other languages, there might be a term that encompasses more than what the English term denotes. Roulon-Doko (2019:) argues that Gbaya (Ubangian, Niger-Congo), a language of the Central African Republic, "has no generic term for 'color'" nor does it lexically distinguish color from the visual aspect, resulting from a variety of parameters. Indeed, this language deploys the word *dàp* 'pattern, drawing' as a generic term and may use *tè* 'body' in construction with a prototypical reference term to talk about color. Similarly, Petrollino (2022) argues that there is no word for color in Hamar, an Omotic language of Southwest Ethiopia. The Hamar use the word *bíshi* 'outer surface, e.g., skin of things; appearance'. Payne (2003) reports that Maa (Kenya, Tanzania, Nilotic) has a word *eɱúá* which covers a broader category. It includes both terms defined by hue, saturation, and brightness, i.e., 'color', and also those that describe color plus design or pattern, e.g., *arûss* 'spotted black and white' (see Segerer and Vanhoeve 2019).

In some languages, the so-called superordinate term for 'color' may refer to a narrower domain. In Ewe there is a polysemous term *ama* which denotes herbs, medicinal plants, and leafy green vegetables in one reading. It is also used to characterize saturation and tone rather than hue or brightness. As this term does not cover hue, Ewe speakers borrow the English term as *kɔla* to designate the domain. This is used in the descriptive term for BROWN, namely, *avu-mí-kɔla* 'dog-shit-color'. Thus, languages without a term for the color domain as understood in the research tradition may either borrow a term, use a broader or narrower term, or not apply superordinate terms at all, as is the case in Chumburung (Guang, Kwa, Ghana).

In many languages, color terminology varies according to the frame. This is most pronounced in bovine cultures. The anthropological literature on the pastoralists of East Africa, for instance, indicates that cattle color terms rarely refer to pure colors or shades of colors. They refer to configurations of colors or patterns (see Coote 2012). Apart from this, the color terminologies of these peoples seem to comprise two systems, where the terms for the non-bovine world are derived from those of the cattle terms. However, these two terms are not referentially isomorphic. For example, in Chai (a Surmic language of Ethiopia), the term *cá!gí* refers to grass and trees (green) in the non-bovine frame, but when used of cows designates reddish brown (Last 1995: 113; cf. Dimmendaal 1995; see also Maffi 1984, 1990 on Somali color terms).

One of the characteristics of basic color terms proposed by Berlin and Kay is that the terms should share the same grammatical class. In many African languages, color terms fall into different form classes. In other words, the languages tend not to treat words that refer to color as belonging to one domain. Dimmendaal (1995) argues that in Turkana (Nilotic), color words fall into at least two classes, verbs and adjectives. Similarly, Payne (2003) describes Maa (Nilotic) color words as belonging to two classes: adjective and verbs. Hansford (2010) shows that Chumburung (Guang, Kwa) color terms are either verbs, such as the word for 'red', or adjectives or nouns where they participate in the nominal class system. For Ewe (Gbe, Kwa), Ameka (2001, 2012) demonstrates that words for focal red *dzĩ* and focal white *ɣé* are simple underived adjectives, while the term for focal black *yibɔɔ* is an ideophonic adjective. The terms for the macro-color counterparts of these are verbs, while there are ideophonic modifiers for the various colors. In several domains the term used is vastly distant from the focal color. In a domain such as that of skin pigmentation, the European skin is designated as white in many European languages. In African languages, the European skin pigmentation is designated with a term that refers to macro-red. There are interesting descriptors for the color YELLOW in many African languages (see Segerer and Vanhove 2021); we will cite just two. Van Beek (1977) reports that the Kapsiki of Nigeria and Cameroon describe yellow stimuli with the following expressions, which relate to similarity with something in the natural world.

(3) *kwaxaŋwayaxaŋwaya*   '(like) the color of corn'
   kwarəwurəxwu   'like the flower of rəxwu'
   kwayɛmugwarəyɛmugwarə 'like the waters of Gawar',
   kwadawadawa   'like the vomit of jaundice'

In Asante Twi (Akan, Kwa), the term for yellow is *akokɔsradeɛ* 'chicken fat'. The same conceptualization underlies the terms for yellow in the closely related Ga and Dangme languages: *wuɔfɔ* 'chicken fat' (Ga) and *kungwɔ zɔ* 'chicken fat' (Dangme). The conceptual motivations for this lexicalization are fairly transparent.

In a recent survey of color systems in Africa, Payne (2020) notes that there are few detailed studies of color systems. Nevertheless, based on some of the available data and her survey of 70 languages from the different phyla she observed that there is variation in the areal distribution of different BCTs. There seems to be a historical three-term system in the Niger-Congo languages. Significantly, she observes that salient cultural activities as well as urbanization have had an impact on the distribution. She draws attention to the fact that in some African languages, such as Maa, an East African Nilotic language, there are two words for the color hue RED: *dɔ* 'be dark red' whose protype is related to blood, and *nyokie* 'be.red', which is used to talk about animal pelts and human skin colors. The Maa system illustrates a situation found in pastoralist cultures. In some of those linguacultures, one encounters simple terms that describe color, but more commonly the terms that describe animal coats in such languages may relate to color plus pattern, or just pattern.

The literature on pastoralist cultures is huge, among these the classic works by the Japanese scholar Fukui (1979, 1996). Petrollino (2022) gives a quick overview grouping them according to disciplines. Some ethnographic works that deal with color and pattern terms include Almagor (1983) on Dhaasanach (Ethiopia); Arensen (1992) on Murle (Sudan); Dubosson (2014, 2018) on Hamar (Omotic, Ethiopia); Dyson-Hudson (1966) on Karimojong (Uganda); Eczet (2018, 2019) on Mursi (Nilotic, Ethiopia); Evans-Pritchard (1934, 1940) on Dinka and Nuer (Sudan); Galaty (1989) on Maasai (Tanzania, Kenya); Lienhardt

(1961) on Dinka (Sudan); Ohta (1989, 1986) on Turkana (Kenya); Tornay (1973, 1978) on Nyangatom (Nilotic, Ethiopia); and Turton (1980) on Mursi (Ethiopia). Studies on the semantic and cognitive aspects of livestock color and pattern terms include Eckl (2000) on Herero; Dimmendaal (2015) on various languages; Payne (2003) on Maasai; and Taljard (2015) on Northern Sotho. Koopman (2019) is about Zulu bird lore but he discusses the relationship between cattle patterns and bird names, building on previous work on Zulu cattle color terminology by Oosthuizen (1996).

Some questions that emanate from this large literature concern the semantics of the cattle model color and pattern terms. What kind of visual semantics do they have? In the case of languages that have some terms which seem to relate to color hue and others that combine color and pattern, are they the same category or different? Mixed methods are being used to address these and other questions. Petrollino (2022) reports that "[r]ecent studies in experimental psychology by Jules Davidoff and his colleagues have focused on Himba's categorical perception of livestock's patterns (Goldstein and Davidoff, 2008) and on various aspects of Himba's attention and distractibility in relation to livestock's appearance and other social and cultural factors (Caparos et al., 2012, 2013; Davidoff et al., 2008; Fockert et al., 2007, 2011)".

Using stimulus-based elicitation methods and coloring tasks, combined with textual analysis of cattle-talk discourses, Petrollino (2022) focuses on the meaning and conceptualization of cattle coat terms and patterns used by the Hamar. She finds that features such as brightness, sheen, and (de)saturation, rather than hue, are central to the meanings of at least some "color" terms in the Hamar visual system. The lingering question remains whether there is a psychologically and culturally real distinction between hue color terms and color plus pattern terms in these pastoral cultures. Dimmendaal (2022) suggests that reaction time experiments in these bovine cultures could provide clues.

In terms of further research on color in African languages and cultures, we need detailed studies of the linguistics and ethnography of color in individual languages that investigate both conceptual and symbolic meanings of color terms, as well as appearance terms more generally. There is very little on color-related cultural practices in African societies, even though there are various domains where color and patterns are used, such as in cloth making. We also need a systematic study and comparison of cattle color terms and patterns as well as of the use of color in non-bovine domains to understand the visual semantics of color in these cultures.

3 Ethnosyntax

Ethnosyntax was introduced as a parallel domain of study to ethnosemantics by Anna Wierzbicka (1979) to account for the "[D]irect encoding of cultural meaning in the semantics of morphosyntax" (Enfield 2002: 4). This narrow definition of ethnosyntax has been broadened to cover the exploration of semantic and pragmatic consequences of "typicality" in grammar, e.g., the serial verb constructions where combinations of verbs that would normally be interpretable are not available because they do not describe typical ways of doing things in a culture (see Lovestrand 2021). For instance, a sub-construction of SVCs in Ewe is one where VP1 is a posture and VP2 represents an activity, which can be roughly paraphrased as 'assume/be in a position and do something'. Thus, an expression like *é-nɔ anyí ɖu nú* [3SG-be.atNPRES ground eat thing] 'She sat down and ate' is interpreted as a culturally appropriate typical way of doing things and hence an appropriate SVC. However, a lying down position is not the typical, unmarked way of eating in this culture, and hence the structurally similar form *é-mlɔ́ anyí ɖu nú* [3SG-lie ground eat thing] 'She lay down and ate' is less felicitous as an SVC. The social indexical significance of grammatical choices and culturally determined uses of grammatical constructions, e.g., possessive constructions, fall within the broad scope of ethnosyntax. The idea that "every language embodies in its very structure a certain world-view, a certain philosophy (. . .) while being 'obviously true' (. . .) is at the same time notoriously difficult to prove" (Wierzbicka 1988: 196). That vocabulary or words index culture is evident and axiomatic for many. That grammar encodes and indexes cultural meaning is harder for many to accept. Ken Hale advises that "establishing a connection between a philosophical postulate [world view/cultural theme/value (FKA and AA)] and a principle of grammar requires that the two be established independently" (Hale 1986: 233). This is the principal methodology of ethnosyntactic research, broken down into steps by Simpson (2002: 290–291) as follows:

(i)   Identify the morphosyntactic construction, e.g., possessive construction, serial verb construction, logophoric construction, or nominal classification construction

(ii) Identify a meaning associated with the construction

(iii) Propose a relationship between this meaning and a shared topic of conversation, assumption, or expectation of speakers

(iv) Provide evidence that the shared topic of conversation, assumption, or expectation is or has been highly salient for the speakers

(v) Provide an explanation based in conversational practice as to how the construction came to exist and bear the proposed meaning (or pragmatic inference or function)

(vi) Look at similar constructions in other languages and check whether the proposed connection between conversational practice and grammatical construction holds

In the rest of the section, we report on some instances of cultural meanings embodied in possessive, logophoric, and nominal categorization constructions in some African languages.

3.1 Body part possessive constructions in Ewe

Languages tend to have a number of possessive constructions that are used to code the relationship between entities. In Ewe there are two constructions: a juxtaposed construction where the speaker wishes to indicate a very close relationship between the possessor and the possessed, and a linker construction where the speaker wishes to indicate a conceptual distance between the entities. From this perspective, one expects body part terms which are seen as conceptually close to their owners to occur in the juxtaposed construction. However, in Ewe grammar, body parts must occur in the linker construction (Ameka 1996). Ewe is in a minority crosslinguistically when it comes to the treatment of body parts as being distinct from their owners. Claudi and Heine (1986) find such body part possessive construction to have "peculiar semantics". Ameka (2012 [1991] Chapter 7) argues that this is not peculiar, but rather, that there is a direct encoding of a cultural idea in the semantics of these constructions which relates to whether or not a possessor can do things with the possessed item as they want, which accounts for the distribution of relational and other nouns across the constructions. Ameka proposed a semantics for both constructions as shown in Table 13.2, with the culturally significant components in italics. Spatial relational terms (mainly expressed as postpositions or locative nominals), kinship terms including affinal terms, and significant socio-cultural terms, e.g., *de* 'hometown', *agble* 'farm, garden' occur juxtaposed to their possessors. There are socio-cultural conventions about how to do things with kin, as well as with other culturally important entities. Spatial relations are inherent and cannot be disassociated from their possessors. It follows that their possessors cannot do things with them as they want.

Compare the interpretation of the expressions in (4), where the same nominal entity occurs in both constructions and in the construal of the relationship. In (a), because there is a cultural constraint on what one can do with communally owned

Table 13.2: Ewe (Gbe) adnominal possessive constructions.

Juxtaposed construction NP1 (=X) NP2 (=Y)	Linker construction NP1 (=X) ƒé NP2 (=Y)
One can think of X and Y like this:	One can think of X and Y like this:
When one thinks of Y, one cannot not think of X	Y is a part of X
X and Y are like one thing X and Y are like part of the same thing	X can think of Y/ say something about Y like this: this thing is mine
X cannot do things with Y as X wants	*Because of this, X can do things with Y as X wants*

land, the juxtaposed construction is used. In (b) there is no such constraint and the possessor can use the land as he wishes.

(4) *anyígbá* earth, ground; land
a. Land as communal property: juxtaposed *fo.me nyígbá   yé*
    family land   FOC
    'It is family land'
b. Land as individual property: linker *Kofí ƒé   anyígbá le   Gẽ*
    Kofi POSS land   LOC Accra
    'Kofi's land is in Accra'

Recently, Kpoglu (2021) explained the distribution of kinship terms between the two constructions in Tongugbe, a riverine dialect of Ewe. He shows that ascending collateral and horizontal kin terms occur in the juxtaposed construction; descending collateral terms occur in the linker construction; and lineal kinship terms (both ascending and descending) can occur in either of the two construction types. The argument here is that the kin with whom one can do as one wants, i.e., those under the possessor's control, can occur in the linker construction. However, those kin with whom the possessor cannot do as they like, i.e., cannot control and would have to show respect etc., typically do not occur in the linker construction except when the speaker wishes to show conceptual alienation. This confirms the inherent semantics of the constructions with a cultural postulate as proposed.

3.2 Third party communication – logophoricity and interpretive marking

A socio-cultural norm of speaking in West Africa is "triadic communication – the art of communicating with another through a third party" (Yankah 1995: 2). There are different modes of triadic communication; the main one which has reflexes in various grammatical structures in the languages is the one involving situations where a principal speaks and a mediator transmits the message in embellished form, either through artistic elaboration or paraphrasing. Ameka and Breedveld (2004) propose the following cultural script for triadic communication in (West) Africa:

> [people think like this:]
>> when I want to say something to someone
>> if I think about it like this: "it is not a small thing",
>> it is good if someone else can say it to this person
>>> because of this, it can be good to say to another person: "I want you to do it"

As Levison (1988: 164–165) points out, "[T]here is an interplay between language structure and language use such that usage properties often have effects or correlates in linguistic structure". Some of the correlates and effects of triadic communication include:

(i)   A distinction between different text types depending on the participant roles. For instance, texts addressed to or by a principal would have different features from texts interpreted by a mediator.

(ii) The Principal does not use a reported speech frame. The intermediaries' speech, however, carries signals of reported speech and of represented speech.

(iii) "In his [mediator's] reporting, there is a deictic shift from his principal's first person perspective to third person (in reference to the Principal)" (Yankah 1995:129).

(iv) There is distribution of authorial responsibility and various evidential stance strategies are employed by the intermediaries.

Among the Wolof of Senegal, there is an institutionalized social caste, the griots, who are the mediators for the noble class. Consequently, there are differences between noble-like speech and griot-like speech, as shown in Table 13.3.

Apart from such usage effects, Ameka (2004) argues that the preoccupation with triadic communication has spawned grammatical structures of logophoricity and interpretive markers. Logophoric markers are distinct grammatical forms such as pronouns or verbal markers, used to report the speech, thoughts,

Table 13.3: A comparison of noble-like speech and griot-like speech (Irvine 1990: 144).

	Noble-like speech	Griot-like speech
Emphatic devices		
	Unmarked (subject-verb-object) order of constituents; sparse use of focus markers	Left-dislocation, cleft sentences; heavy use of focus markers (subject focus, object focus, and the 'explicative' verbal auxiliary).
	Sparse use of spatial deictics and determinants	Frequent use of spatial deictics, especially their emphatic forms
	Sparse use of modifiers.	Ideophones (intensifiers) and greater use of the verb complement construction né____, which often convey details of sound and motion
Parallelisms		
	Little use of parallelisms.	Repetitive and parallel constructions (e.g., parallel clauses)
	Few reduplicated forms, especially in verbs; no novel use of morphological reduplication	Frequent use of morphological reduplication, especially in verbs, including novel word formations
Disfluencies		
	Noun classification system: choice of "wrong" or semantically neutral class markers, avoidance of markers when possible; incomplete or inconsistent concord	"Correct" class markers, principles of consonant harmony and semantic subtlety; more use of markers; consistent and complete concord
	Incomplete sentence structures; false starts	Well-formed sentence structures

wants, desires, etc. of an individual other than the speaker (see, e.g., Hagège 1974, Clements 1975, von Roncador 1992, Dimmendaal 2001, Güldemann 2008, Nikitina 2012). In example (5) below from Ewe, a spokesman is relaying a message from a chief who is referred to with the regular 3SG pronoun *é* in the main clause and with the logophoric pronoun *ye* in the reported clause. The suggestion is that this is a structure which allows intermediaries to distinguish the Source/Principal from their own viewpoint.

(5) Example from an Ewe written play based on the Ewe migration story:

É=bé	gafofo	ene	sɔŋ=é	nyé	é=si
3SG=QT	hour	four	INT=aFOC	COP	3SG=this

ye=le		mia-fé	así-nu	dzɔ=mĩ
LOG-be.at:PRES		2PL-POSS	hand-mouth	wait=PROG

ko	*ye=mé-se*		nya	áɖéké	o
only	LOG-NEG-hear		word	INDEF	NEG

'He₍ᵢ₎ says he₍ᵢ₎ has been waiting for signs from you for four whole hours now and he₍ᵢ₎ has not heard anything' (Kwamuar 1997: 15, glosses and translation added)

Those languages that do not have logophoric pronouns use other devices to achieve the same evidential distancing. For instance, Akan, a linguaculture which practises a royal system of third-party communication, does not have logophoric markers. It has forms that have an interpretive function – a complementizer *sɛú* and a clause final interpretive marker *sɛ* that reflect the use of logophoric speech (see Agyekum 2002 on Akan and Blass 1991 on Sissala). A similar utterance-final inferential marker occurs in other languages, such as Likpe, where it is a strategy for indicating authorial responsibility. Here is a case of a communicative practice with its values and usage effects grammaticalized – a clear instance of culture-in-grammar.

3.3 The cultural semantics basis for nominal classification

Another area in African languages where cultural meaning is encoded in morphosyntactic structures is nominal categorization. There is a long-standing debate in African linguistics as to whether the various types of noun classification constructions have a semantic basis. Hurskainen (2000: 667) observes that "there is a widely accepted view that there was a semantic motivation for the emergence of the noun classification" in Niger Congo languages. "It had a semantic basis in the oldest reconstructed layer, the so-called pre-Niger-Congo languages, but it had already become grammaticalized and developed into more formal systems in the intermediate layer, the proto-Niger-Congo (Williamson 1989: 32)". Philosophical constructions of the nominal classification system have been developed on the principle of this historical semantic motivation (Tempels 1959, Jahn 1958, Kagame 1976). With the grammaticalization of the system, the semantic motivation became less transparent and various mergers occurring in present day languages obscure the semantics. However, in recent times. various studies have argued that there is a motivated semantics of noun classes despite the heterogeneity of the nouns that belong to the classes (see, e.g., Contini-Morava 1994, Breedveld 1995a,b, Palmer 1996). Challenges to the semantic basis of the nominal classification systems stem from the search for a single semantic feature to account for the semantics of the class. Indeed, what one feature can account for a class that contains words for trees, medicine, and dances, for example? A prototype and family resemblance approach to categorization can reveal the network of relationships between the members of the noun class. Secondly, cultural motivations as well as experiential features contribute to the explanations of the semantic links between clusters of nouns within a noun class, and these should not be eschewed in the accounts. Selvik (2001) reports on psycholinguistic testing of the hypotheses about the semantics of some Setswana classes. Breedveld (1995a) explores the semantics of the 25 individual classes of Fulfulde. She argues convincingly for network analyses, where the noun classes, being categories, have polysemic structures and the links between the semantic fields within the classes are motivated on the basis of the speakers' experience. The most fascinating thing about Fulfulde is that it is the language of pastoralists and, apart from elaboration in the lexicon, with hundreds of terms for cattle, there is also the encoding of culture-specific cattle semantics in the grammar. There is a cow nominal class, i.e., the -*nge* class. Breedveld (1995b) represents the semantics of this class as follows (Figure 13.2):

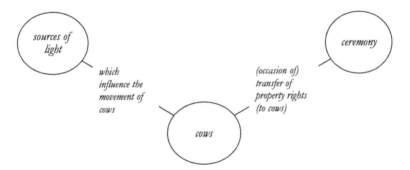

Figure 13.2: Semantic network of the NGE class in Maasina (based on Breedveld 1995b).

Breedveld argues that the words in the NGE class end in the suffix -*nge* and more importantly can be referred to with the NGE concord. She argues that the words can be grouped into three semantic fields, as shown in Figure 13.2. The key term for the class is 'cow', as words for bulls belong to a different class. Apart from the cow field there are the words *yire* 'fire', *yaynge* 'light', and *nange* 'sun' which form a field of sources of light. Breedveld motivates the link between the cow field and the sources of light field as being due to the influence of light on the movement of cows. She supports this from a myth involving a cow and light and from information from consultants. Another word in the class is the word *yannge* 'ceremony, family celebration'. The ceremonies that fall in this field are those during which property rights to cows are transferred, such as name-giving or wedding ceremonies. Breedveld thus uses cultural information to motivate links between the fields of cow, sources of light, and ceremony. We saw earlier the use of the cattle model in a lexical domain (color); here we see the indexing of a bovine cultural theme in the grammar.

4 Ethnopragmatics: Social interaction

A social interaction is an exchange between two or more individuals, reciprocally influencing each other during social encounters. The participants may be co-present at a place or may be at a distance. In the latter case the interaction may be mediated by technology through the use of writing or audiovisual media (see De Jaegher et al. 2010: 442). In interactions in which people are physically present in the same place, different levels of engagement may be involved. Goffman (1963) talks of "unfocused interaction", when "acknowledgment between two or more strangers or familiar others, such as an exchanged nod, smile, or greeting" is involved. These latter types of engagement are the building blocks of society and they reflect the norms, values, and expectations of its members. Communication can involve two parties (a dyadic interaction) or a participant structure involving communication from a principal being relayed through an animator or intermediary, i.e., third party communication. The interaction might also involve multiple parties. In Section 3.2 we discussed effects on grammar of the use of third parties in communication. In the present section, we examine research on greeting forms, contexts of use, and the values attached to greetings as social practices in various African languages. We show that in the enactment of greetings, the values and ideologies of social interaction involved are, among others, "inclusiveness", "hospitality", "harmony" (Ameka 2009), "respect" (Dammers 2010, Paulos 2002 [1956]), and "fertility" (Baxter 1990). Withholding greetings, on the other hand, reflects notions or ideologies of "cleanliness" or "pollution", e.g., not greeting care-takers during burials, and avoidances in caste relations.

4.1 Greetings and parting

Different definitions or characterizations are given to what are regarded as "greetings" in different studies. Firth (1972: 1) characterizes greetings and farewells as "the recognition of an encounter with another person as socially acceptable". Ameka (2009: 127) notes that "[g]reetings and farewells are components of opening and closing access rituals and are not coextensive with them". Taking various language-specific and general definitions into account, Duranti (1997: 67) proposes six recurring features to be used as criteria for the identification of greetings in a speech:

1. near-boundary occurrence, i.e., they are expected to occur at the beginning of a social encounter
2. establishment of a shared perceptual field: interactants' recognition of each other's presence
3. adjacency pair format: typically involves the exchange of two or more sequences of utterances, i.e., greeting and re-greeting
4. relative predictability of form and content; i.e., formulaic speech
5. implicit establishment of a spatio-temporal unit of interaction (different parts of a day may elicit different greetings and different greetings may be appropriate in different places or contexts)
6. identification of the interlocutor as a distinct being worth recognizing

Co-present greeting and parting expressions have received extensive attention in African cultural and linguistic studies. A number of works, including Irvine ([1974] 1989), Youssouf et.al. (1976), Merton (1988), Akindele (1990), Nwoye (1993), Yahya-Othman (1995), Schottman (1995), Yimam (1997), Ameka (2009), and Wojtowicz (2021), are dedicated to the examination of the phenomenon in individual languages or in a comparative perspective. In this section we highlight major issues these studies have addressed concerning the exchange of greetings and parting or farewell expressions.

Generally, greeting is routinely extended to persons one is familiar with before engaging in conversation of any sorts. It is also extended to complete strangers in cases of co-presence e.g., in a service center or when passing by. The latter type of greetings may or may not be followed up by extensive conversation or leave-taking. In greeting non-familiar people, it can suffice to use abridged greeting expressions, e.g., *t'ena yïst'ïllïn* ('may God give (you) health on my behalf'), *sälam* ('peace') in Amharic, and *sáro* ('peace') in Wolaitta (Yimam 1997). The same forms, i.e., *t'ena yïst'ïllïn*, *sälam*, and *sáro*, are used in response to such short salutations, not involving the several turns of greetings and expressions of gratitude that are common when greeting familiar persons.

Akindele (1990: 10) observes a similar use of *e pèlé* (polite) or *pèlé* in Yoruba, and notes that greeting a familiar person with just short forms may be considered "brusque or rude". The same is observed in Wolof (Irvine 1989: 170).

Among familiar persons, elaborate greeting expressions follow the short "initial salutations". The extended greeting forms enquire about the well-being of the addressee and his/her family and livelihood. Some authors claim that the questions in greetings have no propositional content (see Youssouf et al. 1976 on Tuareg greetings). Others argue that these questions are uttered with genuine intent to elicit information about the well-being of others (see Ameka 2009). Indeed, the regularly attested "themes" of greeting questions in African languages relate to "health" and "peace". Nicolas (2005: 888) notes, for Oromo of Ethiopia: "[a] common feature of all Oromo greetings is wishing each other peace (*nagaa*) and asking about each other's well-being". The author further notes that *nagaa*-related greetings and blessings in Oromo invoke 'may you be healthy', 'may you not become ill', 'may you experience no fighting or disagreements with others', 'may you enjoy protection from harm', and 'may you be in proper relationship with God (the sky) and the earth, people and cattle'. The responses to the greetings include an element of gratitude, often invoking a religious element as in *hamdu lilla* 'Praise God' (derived from Arabic) and *igzia-biher yimmesgen* 'May God be praised' in Amharic (Yimam 1997).

Expressing appreciation, solidarity, or good wishes to those exerting physical labor is another central element in greeting and leave-taking expressions across cultures. In Ewe, for example, gratitude expressions involve acknowledging the services that people render to each other daily, as in *etsɔ fe dɔ* 'Thanks for yesterday's work', *mia-wóé le dɔ dzí* 'You (PL) are working', or *mia-wóé le ame ta kpɔ́m̃* 'You (PL) are looking after people'. Such expressions are responded to with *yoo, miawo hã* 'Okay, you too' or simply with *Máwùé* 'it is God' (Ameka 2009: 134–135). According to Akindele (1990: 7), in Yoruba someone engaged in hair dressing is greeted with *e kú ewà* 'greetings to beauty', while one involved in hunting expeditions is addressed with *à rí pa o* 'may your expedition be successful' or 'May you find game to kill'. The responses to these are *oo e sé* 'thank you' and *á á se* 'May it be so'. In Wolaitta (Omotic, Ethiopia), greeting someone who is busy with or on his/her way to physical work, e.g., work on farm, a construction site, etc. can begin with *wolk'á ʔimm-ó* [power give-OPT] 'May (God) give you energy'; someone selling or buying in the market or carrying his/her goods to the market is greeted by first saying: *sintá ʔimm-ó* [face give-OPT] 'May you have good transactions'. Leave-taking can also be done by using these expressions. Similarly, in Zargulla (Omotic, Ethiopia), greeting people occupied with physical work begins with an interjection, *ʔaʃʃám* (described as 'may I share your burden/effort'), and a gesture may be made to help with the work at hand, e.g., by taking on the load that the person is carrying, even if it is only for a few steps (this even when the offer of help may mean changing one's direction of travel, especially when one encounters people carrying a sick person on a stretcher to or from a clinic). In Wolaitta, a formally identical word, *ʔaʃʃám*, is used as an opening in greeting or welcoming family members or neighbors who are returning from work or from a long trip. It implies that the person extending the utterance *ʔaʃʃám* has remained in a familiar, intimate place, i.e., at home or in the neighborhood, while the addressee has been away on business and is coming back to the shared place. It would not be used when the same interlocutors met each other out on the road at a random place, in a market, or at work.

As Duranti (1997: 67) points out, greetings establish implicit spatio-temporal units of interaction. The temporal aspect is reflected in widely reported variations in greeting forms, involving indications of the time of the day at which the greeting takes place. Morning, afternoon, and evening greetings are distinguished, among many others, in Amharic (Yimam 1997), Beja (Morton 1988), Ewe (Ameka 2009), Maale (Amha 2001), and Yoruba (Akindele 1990). The morning greeting seems to be particularly important: Amharic has only one greeting form for the afternoon and evening greetings but it distinguishes two forms in its morning greeting. In a greeting directed to a male person with the same social status as the speaker, one would say *ïndämïn addärk* (lit.: 'how did you spend the night?') at any time between dawn and the early hours of daylight, up to around 9 a.m. Between 9 and 11 a.m., the person would be greeted with *ïndämïn aräffädk* 'how did you spend the late time of morning?' (see Yimam 1997). Nwoye (1993: 39) notes that the Igbo morning greeting *I putago ula* 'have you risen from sleep?' enquires about how the hearer slept the previous night. Although these Igbo greetings are used on the first encounter in a day, unlike the English *Good morning*, they can occur beyond the morning as long as the interactors have not encountered one another previously.

A designated greeting form may be used to reflect special social relations. For example, in Maale an 'ordinary friend' is *láge* and would be greeted with *wozí* 'How?' (i.e., 'how are you?'), *kófi dáa* 'are you well?', or with any of the appropriate daytime greetings, i.e., *kófi wórk'íya/kófi péék'k'íya* 'Did you spend the night/day well?'. But people who have special friends known as *béélla* 'bond friends' (i.e., people who have entered into close friendship through elaborate rituals and the exchange of special gifts), greet each other with *ta béélli béé* 'my friend I greet you' (Amha 2001: 264–265). Different spaces may involve different greeting practices. As Ameka (2009) has shown, greetings in Ewe differ when they are exchanged during a chance meeting at the market or on the road, and when they are exchanged during a visit to someone's house: the former generate minimal exchanges of greetings between the interlocuters. Visits at home, on the other hand, may involve varying lengths as well as different modes of communication depending on whether it is a "flying" visit in which the visitor comes around to say hello and quickly departs, or whether it is a "sitting" visit. The latter type has opening, central, and closing phases of greeting rituals and may involve "triadic communication" (see Section 3.2), widely attested in West Africa, whereby greetings, leave-taking, and the exchange of information between two persons may be mediated by a spokesperson (see Yankah 1995, Ameka 2004, Ameka and Breedveld 2004).

Age, social status, and gender differences of the participants are reflected in the greeting forms and may also determine who might initiate greetings. For example, in Wolof, "ideally one greets up' i.e., one greets adults before greeting children; a low-ranking individual greets the higher-ranking one first, etc." (Irvine 1989: 169). Comparable hierarchy-based greeting roles are reported for Baatombu (Schotman 1995), Bisa (Naden 1980), and Gonja (Goody 1972). In Maale, when a younger person or somebody with a lower social status joins a group of older or respected adults, he does not normally take the initiative to greet them. Instead, one of the elders would say *tá nēná ?éélláne* 'I call you!', to which the person responds with the regular greeting forms, e.g., *?intsí kófi péék'k'íya* 'Did you (2PL or 2SG polite) spend the day well?' (Amha 2001: 266). In Ewe and Ga, greetings are initiated by the visitor(s), irrespective of their social status (Ameka 2009: 134). Outside of the home context, tacit understandings determine who the "visitor" or "host" is. Thus, in West Africa, "a trader in the market, a teacher at school, and a farmer on the farm are all functionally at home" (Ameka 2009: 130).

Among pastoralists and trading communities engaged in long-distance travelling, greeting is intertwined with the exchange of news. Youssouf et.al (1976: 803) note that in Tuareg, "[a] typical greeting exchange goes through three stages, following which questions for specific information may be asked". A similar greeting system in Northern Beja is characterized as a "ceremony" or "ritual" by Morton (1988: 322, 433–434). In this culture, greeting is not restricted to the "boundary edge", i.e., to the opening or closing of conversation; rather, the greeting and information exchange can take place in cycles depending on context. Accordingly, casual greeting, i.e., greeting among people who are in frequent contact, involves the standard *salaamu alekum – alekum salaam* 'peace be with you – with you be peace' and/or other exchanges that indicate times of the day, e.g., *lebabi mehata/ mehawa* 'you have risen fortunate' or *lebabi t'ayima* 'you have passed the noon fortunate'. However, a more elaborate and phased greeting takes place when meeting people after a prolonged separation, distinguishing at least four stages:

I) Initial salutation: this involves a hand shake or a hug while repeatedly and emphatically uttering *ʃop-ʃop-ʃop* or *dehani eta* 'you have come alive', to which the new-comer responds *dehani tisiniena* 'you have stayed well for us'.

II) *sakanab* 'news': possibly with a lapse of some time for the traveler(s) to get settled, this main part of the greeting follows. It comprises rapid sequences of short "questions", which may or may not be answered and which have little or no question intonation. As example (6), from Morton (1988: 428), illustrates, the *sakanab* 'news' enquiries are mainly about the state of the traveler and unidentified 'people' at the source of the travel; they are not direct questions about the well-being of a specific (group of) family members.

(6) A: *dabaiwa*   'are you guarded (by God)?'
     B: *kwatiwa*   'are you happy?'
     A: *mabsutwa*   'are you happy?'
     B: *sikerawa*   'are you strong?'
     A: *afimawa*   'are you happy?'
     B: *lebabiwa*   'are you fortunate?'
     A: *afietawa*   'are you happy?'
     B: *natka heru*   'is all goodness?'
     A: *hamdu lilla*   'praise God.'
     B: *gurha kihain*   'there are no troubles?'
     A: *layif kitbaru* 'you have no troubles?'
     B: *regat kitbaru* 'you have no troubles?'
     A: *hamdu lilla*   'praise God.'
     B: *dabai no eta*   'is it guarded from where you have come?'
     A: *dabai no ean*   'it is guarded from where I have come.'
     B: *udhei lebabi*   'are the people fortunate?'
     A: *udhei lebabi*   'the people are fortunate.'
     B: *awajat kithai* 'there is no harm?'
     A: *hamdu lilla*   'praise God.'

Morton (1988: 428–429) notes that the *sakanab* sequence under (6) above "may be a great deal longer, especially if more than two speakers are involved. It is as much a game as a ritual. There is often an element of competition as the speakers attempt to prolong the exchange without direct repetition or hesitation".

III) Then follows what Morton labels "a *lotanena* sequence", a formal exchange with little possibility for improvization:

(7) Local: *lotanena* 'you have appeared to us'
 Traveler: *baguda* 'do not go astray'
 Local: *dehani lotanena* 'you have appeared alive to us'
 Traveler: *bagiga* 'do not go'

This sequence "is not normally used among the residents of or frequent visitors to one village" (1988: 428) and it is not considered part of *sakanab*. Instead, it is followed by more *sakanab* questions.

IV) The actual invitation to tell the news, using any of the following expressions:

(8) *na sakana* 'what news?'
 sakanab tegubia 'have you uncovered news?'
 sakanab timiriwa 'have you found news?'
 gubia 'uncover!'
 fifa 'pour out!'

The presentation of news is concluded by blessings *hamdi lilla medhanok* 'praise God, your life!', *gudab dehana* 'live long!', etc., which will be followed by more *sakanab* (greetings questions, lit. 'news'). Thus are exchanges of greetings and news intertwined.

The closing of an encounter may involve little verbal exchange, e.g., in Mampruli of northern Ghana, "at the end of business, interactants drift apart without any formal closure" (Naden 1986: 195). The farewell expressions in Amharic, Nuer, Oromo, and Wolaitta involve short jussive or imperative verbs (see Yimam 1997: 113–116). In Ewe, formal or "sitting visits" involve three-phase leave-taking enactments (Ameka 2009: 140–143):

1) a preclosing phase in which one of the participants signals his or her intention to bring the encounter to a close by asking permission to leave;
2) a leave-taking phase enacted through various social rituals such as thanking;
3) the final departure, with the host or someone else assigned to seeing the visitor off, and the exchange of routine expressions.

Verbal greeting is often accompanied by gestures: raising one (the right) or both hands, clapping, head bowing, body lowering, and other demeanors.[4] Ullendorff (1973: 176–177) makes the following observation about greeting gestures in Ethiopia (probably referring to northern and central Ethiopia, but some of the practices are widespread): "A low bow is *de rigueur* in almost all instances. If the *shemma* [large scarf] covers one's head, hood-like, it will be lowered, and at times also the shoulders may be uncovered. Frequently the ground is touched with right hand which is then brought to the lips."

Regarding child-father greeting customs among Amhara and Tigray, Paulos (2002: 116 [reprint from 1956]) writes:

> A child, generally up to the age of fifteen, kisses the feet of his father. He does not do so every time the father comes into the house, but only when the father has been away for some days. [. . .] From fifteen usually up to the age of marriage the son kisses the knees of his father. After marriage he bows down and then proceeds to kiss and to be kissed in the case of the Amharas, and to be kissed in the case of the Tigreans among whom the general rule is that the elder must kiss. This gradual promotion of the son from the feet to the knees and then to offering cheeks is in itself a sign of respect on the part of the father towards his growing son or daughter.

Body contact, involving shoulder-to-shoulder touching among young men, or cheek-to-cheek or mouth-to-cheek kisses (and a now out-of-fashion practice: mouth-to-mouth kiss among women) are noted. Elderly men do "hat tipping or touching" if they wear one. When people are seated together, they usually greet an incoming person by (half) rising from their seats. Another common greeting practice in Ethiopia is hand clasping using the right hand, while the palm of the left hand supporting the forearm or elbow of the right hand symbolizes respect (see Richter 2005, Bustorf 2005, Dammers 2010). Muslims often extend the handshake by kissing the backs of each other's right hands while maintaining the hand clasp.

A greeting type known as *ɨjj mänsat* was formerly widely practiced in Ethiopia. It involves bowing while the right hand is moved towards the left side of the waist or is placed on one's belly or chest; the left hand is retracted to one's lower back, tips ones hat, or uncovers the head-scarf. The term comprises *ɨjj* 'hand' and the verbal-nominal *mänsat*, derived from the verb *nässa*, which is translated as 'deprive of, take away, hold back', with examples like *ɨjj nässa* 'bow down to greet, curtsy, pay one's respects, pay homage', *ɨnkʼɨlf nässa* 'not let sleep, keep

---

4 An anonymous reviewer mentioned that the chiShona speaking people of Zimbabwe clap their hands while expressing greetings and gratitude, especially in formal/polite contexts; male persons clap with flat hands while women clap with cupped hands.

awake', *fit nässa* 'give someone the cold shoulder, act distant towards someone, show disfavor to', etc. (see Leslau 1976: 111). The greeting *ïjj mänsat* received special importance when COVID-19 struck. A song produced in early 2020 to help create awareness about the disease emphasizes how washing the hands and practicing *ïjj mänsat* ("the old, ancestors' custom of greeting") has come back to help people stay healthy.[5] Thus, the definition of *nässa* in Leslau (1976: 111) perfectly matches the body gestures and folk understanding of *ïjj mänsat* (as suggested in the song and in current use of Amharic). However, the Amharic-French dictionary (Baeteman 1929: 502) gives two opposing translations of *nässa (ነሣ):* 1) *leva, saisit, prit, emporta* ['raised, grabbed/held, took'], and 2) *refusa, ne donna pas interdit* ['refused, did not give, forbidden']. And Baeteman's (1929: 502) translation of *ïjj nässa* as *se salua l'un l'autre* ['greeted each other'] does not indicate to which meaning of the verb the practice of greeting is related. Moreover, in his dictionary of Ge'ez, Leslau (1989: 120) translates the formally related verb *näsʔa (ነሥአ)* as 'take, receive, accept, grasp. seize, catch', with *näsʔa ʔïda* [*ʔïda* 'hand'] translated as 'pay homage, greet by shaking hands'. Thus, the Ge'ez dictionary does not help resolve the potential discrepancies in folk understanding of *ïjj mänsat* and the translation of the verb *mänsat (nsʔ)* in Baeteman's (1929) dictionary of Amharic.

Some of the gestures and body contact practices mentioned above could be repeated at the closing of the encounter and leave-taking. In Ewe one of the leave-taking gestures is called *zikpuilélé* [chair-RED-catch] 'holding chairs', in which those that remain in the place take leave of the departing by rising from their seats a little and then sitting down again while simultaneously uttering *hɛ̃* (see Ameka 2009: 142). In Wolaitta, Azeb Amha (p.c.) observes that a similar gesture is used both in welcoming and leave-taking among neighbors and relatives with the same social status: both the host and others who have taken a seat in a house make a gesture of standing up (lifting their bodies briefly with a slight head-bow) and sitting back down again once the incoming or departing person has acknowledged the gesture. If the departing or incoming person is older, has higher status, or if it is a relative who has come from a distant place, all present stand up for leave-taking and the host might accompany the person to the door or gate. Similarly, when the arrival of such a relation is made known, the host would walk to the door or to the gate and welcome the person. These two actions are known by designated verbs in Wolaitta: *mokk-* 'to welcome a visitor by the door or gate' and *moys-* 'to see off a visitor at the door or

---

5 See the varying greeting gestures in the song on YouTube: [https://www.youtube.com/watch?v=JYO2DYtiCB8] (accessed 7 January 2022).

gate' (this can extend to the *karé* 'an open space at the front of houses'). Whether or not people stand up completely and wait until the incoming person has taken a seat or only make the gesture of standing depends on the status, age, or other social markers of the visitor and the host. Similarly, the elderly host may remain seated when leave is taken by a younger person. Otherwise, the visitor may be accompanied to the door, to the gate of the compound, or even farther again, depending on these same social variables. The variables indicate respect relationships among people.

In Amharic speaking areas and more widely in Ethiopia, e.g., in Wolaitta, this same gesture is used (especially by the host but often also by others present) to acknowledge the re-entry of a person who has already been greeted and has taken a seat in a room but who has since vacated the room briefly (it is not commonly used outdoors). This acknowledgment may be repeated several times as the same person or other people leave and re-join the room for various reasons. As they half-rise, those that have remained in the room say *nor* (probably from the verb root *nwr* 'live, exist) in Amharic, upon which the person who is re-entering the room responds *bägzer* ('by God!') while slightly bending and/or "tipping hat" as s/he heads to his/her seat. In a similar context in Wolaitta, the person(s) who have remained in the room make(s) the gesture while simultaneously uttering *nooré* (borrowing of Amharic *nor*), to which the one who is re-entering responds by uttering *deʔá* 'live! exist!' (for one person) or *deʔité* (for more than one person).

Respect and politeness in greeting exchanges are further reflected in customs of addressing people by various names, themes which we address in the next section.

4.2 Restrictions on social interaction: naming and taboos on using names

Naming reveals underlying beliefs, social values, and changes, as well as inequalities. Some practices of naming fade away and new ones are introduced as social changes take place. Numerous studies have been conducted on the ethnography and linguistic aspects of naming practices in African cultures. See, among many others, Leyew (2003) on Amharic in Ethiopia; Okello (2021) on Luo in Kenya; Sebonde (2020) on Chasu in Tanzania; Abarry (1997) on the Ga people in Ghana; Schottman (2000) on Baatonu in Benin; Ideh (2019) on the Igbo in Nigeria; Vilakazi (2002) on Ndebele in South Africa; and McGranaghan (2015) on the San in Southern Africa. From an interactional perspective, of particular interest is the way human personal names are bestowed, and norms in the use or non-use of such names in social interaction.[6]

There are designated naming events among some African societies; for example, the Mijikenda in Kenya have a naming ceremony known as Vyalusa, in which "a child is given a clan name by a grandparent or a clan elder identified by the family. If the child is a boy, he is named after the grandfather, while a girl is named after her grandmother" (Mumbo 2012: 377). The naming ceremony of the Ga people in Ghana, *bi kpojiemo* or *kpojiemo gbi* 'child out-taking', must take place on the eighth day after the birth and involves elaborate rituals. According to Abarry (1997: 367), "If a child dies within those 7 days, the corpse is quickly buried without ceremony and its parents are denied the status of parenthood. On the other hand, should the infant survive for even just a day after *kpojiemo* and receiving a name, the parents will have achieved the status of parents even if they bear no more children". The Ga practice and beliefs are more or less shared across the linguacultures of the Gulf of Guinea. In other African cultures, naming is ancillary to other events, e.g., baptism, or a name may be bestowed with little or no ritual and at the convenience of the parents. In the latter case, children are addressed with so-called "waiting names" or "home names" until they are about school going age.

An individual may have several names that are used in different contexts: proper names, honour or "horse" names, kin names, death-prevention names, and nicknames. A special case of naming among the Oyda (Omotic, Ethiopia) involves whistle names, known as *moyzé sunts*, that are distinct from proper names known as *tseéggo sunts* (calling names). Generally, a *moyzé sunts* of an individual is not the whistled version of his/her proper name. *Moyzé sunts* are used in long-distance communication to get the attention of the name-bearer, and in traditional funeral dirges, to invoke the memory of a deceased person (see Amha, Slotta, and Sarvasy 2021).

The primary function of a name is to single out an individual when referring to or when addressing him/her. However, due to politeness, intimacy, and hierarchies in social relations, there may be restrictions on the use of names. One such restriction in African social interaction is the general avoidance of bare personal names when addressing people one thinks of as being above one in some hierarchy. For example, Ideh (2019: 8) notes that Igbo children are not allowed to call their parents by name. In some areas male in-laws cannot be

---

6 Proper names may be bestowed on household animals. As Storch (2019) shows, the naming of characters in literary works as well as naming objects e.g., small boats in tourist areas, involves great creativity and cultural dynamics. See also the inscriptions of names on vehicles, buildings, and shops which contribute to the semiotic landscape of places all over Africa (e.g., Reh 2004, Makoni and Makoni 2009).

addressed (or even referred to) by their personal names at all. This has far-reaching consequences in language use and in the day-to-day life of some members of society.

Respect and familiarity are among the considerations as to whether or not persons are identified by their proper names in greetings and other social encounters (see Schottman 1995, 2000, Ameka and Breedveld 2004, Sebonde 2020). They underlie the use of honorific pronouns (Abiodun 1992), indirectness (e.g., the switch of indexicality in personal pronouns in Akan, as shown in Obeng 1997 and Schottman 1993), and greeting titles or replacement names (known as "horse names", teknonyms, and nick names). Affixation of certain inflectional or derivational morphology on verbs and nouns in greeting and farewell expressions is also determined by politeness or respect (Yimam 1997). That is, these linguistic forms are used in the observance of norms dictated by cultural values and practices.

Rules of address determined by sex are widespread in African linguacultures. The rules may involve the avoidance of names of affinal relations by women of their male in-laws, as reported, among others, for the Cushitic languages Sidama (Teferra 1987), Kambaata (Treis 2005), and Oromo (Tesfaye 2007), and in Xhosa and related languages of southern Africa (Finlayson 1982). However, among the Datooga of Tanzania, avoided in-laws can include "matrilateral female relatives of the first ascending generation, to the first collateral degree, plus the husband's mother's father" (Mitchell 2015: 197). Married women must avoid not only names but also ordinary words if these are phonologically similar to the names of their in-laws with whom they have taboo relations, affecting communication strategies and language use more broadly (see also Mitchell and Storch, this volume, Fleming, this volume). For example, as Mitchell (2015: 202) shows, in Datooga a "woman who avoids the name *Bálãwa* will predictably avoid words beginning with *bal*, such as *bàláng'da* 'salt', *balool* 'speak', and *bálléanda* 'boy'". The methods of avoidance are varied and they include using alternative words from a conventionalized avoidance vocabulary, circumlocutions ("the son of so-and-so", "the tallest son of so-and-so", etc., to refer to people), using synonyms, initial syllable substitution, etc. Cumulatively, linguistic avoidance might result in women's language being somewhat different from that of men within the same linguistic group. Such a linguistic avoidance system is asymmetrical, affecting only women's language use, and it might reflect the subordinate status of (especially younger) women in society. Transferring the system is also the responsibility of women, since mothers-, sisters-, and/or aunts-in-law are the ones who teach a newly married woman which names to avoid and how to pronounce similar-sounding words. As mentioned in the introduction, the linguistic avoidance system is known by different names in different languages: in

Datooga, a Nilotic language in Tanzania, the avoidance system is called *gíing'á-wêakshòoda*, among the Cushitic languages of Ethiopia it is called *baliʃʃa* in Sidama (Teferra 1987) and Kambaata (Treis 2005), while it is *laguu* in Oromo (Tesfaye 2007). In Xhosa, Sesotho, and related languages of southern Africa, it is known as *ukuhlonipha* or *hlonipha* (Finlayson 1982, 2002).[7] Name avoidance and its implementation involving linguistic manipulation is but one aspect of avoidance behavior to show respect to the other because of one's relations. It has been presented from the perspective of women and affinal relations, but in some cultures, such as the Fulbe, a similar avoidance is practiced between a father and his children (especially the first son), also leading to linguistic manipulations of names (see Ameka and Breedveld 2004 and references therein).

5 Some thoughts for further exploration

In this chapter we have highlighted a number of themes that we consider salient in African linguacultures on which some research has been done. We have drawn attention to some new and understudied topics such as the discussion of the vestibular sense of balance, and questions of ethnosyntax such as the cultural semantic basis of nominal classification. At the same time we have tried to review some of the themes that are at the core of classic studies in anthropological linguistics, such as color terms, names, and greetings. We have focused on these themes because we believe that there is the need for more research in these areas. Take the topic of the senses, especially the sense of balance. It would be good if more language-cultural research is done to investigate this topic in many more communities. In the same vein, we would have liked to discuss the research on other senses, especially of taste and smell, which are thriving but which space did not permit. It is very significant that in Luwo there is a distinct grammatical class for smell terms (Storch 2014). It seems also that there is a "smell area" in a part of Africa which runs from Ethiopia (Almagor 1987) through Sudan to Central Nigeria (Blench and Longtau 1995, Koops 2009), and down into Cameroon (van Beek 1992), Gabon (Hombert 1992), and southern Africa (Demolin et al. 2016). Are there environmental correlates for this? Are

---

7 Analyzing discourse in a South African multilingual court room, Thetela (2003) demonstrates consequences of women's *hlonipha*-influenced speech in the justice system. The author argues that the practice of *hlonipha* influences Sesotho-speaking women to lexical substitution of words (euphemisms) that make explicit mention of sexuality and thereby weaken their testimonies against male defendants, e.g., in trials of rape.

there culture-specific smells and cultural uses of smell such as are found among the Kapsiki that define social groups in other African cultures?

Another topic we would have liked to discuss relates to numerals and cultures of counting and reckoning (see e.g., Zalsvasky 1999). This is a domain in which linguistic practices and cultural activities interact. Attention is given to mathematical operations and their use in the Pan-African Mankala board game called *Bao* in East Africa, *Oware* on the Guinean coast, and *Adito* in the Gulf of Benin. There is a diversity of counting gestures as well as of ways of reckoning in the African linguacultures that needs to be investigated. In relation to this there are other aspects of numerical cognition such as estimation and creating sets, e.g., in markets, that need attention. This domain also relates to time reckoning (see also da Silva Sinha, this volume), which reflects a tension between traditional ways of reckoning and ways introduced through contact. A very clear case is the two calendrical and clock systems that operate in Ethiopia. More generally, there is a tension between the systems for reckoning days, whether based on market days or on other occupational activities and the predominant Gregorian system. This is just the tip of the iceberg of language-culture nexus research in Africa. More explorations are needed to give a more complete picture.

There is a resurgence in the study of the classical topics of ethnoscience/ethnosemantics using new methods that should also be explored in African linguacultures: ethnobiology and kinship, for example. The rising interest in evaluative morphology (see Grandi and Körtvélyessy 2015) should also lead to more studies of the uses of forms such as diminutives and gender marking to express attitudes which tend to be culturally determined. All these topics can be fruitfully integrated in language-culture documentation projects on the continent.

References

Abarry, Abu Shardow. 1997. The naming drama of the Ga people. *Journal of Black Studies* 27 (3). 365–377.

Abiodun, Michael A. 1992. On the restricted spread of the honorific pronoun in Yoruba. A case study of Oǹdó, Ọ̀wọ̀ and Òyì dialects. *African Languages and Cultures* 5 (2). 101–111.

Agar, Michael. 1995. *Language shock. Understanding the culture of conversation*. New York: William Morrow.

Agyekum, Kofi. 2002. The interpretive marker sɛ in Akan. In Felix K. Ameka & E. Kweku Osam (eds.), *New directions in Ghanaian linguistics*, 127–146. Accra: Black Mask.

Akindele, Femi. 1990. A sociolinguistic analysis of Yoruba greetings. *African Languages and Cultures* 3 (1). 1–14.

Almagor, Uri. 1983. Colours that match and clash. An explication of meaning in a pastoral society. *Res: Anthropology and Aesthetics* 5 (19). 49–73.

Almagor, Uri. 1987. The cycle and stagnation of smells: Pastoralists-fishermen relationships in an East African society. *Res: Anthropology and Aesthetics* 13: 106–121.

Ameka, Felix K. 1996. Body parts in Ewe grammar. In Hilary Chappell & William McGregor (eds.), *The grammar of inalienability. A typological perspective on body part terms and the part-whole relation*, 783–840. Berlin: De Gruyter Mouton.

Ameka, Felix K. 2001. Ideophones and the nature of the adjective class in Ewe. In Erhard F. K. Voeltz & Christa Kilain-Hatz (eds.), *Ideophones*, 25–48. Amsterdam: John Benjamins.

Ameka, Felix K. 2002. Cultural scripting of body parts for emotions. On 'jealousy' and related emotions in Ewe. *Pragmatics and Cognition* (Special issue: The body in emotion description) 10 (1/2). 21–45.

Ameka, Felix K. 2004. Grammar and cultural practices. The grammaticalization of triadic communication in West African languages. *Journal of West African Languages* (Special issue: Areal Typology of West African Languages) 30 (2). 5–28.

Ameka, Felix. 2009. Access rituals in West African communities. An ethnographic perspective. In Gunter Senft & Ellen Basso (eds.), *Ritual communication*, 127–151. Oxford & New York: Berg.

Ameka, Felix K. 2012 [1991]. *Ewe. Its grammatical constructions and illocutionary devices* (Outstanding grammars from Australia 10). Munich: LINCOM Europa.

Ameka, Felix K. 2017. Meaning between algebra and culture. Auto-antonyms in the Ewe verb lexicon. In Lisa L. S. Cheng, Maarten Hijzelendoorn, Hilke Reckman, & Rint Sybesma (eds.), *Crossroads semantics. Computation, experiment and grammar*, 227–248. Amsterdam: John Benjamins.

Ameka, Felix & Anneke Breedveld. 2004. Areal cultural scripts for social interaction in West African communities. *Intercultural Pragmatics* 1 (2). 167–187.

Amha, Azeb. 2001. *The Maale language*. Leiden: CNWS Publications.

Amha, Azeb, James Slotta & Hannah S. Sarvasy. 2021. Singing the individual. Name tunes in Oyda and Yopno. *Frontiers in Psychology* 12: 667599. DOI:10.3389/fpsyg.2021.667599

Arensen, Jonathan E. 1992. Mice are men. Language and society among the Murle of Sudan. Dallas, TX: International Museum of Cultures.

Baeteman, J. 1929. *Dictionnaire Amarigna – Français*. Dire-Daoua: Imprimerie Saint Lazare des rr. pp. Capucins.

Barber, Karin. 1991. *I could speak until tomorrow. Oriki, women & the past in a Yoruba town*. Edinburgh: Edinburgh University Press.

Baxter, Paul T. W. 1990. Oromo blessings and greetings. In Anita Jacobson-Widding & Walter van Beek (eds.), *The creative communion. African folk models of fertility and the regeneration of life*, 235–250. Uppsala: Uppsala Studies in Cultural Anthropology.

Berlin, Brent & Paul Kay. 1969. *Basic colour terms*. Berkeley: University of California Press.

Blass, Regina. 1991. *Relevance relations in discourse*. Cambridge: Cambridge University Press.

Blench, Roger & Selbut Longtau. 1995. Tarok ophresiology. An investigation into the Tarok terminology of odours. In E. Nolue Emenanjo & O.-M. Ndimele (eds.), *Issues in African languages and linguistics. Essays in honour of Kay Williamson*, 340–344. Aba: Nigerian Institute of Languages.

Breedveld, Anneke. 1995a. *Form and meaning in Fulfulde*. Leiden: CNWS Research School.

Breedveld, Anneke. 1995b. The semantics of noun class systems. The semantics of the -KI and -NGE classes in Fulfulde. *Journal of West African Languages* 25 (2). 63–74.

Brown, Penelope. 2006. Cognitive anthropology. In Christine Jourdan & Kevin Tuite (eds.), *Language, culture and society. Key topics in linguistic anthropology*, 96–114. Cambridge: Cambridge University Press.

Brown, Roger W. & Eric H. Lenneberg. 1954. A study in language and cognition. *The Journal of Abnormal and Social Psychology* 49 (3). 454–462.

Burenhult, Niclas & Asifa Majid. 2011. Olfaction in Aslian ideology and language. *The Senses & Society* 6. 19–29.

Bustorf, Dirk. 2005. Greetings in body language. In Siegbert Uhlig (ed.), *Encyclopedia Aethiopica*, Vol. 2, 888. Wiesbaden: Harrasowitz Verlag.

Calame-Griaule, Geneviève. 1987. *Ethnologie et langage. La parole chez les Dogon*. Paris: Gallimard.

Caparos, Serge, Lubna Ahmed, Andrew J. Bremner, Jan W. de Fockert, Karina J. Linnell & Jules Davidoff. 2012. Exposure to an urban environment alters the local bias of a remote culture. *Cognition* 122 (1). 80–85.

Caparos, Serge, Karina J. Linnell, Andrew J. Bremner, Jan W. de Fockert & Jules Davidoff. 2013. Do local and global perceptual biases tell us anything about local and global selective attention? *Psychological Science* 24 (2). 206–212.

Chamo, Isa Yusuf. 2011. Cultural scripts. The analysis of Kunya in Hausa. *FAIS Journal of humanities* 5 (1). 121–130.

Claudi, Ulrike & Bernd Heine. 1986. On the metaphorical base of grammar. *Studies in Language* 10 (2). 297–335.

Clements, George N. 1975. The logophoric pronoun in Ewe. Its role in discourse. *Journal of West African Languages* 10 (2). 141–177.

Coetzee, Pieter Hendrik & Abraham Pieter Jacob Roux (eds.). 1998. *The African philosophy reader*. London: Routledge.

Contini-Morava, Ellen. 1994. Noun classification in Swahili.*Virginia: Publications of the Institute for Advanced Technology in the Humanities, University of Virginia*.

Coote, Jeremy. 2012. Marvels of everyday vision. The anthropology of aesthetics and the cattle-keeping Nilotes. In Sandra H. Dudley (ed.), *Museum objects. Experiencing the properties of things*, 245–273. London: Routledge.

D'Andrade, Roy. 1995. *The development of cognitive anthropology*. Cambridge: Cambridge University Press.

Dammers, Kim. 2010. Gestures and body language used in public greetings and departures in Addis Ababa. In Alke Dohrmann, Dirk Bustorf & Nicole Poissonnier (eds.), *Schweifgebiete. Festschrift für Ulrich Braukämper*, 60–65. Berlin: LIT Verlag.

Davidoff, Jules, Elisabeth Fonteneau & Julie Goldstein. 2008. Cultural differences in perception. Observations from a remote culture. *Journal of Cognition and Culture* 8 (3/4). 189–209.

Davies, Ian R. L., Christine Davies & Greville Corbett. 1994. The basic colour terms of Ndebele. *African Languages and Cultures* 7 (1). 36–48.

Davies, Ian R. L. & Greville G. Corbett. 1997. A cross-cultural study of colour grouping. Evidence for weak linguistic relativity. *British Journal of Psychology* 88 (3). 493–517.

De Jaegher, Hanne, Ezequiel Di Paolo & Shaun Gallagher. 2010. Can social interaction constitute social cognition? *Trends in Cognitive Sciences* 14 (10). 441–447.

De Kadt, Elizabeth. 1998. The concept of face and its applicability to the Zulu language. *Journal of Pragmatics* 29 (2). 173–191.

Demolin, Didier, Anthony Traill, Gilles Sicard & Jean-Marie Hombert. 2016. Odour terminology in !Xóõ. In Rainer Vossen & Wilfrid H. G. Haacke (eds), *Lone tree. Scholarship in service of the Koon. Essays in memory of Anthony T. Traill*, 107–118. Cologne: Rüdiger Köppe.

Dimmendaal, Gerrit J. 1995. Studying lexical semantic fields in languages. Nature vs. nurture, or where does culture come in these days? *Frankfurter Afrikanistische Blätter* 7. 1–29.

Dimmendaal, Gerrit J. 2001. Logophoric marking and represented speech in African languages as evidential hedging strategies. *Australian Journal of Linguistics* 21 (1). 131–157.

Dimmendaal, Gerrit J. 2015. *The Leopard's spots. Essays on language, cognition and culture.* Leiden: Brill.

Dimmendaal, Gerrit J. 2022. *Nurturing language. Anthropological linguistics in an African context.* Berlin: De Gruyter Mouton.

Dubosson, Jérôme. 2014. Human 'self' and animal 'other'. The favourite animal among the Hamar. In Felix Girke (ed.), *Ethiopian images of Self and Other*. 83–104. Halle an der Saale: Universitätsverlag Halle-Wittenberg.

Dubosson, Jérôme. 2018. The Hamar. Living by, for and with the cattle. In Timothy Clack & Marcus Brittain (eds.), *The river. Peoples and histories of the Omo-Turkana area*, 125–132. Oxford: Archaeopress Publishing Ltd.

Duranti, Alessandro. 1997. Universal and culture-specific properties of greetings. *Journal of Linguistic Anthropology* 7 (1). 63–97.

Dyson-Hudson, Neville. 1966. Karimojong politics. Oxford: Clarendon Press.

Dzokoto, Vivian Afi. 2010. Different ways of feeling. Emotion and somatic awareness in Ghanaians and Euro-Americans. *Journal of Social, Evolutionary, and Cultural Psychology* 4 (2). 68–78.

Dzokoto, Vivian Afi & Sumie Okazaki 2006. Happiness in the eye and in the heart. Somatic referencing in West African emotion lexica. *Journal of Black Psychology* 32 (2). 117–140.

Eckl, Andreas E. 2000. Language, culture and environment. The conceptualization of Herero cattle terms. In Michael Bollig & Jan-Bart Gewald (eds.), *People, cattle and land. Transformation of a pastoral society in Southwestern Africa*, 401–431. Cologne: Rüdiger Köppe.

Eczet, Jean-Baptiste. 2018. Colours, metaphors and persons. In Timothy Clack, Marcus Brittain (eds.), *The river. Peoples and histories of the Omo-Turkana area*, 65–70. Oxford: Archaeopress Publishing Ltd.

Eczet, Jean-Baptiste. 2019. Ceci n'est pas une couleur. *L'Homme* 230 (2). 117–132.

Enfield, N. J. 2002. Ethnosyntax. Introduction. In N. J. Enfield (ed.), *Ethnosyntax. Explorations in grammar and culture*, 3–30. Oxford: Oxford University Press.

Essegbey, James. 1999. *Inherent complement verbs revisited. Towards an understanding of argument structure in Ewe.* Leiden & Nijmegen: Leiden University & MPI for Psycholinguistics dissertation.

Evans, Nicholas & David P. Wilkins. 2000. In the mind's ear. The semantic extensions of perception verbs in Australian languages. *Language* 76 (3). 546–592.

Evans-Pritchard, Edward E. 1934. Imagery in Ngok Dinka cattle-names. *Bulletin of the School of Oriental and African Studies* 7 (3). 623–628.

Evans-Pritchard, Edward E. 1940. *The Nuer. A description of the modes of livelihood and political institutions of a Nilotic people.* Oxford: Clarendon Press.

Fabian, Johannes. 1991. *Language and colonial power.* Berkeley: University of California Press.

Finnegan, Ruth. 2012. *Oral literature in Africa*. Cambridge: Open Book Publishers.

Finlayson, Rosalie. 1982. *Hlonipha*. The woman's language of avoidance among the Xhosa. *South African Journal for African Languages* 2 (1). 35–60.

Finlayson, Rosalie. 2002. Women's language of respect. Isihlonipho sabafazi. In Rajend Mesthrie (ed.), *Language in South Africa*, 279–296. Cambridge: Cambridge University Press.

Firth, Raymond. 1972. Verbal and bodily rituals of greeting and parting. In J. S. La Fontaine (ed.), *The interpretation of ritual*, 1–38. London: Tavistock.

Floyd, Simeon 2021. Conversation and culture. *Annual Review of Anthropology* 50. 219–240.

Fockert, Jan W. de, Jules Davidoff, J. Fagot, C. Parron & Julie Goldstein. 2007. More accurate size contrast judgments in the Ebbinghaus Illusion by a remote culture. *Journal of Experimental Psychology Human Perception Performance* 33 (3). 738–742.

Fockert, Jan W. de, Serge Caparos, K. J. Linnell & Jules Davidoff. 2011. Reduced distractibility in a remote culture. *PLoS One*, 6 (10). e26337. DOI:10.1371/journal.pone.0026337

Friedrich, Paul. 1989. Language, ideology, and political economy. *American Anthropologist* 91 (2). 295–312.

Fukui, Katsuyoshi. 1979. Cattle color symbolism and inter-tribal homicide among the Bodi. In Katsuyoshi Fukui & David Turton (eds.), *Warfare among East African herders*, 147–177. Osaka: National Museum of Ethnology.

Fukui, Katsuyoshi. 1996. Co-evolution between humans and domesticates. The cultural selection of animal coat-colour diversity among the Bodi. In Ellen Roy & Katsuyoshi Fukui (eds.), *Redefining nature. Ecology, culture and domestication*, 319–386. Oxford & Washington, DC: Berg.

Galaty, John G. 1989. Cattle and cognition. Aspects of Maasai practical reasoning. In Julliet Clutton-Brock (ed.), *The walking larder. Patterns of domestication, pastoralism, and predation*, 214–230. London: Routledge.

Geiger, Lazarus. 1871. *Zur Entwicklungsgeschichte der Menschheit*. Stuttgart: Cotta.

Geiger, Lazarus. 1872. *Ursprung und Entwicklung der menschlichen Sprache und Vernunft*, 2 vols. Stuttgart: Cotta.

Geurts, Kathryn Linn. 2002a. *Culture and the senses. Bodily ways of knowing in an African community*. Berkeley: University of California Press.

Geurts, Kathryn Linn. 2002b. On rocks, walks, and talks in West Africa. Cultural categories and an anthropology of the senses. *Ethos* 30 (3). 178–198.

Goddard, Cliff. 2002. Ethnosyntax, ethnosemantics, ethnopragmatics. In N. J. Enfield (ed.), *Ethnosyntax*, 52–73. Oxford: Oxford University Press.

Goffman, Erving. 1963. Embarrassment and social organization. *American Journal of Sociology* 62 (3). 264–271.

Goody, Esther N. 1972. 'Greeting', 'begging' and the presentation of respect. In J. S. La Fontaine (ed.), *Interpretation of ritual*, 39–72. London: Tavistock.

Goldstein, Julie & Jules Davidof. 2008. Categorial perception of animal patterns. *British Journal of Psychology* 99 (2). 229–243.

Grandi, Nicola & Livia Körtvélyessy (eds.). 2015. *Edinburgh handbook of evaluative morphology*. Edinburgh: Edinburgh University Press.

Güldemann, Tom. 2008. *Quotative indexes in African languages*. Berlin: De Gruyter Mouton.

Gyekye, Kwame. 1996. *African cultural values. An introduction*. Accra: Sankofa Publishers.

Hagège, Claude. 1974. Les pronoms logophoriques. *Bulletin de la Société de Linguistique de Paris* 69 (1). 287–310.

Hale, Ken. 1986. Notes on world view and semantic categories. Some Warlpiri examples. In Pieter Muysken & Henk van Riemsdijk (eds.), *Features and projections*, 233–254. Dordrecht: Foris.

Hansford, Gillian F. 2010. Red is a verb. The grammar of colour in Chumburung. *Journal of West African Languages* 37 (2). 109–137.

Holland, Dorothy & Naomi Quin (eds.). 1987. *Cultural models in language and thought*. Cambridge: Cambridge University Press.

Hombert, Jean-Marie. 1992. Terminologie des odeurs dans quelques langues du Gabon. *Pholia* 7. 61–65.

Hurford, James R. 2014. *Origins of language. A slim guide*. Oxford: Oxford University Press.

Hurskainen, Arvi. 2000. Noun classification in African languages. In Barbara Unterbeck, Matti Rissanen, Terttu Nevalainen & Mirja Saari (eds.), *Gender in grammar and cognition*, 665–688. Berlin: De Gruyter Mouton.

Ideh, Amaka. 2019. Name and politeness. Multiple address term among the Igbo. *Language in India* 19. 1–19.

Idowu, Emanuel B. 1973. *African traditional religion. A definition*. London: Orbis Books.

Irvine, Judith T. [1974] 1989. Strategies of status manipulation in the Wolof greeting. In Richard Bauman & Joel Sherzer (eds.), *Explorations in the ethnography of speaking*, 2nd edition, 167–191. Cambridge: Cambridge University Press.

Irvine, Judith T. 1990. Registering affect. In Catherine Lutz & Al Amin Abu-Manga (eds.), *Language and the politics of emotions*, 126–161. Cambridge: Cambridge University Press.

Jahn, Janheinz. 1958. *Muntu. Umrisse der neoafrikanischen Kultur*. Düsseldorf: E. Diedrichs.

Kagame, Alexis. 1976. *La philosophie bantu comparée*. Paris: Présence Africaine.

Kay, Paul. 2006. Methodological issues in cross-language colour naming. In Chtistine Jourdan & Kevin Tuite (eds.), Language, culture and society, 115–134. Cambridge: Cambridge University Press.

Kay, Paul, Brent Berlin, Luisa Maffi, William R. Merrifield & Richard Cook. 2009. *The world color survey*. Stanford, CA: CSLI Publications.

Kay, Paul, Brent Berlin, Luisa Maffi & William Merrifield. 1997. Color naming across languages. In C. L. Hardin & Luisa Maffi (eds.), *Color categories in thought and language*, 21–57. Cambridge: Cambridge University Press.

Kay, Paul & Luisa Maffi. 1999. Color appearance and the emergence and evolution of basic color lexicons. *American Anthropologist* 101. 743–760.

Kay, Paul & Chad K. McDaniel. 1978. The linguistic significance of the meanings of basic color terms. *Language* 54. 610–646.

Koops, Robert. 2009. *A grammar of Kuteb*. Cologne: Rüdiger Köppe.

Koopman, Adrian. 2019. *Zulu bird names and bird lore*. Pietermaritzburg: University of KwaZulu Natal Press.

Kpoglu, Promise D. 2021. On kinship terms and adnominal possessive constructions. Insights from Tongugbe, a riverine dialect of Ewe. *Journal of West African Languages* 48 (2). 59–71.

Kwamuar, Sebastian. 1997. *Ewɔ moya na Tɔgbi Agɔkɔli* [It surprised Chief Agokoli]. Accra: Bureau of Ghana Languages.

Last, Marco. 1995. *Aspects of Chai grammar*. Leiden: Leiden University MA thesis.

Leslau, Wolf. 1976. *Concise Amharic dictionary*. Wiesbaden: Otto Harrassowitz.

Leslau, Wolf. 1989. *Concise dictionary of Geez (Classical Ethiopic)*. Wiesbaden: Otto Harrassowitz.

Levinson, Stephen C. 1988. Putting linguistics on a proper footing. Explorations in Goffman's concepts of participation. In Paul Drew & A. Wootton (eds.), *Erving Goffman. Exploring the interaction order*, 161–227. Cambridge: Polity Press.

Leyew, Zelealem. 2003. Amharic personal nomenclature. A grammar and sociolinguistic insight. *Journal of African Cultural Studies* 16 (2). 181–211.

Lienhardt, Godfrey. 1961. *Divinity and experience. The religion of the Dinka*. London: Oxford University Press.

Lovestrand, Joseph. 2021. Serial verb constructions. *Annual Review of Linguistics* 7. 109–130.

Lucy, John. 1997. The linguistics of "color". In C. L. Hardin & Luisa Maffi (eds.), *Color categories in thought and language*, 320–346. Cambridge: Cambridge University Press.

Maffi, Luisa. 1984. Somali colour terminology. An outline. In Thomas Labahn (ed.), *Proceedings of the Second International Congress of Somali Studies, University of Hamburg, 1-6 August 1983*, 299–312. Hamburg: Buske.

Maffi, Luisa. 1990. Somali color term evolution. Grammatical and semantic evidence. *Anthropological Linguistics* 32 (3/4). 316–334.

McGranaghan, Mark. 2015. 'My name did float along the road'. Naming practices and |Xam Bushman identities in the 19th-century Karoo (South Africa). *African Studies* 74 (3). 270–289.

Mbiti, John S. 2015. *Introduction to African religion*, 2nd edition. Long Grove: Waveland Press.

Mitchell, Alice. 2015. Words that smell like father-in-law. A linguistic description of the Datooga avoidance register. *Anthropological Linguistics* 57 (2). 195–217.

Morton, John. 1988. SAKANAB. Greetings and information among the Northern Beja. *Africa* 58 (4). 423–436.

Mumbo, Collins Kenga. 2012. Artistic techniques of expression in the performance of the Mijikenda naming ceremony Vyalusa of Kenya. *African Cultures and Literatures: A Miscellany* 41. 377.

Naden, Tony. 1980. How to greet in Bisa. *Journal of Pragmatics* 4 (2) 137–145.

Naden, Tony. 1986. Social context and Mampruli greetings. In George Huttar (ed.), *Pragmatics in non-Western perspective*, 161–199. Dallas: University of Texas at Arlington Press.

Naden, Tony. 2005 Three cheers for red, white and black. In M. E. Kropp Dakubu & E. Kweku Osam (eds.), *Proceedings of the Annual Colloquium of the Legon-Trondheim Linguistics Project, 18-20 January 2005*, Vol. 3. Legon: Linguistics Department, University of Ghana.

Nicolas, Andrea. 2005. Greetings in Oromo. In Sigbert Uhlig (ed.), *Encyclopedia Aethiopica*, Vol. 2, 888. Wiesbaden: Harrassowitz Verlag.

Nikitina, Tatiana. 2012. Logophoric discourse and first person reporting in Wan (West Africa). *Anthropological Linguistics* 54 (3). 280–301.

Nwoye, Onuigbo G. 1992. Linguistic politeness and socio-cultural variations of the notion of face. *Journal of Pragmatics* 18 (4). 309–328.

Nwoye, Onuigbo G. 1993. An ethnographic analysis of Igbo greetings. *African Languages and Cultures* 6 (1). 37–48.

Obeng, Samuel Gyasi. 1997. Indirectness in pronominal usage in Akan discourse. *Journal of Language and Social Psychology* 16 (2). 201–221.

Ohta, Itaru. 1986. Livestock individual identification among the Turkana. The animal classification and naming in the pastoral livestock management. *African Studies Monographs* 8 (1). 1–69.

Ohta, Itaru. 1989. A classified vocabulary of the Turkana in Northeastern Kenya. *African Studies Monographs* (Supplementary issue) 10. 1–104.

Okello, Belindah. 2021. What's in a name? Reinventing Luo naming system in Kenya's ethnopolitical landscape. *African Identities* 19 (1). 77–90.

Okpewho, Isidore. 1992. *African oral literature. Backgrounds, character, and continuity.* Bloomington: Indiana University Press.

Olivier, Lennox. 2010. Greeting rituals as everyday management of differences among Ras-Tafari groups in Stellenbosch. *Anthropology Southern Africa* 33 (3/4). 126–131.

Oosthuizen, Marguerite P. 1996. *Uchibidolo. The abundant herds. A descriptive study of the Sanga-Nguni cattle of the Zulu people, with special reference to colour-pattern terminology and naming-practice.* Pietermaritzburg/Durban: University of Natal dissertation.

Palmer, Gary B. 1996. *Toward a theory of Cultural Linguistics.* Austin: The University of Texas Press.

Paulos, Tilahun. 1956. Forms of greetings and other forms of respect in Ethiopia. *University College of Addis Ababa Ethnological Society Bulletin* 5. 25–31.

Paulos, Tilahun. 2002 (reprint from 1956). Forms of greetings and other signs of respect in Ethiopia. In Alula Pankhurst (ed.), *Ethnological Society Bulletin*, 1 (1-10) & 2 (1). 1953–1961. 116–117. Addis Ababa: Addis Ababa University, Department of Sociology and Social Administration.

Payne, Doris L. 2003. Maa color terms and their use as human descriptors. *Anthropological Linguistics* 45. 169–200.

Payne, Doris L. 2020. Color term systems. Genetic vs. areal distribution in sub-Saharan Africa. In Rainer Vossen & Gerrit J. Dimmendaal (eds.), *The Oxford handbook of African languages*, 704–714. Oxford: Oxford University Press.

Petrollino, Sara. 2022. The Hamar cattle model. The semantics of appearance in a pastoral linguaculture. *Language Sciences* 89. 101448. DOI:10.1016/j.langsci.2021.101448

Ray, Verne F. 1952 Techniques and problems in the study of human color perception. *Southwestern Journal of Anthropology* 8. 251–259.

Reh, Mechthild. 2004. Multilingual writing: A reader-oriented typology—with examples from Lira Municipality (Uganda). *International Journal of the Sociology of Language* 170. 1–41.

Richter, Renate. 2005. Greetings in Amharic. In Sigbert Uhlig (ed.), *Encyclopedia Aethiopica*, Vol. 2, 886–887. Wiesbaden: Harrassowitz Verlag.

Roulon-Doko, Paulette. 2019. Lexicalization patterns in color naming in Gbaya, a Ubanguian language of CAR. In Ida Raffaelli, Daniela Katunar & Barbara Kerovec (eds.), *Lexicalization patterns in color naming. A cross-linguistic perspective*, 133–152. Amsterdam & Philadelphia: John Benjamins.

Saunders, Barbara A. C. & Jaap Van Brakel. 1997. Are there nontrivial constraints on colour categorization? *Behavioral and Brain Sciences* 20 (2). 167–179.

Sebonde, Rafiki Yohana. 2020. Personal naming practices and modes of address in the Chasu speech community. *Nordic Journal of African Studies* 29 (2). 1–18.

Segerer, Guillaume & Martine Vanhove. 2019. Color naming in Africa. In Ida Raffaelli, Daniela Katunar & Barbara Kerovec (eds.), *Lexicalization patterns in colour naming. A cross-linguistic perspective*, 287–330. Amsterdam & Philadelphia: John Benjamins.

Segerer, Guillaume & Martine Vanhove. 2021. Areal patterns and colexifications of colour terms in the languages of Africa. *Linguistic Typology*. DOI:10.1515/lingty-2021-2085

Selvik, Kari-Anne. 2001. When a dance resembles a tree. In Cuyckens, Hubert & Britta E. Zawada (eds.), *Polysemy in cognitive linguistics. Selected papers from the*

International Cognitive Linguistics Conference, Amsterdam, 1997, 161–184. Amsterdam: John Benjamins.

Schottman, Wendy. 1993. Proverbial dog names of the Baatombu. A strategic alternative to silence. *Language in Society* 22. 539–554.

Schottman, Wendy. 1995. The daily ritual of greeting among the Baatombu of Benin. *Anthropological Linguistics* 37 (4). 487–523.

Schottman, Wendy. 2000. Baatɔnu personal names from birth to death. *Africa* 70 (1). 79–106.

Schrock, Terrill. 2017. *The Ik language. Dictionary and grammar sketch*. Berlin: Language Science Press.

Scribner, Sylvia & Michael Cole. 1981. *The psychology of literacy*. Cambridge, MA: Harvard University Press.

Sharifian, Farzad. 2014. Language and culture overview. In Farzad Sharifian (ed.), *The Routledge handbook of language and culture*, 3–18. London: Routledge.

Simpson, Jane. 2002. From common ground to syntactic construction. Associated path in Warlpiri. In N. J. Enfield (ed.), *Ethnosyntax. Explorations in grammar and culture*, 287–307. Oxford: Oxford University Press.

Stoller, Paul. 1989a. *Fusion of the worlds. An ethnography of possession among the Songhay of Niger*. Chicago: University of Chicago Press.

Stoller, Paul. 1989b. *The taste of ethnographic things*. Philadelphia: University of Pennsylvania Press.

Storch, Anne. 2014. *A grammar of Luwo. An anthropological approach*. Amsterdam: John Benjamins.

Storch, Anne. 2019. Games with names. Naming practices and deliberate language change. *Language Dynamics and Change* 9. 162–191.

Strauss, Claudia & Naomi Quinn (eds.). 1998. *A cognitive theory of cultural meaning*. Cambridge: Cambridge University Press.

Sweetser, Eve. 1990. *From etymology to pragmatics. Metaphorical and cultural aspects of semantic structure*. Cambridge: Cambridge University Press.

Taljard, Elsabé. 2015. Cattle and their colours. A synchronic investigation of cattle colour terminology in Northern Sotho. *South African Journal of African Languages* 35 (2). 199–205.

Teferra, Anbessa. 1987. Bališša. Women's speech among the Sidama. *Journal of Ethiopian Studies* 20. 44–59.

Tempels, Placide. 1959. *Bantu philosophy*. Paris: Présence Africaine.

Tesfaye, Wondwosen. 2007. Laguu in the Oromo society. A sociolinguistic approach. In Amha, Azeb, Maarten Mous & Graziano Savà (eds.), *Omotic and Cushitic language studies. Papers from the Fourth Cushitic and Omotic Conference Leiden, 10-12 April 2003*, 245–259. Cologne: Rüdiger Köppe.

Thetela, Pulie. 2003. Discourse, culture and the law. The analysis of crosstalk in the Southern African bilingual courtroom. *AILA Review* 16. 78–88.

Tornay, Serge. 1973. Langage et perception. La dénomination des couleurs chez les Nyangatom du Sud-Ouest éthiopien. *L'Homme* 13 (4). 6694. DOI:10.3406/hom.1973.367381

Tornay, Serge (ed.). 1978. *Voir et nommer les couleurs*. Nanterre: Laboratoire d'ethnologie et de sociologie comparative.

Treis, Yvonne. 2005. Avoiding their names, avoiding their eyes. How Kambaata women respect their in-laws. *Anthropological Linguistics* 47 (3). 292–320.

Turton, David. 1980. There's no such beast. Cattle and colour naming among the Mursi. *Man*, New Series, 15 (2). 320–338.

Ullendorff, Edward. 1973. *The Ethiopians. An introduction to country and people*, 3rd edition. London, Oxford & New York: Oxford University Press.

Van Beek, Walter E. A. 1977. Color terms in Kapsiki. In Roxana Maa Newman & Paul Newman (eds.), *Papers in Chadic linguistics*, 13–20. Leiden: African Studies Centre.

Van Beek, Walter E. A. 1992. The dirty smith. Smell as a social frontier among the Kapsiki/Higi of north Cameroon and north-eastern Nigeria. *Africa* 62 (1). 38–58.

Vansina, Jan M. 1985. *Oral tradition as history*. Madison: University of Wisconsin Press.

Viberg, Åke. 2021. Why is smell special? In Łukasz Jędrzejowski & Przemysław Staniewski (eds.), *The linguistics of olfaction. Typological and diachronic approaches to synchronic diversity*, 35–72. Amsterdam: John Benjamins.

Vilakazi, Herbert W. 2002. African indigenous knowledge and development policy. *Indilinga: African Journal of Indigenous Knowledge Systems* 1 (1). 1–5.

Von Roncador, Manfred. 1992. Types of logophoric marking in African languages. *Journal of African Languages and Linguistics* 13 (2). 163–182.

Westermann, Diedrich. 1973. *Ewefiala. Ewe-English dictionary/Gbesela yeye or English Ewe dictionary*. Berlin: Dietrich Reimer.

Wierzbicka, Anna. 1979. Ethno-syntax and the philosophy of grammar. *Studies in Language* 3 (3). 313–383.

Wierzbicka, Anna. 1988. *The semantics of grammar*. Amsterdam & Philadelphia: John Benjamins.

Wierzbicka, Anna. 2005. There are no "color universals" but there are universals of visual semantics. *Anthropological Linguistics*, 47 (2). 217–244.

Wierzbicka, Anna. 2008. Why there are no 'colour universals' in language and thought. *Journal of the Royal Anthropological Institute* 14 (2). 407–425.

Wierzbicka, Anna. 2014. *Imprisoned in English*. Oxford: Oxford University Press.

Will, Izabela. 2017. Programmed by culture? Why gestures became the preferred ways of expressing emotions among the Hausa. In Anne Storch (ed.), *Consensus and dissent. Negotiating emotion in the public space*, 123–148. Amsterdam & Philadelphia: John Benjamins.

Williamson, Kay. 1989. Niger-Congo overview. In John Bendor-Samuel (ed.), *The Niger-Congo languages*, 3–46. Lanham, New York & London: University Press of America.

Wojtowicz, B. 2021. Cultural norms of greetings in the African context. *Roczniki Hmanistyczne* [Annals of Arts] 69 (6). 173–189.

Yahya-Othman, Saida. 1995. Aren't you going to greet me? Impoliteness in Swahili greetings. *Text & Talk* 15 (2). 209–228.

Yankah, Kwesi. 1995. *Speaking for the chief*. Bloomington: Indiana University Press.

Yimam, Baye. 1997. The pragmatics of greeting, felicitation and condolence expressions in four Ethiopian languages. *African Languages and Cultures* 10 (2). 103–128.

Youssouf, Ibrahim Ag, Allen D. Grimshaw & Charles S. Bird. 1976. Greetings in the desert. *American Ethnologist* 3 (4). 797–824.

Zaslavsky, Claudia. 1999. *Africa counts. Number and pattern in African languages*, 3rd edition. Chicago: Lawrence Hills Books.

Rex Lee Jim & Anthony K. Webster

14 Native North America: Notes towards a dialogical ethnopoetics

> Is this what I deserve: a white anthropologist sitting beside me at a winter ceremony?
>
> Sherwin Bitsui, *"The Northern Sun"*

This chapter returns to a recording of a conversation I had with Navajo poet Rex Lee Jim[1] twenty years ago in February 2001. Combining recent Indigenous critiques of the epistemology and representational practices of linguistics and linguistic anthropology, I engage in, following the work of Dennis Tedlock (1983), a dialogical ethnopoetics. I do this by showing the ways in which I came to know about a poem by Rex Lee Jim in and through our conversation. Such epistemic slippage (Perley 2013a), the ways in which we come to know through talk, resituates the role of ethnography and the ethnographer, from one that positions itself as the expert, to one that places the ethnographer within the inter-subjective experience of coming to know. Working through the transcript by

---

[1] Given the heavy reliance on the transcript from Rex Lee Jim, that he is the authority in the conversation about his poem, it was decided in conversation with Jim that he should be co-author with Webster on the chapter. Jim is responsible for his comments in the transcript and comments made more recently to Webster, which are indicated in the text. Jim is also responsible for the poem and its translation. Webster is responsible for the anthropological framing and his own commentary on the transcript. The "I" of the chapter is Webster.

Acknowledgments: I want to thank again Rex Lee Jim for his patience with me and for attempting to explain things to me over the years. I thank him as well for comments on earlier drafts of this chapter. Thanks to Aimee Hosemann, Arnold Krupat, and Leighton C. Peterson for useful comments on earlier iterations of this paper. Thanks as well to the two anonymous reviewers of this chapter. The chapter is the better for their comments. Thanks as well to Nico Nassenstein and Svenja Völkel for their encouragement about this chapter. Thanks, again, to the many Navajos who have taken the time to talk with me about things language, culture, and poetry. Research on the Navajo Nation was done under permits from the Historic Preservation Office. I thank them. Funding for this research was provided by Wenner-Gren, the American Philosophical Society, and the Jacobs Fund. I thank them all. I dedicate this paper to the memory of my colleague Nora England (1946–2022). Her influence on my thinking was and is profound. She might not have liked all the "anthrobabble" in this chapter, but I think she certainly would have appreciated the larger point of the chapter.

Rex Lee Jim, Diné College Tsaile/United States, e-mail: rexleejim@gmail.com
Anthony K. Webster, University of Texas at Austin/United States, e-mail: awebster@utexas.edu

https://doi.org/10.1515/9783110726626-014

way of ethnographic commentary reveals both the ways that Jim attempted to give some sense of the meaning of the poem, but also the way the poem became a way for Jim to critique the practice of anthropology. Towards the end of this chapter, I offer some further reflections on the transcript and the commentary that accompanies it – suggesting that such commentary continues the conversation. The chapter begins, however, with a discussion of the broader anthropological linguistic and linguistic anthropological tradition of work within Native North America and then turns to a more particular ethnographic and ethnopoetic discussion.

1 Introduction: Native North American beginnings

Linguistic anthropology emerged, came into existence, in a very real sense through an engagement with Indigenous peoples of North America (see Webster and Peterson 2011). The early work of Franz Boas focused on the documenting of Indigenous languages of North America (see Boas 1911). The foundations of this work can be described as "text-centered" (Epps, Webster and Woodbury 2017). Ella Deloria (1954), for example, documented both Dakota texts and conversations. Beyond the documenting of texts, the creation of dictionaries and grammars were also vital to this project (Epps, Webster, and Woodbury 2017). However, such documents were aimed not at Indigenous peoples, but rather as documents of "disappearing" languages for the use of scholars (both Indigenous and non-Indigenous). Boas's (1889) work also meant to critique ostensibly "scientific" – but certainly racist – assumptions about Native American languages (Webster and Peterson 2011). Central, as well, to this early Boasian agenda was a concern with translation and verbal art (see Boas 1911; see also Epps, Webster, and Woodbury 2017). But the Boasian project of linguistic anthropology also, even as it documented Indigenous uses of language through texts, erased actual Native people (see, for example, Berman 1994). The Boasian legacy, like all legacies, is thus a complicated one.

    Concern with Native American languages – if not always with their speakers – also informed later trends in linguistic anthropology. Whorfian concerns with issues of linguistic relativities, were, for example, founded on engagements with Hopi (Whorf 1956), Wintu (Lee 1944), and Navajo (Hoijer 1951). And while it is quite certain, for example, that Whorf's work emerged out of conversations with his Hopi consultant Ernest Naquayouma, there is little trace of such conversations in the work of Whorf.[2] Other work, concerning language change and the then current topic of linguistic acculturation, also focused attention on Native American languages (see, for example, Dozier 1955, 1956, Lee 1943). So too the beginnings of research on varieties and linguistic diversity within Native groups (see Newman 1955, Reichard 1945). Forms of speech play and verbal art continued to be documented by linguistic anthropologists as well (see, for example, Sapir 1932, Reichard 1944).

With the 1960s we find a shift in linguistic anthropology from the texts, grammar, and dictionary tradition to a concern with the ethnography of speaking, which was not as committed to the documenting of texts, though concern with the documenting of texts in contexts became of central concern for the verbal art as performance tradition then emerging in conjunction with the ethnography of speaking (see Epps, Webster, and Woodbury 2017). The foundational edited volume of the ethnography of speaking, Richard Bauman and Joel Sherzer's (1974) *"Explorations in the ethnography of speaking"*, contained a number of chapters that focused on Native North America – some of those chapters would also form the foundations for book-length monographs (see, for example, Philips 1983, Foster 1974). Many of the contributors to Bauman and Sherzer (1974) had come out of the University of Pennsylvania and had been greatly influenced there by Dell Hymes (Murray 1994). The 1970s saw a number of ethnographies of speaking that focused on Native North America. Ronald Scollon and Suzanne Scollon (1979) focused on linguistic convergence at Fort Chipewyan. Keith Basso (1979) examined a genre of joking among Western Apache. In the 1970s and early 1980s, Native American verbal artistic traditions took center stage in discussions concerning ethnopoetics. Hymes (1981), Dennis Tedlock (1983), William Bright (1979), Anthony Woodbury (1985), and Virginia Hymes and Hazel Supah (1992) all focused their ethnopoetic work on narrators and narratives from Native North America. Importantly, it was in ethnopoetic work that one began to see collaborative work between Indigenous intellectuals and anthropologists (discussed below). Ethnopoetics also continued the text-centered tradition of earlier linguistic anthropology – both in focusing on the texts documented by prior generations of anthropological linguists and in the documenting of texts in performance (see Sherzer and Woodbury 1987).

And while the center of gravity of linguistic anthropology has certainly moved away from work with Native North America over the last several decades,

---

2 The same could be said for Witherspoon (1977) – it seems clear that much of what is found in the book emerged through conversations with Navajo intellectuals, there is virtually no trace of those conversations in the book (see also Evers and Toelken 2001: 9).

important work in the linguistic anthropology of Native North America continues to be done (see Valentine and Darnell 1999, Murray 1994). Ethnographies by Paul Kroskrity (1993) and Lisa Valentine (1995) combined concerns with older traditions of linguistic anthropology (language change, the ethnography of speaking, ethnopoetics) with more recent concerns involving questions of, for example, language and identity. Brenda Farnell (1995), in her ethnography of Plains Indian Sign Talk, pushed for a multimodal linguistic anthropology. Keith Basso's (1996) *"Wisdom sits in places"* ushered in a wave of ethnographies that examined place-making and senses of place (see, for example, Palmer 2005, Moore and Tlen 2007, Thornton 2008, Schreyer 2016). Some of this work, including Basso's (1996), was done at the behest of Indigenous groups and concerned land and water rights issues. More recent linguistic anthropology has focused ever more on ethnographies of language revitalization efforts and the language ideologies that inform such efforts (see Goodfellow 2005, Meek 2010, Perley 2011, Nevins 2013, Debenport 2015, Davis 2018, Schwartz 2018, see also Kroskrity and Field 2009, Kroskrity 2012, Kroskrity and Meek 2017). Though research on Whorfian issues (O'Neill 2008), verbally artistic traditions (Shaul 2002, Palmer 2003, Webster 2009, 2015, Field 2019, see also Kroskrity and Webster 2015), and more focused ethnographies of ways of speaking and literacy practices (Klain and Peterson 2000, Bender 2002, Innes 2006, Richland 2007, McIlwraith 2012) continue to be done as well. Much contemporary linguistic anthropology of Native North America attempts to be more attentive to the concerns of Native people, the work more focused on scholarship that is responsive to local concerns. Where previous generations of scholarship often did not make visible such collaborations, more recent work, in response to Indigenous critiques (to be discussed in the next section), have become more attentive to such issues. This chapter explores those issues by way of a dialogical ethnopoetic approach, which links both with an older tradition in the linguistic anthropology of Native North America and with recent critiques of the doing of anthropology by Indigenous scholars.

2 On dialogue and participation

What does it mean to return to a recording of a conversation some twenty years later? To retranscribe that conversation? How might making visible that interaction shed light on anthropology and the ways we come to know in and through ethnography? More specifically, how might a *dialogical ethnopoetics* make anthropology a more responsible, a more humane, discipline? This chapter looks at a transcript of a conversation I had with Navajo poet Rex Lee Jim in early

2001 about his poem *"Na'azheeh/Hunting"*. It has been a part of a larger endeavor on my part to focus my recent work on the conversations that I have had with Navajo poets over the last twenty years (see Webster 2015, 2016, 2017, 2021a, n.d.). Central to this endeavor has been the presenting of the transcripts of those conversations – to make visible the ways that I came to know certain things about Navajo poetry. To acknowledge and make visible the intellectual contributions of the Navajos that have guided my thinking over the years. In returning to these recordings of conversations I have had with Navajo poets over the last twenty years, I have been trying to find ways to write ethnography that acknowledges the voices, the intellectual and epistemological contributions, of those who have taken the time to talk with me, to try and explain things to me. If, as Johannes Fabian (1991: 88–89, see also Fabian 1979) remarked, we need to refigure the ethnography of speaking as *ethnography as speaking,* then our ethnographies need to make visible such speaking.

What I want to do in the rest of this chapter is to place ethnopoetics within concerns about dialogical anthropology – a way of doing ethnography that I think still has much value. The goal then, to take the concerns of ethnopoetics and put them in conversation with a tradition that developed in tandem with some of the early ethnopoetics work, namely, Tedlock's (1979, 1983) view of a dialogical anthropology. My suspicion is that much ethnopoetics that was done in the Tedlockian manner was, simultaneously, dialogical ethnopoetics – even if it was not always visible. Tedlock (1972a: 238) makes this point, I think, when he writes,

> an analysis of the kind presented above depends heavily on 'ethnopoetics,' that is, on the literary criticism offered by Zunis themselves . . . all modes of analysis – social, psychological, structural, or stylistic – could benefit from a greater attention to ethnopoetic considerations.

Yet, too often, the literary criticism offered by Zunis, Puebloan people of the Southwest of the United States, for example, is submerged under the voice of the anthropologist. Actual Zuni views are thus hidden, and, in their place, we find fictions such as "the Zuni".[3] Imaginary whole cultures are thus circumscribed by way of such totalizing visions that obscure the ways that such knowledge was acquired in the first place.

This work is also informed by recent critiques of linguistics and linguistic anthropology by a number of Indigenous scholars (see Adley-Santa Maria 1997. Palmer Jr. 2003, Meek 2011, Leonard 2011, 2021, Perley 2013a, 2013b, 2013c, Davis

---

3 For an enlightening and entertaining Zuni perspective on the anthropological endeavor, see Hughte (1995).

2017, E. Cruz 2021). These scholars have been concerned both with the ways Indigenous languages and people have been represented or erased, but also in the ways that anthropologists and linguists come to know – they have, that is, been concerned with both representation and with epistemology. As Kiowa linguistic anthropologist and poet Gus Palmer Jr. (2003: 31) notes, especially concerning the interpreting of Kiowa narrative traditions, but also more broadly applicable, "I am a little suspicious of outsiders who collect Indian stories and then make claims without giving the Indians a chance to comment". What is needed, according to Palmer (2003: 28), is "dialogue and participation". Here Palmer (2003) echoes early work by Indigenous scholars like Beverly Crum (1980) – with her biting criticism of the work of anthropologist Julian Steward – and Judy Trejo (1974), with her thoughtful discussion of Paiute Coyote narratives and her critique of the work of anthropologist John Greenway.[4] In an insightful article, Maliseet linguistic anthropologist Bernard Perley (2013a: 114–116) links his own attempts at creating "graphic ethnographies", with Johannes Fabian's (2007, 2008) concerns with confrontation and intersubjectivity. Perley (2013a: 115–116) argues, following Fabian (2007), that coming to know occurs in and through an encounter with real people:

> For anthropological knowledge to grow, Fabian argues that it requires a dialectical exchange with Other knowledge systems.
>
> > Anthropological agency, then, is based on our claims to validity on fieldwork, on direct interaction with those whom we study. Ethnographic authority may be said to rest on "having been there," that is, on our presence. But what would our presence count if it were not matched by the presence of those whom we study? Neither presence, ours or theirs, is a natural, physical fact (nor is intersubjectivity as a condition of communicative interaction); it must be achieved and it is always precarious.
> >
> > (Fabian 2007: 5)
>
> Fabian's insight that presence and intersubjectivity themselves are not natural or physical facts can be extended to experimental systems and cultural analyses. "Doing anthropology" implies agency, and that implies engagements with other agents. Fabian states:
>
> > What enables us to communicate with and represent other practices is not (only) our command of contents, which count as data or as our findings; it is our ability to converse with knowers, and that conversation includes confronting each other, arguing with each other, negotiating agreements, stating disagreements, as well as conceiving common projects.
> >
> > (ibid.: 15)

---

4 For other criticisms of Steward's Great Basin work see S. Crum (1999) and Blackhawk (1999), for another contemporary criticism of Greenway see the discussions in Henry (1972).

Ethnography, the doing of ethnography, then, an exercise in what Perley (2013a: 103) calls "epistemic slippage, the process of *knowing*" (emphasis in the original). This chapter, then, an extended example of such epistemic slippage.

In what follows I look at a transcript of a conversation that I had with Rex Lee Jim about the meaning of his poem *"Na'azheeh/Hunting"*. As will become clear, our conversation was about a great deal more than just the meaning of the poem. The poem became, rather, a topic to think through a variety of issues, including, not least among them, the role of the anthropologist and anthropology in relation to Navajos. My goal here is to show how my understanding of the poem emerged in and through this conversation. To make visible "one of anthropology's dirty little secrets" (Whiteley 2018: 231) – namely, "that notwithstanding their claims to distinctive professional expertise, anthropologists depend greatly on the intellectual positions of their interlocutors in order to generate meaningful cultural explanations" (Whiteley 2018: 231). Or, to echo the work of Johannes Fabian (2007, 2008), the epistemological foundation of much of our ethnographic knowledge is to be found in our intersubjective conversations with the people we work with. We come to know in and through the conversations we have with people. A *dialogical ethnopoetics* would, then, be *an ethnopoetics that foregrounds the dialogic emergence of knowledge of and about particular forms of verbal art*. It would attempt to center the comments of those we have worked with. Finally, as Fabian (2008) makes clear, our conversations, these intersubjective experiences, are also confrontations – confrontations of values, of beliefs, of ways of speaking, of knowledge. There will be confrontations in what follows – no dialogical ethnopoetics could be otherwise, there are always limits on what we can and should know, there are always confrontations of values and beliefs (Webster 2020).

3 Dialogical ethnopoetics

A dialogical ethnopoetics, as I envision it, owes its foundations to the work of Tedlock (1983). On the one hand, Tedlock (1983) was one of the leading figures in the ethnopoetics movement in linguistic anthropology. He wrote insightfully about both Zuni and Maya verbal art. He also argued that narratives were better presented as groupings of lines instead of as blocks of prose. Such lines were based on, among other things, breath pausing. He also included changes in loudness and speed and pitch in his presentation of Zuni verbal art. On the other hand, Tedlock (1983) was also one of the key figures in arguing for a dialogic anthropology (see also Tedlock and Mannheim 1995). Here, for example, he argued for making visible the voices of those we worked with, not as data to be mined, but rather as the foundational moments through which we come to know. Tedlock contrasts a dialogical anthropology (a talking across) with an analogical anthropology (a talking above) and notes (1983: 324):

> Judging from the empirical evidence, as we run through the ethnographies on our bookshelves, it is a law of analogical anthropology that the ethnographer and the native must never be articulate between the same two covers. In the classic ethnography, other anthropologists may be quoted at length, but no native ever utters a complete sentence, whether in text or translation. In the exceptional cases, where the natives do speak at some length, they speak only as a group, through excerpts from myths or prayers.

A similar claim, I believe, could still be made about many contemporary ethnographies. A recent ethnography purporting to be based on conversations between the anthropologist and Indigenous people contains no transcripts of those conversations. Rather the stories are told by the anthropologist. Even linguistic anthropological ethnographies, which are often quite full of people speaking, do not include the conversations that the anthropologists had with their hosts.[5] All that talk is data to be mined and explained. This, in fact, was a critique leveled against the ethnography of speaking by both Fabian (1979) and Tedlock (1983) – that linguistic anthropology ran the very risk of falling into the positivistic or analogical anthropology trap.

Ethnopoetics emerged as a named theoretical movement in the 1970s, led by Jerome Rothenberg (see, for example, Rothenberg and Rothenberg 1983) and Tedlock (1972b, 1983), and later by Dell Hymes (1981), it looked to rethink the nature of the verbal artistic traditions of Indigenous peoples.[6] As Robert Moore

---

5 This is a lingering form of positivism, where anthropologists seek to assure us that their "data" is uncontaminated with the presence of the anthropologist. Tedlock (1983) describes this as an example of analogical anthropology. But presence and an intersubjective presence, as Fabian (2007) and Perley (2013a) make clear, is precisely the point. I will return to this topic in what follows.

6 I have always been troubled by some of the ethnopoetic work of Jerome Rothenberg. William Bright (1979), early on, critiqued Rothenberg's translation practices as merely reproducing contemporary Western aesthetics and as being unmoored from the languages being translated from. Hymes's (1981) work focused primarily on narratives that had been documented by prior generations of linguists and anthropologists and seldom focused on narratives that he had been told. Hymes's (1975) *"Breakthrough into performance"* does provide a telling confrontation between Hymes and Philip Kahclamet. For a discussion of a narrative that Hiram Smith told to Hymes, see Hymes (1980). In a number of places, Hymes (1991, 1994, 1998) talks of ethnopoetics as a form repatriation. The work of ethnopoetics, especially when it is done on narratives told in languages no longer actively spoken, reveals poetic structuring, makes visible something of the artistry and craft of such narratives. Recent collaborative work

(2015) has noted, at one level, ethnopoetics is the study of the literary (spoken or written) traditions of others, and, on another level, ethnopoetics became, over time, focused more and more on the techniques of representing such verbal art on the printed page (that is to say, it dealt with questions of transcription and retranscription). This was a point that Donald Bahr (1986: 171) early noted as well:

> much anthropological ethnopoetics (roughly speaking, the study of other peoples' literatures) has been concerned with how to find valid linguistic reasons for dividing previously unwritten texts into lines . . . I hope those writers would agree, however, that ethnopoetics should be more than the study of technique, and that it should include meaning and use.

I agree with Bahr's position, and it has informed much of my own work over the years. Ethnopoetics should be more than the discerning of lines, it should tell us something about meaning and use as well. This, as I have discussed elsewhere (Webster 2020), can most usefully be done in and through ethnography. The ethno- of ethnopoetics, as Barbra Meek suggested to me in 2019, is not so much about "other peoples' literatures", but a reminder of the need for ethnography in such work.[7] Though, in the article by Bahr (1986), there is, in fact, not much dialogue. Other work, for example by Bahr (Bahr et al. 1997), does, indeed, include O'odham voices who disagree with Bahr's interpretations. Indeed, Bahr's work with O'odham singers was part of a trend in the 1980s and 1990s that meant to promote a more dialogical, a more "collaborative ethnopoetics" (the term is actually McDowell's 2000). In, for example, the work of Larry Evers and Felipe Molina (1987) and Molina and Evers (2001), I see the workings of a dialogical ethnopoetics which attempts to shift the locus of authority from some putative "all-knowing" anthropologist to the actual experts who tried to explain something of their lives, their worlds, their poetries to us – so too in the work of Keith Basso (1976). As Billie Jean Isbell (1985) has noted, Basso's (1976) *"Wise words of the Western Apache"*, is an early example of a dialogical anthropology – I would say dialogical ethnopoetics. In that article, Basso (1976: 104–107) provides transcripts of the conversations he has had with

---

by Catharine Mason (Howard 2021), Henry Zenk and Jedd Schrock (Kenoyer 2017) and Nevins (2017), in consultation with Native communities, to produce ethnopoetically analyzed narratives highlights such a possibility for ethnopoetics as a form repatriation. For a useful history of ethnopoetics and issues of translation see Krupat (1992). For a useful critique of Hymes and Tedlock, see Mattina (1987). See also Kinkade and Mattina (1996).

7 Here a dialogical ethnopoetics, one that is founded on ethnography, resonates with Meyers's (2019) recent call for a reviving of ethnography in Native communities.

Apaches about the meanings of "Wise Words". In each case, Basso offers his interpretation of the metaphor and Apaches disagree with that interpretation and offer a more relevant interpretation. As Diné historian Jennifer Nez Denetdale (2007: 19) notes, "Navajos continue to be understood within Western frameworks, thereby contributing to the ongoing distortion of the realities of Native lives, cultures, and histories." If dialogical ethnopoetics is to have any value, it is in seeking a redress of such distortions.

Especially important as a foundational text for a dialogical ethnopoetics is the book edited by Evers and Barre Toelken (2001) – and, indeed, the work was informed by Tedlock's concern with dialogical anthropology (Evers and Toelken 2001: 10–11). Each chapter in the volume is co-authored by an Indigenous intellectual and a non-Native scholar, often with independent contributions by each and then sections co-written by both authors. The goal was to make visible who contributes what to a particular interpretation – to create a dialogue within the article. While earlier work, one thinks of the very fine article by Toelken and Tacheeni Scott (1981) and their retranslation of a Navajo Coyote story told by Yellowman, was co-authored by an Indigenous intellectual and a non-Native academic, there was no sense of what each brought to the analysis, there was no evidence of the conversations that informed such work.[8] The chapter by Yupik scholar Elsie Mather and anthropologist Phyllis Morrow (2001), an especially insightful chapter, makes visible both something of the collaboration between Mather and Morrow, but also places of confrontation, both between Mather and Morrow, and, as Mather says to Morrow, "I find myself fluctuating between wanting to discourage some of your conclusions and at the same time wanting to follow the Yupik way of respecting what others have to say" (Mather and Morrow 2001: 238).

Also arising out of Tedlock's (1983) concern with dialogical anthropology was work on the dialogic emergence of culture (Tedlock and Mannheim 1995). Ethnopoetics was informed by this tradition as well. Bruce Mannheim and Krista Van Vleet (1998) and M. Eleanor Nevins (2015) have attempted to combine a concern with a Bakhtinian dialogism and ethnopoetics. In Mannheim and Van Vleet's (1998) case, they look at the various kinds and levels of dialogues present in Southern Quechua narratives. These range from the formal level, in which narratives often emerge in conversation, to the use of reported speech, to the forms of intertextuality that emerge in such narratives, to the myriad participant frameworks both in the narrating of the narrative, but also within the narrative itself (for a summary, see Mannheim and Van Vleet 1998:

---

8 A similar criticism could be made about the article that Blackhorse Mitchell and I published together (Mitchell and Webster 2011).

240). Nevins (2015) too takes up the question of Bakhtinian dialogism as it relates to the Western Apache genre of *Bá'hadziih*, a way of speaking in which Western Apaches can comment on the present by way of the past, and, as well, point towards a potential future. Besides describing a contemporary example of the use of *Bá'hadziih* by Eva Lupe, Nevins also suggests that Lawrence Mithlo used such a genre in his work with Harry Hoijer (see also Webster 2021b). I consider both these papers to be exceptional analysis of verbal art and ethnopoetics. And yet, and there must always be an 'and yet', for all their talk of dialogics and dialogism, for all their willingness to center the words of Quechua and Apache people, there is a divide as well. We get very little interpretation from Apaches or Quechuas – they tell the stories; anthropologists continue to be the ultimate interpreter. There is no confrontation between narrator and anthropologist, nothing that matches, for example, the confrontation that Kevin Dwyer (1987) reproduces in his "Moroccan dialogues" or the kinds of confrontations that Fabian (2015) reproduces – where the anthropologists is made visible, is, in fact, called out by the people we are talking with, no longer the detached and knowing observer, they are critiqued and challenged. Fully present, as awkward as that may be, in the moment.

Finally, the perspective taken in this chapter is discourse-centered (Sherzer 1987, 1994, 1998) and language-centered (Fabian 2007, 2008, 2015). In both cases, there is a commitment to attending to transcripts, of centering the words of those we are in conversation with. Such a perspective makes certain demands, namely that transcripts are the centerpiece of an article, our commentary of those transcripts is meant to supplement, but not to explain in some totalizing manner. I am not here to solve what Jim told me. Ethnography as commentary is a further iteration of the conversation first begun, in this case, in February 2001.[9]

4 Na'azheeh

Before presenting the transcript, I first briefly discuss the poem that was the topic of our conversation. The poem is written entirely in Navajo, but Jim has translated it into English. The poem was published in Jim's 1989 all-Navajo collection of poetry. It was also published in the 1998 trilingual collection of poetry

---

[9] As work in ethnopoetics has long made clear, transcripts are not neutral, rather they are forms of representation, and thus can highlight and obscure (Hymes 1981, Tedlock 1983, Sherzer 1992). This is why much work in ethnopoetics spends so much time discussing transcription choices – to make explicit the decisions that inform such representations.

in Navajo, English, and Gaelic. More recently it was published in Jim's 2019 bilingual in Navajo and English collection of poetry. Finally, it was published in "*The Diné Reader*" (2021) that Esther Belin, Jeff Berglund, Connie Jacobs and I edited. Here, then, the poem in Navajo and in the English translation by Jim from "*The Diné Reader*" (Belin et al. 2021: 143):

Na'azheeh

> Tłig
> Niyol nee ní'įį'
> Tłig
> Nibeedí nee ní'įį'
> Tłig
> Tséghájooghałii nee ní'įį'
> Tłig
> Nikéyah nee ní'įį'
> Tłig
> Nidiyin nee ní'įį'
> Tłig
> K'ad łáą,
> > dah náá'diit'áhígíí bii' doo
> > áadi sǫ' łichíí' bidáádidoogááł

Hunting

> Click
> I stole your breathing
> Click
> I stole your survival tools
> Click
> I stole your living goods
> Click
> I stole your land
> Click
> I stole your gods
> Click
> Now all is ready
> > For the next shuttle flight
> > The red star will keep it from returning.

Here, now, a few points about the poem. The first thing that strikes a reader, even one that doesn't know Navajo is that the poem is built around a good deal of parallelism. A parallelistic frame is created and repeated throughout the poem: the ideophone comes first, this is followed by a second person possessed noun (e.g., ni + kéyah = your land) and then *nee ní'íí'* which Jim translates as 'I stole'. Though such glossings, like *nikéyah* as 'your land', are misleading in certain respects. In a recent conversation with Jim (2021), he noted that *nikéyah* has a sense of the earth or land beneath one's feet, your footprints, and such land is wherever you are. It isn't just your land, but the very land one walks and that one is responsible for taking care of. Note as well that, *tséghájooghałii* lacks the use of the second person possessive (*ni-*).[10] Jim translates this as 'living goods' above – but has recently (2021) described it to me as a kind of mountain goat, "peeking between the rocks" (which catches something of the morphology of the form) and that the form suggests "having fun, enjoying life".

Following the work of Chatino linguist Hilaria Cruz (2017: 510–511) on parallelism, in this poem, the frame is *tłig ____ nee ní'íí'* and the focus, the thing that comes into focus through repetition with variation, is the noun, often in conjunction with the second person possessive. The frame is repeated five times (though with variation in the third iteration) and then the pattern is broken the sixth time, where *tłig* (the sound of a gun or the sound of a camera) is followed by *k'ad łáá* (now + an emphatic) which Jim translates as 'now all is ready' instead of another noun and *nee ní'íí'*. This, then, is followed by two additional lines. As will become clear, it is these two lines that become a crucial topic in the conversation to follow. Before getting to that, let me just note that Jim here translates the ideophone *tłig* into English as 'click' – the form seems less interwoven (Woodbury 1998) in this poem than it does in other poetry that Jim has written (Jim 1995, Webster 2006, 2020).[11] More importantly for the purposes here, it should be noted, as Jim repeatedly explained to me about this poem, it has the shape – a rhetorical structure – of a "ceremonial prayer". The last line, as will be clear in the following transcript of my conversation with Jim about this poem, is an intertextual reference, a phrase, from a ceremonial prayer.

---

10 Note as well that the second person pronoun *ni-* is homophonous – that is it can pun with – both *ni'* 'earth' and *-ni'* 'mind' (see Webster 2016 and 2018 on the importance of punning in the poetry of Rex Lee Jim).

11 In a conversation with Jim in December of 2021, Jim noted that in this poem, *tłig* was an "unnatural sound" – that is, it was a "man made sound". In the poem, the sound "invades something natural". It is, according to Jim, a "more forceful" sound than the English *click*. Its non-interwovenness thus creates a kind of jarring effect. Indeed, the formatting of the poem by Jim, leaving *tłig* as its own line, seems to reinforce that jarring effect.

5 "But it doesn't negate the possibility":
An ethnographic commentary

I now turn to a transcript of a conversation that I had with Rex Lee Jim about this poem in early 2001.[12] We were in his office at Diné College in Tsaile, AZ. It was early February. It was a Friday. The door was left slightly open. Throughout the tape one can hear the murmur of other conversations in the background. At various points our conversation was interrupted by people needing to ask Jim work-related questions. There were, then, any number of potential overhearers to our conversation. I had had a number of conversations with Jim by this time (this becomes clear in the transcript, since I at various points refer to prior conversations and quote things he has told me). I should add, I would go on to have more conversations with Jim about his poetry (we spoke recently about this poem in October and December 2021). The goal here, really, is to follow Palmer's (2003) point and yield the floor to Jim. I will present the transcript in lines based on breath pausing. I do this not to claim that either Jim or I spoke in poetry, but to highlight the cadence and rhythm of our talk. To highlight as well something of the time such talk takes. I will also provide commentary along the way. I do this to make clearer some of what is being said.[13] One value in ethnography as commentary (Fabian 2008, 2015, Webster 2021a), is that it doesn't demand a final explanation, some final verdict by the anthropologist. Rather, it acknowledges that texts do not speak for themselves, and that commentary puts the transcript into further conversations but without resolving those conversations. Commentary then becomes a further iteration of the ethnographic confrontation.

After a tangled beginning – just as we had begun, we were interrupted by someone sticking their head in the office to ask Jim a question – we begin to discuss some of his poetry. Jim sets the agenda. I begin by offering a tentative interpretation – though I have every reason to suspect that it is misguided and "irrelevant" (Fernandez 1989, see also Basso 1976). I suspect, based on prior conversations, that my interpretation will act as a prompt for our discussion of

---

12 I encourage the interested reader to consult Jim (2000) for more on his views on poetry and language. For a discussion of an earlier conversation I had with Jim, see Webster (2016). I consider this chapter to be a companion piece to that article.

13 In presenting the transcripts, I have followed the work of Tedlock (1983) and Molina and Evers (2001) and presented it according to pauses. Capitalization indicates loudness (for example, THAT is said loudly). A colon indicates the non-phonemic lengthening of sound. Clarifications are included in brackets.

the poem. This is, indeed, what follows. My interpretation of the last line, 'The Red Star will keep it from returning', is clearly misguided and Jim begins to place the poem into a particular intertextual and interpretative context. He notes, as well, that much of the force of the poem occurs in Navajo and not in English. One needs to, as he is doing in our conversation, explain things more directly. This becomes especially clear later in the conversation.

2/2/01 Tsaile

AKW	what were you going to say about your short poems
RLJ	I was going to say
	let's take a look at it
	and see what we need to do
	to get to what it's all about
AKW	this is actually one of my favorite poems
	the 'Hunting' poem
	which seems to me to be on the surface
	about imperialism and colonialism
RLJ	mhm
AKW	but the end of the poem is enigmatic in a way
	it could be the fact that we waste money on going into outer space
	while people on the earth die
	we might have our priorities mixed up
	but the mention of the red star
	and the use of the word red
	seems to be a reference to Native Americans perhaps
RLJ	what's Native American?
AKW	the Red Star will keep it from returning
RLJ	yeah, but what's Native American
	it's too general
AKW	okay yea:h:
	well, what would you say then
RLJ	well in Navajo you say, *sǫ' łichíí' bidáádidoogááł*
	a protection way prayer
	that's very specific to a ceremonial thing that addresses
	certain illnesses that deal with exorcism
AKW	so
RLJ	and when it's prayed he sends the bad stuff to the north
	and say
	into the

```
       what you might consider your
       in your concept hell
AKW    oh
RLJ    and then you just need to block it off and
       the red star has very specific
       whoops [knocked something off desk]
       and because of that language it also
       it taps into the prayer structure
       it taps out a lot of
       um
       ceremonialism
       and how and when it's done and all that
       all those inform
       that expression there
       and you don't get that in English
AKW    right
RLJ    without having to go into detail and explain everything
       any Navajo who has attended the ceremony
       and heard these prayers will automatically connect to them
       "Oh, I know what this is about"
```

I then summarize what I see as the key point that Jim is making about the poem, that they connect to a particular ceremony. Jim agrees but then adds that it isn't just the ceremony, but rather a whole set of ideas and philosophies. He then goes on to point out that both "Native American" and "Navajo" would be, as he says shortly, "too general" because one must be aware of – and in all likelihood attended – the particular ceremony. That there is specificity to the poem, a particularity that can be evoked. Jim makes this point through a tight parallelism. The frame here, that which is "particular" – the focus, those things that are particular.

```
AKW    so then the final two lines
       the final line here
       connects to a ceremony or ceremonies
RLJ    mmhm
       not only to the ceremony but the philosophies and ideas informing
       that
AKW    mm
RLJ    so in that sense then it's very specific
       so that's when I you say when you say something "Native American"
```

AKW right
RLJ I say "what what's Native American"
     you can't even say it's Navajo
AKW right
RLJ because certain Navajos don't even know about this
     it's the particular families
     it's the particular ceremonies
     it's the particular diseases
     it's the particular time and places
     so it's that specific

In what follows, I ask Jim if he wants to expand on what disease might be involved. My expectation, having talked with him before, is that he will not want to explain in detail such things. Jim declines to explain more here. I suspected, rightly, that there was a limit on what I could ask – but I asked in a rather halting fashion anyway. Jim declined to tell me more. Though later in the conversation he does explain something about the ceremony to me. But, and I think this crucial, that explanation is on his terms and not from my request.

AKW so what if it's not
     so what disease is it for
     if that's not to
RLJ I don't want to go into details
AKW I thought you might not
RLJ and that's what I mean by you know
     because I've lived those
     and I continue to live that
     it informs in many ways a lot of my writing
     so even another Navajo cannot possibly say,
     "oh that's Navajo"
     because it's too general

Jim then explains to me more about the poem and its structure. Something as well of the intertextuality of the poem – the way a ceremonial prayer phrase is used in the poem. This is when I learn about the intertextual reference. I want that to be clear. I learned this from Jim, and I learned it from him in this conversation. While by this time in my fieldwork, I could recognize certain poetic structures in Navajo, Jim's explicit linking of the poem to a ceremonial prayer structure, confirmed my own sense of its structure – but, as Jim makes clear, recognizing the structure was not sufficient for understanding the poem. That required participation in the ceremony and "a way of life". Not every Navajo would understand the reference either.

> AKW right
>
> RLJ even if you ask them what's Navajo about it
> they'll probably say the same thing
> "Oh, it's the red star"
> well what's the whole point of the red star
> and then the way it's written
> it's
> comes out of a certain prayer structure
> and part of it is ceremonial prayer phrase
> and that phrase really put it, put it, put it
> in place the ceremonial structure
> and when those prayers are uttered
> I mean you just don't utter that prayer
> in the morning or
> in the evening
> it has to be a certain time of the night
> when certain things happen first
> so many of my poems are like that
> but again like I said
> it's just coming out of a way of life
> I cannot say that it defines Navajo poetry
> the poems just rises out of a certain sense of values
> certain ways of doing things
> and
> and I feel there is anything unique about that
> I don't know
> it certainly isn't unique to me
> or to my other family members
>
> AKW right
>
> RLJ it may different from
> what someone else might write who is not Navajo
> or who is not from my family
> but I would think that whoever has been exposed to that cere-
> mony and who has
> been

> who has heard those ceremonies
> or in fact has been a patient in where they have uttered those
> ceremonies
> and as a result of that they have gotten better
> or something
> happened that they considered as a blessing as an outcome of that
> then how they read that poem will be so different from
> another Navajo whose just been
> a part of the group rather than the patient
> who benefit from it

Here I summarize what I have taken from what Jim has been describing to me. Checking to make sure that I am understanding it. I follow this up by asking a question about "interpretation". What I want to understand is how Jim approaches the question of interpretation. Jim responds by going back to something we had talked about earlier, this question of relationship, and explains that the relationship is dependent on a person's experience and all three interpretations are in certain respects "valid". But circling back to my interpretation from the beginning of our conversation, Jim tells me that if I were to ask him if my interpretation is what he "meant" in his poem, he would tell me plainly, "no". This seems a valuable caution. But then Jim notes that he does not have control over the interpretations of others, that by publishing the poem, he has, in essence, allowed it to be multiply interpreted – and, perhaps, in ways he did not intend. There are other poems, though, that Jim has not published because he does not want them interpreted by others. He wants them, as he says, "to mean what I want them to mean".

> AKW right
> so then
> what you are saying is that there are at least
> three different kinds of interpretations
> that could be given to it by say a Navajo person
> RLJ mhm
> AKW one is that it's just a red star
> RLJ mhm
> AKW the other is that it's
> they get the connection to the particular ceremony
> that they witnessed
> RLJ mhm
> AKW and the third is that they were

	a participant
	they were the subject in the ceremony
RLJ	mhm
AKW	and so it would have an entirely different meaning for them
RLJ	yeah
AKW	now are all three of those correct
	and I hate to use that word
RLJ	I think
	like I said
	it's all the relationship
AKW	mhm
RLJ	that the reader has a relationship to that
	and that relationship depends on the person's experience
	and I think all are valid
	to degree
	that they can
	I don't want to say justify it
	to the degree that they have
	that whatever they are saying about the poem is
	how they're interpreting
	is the experience that they've had
	and that why I sit here and
	allow you to do your Western stuff to it
	okay that's fine
	but if you ask me if that's what I meant
	I'll say "no"
	but after
	the more you think about is
	how about important is that
	people read the way I want them to
	or the way I thought I was doing it
AKW	right
RLJ	and the reality is
	I can't do that
AKW	and you told me one time
RLJ	if I wanted it that way then I'd keep the book to myself
	I don't write it
	I just put it in my journal and then don't publish it
AKW	and you do that with certain poems

RLJ   mhm there are certain poems I keep to myself
         because they're personal
         and I want them to mean what I want them to mean
AKW right
RLJ   also as you grow older
         you say, "I was foolish and silly to hold on to this
         better get rid of it" [laugh]

It would be easy enough for me to end my discussion at this point in the transcript. I have shown Jim explaining the poem to me, shown the ways that my knowledge of the poem emerges out of our conversation. I have made my point: that Jim is, clearly, the expert on the poem, the one with knowledge. But as Julie Cruikshank (1998: 25) notes, "ethnographies always begin as conversations between anthropologists and our hosts [. . .]. If we are fortunate some of these conversations take unexpected turns". I agree with Cruikshank that ethnographies must, by necessity, begin in conversations with those we work with, with, that is, our hosts. It is the unexpectedness of the turns of those conversations that I want to explore now. The conversation that Jim and I were having, did, indeed, take some "unexpected turns". These turns, however, are also part of how I came to understand the poem, how it came to be commentary on the very practice of anthropology. I probably would not have characterized these turns as "fortunate" at the time. Now, twenty years later, I do consider them fortunate because they have forced me to reflect on my work as an anthropologist over the years.

So let us not wait, let us move forward a bit in the conversation. Jim and I have been, for a few minutes, discussing the social and political value of poetry and whether or not it can change the world. Jim suggests that being an artist is dangerous. I challenge that point by suggesting that people in the United States do not care about the arts. It is clear that Jim disagrees. In making his point, Jim will bring the conversation back to the poem "*Hunting*". In what follows, Jim seems to be forcing me to see how his poem "*Hunting*" is a threat and can intimidate me, the white anthropologist, to show how the poem can, in fact, make one (me) uncomfortable. And, to be sure, I was uncomfortable during this stretch of conversation. This is, in the terms of Fabian (2007), a confrontation. My "hmm" (said quizzically) is used as a way of marking disagreement without overtly disagreeing.

RLJ   so somebody could be killed in this country for their art
AKW hmm
         see I say that

> I say that not because I think that America is such a liberal and
> open place
> that that would never happen
> but because I think the arts are so devalued in this country
> that no one would care
>
> RLJ   mhm
> AKW and so my my take is actually a rather cynical perspective

I have long found Jim's response that follows to be an important defense of the
role of art in society – even, or perhaps more precisely, when "no one will give
a shit" about your art. It is the possibility that matters – the possibility that,
indeed, one can make a difference. Make a difference in ways, perhaps, more
substantial, than can an anthropologist or a linguist (in, for example, getting
the anthropologist to see more clearly their own role, their own position, to recognize what they are, in fact, doing). Here too, Jim tells me a bit more about the
ceremony invoked in the poem *"Hunting"*. *Ch'įįdii* translates into English as
something akin to 'ghost(s)'. Jim also obliquely references the Challenger disaster (1986) and the death of the teacher Christa McAuliffe in that explosion (recall that the original version of this poem was published in 1989). He thus links
the poem, and its reference to the shuttle, with the Challenger explosion. Jim
also links the "I" of the poem with the work of anthropologists.

    Jim is also, obviously, right. I was recording our conversation to analyze
later on. We both knew that. My commentary here is a form of analysis. One
goal of ethnography as commentary, of dialogical ethnopoetics, is to make visible Jim's critique – it isn't a unique critique of anthropology (see, for example,
Denetdale 2007), but it is an important critique, and a critique that emerged in
our conversation about this poem. It is a part of how I came to understand this
poem through this conversation. To obscure that, to hide it, to erase it, would
be to ignore the epistemic slippage that occurs here – the confrontation of
knowledges, of ways of knowing. Note too that the parallelism in Jim's comments echoes the parallelism in the poem.

> RLJ   that's what makes being an artist such a courageous act
> that there's always that possibility that no one will give a shit
>
> RLJ   [Overlap]
> AKW [Overlap] no go ahead
> RLJ   but I think
> I still that that art
> any kind

is powerful enough to do a lot of damage
it intimidates threatens
it's probably true that a high percentage of the population doesn't
care

but it doesn't negate the possibility
AKW ah
RLJ and as long as that possibility that hope is still there
then artist will continue to create
they will continue to
express
I mean if you really look at that poem
that 'Hunting'
that ceremony is used when you're thought of as a ghost
Ch'įįdii and evil and all that
and then you throw out
and that simply says
talks about anthropologists
that's what you think of my language
that's what you think of my culture
that's what it comes down to
that's why you're recording it
so you can analyze it
as what it is
and run out with it
and be useless to the people here
that's what that poem is all about
taking photographs
recording
asking questions
with the idea that you want
to think this through and learn from it
and then share that learning with others
but no
you just going to blow it the way you did with those teachers
in that shuttle
[SIDE A ends]

Here SIDE A of the tape ends. Unfortunately, my notes are not particularly good concerning what transpired in the few seconds in which I was flipping the tape over. SIDE B begins with Jim speaking. Neither of us paused our conversation while I flipped the tape over. In what follows, Jim offers a critique of the work of anthropologists and linguists. The poem, then, a challenge to the "little intellectual exercise[s]" that anthropologists engage in. There is more than a hint of irony in the fact that I liked the poem and Jim clearly teases me about that.

> [SIDE B begins]
> RLJ   white anthropologists
> we should add linguists too [laugh]
> AKW [laugh]
> RLJ   well not only anthropologists
> just
> when you begin to seek other peoples' knowledge
> and the way they do things
> if you're really really interested in it
> why not
> go and get yourself a doctorate and live there
> and if you don't commit to that level
> then you're just interested in doing a
> little intellectual exercise
> that's what that poem is [laugh]
> AND I'm glad you LIKED it
> AKW well thank you
> RLJ   [laugh]

After a rather long pause, I, having taken the critique rather personally, attempt to justify myself. This, now, twenty years on, strikes me as an unfortunate response. I don't think a spoken response on my part was needed here – in fact, it seems a mistake to me now. Unsurprisingly, I think, given my graduate training in anthropology in the mid to late 90s, Jim's critique struck rather sharply, because it was an issue that often preoccupied my own thinking about what I was doing. Was my being an anthropologist useless? The question haunts many a would-be anthropologist, and not a few experienced ones as well. It reminded me very much of the kinds of conversations I had been having with my fellow apprentice anthropologists in graduate school. It was an anxiety that was (is still) rather palpable. Here too it was a topic that Jim had raised with me before – the very first time we met (in March of 2000), he had put me on the spot about this issue. I quote him from that conversation in what follows.

AKW no but
       I do
       I mean the first time I met you
       you said,
       "Are you going to be a rapist anthropologist?"[14]
       and ah
       and it is something I think about
       and I worry about that
       I mean that's why I was keen on the grant
       I do want to
RLJ   ease your guilty conscience
AKW exactly
       to put it bluntly
RLJ   as long as you admit you have a conscience
       this is good [laugh]
AKW but it is something that troubles me
       because I will leave here
RLJ   we know that
AKW and the parade will be very nice
RLJ   and you won't be the first or last to be sitting there
       others will come after you
       others have sat there before you

       so
       what is art
       what is poetry
       what's it for
       big questions
       important questions
AKW well they are important questions

---

14 The term implies an anthropologist who takes what they want and then leaves. There is, of course, a violence to the metaphor as well. It was jarring to hear. I suspect, as well, it was meant to be jarring.

Listening again to this conversation, twenty years later, is a difficult experience for me. It seems to me now that I rather missed the point here. But then, learning, learning through talking with people, learning through that intersubjective dialogue, is often a difficult and humbling experience. It is a reminder of how we come to know and that it is not some simple, anthropologist asks questions and consultant responds accordingly. The poem *"Hunting"*, as Jim makes clear can intimidate and threaten. Here it also seems clear now that Jim's commentary was not aimed at me personally, but rather at a broader category of "anthropologists". At the time, and not unsurprisingly, Jim's comments were issues that were often on my mind. I felt the need to justify, perhaps to Jim, more likely to myself, my purpose as an anthropologist. Jim gives me an opportunity to end this line of conversation when he notes that my having a conscience is for the good. I take this as an opportunity to repeat what I've been struggling with, and Jim cuts me off and then makes it clear that I am not unique – it isn't me. After having made his point, he then changes the topic of the conversation and returns to some rather large and unanswerable questions. Jim, it seems clear in listening again to the recording now twenty years later and numerous conversations with Jim since, is teasing me. It is, of course, teasing with a moral point (as much teasing can be) (see, for another example, Webster n.d.). It is also, however, clearly a topic that was causing me a certain amount of anxiety, and I took the teasing rather personally. Jim, it seems to me, was encouraging me to think about these issues. My mistake, and I think it a mistake now, was to try and answer his teasing rather earnestly. I put us both in an uncomfortable situation.[15] The question can't be answered, it can only be lived.

Moving forward a bit in the transcript. Jim and I have continued to discuss the politics of Jim's poetry and I now bring up a conversation that we had had at a mutual friend's house in December 2000. The friend had hosted a poetry reading at his home. Jim, Sherwin Bitsui, and Orlando White read that night. After the reading, Jim, our host, and I had sat around in the kitchen talking about poetry. This was the context of my reference here. The grant that is mentioned, was a grant that I had helped write that was to support some Navajo artists.

---

15 I am reminded of an incident at a film screening at the Navajo Nation Museum of the film *"The return of Navajo boy"* (2000) while I was doing fieldwork in 2000–2001. One of the producers, Diné filmmaker Bennie Klain, was leading a Q & A when a white audience member raised his hand. Klain called on him. The white man then apologized to Klain and the rest of the audience – which was largely Navajo – for colonialism. After a few moments of silence, Klain then asked if there were other questions. At no point did he directly respond to the comment from the white audience member.

AKW you said
      at [name of a mutual friend]'s after the reading
      when we were talking about politics
      you said your poems are political
      BUT your choice of language isn't political
RLJ   mhm
AKW Is that an accurate
RLJ   I don't know if I said that or not
      but it sounds like something I'd say [light laugh]
AKW [light laugh]
RLJ   I think that
      I always say about the language is a design
      which in some sense is like a filter
      where we all certain parts of ourselves to go through
      those words are just being outcomes of who we are in some ways
      but of course those are
      informed by our
      ideologies whether political or otherwise
      and even though the words are not political then
      the expression itself might
      present itself
      in a way that's political
      where's the other person's filtering is much more political
      easily connected
      sort of like a magnet
      "Hey this is a political poem"

      so I think there's not really
      not just one right way
      for your expression to sit here
      and everyone agrees
      that that's the way it is
      you always have different ways because own
      design of language
      and how they use that

      so in that sense my words are not political
      but
      the expression
      the outcome of it

and how people respond to it
THAT can become very political

After Jim describes this way of thinking about the politics of his poetry, I then
want to circle back to the poem '*Hunting*', which strikes me, given our current
conversation, as a political poem. Though I frame this as a question. Jim responds that it does not start as a political poem because it is connected with
ceremonial structures. It can become political through talking about it. I take
up the question of the structure of the poem. This leads again to the final line
of the poem and also to a discussion by Jim of what he did not include in the
poem. He tells me that he has left out the "last part of the prayer" which raises
the possibility of hope – the hope that life will continue for Navajos. There is,
then, something– potentially – quite positive about the poem "*Hunting*". The
poem, according to Jim, can be read as suggesting hope for the future.

AKW but
'Hunting' is a political poem?
RLJ if you read it in Navajo
no it isn't
it becomes a ceremonial
it that follows that pattern
"Oh this is an interesting play on words" and all that
AKW mm
RLJ Then you begin to talk about it and then yes it becomes political
AKW I mean you use a great deal of parallelism
RLJ mhm
AKW you basically change the noun and use the same verbal construction
RLJ mhm
AKW until the end
RLJ mhm
AKW and then
RLJ but then again it follows the same pattern that
that ceremonial prayer follows
[unintelligible]
and I didn't add that last part of that prayer
simply cuz
there's hope
I mean there's
depending on which prayer it is

that after the Red Star will keep it from returning
there are certain expressions where you really kill the sucker on
the other side [laugh]
and others
but I left it out because there's a possibility
yes people may be
anthropologists may be doing this to us
but
there's still hope we might be around hundred years from now
rather that our skeletons hanging in some museum in
Texas is that where you're from
AKW Texas yes
RLJ   yes
AKW I don't know if we have any skeletons
they gross me out [light laughter]
just not a big fan

I suspect at this point there was a bit of a misunderstanding. Jim, I think, was asking about the state I was from (Texas). I was responding about the University of Texas at Austin where I was doing my PhD. The "we" meant the University and the moment after I make that statement, that I didn't know if there were any skeletons hanging up in museums in Texas, I also distance myself from that statement by suggesting my disdain for skeletons. It is and was, of course, the case that the University of Texas at Austin houses the skeletal remains of Indigenous people. This point, which I think crucial, is that Jim was linking me with larger issues (NAGPRA was an often-discussed topic in 2000–2001 when I was living on the Navajo Nation) – I may have wanted to distance myself from such things, but I was clearly implicated in them myself. It is one thing to criticize colonialism and imperialism abstractly, it is quite another thing to acknowledge one's own complicity in such things. We may nod knowingly (and smugly) as we read Vine Deloria's (1988: 78–100) "*Anthropologists and other friends*" at the hubris of the anthropologists and their pure research agenda, but it is quite another thing to be the anthropologist and to be confronted about what you are, in fact, doing. The divide between *those* anthropologists and ourselves is not as clear as we may wish to tell ourselves (see also Perley 2013a, Medicine 2001).

RLJ   so yes I think um
the words themselves

you would think that it's ceremonial all this stuff
but when you really begin to think about it
the outcome of this expression
will touch people in certain ways
and they will because of their own design of language
they will begin
to talk about it in different terms

of course that doesn't mean my intent isn't political

AKW right

RLJ it could be totally political

AKW right

RLJ I think that's one of the good things about poetry
you make it
you can
disguise it in many ways
where when it finally surfaces
it hits hard like that
[hits fist against his other hand]

AKW well and that's

RLJ and sometimes that approach is sorta sneaky but
it's a preferred approach in many ways
and it's a much more forceful approach in many ways
because the person end up talking about it
and discover for him or herself

AKW mhm

RLJ rather than say it directly
I mean I could say it so did I really just give it to you straight
and you could say
"well, you're not supposed to say that, and well it won't be the last
too bad" whereas the other way it begins as way of self-exploration
and that process again the reader
it many ways begin to say "hey wait a minute"
and becomes more convincing
it becomes a little bit more
I don't want to say more important
I guess it becomes more meaningful
because of the experience that that person the reader goes through
the hearer

the listener
do I think through all these things I'm talking about when I write?
absolutely not [laughter]
AKW [laughter]
RLJ it more than enough to keep me from writing
AKW when do they come to you? after you've written it?
RLJ when you ask me the questions [slight laughter]
no I think they are all at play
at a certain level that you're not aware of
but later on when you really think about it
"yeah, I know
and this is why I'm doing it"
and then you say
"oh okay, to make it a little bit more satirical
or bit more strong or political
or whatever
and then I'm going change this word
so it connect with this specific this other set of stories"
AKW mhm

I'll let the transcript of our conversation end there. We talked for a few minutes more, but it was a wrapping up of the conversation. We would talk again, and repeatedly. And my memories of this conversation, ever evocable when I read "*Na'azheeh/Hunting*", continue as well. I do consider "*Na'azheeh/Hunting*" to be a poem that is about, among other things, the doing of anthropology.

The description by Jim of the way he prefers to structure his poetry has greatly influenced my own interpretations of his poetry (see Webster 2016). His poems are "sorta sneaky" and other Navajos have made similar comments about his poetry to me (see Webster 2018). I think it clear, though, that Jim has, of course, earlier in our conversation, actually given it to me rather straight. Sometimes the direct way is needed.

6 Some further reflections

Intersubjective experiences, conversations, are essential for the doing of ethnography. What has struck me over the years in reading any number of ethnographies is how invisible those conversations are. The kind of anthropology that I've engaged in over the years has always been language-centered and discourse-centered. It has meant to center the words of those we are in conversation with. Ethnopoetics, too, has meant to center the narratives, the words, of those we work with, but even here, there has been an interpretative divide – a closing or hiding of those conversations. The narrator tells the story and we the anthropologist interpret it. What becomes obscured is the epistemology, the how and in what ways, we came to know how to interpret the narrative or poem. More often than not, such interpretations emerged in conversations with real people.[16] Seldom are those conversations included in our publications. The anthropologist takes credit for knowing things, for explaining things, that were explained to us in the first place – often awkwardly and unevenly, full of confrontations and misunderstandings.

A dialogical ethnopoetics makes visible how we come to know in and through conversations. It makes visible the confrontations that emerged in the conversation I had with Jim, in our intersubjective experience. As Fabian (2008: 119) notes, "there is no confrontation without presence." And presence, as both Fabian (2007) and Perley (2013a) have noted, means another human being. It isn't enough just to be there; we must also talk with our fellow human beings. Our transcripts evidence of that intersubjective experience, that co-presence, but also, evidence of that epistemic slippage, that coming to know in and through our conversations. Ethnopoetics, it seems to me, has the potential to be irrelevant if we exclude or erase the conversations that inform our interpretative practices. A dialogical ethnopoetics demystifies what we do, it brings it down to a human scale (see Webster 2020). It makes visible the intersubjective coming to know something through situated talk that is the epistemological foundation of ethnography and of a language-centered and discourse-centered anthropology. It makes visible that epistemic slippage. A dialogical ethnopoetics is, to borrow from Gerald Carr and Barbra Meek (2015: 200), an "interactive process" and we should make visible such interactions. One way to recognize voice in and through ethnopoetics (Kroskrity and Webster 2015), is to make visible such interactive processes, such confrontations. A dialogical ethnopoetics might limit our exuberances, our anthropological penchant for "exotic readings" (Keesing 1989). It should be foundational for any humanities of speaking approach as well (Epps, Webster, and Woodbury 2017). There is, of course, still a place for outside analysis, but it must "relate in principled ways" (Sherzer 1998: 175) to the interpretations of those we work with, who are also engaged in that "analytical process" (Sherzer 1998: 175), it must be grounded, that is, in a dialogical ethnopoetics first.

---

16 The phrase "real people" is meant to acknowledge my debt to E.P. Thompson (1978). These are real people as opposed to abstractions.

We have here the poem, and we have the conversation that I had with Jim about the poem. Neither the poem nor the transcript speaks for itself. Our conversation was suffused with intertextuality – of prior conversations, of quotations of each other and of curing ways, of rhetorical structures. As should be clear, the poem became a recurring theme, a way to make sense of our on-going conversation and confrontation, a shared reference point at times. To extract from all this that the poem has the structure of a ceremonial prayer that concerns the expelling of ghosts, that the final line of the poem is from that ceremonial prayer, that other lines are not included because by not including them, the poem leaves open the possibility of hope for a future for Navajos, is to fundamentally miss the ways that I came to know such things – that they emerged in a conversation with Jim. Jim told me those things. But he also told me a great deal more and such extractable "facts" about the poem ignores all of that.[17] That the poem, for example, could be, was in fact, used as a critique by Jim of the very practice of anthropology that I was engaged in at that moment, and that this emerged in and through our conversation. To make this point, I should add, is to ground my discussion in the very kinds of particulars, the kinds of compounding and reverberating relationships, that Jim was describing to me.

7 Coda

Why revisit a recording of a conversation that is twenty years old? I hope by now it is clear that in many ways, I have never completely stopped hearing that conversation. Every time I read again Jim's poem, I hear in it Jim's critique, not just of anthropology, but of my anthropology – the poem a prompt for me to reflect on anthropology and on my own practices as an anthropologist. The poem means many things, and should, but the conversation that I had with Rex Lee Jim very much shaped and shapes my understanding of the poem. Why, then, revisit this conversation? Because the conversation is not yet over – and in that, there is hope for the future, perhaps even for the future of anthropology.

---

17 My thinking about anthropology and extraction has been greatly informed by Kroskrity (2015).

References

Adley-Santa Maria, Bernadette. 1997. White Mountain Apache language. Issues in language shift, textbook development, and Native speaker-university collaboration. In Jon Reyhner (ed.), *Teaching Indigenous languages*, 129–143. Flagstaff: Northern Arizona University Press.

Bahr, Donald. 1986. Pima swallow songs. *Cultural Anthropology* 1 (2). 171–187.

Bahr, Donald, Lloyd Paul & Vincent Joseph. 1997. *Ants and orioles. Showing the art of Pima poetry*. Salt Lake City: University of Utah Press.

Basso, Keith. 1976. "Wise words" of the Western Apache. Metaphor and semantic theory. In Keith Basso & Henry Selby (eds.), *Meaning in anthropology*, 93–122. Albuquerque: University of New Mexico Press.

Basso, Keith. 1979. *Portraits of "The Whiteman."* Cambridge: Cambridge University Press.

Basso, Keith. 1996. *Wisdom sits in places*. Albuquerque: University of New Mexico Press.

Bauman, Richard & Joel Sherzer (eds.). 1974. *Explorations in the ethnography of speaking*. London: Cambridge University Press.

Belin, Esther, Jeff Berglund, Connie Jacobs & Anthony K. Webster (eds.). 2021. *The Diné reader. An anthology of Navajo literature*. Tucson: University of Arizona Press.

Bender, Margaret. 2002. *Signs of Cherokee culture. Sequoyah's syllabary in Eastern Cherokee life*. Chapel Hill: UNC Press.

Berman, Judith. 1994. George Hunt and the Kwak'wala Texts. *Anthropological Linguistics* 36 (4). 482–514.

Blackhawk, Ned. 1999. Julian Steward and the politics of representation. In Richard O. Clemmer, L. Daniel Myers & Mary Elizabeth Rudden (eds.), *Julian Steward and the Great Basin. The making of an anthropologist*, 203–218. Salt Lake City: University of Utah Press.

Boas, Franz. 1889. On alternating sounds. *American Anthropologists* 2. 47–53.

Boas, Franz. 1911. Introduction. *Bureau of American Ethnological Bulletin* 40 (1). 1–83.

Bright, William. 1979. A Karok myth in measured verse. The translation of a performance. *Journal of California and Great Basin Anthropology* 1. 117–123.

Carr, Gerald & Barbra Meek. 2015. The poetics of language revitalization. Text, performance, and change. In Paul V. Kroskrity & Anthony K. Webster (eds.), *The legacy of Dell Hymes. Ethnopoetics, narrative inequality, and voice*, 180–205. Bloomington: Indiana University Press.

Cruikshank, Julie. 1998. *The social life of stories*. Lincoln: University of Nebraska Press.

Crum, Beverly. 1980. Newe Hupia – Shoshoni Poetry Songs. *Journal of California and Great Basin Anthropology Papers in Linguistics* 2. 1–23.

Crum, Steven. 1999. Julian Steward's vision of the Great Basin. A critique and response. In Richard O. Clemmer, L. Daniel Myers & Mary Elizabeth Rudden (eds.), *Julian Steward and the Great Basin. The making of an anthropologist*, 117–127. Salt Lake City: University of Utah Press.

Cruz, Emiliana. 2021. Between the academy and the community. The trickster who dances at the party and shows her tongue. *Language Documentation & Conservation* 23. 105–130.

Cruz, Hilaria. 2017. Prayers for the community. Parallelism and performance in San Juan Quiahije Eastern Chatino. *Oral Tradition* 31 (2). 509–532.

Davis, Jenny. 2017. Resisting rhetorics of language endangerment. Reclamation through Indigenous language survivance. *Language Documentation and Description* 17. 37–58.

Davis, Jenny. 2018. *Talking Indian. Identity and language revitalization in the Chickasaw renaissance*. Tucson: University of Arizona Press.

Debenport, Erin. 2015. *Fixing the books. Secrecy, literacy, and perfectibility in Indigenous New Mexico*. Santa Fe: School for Advanced Research Press.

Deloria, Ella. 1954. Short Dakota Texts, including Conversations. *International Journal of American Linguistics* 20 (1). 17–22.

Deloria Jr., Vine. 1988. *Custer died for your sins. An Indian manifesto*. Norman: University of Oklahoma Press.

Denetdale, Jennifer Nez. 2007. *Reclaiming Diné history. The legacies of Navajo Chief Manuelito and Juanita*. Tucson: University of Arizona Press.

Dozier, Edward. 1955. Kinship and linguistic change among the Arizona Tewa." *International Journal of American Linguistics* 21 (3). 242–257.

Dozier, Edward. 1956. Two examples of linguistic acculturation. The Yaqui of Sonora and Arizona and the Tewa of New Mexico. *Language* 32 (1). 146–157.

Dwyer, Kevin. 1987. *Moroccan dialogues. Anthropology in question*. Prospect Heights: Waveland Press.

Epps, Patience, Anthony K. Webster & Anthony C. Woodbury. 2017. A holistic humanities of speaking. Franz Boas and the continuing centrality of texts. *International Journal of American Linguistics* 83 (1). 41–78.

Evers, Larry & Felipe Molina. 1987. *Yaqui deer songs*. Tucson: University of Arizona Press.

Evers, Larry & Barre Toelken. 2001. *Native American oral traditions. Collaboration and ethnopoetics*. Logan: Utah State University Press.

Fabian, Johannes. 1979. Rule and process. Thoughts on ethnography as communication. *Philosophy of Social Sciences* 9. 1–26.

Fabian, Johannes. 1991. *Time and the work of anthropology. Critical essays 1971–1991*. Philadelphia: Harwood Academic Publishers.

Fabian, Johannes. 2007. *Memory against culture. Arguments and reminders*. Durham: Duke University Press.

Fabian, Johannes. 2008. *Ethnography as commentary. Writing from the virtual archive*. Durham: Duke University Press.

Fabian, Johannes. 2015. *Talk about prayer. An ethnographic commentary*. New York: Palgrave MacMillan.

Farnell, Brenda. 1995. *Do you see what I mean. Plains Indian Sign Talk and the embodiment of action*. Austin: University of Texas Press.

Fernandez, James. 1989. Comment. *Current Anthropology* 30 (4). 470–471.

Field, Margaret (ed.). 2019. *Mii namak nyamak kweyiwpo/Huellas del pasado hacia el futuro/ Footsteps from the past into the future. Jwanya Kumiai Kuwak/Cuentos Kumiai de Baja California/Kumeyaay stories of Baja California. A trilingual collection in Kumeyaay, Spanish, & English*. San Diego: San Diego State University Press.

Foster, Michael. 1974. *From the earth to beyond the sky. An ethnographic approach to four longhouse Iroquois speech events*. (Canadian Ethnology Service Paper 20). Ottaw: National Museums of Canada.

Goodfellow, Anne. 2005. *Talking in context. Language and identity in Kwakwaka'wakw society*. Montreal: McGill-Queen's University Press.

Henry, Jeannette (ed.). 1972. *The American Indian reader. Anthropology*. San Francisco: The Indian Historian Press.

Hoijer, Harry. 1951. Cultural implications of some Navaho linguistic categories. *Language* 27. 111–120.

Howard, Victoria. 2021. *Clackamas Chinook performance art. Verse form interpretations*, edited by Catharine Mason. Lincoln: University of Nebraska Press.

Hughte, Phil. 1995. A Zuni artist looks at Frank Hamilton Cushing. *American Anthropologist* 97 (1). 10–13.

Hymes, Dell. 1975. Breakthrough into performance. In Dan Ben-Amos & Kenneth Goldstein (eds.), *Folklore. Performance and communication*, 11–74. The Hague: Mouton.

Hymes, Dell. 1980. Verse analysis of a Wasco text. Hiram Smith's "At'Unaqa". *International Journal of American Linguistics* 46 (2). 65–77.

Hymes, Dell. 1981. *In vain I tried to tell you. Essays in Native American ethnopoetics*. Philadelphia: University of Pennsylvania Press.

Hymes, Dell. 1991. Custer and linguistic anthropology. *Journal of Linguistic Anthropology* 1 (1). 5–11.

Hymes, Dell. 1994. Ethnopoetics, oral-formulaic theory, and editing texts. *Oral Tradition* 9 (2). 330–370.

Hymes, Dell. 1998. When is oral narrative poetry? Generative form and its pragmatic conditions. *Pragmatics* 8 (4). 475–500.

Hymes, Virginia & Hazel Supah. 1992. How long ago we got lost. *Anthropological Linguistics* 34 (1–4). 73–83.

Innes, Pamela. 2006. The interplay of genres, gender, and language ideology among the Muskogee. *Language in Society* 35 (3). 231–259.

Isbell, Billie Jean. 1985. The metaphoric process. From culture to nature and back again. In Gary Urton (ed.), *Animal myths and metaphors in South America*, 285–313. Salt Lake City: University of Utah Press.

Jim, Rex Lee. 1989. *Áhí Ni' Nikisheegiizh*. Princeton: Princeton Collections of Western Americana.

Jim, Rex Lee. 1995. *Saad*. Princeton: Princeton Collections of Western Americana.

Jim, Rex Lee. 1998. *Dúchas Táá Kóó Diné*. Beal Feirste, Ireland: Au Clochan.

Jim, Rex Lee. 2000. A moment in my life. In Arnold Krupat & Brian Swann (ed.), *Here first*, 229–246. New York: Modern Library.

Jim, Rex Lee. 2019. *Saad Lá Tah Hózhóón. A collection of Diné poetry*. Flagstaff: Salina Bookshelf.

Jim, Rex Lee. 2021. Na'azheeh/Hunting. In Esther G. Belin, Jeff Berglund, Connie Jacobs & Anthony K. Webster (eds.), *The Diné reader*, 143. Tucson: University of Arizona Press.

Keesing, Roger. 1989. Exotic readings of cultural texts. *Current Anthropology* 30 (4). 459–478.

Kenoyer, Louis. 2017. *My life, Louis Kenoyer. Reminiscences of a Grand Ronde reservation childhood*, edited by Jedd Schrock & Henry Zenk. Corvallis: Oregon State University Press.

Kinkade, M. Dale & Anthony Mattina. 1996. Discourse. In Ives Goddard (ed.), *Handbook of North American Indians: Languages*, Vol. 17, 244–274. Washington, DC: Smithsonian Institute.

Klain, Bennie & Leighton Peterson. 2000. Native media, commercial radio, and language maintenance. Defining speech and style for Navajo broadcasters and Broadcast Navajo. *Texas Linguistic Forum* 43. 117–128.

Kroskrity, Paul V. 1993. *Language, history and identity. Ethnolinguistic studies of the Arizona Tewa*. Tucson: University of Arizona Press.

Kroskrity, Paul V. 2015. Discursive discriminations in the representation of Western Mono and Yokuts stories. Confronting narrative inequality and listening to Indigenous voices in Central California." In Paul V. Kroskrity & Anthony K. Webster (eds.), *The legacy of Dell Hymes. Ethnopoetics, narrative inequality, and voice*, 135–163. Bloomington: Indiana University Press.

Kroskrity, Paul (ed.). 2012. *Telling stories in the face of danger. Language renewal in Native American communities*. Norman: University of Oklahoma Press.

Kroskrity, Paul & Margaret Field (eds.). 2009. *Native American language ideologies. Beliefs, practices, and struggles in Indian Country*. Tucson: University of Arizona Press.

Kroskrity, Paul & Barbra Meek (eds.). 2017. *Engaging Native American publics. Linguistic anthropology in a new key*. London: Routledge.

Kroskrity, Paul V. & Anthony K. Webster (eds.). 2015. *The legacy of Dell Hymes. Ethnopoetics, narrative inequality, and voice*. Bloomington: Indiana University Press.

Krupat, Arnold. 1992. On the translation of Native American song and story. A theorized history. In Brian Swann (ed.), *On the translation of Native American literatures*, 3–32. Washington, DC: Smithsonian Institution Press.

Lee, Dorothy. 1943. The linguistic aspect of Wintu' acculturation. *American Anthropologist* 45 (3). 435–440.

Lee, Dorothy. 1944. Linguistic reflection of Wintu' thought. *International Journal of American Linguistics* 10 (4). 181–187.

Leonard, Wesley. 2011. Challenging "extinction" through modern Miami language practices. *American Indian Culture and Research Journal* 35 (2). 135–160.

Leonard, Wesley. 2021. Toward an anti-racist linguistic anthropology. An Indigenous response to White supremacy. *Journal of Linguistic Anthropology* 31 (2). 218–237.

Mannheim, Bruce & Krista Van Vleet. 1998. The dialogics of Southern Quechua narrative. *American Anthropologist* 100 (2). 326–346.

Mather, Elsie & Phyllis Morrow. 2001. There are no more words to the story. In Larry Evers & Barre Toelken (eds.), *Native American oral traditions. Collaboration and interpretation*, 200–242. Logan: Utah State University Press.

Mattina, Anthony. 1987. North American Indian mythography. Editing texts for the Printed Page. In Brian Swann & Arnold Krupat (eds.), *Recovering the word. Essays on Native American literature*, 129–148. Berkeley: University of California Press.

McDowell, John. 2000. Collaborative ethnopoetics. In Kay Sammons & Joel Sherzer (eds.), *Translating Native Latin American verbal art*, 211–232. Washington, DC: Smithsonian Press.

McIlwraith, Thomas. 2012. *"We are still Didene". Stories of hunting and history from Northern British Columbia*. Toronto: University of Toronto Press.

Medicine, Bea. 2001. *Learning to be an anthropologist and remaining "Native". Selected writings*, edited by Sue-Ellen Jacobs. Urbana: University of Illinois Press.

Meek, Barbra. 2010. *We are our language. An ethnography of language revitalization in a Northern Athabaskan community*. Tucson: University of Arizona Press.

Meek, Barbra. 2011. Failing American Indian languages. *American Indian Culture and Research Journal* 35 (2). 43–60.

Meyers, Richard. 2019. Native anthropology, to be a Native scholar, or a scholar that is Native. Reviving ethnography in Indian Country. *Anthropology Now* 11 (1–2). 23–33.

Mitchell, Blackhorse & Anthony K. Webster. 2011. "We don't know what we become". Navajo ethnopoetics and an expressive feature in a poem by Rex Lee Jim. *Anthropological Linguistics* 53 (3). 259–286.

Molina, Felipe & Larry Evers. 2001. Like this it stays in your hands. Collaboration and ethnopoetics. In Larry Evers & Barre Toelken (eds.), *Native American oral traditions. Collaboration and interpretation*, 15–57. Logan: Utah State University Press.

Moore, Patrick & Daniel Tlen. 2007. Indigenous linguistics and land claims. The semiotic projection of Athabaskan directionals in Elijah Smith's radio work. *Journal of Linguistic Anthropology* 17 (2). 266–286.

Moore, Robert. 2015. Rethinking ethnopoetics. In Paul V. Kroskrity & Anthony K. Webster (eds.), *The legacy of Dell Hymes. Ethnopoetics, narrative inequality, and voice*, 11–36. Bloomington: Indiana University Press.

Murray, Stephen O. 1994. *Theory group and the study of language in North America. A social history*. Amsterdam & Philadelphia: John Benjamins.

Nevins, M. Eleanor. 2013. *Lessons from Fort Apache. Beyond language endangerment and maintenance*. Malden: Wiley-Blackwell.

Nevins, M. Eleanor. 2015. "Grow with that, walk with that". Hymes, dialogicality, and text collections. In Paul V. Kroskrity & Anthony K. Webster (eds.), *The legacy of Dell Hymes. Ethnopoetics, narrative inequality, and voice*, 71–107. Bloomington: Indiana University Press.

Nevins, M. Eleanor (ed.). 2017. *World-making stories. Maidu language and community renewal on a shared California landscape*. Lincoln: University of Nebraska Press.

Newman, Stanley. 1955. Vocabulary levels. Zuni sacred and slang usage. *Southwestern Journal of Anthropology* 11 (4). 345–354.

O'Neill, Sean. 2008. *Cultural contact and linguistic relativity among the Indians of Northwestern California*. Norman: University of Oklahoma Press.

Palmer, Andie. 2005. *Maps of experience. The anchoring of land to story in Secwepemc discourse*. Toronto: University of Toronto Press.

Palmer Jr., Gus. 2003. *Telling stories the Kiowa way*. Tucson: University of Arizona Press.

Perley, Bernard. 2011. *Defying Maliseet language death. Emergent vitalities, culture, and identity in Eastern Canada*. Lincoln: University of Nebraska Press.

Perley, Bernard. 2013a. Gone anthropologist. Epistemic slippage, Native anthropology, and the dilemmas of representation. In Gabriela Vargas-Centina (ed.), *Anthropology and the politics of representation*, 101–118. Tuscaloosa: University of Alabama Press.

Perley, Bernard. 2013b. Zombie linguistics. Experts, endangered languages and the curse of undead voices. *Anthropological Forum* 22 (2). 133–149.

Perley, Bernard. 2013c. Remembering ancestral voices. Emergent vitalities and the future of Indigenous languages. In Elena Mihas, Bernard Perley, Gabriel Rei-Doval & Kathleen Wheatley (eds.), *Responses to language endangerment*, 243–270. Amsterdam & Philadelphia: John Benjamins.

Philips, Susan U. 1983. *The invisible culture*. New York: Longman Inc.

Reichard, Gladys. 1944. *Prayer. The compulsive word*. (American Ethnological Society Monograph 7). Seattle: University of Washington Press.

Reichard, Gladys. 1945. Linguistic diversity among the Navaho Indians. *International Journal of American Linguistics* 11. 156–168.

Richland, Justin. 2007. *Arguing with tradition. The language of law in Hopi Tribal Court*. Chicago: University of Chicago Press.

Rothenberg, Jerome & Diane Rothenberg (eds.). 1983. *Symposium of the Whole. A range of discourse toward an ethnopoetics*. Berkeley: University of California Press.

Sapir, Edward. 1932. Two Navajo puns. *Language* 8. 217–219.

Schreyer, Christine. 2016. Taku River Tlingit genres of place as performative stewardship. *Journal of Linguistic Anthropology* 26 (1). 4–25.

Schwartz, Saul. 2018. Writing Chiwere. Orthography, literacy, and language revitalization. *Language and Communication* 61. 75–87.

Scollon, Ronald & Suzanne Scollon. 1979. *Linguistic convergence. An ethnography of speaking at Fort Chipewyan*. New York: Academic Press.

Shaul, David Leedom. 2002. *Hopi traditional literature*. Albuquerque: University New Mexico Press.

Sherzer, Joel. 1987. A discourse-centered approach to language and culture. *American Anthropologist* 89. 295–309.

Sherzer, Joel. 1992. Modes of representation and translation of Native American discourse. Examples from the San Blas Kuna. In Brian Swann (ed.), *On the translation of Native American literatures*, 426–440. Washington D.C.: Smithsonian Press.

Sherzer, Joel. 1994. The Kuna and Columbus. Encounters and confrontations of discourse. *American Anthropologist* 96. 902–924.

Sherzer, Joel. 1998. *Verbal art in San Blas. Kuna culture through its discourse*. Albuquerque: University of New Mexico Press.

Sherzer, Joel & Anthony Woodbury (eds.). 1987. *Native American discourse. Poetics and rhetoric*. Cambridge: Cambridge University Press.

Tedlock, Dennis. 1972a. Pueblo literature. Style and verisimilitude. In Alfonso Ortiz (ed.), *New perspectives on the Pueblos*, 219–242. Albuquerque: University of New Mexico Press.

Tedlock, Dennis. 1972b. *Finding the center*. New York: The Dial Press.

Tedlock, Dennis. 1979. The analogical tradition and the emergence of a dialogical anthropology. *Journal of Anthropological Research* 42 (3). 483–496.

Tedlock, Dennis. 1983. *The spoken word and the work of interpretation*. Philadelphia: University of Pennsylvania Press.

Tedlock, Dennis & Bruce Mannheim (eds.). 1995. *The dialogic emergence of culture*. Urbana: University of Illinois Press.

Thompson, E. P. 1978. *The poverty of theory and other essays*. New York: Monthly Review Press.

Thornton, Thomas. 2008. *Being and place among the Tlingit*. Seattle: University of Washington Press.

Toelken, Barre & Tacheeni Scott. 1981. Poetic retranslation and the "Pretty Languages" of Yellowman. In Karl Kroeber (ed.), *Traditional Literatures of the American Indians*, 65–116. Lincoln: University of Nebraska Press.

Trejo, Judy. 1974. Coyote tales. A Paiute commentary. *Journal of American Folklore* 87 (343). 66–71.

Valentine, Lisa. 1995. *Making it their own. Severn Ojibwe communicative practices*. Toronto: University of Toronto Press.

Valentine, Lisa & Regna Darnell (eds.). 1999. *Theorizing the Americanist tradition*. Toronto: University of Toronto Press.

Webster, Anthony K. 2006. The mouse that sucked. On "translating" a Navajo poem. *Studies in American Indian Literature* 18 (1). 37–49.

Webster, Anthony K. 2009. *Explorations in Navajo poetry and poetics*. Albuquerque: University of New Mexico Press.

Webster, Anthony K. 2015. *Intimate grammars. An ethnography of Navajo poetry*. Tucson: University of Arizona Press.

Webster, Anthony K. 2016. The art of failure in translating a Navajo poem. *Journal de la Société des Américanistes* 102 (1). 9–41.

Webster, Anthony K. 2017. "So it's got three meanings dil dil". Seductive ideophony and the sounds of Navajo poetry. *Canadian Journal of Linguistics/Revue canadienne de linguistique* 62 (2). 173–195.

Webster, Anthony K. 2018. *The sounds of Navajo poetry. A humanities of speaking*. New York: Peter Lang.

Webster, Anthony K. 2020. Learning to be satisfied. Navajo poetics, a chattering chipmunk, and ethnopoetics. *Oral Tradition* 34. 73–104.

Webster, Anthony K. 2021a. "Let them know how I was or something like that, you know". On lingual life histories, remembering and Navajo poetry. *Journal of Anthropological Research* 77 (1). 16–34.

Webster, Anthony K. 2021b. Anthropology at the water's edge. Morris Opler among the Apaches. *Journal of the Southwest* 63 (3). 468–505.

Webster, Anthony K. n.d. "I want people to really see it". On poetry, truth, and the particularities of Blackhorse Mitchell's "The beauty of Navajoland". Unpublished manuscript.

Webster, Anthony K. & Leighton C. Peterson. 2011. Introduction. American Indian languages in unexpected places. *American Indian Culture and Research Journal* 35 (2). 1–18.

Whiteley, Peter. 2018. The Native shaping of anthropological inquiry. In Leigh Kuwanwisiwma, T.J. Ferguson & Chip Colwell (eds.), *Footprints of Hopi history. Hopihiniwtiput Kukveni'at*, 230–246. Tucson: University of Arizona Press.

Whorf, Benjamin Lee. 1956. *Language, thought, and reality*, edited by John Carroll. Cambridge: MIT University Press.

Witherspoon, Gary. 1977. *Language and art in the Navajo universe*. Ann Arbor: University of Michigan Press.

Woodbury, Anthony. 1985. The function of rhetorical structure. A study of Central Alaskan Yupik Eskimo discourse. *Language in Society* 14. 153–190.

Woodbury, Anthony. 1998. Documenting rhetorical, aesthetic, and expressive loss in language shift. In Lenore Grenoble & Lindsay Whaley (eds.), *Endangered languages*, 234–258. Cambridge: Cambridge University Press.

Alexandra Y. Aikhenvald

15 Perspectivism through language: A view from Amazonia

South America, and especially Lowland Amazonia and Circum-Amazonian regions, constitute the locus of extreme linguistic diversity in terms of their "phylogenetic" range (that is, how many genetic groupings are present in an area), "language density" (involving the sheer number of languages or linguistic varieties spoken), and the diversity of linguistic structures. This goes hand-in-hand with cultural diversity, in terms of a rich gamut of societal organizations, norms of social behavior, knowledge, beliefs and customs. And yet we can trace a few typically Amazonian phenomena, which transcend the boundaries of distinct languages and cultures. Among these are the shared ontological stance known as Amazonian perspectivisim – the underlying primordial unity of humans and other entities. This is seen in the choice of linguistic features – genders and classifiers. The transformation of a visual form and its disguise are mirrored in the concept of clothing or outer skin visible to those who have special powers of seeing. The double, or even multiple, nature of entities – including jaguar-shamans and peccary-shamans – is expressed through further grammatical means. The chapter address these and other, putative, instantiations of Amazonian perspectivism in the languages of the region.

1 How Amazonia is special: A backdrop

Lowland Amazonia and the adjacent Circum-Amazonian regions constitute the locus of extreme linguistic diversity in its varied guises – in terms of their "phylogenetic" range, that is, the number of genetic groupings present in an area; in terms of its "language density", that is, a sheer number of languages or linguistic varieties spoken; and in terms of diversity of linguistic structures. This goes

Acknowledgments: I owe a debt of gratutide to R. M. W. Dixon for his incisive comments, to Brigitta Flick and Luca Ciucci for their feedback, and to my Tariana family for sharing their remarkable language with me. Many thanks to Nico Nassenstein and Svenja Völkel, for involving me in this wonderful enterprise.

Alexandra Y. Aikhenvald, Central Queensland University, Cairns/Australia,
e-mail: a.aikhenvald@cqu.edu.au

https://doi.org/10.1515/9783110726626-015

hand-in-hand with cultural diversity, spanning a rich gamut of societal organizations, norms of social behavior, knowledge, beliefs and customs (see Aikhenvald 2015 and also Epps 2020, for an appraisal of different aspects of linguistic and cultural diversity). The linguistic diversity in the Amazon Basin – the world's major river system – is rivalled only by that of the island of New Guinea. The region comprises over 350 extant languages grouped into over fifteen language families, in addition to a number of isolates (Loukotka 1968, Tovar and Tovar 1984, Dixon and Aikhenvald 1999, Aikhenvald 2015: 19–23, 2022). The consensus among archaeologists is that the Americas were first populated approximately 12,000 years ago, possibly in successive waves of migration across the Bering Strait (a brief history and references are in Aikhenvald 2015: 2–17). As a result of population movements, dispersals, and displacement, the linguistic map of Amazonia resembles a patchwork quilt. Most major families – including Arawak, Tupí, and Cariban – are spoken in several disconnected geographical locations.

Intensive language contact between adjacent groups and historically documented migrations have resulted in the creation of numerous linguistic areas across the continent. These include:

- the Vaupés River Basin Linguistic Area, the adjacent regions of the Upper Rio Negro Basin, and the neighboring Caquetá-Putumayo River Basin (known as "the people of the centre of the world": see Aikhenvald 2002, 2015, 2022 on the linguistic picture of Amazonia and a summary of work on the Vaupés River Basin Linguistic Area and neighboring regions, Echeverri 1997 and Wojtylak 2020, 2021 on the Caquetá-Putumayo area);
- the Pre-andine region (see Adelaar 2004 and Wise 2011 on shared cultural and linguistic features across the Pre-andine area and the Andean foothills and Valenzuela 2015);
- the Xingu Park area (see Seki 1999, 2010 on the Xingu region as a cultural area and an incipient linguistic area);
- the Guaporé-Mamoré area (see Crevels and van der Voort 2008);
- and the Gran Chaco area (see Comrie et al. 2010, González 2015, and Ciucci 2020 on the linguistic and cultural diffusion across the region).

Mass language extinction, especially in the areas of the head waters of the Amazon, and eastern Brazil occupied by Europeans soon after the invasion, makes the task of revealing the exact linguistic picture, and the past patterns of language and culture interaction in Amazonia, truly daunting. Over 60% of indigenous languages are estimated to have become extinct since the European conquest (Adelaar 2000, 2004, Loukotka 1968, Hemming 1978a, b, Aikhenvald 2015, 2022). As a consequence of constant pressure from major national, and sometimes other indigenous languages, most languages of Amazonia are currently endangered. The effects of language obsolescence and concomitant loss of traditional culture patterns, plus the influence of national languages and cultures, create further complications for studies of languages and social correlates for the recurrent linguistic parameters.

Shared linguistic and cultural features may be due to a conglomerate of substrata and contact with extinct groups, many of them no longer recoverable. Numerous indigenous groups became depleted – mostly due to epidemics and raids, subsequent to the colonial invasion. Survivors from one group amalgamated with their neighbors of different, and often no longer known groups. Examples include:

- the Tupari, a Tupí-speaking group in northern Brazil (Caspar 1956: 220–221);
- the Palikur, an Arawak-speaking group in the Brazilian state of Amapá and the adjacent regions of French Guiana (Green and Green 2013, Diana Green p.c.);
- the Yucuna, an Arawak-speaking group in Colombia (Fontaine 2008: 48–50, 83–84);
- the Waiwai, a Cariban-speaking group in Brazil and Suriname (see Carlin 2006, 2011 on the Waiwai, and their "nested identities");
- the Yanesha' (or Amuesha), an Arawak-speaking group in Peru (Adelaar 2006);
- the Sorowaha, one of the least known Arawá-speaking groups in southern Amazonia in Brazil (Dixon 2004: 9).

As a consequence, each of these languages display unusual linguistic features, and are divergent from their genetic relatives. In the absence of reliable data and historical records, we will never be able to go beyond mere hypotheses about possible paths of contact-induced change, and the exact reasons for commonalities and for diversification. Amazonia remains a land of historical puzzles.

Despite these pitfalls, the past decades have seen a surge of interest in establishing correlations between linguistic features and the societal characteristics of Amazonian peoples. Against the backdrop of an overwhelming diversity, common features emerge.

This chapter focuses on a number of common features shared by indigenous peoples of the Amazon, especially perspectivism and its reflection in the extant languages.

2 Unity in diversity: In search of common threads

Shared structural features across Amazonian languages have led some scholars to a suggestion that the whole of Amazonia may be considered a linguistic area, setting them apart from the languages of the Andes (see, for instance, Derbyshire and Pullum 1986, Derbyshire 1987, and also Key 1993).[1]

A number of forms are shared by unrelated Amazonian languages. Payne (1990) identified five widespread grammatical forms, including a causative prefix *mV-* and valency-changing affixes of the shape *-ka*, in addition to monosyllabic possessive and nominalizing affixes. The form **koko* 'mother's brother, father-in-law' can be reconstructed for Proto-Arawá; a similar form **kuhko* 'uncle, father-in-law' was reconstructed for Proto-Arawak. In his pioneering study of indigenous languages of Brazil, von Martius (1867, Vol. 1: 359–360) mentioned a few similar forms meaning 'uncle' in unrelated languages including Kariri (Macro-Jê) and Macushi (Carib). He grouped them under the name of "Guck" or "Coco" languages. Further forms shared by genetically unrelated languages include *kanawa* 'canoe', found in Carib and Arawak families, in addition to a number of others (such as Arawá).[2]

A number of mythological motives are shared by Amazonian groups – including jaguar shamans, tapir avoidance and an association between agouti (a large rodent) and the underground magical world, in addition to a pervasive tendency towards twin-avoidance. A discussion of pan-Amazonian mythological motives is in Roe (1982) and Urton (1985). Pan-Amazonian features – both linguistic and cultural – may point towards traces of older, and oftentimes no longer recoverable, language contact patterns which may have played a role in shaping the linguistic landscape of Amazonia as a linguistic continent and are reminiscent of "pan-African" features (along the lines of Heine and Nurse 2008).

A further typically Amazonian phenomenon – which transcends the boundaries of linguistic families and areas – is a shared ontological stance known as Amazonian perspectivism.

---

1 The "Amazonian" linguistic type is contrasted to the "Andean" type in Dixon and Aikhenvald (1999) and Aikhenvald (2015: 74). A putative division of Amazonian languages along a hypothetical East-West divide (e.g., Birchall 2014, and references there) is based on partial investigation of a limited set of languages, and is not borne out by facts (especially in view of extensive language loss in the Eastern areas of the Amazon Basin).
2 See Dixon (2004: 13) for Proto-Arawá, and Aikhenvald (2002) for Proto-Arawak; a number of further forms are addressed by Zamponi (2020) and Aikhenvald (2015: 71, 2022).

2.1 Amazonian perspectivism: A shared ontological stance

One shared feature permeates most if not all traditional Amazonian communities. This concerns "a basic animistic ontological stance whereby humans and animals who share their interiority (*anima*) but differ in their physicality form part of a shared relational frame of interaction" (Carlin 2018: 315, Halbmayer 2012: 12), captured by the notion of "perspectivism". This notion and the term, coined by Viveiros de Castro (1998, 2004a, 2004b), sum up the indigenous conceptions concerning "the configuration of distinctions between humans and nonhumans" (Vanzolini and Cesarino 2018). This is reminiscent of the concept of "animism" discussed by Descola (2005).

According to the understanding of the world common to numerous Amerindian people, in mythological times – or at the beginning of time – various entities shared a general human condition. A speaker of Kari'na, a Cariban language, tellingly referred to stories about those primordial times – of the mythological past – as *isenurupiry ja'konombo aurananon*, freely translated as 'things that happened in the time when everything still spoke to each other, or stories from the time of our beginning' (Carlin 2018: 332).

As this primeval condition suffered a disruption, the varied types of humans transformed into different species of animals and other entities – vegetables, plants, artifacts, etc.; for a detailed discussion of recent anthropological work on this "animism", perspectivism and the ontological turn, see Halbmayer (2012) (with special attention to Cariban languages). The underlying unity of the erstwhile entities in their primeval human condition can still be recognized, albeit in a covert way. It can be uncovered and made clear to those privy to such knowledge in shamanic practices, and also in customs associated with hunting and fishing. Animals, spirits, and also objects "can still reveal an inner human form usually associated with their 'soul' or 'double'" (Vanzolini and Cesarino 2018). "The continuity between species" manifests itself in the way each species sees itself, and how they share culture and language (Costa and Fausto 2010: 94). The importance of visual, rather than aural, perception for the recognition of the nature of entities was made clear by Lewy (2012), and also Halbmayer (2012: 17): this foregrounds the special powers of vision and the importance of visual perception across languages and cultures, in Amazonia and beyond it (see Aikhenvald and Storch 2013). As Rosengren (2006: 810) put it in his analysis of the Matsigenka (a Campa (Arawak)-speaking group of Peruvian Amazon), the net result is "the creation of a community of similars" – spanning humans, shamans, and those behind a non-human disguise, and thus highlighting their similarity.

This nonhuman disguise can be seen as just an outer covering, clothing, or "skin" (see the discussion of a special classifier -*maka* 'extended piece of cloth' in Tariana further on in this section). The form – the clothing – determines the appearance depending on a viewpoint, and often the nature and the intentions of the perceiver. The Amazonian animism operates on the basis of a spiritual unity (of humans and animals) and a corporeal diversity, so that what one sees in physical terms is not necessarily that which it is in essence: a spirit or soul can be wearing "clothes" that mask the underlying essence. "Clothes", or outer form(s), "is a common metaphor in Amazonia to describe not only outward appearances but also attributes and competences associated with beings of that outer appearance. Thus, in the transformative world of Amazonians, where focus is on states of being and changes of state, changing one's 'clothes' entails that appearances may be deceptive" (Carlin 2018: 315). As Rivière (1994) phrased it in the title of his oft-quoted paper, in Amazonia, *"What you see is not what you get"*.

The inherent animism and perspectivism in the sense of an underlying unity of humans and non-humans tend to be reflected in those linguistic categories which are known to be sensitive to societal features and cultural stereotypes (summarized in Aikhenvald, Dixon, and Jarkey 2021). The unity of humans and non-humans reflected in the language is not a uniquely Amazonian feature. Its salience in the grammatical structure of Amazonian languages highlights its special status for the region. Among these are patterns of nominal classification (classifiers and gender) and kinship systems.

The unity of all animate beings is reflected in the assignment of classifiers in Murui, a Witotoan language from the Caquetá-Putumayo region. The fluidity of the distinction between humans and non-humans in Murui noun classification can be understood from the perspective of the people's cosmology (Wojtylak 2021). According to the Murui mythology, at the beginning of time most beings were simultaneously human and non-human. They used to be able to communicate with each other, and at the same time had physical or behavioral traits characteristic of non-humans. Later, they transformed into the present-day species of animals, vegetables, artefacts, and other kinds of beings. *Jimenaki*, Possum Man, once a powerful mythological being who had a characteristic monkey-like speech, is a case in point (see Wojtylak 2020). Punished for burning his children alive, *Jimenaki* was transformed into a species of possum, known as *jimenaki*. Along similar lines, some of the names for species of animals and plants in Murui share the same roots, and are understood by the people to "belong to one another" (Wojtylak 2015: 555, 2021). Many of such original transformations explain similarities in the assignment of Murui classifiers to human and non-human referents with shared forms, and shared histories. Along similar lines, the assignment of grammatical gender to animals and numerous non-human entities in Ayoreo, a Zamucoan language of Paraguay, is associated with the role the protagonists played in myth (Ciucci 2021, and references therein). The same principle applies to most non-human entities in the Campa cosmology (Weiss 1972: 170).

The intrinsic unity of humans and animals is reflected in their integration into the classificatory kinship system. The Vaupés River Basin Linguistic area is a case in point. Languages spoken in this area include the East Tucanoan languages Tucano, Wanano, Desano, Piratapuya, Tuyuca (and a few others), and just one Arawak language, Tariana. Speakers of these languages participate in the traditional exogamous marriage network, which ensures obligatory multilingualism. According to the main principle of linguistic exogamy, one can only marry someone who speaks a different language (see Aikhenvald 2002, 2015: 73–82, and references therein). The classificatory kinship system is the basis for interactions and social relations between the members of the marriage network within the Vaupés River Basin Linguistic Area – as for many other Amazonian groups; kinship system is of Dravidian type (based on cross-cousin marriage). In traditional stories, animals – especially mammals – interact as humans would. They refer to each other as *naí*, a marriageable cousin (e.g., mother's brother's child; see, for instance, Aikhenvald 2003: 513). This is a feature shared by other groups across the region. Similar phenomena were described by Rosengren (2006) for the Matsigenka, and Crocker (1985) for the Macro-Jê-speaking Bororo, within the framework of totemism.

Animals share their essence with humans – and are believed to have been "people-like" at the beginning of it all, but they are to be kept apart. A reason for twin infanticide – a prominent feature of many Amazonian groups, from the Yanomami in the north to the Sorowaha in the south – is "to affirm human distinctiveness vis-à-vis animals" (Marroquín and Haight 2017: 263, Stephen Hugh-Jones p.c.): multiple births are frequently observed among animals, and twins and triplets are considered animal-like and non-quite human (see also Ball and Hill 1996: 856 on an association between twins and wild animals). A twin can be conceptualized as an unwanted and unpredictable "double" – as one dangerous in a society permeated with ambiguous entities which appear in different disguise. We turn to this in Section 2.2.

The ambiguous figure of a Trickster-Creator is another case in point. Across Amazonia, this powerful being combines human and non-human properties. This is reminiscent of the "trickster" among the Kalapalo of the Xingu region in Brazil discussed by Basso (1987), and the grotesque creators across Amerindian domain (Lagrou 2006). The general analytic framework of the concept of "trickster" goes back to Radin (1972 (1956)). Among the Tariana of the Vaupés River Basin, the Trickster-Creator, *Yapi-riku-ri* (lit. bone-LOCATIVE-NOMINALIZER, 'the one on the bone') is often represented as a bird *Wanali* 'carará bird' (*Anhinga Anhinga*) and referred to as *Wanali Yapirikuri*. The figure of *Yapirikuri* shares numerous features with *Iñápi-riku-li* 'Made-from-bone' of the Baniwa of Içana-Kurripako groups (who speak a closely related language). The Trickster-Creator is "an omniscient, powerful being who always anticipates the treachery and deceit of other beings" (Hill 2009: xi) and never offers humans anything in a direct way. For example, to obtain tobacco, the daughter of the Creator has to send her son to Wanali, who then feeds it to him and makes him vomit. The tobacco plant sprouts out of his vomit, and this is how the people obtain the desired goods. Nothing is straightforward – and this takes us to a further aspect of perspectivism: the change of shape or outer covering, disguising or revealing the underlying nature of an entity.

2.2 "Entering the skin": The language of Amazonian disguise

As Carlin (2018: 315) put it, "reading the oral traditions of Amazonian peoples, one runs the gauntlet of trying to determine whether a given protagonist is really that which is expressed by the nominal, that is, is Jaguar really a jaguar or perhaps a spirit in jaguar clothes?".

Transformations and interactions between double, or multiple, realizations of the entity are reflected in the multiple identities of powerful shamans – see, for instance, Lima (1996) on shamans-peccaries among the Juruna of the Xingu region, Reichel-Dolmatoff (1985) on the double nature of tapir as a spirit, and Wright (2013) on jaguar-shamans in Northwest Amazonia.

Amazonian languages employ a number of grammatical mechanisms to express the process of transformation, from one visual form to another. In Carlin's (2018: 316) words,

> built into the Cariban languages, however, is a grammatical truth-tracking system that allows us to know whether a protagonist is in essence that expressed in the noun – for example, jaguar – or whether s/he is intrinsically something else entirely, and simply appearing in jaguar clothes having undergone a transformation of some sort. Such nominal marking for transformation of state has been termed 'similative' or 'facsimile'.

Across the Cariban languages, the meaning of a similative marker is "being for all intents and purposes X but not in essence so" (Carlin 2004: 124). The form is *-me* (or *-pe*) across the family. For instance, the Trio form *wïtoto* means "a human being". If marked with *-me*, the resulting *wïtoto-me* refers to "a manifestly but not inherently a human being" (Carlin 2004: 123–130, 2006: 328–330). The suffix is always used to describe a transient state, especially in constructions involving transformations. An example from Trio is in Example (1).[3]

(1)   kaikui-me   tëmetae   *Trio*
      jaguar-SIMIL   he.transformed
      'He transformed into a jaguar.'

Mawayana, a moribund Arawak language, spoken by a few elders in Trio and Waiwai-speaking villages, has developed a suffix with a similar meaning, out of its own resources. This is illustrated in (2).

(2)   waata-ni   r-ayãd̃ĩyã   *Mawayana*
      oppossum-SIMIL   3sg-transform.PAST
      'He changed into an oppossum.'

The meanings and the functions of the suffix -*ni* in Mawayana mirror those contexts in Trio and in Waiwai where transformations are seen to have occurred between the world of humans and that of spirits in animal disguise.

A transformation from one visual form into another involves entering a "skin" or "clothing". Numerous Amazonian languages with extensive systems of classifiers have a special form for extended piece of cloth which can refer to an "outward appearance" in transformative contexts.

The Tariana classifier -*maka* 'extended piece of cloth' is the case in point. The classifier itself goes back to an independent root Proto-Arawak *-*maka* 'hammock, clothing, flat item'. Incidentally, this is cognate to the well-known word *hammock*, first attested in English in 1555, "a hanging bed, consisting of a large piece of canvas, netting, etc. suspended by cords at both ends; used especially by sailors on board ship, also in hot climates or seasons on land". The word stems from Spanish *hamaca* (first attested in 1519), from the Taino language of Hispaniola, the oldest recorded language of the Arawak family. This form reflects the proto-Arawak root -*maka* 'stretch of cloth; clothing; hammock' and a dummy prefix *(h)a-* (Aikhenvald 2015: 64).

To describe someone changing their outer appearance, one would say (3). This is a way of referring to a person taking on the outer appearance, or entering

---

3 1, 2, 3 – first, second, third person; CL classifier; FOC.A/S focussed subject; PAST past (no abbreviation), sg singular, sgnf singular non-feminine, SIMIL similative, PRES.VIS present visual, REM.PAST.REP remote past reported, REM.PAST.VIS remote past visual, TOP.NON.A/S topical non-subject.

the 'clothing', of an evil spirit. The example comes from a story cast in remote past reported evidential.

(3)   iñe-maka   dhe-pidana   *Tariana*
      evil.spirit-CL:CLOTH   3sgnf+enter.enclosed.space-REM.PAST.REP
      'He took on the appearance of an evil spirit.' (lit. entered the clothing of an evil spirit)

In contrast, if someone changes their nature and becomes something else in their essence, the classifier for 'clothing' is no longer needed. The Tariana are now devout Catholics (Catholicism has been established in the area since the late 19th century). Example (4) describes what happened to a former priest, who subsequently got married and left the priesthood. The man entered 'evil-spirit-hood' for ever – he had changed his nature and not just the outer shape and covering. The speaker had seen the former priest marry and become an evil spirit, hence the use of the remote past visual evidential. Tariana has five evidentials – visual, nonvisual, inferred, assumed, and reported (Aikhenvald 2003: 293–310).

(4)   iñe   dhe-na   *Tariana*
      evil.spirit 3sgnf+enter.enclosed.space-REM.PAST.VIS
      'He has entered evil-spirithood.'

As is typical across the Amazonian northwest, Tariana shamans are known to have the potential of transforming themselves into a jaguar which is not "just" outer covering. A jaguar is their intrinsic "double" (in the sense of Lima 1996) and a facet of their nature (a comprehensive discussion of jaguar-shamans is in Wright 2013). This was described as (5) (from a story cast in the remote past reported evidential).

(5)   yawi   dhe-pidana   *Tariana*
      jaguar 3sgnf+enter.enclosed.space-REM.PAST.REP
      'He became a jaguar; entered jaguar-hood.'

We thus have a grammatical mechanism to express the two facets of transformations. A transformation which involves taking on the visible features, or 'clothing', of something else involves the classifier for 'clothing'. A transformation which involves entering another essence does not require a mention of clothing. The jaguar in Example (5) is the shaman himself, not just an outer appearance.

    Seeing things differently from different perspectives is reflected in another construction in Tariana, which appears to be unique across Amazonian languages.

This involves double marking of syntactic function on a noun phrase. In each instance the noun phrase has a case-marked function in a subordinate clause, and the clause itself is case-marked for a syntactic function in a higher clause. All subordinate clauses in Tariana can take case-markers, especially the marker -*nuku* 'topical non-subject'. The predicate of the topical complement clause is omitted if retrievable from the context. If the subject of a complement clause is contrastive, it can take focussed subject marker -*nhe* followed by -*nuku*, thus creating the situation of a double marking of syntactic function on one noun phrase. The most typical instance of such double marking involves the context "seeing something as something else" when a human's perception is contrasted to that of a shaman or a powerful spirit. The omitted predicate – understood from the general context of disguise and "other's" perspective – is the verb 'see/look'. This is illustrated with Example (6). Square brackets indicate the scope of case marking (see also Aikhenvald 2003: 160–163).

(6) [[iñe-nhe]-nuku]   hemali-pidana   *Tariana*
     [evil.spirit-FOC.A/S]-TOP.NON.A/S] piquiá.fruit-REM.PAST.REP
     'For the evil spirit (looking) it was piquiá fruit.'
     [[chiãli-nhe]-nuku]   mawali-pidana
     [[man-FOC.A/S]-TOP.NON.A/S] snake-REM.PAST.REP
     'For the man (looking) it was a snake.'

In day-to-day conversations, this "perspectivist" construction is used to refer to differences in perception of what one is exposed to, such as different time zones. In Example (7), from a WhatsApp message, the speaker is commenting on the fact that it is night for him in Brazil, and morning for me in Australia.

(7) wha-nhe-nuku   de:pi-naka
     [[1pl-FOC.A/S]-TOP.NON.A/S] night-PRES.VIS
     phia-nhe-nuku   halite-naka
     [[2sg-FOC.A/S]-TOP.NON.A/S] morning-PRES.VIS
     'For us, it is night, for you, it is morning.'

The statement in (7) refers to different perspectives and different time-frames available to different perceivers. This can be seen as an extension of the "perspectivist" double case construction, adjusted to the current communicative needs of the speakers. In each instance, what is seen as one thing by one turns out to be perceived as something else by another.

The double nature of entities can only be discerned by a select few (see Rivière 1994, Wright 2013). The effects of transformations of one visible form into another and the capacity to tease apart the essence and the outer "covering" relate to the shamanic powers. A powerful shaman or a spirit will be able to see what a common human cannot – the human essence of those in non-human disguise, or the other way around. The power of access to visual information correlates with manipulating evidentials, and the ways in which one perceives things.

Evidentiality – grammatical marking of information source – is a common feature of many Amazonian languages (see Aikhenvald 2015: 248–78, for an overview). In Carlin's (2018: 316) words,

> source of information, and in particular visual input, as well as speaker's attitude towards the information given in an utterance is paramount. [. . .] The Cariban languages both afford us, or indeed even demand, a great deal of specification, precision and clarity of reference to states of being, knowledge and source of information.

Obligatory expression of how one knows things in numerous Amazonian languages is a correlate of a requirement of being precise in expressing the information source (see, for instance, Carlin 2018, Eberhard 2018, Stenzel and Gomez-Imbert 2018, Barnes 1984, and a summary in Aikhenvald 2015: 276–278 and 2021: 192–209). The shaman is licensed to use the visual evidential when talking about their own prophetic dreams, their own actions, and events in the spirit world. A common mortal is not – and if they do so, they make themselves vulnerable to potential accusations of hidden access to unseen powers. Across Amazonia, shamanic actions and spirit attacks are described by common mortals as unseen (in contrast to the actions of common mortals, including a priest in Example 3).

Precision in how one knows things can be contrasted by the apparent lack thereof in another domain. A notable feature that sets Amazonian cultures apart from those of the Andean peoples is the consistent lack of a large system of number words, and the lack of a counting routine (see a summary in Aikhenvald 2015: 355–357, Wojtylak 2020). Most Amazonian languages have a small set of lexical numbers, typically, one, two and three. Larger numbers tend to be borrowed. Quite a few languages do not seem to have had a counting system before contact with Europeans. Counting was simply not a cultural practice. What has been reinterpreted as 'one' used to mean 'be alone', as appears to have been the case in Jarawara (Dixon 2004: 559–560, 2012: 71–73), Xavante (a Jê language), and also Matsigenka and other Campa languages (Johnson 2003: 153, Mihas 2015) and Sirionó, a Tupí-Guaraní language of Bolivia (Holmberg 1985: 121), to name a few (see also Aikhenvald 2015: 349–355). What was reinterpreted as 'two' used to mean 'be a pair' as in Jarawara, an Arawá language, or 'be the same', as in Jabutí, a member of the small Jabutí-Arikapu family from Brazil; and so on. The Hixkaryana, speakers of a Cariban language, are reported to use their three basic number words *towenyxa* 'one, alone, singly', *asako* 'two, a couple or so' and *osorwawo* 'three, a few' 'without precision as to quantity' (Derbyshire 1985: 1). The vague application of counting is reflected in the Tariana origin myths: the ancestors of the Tariana – grandchildren of Thunder who emerged out of the drops of his blood – are alternatively referred to as two or three even within the same narrative.

Absence of a counting system and a counting routine does not imply lack of cognitive ability to differentiate quantities. In contrast to speakers of European and Andean languages with their exact counting systems, the Mundurukú, speakers of a Tupí language in northern Amazonia (Brazil), do not have a counting routine; there are no native number words beyond five, and the words translatable as 'one', 'two' or 'three' do not refer to exact quantities (much like the quantifier *couple* in English which may extend to three or more items). A well-known study by a team of psychologists (Pica et al. 2004), directed towards the Mundurukú, led to the conclusion that the people in fact do "have a capacity to mentally represent very large numbers of up to 80 dots, far beyond their naming range, and do not confuse numbers with other variables such as size and density". In other words, "sophisticated numerical competence can be present in the absence of the well-developed lexicon of number words". This competence allows any Mundurukú, be it a bilingual or a monolingual adult, or a young child who never learnt any formal arithmetic, to spontaneously perform addition, subtraction, and comparison of quantities. All humans have an innate capacity to perceive different numbers and different quantities, and ultimately to count. The lack of "crystallized" terms for discrete numbers in many Amazonian languages can be seen a gap in the inventory of cultural items (further discussion of number words and counting systems across Amazonia and other regions, and further references, are in Aikhenvald 2015: 350–359 and Dixon 2012: 71–80). The existence of perceivable gaps could also be the reason why Spanish and Portuguese counting systems are quickly mastered and used by the Amazonian peoples, once exact counting becomes a necessity – for instance, in situations where the use of money is important, or quantities of land and property are disputed, or the exact age of a person has to be indicated for the national census or the issuance of identity cards and old age pensions.

Approximation and deliberate vagueness in approaches to quantity among Amazonians are the reverse of the cultural requirement for precision in how one knows things. One is precise in delineating the source of knowledge – where lack of precision may lead to dangerous accusations. But one remains vague where there is no need to be explicit. Could this be considered another facet of perspectivism at large, across the whole of Amazonia? This is a question for further study.

3 Disguise and transformations: The language of Amazonian perspectivism

Amazonia is undoubtedly the locus of almost unprecedented linguistic and cultural diversity, paralleled only by the island of New Guinea. And yet we can trace a few typically Amazonian phenomena, the common threads which transcend the boundaries of distinct languages and cultures. Among these are the shared ontological stance known as Amazonian perspectivism – the underlying primordial unity of humans and other entities. This is reflected in the choice of linguistic features – genders and classifiers. The transformation of a visual form and its disguise are mirrored in the concept of clothing or outer skin visible – albeit in different representations – to those who have special powers of seeing. The double, or even multiple, nature of entities – including jaguar-shamans and peccary-shamans – is expressed through a number of grammatical means. These include similative markers, specific classifiers, and an unusual double case-construction expressing multiple perspectives for multiple perceivers. The requirement to be precise in how one talks about what one knows permeates Amazonian cultures, alongside its opposite: the vagueness and deliberate lack of precision in determining quantities via poorly developed systems of traditional number words.

The intricate fabrics of traditional languages offer insights into the ways people conceptualize the world around them. The common threads of Amazonian perspectivism form part and parcel of the rich mosaic of concepts, narratives, and communication patterns which can still be documented before they slide into oblivion.

References

Adelaar, Willem F. H. 2000. La diversidad lingüística y la extinción de las lenguas. In Francisco Queixalós & Odile Renault-Lescure (eds.), *As línguas amazônicas hoje*, 29–38. São Paulo: IRD.

Adelaar, Willem F. H. 2004. *The languages of the Andes*. Cambridge: Cambridge University Press.

Adelaar, Willem F. H. 2006. The Quechua impact on Amuesha, an Arawak language of the Peruvian Amazon. In Alexandra Y. Aikhenvald & R. M. W. Dixon (eds.), *Grammars in contact*, 290–312. Oxford: Oxford University Press.

Aikhenvald, Alexandra Y. 2002. *Language contact in Amazonia*. Oxford: Oxford University Press.

Aikhenvald, Alexandra Y. 2003. *A grammar of Tariana, from north-west Amazonia*. Cambridge: Cambridge University Press.

Aikhenvald, Alexandra Y. 2015. *The languages of the Amazon.* Oxford: Oxford University Press.
Aikhenvald, Alexandra Y. 2021. The ways of speaking and the means of knowing. The Tariana of north-west Amazonia. In Alexandra Y. Aikhenvald, R. M. W. Dixon & Nerida Jarkey (eds.), *The integration of language and society*, 175–214. Oxford: Oxford University Press.
Aikhenvald, Alexandra Y. 2022. The Amazon basin. Linguistic areas and language contact. In Salikoko S. Mufwene & Anna María Escobar (eds.), *The Cambridge handbook of language contact*, 232–60. Cambridge: Cambridge University Press.
Aikhenvald, Alexandra Y., R. M. W. Dixon & Nerida Jarkey. 2021. The integration of language and society. A cross-linguistic perspective. In Alexandra Y. Aikhenvald, R. M. W. Dixon & Nerida Jarkey (eds.), *The integration of language and society*, 1–57. Oxford: Oxford University Press.
Aikhenvald, Alexandra Y. & Anne Storch. 2013. Perception and cognition in typological perspective. In Alexandra Y. Aikhenvald & Anne Storch (eds.), *Perception and cognition in language and culture*, 1–46. Leiden: Brill.
Ball, Helen L. & Catherine M. Hill. 1996. Reevaluating "twin infancitide". *Current Anthropology* 37. 856–863.
Barnes, Janet. 1984. Evidentials in the Tuyuca verb. *International Journal of American Linguistics* 50. 255–271.
Basso, Ellen B. 1987. *In favor of deceit. A study of tricksters in an Amazonian society.* Tucson: The University of Arizona Press.
Birchall, Joshua. 2014. Verbal argument marking patterns in South American languages. In Loretta O'Connor & Pieter Muysken (eds.), *The Native Languages of South America*, 223–249. Cambridge: Cambridge University Press.
Carlin, Eithne B. 2004. *A grammar of Trio, a Cariban language of Suriname.* Frankfurt: Peter Lang.
Carlin, Eithne B. 2006. Feeling the need. The borrowing of Cariban functional categories into Mawayana (Arawak). In Alexandra Y. Aikhenvald and R. M. W. Dixon (eds.), *Grammars in contact. A cross-linguistic* typology, 313–332. Oxford: Oxford University Press.
Carlin, Eithne B. 2011. Nested identities in the Southern Guyana-Suriname corner. In Alf Hornborg & Jonathan D. Hill (eds.), *Ethnicity in ancient Amazonia*, 225–236. Denver: University Press of Colorado.
Carlin, Eithne B. 2018. Evidentiality and the Cariban languages. In Alexandra Y. Aikhenvald (ed.), *The Oxford handbook of evidentiality*, 315–332. Oxford: Oxford University Press.
Caspar, Franz. 1956. *Tupari.* London: Bell.
Ciucci, Luca. 2020. Matter borrowing, pattern borrowing and typological rarities in the Gran Chaco of South America. *Morphology* 30 (4). 283–310.
Ciucci, Luca. 2021. How grammar and culture interact in Zamucoan. In Alexandra Y. Aikhenvald, R. M. W. Dixon & Nerida Jarkey (eds.), *The integration of language and society*, 235–287. Oxford: Oxford University Press.
Comrie, Bernard, Lúcia Golluscio, Hebe González & Alejandra Vidal. 2010. El Chaco como área lingüística. In Zarina Estrada Fernández & Ramón Arzapalo (eds.), *Estudios de lenguas amerindias 2: Lenguas indígenas*, 88–130. Hermosillo: Universidad de Sonora.
Costa, Luiz & Carlos Fausto. 2010. The return of the animists. Recent studies in Amazonian ontologies. *Religion and Society: Advances in Research* 1. 89–109.
Crevels, Mily & Hein van der Voort. 2008. The Guaporé-Mamoré region as a linguistic area. In Pieter Muysken (ed.), *From linguistic areas to areal linguistics*, 151–179. Amsterdam & Philadelphia: John Benjamins.

Crocker, Jon Christopher. 1985. *Vital souls: Bororo cosmology, natural symbolism, and shamanism*. Tucson, AZ: University of Arizona Press.

Derbyshire, Desmond C. 1985. *Hixkaryana and linguistic typology*. Dallas: SIL and the University of Texas at Arlington.

Derbyshire, Desmond C. 1987. Morphosyntactic areal characteristics of Amazonian languages. *International Journal of American Linguistics* 53. 311–326.

Derbyshire, Desmond C. & Geoffrey K. Pullum. 1986. Introduction. In Desmond C. Derbyshire & Geoffrey K. Pullum (eds.), *Handbook of Amazonian languages*, Vol. 1, 1–28. Berlin: De Gruyter Mouton.

Descola, Philippe. 2005. *Par-delà nature et culture*. Paris: Gallimard.

Dixon, R. M. W. 2004. *The Jarawara language of southern Amazonia*. Oxford: Oxford University Press.

Dixon, R. M. W. 2012. *Basic Linguistic Theory*, Vol. 3: *Further grammatical topics*. Oxford: Oxford University Press.

Dixon. R. M. W. & Alexandra Y. Aikhenvald. 1999. Introduction. In R. M. W. Dixon & Alexandra Y. Aikhenvald (eds.), *The Amazonian languages*, 1–22. Cambridge: Cambridge University Press.

Eberhard, David M. 2018. Evidentiality in Nambikwara languages. In Alexandra Y. Aikhenvald (ed.), *The Oxford handbook of evidentiality*, 333–356. Oxford: Oxford University Press.

Echeverri, Juan Alvaro. 1997. *The people of the center of the world. A study in culture, history and orality in the Colombian Amazon*. New York: New School for Social Research dissertation.

Epps, Patience. 2020. Amazonian diversity and its sociocultural correlates. In Mily Crevels & Pieter Muysken (eds.), *Language dispersal, diversification, and contact. A global perspective*, 275–290. Oxford: Oxford University Press.

Fontaine, Laurent. 2008. *Paroles d'échange et règles sociales chez les indiens yucuna d'Amazonie colombienne*. Paris: L'Harmattan.

González, Hebe A. 2015. El Chaco como área lingüística: una evaluación de los rasgos fonológicos. In Bernard Comrie & Lucía Golluscio (eds.), *Language contact and documentation*, 193–266. Berlin: De Gruyter Mouton.

Green, Lesley & David R. Green. 2013. *Knowing the day, knowing the world. Engaging Amerindian thought in public archaeology*. Tucson: The University of Arizona Press.

Halbmayer, Ernst. 2012. Debating animism, perspectivism and the construction of ontologies. *Indiana* 29. 9–23.

Heine, Bernd & Derek Nurse. 2008. Introduction. In Bernd Heine & Derek Nurse (eds.), *A linguistic geography of Africa*, 1–14. Cambridge: Cambridge University Press.

Hemming, John. 1978a. *Red Gold. The conquest of the Brazilian Indians*. Cambridge, MA: Harvard University Press.

Hemming, John. 1978b. *The search for El Dorado*. London: Book Club Associates.

Hill, Jonathan D. 2009. *Made-from-bone. Trickster myths, music, and history from the Amazon*. Urbana and Chicago: University of Illinois Press.

Holmberg, Allan R. 1985. *Nomads of the long bow. The Sirionó of eastern Bolivia*. Prospect Heights, IL: Waveland Press.

Johnson, Allen. 2003. *Families of the forest. The Matsigenka Indians of the Peruvian Amazon*. Berkeley: University of California Press.

Key, Mary Ritchie. 1993. Situación actual, tareas y problemas de la clasificación de las lenguas indígenas en Suramérica. In María Luisa Rodríguez de Montes (ed.), *Estado actual de la clasificación de las lenguas indígenas de Colombia*, 25–48. Santafé de Bogotá: Insttuto Caro y Cuervo.

Lagrou, Elsje. 2006. Laughing at Power andf the Power of Laughing in Cashinawa narratives and performance. *Tipití: Journal of the Society for the Anthropology of Lowland South America* 4. 33–56.

Lewy, Matthias. 2012. Different "seeing" – similar "hearing". Ritual and sound among the Pemón (Gran Sabana/Venezuela). *Indiana* 29. 53–71.

Lima, Tánia Stolze. 1996. O dois e seu múltiplo. Reflexões sobre o perspectivismo em uma cosmologia tupi. *Mana* 2. 21–47.

Loukotka, Chestmír. 1968. *Classification of South American Indian languages*. Los Angeles: Latin American Centre, University of California.

Marroquin, Andrés & Colleen Haight. 2017. Twin-killing in some traditional socieities. An economic perspective. *Journal of Bioeconomics* 19. 261–279.

Martius, Karl F. P. von. 1867. *Beiträge zur Ethnographie und Sprachenkunde Amerikas, zumal Brasiliens*. 2 Volumes. Friedrich Fleischer: Leipzig.

Mihas, Elena I. 2015. *A grammar of Alto Perené (Arawak)*. Berlin: De Gruyter Mouton.

Payne, David Lawrence. 1990. Morphological characteristics of Lowland South American languages. In Doris L. Payne (ed.), *Amazonian linguistics. Studies in Lowland South American languages*, 213–241. Austin: University of Texas Press.

Pica, Pierre, Cathy Lemer, Véronique Izard & Stalislas Dehaene. 2004. Exact and approximate arithmetic in an Amazonian Indigene group. *Science* 306. 499–503.

Radin, Paul. 1972 (1956). *The trickster. A study in Native American Indian mythology*. New York: Philosophical Library.

Reichel-Dolmatoff, Gerardo. 1985. Tapir avoidance in the Colombian Northwest Amazon. In Gary Urton (ed.), *Animal myths and metaphors in South America*, 107–144. Salt Lake City: University of Utah Press.

Rivière, Peter 1994. WYSINWYG in Amazonia. *Journal of the Anthropological Society of Oxford* 25. 255–262.

Roe, Peter. 1982. *The cosmic zygote. Cosmology in the Amazon Basin*. New Brunswick: Rutgers University Press.

Rosengren, Dan 2006. Transdimensional relations. On human-spirit interaction in the Amazon. *Journal of the Royal Institute (N.S.)* 12. 803–816.

Seki, Lucy. 1999. The Upper Xingu as an incipient linguistic area. In R. M. W. Dixon & Alexandra Y. Aikhenvald (eds.), *The Amazonian languages*, 417–430. Cambridge: Cambridge University Press.

Seki, Lucy. 2010. Alto Xingu. Uma sociedade multilíngue? In Bruna Franchetto (ed.), *Alto Xingu. Uma sociedade multilíngue*, 57–86. Rio de Janeiro: Museu do Índio.

Stenzel, Kristine & Elsa Gomez-Imbert. 2018. Evidentiality in Tukanoan languages. In Alexandra Y. Aikhenvald (ed.), *The Oxford Handbook of evidentiality*, 357–87. Oxford: Oxford University Press.

Tovar, Antonio & C. L. De Tovar. 1984. *Catálogo de las lenguas de América del Sur*. Madrid: Editorial Gredos.

Urton, Gary. 1985. Introduction. In Gary Urton (ed.), *Animal myths and metaphors in South America*, 3–12. Salt Lake City: University of Utah Press.

Valenzuela, Pilar M. 2015. ¿Que tan "amazónicas" son las lenguas kawapana? Contacto con las lenguas centro-andinas y elementos para una área lingüística intermedia. *Lexus* XXXIX: 5–26.

Vanzolini, Marina & Pedro Cesarino. 2018. Perspectivism. *Oxford Bibliographies Online*. New York: Oxford University Press. [https://www.oxfordbibliographies.com/view/docu ment/obo-9780199766567/obo-9780199766567-0083.xml] (accessed 12 June 2021).

Viveiros de Castro, Eduardo B. 1998. Cosmological deixis and Amerindian perspectivism, *Journal of the Royal Anthropological Institute* (N.S.) 4 (3). 469–488.

Viveiros de Castro, Eduardo B. 2004a. Exchanging perspectives. The transformation of objects into subjects in Amerindian ontologies. *Common Knowledge* 10. 463–484.

Viveiros de Castro, Eduardo B. 2004b. Perspectival anthropology and the method of controlled equivocation. *Tipití: Journal of the Society for the Anthropology of Lowland South America* 2. 3–22.

Weiss, Gerard. 1972. Campa cosmoplogy. *Ethnology* 11. 157–172.

Wise, Mary Ruth. 2011. Rastros desconcertantes de contactos entre idiomas y culturas a lo largo de los contrafuertes orientales de los Andes del Perú. In Willem F. Adelaar, Pilar Valenzuela Bismarck & Roberto Zaqiquiey Biondi (eds.), *Estudios sobre lenguas Andinas y Amazónicas. Homenaje a Rodolfo Cerrón-Palomino*, 305–316. Lima: Fondo Editorial Ponfiticia. Universidad Católica del Peru.

Wojtylak, Katarzyna I. 2015. Fruits for animals. Hunting avoidance speech style in Murui (Witoto, Northwest Amazonia). In *Proceedings of the 41st Annual Meeting of the Berkeley Linguistic Society. University of California at Berkeley*, 545–561.

Wojtylak, Katarzyna I. 2020. *A grammar of Murui (Bue), a Witotoan language of Northwest Amazonia*. Leiden: Brill.

Wojtylak, Katarzyna I. 2021. Links between language and society among the Murui of north-west Amazonia. In Alexandra Y. Aikhenvald, R. M. W. Dixon & Nerida Jarkey (eds.), *The integration of language and society*, 215–234. Oxford: Oxford University Press.

Wright, Robin M. 2013. *Mysteries of the Jaguar shamans of the Northwest Amazon*. Lincoln: University of Nebraska Press.

Zamponi, Raoul. 2020. Some pre-contact widespread lexical forms in the languages of Greater Amazonia. *International Journal of American Linguistics* 86. 527–573.

Alan Rumsey, Ruth Singer & Matt Tomlinson

16 Recent research on language and culture in Australia and Oceania

In this chapter we identify prominent strands of current research on language and culture in Australia and Oceania. The themes are: 1. Australia's remarkably elaborate systems of kin classification, and some new developments in the study of them; 2. multilingualism in Indigenous Australia, the complex patterns of alternation among the languages in the course of people's everyday interaction, and their significance for questions of social and territorial identity; 3. the emergence of more collaborative approaches to producing, storing and accessing Indigenous digital heritage; 4. new studies of Indigenous Australian children's language socialization, and the associated rise of new languages resulting from interactions between northern Australian creole English (Kriol) and Indigenous languages; 5. new studies of children's language socialization in various parts of Oceania and the relation between their findings and those of other anthropological studies there; 6. the political effects of language ideologies across multiple scales of interaction in the Solomon Islands, Tokelau and Papua New Guinea; 7. practices of translation in Christianity within Oceania, and the ways in which the process of translation models other kinds of transformation; 8. the rise of new media and communication technologies in Oceania, and studies of the social changes prompted by and reflected in their use. The new work on these topics is notable for the way in which it draws on long traditions of close attention to language's imbrication with culture, and points to new directions for research.

1 Introduction

In this chapter we discuss several strands of recent research on language and culture in Australia and Oceania by linguists and linguistic anthropologists. "Oceania" here refers to the the islands of the central and southern Pacific,

Alan Rumsey, The Australian National University, Canberra/Australia,
e-mail: alan.rumsey@anu.edu.au
Ruth Singer, University of Melbourne/Australia, e-mail: rsinger@unimelb.edu.au
Matt Tomlinson, The Australian National University, Canberra/Australia,
e-mail: matt.tomlinson@anu.edu.au

https://doi.org/10.1515/9783110726626-016

including the regions known as Micronesia, Melanesia, Polynesia. The sections on Australia within the chapter deal exclusively with Indigenous Australia, mainly because it has been the focus of most of the research on language and culture that has been done within Australia by linguists and linguistic anthropologists. Of the bodies of research that we discuss, three are focussed on Australia, three on Oceania, and one pertains to both regions. Any such selection of topics and researchers is bound to be arbitrary to a certain extent – especially in this case where it pertains to such a vast region and range of relevant literature. Our main basis for selection of topics to include is that there has recently been much lively discussion of them, either as new research topics or in ways that take them in interesting new directions.

We begin with a topic of the latter kind: Australia's remarkably elaborate, anthropologically renowned systems of kin classification, and some new developments in the study of them. Then we turn to another remarkable aspect of the Australian Aboriginal language scene: the high rates of multilingualism among their speakers, the complex patterns of alternation among the languages in the course of people's everyday interaction, and their significance for questions of social and territorial identity. This is followed by a discussion of collaborative approaches to the management of Indigenous intangible heritage. These new approaches are motivated by the experiences of Indigenous and non-Indigenous people working together to document and revitalize Indigenous languages, and music and dance traditions.

Next we turn to a topic on which there has been extensive new research within the past decade within both Aboriginal Australia and Oceania: children's language acquisition and socialization. Within the Australian field this links up to the topic of kinship, in that some of the language-acquisition research has focused on Aboriginal children's acquisition of kin terms. It also relates to the topic of multilingualism, in that all of the environments in which children are learning Aboriginal languages are multilingual ones, in some cases resulting in the rise of new hybrid languages that incorporate features of the multiple ones that children are exposed to, and develop in ways that are actively shaped by the children.

An interestingly comparable process has taken place in one of the research settings that are discussed in the next section of the chapter, on children's language socialization in Oceania: Rapa Nui (a.k.a. Easter Island), where indigenous children are nowadays exposed to both the (Polynesian) Rapa Nui language and Chilean Spanish. Likewise, an in-depth study of children's language socialization in the Marshall Islands shows how children play an active role not only in the reproduction of a particular way of life, but in its transformation.

The other three chapter sections on Oceania all focus on instances of a phenomenon that has been a central focus of linguistic anthropology in recent decades: "language ideology", that is, more-or-less shared (but frequently also contested) bodies of common-sense notions about the nature of language in the world (Schieffelin et al. 1998, Gal and Irvine 2019). Topics treated include: ideologies held by middle-class speakers of Pijin, the lingua franca of the Solomon Islands, and their political effects; ideologies about the linguistic dimensions of authority that are tied up with perceived differences between English, Samoan and Tokelauan, the indigenous Polynesian language of New Zealand's territory of Tokelau; ideas about the importance of listening for self-determination among inhabitants of the Yopno Valley in Papua New Guinea. This is followed by a discussion of language ideologies in relation to ideologies of mediation and effects of new media, including mobile phones in the Sepik region of Papua New Guinea, texting in Tok Pisin, and Facebook in Tonga.

While this selection of topics can do no more than scratch the surface of recent linguistic-anthropological literature on Indigenous Australia and Oceania, we hope that for anyone interested in exploring that literature and learning more about the scope of such research, our survey will provide some useful starting points.

2 Indigenous Australia

2.1 New research on Australian kinship systems

One of the most striking aspects of Indigenous Australian cultures is the complexity and universal scope of their kinship systems (Dousset 2011). The same terms by which Aboriginal people refer to their immediate family and other close relatives ('father', 'mother', 'uncle', etc.) are also used for an open-ended set of other people who are classified in the same way. One of the main logical principles behind this is the equivalence of siblings of the same sex, both as relatives in their own right and as links to other relatives. So, for example, the brother of my father is also classified as my father, and his children are accordingly classified as my brothers and sisters. By contrast, my father's sister, as his opposite-sex sibling, is treated differently from him as a linking relative (my aunt), and her children are therefore classified differently from those of my father's brother – as my cousins. This principle of the equivalence of same-sex siblings is potentially a very powerful one for creating extensive kin classes. This can be seen, for example, from the fact that the people it treats as my siblings include not only my father's brother's children, but my father's father's brother's son's children, my father's father's father's brother's son's son's children, etc. Likewise for my mother's mother's sister's daughter's children, etc.

Australian Aboriginal kinship systems are by no means unique in these respects. All kinship systems are "classificatory" in grouping people into relational categories, and many of them (especially non-Western ones) make use of the same principles, including the equivalence of same-sex siblings. But in the profusion and composition of their categories, Australian kinship systems include some of the world's most complex ones. They are also unusual in being understood by their users to be universal in scope, that is, capable of fitting any person within a given speaker's social universe into some particular kin category.

Australian kinship systems were extensively studied by anthropologists over most of the twentieth century, to the point where it could be rightly claimed in 1982 by linguist Jeffrey Heath that "the literature on [Australian Aboriginal] kinships systems is vast" and "has now reached the point where the major thrust of research seems to be in collating, organizing and interpreting materials already gathered and published" (Heath 1982: 1). But Heath immediately went on to declare that "such synthesizing is premature" (ibid.). For in the previous few years the first extensive fieldwork had been done in Australia by researchers with training in both linguistics and anthropology whose focus on language and its uses had turned up many other kinds of kin terms and usages besides the ones which had been focused on in previous anthropological accounts.[1]

Particularly striking examples of such usage are the so-called "triangular" or "trirelational" terms. By nature all kin terms involve a relation between two people: the one to whom the term refers – the "referent" – and the one to whom that person is related – the "propositus" or "anchor". So for example when someone says 'my mother', the speaker is the anchor and their mother is the referent. In many Aboriginal languages there are also terms that simultaneously take account of *three* different relations – among the speaker, the referent and the addressee. An example from the Bininj Kunwok language of western Arnhem land is the term *berlunghkowarr*, which means 'my sister, [who is] your mother's elder sister [and] you are my sister's child' (Garde 2013: 97).

During the past two decades, trirelational terms and other such long-unrecognized complexities of Australian kinship systems have been the subject

---

1 For a wide-ranging data base that has been compiled from this literature and earlier sources see [http://www.austkin.net/index.php] (accessed 18 March 2022).

of new research that has benefitted greatly from cross-fertilization between linguistics and anthropology (e.g., McConvell et al. 2018, Green 2019, Gaby 2017). A study of that kind that includes extensive treatment of trirelational kin terms is the one by Murray Garde from which the above example is taken, entitled *"Culture, interaction and person reference in an Australian language"* (Garde 2013). The book is based on over twenty years of fieldwork with Bininj Kunwok speakers. Most studies of Australian kin classification (as elsewhere) are based mainly on elicited data. But given their grounding in subtle aspects of face-to-face interaction, trirelational terms have proven very difficult to study in that way. Drawing on his full fluency in Bininj Kunwok, and interactions with other speakers over many years, Garde was able to note many instances of trirelational terms and other forms of person reference in everyday conversation, and discuss their range of uses with people in their own language. Based on that data, and an analytical framework drawing on the linguistic-anthropological concept of social indexicality, Garde developed one of the most thorough and insightful treatments of person reference anywhere.

An enabling condition of Garde's work is that the Bininj Kunwok region is one of the few anywhere in Australia where Indigenous languages continue to be spoken as the main ones, and are still being learned by children (who figured importantly in his study). The same is true of another locale about 500 km to the west of there – Wadeye, where the Murrinhpatha language is spoken by about 2,500 people of all ages. Over the past 16 years, linguistic research on many different topics has been carried out there by a team of researchers based mainly at the University of Melbourne. One of those researchers, Joe Blythe, is a specialist in conversational interaction, and has studied forms of person reference based on a corpus of over 60 hours of interaction among Murrinhpatha speakers of all ages.

Like Bininj Kunwok, Murrinhpatha has a set of trirelational kin terms in addition to its "ordinary" ones. But it is a much smaller and less comprehensive set than the Bininj Kunwok one, with only eight trirelational terms that are single-word lexical items (Blythe 2018: 441–442), while Bininj Kunwok has approximately 170 of them (Garde 2013: 98). But through close examination of Murrinhpatha conversations, Blythe has turned up what appears to be an alternative version of trirelational kin terms. As elsewhere in Aboriginal Australia, Murrinhpatha speakers show a marked dispreference for the use of personal names. Instead, when an ordinary kin term fails to make it clear who is being referred to, for greater specificity, they regularly use more-or-less improvised multi-word expressions that identify that person in relation to both the speaker and the addressee. As an example of this, Blythe discusses a conversation in which one speaker refers to a woman whose identity he seeks to clarify for his addressee by saying *nekika kaka mamnyewurran*, which means '[she] calls you and me "uncle"', where the speaker and addressee are classificatory brothers (Blythe 2018: 448–449).

Blythe shows that the form of the (single-word) trirelational terms in Murrinhpatha provides good evidence of their having developed out of multi-word expressions such as the one above, and argues, more speculatively, that the same could be true elsewhere in Australia, as "the non-intended outcome of routine conversational practices" (Blythe 2018: 454). Perhaps so, but the resulting semantically and pragmatically complex single-word expressions are salient for their users, not just for their referential specificity and economy, but as a kind of "verbal art" (Garde 2013: 258). For example, when an international delegation from the World Heritage Committee in Paris visited Kakadu National Park in Bininj Kunwok country, their local Aboriginal host Yvonne Margarula in her welcoming address "focused on the complexity of the triadic kinship reference system in her language as an extraordinary example of local intangible cultural heritage" (ibid.: 95).

2.2 Multilingualism

Australia was one of the most multilingual areas in the world before colonization, home to hundreds of small languages, each with fewer than 5,000 speakers. In the absence of lingua francas, multilingualism enabled communication across language areas (Vaughan 2022). In many parts of Australia, Indigenous people are still multilingual in a number of ancestral Indigenous languages, each of which is seen to belong to a different area of land (Rumsey 1993). Contemporary Indigenous multilingualism also involves new languages that emerged since colonization: Australian Kriol, Indigenous varieties of English, and mixed languages which combine new languages with ancestral languages. Indigenous Australian language ecologies also include different modalities such as sign, gesture and sand drawing and different registers such as baby talk and ritual languages.

In the past few decades, approaches to language documentation have broadened from a single–language focus to the documentation of multilingual language ecologies. Projects in northern Australia have shown how the many small Indigenous languages still spoken are supported by a kind of multilingualism known as "small-scale multilingualism". This kind of multilingualism is relatively understudied and is substantially different from the more often studied kind of multilingualism found in migrant communities in largely monolingual nations (Lüpke 2016). In small-scale multilingual contexts, an emphasis on social differentiation via language and language ideologies that value the use of many languages offsets pressures to shift to a single common code. Many languages are used in the same domain, such as home and work, challenging the assumption that separation of domains is required to create a stable kind of societal multilingualism that supports minority languages (Fishman 1967).

In western Arnhem Land, a region of small-scale multilingualism, many languages have only a few hundred speakers and continue to be learned by children growing up in multilingual households. Interviews with community members and analyses of multilingual conversations have identified language practices that may be crucial to the co-existence of many small languages. For example receptive multilingualism is widespread, the use of different languages by interlocutors who understand one another's languages but may not speak them. Surprisingly, people often chose to speak their own language in a conversation, even if they can also speak the language of their interlocutor. Receptive multilingualism allows people who identify with very small languages, spoken by only a few hundred people, to continue using them while living amongst speakers of larger Indigenous languages (Singer and Harris 2016).

In keeping with the findings of Sutton (1997) about Aboriginal Australia in general, in western Arnhem Land, harmonious relations between groups are seen to depend on their social and linguistic differentiation. It has been argued that the intentional cultivation of diversity underpins the continued use of many small languages across sites of small-scale multilingualism around the world (Vaughan and Singer 2018, Evans 2018). Linguistic differentiation may operate at a number of scales. For example clan-level speech varieties of Bininj Kunwok are distinguished by a small set of features (Vaughan, Singer and Garde 2022) as are varieties of a language labeled "Burarra" by linguists (Vaughan 2018). In both cases, differences between the varieties are heard more when group affiliations are relevant to the topic of conversation. Cumulatively, the tendency to differentiate small groups via language seems to have led over time to the great differences between languages that we find in regions of small-scale multilingualism (see also Rumsey 2018, Marley 2020, Sutton 1978).

Another area of research within the study of multilingual language ecologies looks beyond speech to include other modalities: sign, gesture, song and drawing. Alternate sign languages, which are used by people who can hear, are a ubiquitous feature of Indigenous Australian language ecologies (Green and Wilkins 2014). Like gesture, which is less conventionalized than sign, alternate sign languages are used to accompany speech, but may also be used alone when speech is difficult, e.g., across large distances or when speech is culturally proscribed. An example of the latter is that widows traditionally used only sign for up to a year after the death of their husband in central Australia. The use of sign rather than speech creates a sense of "indirectness" which is associated with politeness (Kral and Ellis 2020). Recent work comparing signs across Australian Indigenous communities has found substantial commonalities between signs used in communities with quite different spoken languages (Green and Jorgensen 2021). This suggests that sign can facilitate communication between people who have little in common in their spoken language repertoires.

Green (2014) has analyzed how sign, gesture and drawings made in the sand accompany central Australian women's storytelling. Her research shows how multiple modalities are integrated into a single speech event such as a narrative. In northeast Arnhem Land, there has also been new research on signs used by speakers of Yolngu-matha varieties (Bauer 2014, Adone and Maypilama 2013). Jennifer Green, Elizabeth Marrkilyi Ellis, and Inge Kral recently completed the Western Desert Verbal Arts Project, an ambitious documentation project on sign, gesture, sand drawing, verbal arts, speech styles and respect speech registers among Ngaanyatjarra speakers of the Western Desert region. These aspects of communication are highly valued by Ngaanyatjarra people and Ngaanyatjarra communities are working hard to keep them going across the generations.

The language ecology in the Western Desert allows people to draw on a number of semiotically different modes, engaging the whole body in communication and artistic expression. As Ngaanyatjara linguist Elizabeth Marrkilyi Ellis notes, "[i]t's best to talk in many different ways, not just by words [. . .] It makes it more creative, and it also gives the brain that extra thing, you know" (Ellis et al. 2019: 94). All these different semiotic systems make up the whole that is called *wangkarra* 'communication' in Ngaanyatjara as illustrated by Ellis in Figure 16.1.

Australian Indigenous communities have long celebrated their rich diversity in ways of communicating; multilingual, multivarietal and multimodal. Working with more than one language or modality calls for a collaborative approach to language documentation and the Western Desert Verbal Arts project is an inspiring example of this. Key elements of the project were: Indigenous leadership, productive partnerships across the Ngaanyatjarra Lands and engagement with all generations, including elders and youth. The recordings created during the project capture three-dimensional, dynamic modalities and are archived along with explanatory files. This kind of careful documentation of multilingual language ecologies is of great value to both researchers and communities (see Ellis, Green and Kral 2014, Kral and Ellis 2020, Kral, Green, and Ellis 2020).

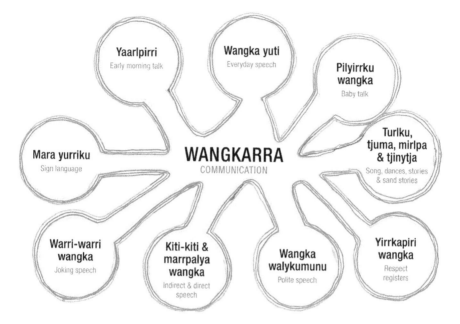

Figure 16.1: The network of communicative practices found in Ngaanyatjarra communities (reprinted with permission from Elizabeth Marrkilyi Ellis (original design) and Christine Bruderlin (artwork)) (Kral and Ellis 2020: 50).

2.3 Collaborative approaches to the management of Indigenous intangible heritage

In response to challenges from Indigenous Australian scholars and activists (Treloyn and Charles 2014), more collaborative approaches to producing, storing and accessing Indigenous digital heritage have developed over the past few decades, changing research practices for the better. Discussions about how to improve research have occurred across the boundaries of disciplines, between linguistics, anthropology, musicology and archival science. The Western Desert Verbal Arts Project is an example of how Indigenous Australian communities and researchers of language and culture have created new ways of working collaboratively. The first work on sign and sand drawing in the Western Desert in the 1930s was stored in researchers' notebooks and collections of recordings with no consideration for community needs (Ellis et al. 2019). As was typical for the time, communities did not even know about the existence of their records for many decades.

Australian researchers of language and music have embraced digital archives as a way to make materials more accessible to both Indigenous communities and scholars. Providing digital material online is one way of repatriating archival materials to communities, often understood to be part of the process of decolonizing disciplines and their archives (Barwick et al. 2019). Even today, Indigenous people are often unable to get access to archived materials made by their ancestors (Croft et al. 2019). On the other hand, Indigenous Australian communities need to be able to control access to their data, so access must be managed and sometimes restricted. Indigenous scholars Clint Bracknell and Kim Scott explain the motivation for the Wirlomin Noongar group to restrict access to a set of archival materials, at least initially, to a group of 100 descendants of the people in the recordings: "The circumstances in which Noongar cultural heritage was decimated demand that language revitalisation be undertaken as part of a process to empower Noongar people. This is possible by starting with a small 'home community' and progressively sharing with ever-widening circles" (Bracknell and Scott 2019: 335). The Noongar are a group of around 20,000 people and their language Noongar is associated with the south-west region of Western Australia.

Bracknell and Scott elaborate that Wirlomin Noongar need to work on the songs and language themselves first to piece them back together, before they can share them more widely with other Noongar and non-Indigenous people. They relate the joy that a group of Wirlomin members feel when they work out, after extensive analysis, that one song is about an eagle. These rewards of scholarship and often the resulting knowledge were once solely the privilege of non-Indigenous researchers but now Indigenous people are claiming their right to do the analysis first:

> The fragmented and incomplete nature of archival records relating to the Noongar language emphasises the need for those within its home community of origin to make corrections, add missing metadata and make informed decisions about their cultural heritage material. In revitalising language by running it through living Wirlomin Noongar bodies, we make ourselves instruments for this deep, spiritual heritage that thousands of generations have entrusted to us in this part of the world.   (Bracknell and Scott 2019: 335)

Bracknell and Scott conclude by emphasizing that the process of renewing archival records independently brings strength and wellbeing to members of their Wirlomin group.

Much of the work that is done now, like the work of the Wirlomin group, creates a circular relationship between communities, researchers and the archives. Digital archives are not just repositories where researchers store materials at the end of a research project, or simply places where material is accessed.

Much research now involves returning archival materials to the community, then enriching the archive with more information about the materials and often new recordings as part of an ongoing documentation cycle. These practices create opportunities for younger generations to learn from archival materials in documentation projects and thus contribute not only to documentation of language and culture but also to revitalization. Festivals and workshops provide opportunities to engage with archival records as a group and promote the renewal and intergenerational transmission of ancestral knowledges (Treloyn and Charles 2014).

Christen points out that archives were traditionally the endpoint of colonial practices that sought to extract, classify, and possess the knowledges of Indigenous people (Christen 2018). Meaningful relations between the archive and communities are thus not inherent to the archive (Brown and Treloyn 2017). In fact, most archives do not currently have the resources to maintain close relationships with communities. As a result, researchers often find themselves acting as intermediaries between Indigenous communities and archives. At times this can be quite an uncomfortable role but regardless, researchers have played a role in helping archives to be more responsive to community needs. The next step is to re-imagine archives as truly relational institutions, which are centered on the relations that Indigenous communities have with their ancestors, their knowledge, and their land.

2.4 Child language

The last fifteen years have seen a burgeoning of studies of Indigenous Australian children's language acquisition and the part it has played in language change. The biggest concentration of the work on language acquisition has been at Wadeye, by a team of seven researchers from Melbourne University focusing on a wide range of topics. These have included Joe Blythe, who has headed a project on Murrinhpatha children's learning of kin terms. That research is innovative in at least two ways. First, while the development of children's understanding of kin relationships and terminology has been studied elsewhere, very little of the research has been focused on systems which are of universal scope in the sense discussed above. The mastery of these systems would seem to present children with special challenges, since the range of people they must learn to classify includes not just a small set of genealogically close relatives, but everyone in the child's social universe.

Another challenge presented by Murrinhpatha kin categories is that they figure in the language not only as words, but in the grammar of the language.

All Murrinhpatha verbs include prefixes that specify the person and number of their subject (and of their object in the case of transitive verbs). The number categories include singular, dual, paucal (for a set of referents which is small but more than two), and plural. Where the referents are people, and there are two or a few of them (i.e., within the dual or paucal category rather than the plural one), the prefix varies in form according to whether the people referred to are related to each other as 'male non-brothers', 'feminine non-siblings', or 'siblings'[2] (Blythe et al. 2020: 669). This is an instance of the integral relationship between kinship and grammar that has been found in many Indigenous Australian languages, and studied under the rubric of "kintax" (Evans 2003).

Working in collaboration with linguistic anthropologist Alice Mitchell, cognitive scientist Péter Rácz and Murrinhpatha speaker Jeremiah Tunmuck,[3] Blythe and his colleagues devised two sets of experimental tasks using pictures of people at Wadeye, and administered them to children of various ages. The first set of tasks tested the extent to which children's assignment of 24 people to kin classes was "correct" (i.e., adult-like). It was found, as predicted, that this correlated directly to the age of the child and to the closeness of their relation to the person in the photo. The second set of tasks tested 39 children's ability to match hypothetical uses of kinship-inflected verbs in reference to particular combinations of people shown in the photos. This too was found to relate directly to the children's age. But unexpectedly, the kinship-based aspects of Murrinhpatha verb morphology turned out not to present any special learning difficulties to the children. The verb morphology is extraordinarily complex in many ways besides its indexing of kin relationships – so much so that people do not fully master it until they are into their late teens, by which time their constant exposure to the universal use of kin terms in everyday life has already equipped them for the mastery of "kintax" (Blythe et al. 2020: 687).

Blythe et al.'s study does not address the question of *how* children gradually master the complexities of the Murrinhpatha kinship system, focusing instead on *how much* they know and can do at various ages, but it breaks new

---

2 Strictly speaking, these three categories do not include all of the logically possible combinations. The authors explain that "[w]hereas 'masculine nonsibling' denotes male-only nonbrothers, 'feminine nonsibling' denotes groups that include at least one female. 'Feminine nonsibling' is the unmarked (default) category, used for reference to families, households, and so forth that are likely to comprise males and females" (Blythe et al. 2020: 669, note 10).

3 Tunmuck has participated in this research both at Wadeye and in Melbourne. In 2018 he gave what was perhaps the first academic seminar at the University of Melbourne to be presented in an Indigenous Australian language: [https://www.dynamicsoflanguage.edu.au/news-and-media/latest-headlines/article/?id=historic-seminar-in-an-indigenous-language] (accessed 18 March 2022).

ground as "the first quantitative experimental study of the acquisition of classi-ficatory kinship principles and the first comprehensive study of the acquisition of kinship-related morphosyntax in any of the world's languages" (Blythe et al. 2020: 687). For addressing the "how" questions, more anthropological ap-proaches are called for, including ethnographic study of children's daily lives and longitudinal analysis of transcribed video recordings of their everyday in-teractions. Fortunately, a wealth of data of those kinds is available through work of others on the Melbourne Murrinhpatha research team. Extensive longi-tudinal video data has been recorded and transcribed by William Forshaw and Lucinda Davidson (Forshaw et al. 2017). Ethnographic study of Murrinhpatha children's interactions with adults and other children has been done by David-son, informed by the "language socialization" approach which treats language learning as part of the more general process by which children become social-ized into particular cultures.[4] This has resulted in an innovative study of eight Wadeye children's emerging sense of social relatedness, alliance and alterity (Davidson 2018).[5]

In addition to long-standing Aboriginal languages such as Murrinhpatha, within the past century another language has arisen over much of northern Australia which is now called "Kriol" (Harris 1993). Kriol is a "mixed" language in that its vocabulary comes mainly from English, while aspects of its grammar and semantics are influenced by widespread features of the pre-existing Aborig-inal languages. In some of the areas where Kriol is spoken, the interaction be-tween it and local languages in the speech of children has given rise to a new generation of mixed languages that draw both on Kriol and the local languages. In comparative terms, such new mixed languages are important because, as Carmel O'Shannessy has put it "they lead to richer understandings of the mech-anisms and outcomes of contact-induced language change in different types of context, and they allow us to examine whether unusual outcomes result from unusual or commonly occurring processes" (O'Shannessy 2020: 326).

Recent Australian research on such languages and processes has contributed greatly to that enrichment. One example is the work of O'Shannessy herself on

---

4 For details about this approach and its relation to the overall field of child language acquisi-tion studies, see this volume, Chapter 2.
5 Other Melbourne University-based Murrinhpatha researchers besides the ones referred to above have included Gillian Wigglesworth, Rachel Nordlinger, Barbara Kelly, and John Mans-field. In addition to the research on children's acquisition of Murrinhpatha at Wadeye, Mel-bourne University has also hosted ground-breaking longitudinal research by Rebecca Defina on the acquisition of another, very different Aboriginal language, Pitjantjatjara, about 1200 km to the south in Central Australia (e.g., Defina 2020).

"Light Warlpiri" (O'Shannessy 2013). Another is the work of Patrick McConvell and Felicity Meakins on Gurindji Kriol (McConvell and Meakins 2005). In a general formulation intended to apply to both of those cases among others, Patrick McConvell observes that

> [c]hildren and teenagers may deliberately choose not to emulate parents or the old language. Instead they select or build a language variety of their own from among the models available. If there is no counter-weight from the old language, then this peer-group talk can form the basis of the language of the rising generation.   (McConvell 2008: 240)

In line with this formulation, Gurindji and Warlpiri children have played an active role in the birth of new languages, in effect creating unified systems out of the alternation between Kriol and Warlpiri or Gurindji that they were exposed to in the speech of adults. This seems to have been in part a conscious process of identity creation.

3 Oceania

3.1 Child language

Although there is only a partial overlap between the community of scholars working on anthropological-linguistic topics in Oceania and those focusing on such topics in Indigenous Australia, there have been some parallel developments between them in recent years. One such topic is child language acquisition. In the Mount Bosavi region of Papua New Guinea (PNG), Bambi B. Schieffelin carried out a longitudinal acquisition study among the Kaluli during 1975–1977 which was foundational for the development of the language socialization approach (Schieffelin 1990, Ochs and Schieffelin 2012). Such studies have stressed the importance of cross-cultural differences in the language-learning environments that children grow up in. Although there is enormous linguistic and cultural diversity within Papua New Guinea itself, no other longitudinal acquisition studies were done there until the early 2000s, at around the same time they started up in Australia. These studies have been carried out in three quite different parts of PNG: among Ku Waru speakers in Western Highlands of PNG's main island by Alan Rumsey and his team at Australian National University, among Nungon speakers on the Huon Peninsula about 250 kilometers to the east by Hannah Sarvasy of Western Sydney University, and among speakers of Qaqet Baining on the Island of New Britain about 600 kilometers further to the east by Birgit Hellwig and her team at the University of Cologne (see Hellwig, this volume).

One of the many comparative issues on which these studies have turned up relevant evidence is the nature of so-called "child-directed speech", i.e., the kind of speech that is used by adults when addressing children, and the question of how and to what extent it differs from how they speak when addressing other adults. This is important because until fairly recently it had been widely assumed that certain features of child-directed speech are cross-culturally universal, and essential for children's language development. These features were thought to include special "baby talk" vocabulary, simplified grammar and speech sounds, slower speech, higher pitch, exaggerated vowel contrasts, and exaggerated pitch contours (wider swings between the highest and lowest pitch within utterances) (Ferguson 1977).

Schieffelin's (1990) study showed that many of those features were absent from the speech used by caregivers to Kaluli children. She related this fact to Kaluli people's view that the right way to teach children to talk is to address them with "hard speech" that will fully model competent adult speech for them. Caregivers' views differ about this in the three more recent PNG acquisition studies, but child-directed speech in all of them has been found to differ in some ways from what had been taken to be its universal or canonical form as described above (Rumsey et al. 2020: 20, 24, 26, Sarvasy et al. 2019: 3157, Frye 2019: 121, 177); while conforming to it in some others (Rumsey 2017, Sarvasy 2019: 1078, Frye 2019: 182–183). The same is true of another study of child-directed speech carried out elsewhere in Island Melanesia, on the island of Tanna in Vanuatu, by Tanya Broesch (Broesch and Bryant 2018).

As elsewhere in the world, studies of children's language learning in the Pacific have varied in the extent to which they have treated it in relation to the sociocultural orders in which it takes place, and how they get reproduced and transformed in the process. An outstanding recent example of a study which treats these relationships and transformations in detail is Elise Berman's (2019) book "*Talking like children: Language and the production of age in the Marshall Islands*". Berman's research methods included participant observation, video and audio recordings, interviews, and children's drawings, yielding a corpus including over 80 hours of recorded naturalistic social interaction. She analyzes a variety of interactions, all involving exchange – a key activity in many Pacific societies, but one which has almost never been studied with a focus on children. Based on close analysis of everyday interaction, Berman shows that children play an important role in Marshallese exchange because they are expected to do things that adults are not allowed to – e.g., to speak openly and shamelessly – thereby enabling them to act as intermediaries, conveying messages that would sound inappropriately confrontational between adults.

Accordingly, although grounded in the language socialization approach, Berman's study leads her to call for a rethinking of one of its key premises. "Socialization" within that approach is generally understood as a process of transition from the position of "novice" to one of full "cultural competence". Based on her Marshallese research, Berman argues to the contrary that "[. . .] cultural reproduction requires people who, before they learn to be like their elders, learn to be different from them. Socialization, therefore, is not the acquisition of cultural practices by children and other novices but, rather, the constant and continuous production of differences" (ibid.: 135).

In the discussion of child-language studies in Indigenous Australia in Section 2.4 we referred to work on Light Warlpiri and Gurindji Kriol in which it was shown that children had played an active part in the creation of new "mixed languages" from pre-existing ones. A somewhat similar development has taken place on the other side of the Pacific, in Rapa Nui (a.k.a. Easter Island), as described by Miki Makihara (2005a, 2005b). The island's original Polynesian language was widely spoken there, including by children, until the 1980s, when it was overtaken by Spanish, after the influx of increasing numbers of Chileans and fuller integration of Rapa Nui into the national and global economy. Among first-language speakers of the indigenous language, a distinct Rapa Nui variety of Spanish emerged with simplified grammar and partial assimilation of the phonology of Chilean Spanish grammar to that of Rapa Nui (Makihara 2005a: 733–737).

Importantly, even though most bilingual Rapa Nui adults are now fluent speakers of Chilean Spanish, many of them continue to speak varieties of Rapa Nui Spanish in certain contexts, apparently as "interactional diacritics of the speaker's identity which serve to underline solidarity and to authenticate Rapa Nui identity, or to polarize ethnic differences in a community where heritage tourism and a politicized indigenous movement are both salient" (Makihara 2005a: 730). This has been taken further by Rapa Nui children, who "are developing their own Rapa Nui ways of speaking Spanish, which are structurally distinct from older Rapa Nui Spanish" (ibid.: 731), and include the use of some Rapa Nui words within otherwise Spanish utterances (Makihara 2005b: 127). Close analysis of the situated uses of this new speech variety has led Makihara to a conclusion which compares interestingly with the ones reached by O'Shanessy, McConvell and Meakins regarding the rise of new languages in Northern Australia (Section 2.4), and by Berman regarding the Marshall Islands, namely, that "[c]hildren are not just passive learners who are only at the receiving end of language socialization, but can be competent interpreters of the social world around them and their own place within it, and they play a role in socializing the adults in their lives and raising their consciousness" (Makihara 2005b: 130).

3.2 Language ideologies

Insightful new work in the linguistic anthropology of Oceania addresses the political effects of language ideologies across scales of interaction. For example, Christine Jourdan and Johanne Angeli (2014) analyze connections among different language ideologies held by middle-class speakers of Pijin, the Solomon Islands' lingua franca, in the capital city of Honiara. They identify four co-present ideologies: "reciprocal multilingualism", in which the nation's more than seventy indigenous languages are considered equally valuable; "hierarchical multilingualism", the colonial promotion of English as both elite and uniquely legitimate; "linguistic pragmatism", in which English's utility is emphasized; and "linguistic nationalism", the promotion of a national standard. The last of these has not gained firm purchase in the Solomons because many people believe there are "too many vernacular languages" to choose one as a standard, and Pijin, the social standard, is thought to be "too 'artificial' and 'inauthentic' to warrant its protection as part of Solomon[s] culture" (2014: 276).

Jourdan and Angeli argue that Pijin and English are evaluated in relation to each other in changing ways. Whereas English was once valued because it was promoted as inherently superior and the only way to make progress within the colonial order, younger speakers now value it for its international utility but also criticize Solomon Islanders who use it in informal settings as being snobbish. Solomons Pijin is subject to local critique on two related counts. First, Pijin as currently spoken is heard to be heavily influenced by English, and speakers idealize older Pijin as a "pure" form. Second, speakers of Solomons Pijin believe that the closely related Tok Pisin of Papua New Guinea (PNG) and Bislama of Vanuatu "are at least 'real' Melanesian Pidgin" (2014: 278). The authors describe Pijin as having "social legitimacy" but not "linguistic legitimacy", and conclude that "linguistic ideologies are not replacing each other, but accumulate and interact" (2014: 282).[6]

Another consideration of the ideological relationships between languages is presented by Ingjerd Hoëm (2015) in her analysis of governance in the territory of Tokelau. New Zealand had been administratively preparing Tokelau for independence, but the territory's citizens voted against it in referenda in 2006 and 2007. Hoëm examines the linguistic dimensions of conflicting expectations of authority. She observes that the Samoan language is generally associated

---

6 In related work, Jourdan has examined the ideological dimensions of vernacular-language education in Oceania (Jourdan and Salaün 2013) and the preparation of a Pijin dictionary (Jourdan 2020).

with "high culture" in Tokelau, English with modernity, and Tokelauan with "social belonging and identity" (2015: 57). Analyzing the use of these languages within government systems, she describes decades-long dialogues over how Tokelau should be governed as intertextual processes of adoption, resistance, and transformation. Hoëm suggests that these intertextual articulations have given Tokelauans an expanded sense of space but a contracted sense of time. In other words, Tokelauans have developed new transnational connections, but audit culture associated with governance in places like New Zealand (and espoused by the United Nations) has led to a situation in which "local control over time, at least in the sense of the orchestration of activities engaged in by people associated with the atolls, can be said to have diminished incrementally" (2015: 85).

Hoëm points out that key terms and concepts in global governance – growth, transparency, accountability – have strikingly different connotations in different contexts. For example, she notes that English-language "transparency" refers to "a bureaucratic check on procedures of appointing people to positions on the basis of acquired skills", a process which can clash with Tokelauan expectations of people's ascribed social roles (2015: 97). Yet to argue that transparency is a foreign concept in Tokelau would be to overlook the fact that Tokelauans endorse a kind of hyper-transparency, one in which public-private distinctions do not make sense because nearly everything is public. Indeed, people cultivate a "sense of absolute social visibility" (2015: 97). Governance in Tokelau can thus be seen as an ever-evolving process in which different languages, terms, and linguistic features are evaluated and given ideological weight.

Working at a village level, James Slotta (2015, 2017) analyzes how listening is considered more effective for self-determination than speaking for inhabitants of the Yopno Valley in PNG. He notes that theorists as diverse as Kant, Rousseau, Habermas, Spivak, and Butler have characterized speaking as self-determinative action and listening as submission to such action. He then points out that Yopno residents think and communicate differently: for them, listening is an expression of agency and an effective means toward self-determination, or "the capacity to shape one's future" (Slotta 2017: 333). Speakers offer words which listeners receive and metaphorically break up and sort out as if they were food to be distributed, the talk evaluated as good or bad, true or false (Slotta 2015: 535).

Yopno communicators believe that reality can be "opaque", Slotta observes. Expertise comes from many sources – schoolteachers, church pastors, overseas NGO representatives – and witches and evil spirits deceive people (2017: 332–336; see also Slotta 2014). Accordingly, a listener must guard against deception and listen to the right experts. In political contexts, Yopno speakers often suggest that what listeners think they are doing is mistaken, and they must learn to listen in a more effective way (2017: 332). Discernment and authority, Slotta writes, ultimately lie with listeners: "The relatively acephalous political organization . . . is reinforced by conceptions and practices that stress the agentive role of recipients in swaying the outcome of communicative events. A would-be leader's word is nobody's command" (2015: 544).

3.2.1 Translation and transformation

Anthropologists working in Oceania have also analyzed language ideologies with reference to translation and Christian models of transformation. Christianity is a profound social force in the Pacific Islands, and religious understandings of language, person, and society are entwined in personal and political projects from local to national and transnational levels (Tomlinson and McDougall 2013). Courtney Handman has developed the argument that schism among Protestant churches should be seen as a constructive process of critique, a socially constructive way of being "separate together with others" (Handman 2015: 14; emphasis deleted). Her research interlocutors, Guhu-Samane speakers in PNG, belong to three main churches: Lutheran, New Life (who split from the Lutherans in the 1970s), and Reformed Gospel (who split from New Life in the 1990s). The churches strive to distinguish themselves from each other, and language (and more broadly semiotic) ideologies play a key part in shaping their critical stances. In contrast to the past's recalled or imagined silence and monological norms, today "one must speak one's self to be Christian, [which] for many people means that there are too many speakers and not enough listeners" (2015: 179; see also Robbins 2001, and recall Slotta's description of the agency of Yopno listeners). Handman argues that translation between languages (including Guhu-Samane, Tok Pisin, and English) "engenders critical discussion" by raising possibilities of comparison, differentiation and equivalence; it also serves as a "productive figure of transformation", modelling the change of a person or community from one state to another (2015: 19–20, 36, 191–214).[7]

Similarly, Debra McDougall (2012) observes that when a vernacular language is promoted as the truest way to understand Christianity, colonial language ideologies can be inverted and values of local identity reevaluated. McDougall describes the efforts of a theologian and linguist, Alphaeus Graham Zobule, on

---

7 See also Schieffelin (2014) on missionaries' ideological separation of culture and language – the former to be replaced, the latter retained – which helped change how Bosavi of PNG constitute community and relate to place; and Tomlinson (2012) on incomprehensible language modelling human relations with God.

behalf of the language of Luqa in Ranongga, Solomon Islands. Zobule completed the translation of the New Testament into Luqa, then established a language institute to train Solomon Islanders in linguistic study. He insists that knowledge of local languages' grammar is key to "unlock[ing] the treasures hidden in the vernacular" and also understanding English better, as English is often the only language in which younger Ranonggans are literate (2012: 322–323). "By lifting up Luqa", McDougall writes, "Zobule and other Ranonggans [. . .] hope to transform their colonially induced shame in being 'local' into pride [. . .] revers[ing] nearly a century of linguistic, social, economic and political marginalisation" (2012: 323; see also McDougall 2019). Ryan Schram (2016) adds the crucial point that some missionaries, despite recognizing the missiological significance of mother tongues, have historically positioned themselves as the only speakers capable of creating mutual comprehension in multilingual mission encounters. Analyzing the writings of Methodist missionaries in the colony of British New Guinea, Schram argues that these authors "parodied" indigenous speakers, quoting them in ways which characterize them as ignorant, capable only of imitation in word and gesture rather than true Christian understanding.

3.2.2 New media

Entangled with ideologies of language and semiosis are ideologies of mediation and, today, meanings and effects of new media. As Ilana Gershon (2010) and others have pointed out, a key step in adopting new technologies is figuring out how to evaluate the relationships that new media helps to configure. "Media ideologies" may intersect with expressions of power and spirituality of the sort discussed above. For example, Christiane Falck (2016) argues that although mobile phones have meshed with existing ideas of spirit communication for Nyaura speakers of Timbunmeli village in PNG's East Sepik Province, they have also opened up new communicative possibilities. Some possibilities are decidedly this-worldly, such as downloading pornography and trying to make easy money while being wary of financial scams. When it comes to speaking with spirits, members of one Christian group, the Thomas Souls Ministry, make a point of keeping separate mobile phones: a 'bridge phone' or 'heaven phone' is strictly for speaking with deceased relatives, whereas a 'ground phone' is for contacting the living.[8]

---

8 Compare Jorgensen (2018) and Hobbis (2020, chapter 6 therein) on anxieties about new media's religious and magical powers in PNG and Solomon Islands, respectively.

New media technologies do not change anything by themselves, but are pulled into existing relationships and practices whose values people might seek to reaffirm and reshape at the same time (see Good [2021, n.d.] on Tongan youths' use of Bebo and Facebook in this regard). One area in which new media's effects are especially notable is the transformation of language ideologies themselves. Leslie Vandeputte-Tavo (2013) describes how Bislama in Vanuatu has gone from being considered a "plantation language" to one associated with urban modernity thanks to its use in social media. A colony jointly administered by the United Kingdom and France, Vanuatu has long positioned English and French as languages of prestige and education alongside more than one hundred indigenous vernaculars. Within this linguistic mix, Bislama, the national lingua franca, has become the main choice for sending text messages and posting comments on Facebook. Vandeputte-Tavo observes that the association of mobile phones and the Internet with "power and modernity" in Vanuatu mean that these technologies – and Bislama with them – do not just symbolize power and modernity but "incarnate" it (2013: 170). As social media use increases, Bislama gains social value and legitimacy – and also the quirky shorthand standardization typical of online communication, for example, shortening *givim* ('give') to *gim* and replacing *stret* ('OK') with *z*.[9]

Handman (2013) also takes up the topic of text messaging's shorthand codes. She demonstrates how orthography and language ideology are historically entangled in PNG's national language Tok Pisin. The first orthographies developed for Melanesian pidgins were based on English standards; later orthography was meant to reflect local phonology and establish Tok Pisin as an independent language. In this historical shift, the representation of vowels was simplified, doubled consonants were reduced to single consonants, and epenthetic vowels were inserted to break up consonant clusters and reflect PNG speakers' pronunciation. Hence the older pidgin phrase *Missionary, suppose you hungry* (meaning 'Missionary, if you are hungry') was to be written in Tok Pisin as *Misonari, sapos yu hangere*.

Linguists hoped to emphasize Tok Pisin's independence from English. In doing so, they wanted to create an icon of PNG's eventual independence from Australia and also to foster pride in a regional Melanesian Way. Today, however,

---

9 For Vanuatu, compare Levisen (2017) on Bislama's link to reggae, with both forms indexing youth, illegitimacy/transgression, and Black identity; Kraemer (2017) on young people in Port Vila using mobile phones to get "evidence" of others' activities and disconnect from romantic partners; and Dick and Doyle (2021) on young media artists developing a sense of "screen sovereignty", or power to create new art forms through *rimix* (Bislama for 'remix') of foreign and local elements.

people sending text messages disrupt this project, combining Tok Pisin and English with internationally recognized shorthands like @, *2* for 'to', and so forth. Consonant clusters reappear (e.g., second-person plural *yupela* becomes *u pla*), and *z* and *x* see "heavy use", especially in nicknaming (Handman 2013: 278–280). "Not concerned with separating out a unique Melanesian Way of social life, as was so crucial during the independence era", Handman writes, "young people [. . .] are forming connections to world Englishes and to international text message protocols while they also undo the forms that produced Tok Pisin language-ness in the first place" (2013: 280).

As we stated at the beginning of this chapter, our selection of topics and researchers for discussion is partial. Much more could be said about other strands of research on language and culture in Australia and Oceania, but we consider these studies of language ecologies and ideologies, multilingualism and multimodal sign systems, kintax, children's language, translation, and new media to be notable for the way they draw on long traditions of close attention to language's imbrication with culture and point to new directions for research.

References

Adone, Marie & Elaine Maypilama. 2013. *A grammar sketch of Yolngu Sign Language*. Cologne: University of Cologne Press.

Barwick, Linda, Jennifer Green, Petronella Vaarzon-Morel & Katya Zissermann. 2019. *Conundrums and consequences. Doing digital archival returns in Australia*. In Linda Barwick, Jennifer Green & Petronella Vaarzon-Morel (eds.), *Archival returns. Central Australia and beyond* [Language Documentation & Conservation Special Publication 18], 1–27. Honolulu: University of Hawai'i Press.

Bauer, Anastasia. 2014. *The use of signing space in a shared sign language of Australia* [Sign Language Typology 5]. Berlin & Boston: De Gruyter Mouton.

Berman, Elise. 2019. *Talking like children. Language and the production of age in the Marshall Islands*. Oxford: Oxford University Press.

Blythe, Joe. 2018. Genesis of the trinity. The convergent evolution of trirelational kinterms. In Patrick McConvell, Piers Kelly & Sébastien Lacrampe (eds.), *Skin, kin and clan. The dynamics of social categories in Indigenous Australia*, 441–471. Canberra: ANU Press.

Blythe, Joe, Jeremiah Tunmuck, Alice Mitchell & Péter Rácz. 2020. Acquiring the lexicon and grammar of universal kinship. *Language* 96 (2). 661–695.

Bracknell, Clint & Kim Scott. 2019. Ever-widening circles. Consolidating and enhancing Wirlomin Noongar archival material in the community. In Linda Barwick, Jennifer Green & Petronella Vaarzon-Morel (eds.), *Archival returns. Central Australia and beyond* [Language Documentation & Conservation Special Publication 18], 325–338. Honolulu: University of Hawai'i Press.

Broesch, Tanya & Gregory A. Bryant. 2018. Fathers' infant-directed speech in a small-scale society. *Child Development* 89 (2). e29–e41.

Brown, Reuben & Sally Treloyn. 2017. Relationships and the repatriation of legacy song recordings in Australia. *University of Melbourne Collections* 20. 50–61.

Christen, Kimberly. 2018. Relationships, not records. In Jentery Sayers (ed.), *The Routledge companion to media studies and digital humanities*, 1st edition, 403–412. New York: Routledge.

Croft, Brenda L., Sandy Toussaint, Felicity Meakins & Patrick McConvell. 2019. "For the children . . . ". Aboriginal Australia, cultural access, and archival obligation. In Linda Barwick, Jennifer Green & Petronella Vaarzon-Morel (eds.), *Archival returns. Central Australia and beyond*, 173–192. Honolulu & Sydney: University of Hawai'i Press and Sydney University Press.

Davidson, Lucinda. 2018. *Allies and adversaries. Categories in Murrinhpatha speaking children's talk*. Melbourne: University of Melbourne dissertation. [https://minerva-access.unimelb.edu.au/handle/11343/219709] (accessed 18 March 2022).

Defina, Rebecca. 2020. Acquisition of Pitjantjatjara clause chains. *Frontiers in Psychology* 11. 1–18.

Dick, Thomas, & Sarah Doyle. 2021. Screen sovereignty. Urban youth and community media in Vanuatu. In Keith L. Camacho (ed.), *Reppin'. Pacific Islander youth and native justice*, 109–128. Seattle: University of Washington Press.

Dousset, Laurent. 2011. *Australian Aboriginal kinship. An introductory handbook with particular emphasis on the Western Desert*. Marseille: Pacific-Cred.

Ellis, Elizabeth Marrkilyi, Jennifer Green & Inge Kral. 2014. Documentation of the verbal arts of the Western Desert people of Australia (collection WDSSS-kral-0342), 2010–2013. *Endangered Languages Archive*. [http://hdl.handle.net/2196/00-0000-0000-000A-0C05-A (collection WDSSS-kral-0342)] (accessed 25 November 2021).

Ellis, Elizabeth Marrkilyi, Jennifer Green, Inge Kral & Lauren W. Reed. 2019. "Mara yurriku". Western Desert sign languages. *Australian Aboriginal Studies* 2019 (2). 89–111.

Evans, Nicholas. 2003. Context, culture, and structuration in the languages of Australia. *Annual Review of Anthropology* 32. 13–40.

Evans, Nicholas. 2018. The dynamics of language diversity. In Rajend Mesthrie & David Bradley (eds.), *The dynamics of language. Plenary and focus lectures from the 20th International Congress of Linguists*, 12–35. Cape Town: UCT Press.

Falck, Christiane. 2016. *Calling the dead. Spirits, mobile phones, and the talk of God in a Sepik community (Papua New Guinea)*. Cairns & Aarhus: James Cook University & Aarhus University dissertation.

Ferguson, Charles. 1977. Baby talk as a simplified register. In Catherine E. Snow & Charles A. Ferguson (eds.), *Talking to children*, 209–235. Cambridge: Cambridge University Press.

Fishman, Joshua. 1967. Bilingualism with and without diglossia. Diglossia with and without bilingualism. *Journal of Social Issues* 23. 29–38.

Forshaw, Bill, Lucinda Davidson, Barbara Kelly, Rachel Nordlinger, Gillian Wigglesworth & Joe Blythe. 2017. The acquisition of Murrinhpatha (Northern Australia). In Michael Fortescue, Marianne Mithun & Nicholas Evans (eds.). *The Oxford handbook of polysynthesis*, 473–494. Oxford: Oxford University Press.

Frye aus Schwerte, Henrike. 2019. *Child-directed speech in Qaqet. A language of East New Britain, Papua New Guinea*. Cologne: University of Cologne dissertation.

Gaby, Alice 2017. Kinship semantics. Culture in the lexicon. In Farzad Sharifian (ed.), *Advances in Cultural Linguistics*, 173–188. New York: Springer.

Gal, Susan & Judith T. Irvine. 2019. *Signs of difference. Language and ideology in social life.* New York: Cambridge University Press.

Garde, Murray. 2013. *Culture, interaction and person reference in an Australian language.* Amsterdam & Philadelphia: John Benjamins.

Gershon, Ilana. 2010. Media ideologies. An introduction. *Journal of Linguistic Anthropology* 20 (2). 283–293.

Good, Mary K. 2021. "Holla mai! Tongan 4 life!" Transnational citizenship, youth style, and mediated interaction through online social networking communities. In Keith L. Camacho (ed.), *Reppin'. Pacific Islander youth and native justice*, 129–149. Seattle: University of Washington Press.

Good, Mary K. n.d. Relational status and multi-faceted profiles. Facebook use among Tongan youth and the presentation of selfhood. Unpublished manuscript.

Green, Jennifer. 2014. *Drawn from the ground. Sound, sign and inscription in Central Australian sand stories.* Cambridge: Cambridge University Press.

Green, Jennifer. 2019. Embodying kin-based respect in speech, sign, and gesture. *Gesture* 18 (2–3). 370–395.

Green, Jennifer & Eleanor Jorgensen. 2021. Same, similar or different? Lexical overlap in Australian Indigenous sign languages. Paper presented at the *Australian Linguistics Society conference*, 7–9 December 2021, La Trobe University (online).

Green, Jennifer & David P. Wilkins. 2014. With or without speech. Arandic Sign Language from Central Australia. *Australian Journal of Linguistics* 34. 234–261.

Handman, Courtney. 2013. Text messaging in Tok Pisin. Etymologies and orthographies in cosmopolitan Papua New Guinea. *Culture, theory and critique* 54 (3). 265–284.

Handman, Courtney. 2015. *Critical Christianity. Translation and denominational conflict in Papua New Guinea.* Berkeley: University of California Press.

Harris, John W. 1993. Losing and gaining a language. The story of Kriol in the Northern Territory. In Michael Walsh & Colin Yallop (eds.), *Language and culture in Aboriginal Australia*, 145–154. Canberra: Aboriginal Studies Press.

Heath, Jeffrey. 1982. Introduction. In Jeffrey Heath, Francesca Merlan & Alan Rumsey (eds.), *Languages of kinship in Aboriginal Australia*, 1–18. Sydney: Oceania Publications.

Hobbis, Geoffrey. 2020. *The digitizing family. An ethnography of Melanesian smartphones.* Cham: Palgrave Macmillan.

Hoëm, Ingjerd. 2015. *Languages of governance in conflict. Negotiating democracy in Tokelau.* Amsterdam & Philadelphia: John Benjamins.

Jorgensen, Dan. 2018. Toby and "The mobile system". Apocalypse and salvation in Papua New Guinea's wireless network. In Robert J. Foster & Heather A. Horst (eds.), *The moral economy of mobile phones. Pacific Islands perspectives*, 53–71. Canberra: ANU Press.

Jourdan, Christine. 2020. Restituting language. Ethics, ideology and the making of a dictionary. *Journal de la Société des Océanistes* 151. 285–296.

Jourdan, Christine & Johanne Angeli. 2014. Pijin and shifting language ideologies in urban Solomon Islands. *Language in Society* 43 (3). 265–285.

Jourdan, Christine & Marie Salaün. 2013. Vernacular and culturally based education in Oceania today. Articulating global, national and local agendas. *Current Issues in Language Planning* 14 (2). 205–216.

Kraemer, Daniela. 2017. "Do you have a mobile?" Mobile phone practices and the refashioning of social relationships in Port Vila Town. *The Australian Journal of Anthropology* 28 (1). 39–55.

Kral, Inge, Jennifer Green & Elizabeth Marrkilyi Ellis. 2020. *i-Tjuma. Ngaanyatjarra stories from the Western Desert of Central Australia*. Perth: University of Western Australia Press.

Kral, Inge & Elizabeth Marrkilyi Ellis. 2020. *In the time of their lives. Wangka kutjupa-kutjuparringu. How talk has changed in the Western Desert*. Perth: University of Western Australia Publishers.

Levisen, Carsten. 2017. The social and sonic semantics of reggae. Language ideology and emergent socialities in postcolonial Vanuatu. *Language & Communication* 52. 102–116.

Lüpke, Friederike. 2016. Uncovering small-scale multilingualism. *Critical Multilingualism Studies* 4. 35–74.

Makihara, Miki. 2005a. Rapa Nui ways of speaking Spanish. Language shift and socialization on Easter Island. *Language in Society* 34. 727–762.

Makihara, Miki. 2005b. Being Rapa Nui, speaking Spanish. Children's voices on Easter Island. *Anthropological Theory* 5 (2). 117–134.

Marley, Alexandra. 2020. *Kundangkudjikaberrk. Variation and change in Bininj Kunwok, a Gunwinyguan language of Northern Australia*. Canberra: Australian National University dissertation.

McConvell, Patrick. 2008. Language mixing and language shift in Indigenous Australia. In Jane Simpson & Gillian Wigglesworth (eds.), *Children's language and multilingualism. Indigenous language use at home and school*, 237–260. London: Continuum Publishing Company.

McConvell, Patrick, Piers Kelly & Sébastien Lacrampe (eds.). 2018. *Skin, kin and clan. The dynamics of social categories in Indigenous Australia*. Canberra: ANU Press.

McConvell, Patrick & Felicity Meakins 2005. Gurindji Kriol. A mixed language emerges from code-switching. *Australian Journal of Linguistics* 25 (1). 9–30.

McDougall, Debra. 2012. Stealing foreign words, recovering local treasures. Bible translation and vernacular literacy on Ranongga (Solomon Islands). *The Australian Journal of Anthropology* 23 (3). 318–339.

McDougall, Debra. 2019. *Reviving the spirit of vernacular languages in Solomon Islands*. Canberra: ARC Centre of Excellence for the Dynamics of Language. [http://www.dynamicsoflanguage.edu.au/news-and-media/latest-headlines/article/?id=reviving-the-spirit-of-vernacular-languages-in-solomon-islands] (accessed 16 February 2021).

O'Shannessy, Carmel 2013. The role of multiple sources in the formation of an innovative auxiliary category in Light Warlpiri, a new Australian mixed language. *Language* 89 (2). 328–353.

O'Shannessy, Carmel 2020. Mixed Languages. In Evangelia Adamou & Yaron Matras (eds.), *The Routledge handbook of language contact*, 325–348. London: Routledge.

Ochs, Elinor & Bambi B. Schieffelin. 2012. The theory of language socialization. In Alessandro Duranti, Elinor Ochs & Bambi B. Schieffelin (eds.), *The handbook of language socialization*, 1–21. Malden: Wiley Blackwell.

Robbins, Joel. 2001. God is nothing but talk. Modernity, language, and prayer in a Papua New Guinea society. *American Anthropologist* 103 (4). 901–912.

Rumsey, Alan. 1993. Language and territoriality in Aboriginal Australia. In Michael Walsh & Colin Yallop (eds.), *Language and culture in Aboriginal Australia*, 191–206. Canberra: Australian Institute of Aboriginal and Torres Strait Islander Studies Press.

Rumsey, Alan. 2017. Dependency and relative determination in children's language acquisition. The case of Ku Waru. In N. J. Enfield (ed.), *Dependencies in language. On the causal ontology of linguistic systems*, 97–114. Berlin: Language Science Press.

Rumsey, Alan. 2018. The sociocultural dynamics of indigenous multilingualism in northwestern Australia. *Language & Communication* 62. 91–101.

Rumsey, Alan, Lauren W. Reed & Francesca Merlan. 2020. Ku Waru clause chaining and the acquisition of complex syntax. *Frontiers in Communication* 5. DOI:10.3389/fcomm.2020.00019

Sarvasy, Hannah. 2019. The root nominal stage. A case study of early Nungon verbs. *Journal of Child Language* 46 (6). 1073–1101.

Sarvasy, Hannah, Jaydene Elvin, Weicong Li & Paola Escudero. 2019. An acoustic analysis of Nungon vowels in child-versus adult-directed speech. In Sasha Calhoun, Paola Escudero, Marija Tabain & Paul Warren (eds.), *Proceedings of the 19th International Congress of Phonetic Sciences, Melbourne, Australia 2019*, 3155–3159. Canberra, Australia: Australasian Speech Science and Technology Association Inc.

Schieffelin, Bambi B. 1990. *The give and take of everyday life. Language socialization of Kaluli children*. Cambridge: Cambridge University Press.

Schieffelin, Bambi B. 2014. Christianizing language and the dis-placement of culture in Bosavi, Papua New Guinea. *Current Anthropology* 55. S226–S237.

Schieffelin, Bambi B., Kathryn A. Woolard & Paul V. Kroskrity (eds.). 1998. *Language ideologies. Practice and theory*. Oxford: Oxford University Press.

Schram, Ryan. 2016. "Tapwaroro is true". Indigenous voice and the heteroglossia of Methodist missionary translation in British New Guinea. *Journal of Linguistic Anthropology* 26 (3). 259–277.

Singer, Ruth & Salome Harris. 2016. What practices and ideologies support small-scale multilingualism? A case study of unexpected language survival in an Australian Indigenous community. *International Journal of the Sociology of Language* 241. 163–208.

Slotta, James. 2014. Revelations of the world. Transnationalism and the politics of perception in Papua New Guinea. *American Anthropologist* 116 (3). 626–642.

Slotta, James. 2015. The perlocutionary is political. Listening as self-determination in a Papua New Guinea polity. *Language in Society* 44 (4). 525–552.

Slotta, James. 2017. Can the subaltern listen? Self-determination and the provisioning of expertise in Papua New Guinea. *American Ethnologist* 44 (2). 328–340.

Sutton, Peter. 1978. *Wik. Aboriginal society, territory and language at Cape Keerweer, Cape York Peninsula*. Brisbane: University of Queensland dissertation.

Sutton, Peter. 1997. Materialism, sacred myth and pluralism. Competing theories of the origin of Australian languages. In Francesca Merlan, John Morton & Alan Rumsey (eds.), *Scholar and sceptic. Australian Aboriginal Studies in honour of L.R. Hiatt*, 211–242. Canberra: Aboriginal Studies Press.

Tomlinson, Matt. 2012. God speaking to God. Translation and unintelligibility at a Fijian Pentecostal crusade. *The Australian Journal of Anthropology* 23 (3). 274–289.

Tomlinson, Matt & Debra McDougall (eds.). 2013. *Christian politics in Oceania*. New York: Berghahn.

Treloyn, Sally & Rona Googninda Charles. 2014. How do you feel about squeezing oranges? Dialogues about difference and discomfort in intercultural ethnomusicological research collaboration in the Kimberley. In Katelyn Barney (ed.), *Collaborative ethnomusicology*.

New approaches to music research between indigenous and non-indigenous Australians, 169–186. Melbourne: Lyrebird Press.

Vandeputte-Tavo, Leslie. 2013. New technologies and language shifting in Vanuatu. *Pragmatics* 23 (1). 169–179.

Vaughan, Jill. 2018. "We talk in saltwater words". Dimensionalisation of dialectal variation in multilingual Arnhem Land. *Language & Communication* 62. 119–132.

Vaughan, Jill. 2022. Multilingualism. In Claire Bowern (ed.), *The handbook of Australian languages*. Oxford: Oxford University Press.

Vaughan, Jill & Ruth Singer. 2018. Indigenous multilingualisms past and present. *Language & Communication* 62. 83–90.

Vaughan, Jill, Ruth Singer & Murray Garde. 2022. Language naming in Indigenous Australia. A view from western Arnhem Land. *Multilingua*. DOI:10.1515/multi-2021-0005

N. J. Enfield & Jack Sidnell

17 Language and culture in Mainland Southeast Asia

In the early decades of the twentieth century, Franz Boas argued for the central importance of language to an understanding of culture. Specifically, Boas noted that certain aspects of linguistic structure, such as grammatical categories, rarely become objects of conscious reflection. Because of this, he proposed, these aspects of language provide a window onto primary ethnological phenomena (or "fundamental ethnic ideas"; see Stocking 1966, Silverstein 1979). In contrast, aspects of custom and tradition more available to conscious reflection are subject to secondary explanation and reanalysis, and get caught up in higher-order subjective schemes of social evaluation (as, e.g., "high", "popular", "traditional", "noble" and so on, see Sapir 1924). In recent years, linguistic anthropologists have focused on differences in the degree to which cultural phenomena are available to conscious awareness, finding here not a reason to privilege some kinds of data over others but rather a central mechanism of cultural dynamism. In what follows, we explore these issues at the heart of the language/culture relationship – and some of the associated complexities of current semiotic theory – through a consideration of the language-culture nexus in two settings in mainland Southeast Asia: historical developments in twentieth century Vietnam and contemporary life in rural communities of lowland Laos. We evaluate the implications of these case studies for directions in linguistic anthropology broadly, as well as for research on language and culture in mainland Southeast Asia.

1 Introduction

The relation between language and culture is central to linguistic anthropology. This is especially so if we take "culture" in the most general way to include any form of non-instinctive, patterned behavior that is transmitted via social learning across generations and supported by rules or norms (see Sahlins 1976, Trouillot 2003). This would encompass diverse forms of human behavior, not only those described as economic, political, legal, religious, and scientific, but also knowledge and practices of language. This presents a problem: How can

N. J. Enfield, University of Sydney/Australia, e-mail: nick.enfield@sydney.edu.au
Jack Sidnell, University of Toronto/Canada, e-mail: jack.sidnell@utoronto.ca

https://doi.org/10.1515/9783110726626-017

we isolate "language" from "culture" such that we might be able to determine the relation between them? On the one hand, it is all but impossible to think about, say, economics without linguistically-mediated contracts, politics without linguistically-mediated attempts at persuasion, or religion without linguistically-mediated acts of prayer, myth-telling, or performances of piety. On the other hand, where can we possibly hope to find an instance of language that has no connection to the culture of its speakers? Such considerations suggest that there are no clear lines which divide language from culture, that language is a part of culture and culture is a part of language.

But if we bracket such problems for a moment and, like Geertz (1973: 4), try to cut "the culture concept down to size", perhaps we can think about the relationship in a more productive way. It is possible to discern at least four approaches to the relation between language and culture in the literature. For simplicity, we can describe these as 1. No significant relation, 2. Direct coding, 3. Ways of speaking, and 4. Reflexive semiosis.

Here we consider these approaches to the language-culture relationship in light of linguistic and anthropological research on mainland Southeast Asia, which we define as the region east of the Indian subcontinent, south of China, bordered by the Indian Ocean to the west and the Pacific Ocean to the east, and including the countries of Cambodia, Laos, Myanmar, Peninsular Malaysia, Thailand and Vietnam (Enfield 2021, Chapter 1 therein). This is an extraordinarily diverse area in which languages from five families are spoken across social groupings ranging in size and complexity from small bands of semi-nomadic horticulturalists and hunter-gatherers in the Malaysian rainforest to cities of millions in urban Thailand and Vietnam. Despite this remarkable diversity it is nevertheless possible to identify relatively widespread areal characteristics in the languages (see Enfield 2021 for a detailed survey).

2 Four approaches to the language and culture relationship

2.1 No significant relation between language and culture

For many professional linguists, language is a manifestation of universal and innate properties of the human mind and its capacity to form and manipulate representations. In this conception, links between language and culture (as well as society, history, demography, and more) are irrelevant to the concerns of linguistic science. And for many professional anthropologists an altogether complementary view either denies or overlooks the idea that human social life is semiotic in character. On this view, language, speech and other aspects of human semiosis are held to have little bearing on matters such as the division of labor, the exercise of political power, or the expression of human emotion, which in turn may be regarded as central to culture. We will not give further consideration here to the views of specialists either of culture or of language who suppose that the other's specialization is not relevant to them (for analogous arguments with respect to other specializations, see Sapir 1949 [1938], Hymes 1967). Instead, we turn to perspectives on the possible ways in which language and culture may be meaningfully connected.

2.2 Culture is directly coded in language

The locus classicus for the view that language encodes culture is the introduction to "*The Handbook of American Indian Languages*" in which Boas set out the basic principles of the modern approach to linguistic relativity. This approach that would later be developed by Sapir, Whorf and more recently by Lucy and Levinson among others (see Lucy 1992, Gumperz and Levinson 1996, Levinson 2003, Enfield 2015b, inter alia). Boas begins with a conceptual argument:

> Since the total range of personal experience which language serves to express is infinitely varied, and its whole scope must be expressed by a limited number of phonetic groups, it is obvious that an extended classification of experiences must underlie all articulate speech.
>
> (Boas 1911: 24)

With the necessity of semantic classification by language so established, Boas then formulates a principle of relativity as a logical consequence:

> Thus it happens that each language, from the point of view of another language, may be arbitrary in its classifications; that what appears as a single simple idea in one language may be characterized by a series of distinct phonetic groups in another. (Boas 1911: 26)

Boas's argument goes to the heart of the larger anthropological enterprise. The conceptual classifications that are written into grammar are a key source of ethnological data for the anthropologist precisely because they rarely rise to the level of conscious awareness (this being, to some extent, possible only from a comparative perspective). The ontological assumptions encoded by language are in this way naturalized.

> If the phenomena of human speech seem to form in a way a subject by itself, this is perhaps largely due to the fact that the laws of language remain entirely unknown to the speakers, that linguistic phenomena never rise into the consciousness of primitive man,

while all other ethnological phenomena are more or less clearly subjects of conscious thought.

(Boas 1911: 63)

The idea is this. Culture is directly coded in the grammatical organization of a language and this, insulated from the distorting effects of native-speaker awareness and reanalysis, provides the anthropologist with a kind of "primary ethnological data" (see Silverstein 1979). Boas makes this argument even more explicit in the following passage:

> It has been mentioned before that in all languages certain classifications of concepts occur. To mention only a few: we find objects classified according to sex, or as animate and inanimate, or according to form. We find actions determined according to time and place, etc. The behavior of primitive man makes it perfectly clear that all these concepts, although they are in constant use, have never risen into consciousness, and that consequently their origin must be sought, not in rational, but in entirely unconscious, we may perhaps say instinctive, processes of the mind. They must be due to a grouping of sense-impressions and of concepts which is not in any sense of the term voluntary, but which develops from quite different psychological causes. It would seem that the essential difference between linguistic phenomena and other ethnological phenomena is that the linguistic classifications never rise into consciousness, while in other ethnological phenomena, although the same unconscious origin prevails, these often rise into consciousness, and thus give rise to secondary reasoning and to reinterpretations.
>
> (Boas 1911: 63)

In the literature on languages of Mainland Southeast Asia, perhaps the most obvious application of such an idea is to numeral classifiers, an areal feature attested in languages from diverse families of the area (Enfield 2021, Section 6.2.1). In a classic statement of this approach, Becker (1975) suggests that the Burmese system organizes the things talked about according to the cosmology of its speakers.[1] More specifically, rather than convey shape, size and other physical attributes the way classifiers in languages such as Vietnamese do, Becker proposes that, in Burmese, classifiers form a series of concentric circles. The centre is occupied by the Buddha and objects related to him, such as Buddha images, pagodas, and relics.[2] The classifier used for anything occupying this sacred centre is *shu*. In the first orbit around the center are saints, monks and royalty. Anything included here is classified by *'pa*, which means 'closeness' or 'cheek'. In the second orbit are "people of status" such as teachers and scholars. Such persons are classified with *u*, a word meaning 'head' and 'first'.

---

1 Burmese classifiers have been the object of many studies – see, Haas (1951), Burling (1965), Hla Pe (1965), also Jenny (2000) who responds specifically to the arguments of Becker. For a somewhat related approach to materials from Northern Thailand which focuses not on classifiers but on certain "prefixes" that appear in address, see Wijeyewardene (1968b).

2 Also fishing nets, mosquito nets and staircases (see Becker 1975 for a possible explanation).

In the third orbit are ordinary humans. The classifier used is *yauʔ*, likely cognate with Tibetan *yog* 'servant'. Finally, in the outermost circle are animals, ghosts, dead bodies, deprived people, and children. These are classified with *kuang*.

Becker notes that the choice of which classifier is used for a specific person or object is not completely fixed but depends, at least in part, on the speaker's feelings about the person/object as well aspects of the extra-linguistic context. Apart from those at the very center, occupants can be transferred from one circle to another to show contempt or respect, depending on the direction of movement (see Becker 1975: 115, Burling 1965: 246–247). Becker then goes on to describe a similarly organized classifier system for inanimate objects. In this case the center is occupied by "self" and then radiating outwards are a series of orbits distinguished as inalienable, alienable, near to self, far from self.[3]

We do not want to enter into a discussion of the merits of Becker's interesting analysis (for that, see Jenny 2000). Our summary is meant only to illustrate one way in which the relation between language and culture has been understood in work on mainland Southeast Asia. But note this. Whatever is the case for Burmese, this kind of analysis runs the risk of attributing meaningful connections to data based on surface appearance. In the numeral classifier system of Vietnamese, for example, both river, *sông*, and road, *đường*, are classified with *con*, i.e., the classifier typically restricted to animals (Nguyễn 1957). Does that mean that rivers and roads are "animals" in the local ontology?[4] Or in the Chewong language of Malaysia, references to the emotions make explicit reference to the liver, in an area-wide pattern known as the "psycho-collocation" (Enfield 2021, Section 5.6 therein): If the Chewong way of saying "I was ashamed" is literally translated as "my liver was tiny", does this mean that the blood-producing organ is "the seat of all consciousness" (Howell 1981: 142–3) for Chewong speakers? Care must be taken when interpreting figurative language.

A distinct approach to "direct coding" was promoted by the linguist Ken Hale (1986), who distinguished between two ways of conceiving the relation between language and "world view". In what he calls World-View 1, "the central

---

3 Each of these is subdivided by height (head and body), where head is associated with round and body with straight. Becker (1975: 120) writes: "The Burmese classifier system is coherent because it is based upon a single, elementary semantic dimension: deixis. On that dimension, four distances are distinguished, distances which metaphorically substitute for other conceptual relations between people and other living beings, people and things, and people and concepts."
4 See the literature on "ontologies" deriving, in part from Hallowell's (1960) insights about Ojibwa classifiers, which sometimes seems committed to such a literalist view.

propositions or postulates in a people's theory of how things are in the world" are either explicitly formulated in doctrine or implicitly conveyed in "certain cultural institutions and art forms, whether verbal, such as poetry and myth, or non-verbal, such as painting and dance" (Hale 1986: 233). The connection to language, Hale suggests, is mostly superficial and reflected in the elaboration of lexical domains or in "manners of speaking" (see below). The elements of such a world view may be shared to some extent among the speakers of the language. World-View 1 is thus "learned separately from the grammar of a language, as a result of instruction or as a result of participation in the activities of the associated culture" (Hale 1986: 233).

In contrast, World-View 2, "consists in the 'analysis of phenomena' embodied in the system of lexico-semantic themes or motifs which function as integral components in a grammar" (Hale 1986: 234). Such a World-View 2 is shared by all speakers of a language since its acquisition is a necessary consequence of knowing that language. Moreover, it is intimately connected to the grammar, indeed is essentially a part of that grammar, as no distinction is made between grammatical knowledge and world view. Hale further argues that world view in this sense is universal, "a part of the innate linguistic capacity of human beings – albeit instantiated in different ways and in different proportions in different languages" (Hale 1986: 235). Hale illustrates World-View 2 with examples from Warlpiri in which the grammar is organized in terms of distinctions between central and non-central coincidence. This is seen for instance in local cases (locative, perlative, allative, elative), in directional verb enclitics (*by, past, hither, thither*), finite and non-finite complementizers, aspect, and in the distinction between depictive and translative predication.

Hale's World-View 2 idea is that any given language will foreground specific semantic themes or motifs and that these will be manifest in diverse and otherwise unrelated grammatical subsystems. For an MSEA example, we might consider the pervasive evaluative distinctions that run through Vietnamese grammar. This is clearly a universal distinction made in some way in all languages, though what gets coded as a positive and what as a negative varies.[5] In Vietnamese, it is a pervasive ordering principle. Consider three manifestations. First, and best-documented, are the quasi-passive expressions constructed around a verb meaning either 'acquire' or 'suffer' (other verbs are used, but these are the most

---

5 In the Vietnamese case, one principle of evaluation that underlies the system appears to be, something like, "culture as human appropriation of nature is good", whereas "natural encroachment on any kind of human cultivation (in the broadest sense, i.e., not just agricultural cultivation) is bad". So, for instance, native speakers insist that a piece of cultivated land which has been abandoned, must be described using *bị*, literally 'suffer', rather than *được*, as in, *bãi đất bị bỏ hoang*, [CL land PASS/N uninhabited] 'abandoned land'.

common; see, inter alia, Nguyễn Hồng Cổn 2009, Nguyễn Đình Hòa 1997, Simpson and Tâm 2013).[6]

(1) *Anh ấy bị   người ta   đánh.*
     EB   3   suffer person PL   beat
     He has been beaten by someone (Thompson 1965: 229)

(2) *Tiếng con chim sơn ca bị   át đi bởi tiếng còi   tàu rúc*
     Sound CL bird lark suffer drown by sound whistle train hoot.
     The lark's singing is drowned out by the train's whistle. (Nguyễn Hồng Cổn 2009: 112)

(3) *Loan hiện đang   bị   bố mẹ   ép   lấy một người mà*
     Loan now PROG suffer parents force take one person COMP
     Loan không thuận
     Loan NEG agree
     Loan was being forced by her parents to marry someone she did not want.
     (Nhất Linh, *Đoạn Tuyệt*: 2)

(4) *Em học sinh này được cô giáo   khen*
     YS student this get teacher praise
     This student is praised by the teacher. (Nguyễn Hồng Cổn 2009: 107)

(5) *Ngôi nhà   này được xây dựng bởi những tay thợ lành nghề*
     CL   house this get build   by PL   worker skilled
     This house is built by skilled workers. (Nguyễn Hồng Cổn 2009: 112)

An analagous distinction is made with the adjectival modifier indicating 'quite', 'somewhat' or 'a little'. Thus we find,

(6) a. *khá hay*, 'quite interesting'
     b. *khá tốt*, 'quite good'
     c. *khá giỏi*, 'quite well'

---

6 Nguyễn Đình Hòa (1997: 111–112) writes: "Because they carry a sense of submissiveness or passivity, the verbs *bị, phải, chịu, mắc* are often used to translate the "passive" construction in a Western language. Actually each of them is just the head of a pattern of complementation denoting an unpleasant experience and sometimes even qualified with the degree marker *rất* 'very'." And he concludes, "The label 'submissive verb' is definitely better than 'passive verb' (. . .) since the language does not have the passive voice as such." (ibid.: 112).

But,

(7) a. *hơi lạnh*, 'a bit cold'
    b. *hơi nóng*, 'a bit hot'
    c. *hơi mệt*, 'a bit tired'

Finally, we find a similar distinction marked in the derivation of nouns from adjectives expressing emotions. "Positive" emotions combine with *niềm* as in, for example, *niềm vui* 'cheerfulness', *niềm hạnh phúc* 'happiness'. "Negative" emotions, on the other hand, combine with *nỗi* as in, *nỗi buồn* 'sadness', *nỗi sợ* 'fear', *nỗi tức giận* 'anger', *nỗi lo lắng* 'worry'. On the basis of these admittedly somewhat speculative observations about the system of meaning oppositions, we could hypothesise about ways in which World-View 2 is elaborated within Vietnamese grammar, and could continue to identify additional evidence that either supports the claim or calls for modification of it.

2.3 Culture inheres in ways of speaking

A third stance on the language-culture relation resembles Hale's World-View 1. In this approach, the emphasis is less on structural aspects of language than on the culturally specific ways in which language is used. Pioneered in the 1960s and 70s by anthropologists such as Dell Hymes, Joel Sherzer, and Richard Bauman, this strand of research employs notions of speech event and genre in an attempt to describe the social uses of speech in context. In MSEA, Leach's (1964) analysis of Kachin terms of verbal abuse and the cultural assumptions that these reveal can, perhaps, be seen as a precursor to this line of research. However, this approach has not been widely applied to MSEA speech communities. While the "ways of speaking" approach was in its heyday, from about 1965 to about 1980, Indochina was difficult for foreign researchers to access.[7] By historical accident, work in Thailand (by, e.g., Moerman 1988 and Bilmes 1992) tended to be more conversation analytic and ethnomethodological in nature (though see, Wijeyewardene 1968a). And while Becker conducted extensive research in Myanmar, on Burmese, his work does not really exemplify the ways-of-speaking approach. Research in peninsular Malaysia was mostly dominated

---

[7] We note that during this period, there was notable US state-sponsored linguistic and ethnographic research. The scope and nature of this work was constrained by its function as part of the war effort.

by British anthropologists with little interest in language (though see the work of Geoffrey Benjamin for an important exception, e.g., 1968, 1993, 1999, 2014) and there was almost no work done in Laos on language and culture until the twenty-first century (Enfield 2007, Chapter 2 therein). This said, we can imagine many projects in MSEA that would adopt this perspective. The ethnography of speaking has typically focused on specialized, extraordinary modes of speaking. In the Vietnamese context, the event of "soul calling" (gọi hồn) would provide an obvious topic for research in this tradition (see Nguyen Duong 2020, Badenoch 2022).[8] Throughout MSEA there are special registers used in speaking to monks and this too could make for an interesting topic of such ethnographic research.

2.4 Reflexive semiosis

A fourth approach to the relation between language and culture turns on the possibility of language being "about itself", as, for example, when we quote others' speech, pass judgment on their accents, praise them for their eloquence, or correct their turns of phrase. This *reflexive* property is unique to language as a communicative system. The fourth approach to the language-culture relationship we discuss here centres on this property, focusing on the dynamic intersection of language form (structure), language use (practice), and reflective reanalysis of structure and practice (ideology). To define and characterize this approach, it is useful to begin by clarifying what the approach is *not*.

No telepathy: Culture has a cognitive component – people must learn it – but its socially distributed nature means that it must be transmitted and maintained by semiotic means. Culture is necessarily communicated. For culture to cumulate, it must pass through the "bottleneck" of communicative practice in social interaction (Enfield and Sidnell 2022).

No simple symbolism: Culture is composed of different kinds of signs. When a sign serves its function of signifying something else it does so through various types of *ground*, as Peirce (1955) put it, often in combination. The sign may resemble what it stands for (an iconic relation), it may be connected to what it stands for (an indexical relation), or it might have the meaning it has because

---

8 There is of course a large and relevant literature from outside anthropology and linguistics. For instance, there is an extensive literature on Vietnamese poetry and poetics much of which clearly intersects with the themes we develop in the current essay (see, especially, Huỳnh Sanh Thông 1979, 1986).

people in a community agree that it does (a symbolic relation). Further, signs may be thought of as populating a possibility space of sorts: we can distinguish qualisigns (what could possibly be a sign to us), sinsigns (what happens to be realized as a sign) and legisigns (what will necessarily be taken as a sign). (See Peirce 1955, Parmentier 1994, Kockelman 2005 for explication of these concepts.) This means that a fish trap, a highway and a hand gesture are just as much signs, and constituents of culture, as a religious image or a table setting. Semiotic mediation happens both as "residence" and as "representation" (Kockelman 2013).

No culture without society: Culture is socially distributed across populations. Some persons are familiar with the constitutive signs while others are not (Agha 2007). Some may have a passive competence that allows them to recognize a given set of signs but are not themselves able to competently (re)produce them (or may not be entitled to do so; implying a higher order social organization of lower order signs). Moreover, signs are always socially embedded. Consider, for instance, money. Clearly, any currency consists of signs that stand for values arrived at through complex processes of evaluation and practice. Money is socially embedded not only in international financial markets but also state legal systems and banking practices, as well the countless ground-level occasions in which it is exchanged. Any socially significant set of signs is embedded in this way so an analysis of culture as an effervescent superstructure somehow floating above the practicalities of daily social life is necessarily inadequate.

No behaviorism: Just as culture cannot exist without being publicly distributed, it is also mediated by minds. All aspects of culture as semiosis are, to varying degrees, subject to reflexive processes and reanalysis and this is partly constitutive of their significance. To take a simple example: the use, meaning and appropriateness of a pronominal form cannot be properly understood without reference to the ways in which users think and talk about the use, meaning and appropriateness of that pronominal form (see, inter alia, Chirasombutti and Diller 1999). While, as Silverstein (1981) argued, functional aspects of language use are not equally accessible to native speaker awareness and report, under some conditions – the extreme case being comparative linguistic analysis – some degree of awareness is always possible. And, of course, there are ways in which both awareness and report are subject to systemic distortion. Finally, metasemiotic activity – whether implicit or explicit, proximate or distal, vernacular or expert – is itself subject to metasemiotic construal, resulting in n^{th} level reflexive reanalysis.

Put more positively, a semiotic conception of culture insists on a set of interplays: between public practice and private cognition, between natural affordances and conventional values, between actions and evaluations, between populations and identities. And crucially, we argue that these interplays are mediated by a single interface: the real-time locus of interpersonal interaction (Enfield and Sidnell 2022). This is the conception of culture that we adopt.

This semiotic conception of culture has two consequences. First, it provides a straightforward solution to the problem of the language–culture relationship. Much of culture consists of language (e.g., pronouns, polemics, political speeches, parody). And *all* cultural phenomena are partially constituted through the modes of representation to which they are subject, language being the primary means in this respect (e.g., pronouns used only with one's son-in-law, polemics about parents, political speeches that promote nationalism, parodies of political speeches that promote nationalism, etc.). Second, it suggests, in an apparent reversal of Boas, that the most interesting aspects of culture are not those invisible to native speaker awareness but, rather, those most elaborated in and through metasemiotic processes. But this would be too strong. While metasemiotic processes often point to phenomena of particular concern, they themselves are shaped by the very forms of distortion and limits of awareness that Boas pointed to. We will attempt to show how this is so in our discussion of two case studies below.

But that notwithstanding, this perspective encourages us to balance the Boasian (and Whorfian) concern with what Silverstein characterized as "primary ethnological data" (i.e., those aspects of culture that appear coded as basic ontological assumptions in the grammar of a language) with "key symbols" or "cultural focus". Ortner describes key symbols as those which "extensively and systematically formulate relationships [. . .] between a wide range of diverse cultural elements" (Ortner 1973: 1343). For Herskovits, cultural focus is an "area of activity or belief where the greatest awareness of form exists, the most discussion of values is heard, the widest difference in structure is to be discerned" (Herskovits 1955: 485).

Once culture is conceptualized in this way, a number of consequences follow for how we conceptualize the language–culture relationship. The core idea may be put simply as follows: linguistic practice is partially constituted by the ways in which it is construed by those that employ it. This construal may be proximate or distal. This construal may be of tokens and/or types. It may be implicit or explicit. It may be articulated by socially defined experts or ordinary folk.

Adopting the above-defined fourth stance on the language–culture relationship, we now explore this conception in relation to two highly unalike case studies from mainland Southeast Asia. The first, from Vietnamese, starts with a set of functional structures in language – ways of referring to the participants in a communicative encounter – and seeks to understand how they relate to their cultural context in a reflexive semiotic manner. The second, from Lao, starts with a set of functional structures in material culture – devices for catching fish – and seeks to understand how the ways of referring to, and talking about the structures are implicated in their existence as cultural artefacts. By coming from two directions, we seek to converge on a semiotic conception of the language-culture relationship that opens new avenues for research in the anthropology of language in mainland Southeast Asia.

3 Case study I: *Vietnamese interlocutor reference*

By interlocutor reference we mean the practices by which reference to speaker and addressee of an utterance is accomplished (Fleming and Sidnell 2020). This excludes so called "vocative" reference which is typically not grammatically obligatory. So, in English, interlocutor reference is almost always accomplished using the first and second person pronouns. Use of cryptotypic third person forms such as kinterms like *mommy* and *daddy* and personal names is inferentially rich, indexing a shift in register (baby talk), or footing (illeism). In contrast, in Vietnamese, pronouns are rarely used and, in most situations, speakers refer both to themselves and their addressees using kin terms, even when they are not genealogically related. These terms are differentiated according to relative age, generation and sometimes gender and are, generally, not reciprocally usable (see Sidnell and Shohet 2013 for one exception). Two consequences of this are, 1) participants in interaction are identified not according to shifting interactional roles (i.e., speaker, addressee) but according to more perduring, sometimes institutionalized statuses such as "older brother" or "mother's brother" and so on, and, 2) a single utterance may map onto an interactional situation in a number of different ways. Consider a well-known example from Luong (1990: 11–12):

(8)   *Mẹ*   *đã*   *mua*   *cho*   *bố*   *cái mũ hôm qua*   *rồi*
      Mother   PST   bought   BEN   father   CL   hat   yesterday   already

In this example, the sentence can, depending on the institutionalized role relations of the speaker and addressee, mean any of the following:
(a) 'I already bought the hat for you yesterday.'
(b) 'You already bought the hat for me . . .'
(c) 'I already bought the hat for father . . .'
(d) 'Mother already bought the hat for me . . .'
(e) 'You already bought the hat for father . . .'
(f) 'Mother already bought the hat for you . . .'
(g) 'Mother already bought the hat for father . . .'

Generally, in casual conversation, there is a tendency to minimize hierarchical differences and the use of sibling terms between persons who differ in age by 20 years is not uncommon. At the same time, there is a sense in which the use of kin terms indexes and invokes the family as a model for all social relations (see Luong 1990, Sidnell 2022). Linked to one another by such fictive, and often momentary, bonds of "kinship", participants in interaction cast themselves as 'elder brother' and 'younger sibling', 'niece' and 'uncle', and so on. This widespread cultural idealization in which respect combines with mutual obligation is captioned by the oft-cited expression *kính trên, nhường dưới* 'respect those above, yield to those below' (see Sidnell 2022, Shohet 2021).

Because the forms used in interlocutor reference are non-deictic, they allow for various kinds of transposition. For instance, a father may address his elder daughter as *chị* 'elder sister' thereby adopting the persepctive of her younger sibling, the speaker's younger daughter. Such shifts of perspective are pervasive and, Luong (1984, 1990) suggests, in some contexts normatively required. They are also frequently "conventionalized" in various ways, effected in cases where the person whose perspective is adopted is not present or even, indeed, does not exist. For instance, a man of 35 who does not have children may address his slightly younger friend as *chú* 'father's younger brother' thereby adopting the perspective of his own non-existent child (see Luong and Sidnell 2020). It is well known that this was the preferred mode of address with Hồ Chí Minh. His compatriots would address him as *bác* 'father's elder brother' and he would address them as *chú* thereby suggesting a relationship between older and younger brothers as mediated by their children. One thing such practices often do, then, is to formulate the dyadic relationship between speaker and addressee as a triadic or polyadic relation which connects two or more generations.

The practices of interlocutor reference are subject to extensive metasemiotic elaboration. As Luong (1990) writes: "In the metalinguistic awareness of virtually all native speakers, person reference constitutes the most salient domain through which interactional contexts are structured and partly in terms which the native sociocultural universe is reproduced and transformed." Consider, for instance, regulations for the National Armed Forces released in 1946. These dealt quite meticulously with certain aspects of language. Article 40 of ordinance 71, dealt specifically with address and self-reference:

Quân nhân tất cả các cấp coi nhau như anh em. Trong khi làm công vụ không ai xưng hô "mày", "tao", mặc dầu là ngang hàng với nhau. Quân nhân cấp dưới gọi cấp trên bằng ông hoặc anh tuỳ trường hợp. Quân nhân cấp trên gọi cấp dưới bằng anh. Lúc thưa trình với người chỉ huy của mình thì dùng chức vụ mà gọi "thưa tiểu đội trưởng, thưa trung đoàn trưởng [. . .]" Quân nhân tự xưng là "tôi".

> Soldiers at all levels should treat one another like brothers. While on duty no one should address another as "mày" or self-refer with "tao", even {though/if} they are on equal footing. Lower-ranking soldiers should address their superiors as grandfather or brother, depending on the circumstances. High-ranking soldiers should address their subordinates as elder brother. When speaking to his commander, a soldier should use his official title to address him: "honorable platoon leader," "honorable regiment commander [. . .]" The soldier should refer to himself as "tôi".[9]

Such regulations were meant to institutionalize a particular vision of polite civility, discouraging interpersonal modes that might be construed as unconstrained and overly familiar (*mày – tao*, i.e., bare, non-honorific pronouns) while also minimizing hierarchical relations not premised on officially recognized military distinctions.

The mention of *tôi* is important. About 15 years earlier, editorialist and general man of letters, Phan Khôi had advocated for the use of this pronoun in public discourse as a neutral means of self-reference, one that conveyed nothing about the relation between the interlocutors, or between writer and audience (Sidnell, frth). These arguments cast Vietnamese of the day as a pre-modern language which, in comparison with French and Chinese, forced interlocutors to continuously position themselves in relation to one another. This, Phan Khôi suggested, had emerged as particularly inconvenient with the rise of print mediated communications and he argued that it, along with other traditional practices of speaking (such as a strict taboo on the use of a senior party's personal name), had to be reformed if the Vietnamese hoped to modernize their language and public life more generally. Part of the problem that Phan Khôi faced here resulted from the fact that *tôi* was derived from a word meaning "subject of the king" and had been used up until the beginning of the 20th century to convey humility. However, in the first decades of the twentieth century, literacy in *chữ quốc ngữ*, the romanized script in use today, was on the rise and Vietnamese intellectuals began to translate works of European, especially French, literature. Faced with the problem of how to translate *Je*, they turned to *tôi* and, it seems, this usage gradually caught on, perhaps being understood as a means for approximating the self-consciously modern subjectivity of French and European others.

A few years later, in 1936, Vũ Trọng Phụng published his biting satire of Vietnamese elite life in the late colonial period – "*Số đỏ*" (translated as "*Dumb Luck*"). Near the beginning of the novel the hero, red-haired Xuan, is working as a ball boy at the tennis courts and is called to come play with the members Mr. and Mrs. Civilization and Mrs. Deputy Customs Officer. He greets them in the normal,

---

9 *mặc dầu* could be taken to mean either "even though" or "even if", quite a consequential difference in this context.

traditional way, using kinship terms that are calibrated to their relative age and social position. So, he uses *cụ lớn* (literally 'great grandparent' + 'big') for Mrs. Deputy Customs Officer who is the oldest of the three and *ông* 'grandfather' and *bà* 'grandmother' for the other two. After he is chided by Mrs. Deputy Customs Officer, he substitutes *bà lớn* in correcting himself.

> *"Good afternoon, Grandmother (cụ lớn). Good afternoon, Sir (ông). Good afternoon, Madame (bà)."*
>
> Mr. and Mrs. Civilization nodded their heads in acknowledgment, but Mrs. Deputy Customs Officer turned away in disgust. The younger woman grinned knowingly at her husband.
>
> *"My aunt does not approve of such formal language," he said sternly to Xuan.*
>
> *"You stupid ass!" Mrs. Deputy Customs Officer chimed in bitterly. "Who are you calling Grandmother? I'm no older than your mother. Do I look old enough to have delivered your mother? Why, I bet your mother is nothing more than a – "*
>
> *"Yes, yes, Madame (bà lớn). I was mistaken. Please forgive me."*

While Mrs. Deputy Customs Officer complains about the difference of age implied, notice that her nephew describes the matter in terms of not approving of "formal language". These expressions, in other words, are caught up in multiple systems of evaluation. First, use of a senior kin term implies respect, it is honorific. Second, the same term can be read, literally, as implying the addressee is very old relative to the speaker. Third, such practices are evaluated as "traditional" and "old fashioned" or "modern" etc. This last mode of evaluation is suggested by the description of "formal language" and is even more obvious in the next passage in which Mr. Civilization is talking with his father:

> Mrs. Deputy Customs Officer offered her arm to Grandpa Hong. With her assistance, he took his seat-but gingerly, like a genuine great-grandpa.
>
> *"When did toa arrive here?" he asked his son.*
>
> *"A while ago," Mr. Civilization answered, as if not addressing anyone in particular.*
>
> *"Moa has some business with toa. Our via (vieux, 'old man') seems on the verge of . . . going . . . of leaving us. Perhaps we ought to find a medical doctor so that old via can enjoy a little French science before he dies . . ."*

Here the use of invariant French pronouns *toa* and *moa* between a father and his son indexes a self-conscious European modernity, one that was explicitly espoused by the real person upon whom Vũ Trọng Phụng based the character of Mr. Civilization, Nhất Linh the co-founder of the avant garde *Tự Lực Văn Đoàn* 'Self-Strengthening Literary Group'.[10]

---

10 See Agha (2007: 136–139, 174–177) on the way speakers "inhabit distinct register-mediated social personae" (2007: 165).

Clearly, these forms are highly salient and the object of extensive meta-semiotic elaboration in literature, language reform, government policy and so on. Skipping ahead to the contemporary period, we find many instances of such elaboration across a broad swath of different media types. As one example, consider a recent article titled "*Xưng hô ông bà hay bố mẹ khi đã có con?*" (Address as grandfather and grandmother or father and mother when one has children?). This article asks whether persons should, in talking to their parents, adopt the perspective of their own children and so address them as grandfather and grandmother, a practice which is commonly rationalized as a means to socialize children in the appropriate use of kin terms and normatively expected modes of deferential conduct towards senior members of the family. The article tells the story of 75 year old Mrs. Nguyễn Thị Thìn of Hanoi whose three children are married and have children of their own. While in the past they would address her as 'mother', since their children were born, they have begun to call her 'grandmother', even when the children are not present. This has left her 'heartbroken' (*chạnh lòng*) – she wants them to continue to call her mother which she sees as more affectionate (*tình cảm hơn*). Finally, Mrs. Nguyễn Thị Thìn, reports she was led to remind her children – "We are your parents, not your grandparents, why do you call us grandparents!". At this point in the article, Associate Professor Lê Ngọc Văn of the Institute of Family and Gender Studies is brought in to comment: "in the presence of grandchildren, it is acceptable for children to address their parents as 'grandparents' as a way of teaching their children. But when the children are not present, it is better to address one's parents as 'mother' and 'father' so as to foster a better and more emotional relationship."

Interlocutor reference represents, then, an important node in the language culture nexus in Vietnamese. Minimally, its description requires that we look at the intersection of language form (structure), language use (practice), and metasemiotic elaboration, reflexive awareness and construal (ideology).

4 Case study II: Fish traps of Laos

The device shown in Figure 17.1 is a type of fish trap belonging to the family of traps called *toum* in Lao (see Enfield 2007).

This one is used in the deep waters of the Mekong River, just downstream of the Lao capital, Vientiane. The *toum* is one among many kinds of trap made and used by Lao speakers across Laos and neighboring areas of Thailand and Cambodia (Claridge et al. 1997, Enfield 2009 Chapter 5 therein). These types of

Figure 17.1: A *toum* fishtrap on the Mekong River, near Vientiane, in Laos
(Photo by N. J. Enfield).

trap are also made and used in hundreds of other language communities across
mainland Southeast Asia (Enfield 2021).

The craft and technology of fish traps could be considered material culture
par excellence. Classical ethnographies of cultures around the world describe
the tools and devices that community members build and use as part of their
economic livelihoods (on fish trap technology in another MSEA community; see
Hickey 1964: 158–165). The designs and skills embodied in these artifacts persist because the knowledge for making and using them is successfully transmitted in communities. That knowledge is also passed between different culture
groups, in processes of inter-group contact. Cultural knowledge around material artifacts is no doubt embodied in bodily dispositions, but this knowledge
would not be *cultural* without the socialization and regulation that linguistic
commentary provides.

A *toum* is like a lobster trap. It is a chamber made from bamboo strips woven together, with an opening at the base, usually on the side (but sometimes, as with the giant *toum* in Figure 17.1, in the base). Fish find it easy to get into the chamber but difficult or impossible to get out. The *toum* is lowered into water and secured with a stake to the floor of a river or pond. Bait is placed inside the chamber. One then leaves the trap, visiting it later to collect any fish that are caught. The size and shape of various types of *toum* varies depending on the type of fish it is intended to catch.

We can think of the *toum* as a problem-solving device. The problem it solves is simple. Fish are an abundant source of protein for humans but they are difficult to catch by hand. The *toum* is a purpose-designed structure that manipulates its victims (the fish) into doing as its designers (the humans) want them to do, to their unknowing detriment. As described by Krebs and Dawkins (1984) in their analysis of the fundamental logic of animal communication, the trap works by exploiting the victim's attention and natural incentives and then using its own muscle power against it. The trap itself does nothing. The victim does all the work. When the trap-setter returns, he retrieves the fish at his leisure.

Let us consider the three relationships between the three entities involved in the fish-trapping scenario. First, there is the relation between the fish and the trap, as just described. The trap is a sign that fish respond to in a reliable way. It incorporates the fundamental semiotic relation of *affordance* (Gibson 1979): the trap incorporates features that lure or "invite" the fish to act in a certain way (such features are also called "demand characters"; Koffka 1935, Kiverstein et al. 2021: 2286ff). Second, there is the relation between the fish and the human, as mediated by the trap. This relation is more distal, brutal and utilitarian. Neither of these two relations involve language per se (though of course the human-to-fish relationship is linguistically elaborated through the descriptive resources of the Lao language for describing fish anatomy and behavior, and for classifying fish and related creatures). Here, we focus on the third relationship, that between human and trap.

The *toum* is part and parcel of the riverine livelihood that characterizes rural lowland Lao-speaking culture. While the physical, artifactual nature of this piece of material culture may suggest it would be the last place to look for a language-culture relation, we argue that even textbook material culture is nothing without language. Let us consider three ways in which language is implicated: reference, coordination, and accounting.

Reference: In the first language-culture connection, there is an extensive vocabulary in the Lao language for labeling and describing the object, including the word *toum* and specific words for sub-types (e.g., the giant *toum thoong* depicted in Figure 17.1) as well as the names of the component parts of the device (e.g., *ngaa*, the inward-pointing 'tusks' in the trap's opening that allow the fish to swim in but not out), terms for the various actions of constructing the trap (and the terms for the materials used in doing so), setting it and retrieving it, and the trap's status within a larger vocabulary for fishing technologies, their production, usage, and value.

For example, one could not explain the trap's workings, as when instructing an apprentice, without using specific vocabulary. The word for 'setting' the trap in place is *vaang1*, a general term meaning to lay something down, to place it in a location. The action of going to 'check' the trap is described in Lao as *jaam3*, a verb meaning 'to visit', as when one visits relatives in a distant village. To be a functioning member of the culture of people who make and use these traps, one must not only know how the traps are made and used, but also how they are normally spoken about, including the relevant connotations and associations introduced by such ways of speaking (e.g., that the captured fish are 'visited' rather than 'checked').

We emphasize that the language around the culture of fish traps involves much more than a few appropriate nouns and verbs. In discourse around the use of *toum* traps, one also needs to command vocabularies that refer to all associated referential and conceptual domains, including the plants and plant products used for constructing the device, and the kinds of waterscapes in which the trap should be placed, entailing ways of talking about depth, current, temperature, and more. This in turn is tied to topological and geographical knowledge that is similarly language-dependent, encompassing landscape terms and place names (Enfield 2015a, Chapter 4 therein, esp. 74–100). Also, we emphasize that teaching and describing the ins and outs of the *toum* not only involves extensive vocabulary but also the choice of appropriate grammatical constructions (e.g., for expressing actions, part-whole relations, purposes, and for structuring discourses of explanation and narrative that provide the necessary coherence and cohesion for textual comprehension).

For these reasons, a seemingly simple stand-alone physical object will demand much more than a "label". It will be tied to a vast network of words and constructions that moor it to human activities and purposes, as well as to a vast array of related non-human entities, both concrete and abstract.

Coordinating: Many things in our worlds are named, and common sense tells us that this is because we need to talk about them (Zaslavsky et al. 2019). But common sense doesn't explain why the vast majority of things in our lives go *without* labels (Berlin 1992). If something is named, this needs to be explained, or at least made more concrete than a simple claim that the existence of words reflects "communicative need" (Enfield 2015a, 2022). What does such a need actually look like?

If the making and setting of traps were exclusively solitary activities, then an individual could presumably have the required thoughts, and carry out the required actions, without needing to refer to them using the public medium of words. But once we need to socially *coordinate* our actions, then language is the most important tool we have (Enfield 2022, O'Madagain and Tomasello 2022). The "communicative need" implied by the existence of the words is not the need to refer to things but the need that is *served by* such acts of referring: namely, the need to coordinate our behavior and actions around the things we refer to. When the word *toum* is used in Lao-speaking village life, it is not merely to point something out. (And indeed, no act of pointing-out is "merely" for pointing out; it will at the very least in turn serve to elicit or provide help, or to share experience; Tomasello 2006, 2008.) Such pointing-out will be incorporated in a speech act that is in the service of eliciting some response from someone: for example, in reminding a companion to bring a *toum* along on our walk to the creek, in asking if there is a *toum* at the field hut near the river bend where we're going, or in asking to borrow someone's *toum*. Referring to a *toum* may also serve less direct coordinating functions. For example, in answer to the question "Where is Kham?", one could answer "He's taken his *toum*" as a way to convey what kind of place he's likely to be at, what kind of activity he's engaged in, or how long he's likely to be. And there are many other kinds of social activity that will be facilitated by the use of language relating to the *toum*, ranging from the above-mentioned kinds of teaching activities to conversation about the diverse types of fish traps encountered in travels to distant villages, to storytelling about incidents that occurred during fishing activities.

A century ago, Malinowski described the central role of language in coordination, from the "technical references" to the "telling exclamations" that men use in coordinating their actions in coral lagoon fishing parties on Kiriwina Island in Papua New Guinea. He argued that "technical language, in matters of practical pursuit, acquires its meaning only through personal participation in this type of pursuit. It has to be learned, not through reflection but through action" (Malinowski 1923: 311–312). Such use of references and exclamations in coordinated action is arguably the central function of language. Any form of material culture will implicate such use of language in so far as material culture requires the coordination of human behavior, both in cultural transmission (teaching and learning) and in concerted action (which most material culture implies).

Accounting: A third main function that language serves in relation to material culture is to enable the regulation, regimentation, and calibration of collective knowledge, practice, and understanding of that material culture through practices of language-mediated social accountability. People uphold norms through acts of sanctioning others (both praising and criticizing) using the categories en-coded in language. When people hold others to account for claims and actions (including linguistic actions) made in connection with the artifacts in question, they make public the "rules" that apply to those artifacts. This is easiest to see in practices of socialization. When an experienced/authoritative community mem-ber schools (or scolds) an apprentice, their usual tool will be language. Consider an example in which a village man is preparing to walk with his young son to his rice fields, which are near deep river pools that are good for placing *toum* traps. He asks his son to retrieve a *toum* but when the boy appears with a *sai* – a differ-ent kind of trap, for placing in different waterscapes – the father says "That's not a *toum*, that's a *sai!*". (Compare the situation in which a child in a middle-class Toronto household sits on the kitchen table and is told by a parent: "That's not a chair, it's a table!". This is language-mediated normative regimentation of the functions of material culture.) Or when the father and son arrive at the river pool and the boy begins setting the *toum* in place: the father sees that the boy is laying the *toum* down on its side rather than upright, "It's not a *sai* it's a *toum!* Set it upright." Such exchanges can be multiplied by the number of kinds of opportu-nity people have to observe and remark on normatively right or wrong ways to interact with the artifact (including right or wrong ways to talk about it). (And of course there are only a few right ways and an infinite number of wrong ways.) We can think of practices involved not only in the selection of the right trap for a specific context (time of day, location, etc.) but in how a trap is placed, stored, cleaned, repaired, and constructed, how bait is set and how prey is retrieved, the value of traps for purchase and exchange, various cultural beliefs about traps (for example, woven traps are often hung decoratively in Lao village households as a symbol of bounty), among much more.

All of these things are learned in large part through the ways in which in-siders and experts talk. The novice can say "I'm hanging up the *toum*" and the expert can say, "No, do it like this". These utterances seem like simple acts of instruction but they point to the role of language as the mediating link between material culture and sociocultural norms. The accountability of sociocultural membership is introduced with the infrastructure that is the vocabulary.

The *toum* is a physical structure with an ostensible function – to catch fish – that involves no language at all. Indeed, a solitary man could decide to build one, collect and process the raw materials, construct it, deploy it, and consume its catch all without words. But that chain of events could never have become possible without language. The man in this tale could not have ac-quired the requisite skills and knowledge without language, nor could those skills and knowledge have achieved their stability over time and space without language as an instrument for instruction and regimentation.

The relations between language and material culture that we have re-viewed – using the example of a type of fish trap in widespread use across Laos and mainland Southeast Asia – generate a second-order function of language in relation to material culture that goes beyond localized social interactions. This is the function of cultural transmission across time and space. Across time, generations of Lao speakers have built and used *toum* traps, just as across space, the technology of the traps and their usage has diffused throughout the mainland Southeast Asia area and beyond. There would be no cumulative transmission of material culture without language. (Claims that nonlinguistic creatures have "culture" – see Whiten 2021 – are working with a concept of "culture" that is qualitatively distinct from what we mean here. Whiten's defini-tion of culture, as "the inheritance of an array of behavioral traditions through social learning from others", does not capture the cumulative, structured, norm-governed quality of human culture that allows it to become so vastly elaborated across societies and through time.) Such transmission is effected by interactions such as those we have reviewed above, not only directed acts of teaching, but also in any discourse that can be observed by learners who are motivated to attend to cultural practices in their midst as they strive to become full members of society.

With the example of the *toum* we want to convey that the language-culture relationship is not restricted to a narrow range of cultural matters that are obvi-ously language-dependent, such as the language-instantiated practices of ver-bal art, poetry, and oratory. The truth is that little if anything in culture is language-independent. Even in the case of fish traps – which appear more lan-guage-independent than other physical structures such as Buddhist temples – the thing cannot acquire cultural significance without the possibility of ac-countable description and social coordination.

5 Conclusion

We began with an overview of four approaches to the language-culture relation-ship, with some reference to materials from MSEA speech communities. We ar-gued in favor of the fourth of these approaches, a theory of culture as a semiotic system, and we laid out some of the implications of this view for an understand-ing of the language-culture nexus. Then, in our two case studies, we explored the language-culture relationship from distinctly different directions. In our discus-sion of Vietnamese interlocutor reference, we explored some dimensions of the *cul-ture of language* in this setting (for other work in this general area from other parts of MSEA see, for instance, Diffloth 1980, Diller 1985, 1988, 2006, Diller and Junta-namalaga 1990, Zuckerman and Enfield 2020). In the discussion of fish traps from Laos we emphasized the dependence of material culture on language and language use in a wide range of contexts (see also Zuckerman and Enfield 2022).

Contemporary linguistic anthropology has centrally been concerned with ways in which language and discourse (usually *about* language and discourse) shapes human identity, activity, social relations, history, thought, and language itself. But questions about overarching systems of culture and worldview have been largely sidestepped, and to some degree regarded as old fashioned. While it may seem surprising that such an old idea could be a new direction for the field, we submit that if linguistic anthropology is to be truly comprehensive, it will need to offer a coherent account of the foundational concept of anthropology itself: culture.

References

Agha, Asif. 2007. *Language and social relations*. Cambridge: Cambridge University Press.

Badenoch, Nathan. 2022. Speaking like a ghost. Registers of intimacy and incompatibility in the forests of Northern Laos. *Journal of the Siam Society* 110 (1). 103–150.

Becker, Alton L. 1975. A linguistic image of nature. The Burmese numerative classifier system. *Linguistics* 13 (165). 109–22.

Benjamin, Geoffrey. 1968. Temiar personal names. *Bijdragen tot de Taal-, Land- en Volkenkunde* 124. 99–134.

Benjamin, Geoffrey. 1993. Grammar and polity. The cultural and political background to Standard Malay. In William A. Foley (ed.), *The role of theory in language description*, 341–392. Berlin: De Gruyter Mouton.

Benjamin, Geoffrey. 1999. Temiar kinship terminology. A linguistic and formal analysis. *Occasional Papers, Academy of Social Sciences, Penang* 1. 1–29.

Benjamin, Geoffrey. 2014. Aesthetic elements in Temiar grammar. In Jeffrey Williams (ed.), *The aesthetics of grammar. Sound and meaning in the languages of Mainland Southeast Asia*, 36–60. Cambridge: Cambridge University Press.

Berlin, Brent. 1992. *Ethnobiological classification. Principles of categorization of plants and animals in traditional societies*. Princeton, NJ: Princeton University Press.

Bilmes, Jack. 1992. Dividing the rice. A microanalysis of the mediator's role in a Northern Thai negotiation. *Language in Society* 21. 569–602.

Boas, Franz. 1911. Introduction. *Handbook of American Indian languages*, Vol. 1 (Bureau of American Ethnology, Bulletin 40), 1–83. Washington: Government Print Office.

Burling, Robert. 1965. How to choose a Burmese numeral classifier. In Melpord Spiro (ed.), *Context and meaning in cultural anthropology*, 243–264. New York: The Free Press.

Chirasombutti, Voravudhi & Anthony V. N. Diller. 1999. "Who am 'I' in Thai?" The Thai first person: self-reference or gendered self. In Peter A. Jackson & Nerida M. Cook (eds.), *Genders and sexualities in modern Thailand*, 114–33. Chiang Mai, Thailand: Silkworm Books.

Claridge, Gordon F., Thanongsi Sorangkhoun, Ian G. Baird & Hansai Sisomphone. 1997. *Community fisheries in Lao PDR. A survey of techniques and issues*. Vientiane: IUCN.

Diffloth, Gérard. 1980. To taboo everything at all times. *Berkeley Linguistic Society* 6.157–165.

Diller, Anthony V. N. 1985. High and low Thai. Views from within. In David Bradley (ed.), *Papers in South-East Asian linguistics* 9 (Pacific Linguistics A 67), 51–76. Canberra: Australian National University.

Diller, Anthony V. N. 1988. Thai syntax and "National Grammar". *Language Sciences* 10 (2). 273–312.

Diller, Anthony V. N & Preecha Juntanamalaga. 1990. "Full hearts" and empty pronominals in Thai. *Australian Journal of Linguistics* 10 (2). 231–255.

Diller, Anthony V. N. 2006. Polylectal grammar and Royal Thai. In Felix K. Ameka, Alan Dench & Nicholas Evans (eds.), *Catching language. The standing challenge of grammar writing*, 565–608. New York: De Gruyter Mouton.

Enfield, N. J. 2007. *A Grammar of Lao*. Berlin: Mouton de Gruyter.

Enfield, N. J. 2009. *The anatomy of meaning*. Cambridge: Cambridge University Press.

Enfield, N. J. 2015a. *The utility of meaning*. Oxford: Oxford University Press.

Enfield, N. J. 2015b. Linguistic relativity from reference to agency. *Annual Review of Anthropology* 44. 207–224.

Enfield, N. J. 2021. *The languages of Mainland Southeast Asia*. Cambridge: Cambridge University Press.

Enfield, N. J. 2022. *Language vs. reality*. Cambridge, MA: MIT Press.

Enfield, N. J. & Jack Sidnell. 2022. *Consequences of Language: From Primary to enhanced intersubjectivity*. Cambridge, MA: MIT Press.

Fleming, Luke & Jack Sidnell. 2020. The typology and social pragmatics of interlocutor reference in Southeast Asia. *The Journal of Asian Linguistic Anthropology* 2 (3). 1–20.

Geertz, Clifford. 1973. Thick description. Toward an interpretive theory of culture. In Clifford Geertz (ed.), *The interpretation of cultures*, 3–30. New York: Basic Books.

Gibson, James J. 1979. *The ecological approach to visual perception*. Boston: Houghton Mifflin.

Gumperz, John J. & Levinson, Stephen C. 1996. *Rethinking linguistic relativity*. Cambridge: Cambridge University Press.

Haas, Mary R. 1951. The use of numeral classifiers in Burmese. In Walter J. Fischel (ed.), *Semitic and Oriental studies. A volume presented to William Popper on the occasion of his seventy-fifth birthday, October 29, 1949* (University of California Publications in Semitic Philology 11), 191–200. Berkeley and Los Angeles: University of California Press. [Reprinted in: Dil, Anwar S. (ed.). 1978. *Language, culture, and history. Essays by Mary R. Haas*, 65–81. Stanford: Stanford University Press.].

Hale, Kenneth. 1986. Notes on world view and semantic categories. Some Warlpiri examples. In Peter Muysken & Henk van Riemsdijk (eds.), *Features and projections*, 233–254. Dordrecht, The Netherlands: Foris.

Hallowell, A. Irving. 1960. Ojibwa ontology, behavior, and world view. In Stanley Diamond (ed.), *Culture in history*, 19–52. New York: Columbia University Press.

Herskovits, Melville J. 1955. *Cultural anthropology*. New York: Alfred A. Knopf.

Hickey, Gerald C. 1964. *Village in Vietnam*. New Haven: Yale University Press.

Hla Pe, Maung. 1965. A re-examination of Burmese "classifiers". *Lingua* 15. 163–185.

Howell, Signe. 1981. Rules not words. In Paul Heelas and Andrew Locke (eds), *Indigenous psychologies. The anthropology of the self*, 133–143. London: Academic Press.

Huỳnh Sanh Thông. 1979. Introduction. *The heritage of Vietnamese poetry*, translated and edited by Huỳnh Sanh Thông. New Haven: Yale University Press

Huỳnh Sanh Thông. 1986. Fishes and fisherman. Females and males in Vietnamese folklore. *Vietnam Forum* 8. 240–276.

Hymes, Dell. 1967. Why linguistics needs the sociologist. *Social Research* 34 (4). 632–647.

Jenny, Mathias. 2000. A linguistic image of nature? The Burmese numerative classifier system reviewed. *The 33rd international conference on Sino-Tibetan languages and linguistics*, 43–51. Bangkok, Thailand: Ramkhamhaeng University.

Kiverstein, Julian, Ludger van Dijk & Erik Rietveld. 2021. The field and landscape of affordances. Koffka's two environments revisited. *Synthese* 198. 2279–2296.

Kockelman, Paul. 2005. The semiotic stance. *Semiotica*, 157 (1/4), 233–304.

Kockelman, Paul. 2013. *Agent, person, subject, self. A theory of ontology, interaction, and infrastructure*. Oxford: Oxford University Press.

Koffka, Kurt. 1935. *Principles of Gestalt psychology*. New York: Harcourt Brace.

Krebs, John R. & Richard Dawkins. 1984. Animal signals. Mind reading and manipulation. In John R. Krebs & Nicholas B. Davies (eds.), *Behavioural ecology. An evolutionary approach*, 2nd edition, 380–405. Oxford: Blackwell.

Leach, Edmund R. 1964. Anthropological aspects of language. Animal categories and verbal abuse. In Eric H. Lenneberg (ed.), *New directions in the study of language*, 151–165. Cambridge, MA: MIT Press.

Levinson, Stephen C. 2003. *Space in language and cognition. Explorations in cognitive diversity*. Cambridge: Cambridge University Press.

Lucy, John. 1992. *Language diversity and thought. A reformulation of the linguistic relativity hypothesis*. Cambridge: Cambridge University Press.

Luong, Hy Van. 1984. "Brother" and "uncle". An analysis of rules, structural contradictions, and meaning in Vietnamese kinship. *American Anthropologist* 86 (2). 290–315.

Luong, Hy Van. 1990. *Discursive practices and linguistic meanings. The Vietnamese system of person reference*. Amsterdam: John Benjamins.

Luong, Hy Van. & Jack Sidnell. 2020. Shifting referential perspective in Vietnamese speech interaction. *Journal of the Southeast Asian Linguistics Society* (Special publication 6: *Studies in the anthropology of language in Mainland Southeast Asia*, edited by N. J. Enfield, Jack Sidnell & Charles H. P. Zuckerman). 11–22.

Malinowski, Bronislaw. 1923. The problem of meaning in primitive languages. In Charles K. Ogden & Ivor A. Richards (eds.), *The meaning of meaning. A study of the influence of language upon thought and of the science of symbolism*, 296–336. New York: Harcourt, Brace.

Moerman, Michael. 1988. *Talking culture. Ethnography and conversation analysis*. Philadelphia: University of Pennsylvania Press.

Nguyễn, Đình-Hoà. 1957. Classifiers in Vietnamese. *Word* 13 (1). 124–152.

Nguyễn, Đình-Hoà. 1997. *Vietnamese. Tiếng Việt Không Son Phẩn*. Amsterdam: John Benjamins.

Nguyen, Duong. 2020. Talking with the ancestors. Register and repair in the Vietnamese soul-calling ritual (gọi hồn). *Journal of the Southeast Asian Linguistics Society* (Special publication 6: *Studies in the anthropology of language in Mainland Southeast Asia*, edited by N. J. Enfield, Jack Sidnell & Charles H. P. Zuckerman). 53–64.

Nguyễn, Hồng Cổn. 2009. Vietnamese passive sentences from a typological perspective. *Journal of the Southeast Asian Linguistics Society* 2. 105–118.

Ortner, Sherry. 1973. On key symbols. *American Anthropologist* 75. 1338–1346.

O'Madagain, Cathal & Michael Tomasello. 2022. Shared intentionality, reason-giving and the evolution of human culture. *Philosophical Transactions of the Royal Society B: Biological Sciences*, 377 (1843). DOI:10.1098/rstb.2020.0320

Parmentier, Richard J. 1994. *Signs in society. Studies in semiotic anthropology.* Bloomington & Indianapolis: Indiana University Press.

Peirce, Charles S. 1955. *Philosophical writings of Peirce.* New York: Dover Publications.

Sahlins, Marshall. 1976. *Culture and practical reason.* Chicago: Chicago University Press.

Sapir, Edward. 1924. Culture, genuine and spurious. *American Journal of Sociology* 29 (4). 401–429.

Sapir, Edward. 1949 (1938). Why cultural anthropology needs the psychiatrist. In David Mandlebaum (ed.), *Selected writings of Edward Sapir in language, culture and personality*, 569–577. Berkeley: University of California Press.

Shohet, Merav. 2021. *Silence and sacrifice. Family stories of care and the limits of love in Vietnam.* Oakland: University of California Press.

Sidnell, Jack. 2022. "Respect those above, yield to those below". Civility and social hierarchy in Vietnamese interlocutor reference. In Dwi Noverini Djenar & Jack Sidnell (eds.), *Signs of deference, signs of demeanour. Interlocutor reference and self-other relations across Southeast Asian speech communities.* Singapore: National University of Singapore (NUS) Press.

Sidnell, Jack & Merav Shohet. 2013. The problem of peers in Vietnamese interaction. *Journal of the Royal Anthropological Institute* 19 (3). 618–638.

Sidnell, Jack. 2023. The inconvenience of tradition: Phan Khôi's pragmatism and his proposals for modernizing language reform. *Journal of Vietnamese Studies.*

Silverstein, Michael. 1979. Language structure and linguistic ideology. In Paul Clyne, William Hanks & Carol Hofbauer (eds.), *The elements. A parasession on linguistic units and levels*, 193–247. Chicago: Chicago Linguistic Society, University of Chicago.

Silverstein, Michael. 1981. *The limits of awareness* (Working Papers in Sociolinguistics 84). Austin, Texas: Southwest Educational Development Laboratory.

Simpson, Andrew & Hồ Hảo Tâm. 2013. Vietnamese and the typology of passive constructions. In Daniel Hole & Elisabeth Löbel (eds.), *Linguistics of Vietnamese. An international survey*, 155–184. Berlin & Boston: De Gruyter Mouton

Stocking, George. 1996. Franz Boas and the culture concept in historical perspective. *American Anthropologist* 68 (4). 867–882.

Thompson, Laurence C. 1965. *A Vietnamese grammar.* Seattle & London: University of Washington Press.

Tomasello, Michael. 2006. Why don't apes point? In N. J. Enfield & Stephen C. Levinson (eds.), *Roots of human sociality. Culture, cognition, and interaction*, 506–524. London: Berg.

Tomasello, Michael. 2008. *Origins of human communication.* Cambridge, MA: MIT Press.

Trouillot, Michel-Rolph. 2003. Adieu, culture: A new duty arises. In Michel-Rolph Trouillot (ed.), *Global transformations.* Hoboken: Palgrave Macmillan.

Vũ, Trọng Phụng. 2002 (1936). *Số Đỏ* (translated as *Dumb Luck*). A novel edited and translated by Nguyễn Nguyệt Cầm and Peter Zinoman. Ann Arbor: University of Michigan Press.

Whiten, Andrew. 2021. The burgeoning reach of animal culture. *Science* 372 (6537). DOI:10.1126/science.abe6514

Wijeyewardene, Gehan. 1968a. The language of courtship in Chiengmai. *The Journal of the Siam Society* 56 (1). 21–32.

Wijeyewardene, Gehan. 1968b. Address, abuse and animal categories in Northern Thailand. *Man*, New Series, 3 (1). 76–93.

Zaslavsky, Noga, Charles Kemp, Naftali Tishby & Terry Regier. 2019. Communicative need in colour naming. *Cognitive Neuropsychology* 37 (10). 1–13.
Zuckerman, Charles. H. P. & N. J. Enfield. 2020. Heavy sound light sound. A Nam Noi metalinguistic trope. *Journal of the Southeast Asian Linguistics Society* (Special publication 6: *Studies in the anthropology of language in Mainland Southeast Asia*, edited by N. J. Enfield, Jack Sidnell & Charles H. P. Zuckerman). 85–92.
Zuckerman, Charles. H. P. & N. J. Enfield. 2022. The unbearable heaviness of being Kri: house construction and ethnolinguistic transformation in upland Laos. *Journal of the Royal Anthropological Institute* 28 (1). 178–203.

James W. Underhill & Adam Głaz

18 Research on language and culture in Europe

The chances of developing a coherent pan-European concept of cultural linguistics or ethnolinguistics appear to be fraught with difficulties. Can we provide a common European set of definitions, a shared methodology, and a shared set of aims when we inquire into how language shapes the way we understand and express ourselves? What are the main trends in the endeavors of scholars working in the field in Europe? Are those endeavors likely to continue in the same course they are taking today or will a post-colonial, global cultural linguistics replace the European model? In this chapter, we argue that European cultural linguistics often works with a methodology and objectives different from those of cultural linguistics as it is practiced in the Anglo community in the United States and Great Britain. European scholars are likely to continue playing a shaping role in the way peoples understand themselves, sustain their communities, and celebrate their identities and heritages. Philology, the love of language, and cultural linguistics, the study of language, worldviews, values, and identities, show no sign of weakening in the twenty-first century. In the face of a vast field of competing and contrasting schools of thought and research investigations, we make a meaningful attempt to bring some kind of order to this creative field of research. We frame the debate in terms of a small number of key groups sharing similar concerns and practicing a comparable and compatible methodology. A short summary of the main objectives is offered, some or all of which are shared by the major players. We also outline a series of pitfalls that cultural linguistics can fall into if it does not respect alterity but tries to frame other worldviews in terms of their own. These are discussed against the historical backdrop of European anthropology (Bronislaw Malinowski) and Europe's influence on American scholarship (Franz Boas, Edward Sapir, and Benjamin Lee Whorf). The work of Wilhelm von Humboldt (1767–1835), with his key concept of *Weltansicht* as language-bound worldview, and his concern for the cultivation of the individual's sensibility, has the potential of reconciling academic disciplines working with very different understandings of the relationship between language and worldview. Europe's unique facets are noted, such as concern with folk cultures, comparative research, the linguistics of color, intercultural pragmatics, the study of

James W. Underhill, University of Rouen/France, e-mail: james-william.underhill@univ-rouen.fr
Adam Głaz, Maria Curie-Skłodowska University, Lublin/Poland, e-mail: adam.glaz@mail.umcs.pl

https://doi.org/10.1515/9783110726626-018

conversation in real-life settings, comparative approaches to emotion, acculturation and bilingualism, or linguistic and cultural identity. These contributions are integrated into a wide panorama of a rich field of scholarship in which various approaches paint different pictures of Europe and the world. Research in Europe has also reacted to current events of a socio-political nature which are also linguistically mediated and culturally pregnant, such as the "migrant crisis" and Brexit. Important research has been carried out on cultural aspects of cognition, cultural metaphor, and cognitive sociolinguistics. Research on language and culture in Europe thus both elaborates on the ideas proposed in the 19th and early 20th century, and explores new areas.

1 Language and culture in Europe: objectives and methodologies

Given that *language* and *culture*, in English, and *Sprache* and *Kultur* in German, do not coincide any more than *jazyk* and *kultur* in Czech, *język* and *kultura* in Polish, *lengua* and *cultura* in Spanish, or *langue* and *culture* in French, the chances of developing a coherent pan-European concept of cultural linguistics certainly appear to be slim. An ultimate synthesis of the research on language and culture in Europe may prove to be over-ambitious, but surely that should not stop us from trying to form an overview of scholarship published in Europe in the fields of linguistic anthropology, anthropological linguistics, ethnolinguistics, cultural linguistics, philology and translation studies? After all, only when we have formed an overall impression of what is distinctive about the objectives, paradigms, methodologies and terms of the European varieties of work being carried out within those fields, can we hope to compare and contrast them with work being done in North America and around the world. The ultimate synthesis will, therefore, be posited, not as a goal to be realized, but rather an ideal to which we must direct the efforts of our imagination.

Nobody working in the field today would contest the significance of the work of Boas (1911) and Whorf (see Whorf 1956, and Penny Lee on Whorf in Lee 1996) when it comes to discussing words and how they work within worldviews. And, arguably the work of Sapir (1921, 1985 [1949]) and Hymes (Gumperz and Hymes 1986, Hymes 2003) offer a whole range of untapped inspiration when it comes to describing personality, linguistic expression and personal style. Doubtless, it would be absurd to set up an opposition between Anglo-American linguistic anthropology, that is, work framed within the model of Boas, Sapir and Whorf, on the one hand, and work on language and culture as it is carried out in Europe, on the other: they share too much to be considered rivals or even separate endeavors.

Nonetheless, positing differences between the two as a working hypothesis should enable us to draw some fundamental distinctions between Anglo-American and European contributions to cultural linguistics and ethnolinguistics. Gaining insights into the major directions and trends will serve to both celebrate the efforts of Europe-based scholars and highlight where their work can stimulate research around the world, enabling us all to question our own approaches, to reappraise the scope of our questions and the limits of our concepts and paradigms.

This chapter should, therefore, be seen as an invitation to speculate about the fundamental founding questions that have shaped approaches to language and culture which are often referred to (justifiably or not) as "Humboldtian" in that they share with Wilhelm von Humboldt (1767–1835) the desire to establish how words help human beings give form and shape to their conception of the world thanks to the sustained creative efforts of individuals and communities grappling with words (see Trabant 1990, 2015, Underhill 2009, Joseph 2017, Pajević 2017).

2 A shared European approach?

Can we provide a common set of definitions, a shared methodology, and a shared set of aims and objectives when we set about trying to understand how language shapes the way we understand the world and express ourselves in groups? Is there a common European cultural linguistics or ethnolinguistics? What are the main trends shaping the endeavors of scholars working in the field in Europe? How are recent events and developments changing the paradigms we think with? And how are scholars in Europe working within the context of a European Union that celebrates as its mantra "Unity in Diversity", investigating, celebrating and critically appraising, not only different languages, but the discourse of various linguistic communities and subcultures? Are those endeavors likely to continue in the same course they are taking today, or will a post-colonial, global cultural linguistics replace the European model linked too much with military and political hegemonies that are doomed to weaken with time or fall apart? We will touch on these questions but not resolve them. We do, however, maintain that it is crucial to bear such questions in mind as fundamental concerns relating to language, culture and the way Europeans live together and understand their lifestyles.

Where should we start when considering the origins of contemporary European thought on language and culture? For many people around the world, linguistics begins with the Swiss linguist, Ferdinand de Saussure (1857–1913), and what could be more European than that for a beginning to our story? However, language study already had a long tradition in Europe (see Trabant 2003 and François 2017, 2020), and even contemporary specialists of Saussure such as John E. Joseph (2012, 2017) recognize that Wilhelm von Humboldt was already far ahead of the Swiss linguist in understanding the relativity of language, the relationship between language and culture, or between words and cognition. Johann Georg Hamann (1730–1788) and Johann Gottfried Herder (1744–1803) had already largely anchored the idea of an inseparable bond between speaking and thinking in the German eighteenth century tradition, and Wilhelm von Humboldt consolidated the idea that language and worldview (*Weltansicht*) were part and parcel of the same process by which individual human beings (*Menschen*) and linguistic communities or cultures (*Nationen*) evolve by shaping the way human beings perceive and conceive the world (see Underhill 2009).[1]

If, on the other hand, we begin our discussion by focusing on anthropology, then it would seem reasonable to begin with the European school rather than following an American heritage starting with Boas, down to Dell Hymes, passing through Sapir and Whorf, as our American colleagues do. After all, historically speaking, research on language and culture in Europe parallels the development of European anthropology that grew up around the ground-breaking investigations of Bronislaw Malinowski outside of Europe (Malinowski 1922, 1935, 1952 [1923]). Malinowski's contribution, in terms of the global geography of scholarship, is two-directional. Firstly, he brought his European mind-frame to bear in his fieldwork of the Trobriands by developing a uniquely participant-observation approach that he hoped would enable him to overcome the Euro-centric worldview. Secondly, that approach became global through his influence on American

---

1 Although inspired by Humboldt, Slavic ethnolinguistics also owes its development to the Tartu-Moscow school of semiotics, where language, literature, art, religion, custom, and myth were all viewed as organized sign systems. This idea was pursued in the 1960s by Nikita Tolstoy, when he launched his large-scale dialectological research into folk cultures (cf. Tolstoy 1995), which eventually produced a monumental five-volume dictionary, the "*Slavic antiquities*" (*Slavyanskiye Drevnosti* 1995–2012). This Moscow school of ethnolinguistics continues to be a major player, often serving as inspiration for other projects, such as the "*Polish Dictionary of Folk Stereotypes and Symbols*" (*Słownik stereotypów i symboli ludowych* 1996–2021, a multi-volume work in progress), or, more indirectly, the linguistic worldview research in the Czech Republic and Poland (Vaňková 2001).

scholars, whose work in turn subsequently had a great impact on anthropology in and beyond the coastlines of North America.[2]

In fact, Malinowski continues to inspire inquiry into Polynesian "langua-cultures", to use Michael Agar's (1995) term. The following are only a handful of relatively recent contributions. Gunter Senft follows in Malinowski's footsteps in his research in the Trobriand Islands with his work on Kilivila (Senft 2010, 2015). Svenja Völkel inquires into Tongan (Völkel 2010, 2016); Carsten Levisen focuses on Bislama (Levisen 2017) and Tok Pisin (Levisen and Priestly 2017). The Surrey Morphological Group (Franjieh, Corbett, and Grandison 2020) deals with classifiers and categorization in North Ambrym (Vanuatu) and Iaai (New Caledonia). Nassenstein and Bose's (2016) description of Kivu Swahili in Congo, as well as Sinha et al.'s (2011) or Silva Sinha's (2019) research on Amondawa, Awetý, Kamaiurá, and Hatxa Kuĩ in Brazil also demonstrates the way European scholars are contributing to inquiry into the world's languages today.

3 Does mapping work for language and culture in Europe?

These works demonstrate the degree to which it becomes impossible to disentangle European research from studies of languages and cultures around the world. But a methodological problem emerges as soon as we turn our gaze back to Europe, with a desire to catalogue and arrange its languages. Linguistic anthropology as a discipline tends to "map" the languages of the world and the present volume is no exception in this respect. Is this an inevitable approach or a hangover from the colonial era, when Europeans set out to chart and carve up the world, its peoples, their cultures and their languages? On the one hand, it certainly makes sense for us to compare and contrast the way the seven thousand or so languages can be studied around the globe, and a "cartography" of approaches may well prove invaluable in this respect. But on the other, we must

---

2 Another towering figure is that of Bronisław Piłsudski (1866–1918), a Polish exile to Sakhalin under Tsarist Russia. Piłsudski is less well-known than Boas or Malinowski, probably because he did not produce a theoretical synthesis of his findings, and most English translations of his work have only appeared recently (Piłsudski 1998-2011). Piłsudski researched the Ainu and several other peoples of Sakhalin and Hokkaido; he collected linguistic and ethnographic data, as well as making audio and video recordings. The audio files have now been digitalized and made public at [http://www.icrap.org] (accessed 30 April 2021).

begin by highlighting some inevitable misunderstandings, contradictions and confusions that must be cleared up if we are to make any sense of the distinct ways Europeans study language, as opposed to the linguistic anthropologists working in the Anglo-American tradition. Some (but not all, of course) of the distinctions can be resumed fairly succinctly in the eight key points listed below:

1. English is a European language and the American tradition has evolved inseparably from the British culture. Similarly, the American tradition has been heavily influenced in the eighteenth, nineteenth and twentieth centuries by German and French thinkers. Consequently, the very idea of a separate American tradition has to remain a tenuous working hypothesis which soon breaks down under close scrutiny.

2. Europe's influence on American anthropology, of course, extends far beyond Malinowski and in fact does not begin with him because the father of American anthropology, Franz Boas, was both German-born and German-educated, though it was in America that he developed his ground-breaking approach. His student Edward Sapir, whose career was all-American, was also a Jewish immigrant who moved to the United States at the age of five and whose mother tongue was Yiddish. In the post-war period, it was the work of Sapir and his student Whorf that crystalized into the somewhat reductive "Sapir-Whorf hypothesis", a misnomer coined by later scholars. Ironically, in the post-war period this approach tended to be welcomed more warmly in Europe than in the American homeland. Despite the conviction and originality of the two researchers, as well as the richness of their work on native American languages, linguistic anthropology has remained a marginal discipline within American universities. At the outset and to some extent down to this day, philology and languages – both the native language and foreign languages (French, English, Spanish, German studies or Slavic studies) – are central pillars in European universities. Nothing approaching such a philology of Amerindian languages can be said to form the cornerstone of American universities today.

3. Many key European languages have not been strictly speaking "European" for several centuries: they are world languages. French and Spanish are obvious examples with Canada and South and Central America. There are now more French speakers in Africa than in France. And increasingly, with immigration and the Latino population boom, Spanish is clearly becoming the second language of the United States of America. Dutch and German remain predominantly European but both had the potential to become world languages at one point, given their geopolitical influence in Europe and South Africa. Portuguese, Spanish and English follow parallel trajectories in exporting their languages and cultures without their

exponents assimilating into the continents that the British, the Portuguese and the Spanish colonized. Indeed, such was the success of these European colonial endeavors that the cultural, geopolitical centers of Spanish, Portuguese and English are now based in South, Central, and North America.[3]

4. Most American linguists working within the Boas-Sapir linguistic anthropology paradigm or the Hymes sociolinguistics paradigm are Anglophones who spend extensive periods of fieldwork mastering the language, the key concepts, the customs and the worldview. Humboldt and Malinowski would no doubt have approved of such projects. They are, nonetheless carried out by outsiders, generally speaking; Anglophones writing predominantly in English for Anglophones or readers of World English. In effect, anthropology and anthropological linguistics remain dominated by English-speakers in publications and in faculties in Australia, Britain and the US. This contrasts with European scholars who begin with a multilingual paradigm, informed by publications in various languages. In comparison, the bibliographies of even the most erudite and enlightening Anglophone scholars – such as Gumperz and Hymes (1986 [1972]), Lucy (1992) or Levinson and Wilkins (2006) – are practically monolingual. In the same way, online sites defining and promoting linguistic anthropology are massively English. Indigenous speakers of the languages under study appear either unable or reluctant to pursue a career in linguistics. As the specialist of Aboriginal art and culture, Howard Morphy explained, given the pressing needs of endangered linguistic communities that have often between fifty and five hundred members, those members see a more urgent need for doctors, engineers and scientists if they pursue higher education.[4] The Internet has given a forum for minority languages to assert themselves and the major lingua francas, such as Spanish, Portuguese, French, Russian and Hindi, and the Chinese (through Baidu) make ample use of the Internet as a forum for exchanging ideas and promoting cultures. But using any search engine will make it perfectly clear – from Wikipedia to Ted Talks, from

---

3 One can also mention Lusophone Africa, or six African countries where Portuguese is the official language (*Países Africanos de Língua Oficial Portuguesa*): Angola, Cape Verde, Guinea-Bissau, Mozambique, São Tomé and Príncipe, and Equatorial Guinea. This colonialism contrasts with the way, for example, the Scandinavian Vikings assimilated into France, German-speaking countries, and the British Isles. For a critical stance on and an attempt to "disinvent" the notion of European languages being imposed on speakers outside Europe, see Makoni and Pennycook (2006).
4 Howard Morphy, author of "*Becoming art. Exploring cross-cultural categories*" (2007) in private conversation with James Underhill, June 2017, Canberra.

online linguistic glossaries and linguistic, sociological or philosophical websites, and from online dictionaries, encyclopaedias to online corpora – that anthropological studies in English are still primarily concerned with ethnic minorities, be they found within Anglo communities or around the world. In this respect, it should be underlined that when one of the main Polish ethnolinguists, Jerzy Bartmiński, uses the term *ethnolinguistics* (2009), he strives to maintain an emic stance as a member of a linguistic community, aspiring to objectivity as he analyzes the way his language is used around him. Ethnolinguistics in this sense is a neutral term, applicable to all linguistic communities, not simply Polish. When Underhill, a Franco-Scottish linguist, uses it (2012) in the title of a book comparing Czech, French, German and English keywords, written for an anglophone public, it is rightly perceived as an act of defiant provocation. The English and the French tend to go abroad to do anthropology and ethnolinguistics, and they rarely perceive themselves and their languages as "objects" studied by outsiders. Ethno- and ethnic are for "others", minorities or foreigners (Africans, Asians, or East Europeans); it never applies to the dominant world language communities, the English or the Americans, as any major online linguistic corpus demonstrates (see BNC or COCA). This, of course, is deeply problematic.[5]

5. The crucial question of alterity – so fundamental for translation studies, and central to the debates in anthropology as to whether studies should be etic or emic, carried out by outsiders looking in, or insiders looking out – has little significance for European scholars, since they are invariably insiders writing in their own language for the speakers of that language. This shapes the way the Prague Linguistic Circle or the Tartu-Moscow school formulate their questions and hypotheses, or the way historical linguistic traditions are conceived and described by linguists such as Johann Jakob Grimm, or the way he and his brother, Wilhelm, understood the significance of the famous fairy tales they gathered together. Ethnolinguists and cultural linguists in Lublin, Prague or Rouen are interested in preserving the living culture and language of the community in itself for itself, rather than defining the place of their language within a map of world languages or safeguarding its founding myths or keywords.

6. Europe offers a language-friendly environment for scholarship. The Anglo world is vast and global. Paradoxically, however, most researchers receiving funding in the Anglo world must apply to national bodies that offer grants to

---

5 The same point in made forcefully in Anna Wierzbicka's (2010, 2014) extensive analyses of English as a non-neutral, culturally grounded language.

British, US-American, Canadian or Australian applicants. In contrast, the nation state is no longer the context within which much European publications are generated, funded and sustained. The European Union is in essence a multilingual and multicultural project. The language of each of the twenty-seven member states is respected and represented in the Union's day-to-day management and its legislation; twenty-four languages are represented on the official EU website.[6] True, the EU linguistic policy of cultivating individuals who speak their mother tongue plus two further European languages has met with some scepticism in the major post-colonial countries – England, France and even Germany. It is, nonetheless, now perfectly commonplace for European youths to have a good grasp of two foreign languages (one of which, admittedly, tends to be English). In this respect, a multicultural and multilingual Europe has been a great success. The Erasmus generation has consolidated this trend. In generations to come, European research will be funding Europeans to study European languages and their interaction, rather than funding individuals to leave their largely monolingual communities to investigate the languages of other nations, the way the English or the Americans go for a "gap year" abroad.

7. The place of English as a shared lingua franca among Europeans (and Erasmus students) has been consolidated over the past thirty years. Nonetheless, multilingual conferences remain widespread within Europe, a practice which serves to remind linguists that we cannot frame all our grammatical, semantic, cultural and political questions in English. Ultimately, the specificity of each language is not defined in terms of an "alterity" to be respected, but rather as an "identity" to be discovered: European identities are affirmed, discussed and integrated into wider debates on culture and politics. When the majority speaks English as a second language in European debates, there is little danger of falling into an Anglo mode of "universalizing thinking", as can happen in an English-speaking country: the majority of speakers are making an effort to translate both their words and their worldviews. And when this is the case, Sapir's idea that languages represent radically different modes of conceptualizing the world and Whorf's intuition that we must consider not only words but "linguistic patterning" (see Whorf 1956, Lee 1996, and Underhill 2009) become not a hypothesis but a palpable truth. No arguments are needed to defend the case that linguistic patterning affects the way we form our thoughts when the speakers interacting must struggle to express their lived realities in a shared second language.

---

6 See [http://www.europa.eu] (accessed 28 April 2021).

8. Philology and translation studies in Europe are concerned with the ways Europe's literary traditions emerge and condition one another via translating. Theirs is an interactive model which has created a vast literature. For example, specialists such as the Czech Jiří Levý (2011 [1963]) and the Russian Michael Gasparov (1996) envisage the complex ways that Italian, English, French and German metrical structures and traditions, or the verse structures of the Polish, the Germans and the Russians influence one another through translations that leave their mark on the way poems are written in those languages thereafter. Hymes (2003), among others, makes a valid and important contribution to ethnopoetics within the American Indian languages. But translation studies still has to make headway in the United States, if it is to produce an equally well-documented tradition of cross-fertilization among American Indian languages.

This list is not exhaustive; neither is it designed as a provocation or a critique. It should simply serve to make it perfectly clear that there are significant differences in the questions that are being conceived, the paradigms that are being explored, and the publications that are being written and read in European approaches to language and culture, on the one hand, and in the Anglo-American tradition of linguistic anthropology, on the other.

4 Distinctive European approaches

The extent of interactive work between Europe and the Anglo world is vast, of course, but for our purposes it is worth highlighting eight fields of scholarship in which the dialogue is working well, areas in which Europe contributes its unique insights, making an impact on the development of ideas:

1. Cognitive sociolinguistics
2. Translation studies and worldview
3. Translatables and untranslatables
4. Languages and values
5. Languaculture
6. Cultural aspects of cognition
7. Multilingual subjects and second language acquisition
8. Keywords and culture

4.1 Cognitive sociolinguistics

In this field, culture is viewed in terms of social variation and socially-mediated linguistic behavior. Contributions in Kristiansen and Dirven (2008) explore social aspects of language variation, including linguistically-mediated ideologies of socio-political and socio-economic systems. In Geeraerts, Kristiansen, and Peirsman (2010), the authors inquire into parameters of lexical convergence and divergence between language varieties, religious names, socio-cultural aspects of gender and the socio-cognitive aspects of grammar and pronunciation. Geeraerts (2018) provides a comprehensive overview of cognitive sociolinguistics, with a major focus on metaphor and culture, stereotypes, cultural models, and language variation.

4.2 Translation studies and worldview

A decade ago, one of the leading American specialists of translation studies, Lawrence Venuti, included sections from Vinay and Darbelnet's *"Stylistique comparée de l'anglais et du français"* (1977 [1958]) in his *"Routledge translation studies reader"* (Venuti 2012). This might appear somewhat anachronistic for a contemporary approach: after all, this was the third edition, and the revolutionary text in textual stylistics and translation studies was published by the two Canadian scholars back in 1958. However, the comparative stylistics that Vinay and Darbelnet developed was to have an enormous impact on the French tradition with a vast wave of rigorous comparative research striving to ascertain what options were open to translators who found it necessary to modulate between various grammatical units, for example translating nouns by verbs in English, or English adverbs by *avec* + noun or *sans* + noun. Guillemin-Flescher extended this in her work on comparative syntax (1981), and Chuquet and Paillard (2002) wrote a definitive revision of the comparative stylistics translation studies approach that remains to this day the key text used in French State's translation exams (CAPES and AGREG). Vinay and Darbelnet inspired a German response early on in Malblanc's *"Stylistique comparée du français et de l'allemand"* (1963).

In parallel, from the early 1970s to the early 2000s, the prolific French poet, linguist, translator and essayist, Henri Meschonnic, was challenging the reigning structuralist models emerging in the French system, along with both the linguistic approach to translation, on the one hand, and, on the other, reductive models of language as a means of communication that dominate the Anglo world. In contrast to this information-centered approach, Meschonnic (1982) proposed his own *"linguistique anthropologique"* by defending a Humboldtian approach to poetics and claiming that individuals invent themselves in language, that language is a means of living and becoming together in dialogue rather than a simple means of expressing information and ideas. This explains why Meschonnic saw the role of the translator, not in terms of serving the original in a slavish manner, but rather as the active response of an organizing sensibility. He believed that the true vocation of the translator was to create great works, great examples (*"traductions-textes"*, as he called them) capable of transforming their cultures, such as the King James Bible or *"One thousand and one nights"*. Poetry in general and poetry translation were seen as crucial dimensions of linguistic, cultural and subjective expression in both the culture and the life of languages and communities. Although he died in 2009, Meschonnic's influence seems to have outlived him: Marko Pajević recently edited both a Meschonnic Reader (Pajević 2019) and, with David N. Smith, a collection of critical articles on his work (Pajević and Smith 2018). More significantly, Venuti, one of the leading contemporary voices on translation studies, recognizes his debt to Antoine Berman in generating his own ideas on "foreignizing translations" that can resist what he calls "domestication" by challenging the cannon. Antoine Berman was one of Meschonnic's leading doctoral students in the 1980s and, arguably, most of his translation strategies are directly derived from the work published by Meschonnic in the early 1970s, even if it was in his final work, *"Poétique du traduire"* (1999), that Meschonnic gave greater scope and crystallisation to those principles.

4.3 Translatables and untranslatables

Barbara Cassin (2004, 2014) in another neo-Humboldtian project, shows that translating is always ultimately a philosophical question. She reminds us that Humboldt was proposing a philosophy of language when he said – a hundred years before Sapir – that words are not reducible to universal concepts because concepts evolve within the worldviews of linguistic communities.[7] Quoting Humboldt, Cassin (2014: xix) stresses that language always manifests itself in "multiplicity" in terms of perspectives, varieties of "visions of the world". It is for this reason that Cassin's encyclopaedia of "untranslatables" represents a radical Humboldtian critique of the way philosophers treat language. Ultimately, Jean-François Groullier and Fabienne Brugère remind us in their section (in Cassin

---

7 In some approaches (e.g., see Apresyan 2006 on the Russian context), this means that linguistic worldviews emerge from an everyday, colloquial (or "naive") use of language. Cassin's project does not run counter to this claim but rather shows that this is not the whole story.

2014: 84) that words like *bellezza* and *vaghezza* in Italian, or *beauty* and *grace* in English, are framed and filtered through the prisms of very different worldviews. Similarly, Jean-François Courtine (in Cassin 2014: 298–310) explains that *essence* presents similar problems for translation; even *denegation*, *description* and *depiction* (Cassin 2014: 204) prove to be keywords that evolve within distinct European traditions in their various forms.

The fact that Cassin was elected member of the *Académie Française* in 2017 and that her encyclopaedia was translated by Princeton University Press, making waves since it was published in 2014, shows not only the strength of Humboldt's thought for reframing debates in philosophy and culture – it also shows how the Anglo world with its concern for alterity is ready for a celebration of difference and diversity. This is only one more example that serves to prove that there is, ultimately, no "transatlantic divide". Thinking in language is part of an ongoing global debate today in which European scholars are pulling their weight and finding an audience.

4.4 Languages and values

These approaches stress the relativity of language. However, many studies of linguistic diversity emphasize the hierarchies and configurations of the value systems that words evolve within. Blumczynski and Gillespie (2016), for example, bring together several contributions on how translational strategies and practices affect cultural values. Scholars edited in Głaz (2019) explore, more broadly, the diverse consequences of translation, as a process and a product, for the shaping of specific linguistic worldviews, with a focus on the role of translation in linguistic worldview research. Nergaard (2021) proposes to view translation as a personal experience that is inherent in multicultural contexts of migration as a space within which migrants "perform" their lives. Dedenbach-Salazar Sáenz (2019), in turn, provides a rich survey of how religious traditions are communicated across the boundaries of time, space, and culture. The book's very title, "*Translating wor(l)ds*", makes a poignant claim, which the other publications mentioned here also develop: translation is not innocent, it is part-and-parcel of a cultural activity with consequences for people's lives.

4.5 Languaculture

Over time, as language-and-culture research in the USA evolved, a holistic view of *linguaculture* or *languaculture* was proposed, to replace the relational view of language *vs.* culture, language *and* culture, language *in* culture, culture *in* language etc. The notion of *linguaculture* was proposed by Paul Friedrich, who refers to it as "a single universe of its own kind" (1989: 306). A few years later, Michael Agar (1995) renamed it as *languaculture* so as to place language and culture on an equal footing. This idea was pursued in Europe as well (notably in Slavic scholarship), to a large extent as a result of independent developments.[8] The terminology is secondary and different authors prefer different terms, sometimes for aesthetic reasons. The crucial point is that a holistic, rather than a relational view is being practiced in ongoing research, as in Underhill and Gianninoto (2019), who use the term *language-culture* in their study of "migrating meanings". Similarly, in Spanish, Bernárdez (2008) very tellingly talks about *el lenguaje como cultura*, arguing that language arises "from the cooperation between innumerable individuals over many millennia, pushed by real life and especially by what is most real in life, culture" (Bernárdez 2008: 21).[9] Other authors advocate a multidisciplinary perspective, such as Karen Risager (2006, 2015), who proposes a combined anthropological-linguistic approach.[10] This is grounded in the idea of transnational cultural flows, whereby lifestyles, music, food, images, films etc. are linked in global social networks. These flows are also linguistic, which makes them, not cultural *and* linguistic, but linguacultural. If, on the other hand, many authors still find the relational view to be functional in that it proves convenient for analytical purposes, the relationship is nevertheless viewed as involving an intimate, or even a somewhat paradoxical "reciprocal dependence" between the linguistic and cultural domains (see Bartmiński 2017: 23).

---

8 This has been the case in Russian linguistics, with its notion of *lingvokultorologya* 'linguacultural studies', which has also spread throughout Slavic scholarship. In Polish terminological practice, in turn, it has recently become standard to talk about *lingwokultura* 'linguaculture/languaculture'.

9 Original: "[. . .] *de la cooperación entre innumerables individuos a lo largo de muchos milenios, empujados por la vida real y, muy especialmente, por lo más real de la vida: la cultura*". Bernárdez understands culture in Bourdieu's terms as a 'specific, socially sanctioned ways of doing things' ("*formas específicas, socialmente sancionadas, de hacer cosas*", Bernárdez 2008: 268) – and so, given the variety of the opportunities available to an individual, it is normal for one to live in more than one language-as-culture.

10 A different example of ethnolinguistics and anthropology working in tandem is Ilaria Micheli's (2018) report on their practical, non-academic applications. One of the projects in which Micheli participated was designed to restore and develop traditional forms of bee-keeping among the Ogiek in Kenya. Through interviews, Micheli was able to establish the key categories, concepts and vocabulary, relatively quickly building mutual trust, pre-empting potential points of tension and activating a sense of identity in the people. As a result, more in-depth anthropological and social analyses could then be performed, followed by practical action of Italian and Kenyan NGOs and spending of the resources allocated.

4.6 Cultural aspects of cognition

Three related aspects to cognition in culture and language studies have been defined and gained wide recognition in ongoing research and debates. The first is what became known as *cultural cognition*, an idea that was developed in American scholarship going back to D'Andrade (1981), who advocated that culture be incorporated into the framework of cognitive science. Hutchins (1995) and Duranti (1997) went on to demonstrate that knowledge not only resides in individual minds, but extends throughout the environment, the tools people use, their common actions, as well as the institutions that formalize people's interactions and relationships (see Clark and Chalmers 1998 on the extended mind). These views have evolved into the concept of "cultural cognition", the idea of a community as a collective cognizing subject, a key notion in Sharifian's (2017) Cultural Linguistics developed in Australia, but also emerging independently in Europe in the form of "cognitive ethnolinguistics" (see Bartmiński 2009, 2017). In Prague, Irena Vaňková has set up a Czech school of cognitive-cultural linguistics (see Vaňková, Vondrážková and Zbořilová 2017, Vaňková and Šťastná 2018), collaborating closely with the Lublin School of Ethnolinguistics and other Polish scholars (see Vaňková 2001, Vaňková and Viendl 2012).

The second aspect is a reflection on language-as-culture at a higher level of generalization (see e.g., Sinha 2021). For instance, in their Motivation & Sedimentation Model, Devylder and Zlatev (2020) have proposed three levels to meaning-making: situated (where language use is contextualized in situations), sedimented (where linguistic patterns are conventionalized through frequent use), and embodied (through perceptual, tactile and other bodily interactions). This kind of general reflection is also practiced in research on color, such as the Progress in Colour Studies conference series, initiated in 2004 at Glasgow University by Carole Biggam and Christian Kay. The publications produced in their wake focus on linguistic and non-linguistic aspects of color – see MacDonald, Biggam, and Paramei (2018) for recent contributions.

Finally, Chris Sinha (2009, 2015) seeks to forge links between psychology, Darwinian biology, language evolution, and semantics in a model of language as a "symbolic biocultural niche". The model rests on the idea that various biological species construct quasi-artifactual material niches, such as nests, dams, and suchlike. But niches can also be behavioral, such as birdsongs or mating strategies. By extension, Sinha posits that in the case of humans, niche construction not only creates conditions favorable to language but that language itself can be conceptualized as a symbolic biocultural niche for people to pursue their lives.

4.7 Multilingual subjects and second language acquisition

Claire Kramsch, a French scholar specializing in German, who spent her whole career teaching English as a Second Langue in California at Berkeley, developed a revolutionary approach to second language acquisition, when she realized three crucial things. Our first languages condition and shape the way we learn, interpret, physically appropriate and experience the languages we learn. Secondly, multilinguals bring a fertile imagination to language learning. And thirdly, becoming multilingual is an experience which profoundly changes the way we think and feel about the world, about words and about expressing ourselves. It is the richness that multilinguals bring to language-learning and communication that Kramsch (2009, 2012) seeks to promote and celebrate, in a student-focused approach to second language acquisition. Her approach does not aim at merely producing competent speakers of English, but expressive multilinguals capable of tapping into a wide variety of modes of expression (concepts, metaphors, narratives and cultural knowledge).

In Europe, multilingual language learning enjoys attention from a rich range of approaches. One of them addresses issues and challenges that face teachers (see, for example, Brookie 2018 on the context of immigration in the Swedish system). But for many European researchers, linguistic and cultural identity are much broader concepts, not limited to bilingualism and second language contexts. In the Slavic world, Alekseev et al. (2016) bring together inquiries into the spiritual culture of the Slavs. Kretschmer et al. (2019) collect a number of studies on the linguistic and cultural identities of minorities. Nor is European reflection limited to ethnic or national identities. Research covers social or gender issues: for the former, see Dray (2017) on students' identities in British secondary education, while the latter is explored by Kotthoff (2000) in the context of German academics and the discourse of humor. Kotthoff's study is also interesting in terms of its content and methodology: the author constructed her own corpus of informal dinner conversations. Adopting a similar methodology, Zinken (2016) addresses identity in the sense of one's role within the family: he analyzes everyday linguistic behavior, in video-recordings of English and Polish families in contexts of requesting responsibility. This attention to multilingual interaction is fundamental to Europe as a cultural and political project. In this light, we find it parallels and consolidates ongoing European research. So while Kramsch is bringing about a revolution in English teaching in America, her approach is perfectly in tune with various trends that are currently asserting themselves in European academia.

4.8 Keywords

A variety of dynamic overlapping traditions explore keywords and culture in Europe. In English-speaking countries, the keyword approach brings together, to a greater or lesser extent, work generated from two main sources. On the one hand, the keywords approach was cultural, ideological, and initially Marxist in origin, deriving from Raymond Williams' (1985 [1976]) truly groundbreaking work on critical thinking in language and cultural studies. Williams' 155 keywords encouraged a whole generation of critical thinking, forcing social scientists, philosophers and literary scholars to face up to the implicitly ideological frameworks that everyday words like *common*, *democracy*, or *private* and *public* function within. This generation in turn went on to have a big impact on the way Critical Discourse Analysis developed (see Musolff, Shäffner, and Townson 1996, Musolff 2016, 2017, Goatly 2007, Underhill 2011). All of these authors were closely connected to the development of what might be called Multilingual Metaphor Theory, a European response to developments in Conceptual Metaphor Theory in North America, whose best known exponents were composed of the two tandems, Lakoff and Johnson, and Fauconnier and Turner.[11]

Critical Discourse Analysis was not at the outset particularly well-informed linguistically-speaking, however, with Raymond Williams himself and the greater part of those who developed cultural studies within the Anglo world not paying much attention to individual languages. They did not tend to focus on specific differences in individual languages or the way those differences frame thinking. Sociologists and specialists of political science often tend to highlight the way the language of dominant ideologies constrain thought and limit critical thinking. The concept of language that inspired Boas, Sapir, Whorf, Hymes and the vast majority of specialists working on culture and language was fundamentally different, and ultimately closer to the Humboldtian idea of language as a shared space for subjective individuals to create themselves within communities in their everyday exchanges and their literary works. Without wishing to deny that all language is by essence "political", in that it takes place within society and within social hierarchies and social dynamics, the majority of scholars and researchers working on culture and language in Europe tend to envisage languages as shared cultural

---

11 The European response to an understanding of metaphor and metonymy has indeed been vast, varied and innovative in several respects, both in terms of the issues covered and theoretical developments proposed – for just a handful of examples see Benczes, Barcelona, and de Mendoza Ibáñez (2011), Littlemore (2019) or Kövecses (2005, 2020). A truly dialogic project is Kóczy's (2018) focus on cultural metaphors – as they are understood in Sharifian's (2017) Cultural Linguistics – in an in-depth study of Hungarian folk songs.

spaces that allow the development of the individual mind and the shared modes of communication and cultural expression. This emphasis on linguistic communities, their creative, speculative thought, and the patterned forms that individuation takes as members of a linguistic community are socialized, does not animate the early work in Critical Discourse Analysis of cultural studies. But many researchers would agree that the two approaches are, ultimately, perfectly compatible.

The best-known exponent of the multilingual approach to keywords in the Anglo world today remains the Polish linguist, Anna Wierzbicka, born and educated in Warsaw, but based in Canberra, Australia since the 1970s. Wierzbicka has set up the Natural Semantic Metalanguage with a generation of scholars working within European and non-European languages. Over the last four decades, her research has tended to move away from the culture-based approach kept alive by a vast array of philological and linguistic traditions that are being followed in Europe. Jerzy Bartmiński, Alicja Nagórko (see Nagórko 2004), Carsten Levisen, James Underhill and Irena Vaňková (to name but a few) all have their place in celebrating linguistic specificity and individual expression in terms of cultural keywords. In contrast, in recent years, the work of Wierzbicka and her colleagues has focused on the dangers of assuming that Anglo concepts and frameworks of thinking can suffice to investigate human experience encoded in terms such as *space, time, kinship, friendship, sense, experience* and *emotion* (see Wierzbicka 2010 and the video conversations between Wierzbicka and Underhill, Wierzbicka 2018a, 2018b).

The Australian school remains deeply attached to multilingual studies, focusing on indigenous Australian languages, Chinese, French, and the languages of the Pacific, as can be seen in the book edited by Bert Peeters (2019), a Flemish member of the NSM group, Heart- and Soul-like Constructs across Languages, Cultures, and Epochs. However, inevitably, given the target readership of NSM within the global Anglo world, the school's work has been focusing on reflecting on how linguistic communities around the world can develop a "minimal English" based on NSM principles, as set out in Goddard (2018). This not only underlines the difficulty of making clear-cut boundaries between the Anglo world and European research, it also raises the question of how Europeans and other cultures must respond to one another in English within the present-day global culture and global economy.[12] In contrast to this, some

---

12 This is not to say that Wierzbicka's NSM has to be reduced to minimal English. In fact, the opposite point is usually stressed: NSM can assume parallel shapes in any language, allowing us to construct comparable explications in each. For European examples, cf. Levisen (2012) on Danish, Bułat-Silva (2020) on English, Portuguese and Polish, or Peeters (2012) on English vs. French.

recent European work on keywords focuses on how meanings migrate to other cultures. Underhill and Gianninoto (2019), for example, study how European words such as *citizen* and *individual* are exported and transformed by the cultures that adopt and adapt them.[13]

5 European cultural linguistics and friends in the English-speaking world: combat, response or dialogue?

How do European scholars react to the Anglo-American culture that asserts itself around the world? Within this bigger picture, how do European approaches to language and culture respond to research on language in North America? We have already considered a certain number of ongoing dialogues; and where things prove more complex, it would be absurd to make sweeping statements or to reduce individual cultures to a single position. The sensibilities of European cultures differ from nation to nation and among the various linguistic communities that inhabit Europe, of course, which often makes it difficult to understand the way they react to ongoing debates on language and culture. And this causes much confusion for European cultures among themselves.

The ways Europeans and European nations remain attached to certain attitudes and fall victim to prejudices often seems deeply perplexing, absurd, or simply incomprehensible to non-Europeans and Europeans alike. For this reason, it is worth highlighting some of the more striking examples of attitudes to language and culture among specialists that have arisen in recent decades in order to explain how the specific historical and cultural contexts have contributed to their existence. These cases might be considered "emblematic examples", symptomatic of deeper running trends. But they should not be considered to be entirely representative of the cultures they arise in; and, above all else, they should not be used to consolidate caricatures or perpetuate prejudice. If viewed as indications of underlying inclinations, in a myriad of diverse and often very contrasting attitudes, this short summary may be considered to be of some use, not as an explicative model, but as a series of signposts to cultural sensibilities.

---

13 Keywords that have gained global usage after being exported from other cultures are discussed by many authors. For example, see *"Keywords for India. A conceptual lexicon for the 21st century"* (Nair and deSouza 2020).

The four attitudes that will be considered are:
1. Openness
2. Defence and combat
3. Ambivalence
4. Dialogues and one-way streets.

5.1 Openness

To a large extent the liberation of Europe in 1945 predisposed European nations favorably to North American culture, so that in the 1940s, 1950s and 1960s, various cultural waves moved across Europe. The intellectual and cultural exchanges were perhaps more complex, but the Cold War tended to cultivate a climate that was conducive to reading American authors and linguists. From Chomsky's Generative Grammar to, a few decades later, the cognitivists' work on conceptual metaphor and grammar, Britain, France, Germany and many other European nations have avidly read their American counterparts.

However, the end of the Cold War had a remarkable effect on Central and East-European linguistics. Within the course of a few years, the great enthusiasm that came with the breakdown of the Soviet Block went hand in hand with a renewed openness to American culture, music, language and linguistics throughout many Central and East European nations. The enthusiasm of the 1990s consolidated itself into an academic culture that by the 2000s was already ardently promoting various North American schools and approaches. Among the most startling and effervescent influences was the revolution in Czech Sign Language, which helped develop a whole community of signing thanks to the founding impact of American teachers after the Velvet Revolution in 1989.

Towards the end of the 2000s, it appeared that students were so fascinated by Western (and primarily North American) influences that they tended to neglect their own traditions in linguistics. Indeed, it is true that Czech and Polish students sometimes feel more at ease working within cognitive approaches inspired by English-speaking authors than they do with the founding authors of the Prague Linguistic Circle or with Polish semantics. But generally speaking, this trend has been attenuated and, today, Czech and Polish scholars quote works in English, German, and their mother tongue as their sources. Central European scholars appear to think flexibly by moving freely between various North American and European traditions, while remaining grounded in the publications of authors from their own respective cultures.

5.2 Defence and combat

If Europe is, in most practical senses of the word, a global phenomenon – if not a political ideal, as some would have it – then it is important to understand that European scholars see it as their vocation to participate actively in debates going on within the Anglo-American world, that is, within the various spheres in which English has set itself up as the language of education, business, politics, and the media. However, they do not necessarily do it with enthusiasm and certain "reactionary tendencies" within Europe see the spread of English as a direct or implicit threat to the cultural colonialism of their own linguistic communities. This trend grew in force towards the end of the twentieth century.

One of the most ardent and erudite among the French exponents of this movement (or fashion) was the polyglot Claude Hagège, the author of a much celebrated work on the faculty of language, "*L'homme de paroles*" (1985), and several other influential works: "*Le Souffle de la langue*" (1992), "*Le français: histoire d'un combat*" (1996), and "*Halte à la mort des langues*" (2000). Often adulated in the French press, the titles of Hagège's books make it perfectly plain that he sees himself as a post-colonial patriot, defending the cultural and political ideal of the Enlightenment through the spread of French. The terms of his arguments are anything but neutral (see Underhill 2011: 199–206). Hagège has a vast erudition and a dithyrambic style that has endeared him to many French readers (though less to French linguists). But in his paradigm, English represents the invasion of uniformity, the domination of other cultures, and constitutes a threat to diversity by imposing a single barren and sterile worldview. In contrast, French – according to Hagège – has a vocation to defend diversity.

Ever since the eighteenth century, French has been a language of culture that "flourishes" on foreign soil, Hagège affirms (1992: 118). This enables the author to simultaneously seek supporters among the growing global ecolinguistics movement and anchor his cherished mother tongue within the most conventional nationalistic ideals of French with its pretentions to "universality" (*universalité*, Hagège 1992: 118). Promoting the richness of the French language (the Francophonie project) and celebrating linguistic diversity around the world go hand in hand in the marriage that Hagège is arranging here. In this hymn to French, his mother tongue "animates" the cultures of the world, by its capacity for "shining" (*rayonnement*) throughout the world and cultivating the fertile soils of the cultures in which it takes root (see Hagège in Underhill 2011: 204).

French rhetoric often flirts with regal metaphors to celebrate its own revolutionary and republican ideals, thereby setting its English neighbors up in the tradition-bound pre-Enlightenment period. But here it will be clear that if Hagège dreams of French as a kind of crusader defending diversity and dying linguistic communities, it is more in the role of the *"Roi Soleil"*, the Sun-King, whose rays bless the earth. This enables him to borrow the somewhat naïve ecolinguistic metaphors and harness them in a celebration of language as a "life principle" (*principe vitale*), a "breath that defies death" (Hagège 2000: 21), in order to assert that it is through defending diversity that French will 'keep its rank' (*"conserver son rang"*, 1996: 167). This explains the curious, tortuous rhetoric that leads Hagège, in his 2006 book, to marry ecolinguistics and patriotic prejudice. Two fights became one, allies were aligned in the age-old strategy "the enemy of my enemy is my friend" when he titled his 2006 book *"Combat pour le français. Au nom de la diversité des langues et des cultures"* (The combat for French. In the name of the diversity of languages and cultures). This may seem like a long detour to end up in a cul-de-sac, a dead end for linguistic anthropology, and it would hardly be worth citing Hagège unless the temptation to celebrate exotic worldviews and preach to the choir at home were not both practiced by academics and approved of by establishments in large and small countries alike.[14]

5.3 Ambivalence

A very different but equally disconcerting relationship with the language of the nation and English as the world language can be observed in Germany. In German universities, we often find an ambiguous relationship with English, one that appears to be complex, paradoxical, and ambivalent, but both deeply felt and widespread throughout the academic community. Two self-imposed ruling principles seem to have established themselves: on the one hand it has become *de rigueur* to ape the Anglo world by adopting the market principle of "publish or perish", and, on the other, this principle has asserted itself in the vehemently monolingual policy endorsed by all global ranking systems and adopted by universities: "publish in English!". The contemporary specialist on Wilhelm von Humboldt, Jürgen Trabant, explains this complex sensibility in his polemical treatise, *"Globalesisch oder was? Ein Plädoyer für Europas Sprache"* ('Global English or else? A defence of Europe's languages', Trabant 2014).

---

14 The rightly-esteemed encyclopaedist, David Crystal, falls prey to the same temptation as Hagège in simultaneously celebrating global English and its contribution to the world, and denouncing language death – see Underhill (2011: 207–230) and Crystal (2000, 2003). And in post-Brexit Britain, it is likely that publishers will continue to promote everything England exports to the world in terms of culture, language, literature, and films and series.

Like Hagège (but with far greater sincerity and legitimacy), Trabant celebrates multilingualism (*Mehrsprachigkeiten*, Trabant 2014: 103–112) and "*la merveilleuse variété*" so dear to Leibniz (Trabant 2014: 80–81) that inspired Herder, Hamman, and Humboldt. Humboldt defended the German nation as a linguistic community, in the context of the Napoleonic campaigns, by founding the University of Berlin as an institute in which the language of the people was placed at the very center of every other discipline as the worldview generated by shared and interactive cultural and linguistic productions. This is very different from Hagège's "combat": this was Prussia striving to survive the attempts to assert the hegemony of France, French culture and the French language as the language of Universal Culture, with Napoléon's Universal University.

In our times, it may seem natural and laudable to defend linguistic diversity and multilingual language policies. But this is exactly what is going wrong, as Trabant eloquently demonstrates. Leibniz, Herder, and Humboldt have been turned on their heads and multilingualism is perversely paving the way towards a monolingual language policy in Germany. Trabant's conclusion (2014: 205–208) is a sombre parody of Hagège's belligerent modern rendition of "*l'audace, l'audace, toujours de l'audace!*". Trabant argues that the semblance of a multilingual language policy in Germany has come to be understood in terms of German plus English by both the state and the vast majority of citizens.

There are two phases to this process. Firstly, we can observe the emergence of the stance that can be defined as "English-is-enough", a stance that has asserted itself to the detriment of all other European languages. Then the mother tongue falls prey to the logic of efficient communication in the global world. The disastrous consequences of this process form part of a tripartite logic. English becomes the de facto option of the majority, other languages are neglected, and English increasingly becomes a simple reductive tool of communication (*Mittel zur Kommunikation*, Trabant 2014: 206). The whole cultural and intellectual content of the language, the very quality that Humboldt celebrated, begins to appear irrelevant and superfluous. Once this logic asserts itself, both Humboldt and German become progressively difficult to defend. Evaluated in these global, external terms, German itself comes to seem like a secondary means of communication.

The tragic tone of Trabant's conclusion contrasts with his own elegant style and erudite defences of linguistic diversity in German, French, Italian, and of course English. But the question he raises is an essential and an urgent one. It also contrasts with the French sensibility and serves to highlight two post-Humboldtian perspectives on defending languages, communities and worldviews. French linguists rarely succumb to nationalistic defences of their language, as Hagège does, but the French élite are, indeed, susceptible to celebrating their past, their culture and its "universal vocation". In direct contrast, German academics tend to be very uncomfortable when it comes to notions such as *Volk, Volksprache* and *Nation.*

This represents a cultural and existential dilemma, because these concepts were fundamental to both Herder and Humboldt. But since the 1930s and 1940s saw the celebration of the German language and culture in the context of national socialism, post-war Germans down to this day tend to feel somewhat ill-at-ease in celebrating "national ideals" and the vocation of the German people. This is reflected in all the rich and varied publications of the Berlin Academy and the wonderful group of scholars that have gathered around the "Humboldtian Renaissance" (Kurt Müller Vollmer, Jürgen Trabant, Manfred Ringmacher, Ute Tintemann, Markus Messling, among others).

The Germans as academics and political actors are, of course, eager to celebrate German *Kultur,* and recent celebrations of Alexander von Humboldt and Wilhelm von Humboldt confirm this. Regrettably, however, this celebration has often eclipsed the celebration of the German people and their *Sprache*, which, ironically, was the *raison d'être* and vocation of the Berlin University founded by Wilhelm von Humboldt. While the French celebrate French first and diversity second (*Naturellement!*), the Germans have to a large extent consolidated English by their publications. In stark contrast to Hagège, they may well approve of diversity in principle, but do not necessarily see defending the specific destiny of the German language and culture as their first priorities.[15]

Fortunately, things do appear to be changing; since the beginning of the 21st century, generally speaking, most German scholars today have moved on. Many adopt a pro-European multilingual perspective, as world citizens publishing in English, German and the languages they specialize in. In the coming generations, therefore, if there is a "combat" to be carried out in the fields of ethnolinguistics, cultural linguistics, or linguistic anthropology, it seems reasonable to hope that it will be a combat "for" and not "against", as the one Hagège championed in the 1980s. It is in this spirit that most European scholars throughout the twentieth century, and increasingly since the Cold War came to an end, have engaged with publications on language and culture in the Anglo world.

---

15 Words like *combat* still appear to remind Germans of a certain generation of works like those of Goebbels, "*Der Angriff*" ('The attack', 1935), (see Underhill 2011: 156–164). And even defences of a German "sensibility" (*Gefühl*) came to be tainted by the perverse neoromantic versions that transformed the German into a warrior conqueror with a calling for world domination (see Klemperer 1975: 338, 2006 [2000]: 246). Surely it is time to move on?

5.4 Dialogues and one way streets

Openness would seem to be facilitating dialogue. But is this a true dialogue or simply a response? Are American, Canadian, British and Australian scholars responding to the European responses to their work and engaging in dialogue themselves?[16] This remains an open question. Inevitably, the "dialogue" between European and North American scholars can at times appear somewhat one-sided. Despite an ongoing fundamental adherence to European culture and traditions in the Ivy League universities, there is clearly more interest for contemporary American scholars in Europe than for contemporary European scholars in North America.

The vast number of Europeans working in the Anglo world, from Anna Wierzbicka (Polish) to Gilles Fauconnier (French), make it plain that dialogue is implicit to the Anglo world as a locus for projects, debate, and publications on language and culture. Study of cultural metaphor is one of the areas of global import, with European scholars based in the United States or in constant dialogue with their colleagues elsewhere. Zoltán Kövecses is based in Budapest, James W. Underhill is based in Rouen, France, and Andrew Goatly was based at Lingnan University in Hong Kong. And one of the most dynamic forums for cross-lingual interdisciplinary research on metaphor and metonymy, metaphorik.de, is based in Germany.[17]

However, two crucial questions should be borne in mind when we consider whether there really is an ongoing dialogue between scholars working on each side of the Atlantic. Firstly, how many foreign language publications make it into the bibliographies of North American researchers? And secondly, how many of the language-specific forms or traits (from diminutives to gender, declination, compounding, and tense systems) that challenge the conceptual paradigms and linguistic terminologies of North American linguists ever come to be taken on board by North American researchers, when they set up and explore the linguistic frameworks within which they work? Ultimately, perhaps Anna Wierzbicka is right to claim that it is precisely those specialists – who should

---

16 A possible area for a systematic and systemic dialogue between various approaches to linguacultural worldviews is discussed in, for example, Głaz (2017).

17 The website [http://www.metaphorik.de] has an interface in three languages: German, English and French. Most of the contributions to this website journal are in English and German, some are in French and so far one in Italian (accessed on 16 December 2021). But the range of languages analyzed (apart from the ones mentioned) is wider, including Arabic, Basque, Hungarian, Polish, Spanish and possibly others.

know better – who tend to compound confusion when they refuse to recognize that they are thinking within culturally-bound frameworks. If this is indeed the case, then perhaps Wierzbicka is justified in claiming that such academics are "imprisoned in English" (Wierzbicka 2014).

6 Conclusion

Europe may not have been living up to its principles of unity and diversity over the past decade. An influx of migrants from North Africa, Libya and Syria gave rise to what was experienced as a "migrant crisis".[18] And Greece has been in crisis for more than a decade. Britain has broken free from the European Union, while Scotland is contemplating breaking free from Britain. And though the Basques have been placated, Catalonia is increasingly disillusioned by Spain's hegemony. These questions will all affect what languages are learned in Europe and how we feel about linguistic diversity here. Germany's "prudent" attitude to the promotion of its own language and the adoption of English by its elite has brought about a curious state of affairs: now the language of around a quarter of Europeans is learned by only a minority of them, while the language of a minor Member State, Republic of Ireland, with a population of less than five million, around 1% of European citizens – English – is now the lingua franca of most negotiations in the EU. The entry of the Eastern European nations consolidated the hold of German banks and German business, and France followed Germany in welcoming those nations into the EU. But ironically, the entry of Portugal, Finland, Slovakia, Slovenia and the Czech Republic has tended to comfort English in its dominant role, undermining the prestige of both French and German in Brussels and Strasbourg. This is supremely ironic, since, up until a few years ago, British European MPs could not hope to have a career without mastering at least one of those languages.

How changes in Europe will affect how we learn languages, and how we perceive the relationship between language and culture, remains unclear. What will the middle-term and long-term effects of Brexit be?[19] The single market, the

---

18 European cultural linguists were quick to react to these events; cf. Torkington and Ribeiro (2019) on the representation of migrants in Portuguese press, Krzyżanowski (2018) on politicization and mediatization of the refugee crisis in Polish national politics, or Jiménez-Ivars and León-Pinilla (2018) on interpreting in the refugee context.
19 As a major social and political event, Brexit quickly became the focus of research and reflection among cultural linguists; see e.g., Musolff (2017), Buckledee (2018), Charteris-Black (2019) or Tincheva (2019) for analyses and perspectives.

breakdown of economic and cultural barriers, mixed marriages, and commuting across the borders of linguistic communities previously divided by national boundaries and frontiers will all shape the future of Europe, but how will that influence make itself felt? Europe is an ongoing experiment in unity and diversity when it comes to language and culture, and being an experiment, it will inevitably have to contend with various challenges. How will outsiders be assimilated? How will cultures continue to flourish within Europe? What creoles will crop up? How will Turkish be integrated into German, Arabic into French, or Polish into Scottish English? (By 2015, the Polish community had grown to 86,000, as opposed to 300,000 speakers of Gaelic in Scotland.) How will Russian survive in Estonia, Slovenian in northern Italy, or Hungarian in Slovakia?[20]

There is a vast literature on contact languages, creoles, hybridity, and the reinvention of European languages. But the cases above are ongoing sagas, and many of these tales cannot yet be told, since the destinies of the linguistic communities are constantly being reshaped by global cultural and economic forces. Will the dimensions of life explored by the languages of diasporas wither and shrink? Or will those minority cultures resist and persist? In the end, will they even gain a pride of place within the dominant culture, as Picasso has added color to the collage of France, or as Kafka has become emblematic of the culture of Prague? Perhaps we shall understand more fully these developments, if we ponder deeply the way languages and cultures continue to emerge within individual sensibilities and within communities as complex shared identities.

This brief tour of ongoing approaches to language and culture being carried out in Europe has enabled us to posit that there are a certain number of key principles that animate them. It will be self-evident that the various schools we have discussed cannot fully substantiate the claim that there is a common framework for European scholars working in the field. Studies of greater depth and scope will be required to verify and modify the working hypotheses that we have set out here. Linguistic anthropologists working within the frameworks of both the Boas-Sapir-Whorf model and Dell Hymes' sociolinguistics will, it is hoped, respond by defending or redefining their aims and ambitions.

We all have much to gain from the sustained exchange between scholars and fieldworkers, and between the speakers of the languages of Europe and

---

20 Linguistic interaction is, of course, nothing new. As Hugo Schuchardt put it in 1884, "*Es gibt keine völlig ungemischte Sprache*" ('No completely unmixed language exists', Schuchardt 1884: 5). As we are writing this, in May 2022, the questions we have asked here must be supplemented with considerations of the status of the Ukrainian and Russian languages, as well as the speakers of Ukrainian, Russian and Belarusian in Europe, in the wake of the Russian aggression on Ukraine in February 2022.

communities around the world. But that debate must start somewhere – and we have proposed to start here and now by outlining five key principles and highlighting to what degree present studies of language and culture adhere to them. Listing a revised set of principles that animate cultural linguistics in Europe will, it is believed, aid further studies. They are posited here, let us repeat, as no more than a working hypothesis regarding a distinctly European methodology:

1. Linguistic study cannot be based on translations. Rather, linguists should go beyond what Humboldt called the skeleton of languages – their grammars and formal structures – to investigate the worldviews of the linguistic communities.

2. Words must be understood as cultural keywords evolving within value systems and hierarchies. As such, the study of keywords are both personal and political.

3. Words cannot be understood as universal concepts and it is essential to avoid projecting our own frameworks of understanding upon the languages we study (including terms such as *gender, kinship, sense, God, religion, space* and *time* used to investigate "universal" human experience).

4. Language is not simply a means of communication, a tool, but a means of living, existing, and understanding each other together as a community.

5. Metaphor and symbolic frameworks form part of what Whorf would have called the "patterning" of language (and what Humboldt called the "interaction", *Wechselwirkung*). They take form in elaborate constructions that are constantly being reactivated, revived and revised. They have fundamental structuring force that animates the way experience is framed, understood and expressed in language.

European scholars are involved in a vast range of approaches to culture and language, but they are not primarily concerned with mapping languages; nor do they focus on describing, explaining and defending their languages to others. In this respect, most work going on in Europe on language and culture is very different from work being carried out by linguistic anthropologists around the world. Nonetheless, we feel confident that linguistic anthropologists who rightly claim to adhere to the principles of Boas, Sapir and Whorf, will cherish many of the principles set out above. And no doubt they share the belief held by many European linguists that language is at all levels a creative process. Direct speech, conversation, jokes, exchanges, poetry, and translating, all form part of the constant reactivation of language's essential creativity. And it is at this point that the "prison house of language" paradigm begins to fall apart. Languages remain flexible and expressive because they are animated and sustained by creative interpersonal communication. Speaking together spontaneously and thinking together intuitively both enable us to define ourselves in terms of one another. On this point, linguists in Europe no doubt concur with their counterparts working throughout the world.

References

Agar, Michael. 1995. *Language shock. Understanding the culture of conversation*. New York: William Morrow.

Alekseev, Anatolij A., Nikolaj P. Antropov, Anna Kretschmer, Fedor Poljakov & Svetlana M. Tolstaja (eds.). 2016. *Славянская духовная культура: этнолингвистические и филологические исследования. Часть 1: К 90-летию со дня рождения Н. И. Толстого* [Slavic spiritual culture: Ethnolinguistic and philological studies. Part 1: For the 90th birthday of N. I. Tolstoy]. 2 vols. Frankfurt am Main: Peter Lang.

Apresyan, Yuriy D. (ed.). 2006. *Yazykovaya kartina mira i sistemnaya leksikografiya* [Linguistic worldview and systemic lexicography]. Moskva: Yazyki slavyanskikh kultur.

Bartmiński, Jerzy. 2009. *Aspects of cognitive ethnolinguistics*, edited by Jörg Zinken, translated by Adam Głaz. London & Oakville, CT: Equinox.

Bartmiński, Jerzy. 2017. Ethnolinguistics in the year 2016. *Etnolingwistyka/Ethnolinguistics* 28. 9–31.

Benczes, Réka, Antonio Barcelona & Francisco José Ruiz de Mendoza Ibáñez (eds.). 2011. *Defining metonymy in cognitive linguistics. Towards a consensus view.* Amsterdam & Philadelphia: John Benjamins.

Bernárdez, Enrique. 2008. *El lenguaje como cultura*. Madrid: Alianza.

Blumczynski, Piotr & John Gillespie (eds.). 2016. *Translating values. Evaluative concepts in translation*. London: Palgrave Macmillan.

BNC. British National Corpus. [https://www.english-corpora.org/bnc/] (accessed 15 January 2021).

Boas, Franz. 1911. Introduction. *Handbook of American Indian languages*, Vol. 1, (Bureau of American Ethnology, Smithsonian Institution, Bulletin 40), 1–83. Washington, D.C.: Government Printing Office.

Brookie, Hanna. 2018. Controversial topics and teacher answerability in Swedish for immigrants classes for refugees. *Linguistics and Education* 47. 84–92.

Buckledee, Steve. 2018. *The language of Brexit. How Britain talked its way out of the European Union*. London: Bloomsbury Academic.

Bułat-Silva, Zuzanna. 2020. Lexical-semantic analysis of "comfort". A contrastive perspective of English, European Portuguese, and Polish. In Dorothee Birke & Stella Butter (eds.), *Comfort in contemporary culture. The challenges of a concept*, 21–42. Bielefeld: Transcript-Verlag.

Cassin, Barbara (ed.). 2004. *Vocabulaire européen des philosophes. Dictionnaire des intraduisibles*. Paris: Robert.

Cassin, Barbara (ed.). 2014. *A dictionary of untranslatables. A philosophical lexicon*. Princeton: Princeton University Press.

Charteris-Black, Jonathan. 2019. *Metaphors of Brexit. No cherries on the cake?* Cham: Palgrave MacMillan.

Chuquet, Hélène & Michel Paillard. 2002. *Approche linguistique des problèmes de traduction anglais-français*. Paris: Ophrys.

Clark, Andy & David J. Chalmers. 1998. The extended mind. *Analysis* 58. 7–19.

COCA. Corpus of Contemporary American English. [https://www.english-corpora.org/coca/] (accessed 15 January 2021).

Crystal, David. 2000. *Language death*. Cambridge: Cambridge University Press.

Crystal, David. 2003. *English as a global language*, 2nd edition. Cambridge: Cambridge University Press.

D'Andrade, Roy. 1981. The cultural part of cognition. *Cognitive Science* 5. 179–195.

Dedenbach-Salazar Sáenz, Sabine (ed.). 2019. *Translating wor(l)ds. Christianity across cultural boundaries*. Baden-Baden: Academia Verlag Richarz Gmbh.

Devylder, Simon & Jordan Zlatev. 2020. Cutting and breaking metaphors of the self and the Motivation & Sedimentation Model. In Annalisa Baicchi (ed.), *Figurative meaning construction in thought and language*, 253–282. Amsterdam & Philadelphia: John Benjamins.

Dray, Susan. 2017. Identity matters. Language, practices and the (non)performance of rudeness in a pupil referral unit. *Linguistics and Education* 38. 44–54.

Duranti, Alessandro. 1997. *Linguistic anthropology*. Cambridge: Cambridge University Press.

François, Jacques. 2017. *Le Siècle d'or de la linguistique en Allemagne. De Humboldt à Meyer-Lübke*. Limoges: Lambert-Lucas.

François, Jacques (ed.). 2020. *Les linguistes allemands du XIXème siècle et leurs interlocuteurs étrangers*. Paris: Société de linguistique de Paris.

Franjieh, Michael, Greville G. Corbett & Alexandra Grandison. 2020. How classifiers become gender in Oceania. An experimental approach. *Open Science Framework*, August. [https://osf.io/7d8jn/] (accessed 1 March 2021).

Friedrich, Paul. 1989. Language, ideology, and political economy. *American Anthropologist* 91 (2). 295–312.

Geeraerts, Dirk. 2018. *Ten lectures on cognitive sociolinguistics*. Leiden: Brill.

Geeraerts, Dirk, Gitte Kristianssen & Yves Peirsman (eds.). 2010. *Advances in cognitive sociolinguistics*. Berlin & Boston: De Gruyter Mouton.

Głaz, Adam. 2017. Promoting dialogue. Two traditions in language and culture research. In Joanna Ziobro-Strzępek & Władysław Chłopicki (eds.), *Across borders 6. The West looks East*, 41–58. Krosno: PWSZ im. Stanisława Pigonia.

Głaz, Adam (ed.). 2019. *Languages – cultures – worldviews. Focus on translation*. Cham: Palgrave Macmillan.

Gasparov, M. L. 1996. *A history of European versification*, translated by G. S. Smith & Marina Tarlinskaja, edited by G. S. Smith & L. Holford-Strevens. Oxford: Clarendon Press.

Goatly, Andrew. 2007. *Washing the brain. Metaphor and hidden ideology*. Amsterdam & Philadelphia: John Benjamins.

Goddard, Cliff (ed.). 2018. *Minimal English for a global world*. Cham, Switzerland: Palgrave Macmillan.

Guillemin-Flescher, Jacqueline. 1981. *Syntaxe comparée du français et de l'anglais. Problèmes de traduction*. Paris: Ophrys.

Gumperz, John & Dell Hymes. 1986 (1972). *Directions in sociolinguistics. The ethnography of communication*. Oxford: Basil Blackwell.

Hagège, Claude. 1985. *L'homme de paroles. Contribution linguistique aux sciences humaines*. Paris: Fayard.
Hagège, Claude. 1992. *Le souffle de la langue. Voies et destins des parlers d'Europe*. Paris: Odile Jacob.
Hagège, Claude. 1996. *Le français. Histoire d'un combat*. Paris: Editions Michel Hagège.
Hagège, Claude. 2000. *Halte à la mort des langues*. Paris: Odile Jacob.
Hutchins, Edwin. 1995. *Cognition in the wild*. Cambridge, MA: MIT Press.
Hymes, Dell. 2003. *Now I know only so far. Essays in ethnopoetics*. Lincoln & London: University of Nebraska Press.
Jiménez-Ivars, Amparo & Ruth León-Pinilla. 2018. Interpreting in refugee contexts. A descriptive and qualitative study. *Language & Communication* 60. 28–43.
Joseph, John E. 2012. *Saussure*. Oxford: Oxford University Press.
Joseph, John E. 2017. The reception of Wilhelm von Humboldt's linguistic writings in the anglosphere, 1820 to the present. *Forum for Modern Language Studies* 53 (1). 7–20.
Klemperer, Victor. 1975. *LTI: Notizbuch eines Philogen*. Leipzig: Reklam Verlag.
Klemperer, Victor. 2006 (2000). *The language of the Third Reich, LTI Lingua Tertii Imperii*, translated by Martin Brady. London & New York: Continuum.
Kotthoff, Helga. 2000. Gender and joking. On the complexities of women's image politics in humorous narratives. *Journal of Pragmatics* 32 (1). 55–80.
Kóczy, Judit Baranyiné. 2018. *Nature, metaphor, culture. Cultural conceptualizations in Hungarian folksongs*. Singapore: Springer.
Kövecses, Zoltán. 2005. *Metaphor in culture. Universality and variation*. Cambridge: Cambridge University Press.
Kövecses, Zoltán. 2020. *Extended Conceptual Metaphor Theory*. Cambridge: Cambridge University Press.
Kramsch, Claire. 2009. *The multilingual subject*. Oxford: Oxford University Press.
Kramsch, Claire. 2012. Authenticity and legitimacy in multilingual second language acquisition (SLA). [https://www.youtube.com/watch?v=VHxxpdc2PoE] (accessed 20 April 2021).
Kretschmer, Anna, Gerhard Neweklowsky, Stefan-Michael Newerkla & Fedor Poljakov (eds.). 2019. *Minderheiten in der slawischen Welt. Sprachkontakte und kulturelle Identitäten* (Philologica Slavica Vindobonensia). Berlin: Peter Lang.
Kristianssen, Gitte & René Dirven (eds.). 2008. *Cognitive sociolinguistics. Language variation, cultural models, social systems*. Berlin & New York: De Gruyter Mouton.
Krzyżanowski, Michał. 2018. Discursive shifts in ethno-nationalist politics. On politicization and mediatization of the "refugee crisis" in Poland. *Journal of Immigrant & Refugee Studies* 16 (1–2). 76–96.
Lee, Penny. 1996. *The Whorf theory complex. A critical reconstruction*. Amsterdam & Philadelphia: John Benjamins.
Levinson, Stephen C. & David Wilkins. 2006. *Grammars of space. Explorations in cognitive diversity*. Cambridge: Cambridge University Press.
Levisen, Carsten. 2012. *Cultural semantics and social cognition. A case study on the Danish universe of meaning*. Berlin & Boston: De Gruyter Mouton.
Levisen, Carsten. 2017. The social and sonic semantics of reggae. Language ideology and emergent socialities in postcolonial Vanuatu. *Language and Communication* 52. 102–16.
Levisen, Carsten & Carol Priestly. 2017. Social keywords in postcolonial Melanesian discourse. *Kastom* "traditional culture" and *tumbuna* "ancestors". In Carsten Levisen &

Sophia Waters (eds.), *Cultural keywords in discourse*, 83–106. Amsterdam & Philadelphia: John Benjamins.

Levý, Jiří. 2011 (1963). *The art of translation*, translated by Patrick Corness, edited by Zuzana Jettmarová. Amsterdam & Philadelphia: John Benjamins.

Littlemore, Jeannette. 2019. *Metaphors in the mind. Sources of variation in embodied metaphor*. Cambridge: Cambridge University Press.

Lucy, John, A. 1992. *Language diversity and thought. A reformulation of the linguistic relativity hypothesis*. Cambridge: Cambridge University Press.

MacDonald, Lindsay W., Carole P. Biggam & Galina V. Paramei (eds.). 2018. *Progress in colour studies. Cognition, language and beyond*. Amsterdam & Philadelphia: John Benjamins.

Makoni, Sinfree & Alistair Pennycook (eds.). 2006. *Disinventing and reconstituting languages*. Clevedon: Multilingual Matters.

Malblanc, Alfred. 1963. *Stylistique comparée du français et de l'allemand*. Paris: Didier.

Malinowski, Bronislaw. 1922. *Argonauts of the Western Pacific. An account of native enterprise and adventure in the archipelagos of Melanesian New Guinea*. New York: E. P. Dutton & Company Ltd.

Malinowski, Bronislaw. 1935. *Coral gardens and their magic. A study of the methods of tilling the soil and of agricultural rites in the Trobriand Islands*. London: Allen & Unwin.

Malinowski, Bronislaw. 1952 (1923). The problem of meaning in primitive languages. In Charles Kay Ogden & Ivor Armstrong Richards (eds.), *The meaning of meaning*, 10th edition, 296–336. New York & London: Harcourt, Brace & Company/Routledge & Kegan Paul Ltd.

metaphorik.de. Ein Forum der wissenschaftlichen Diskussion über Metapher und Metonimie. [http://www.metaphorik.de/] (accessed 30 April 2021).

Meschonnic, Henri. 1999. *Poétique du traduire*. Paris: Verdier.

Meschonnic, Henri. 1982. *Critique du rythme. Anthropologie historique du langage*. Paris: Verdier.

Micheli, Ilaria. 2018. When ethnolinguistics breaks out of academia. A report from Africa and international cooperation. *Antropologia Pubblica* 4 (1). 137–151.

Morphy, Howard. 2007. *Becoming art. Exploring cross-cultural categories*. Oxford & New York: Routledge.

Musolff, Andreas. 2016. *Political metaphor analysis. Discourse and scenarios*. London: Bloomsbury Academic.

Musolff, Andreas. 2017. Truths, lies and figurative scenarios. Metaphors at the heart of Brexit. *Journal of Language and Politics* 16 (5). 641–657.

Musolff, Andreas, Christina Schäffner & Michael Townson. 1996. *Conceiving of Europe. Diversity in unity*. Suffolk: Dartmouth Publishing Company.

Nagórko, Alicja. 2004. Etnolingvistika i kulturemi u međujezičnom prostoru [Ethnolinguistics and culturemes in interlinguistic space]. *Rasprave: Časopis Instituta za hrvatski jezik i jezikoslovlje* 30. 131–143.

Nair, Rukmini Bhaya & Peter Ronald deSouza (eds.) 2020. *Keywords for India. A conceptual lexicon for the 21st century*. London: Bloomsbury Publishing.

Nergaard, Siri. 2021. *Translation and transmigration*. New York: Routledge.

Nassenstein, Nico & Paulin Baraka Bose. 2016. *Kivu Swahili texts and grammar notes*. Munich: LINCOM.

Pajević, Marko. 2017. Humboldt's "Thinking language". Poetics and politics. *Forum for Modern Language Studies* 53 (1). 95–107.

Pajević, Marko & David Nowell Smith (eds.). 2018. Thinking language with Henri Meschonnic. *Comparative Critical Studies* 15 (3).

Pajević, Marko (ed.). 2019. *The Henri Meschonnic reader. A poetics of society*. Edinburgh: Edinburgh University Press.

Peeters, Bert. 2012. L'interculturel servi à la sauce MSN, ou à quoi sert la métalangue sémantique naturelle? In Nathalie Auger, Françoise Demougin & Christine Béal (eds.), *Interactions et interculturalité. Variété des corpus et des approches*, 149–180. Bruxelles, Bern & Berlin: Peter Lang.

Peeters, Bert (ed.). 2019. *Heart- and soul-like constructs across languages, cultures, and epochs*. New York: Routledge.

Piłsudski, Bronisław. 1998-2011. *The collected works of Bronisław Piłsudski*, Vols. 1-4, translated & edited by Alfred F. Majewicz with the assistance of Elżbieta Majewicz, Larysa V. Ozoliņa, Mikhail D. Simonov, Tatyana Bulgakova, Tatyana P. Roon, Tomasz Wicherkiewicz & Werner Winter. Berlin & Boston: De Gruyter Mouton.

Risager, Karen. 2006. *Language and culture. Global flows and local complexity*. Clevedon, Buffalo & Toronto: Multilingual Matters.

Risager, Karen. 2015. Linguaculture. The language–culture nexus in transnational perspective. In Farzad Sharifian (ed.), *The Routledge handbook of language and culture*, 87–99. London & New York: Routledge.

Sapir, Edward. 1921. *Language. An introduction to the study of speech*. New York: Harcourt, Brace & Company.

Sapir, Edward. 1985 (1949). *Selected writings in language, culture, and personality*, edited by David G. Mandelbaum. Berkeley: University of California Press.

Senft, Gunter. 2010. *The Trobriand islanders' ways of speaking*. Berlin & Boston De Gruyter Mouton.

Senft, Gunter. 2015. *Tales from the Trobriand Islands of Papua New Guinea. Psycholinguistic and anthropological linguistic analyses of tales told by Trobriand children and adults*. Amsterdam & Philadelphia: John Benjamins.

Sharifian, Farzad. 2017. *Cultural Linguistics*. Amsterdam & Philadelphia: John Benjamins.

Silva Sinha, Vera da. 2019. Event-based time in three indigeneous Amazonian and Hinguan cultures of Brazil. *Frontiers in Psychology* 10 (454). DOI:10.3389/fpsyg.2019.00454

Sinha, Chris. 2009. Language as a biocultural niche and social institution. In Vyvyan Evans & Stéphanie Pourcel (eds.), *New directions in cognitive linguistics*, 289–309. Amsterdam & Philadelphia: John Benjamins.

Sinha, Chris. 2015. Language and other artifacts. Socio-cultural dynamics of niche construction. *Frontiers in Psychology* 6 (1601). DOI:10.3389/fpsyg.2015.01601

Sinha, Chris. 2021. Culture in language and cognition. In Xu Wen & John R. Taylor (eds.), *The Routledge handbook of cognitive linguistics*, 387–407. New York: Routledge.

Sinha, Chris, Vera da Silva Sinha, Jörg Zinken & Wany Sampaio. 2011. When time is not space. The social and linguistic construction of time intervals and temporal event relations in an Amazonian culture. *Language and Cognition* 3 (1). 137–169.

Slavyanskiye drevnosti. Etnolingvisticheskiy slovar' v 5 tomakh. 1995. [Slavic antiquities. An ethnolinguistic dictionary in 5 volumes], edited by Nikita I. Tolstoy. Moskva: Mezhdunarodnyye otnosheniya.

Schuchardt, Hugo. 1884. *Slavo-deutsches und Slavo-italienisches*. Graz: Leuschner & Lubensky.

Słownik stereotypów i symboli ludowych. 1996–2021. [Dictionary of folk stereotypes and symbols], edited by Jerzy Bartmiński & Stanisława Niebrzegowska-Bartmińska. Lublin: Wydawnictwo UMCS.

Tincheva, Nelly. 2019. Conceptualizing Brexit. First post-referendum days' dynamics in metaphorization. *International Journal of Language and Culture* 6 (2). 255–278.

Tolstoy, Nikita I. 1995. *Yazyk i narodnaya kul'tura. Ocherki po slavyanskoy mifologii i etnolingvistike* [Language and folk culture. Essays in Slavic mythology and ethnolinguistics]. Moskva: Indrik.

Torkington, Kate & Filipa Perdigão Ribeiro. 2019. "What are these people: Migrants, immigrants, refugees?" Migration-related terminology and representations in Portuguese digital press headlines. *Discourse, Context & Media* 27. 22–31.

Trabant, Jürgen. 1990. *Traditionen Humboldts*. Frankfurt: Suhrkamp.

Trabant, Jürgen. 2003. *Mithridates im Paradies. Kleine Geschichte des Sprachdenkens*. München: C.H. Beck.

Trabant, Jürgen. 2014. *Globalesisch, oder was? Ein Plädoyer für Europas Sprachen*. München: C.H. Beck.

Trabant, Jürgen. 2015. The Jürgen Trabant Wilhelm von Humboldt lectures. Rouen Ethnolinguistics Project. [https://rep.univ-rouen.fr/content/films-trabant] (accessed 10 April 2021).

Underhill, James W. 2009. *Humboldt, worldview and language*. Edinburgh: Edinburgh University Press.

Underhill, James W. 2011. *Creating worldviews. Metaphor, ideology and language*. Edinburgh: Edinburgh University Press.

Underhill, James W. 2012. *Ethnolinguistics and cultural concepts. Truth, love, hate and war.* Cambridge: Cambridge University Press.

Underhill, James W. & Mariarosaria Gianninoto. 2019. *Migrating meanings. Sharing keywords in a global world*. Edinburgh: Edinburgh University Press.

Vaňková, Irena. (ed.) 2001. *Obraz světa v jazyce* [Worldview in language]. Praha: Univerzita Karlova, Filozofická fakulta.

Vaňková, Irena & Jan Weindl (ed.). 2012. *Tělo, smysly, emoce, v jazyce i v literatuře* [Body, senses, emotions in language and literature]. Praha: Univerzita Karlova, Filozofická fakulta.

Vaňková, Irena, Veronika Vondrážková & Radka Zbořilová. (eds.) 2017. *Horizonty kognitivně-kulturní lingvistiky I* [Horizons in cognitive-cultural linguistics I]. Praha: Univerzita Karlova, Filozofická fakulta.

Vaňková, Irena & Lucie Šťastná (eds.). 2018. *Horizonty kognitivně-kulturní lingvistiky II* [Horizons in cognitive-cultural linguistics II]. Praha: Univerzita Karlova, Filozofická fakulta.

Venuti, Lawrence (ed.). 2012. *The Routledge translation studies reader*, 3rd edition. New York: Routledge.

Vinay, Jean-Paul & Jean Darbelnet. 1977 (1958). *Stylistique comparée du français et de l'anglais*. Paris: Didier.

Völkel, Svenja. 2010. *Social structure, space and possession in Tongan culture and language. An ethnolinguistic research*. Amsterdam & Philadelphia: John Benjamins.

Völkel, Svenja. 2016. Tongan-English language contact and kinship terminology. *World Englishes* 35 (2). 242–258.

Whorf, Benjamin Lee. 1956. *Language, thought, reality. Selected writings of Benajmin Lee Whorf*, edited by John B. Carroll. New York & London: The MIT Press & John Wiley and Sons, Inc.

Wierzbicka, Anna. 2010. *Experience, evidence and sense. The hidden cultural legacy of English*. Oxford: Oxford University Press.

Wierzbicka, Anna. 2014. *Imprisoned in English. The hazards of English as a default language*. Oxford & New York: Oxford University Press.

Wierzbicka, Anna. 2018a. *In conversation with Anna Wierzbicka – How English shapes our Anglo world*, interviewed by James W. Underhill. [https://www.youtube.com/watch?v=jCw3dfmgP-0&t=7s] (accessed 29 April 2021).

Wierzbicka, Anna. 2018b. *In conversation with Anna Wierzbicka – The philosophical foundations of NSM*, interviewed by James W. Underhill. [https://www.youtube.com/watch?v=p9fdAbII7-E] (accessed 29 April 2021).

Williams, Raymond. 1985 (1976). *Keywords. A vocabulary on culture and society*. New York: Oxford University Press.

Zinken, Jörg. 2016. *Requesting responsibility. The morality of grammar in Polish and English*. Oxford: Oxford Universiry Press.

Part IV: **Outlook**

Andrea Hollington
19 The language-culture dimension: A space for challenges and opportunities

Research that concerns the intersection of language and culture is diverse, interdisciplinary, and often contested. While many fields and domains have been discussed extensively (such as the connection between language and cognition, initiated under the controversial theory of linguistic relativity), others constitute new and still understudied approaches (such as the role of culture in language acquisition; see Hellwig, this volume, Rumsey, Singer, and Tomlinson, this volume). There are not only different domains and themes in the study of language and culture, but also different conceptions of the very notions of language and culture, and the relationship between them (as discussed by Nassenstein and Völkel in the introduction to this volume). And that's before one even begins to consider the great linguistic and cultural diversity on this planet. With regard to the African continent, for example, Axel Fleisch (2020: 780) states: "A vast field of study like that of African languages and cultures is necessarily fragmented, diverse, and characterized by manifold research approaches with their specific theoretical preferences and methodologies." A similar statement is found at the beginning of Ameka and Amha's contribution on language and culture research in Africa in this volume. For the European context, Underhill and Głaz (this volume) note, likewise, that given the great amount of diverse language and cultural practices, "the chances of developing a coherent pan-European concept of cultural linguistics certainly appear to be slim". Similarly, other parts of the world exhibit enormous linguistic diversity in general and great variety in the ways in which language(s) and culture(s) interact and in the ways these interactions are studied and analyzed, as the contributions to this volume testify (see Enfield and Sidnell, this volume, Aikhenvald, this volume, Rumsey, Singer, and Tomlinson, this volume).

Considering Enfield and Sidnell's (this volume) statement that "[l]anguage is a part of culture and culture is a part of language", and given the fact that both language and culture are dynamic and ever changing, the possible relations, interactions, and mutual influences between language and culture, and the domains and aspects that could be studied, extend to infinity.

What this book has shown with all its insightful contributions is that, on the one hand, the themes and domains to be studied by anthropological linguists

Andrea Hollington, Johannes Gutenberg University of Mainz/Germany,
e-mail: andrea.hollington@yahoo.de

https://doi.org/10.1515/9783110726626-019

and linguistic anthropologists (a historically derived dichotomy that does not seem to be very helpful when it comes to studying the relation between language and culture in various contexts)[1] are manifold, if not infinite, as cultural and linguistic behavior and practices are ever-changing. On the other hand, specific domains and themes of the language-culture nexus that have been studied show that there is great variety with regard to concepts, scope, general approaches, interpretations, applied methodological frameworks, and theoretical backgrounds (including interdisciplinary theoretical approaches). For example, emotion can be regarded as one of the core themes in anthropological linguistics, yet the very concept and scope of the notion has been defined very differently by scholars who study emotional language (Ponsonnet, this volume).

As even the well-established core themes of anthropological linguistics (such as linguistic relativity, color terms, the linguistics of kinship, taboo etc.) constitute a broad range of domains and applied approaches, the true dimension of the language and culture nexus will begin to unfold when we take the numerous interdisciplinary perspectives that look at actual language practices, communicative performances, ideologies, metalinguistic awareness, and language philosophies, in their respective socio-cultural contexts, into account. This volume takes a huge step in this direction: rather than merely summarizing and presenting current themes and approaches, the contributions in this volume also include intersections of established theoretical approaches that lead to new paths, new fields of research, and topics that have fallen into oblivion. We realize that a multitude of understandings of how humans use language is yet to be uncovered when we consider how speech styles and communicative styles emerge in contexts of language contact (Dimmendaal, this volume). Given the fact that multilingualism and language contact scenarios are the norm in many parts of the world, it is obvious that the emergence of new language practices (which is sometimes underestimated in light of the focus on endangered languages among linguists; see also the discussion in Bradley, this volume) requires much more scholarly attention and careful investigation.

An important domain for the study of the language and culture relationship, in which ever new multimodal linguistic and communicative practices evolve, is constituted by artful language, orature, literature, and music (see for instance Finnegan 2012, Bemile 2020, Vierke 2020, to name just a few). Many parts of the world, especially those characterized by contact, linguistic pluralism, and cultural diversity,

---

1 This, however, is a big discussion that will not form a part of this short afterword (see the discussion in the introduction to this volume). In the following, I will mainly use the term anthropological linguistics or speak about the language-culture nexus, for the sake of convenience.

exhibit rich genres and performances that illustrate creative ways with language and other communicative practices that can provide us with more insights into the language and culture nexus. Multivocality, narrative styles, rhetoric, rhythm, rhyme, and ritual language (apart from everyday speech, of course) are among the communicative practices that enrich and make people's cultural worlds.

The Caribbean, a place characterized by histories of migration, slavery, colonialism, contact, revolution, shifting power relations, memories, transatlantic solidarities, and much more, provides a rich repertoire of cultural communicative performances and writings. Hubert Devonish (forthcoming), for example, analyzes identity discourses in popular music from Trinidad and Tobago by employing speech act theory. He shows that linguistic and musical performances employ strategies such as ambiguity to engage in discourses of nation and ethnicity in the complex postcolonial Tribagonian scenario. The postcolonial societies of the Caribbean, their complex and multilayered histories, and the many examples of revolt against slavery and oppression, of remembering, identifying, and remaking, the roots and routes of migration and diaspora communities, require a linguistic perspective that takes the agency of speakers into account (see Faraclas 2012). And in this context, anthropological linguistic perspectives on so-called Creole languages in the Caribbean may help to overcome the reverberations of the strong dichotomies that have dominated Creole Studies since the second half of the 20th century, such as the dichotomy between universalists and substratists, or the one between those who believe in "creole exceptionalism" and those who advocate for a view that treats Creole languages and other contact languages as a unified object of study. Bettina Migge suggests that we develop open, hospitable, and decolonial research practices as linguists, following critical perspectives in anthropology and other disciplines (Migge 2020). Anthropological-linguistic accounts of Jamaican, for example, enable such perspectives as they shed light on African agencies in systems of oppression, slavery, and colonialism, help to understand transatlantic ties due to shared, negotiated, and rebuilt cultural knowledge, and open our eyes to linguistic practices beyond the classical themes in creole linguistics, such as cultural conceptualizations or the expression of emotion (see Hollington 2015, 2017).

In fact, cultural conceptualizations, as an interdisciplinary field of studies (see Sharifian 2011), provide important insights into the language and culture nexus, as they unveil the cognitive foundations of how "[p]eople in diverse settings have ways of doing things, ways of thinking, ways of feeling, and employ a variety of discourses to express them" (Silva Sinha, this volume). This becomes evident in so many different domains of daily life and human conviviality, such as the ways in which humans structure, conceptualize, and talk about time (ibid.). As several scholars noted, time is conceptualized differently across cultures, despite the fact that disciplines such as psychology, philosophy, and cognitive science have, for a long time, focused on the time concepts of WEIRD (Western, Educated, Industrialized, Rich, Democratic) people (Widlok forthcoming, based on Henrich, Heine, and Norenzayan 2010). Importantly, Silva Sinha's chapter points to these contested and problematic aspects of speaking and writing about time in the discipline of anthropology as well, and specifically to the ways in which time conceptualizations and denied coevalness have produced *Othering* (Fabian 1983). In this context, the author alludes to epistemology, which highlights the problematic nature of knowledge production in Western dominated academia. Related to this observation is an issue raised by Underhill and Głaz (this volume), who discuss another bias in the discipline of anthropological linguistics (which is also, and especially in Europe, called ethnolinguistics; see Nassenstein and Völkel, this volume): summarizing works on language in culture produced by European scholars, Underhill and Głaz state that ethnolinguistics, or in fact anything "ethno", implicitly refers to Western scholars studying non-Western languages and cultures, a bias that has colonial roots as well.

In attempts to overcome the ongoing bias rooted in colonial, historical, and imperial academic ideologies and ways of producing knowledge, anthropologists and cultural linguists (in the sense of Palmer's cultural linguistics, 1996) have begun to make efforts to take other ways of knowing, sharing, experiencing, and communicating into account by highlighting the socio-historical and cultural contexts of these practices. However, decolonial approaches have yet to become an established pillar of anthropological linguistics and related disciplines. Yet, many linguists would nowadays agree that studying communicative practices, styles, and genres within their cultural contexts and situational usage also reveals a lot about knowledge production and cultural epistemologies (Brühwiler and Hollington forthcoming). This is also expressed by Meyer and Quasinowski (this volume), who examine genres and conversational organization by showing not only the diversity of genres, but also the multilayeredness of different modes of analysis in the study of communicative practices and their sociocultural embeddedness. Examining ritual, Tavárez (this volume) discusses communicative performances of authority in various sociocultural contexts and highlights the role of local epistemological framing in foregrounding and simplifying processes of semiosis and metasemiosis. Pointing to the significance of multimodality (see below, as well as Mohr and Bauer, this volume), he states that speech in the context of ritual necessarily becomes a "broad rubric that includes structured verbal and bodily performances, along with silences and omissions".

This illustrates that when we consider questions of how we know what we know by looking at ways in which communities create, negotiate, and transmit knowledge, we can hardly underrate the role of language and communication in philosophical views. Linguistic anthropologies of world views and how they are constituted and taught in cultural expressions, social behavior, and linguistic practices may also contribute to a decolonization of philosophy and theories of knowledge, which is still highly dominated by Western schools of thought. This issue is also, in a very demonstrative way, addressed by Jim and Webster (this volume), who use the concept of "epistemic slippage" to describe a process in which an epistemological shift takes places that creates space for the inversion of the researcher and the researched, a space where the assumed expert becomes the learner and the supposed researched subject becomes the true expert. This shift calls for the change of perspective demanded by the decolonial approaches mentioned above. More collaborative work in anthropological linguistic field-work and knowledge production has also yielded new research approaches in studying Australian indigenous languages, such as the development of circular relationships between communities, researchers, and archives, as reported by Rumsey, Singer, and Tomlinson (this volume).

The multidimensionality not only of perspectives, speech styles, and communicative practices, but also of positionalities, intercultural awareness, and multilayered metapragmatic knowledges relates to cultural epistemologies and shared knowledges as well. As Mitchell and Storch (this volume) illustrate by drawing on complex examples in research contexts, dealing with taboo and the unspoken involves hospitality, metapragmatic and (inter)cultural awareness, and conscious positioning. Taking such aspects into account will not only draw a more holistic picture of communicative behavior in cultural contexts, but will also involve an incorporation and reflection of the research contexts in which knowledge on anthropological linguistic topics is being produced.

Connected to this is also the creation of a general approach to and understanding of language, including all its multimodal forms. This is of particular importance as human communication is usually multimodal and humans make use of different modalities at the same time in the process of meaning making (Mohr and Bauer, this volume). As Mohr and Bauer discuss (building on Ferrara and Hodge 2018), in human communicative practices (whether speaking or signing), we manage to employ and coordinate a great diversity of resources from our semiotic repertoire which are expressed in different modalities and through different channels (ibid.). Taken from such a broad angle, communication, even in seemingly simple cases, becomes extremely complex as it includes the co-occurrence of different acoustic and visual signs, gestures, gaze, posture, and so on. As linguists are only beginning to take these complex modes and channels of human interaction into consideration, this constitutes a fairly new field in anthropological linguistics as well (although there are certainly numerous older studies that deal with, for instance, gestures in cross-cultural perspectives). However, many of the past studies on the multimodality of communication either look at Western contexts or apply Western models and theories to communicative practices in other cultures. To arrive at true decolonial approaches to the multimodality of meaning-making, more studies of these complex communicative phenomena in different societies of the world are needed (and Mohr and Bauer offer a great contribution here), but also an inclusion of indigenous and local metalinguistic theories of meaning-making and multimodal practices on a par with the existing models of social semiotics.

Speaking of meaning-making and semiotics, an important level on which meaning is created and transported is that of social indexicalities. This refers to the fact that linguistic signs always also express social meanings in addition to their propositional content, i.e., in non-referential ways (Fleming, this volume). Since these kinds of social indexicalities are always interactionally emergent and manifest in the contexts of their occurrence (ibid.), it becomes even more important to pay attention to the cultural patterns and shared knowledge that contribute to the collective identities or worldviews that are indexed by certain signs. Fleming provides a thorough discussion of a theoretical approach to (stereotyped) social indexicalities by discussing how social gender is indexed in various linguacultures. Like with multimodalities, more in-depth studies of semiotic practices in non-Western contexts are necessary to test, elaborate, and redefine existing models of social indexicalities, given the complex ways in which communicative signs are meaningful on multiple levels.

A topic that has been controversially discussed in cultural conceptualizations and cognitive linguistics, and hence, in meaning-making, is that of awareness (see Hollington 2015). An important contribution to our understanding and rating of metalinguistic knowledge, awareness, and agency lies in the study of language ideologies. Kroskrity (this volume) discusses language ideologies with regard to social identities and distinguishes between indigenous language ideologies, ideologies in contact scenarios, and imposed language ideologies, presenting numerous examples from different parts of the world. In his concluding section, he makes important remarks about linguistic racism and raciolinguistics. The Caribbean, a culturally and linguistically heterogeneous area with a long, fragmented, and pluralistic history of colonialism, oppression, migration, and slavery, as mentioned above, is home to many communities and therefore features language ideologies from all three categories outlined by Kroskrity. It is significant that Rastafari, a movement originating in Jamaica and prominent in the Caribbean, as well as in other parts of the world, pronounces and promotes its own distinct language ideologies, which emerged in a racialized colonial context as explicitly anti-colonial language ideologies. Rastafari, at least on the ideological level, reject the English language as the language of the colonizer and create their own language by "correcting" the deceitful language of the oppressor based on their ideological principles of congruence between word, sound, and meaning (Schrenk 2015, Hollington 2016). These ideologies and conscious language practices are negotiated in a multilingual context that has, within traditional Creole Studies, often been described as diglossia. And while Rastafari may not "qualify" as indigenous in Kroskrity's sense (as he depicts indigenous language ideologies as "old" in his chapter, and Rastafari emerged in the 1930s), Rastafari are recognized as one of Jamaica's indigenous cultural groups by the United Nations. In light of this example and Rastafari's distinct and conscious language ideologies, which seem to incorporate aspects of all three of Kroskrity's categories, a further discussion of the interplay of multilayered language ideologies, multilingual contexts, and colonialism and its discourses promises to yield better insights into linguistic practices and ideologies in linguistically diverse contexts of unequal power relations.

This volume testifies to the fact that the language-culture nexus, in terms of its disciplinary, thematic, and theoretical plurality, is full of challenges and controversies but also opportunities and innovations. While it is sometimes not an easy task to find one's own positioning as a researcher in this broad interdisciplinary and ever-changing field, the editors of this volume offer words of encouragement in their introduction: "Despite or even because of all these fundamental issues, it is important not to get lost in theoretical considerations but to investigate the interplay between language and culture step by step in multiple contexts and from various perspectives". Regardless of the theoretical background or methodological approach chosen, our planet exhibits an amazing diversity of cultural and linguistic (in a broader sense including semiotic and communicative) practices whose study will help us to better understand not only the relationship between language and culture, but humanity at large.

References

Bemile, Sebastian K. 2020. Proverbs. In Rainer Vossen & Gerrit J. Dimmendaal (eds.), *The Oxford handbook of African languages*, 994–1015. Oxford: Oxford University Press.
Brühwiler, Agnes & Andrea Hollington. Forthcoming. *Utu* as epistemology and conviviality in Kiswahili culture: anthropological linguistic perspectives on living together. In Andrea Hollington, Alice Mitchell & Nico Nassenstein (eds.), *Anthropological linguistics. Perspectives from Africa*. Amsterdam: John Benjamins.
Devonish, Hubert. Forthcoming. Discur*sing* the state of a Caribbean nation. In Andrea Hollington, Joseph Farquharson & Byron Jones (eds.), *Contact languages and music*. Kingston, JA: University of the West Indies Press.
Fabian, Johannes. 1983. *Time and the other. How anthropology makes its object*. New York: Columbia University Press.

Faraclas, Nicholas (ed.) 2012. *Agency in the emergence of Creole languages. The role of women, renegades, and people of African and Indigenous descent in the emergence of the colonial era Creoles*. Amsterdam: John Benjamins.

Finnegan, Ruth. 2012 [1970]. *Oral literature in Africa*. Cambridge: Open Book Publishers.

Fleisch, Axel. 2020. Cognition and language. In Rainer Vossen & Gerrit J. Dimmendaal (eds.), *The Oxford handbook of African languages*, 780–794. Oxford: Oxford University Press.

Henrich, Joseph, Steven J. Heine & Ara Norenzayan. 2010. The weirdest people in the world? *Behavioral and Brain Sciences* 33 (2–3). 61–83.

Hollington, Andrea. 2015. *Traveling conceptualizations. A cognitive and anthropological linguistic study of Jamaican*. Amsterdam: John Benjamins.

Hollington, Andrea. 2016. Movement of Jah people. Language ideologies and music in a transnational contact scenario. *Critical Multilingualism Studies* 4 (2). 133–153.

Hollington, Andrea. 2017. Emotions in Jamaican. African conceptualizations, emblematicity and multimodality in discourse and public spaces. In Anne Storch (ed.), *Consensus and dissent. Negotiating emotion in the public space*, 81–104. Amsterdam: John Benjamins.

Migge, Bettina. 2020. Book review: John H. McWhorter. The Creole debate. Cambridge University Press, 2018, Ppvi, 173. *Journal of Language Contact* 12. 857–863.

Palmer, Gary B. 1996. *Toward a theory of cultural linguistics*. Austin, TX: University of Texas Press.

Schrenk, Havenol M. 2015. The positive-negative phenomenon and phono-semantic matching in Rasta talk. In Nico Nassenstein & Andrea Hollington (eds.), *Youth language practices in Africa and beyond*, 271–291. Berlin: De Gruyter Mouton.

Sharifian, Farzad. 2011. *Cultural conceptualisations and language. Theoretical framework and applications*. Amsterdam: Benjamins.

Vierke, Clarissa. 2020. Poetry. In Rainer Vossen & Gerrit J. Dimmendaal (eds.), *The Oxford handbook of African languages*, 1016–1025. Oxford: Oxford University Press.

Widlok, Thomas. Forthcoming. The cultural, linguistic and cognitive relativity of time concepts. In Andrea Hollington, Alice Mitchell & Nico Nassenstein (eds), *Anthropological linguistics. Perspectives from Africa*. Amsterdam: John Benjamins.

About the contributors

Alexandra Y. Aikhenvald is Adjunct Professor at the Centre for Indigenous Health Equity Research at Central Queensland University and Australian Laureate Fellow. She is a major authority on languages of the Arawak family, from northern Amazonia, and has written several grammars of Amazonian and Papuan languages, in addition to studies of language contact in Amazonia and across the world. Her further work covers numerous grammatical topics including serial verbs, evidentials, imperatives and commands, genders and classifiers, grammatical and phonological word, and the principles of grammar writing and immersion fieldwork. Her current focus is on the integration of language and society and the ways of conceptualizing disease and well-being in minority languages and cultures.

Felix K. Ameka is Professor and CIPSH/CIPL Chair of Ethnolinguistic Vitality and Diversity at Leiden University. He is a socio-cultural-cognitive linguist with interest in language documentation and description, semantics and pragmatics, anthropological and contact linguistics, sociolinguistics of development multilingualism and multilingual socialization, comparative and socio-cultural language studies. He has also become interested in digital humanities, and in language technologies for lesser-resourced languages. His area focus is West Africa. He is Editor-in-Chief (with Azeb Amha) of the Journal of African Languages and Linguistics. He continues to train young African scholars in documentary linguistics mostly through a series of Summer Schools that he initiated in 2008 and organizes in different parts of Africa. A recent publication is a co-edited book with Deborah Hill:*Languages, linguistics, and development practices*, Palgrave, 2022.

Azeb Amha is a researcher at the African Studies Center Leiden (ASCL), Leiden University. Her research focuses on language-culture interface in Ethiopia, especially in the Omotic language family. Azeb's research and teaching also address discourse and rhetoric of inclusion and alienation in (public) speeches, as part of the ASCL Collaborative Research Group *Fighting with words*. In the past years, Azeb has been engaged in ethnolinguistic documentation of Oyda, and Wolaitta. She is currently working on a multi-modal documentation of Zargula, an endangered language that is spoken in South-west Ethiopia. Azeb's publications include *The Maale Language* (2001), several articles on the grammar and typology of Omotic languages, and three co-edited books. Since 2005, Azeb is co-editor (with Felix Ameka) of the *Journal of African Languages and Linguistics*.

Anastasia Bauer is a Postdoctoral researcher at the University of Cologne. Her research interests lie in the domains of Slavic linguistics as well as multimodal language, and in contact between languages of different modalities. Her dissertation explores the spatial grammar in an endangered Aboriginal sign language used in the Yolŋu communities in Northern Australia. Her current postdoctoral project focuses on two cross-modal language contact phenomena in Russian Sign Language, i.e., mouthings and fingerspellings.

David Bradley has made a major contribution to linguistic theory and work on endangered languages. He has documented a number of languages of Asia, worked with various communities there to maintain and revitalize their languages, and trained and supported large numbers of scholars to do similar work around the world. He has taken many leadership

https://doi.org/10.1515/9783110726626-020

roles in the discipline, notably as President of the UNESCO Comité International Permanent des Linguistes (CIPL, International Permanent Committee of Linguists) for ten years 2014–2023 and as editor of several journals. His books include the 2019 Cambridge volume *Language Endangerment* and more than twenty others. He is Emeritus Professor of Linguistics at La Trobe University, Australia and honorary professor at four other universities around the world.

Gerrit J. Dimmendaal has been working on three different language families on Africa, Afroasiatic, Niger-Congo and Nilo-Saharan (with a special focus on the latter family). His main interests lie in the documentation of lesser known languages, anthropological linguistics and historical linguistics. His more recent publications include *The Leopard's Spots – Essays on Language, Cognition and Culture* (2015), *Nuba Mountain Language Studies – New Insights* (co-edited with Gertrud Schneider-Blum and Birgit Hellwig; 2018), and *The Oxford Handbook of African Languages* (co-edited with Rainer Vossen; 2019).

N. J. Enfield is Professor of Linguistics at the University of Sydney. His work on language and human sociality is based on regular fieldwork in mainland Southeast Asia, especially Laos. Among his books are *Relationship Thinking: Agency, Enchrony, and Human Sociality* (2013), *Natural Causes of Language* (2014), *The Utility of Meaning* (2015), *The Cambridge Handbook of Linguistic Anthropology* (2014, co-edited with Paul Kockelman and Jack Sidnell), *The Concept of Action* (2019, co-authored with Jack Sidnell) and *The Languages of Mainland Southeast Asia* (2021).

Luke Fleming is a linguistic anthropologist whose research and writing seeks to articulate a comparative approach to the study of speech registers. He has written on sundry topics, from the 'mother-in-law languages' employed in Indigenous Australian communities to the honorific vocabularies found in Austronesian languages to gender-indexing speech styles in the Native Americas. He hopes that his book on the sociolinguistic mediation of kinship-based avoidance relationships, entitled *On Speaking Terms: Avoidance Registers and the Sociolinguistics of Kinship*, will be published in the near future by the University of Toronto Press.

Adam Głaz, affiliated with Maria Curie-Skłodowska University (UMCS) in Lublin, Poland, researches in cognitive and cultural linguistics, linguistic worldview, and translation. He has authored three monographs: *The Dynamics of Meaning* (2002), *Extended Vantage Theory in Linguistic Application* (2012), both published by UMCS Press, and *Linguistic Worldview(s): Approaches and Applications* (2022, Routledge), as well as several dozen articles. He has edited or co-edited ten volumes, most recently *Languages – Cultures – Worldviews: Focus on Translation* (Palgrave Macmillan, 2019). Głaz has also been translating in linguistics and general humanities, including two monographs (Anna Wierzbicka's *Semantyka. Jednostki elementarne i uniwersalne*, 2004 – into his native Polish, and Jerzy Bartmiński's *Aspects of Cognitive Etnholinguistics*, 2009 – into English).

Birgit Hellwig is based at the Department of Linguistics, University of Cologne, where she combines language documentation with psycholinguistic and anthropological approaches, researching language acquisition and socialization in diverse socio-cultural settings. She is currently working with the Qaqet in Papua New Guinea, and she continues to be interested in the documentation and description of the adult language, researching Goemai (a Chadic language of Nigeria), Katla (a Niger-Congo language of Sudan) and Tabaq (a Nilo- Saharan language of Sudan).

Andrea Hollington is a scholar with a background in African Studies. Her research interests include anthropological linguistics, sociolinguistics, ethnomusicology, post- and decolonial studies, youth language practices and studies on repertoires, identity, creativity, and agency. She has focused on cultural, linguistic, and musical practices in Africa and the African Diaspora, and in particular on African – Caribbean connections and carried out research in Ethiopia, Zimbabwe and Jamaica. She is the author of *Traveling Conceptualizations – A cognitive and anthropological linguistic study of Jamaican* (Benjamins) and she has published a wide range of papers on various topics of her multifaceted research interest in journals and edited volumes and co-edited several books and special issues.

Rex Lee Jim First and foremost, Rex Lee Jim loves to play with his grandkids. He enjoys telling stories to his grandkids and loves to travel with them. He enjoys being a grandfather. He is a poet, playwright, and essayist. He is also a medicine man, practicing ceremonies weekly for Navajo families and the land. He lives in southwest Rock Point, a small ranching and farming community, where he was born and raised.

Paul V. Kroskrity is Professor of Anthropology and American Indian Studies at the University of California, Los Angeles. Earning his undergraduate degree from Columbia in 1971, he went on to obtain his Ph.D. in Anthropology from Indiana University in 1977. He is a linguistic anthropologist who continues to conduct long term research with two different Native American language communities – the Village of Tewa (a Kiowa-Tanoan language) in Northern Arizona and the Western Mono (a Uto-Aztecan language) of Central California. His published works include many journal articles as well as the following books: *Language, History, and Identity* (1993); *Language Ideologies: Practice and Theory* (1998, with B. Schieffelin and K. Woolard); *Regimes of Language: Ideologies, Polities, and Identities* (2000); *Native American Language Ideologies* (2009, with M. Field); *Engaging Native American Publics* (2017, with B. Meek) and *The Oxford Handbook of Language and Race* (2020, with H. S. Alim and A. Reyes).

Christian Meyer is a professor of sociology at the University of Konstanz, Germany. He has published extensively on conversational organization, embodied interaction, multimodal interaction analysis, rhetoric, and social theory. Recent books are *Culture, Practice, and the Body* (Metzler 2018) and *Intercorporeality* (Oxford University Press 2017; co-edited with J. Streeck and S. Jordan) as well as a Special Issue of *Human Studies* on Harold Garfinkel's *Studies in Ethnomethodology* (2020; co-edited with M. Endress and S. Nicolae).

Alice Mitchell is currently a Junior Professor in the anthropological linguistics of Africa in the Institute for African Studies at the University of Cologne. She is interested in the diversity of ways in which people use language to mediate their relationships with others. To study language and sociality, she favours approaches that combine ethnography with micro-level analysis of naturally occurring interaction. Her work has mainly focused on person reference practices among Datooga speakers in Tanzania, including topics such as in-law name avoidance and the affective use of kin terms. In recent work she has also been studying children's speech to see how children learn about and negotiate kinship concepts in everyday interaction.

Susanne Mohr is Professor in English Sociolinguistics at the Norwegian University of Science and Technology. She obtained her PhD from the University of Cologne for her work on mouth actions in Irish Sign Language and a postdoctoral degree from the University of Bonn with a thesis on nominal pluralization and countability in African varieties of English. Her research interests are multilingualism, language contact, multimodality, language and globalization and methods in sociolinguistics.

Nico Nassenstein is Junior Professor for African Languages and Linguistics (tenure) at Johannes Gutenberg-Universität Mainz at the Department of Anthropology and African Studies. He holds a PhD from the University of Cologne and works mainly in the fields of Anthropological Linguistics, Sociolinguistics and Pragmatics with a regional focus on Central and East Africa. His research interests include verbal taboo, politeness, the language of violent conflict, swearing and cursing practices, linguistic ethnography, emerging language practices in Africa and metalanguage around sexuality and body parts. Two of his recent books include *Swearing and Cursing: Contexts and Practices in a Critical Linguistic Perspective* (co-ed. with Anne Storch, De Gruyter Mouton, 2020) and *Metasex: The Discourse of Intimacy and Transgression* (co-authored with Anne Storch, John Benjamins, 2020).

Maïa Ponsonnet is a descriptive and anthropological linguist currently based at Centre National de la Recherche Scientifique (CNRS, Dynamique Du Langage, Lyon). She holds a PhD in Linguistics from the Australian National University (Canberra, 2014), with additional background in Philosophy (PhD Université Paris-8, 2005). Maïa's research concerns expressive language, how emotions are linguistically encoded across the world's languages, and whether emotional language may channel people's experience and management of emotions. She has extensive experience working with speakers of Indigenous Australian languages in northern Australia. She is the author many articles and books, in particular a 2014 monograph on the encoding of emotions in Dalabon (Gunwinyguan, norther Australia) and a 2019 monograph on a comparison between Dalabon and Kriol, the creole that has replaced Dalabon.

Benjamin Quasinowski is a research assistant at the research data center Qualiservice, University of Bremen. His research interests are in multimodal conversation analysis, interaction in (bio-)medical settings, intercultural communication, and the methodology of qualitative research methods. He obtained his PhD from the University of Konstanz for his work on conversational organization in the context of a rural hospital in Kazakhstan. He was a member of the DFG-funded research project "Travelling knowledge: The glocalization of medical professional knowledge and practice", which comparatively investigated physician-patient interaction in four university hospitals in Turkey, The Netherlands, China, and Germany.

Alan Rumsey is an Emeritus Professor in the in the College of Asia and the Pacific at The Australian National University, and Chief Investigator in the Australian Research Council Centre of Excellence for the Dynamics of Language. His research fields are highland Papua

New Guinea and Aboriginal Australia, with a focus on linguistic anthropology, comparative poetics, and child language socialization. He is a Fellow of the Australian Academy of Humanities and past president of the Australian Anthropological Society. His publications include "The sociocultural dynamics of indigenous multilingualism in northwestern Australia" (in *Language & Communication,* volume 62, 2018), "Melanesia as a zone of linguistic diversity" (Hirsch, Eric and Will Rollason eds. 2019 *The Melanesian World*) and "Intersubjectivity and engagement in Ku Waru" (*Open Linguistics* volume 5, 2019).

Jack Sidnell is Professor in the Department of Anthropology at the University of Toronto. His research focuses on the structures of talk and interaction. In addition to research in the Caribbean and Vietnam, he has examined talk in court and among young children. He is the author of *Conversation Analysis: An Introduction* (2010) and *The Concept of Action* (with N. J. Enfield) and is the editor of *Conversation Analysis: Comparative Perspectives* (2009) and co-editor of *Conversational Repair and Human Understanding* (2013), *The Handbook of Conversation Analysis* (2012), and *The Cambridge Handbook of Linguistic Anthropology* (2014).

Vera da Silva Sinha is an anthropologist and linguist who seeks to understand how the human mind is shaped by culture and language. She holds a PhD in Linguistics from the University of East Anglia and Master's degrees in Anthropology and International Criminal Justice. She has worked with different indigenous communities in Brazil, in particular Amondawa, Huni Kui, Awety and Kamaiura, using methods from anthropology, linguistics, and psychology. Her current research focuses on how time, number and length are conceptualised and talked about in different cultural settings. She has presented a TEDx talk What is Event-Based Time? (https://youtu.be/EWCGeHhxBh0). She is Co-Editor-in-Chief of the International Journal of Language and Culture. She is involved in several capacity-building, language documentation, and revitalisation projects in partnership with indigenous researchers, for details, go to: https://verasinha.com.

Ruth Singer is an ARC Future Fellow at the Research Unit for Indigenous Languages at the University of Melbourne. She researches multilingualism in collaboration with Warruwi Community, an Indigenous community in Australia's Northern Territory. She is currently exploring how local ways of being multilingual may have played a role in creating high levels of linguistic diversity in western Arnhem land. She is also working on the development of digital resources with Warruwi community; making films with young people and creating online language courses and dictionaries. Earlier research focussed on the semantics of Mawng's system of grammatical gender and idioms formed via verb agreement. Mawng is one of a number of small languages that are still being widely used and passed on to children at Warruwi.

Anne Storch is Professor of African Linguistics at the University of Cologne. Her work combines contributions on cultural and social contexts of languages, the semiotics of linguistic practices, colonial linguistics, heteroglossia and register variation, epistemic language and metalinguistics, as well as linguistic description. Her publications include *Secret Manipulations* (2011), *A Grammar of Luwo* (2014), and several other volumes. She is co-editor of the journal The Mouth (https://themouthjournal.com/).

David Tavárez, Professor of Anthropology at Vassar College, is a historian, linguistic anthropologist, and Mesoamericanist whose interests include religion, calendars and ritual, colonial Nahuatl and Zapotec texts, Indigenous intellectuals, and the Indigenous repurposing of Christianity in the Americas. He is the author of *The Invisible War* (Stanford, 2011), *Rethinking Zapotec Time* (Texas, 2022), and more than 50 peer-reviewed articles and chapters. He is also the editor of *Words and Worlds Turned Around,* and a co-author of the volumes *Painted Words* (Dumbarton Oaks, 2016), and *Chimalpahin's Conquest* (Stanford, 2010). His work has been funded by awards from the John S. Guggenheim Foundation, the National Science Foundation, the National Endowment for the Humanities, and the Mellon Foundation, among other institutions.

Matt Tomlinson is an anthropologist who studies ritual. He has published books on Christian religious politics in Fiji (*In God's Image*, 2009), persistent patterns of ritual form (*Ritual Textuality*, 2014), and new indigenous theologies in the Pacific Islands (*God Is Samoan*, 2020). He has also coedited books on the limits of meaning in Christian ritual (*The Limits of Meaning*, with Matthew Engelke, 2006), the concept of *mana* or spiritual power within and beyond Pacific Islands societies (*New Mana*, with Ty P. Kāwika Tengan, 2016) and monologic tendencies in religious and political speech (*The Monologic Imagination*, with Julian Millie, 2017). He is Associate Professor of Anthropology at the Australian National University.

James W. Underhill was born in Glasgow in 1967. He is Full Professor and lectures on Translation and Ethnolinguistics in Rouen, at Normandy University. He has worked as a full-time translator of French and translated Czech in Prague in the early 1990s. Underhill's work focuses on poetics, translation studies and linguistic philosophy and the relationship between culture. His approach to language and culture explores linguistic worldviews and the essential creative impulse by which individuals assimilate, stimulate, and transform the shared language of the community. He is the author of *Ethnolinguistics and Cultural Concepts: Truth, Love, Hate and War,* Cambridge University Press (2012), *Voice & Versification*, Ottawa University Press (2016), and *Migrating Meanings: Sharing Keywords in a Global World,* Edinburgh University Press (2019). He is the Founder and Director of the Rouen Ethnolinguistics Project.

Svenja Völkel is scientific assistant at the Institute of Language Typology (Johannes Gutenberg-University, Mainz/Germany) and she was a lecturer at the Institute of Cultural Anthropology (Ruprecht Karls-University Heidelberg/Germany). She holds a PhD from the University of Mainz and works in the fields of Anthropological Linguistics, Language Typology, Cognitive Linguistics, Language Contact, and Cognitive Anthropology with a regional focus on Polynesia/Oceania, where she has conducted several long-term field research. Among others, she is author of the book "*Social Structure, Space and Possession in Tongan Culture and Language*" (John Benjamins, 2010) and co-author of the book "*Introducing Linguistic Research*" (Cambridge University Press, 2021). Since 2014, she is co-head of the working group "Cognitive and Linguistic Anthropology" within the German Society for Cultural and Social Anthropology (DGSKA).

Anthony K. Webster is a linguistic anthropologist who focuses on Navajo ethnopoetics. He has worked with Navajo poets since 2000. He is the author of the books, *Explorations in*

Navajo Poetry and Poetics (UNM Press 2009), *Intimate Grammars: An Ethnography of Navajo Poetry* (U of Arizona Press 2015), and *The Sounds of Navajo Poetry: A Humanities of Speaking* (Peter Lang 2018). With Paul Kroskrity, he is the editor of *The Legacy of Dell Hymes: Ethnopoetics, Narrative Inequality, and Voice* (IU Press 2015). Most recently, with Esther Belin, Jeff Berglund and Connie Jacobs, he is the editor of *The Diné Reader: An Anthology of Navajo Literature* (U of Arizona Press 2021). He lives in southern Illinois.

Index

Printed in the USA
CPSIA information can be obtained
at www.ICGtesting.com
JSHW011940240724
66998JS00002B/3